Lecture Notes in Computer Science 16063

The series Lecture Notes in Computer Science (LNCS), including its subseries Lecture Notes in Artificial Intelligence (LNAI) and Lecture Notes in Bioinformatics (LNBI), has established itself as a medium for the publication of new developments in computer science and information technology research, teaching, and education.

LNCS enjoys close cooperation with the computer science R & D community, the series counts many renowned academics among its volume editors and paper authors, and collaborates with prestigious societies. Its mission is to serve this international community by providing an invaluable service, mainly focused on the publication of conference and workshop proceedings and postproceedings. LNCS commenced publication in 1973.

Kairit Tammets · Sergey Sosnovsky ·
Rafael Ferreira Mello · Gerti Pishtari ·
Tanya Nazaretsky
Editors

Two Decades of TEL

From Lessons Learnt to Challenges Ahead

20th European Conference
on Technology Enhanced Learning, EC-TEL 2025
Newcastle upon Tyne and Durham, UK, September 15–19, 2025
Proceedings, Part I

Springer

Editors
Kairit Tammets
Tallinn University
Tallinn, Estonia

Sergey Sosnovsky
Utrecht University
Utrecht, The Netherlands

Rafael Ferreira Mello
Universidade Federal Rural de Pernambuco
Recife, Brazil

Gerti Pishtari
University for Continuing Education Krems
Krems an der Donau, Austria

Tanya Nazaretsky
École Polytechnique Fédérale de Lausanne
Lausanne, Switzerland

ISSN 0302-9743 ISSN 1611-3349 (electronic)
Lecture Notes in Computer Science
ISBN 978-3-032-03869-2 ISBN 978-3-032-03870-8 (eBook)
https://doi.org/10.1007/978-3-032-03870-8

This Springer imprint is published by the registered company Springer Nature Switzerland AG
The registered company address is: Gewerbestrasse 11, 6330 Cham, Switzerland

Preface

Welcome to the proceedings of the *20th European Conference on Technology Enhanced Learning* (ECTEL 2025) – the largest event of the European Association of Technology Enhanced Learning (EATEL). This year, Newcastle and Durham Universities hosted ECTEL 2025 from September 15–19, 2025.

This year's conference theme was *Two Decades of TEL: from Lessons Learnt to Challenges Ahead.* Over the past twenty years, Technology Enhanced Learning (TEL) has developed into a dynamic interdisciplinary field, bridging pedagogy, educational psychology and digital technology. It has consistently addressed the challenges of innovation in education from online platforms to social media, from learning analytics to generative AI, while keeping a strong focus on pedagogical soundness, fairness, and sustainability. ECTEL 2025's theme invited the community to look both backward and forward: to reflect on past achievements and limitations, to critically examine how TEL research and practice have influenced educational practices, and to explore how they might continue to evolve in an era of accelerating technological and societal change.

The TEL community finds itself at a moment marked by rapid advancements, particularly driven by Generative AI, and the need for critical reflection on both successes and setbacks becomes ever more important. While organizations worldwide reevaluate their educational practices and policies to adapt to this technological shift, others actively pursue meaningful AI integration strategies aimed at enhancing teaching and learning experiences. This context calls upon the TEL community to assume a leading role in shaping education's trajectory, guided by sound pedagogical principles more than by shifting technological trends. History shows that substantive educational transformation is contingent not only on technological proficiency but also on deep pedagogical insight, ethical awareness, and social context. That is why this anniversary conference theme combined a forward-looking vision for TEL with a call to reflect on our past experiences. This dual perspective is key to equipping us with the insight needed to navigate future waves of innovation more wisely, focusing on what truly benefits learners and educators.

For ECTEL 2025, we received 155 submissions to the main research track, considering regular, blue sky, milestone, and industry papers, a 10% increase compared to last year. All submissions went through a double-blind review process, with at least three members of the TEL community reviewing each paper. The individual reviews were followed by discussions and a meta-review provided by a senior member of the program committee. As a result, 43 papers were accepted for presentation at the conference, resulting in a 27% acceptance rate. Additionally, 32 posters and 16 demonstration papers were selected to be presented at the conference to encourage discussions among the attending researchers and practitioners. All the research, poster, and demo papers are included in these two volumes. Furthermore, the conference featured eight workshops and a doctoral consortium as pre-conference activities held on September 15–16, 2025.

We would like to thank all the colleagues involved in organizing, writing, and reviewing the contributions to this year's conference. We are grateful to each member of the program committee who contributed reviews on submitted manuscripts, engaged in discussions, and supported the decision-making regarding their acceptance. We would particularly like to thank the keynote speakers Dragan Gašević and Mike Sharples for their valuable contributions to the conference program. Additionally, we extend a big thank you to the workshop chairs Irene-Angelica Chounta and Justin Edwards, the doctoral consortium chairs Ilona Buchem, Mutlu Cukurova, and Carrie Demmans Epp, the communication chairs Kateryna Zabolotna and Jindi Wang, the website chairs Bhoomika Agarwal and Zhaoxing Li, the proceedings chairs Elyda Freitas and Edna Milena Sarmiento Marquez, the Practitioner & Industry Chairs Qi Zhou and Daniel Spikol, and the steering committee representatives Marcus Specht and Tobias Ley, for their efforts, ideas, and time dedicated to assembling the conference program. We are deeply grateful to the local chairs, Alexandra I. Cristea and Lei Shi, for their exceptional dedication and invaluable work that made ECTEL 2025 a success. Thank you!

In this reflective moment for the TEL community, we also remember and honour those who have shaped our field over the years, among them Erik Duval, Martin Wolpers, and Ralf Klamma, whose contributions continue to inspire our work.

July 2025

Kairit Tammets
Sergey Sosnovsky
Rafael Ferreira Mello
Tanya Nazaretsky
Gerti Pishtari

Organization

General Chair

Rafael Ferreira Mello	Rural Federal University of Pernambuco, Brazil

Program Committee Chairs

Kairit Tammets	Tallinn University, Estonia
Sergey Sosnovsky	Utrecht University, Netherlands

Poster / Demo Chairs

Gerti Pishtari	Danube University Krems, Austria
Tanya Nazaretsky	École Polytechnique Fédérale de Lausanne, Switzerland

Workshop Chairs

Irene-Angelica Chounta	University of Duisburg-Essen, Germany
Justin Edwards	University of Oulu, Finland

Doctoral Consortium Chairs

Carrie Demmans Epp	University of Alberta, Canada
Ilona Buchem	Berlin University of Applied Sciences, Germany
Mutlu Cukurova	University College London, UK

Website Chairs

Bhoomika Agarwal	Open University of the Netherlands, Netherlands
Zhaoxing Li	University of Southampton, UK

Communication Chairs

Kateryna Zabolotna	University of Oulu, Finland
Jindi Wang	Durham University, UK

Proceedings Chairs

Elyda Freitas	Universidade de Pernambuco, Brazil
Edna Milena Sarmiento Marquez	Tallinn University, Estonia

Practitioner and Industry Chairs

Qi Zhou	University College London, UK
Daniel Spikol	University of Copenhagen, Denmark

Local Organization Chairs

Lei Shi	Newcastle University, UK
Alexandra I. Cristea	Durham University, UK

Steering Committee Representatives

Tobias Ley	Danube University Krems, Austria and Tallinn University, Estonia
Marcus Specht	Delft University of Technology, Netherlands

Senior Program Committee

Abelardo Pardo	University of Adelaide, Australia
Alejandro Ortega-Arranz	Universidad de Valladolid, Spain
Angela Fessl	Know-Center, Austria
Bert Bredeweg	University of Amsterdam, Netherlands
Birgit Rognebakke Krogstie	Norwegian University of Science and Technology, Norway
Blazenka Divjak	University of Zagreb, Croatia
Carlos Santos	University of Aveiro, Portugal
Cristian Cechinel	Federal University of Santa Catarina, Brazil

Daniel Schiffner	DIPF I Leibniz Institute for Research and Information in Education, Germany
David Joyner	Georgia Institute of Technology, USA
Davinia Hernandez-Leo	Universitat Pompeu Fabra, Spain
Denis Gillet	École Polytechnique Fédérale de Lausanne, Switzerland
Dragan Gasevic	Monash University, Australia
Fridolin Wild	Open University, UK
Irene-Angelica Chounta	University of Duisburg-Essen, Germany
Jakub Kuzilek	Humboldt-Universität zu Berlin, Germany
Jelena Jovanovic	University of Belgrade, Serbia
Joshua Weidlich	Deutsches Institut für Internationale Pädagogische Forschung, Germany
Luís Pedro	University of Aveiro, Portugal
Manuel Caeiro Rodríguez	University of Vigo, Spain
Marcus Specht	Delft University of Technology, Netherlands
Matthias Ehlenz	RWTH Aachen University, Germany
Merike Saar	Tallinn University, Estonia
Miguel Ángel Conde	University of León, Spain
Milos Kravcik	DFKI GmbH, Germany
Mohamed Amine Chatti	University of Duisburg-Essen, Germany
Mohammed Saqr	University of Eastern Finland
Monica Divitini	Norwegian University of Science and Technology, Norway
Mutlu Cukurova	University College London, UK
Nardie Fanchamps	Open University of the Netherlands, Netherlands
Nikol Rummel	Ruhr-Universität Bochum, Germany
Olga Viberg	KTH Royal Institute of Technology, Sweden
Patricia Santos	Universitat Pompeu Fabra, Spain
Paul Libbrecht	IUBH Fernstudium, Germany
Philippe Dessus	Université Grenoble Alpes, LaRAC, France
Rafael Amorim	CESAR School, Brazil
Riichiro Mizoguchi	Japan Advanced Institute of Science and Technology, Japan
Rogers Kaliisa	University of Oslo, Norway
Sambit Praharaj	Cais Research, Germany
Sarah Howard	University of Leeds, UK
Srecko Joksimovic	University of South Australia, Australia
Srinath Srinivasa	International Institute of Information Technology, Bangalore, India
Styliani Kleanthous	CYENS CoE and Open University of Cyprus, Cyprus

Taciana Pontual Falcão	Universidade Federal Rural de Pernambuco, Brazil
Tobias Ley	University for Continuing Education Krems, Austria
Tomaž Klobučar	Jožef Stefan Institute, Slovenia
Tore Hoel	Oslo Metropolitan University, Norway
Vanda Luengo	Sorbonne Université - LIP6, France
Vanessa Echeverria	Monash University, Australia
Vincent Aleven	Carnegie Mellon University, USA
Yvan Peter	Université de Lille, France
Zach Pardos	University of California, Berkeley, USA

Program Committee

Abílio Barros	Universidade Federal Rural de Pernambuco, Brazil
Ademar Aguiar	University of Porto, Portugal
Agathe Merceron	Berliner Hochschule für Technik, Germany
Agustin Caminero	Universidad Nacional de Educación a Distancia, Spain
Ainhoa Alvarez	University of the Basque Country, UPV/EHU, Spain
Alan Berg	University of Amsterdam, Netherlands
Aleksandra Klasnja-Milicevic	University of Novi Sad, Serbia
Alessandro Pagano	University of Bari, Italy
Alex Sandro Gomes	Universidade Federal de Pernambuco, Brazil
Alexander Tillmann	Goethe-Universität Frankfurt, Germany
Alexander Streicher	Fraunhofer IOSB, Germany
Alexander Nussbaumer	Graz University of Technology, Austria
Alona Strugatski	Weizmann Institute of Science, Israel
Álvaro Becerra	Universidad Autónoma de Madrid, Spain
Álvaro Sobrinho	Federal University of the Agreste of Pernambuco, Brazil
Ana Loureiro	Lisbon Open University, Portugal
Ana Luísa Mateus Oliveira Chança Torres	Instituto Politécnico de Santarém, Brazil
Ana Raquel Carvalho	University of Aveiro, Portugal
Anders Kluge	University of Oslo, Norway
Anderson Pinheiro Cavalcanti	Universidade Federal Rural de Pernambuco, Brazil
André Nascimento	Universidade Federal Rural de Pernambuco, Brazil

Andrea Vázquez-Ingelmo	University of Salamanca, Spain
Andreas Schmidt	Karlsruhe University of Applied Sciences, Germany
Andreas Lingnau	Deutsche Hochschule für angewandte Wissenschaften, Germany
Andri Ioannou	Cyprus University of Technology, Cyprus
Andrzej M. J. Skulimowski	AGH University of Kraków, Poland
Ángel Hernández-García	Universidad Politécnica de Madrid, Spain
Anna Nicolaou	Cyprus University of Technology, Cyprus
Antigoni Parmaxi	Cyprus University of Technology, Cyprus
Antonio Balderas	University of Cádiz, Spain
Armin Weinberger	Saarland University, Germany
Arun Balajiee Lekshmi Narayanan	University of Pittsburgh, USA
Atezaz Ahmad	DIPF | Leibniz Institute for Research and Information in Education, Germany
Audrey Serna	LIRIS, INSA Lyon, France
Audrey Cooke	Curtin University, Australia
Aurelio Lopez-Lopez	INAOE, Mexico
Bahtijar Vogel	Malmö University, Sweden
Bernardo Tabuenca	Universidad Politécnica de Madrid, Spain
Birte Heinemann	RWTH Aachen University, Germany
Bruno Alexandre Rosa	CESAR School, Brazil
Christine Michel	SRH University of Applied Sciences for Health, Germany
Clara Schumacher	Humboldt Universität zu Berlin, Germany
Cleon Xavier	Instituto Federal Goiano, Brazil
Covadonga Rodrigo	Universidad Nacional de Educacion a Distancia, Spain
Danial Hooshyar	University of Tartu, Estonia
Danielle R. Thomas	Carnegie Mellon University, USA
Demetrios Sampson	Curtin University, Australia
Diego Dermeval	Federal University of Alagoas, Brazil
Dominique Lenne	Heudiasyc, Université de Technologie de Compiègne, France
Domitile Lourdeaux	CNRS, France
Edna Milena Sarmiento-Márquez	Tallinn University, Estonia
Eduardo Gómez-Sánchez	Universidad de Valladolid, Spain
Eelco Herder	Utrecht University, Netherlands
Ekaterina Shved	EPFL, Switzerland
Elaine Harada	Universidade Federal do Amazonas, Brazil
Elis Kakoulli Constantinou	Cyprus University of Technology, Cyprus
Élise Lavoué	iaelyon, Université Jean Moulin Lyon 3, LIRIS, France

John Stamper	Carnegie Mellon University, USA
John Saint	Regent's University London, UK
Jorge Munoz-Gama	Pontificia Universidad Católica de Chile, Chile
Juan A. Muñoz-Cristóbal	Universidad de Valladolid, Spain
Juan I. Asensio-Pérez	Universidad de Valladolid, Spain
Juan Manuel Dodero	Universidad de Cádiz, Spain
Julien Broisin	IRIT, Université Toulouse III - Paul Sabatier, France
Julio Guerra	Universidad Austral de Chile, Chile
Kamil Akhuseyinoglu	University of Pittsburgh, USA
Karim Sehaba	LIRIS CNRS, France
Konstantinos Michos	EPFL, Switzerland
Koula Charitonos	Open University, UK
Laia Albó	Universitat Pompeu Fabra, Spain
Lele Sha	Monash University, Australia
Leonardo Brandão Marques	Federal University of Alagoas, Brazil
Liron Levy-Nadav	Open University of Israel, Israel
Lisa Lim	University of Technology Sydney, Australia
Luciano Cabral	CESAR School, Brazil
Luis P. Prieto	Universidad de Valladolid, Spain
Luiz Rodrigues	Universidade Tecnologica Federal do Paraná, Brazil
Luiz Barboza	CESAR School, Brazil
M. Cristina Rodriguez-Sanchez	Rey Juan Carlos University, Spain
Maartje Henderikx	Open Universiteit, Netherlands
Maher Elshakankiri	University of Toronto, Canada
Maka Eradze	University of L'Aquila, Italy
Manuel Leon	University of Southampton, UK
Manuel Valle Torre	Delft University of Technology, Netherlands
Manuel Jesus Gomez Moratilla	Universidad de Murcia, Spain
Mar Pérez-Sanagustín	Université Paul Sabatier Toulouse III, France
Marco Temperini	Sapienza - Università di Roma, Italy
Marco Kalz	Heidelberg University of Education, Germany
Maren Scheffel	Ruhr University Bochum, Germany
Margarida Lucas	University of Aveiro, Portugal
Maria Perifanou	University of Macedonia, Aristotle University of Thessaloniki, Hellenic Open University, Greece
María Jesús Rodríguez-Triana	Universidad de Valladolid, Spain
Maria Victoria Soule	University of Cyprus, Cyprus
Mariano Albaladejo-González	Universidad de Murcia, Spain
Marie Lefevre	LIRIS - Université de Lyon, France

Marina Lepp	University of Tartu, Estonia
Markel Vigo	University of Manchester, UK
Marlene Wagner	University for Continuing Education Krems, Austria
Martin Hlosta	Swiss Distance University of Applied Sciences, Switzerland
Martín Llamas-Nistal	Universidad de Vigo, Spain
Michael Kickmeier-Rust	Graz University of Technology, Austria
Miguel Ángel Conde	University of León, Spain
Miguel L. Bote-Lorenzo	Universidad de Valladolid, Spain
Mikhail Fominykh	Norwegian University of Science and Technology, Norway
Minghao Cai	University of Alberta, Canada
Mirko Marras	University of Cagliari, Italy
Mohsen Saadatmand	University of Helsinki, Finland
Mónica Aresta	University of Aveiro, Portugal
Monique Grandbastien	LORIA, Universite de Lorraine, France
Nardie Fanchamps	Open University of the Netherlands, Netherlands
Natalie Kiesler	Nuremberg Tech, Germany
Newarney Torrezão da Costa	Instituto Federal Goiano, Brazil
Ngoc Buu Cat Nguyen	University West, Sweden
Nicolas Ballier	Université de Paris Cité, France
Nicoletta Di Blas	Politecnico di Milano, Italy
Niels Seidel	FernUniversität in Hagen, Germany
Niels Pinkwart	Humboldt-Universität zu Berlin, Germany
Nikos Palavitsinis	Eummena Foundation, Greece
Olga Firssova	Open University of the Netherlands, Netherlands
Onuralp Ulusoy	Utrecht University, Netherlands
Pablo García-Zarza	Universidad de Valladolid, Spain
Panagiotis Kosmas	University of Limassol, Cyprus
Pankaj Chejara	Tallinn University, Estonia
Paraskevi Topali	Radboud University, Netherlands
Patricia Jaques	UFPR, Brazil
Paulo Carvalho	Carnegie Mellon University, USA
Pedro J. Muñoz-Merino	Universidad Carlos III de Madrid, Spain
Pedro Manuel Moreno-Marcos	Universidad Carlos III de Madrid, Spain
Péricles Miranda	Universidade Federal Rural de Pernambuco, Brazil
Piret Luik	University of Tartu, Estonia
Polina Häfner	Karlsruhe Institute of Technology, Germany
Rafael D. Araújo	Universidade Federal de Uberlandia, Brazil
Ranilson Paiva	Universidade Federal de Alagoas, Brazil

Contents – Part I

Research

Contents – Part II

Blue-sky

Industry

Poster

Demo

Research

Detect and Remedy Deceptive Overgeneralization in Adaptive Learning

Marshall An(✉) and John Stamper

Carnegie Mellon University, Pittsburgh, PA 15213, USA
haokanga@andrew.cmu.edu, jstamper@andrew.cmu.edu

Abstract. Adaptive learning technologies observe learner performance, infer mastery, and dynamically tailor instruction. However, this approach can fall short when encountering a learning phenomenon we term "deceptive overgeneralization", where learners perform correct actions based on incomplete understanding. This phenomenon "deceives" adaptive systems into prematurely stopping necessary practice, leaving overgeneralization unaddressed. To address this, we empirically investigated the mechanisms, risks, and remediation strategies for deceptive overgeneralization through experiments using Intelligent Tutoring Systems (ITSs) for Riichi Mahjong. Experiment 1 provided evidence supporting the effectiveness of ITSs in teaching Riichi Mahjong, showing a large effect size. However, despite their overall effectiveness, Experiment 2 revealed that ITSs may fall short in cases of deceptive overgeneralization, as learners, after demonstrating seemingly satisfactory performance during initial practice, subsequently misapplied learned actions "confidently" in scenarios that did not warrant them. Experiments 3–4 replicated this finding and further revealed that adaptive learning systems relying on observed correctness can prematurely cease practice, leaving deceptive overgeneralization unaddressed. Experiments 5–6 replicated the findings of Experiments 3–4, and also extended the methodology by incorporating tailored practice designed via our systematic detection/remediation procedure, which successfully addressed deceptive overgeneralization. This study contributes both theoretically and practically to enhancing the precision of adaptive learning, enabling more accurate mastery assessments and improved learning outcomes.

Keywords: Intelligent Tutoring Systems · Adaptive Learning · Bayesian Knowledge Tracing · Deceptive Overgeneralization

1 Introduction

Adaptive learning technologies dynamically adjust instruction based on learner performance, aiming to optimize learning efficiency and mastery [3]. Their effectiveness is well-supported by various theoretical perspectives, including Vygotsky's zone of proximal development [32], cognitive apprenticeship [14], the expertise reversal effect [16], and the assistance dilemma [17]. However, adaptivity

K. Tammets et al. (Eds.): EC-TEL 2025, LNCS 16063, pp. 3–17, 2026.
https://doi.org/10.1007/978-3-032-03870-8_1

inherently depends on learning data to infer skill mastery [3, p. 523]. Therefore, the completeness of learning data and how well it reflects actual skill mastery are critical—yet there are scenarios where learning data may fall short, particularly in cases of a learning phenomenon we term *deceptive overgeneralization*.

The definition and theoretical modeling of deceptive overgeneralization are grounded in Adaptive Control of Thought–Rational (ACT-R) [7,8] and the Knowledge–Learning–Instruction (KLI) framework [22]. Deceptive overgeneralization occurs when a learner acquires a partial understanding of a skill—retaining an incomplete subset of the necessary conditions while omitting critical application constraints—yet still produces correct actions. This learning phenomenon is "deceptive" because it creates an illusion of mastery: learners appear to perform the expected action, even though their understanding remains flawed. Since adaptive learning systems typically rely on observed actions to infer mastery, deceptive overgeneralization poses a significant challenge: it can mislead adaptive systems into prematurely stopping necessary practice, leaving overgeneralization unaddressed.

To investigate deceptive overgeneralization, we conducted a series of six experiments using Intelligent Tutoring Systems (ITSs) developed with Cognitive Tutor Authoring Tools (CTAT) [1], designed to teach Riichi Mahjong, a domain featuring complex skills with composite conditions but singular observable actions. Experiment 1 evaluated whether ITSs improve learning outcomes of complex skills in this domain. Experiment 2 tested whether learners exhibit deceptive overgeneralization by confidently misapplying acquired actions under conditions where they are no longer appropriate. Experiments 3–4 were designed to replicate Experiment 2's observations and further investigate whether adaptive learning exacerbates the issue by prematurely ceasing practice. Experiments 5–6 replicated the methodology of Experiments 3–4, and also incorporated tailored practice designed in accordance with our systematic detection/remediation procedure to empirically test its efficacy in addressing deceptive overgeneralization. This work substantially extends our prior conference paper [4], which introduced a testable model of deceptive overgeneralization and reported preliminary findings. In this paper, we: (1) present the full experimental methodology for six studies to enable scientific replication; (2) empirically validate a set of skills highly susceptible to deceptive overgeneralization; and (3) provide empirical evidence that our instructional design procedure detects and effectively remedies deceptive overgeneralization.

This paper makes two key contributions: empirical evidence of deceptive overgeneralization and its implications for adaptive learning, and an instructional design procedure to systematically address this phenomenon. We provide empirical evidence showing that learners can appear competent during practice but later misapply learned actions confidently in inappropriate contexts, and that adaptive systems relying solely on correctness risk stopping practice prematurely. Furthermore, we propose and validate a procedure to help educators detect and remedy deceptive overgeneralization when teaching complex skills.

2 Related Work

2.1 Deceptive Overgeneralization vs. General Misconceptions

It is important to distinguish deceptive overgeneralization from the broader category of misconceptions. For example, a well-documented misconception observed in middle school students learning decimals is the belief that "longer decimals are larger" [25]. Learners might erroneously conclude that 0.213 is greater than 0.51 simply because the former has more digits, despite 0.51 being the larger number. Such misconceptions lead to actions that are clearly incorrect, allowing for immediate observation, feedback provision, and tailored subsequent training. In contrast, deceptive overgeneralization involves learners who, during closely monitored learning sessions, apply correct actions that are based on incomplete understanding of the necessary conditions. These learners may later inappropriately apply these actions under unsuitable circumstances, often beyond the scrutiny of the initial learning. This highlights why deceptive overgeneralization is particularly "deceptive": learners are still observed to take correct actions, despite their misconceptions.

2.2 Deceptive Overgeneralization vs. Shallow Problem Features

Furthermore, this study differs from prior research that has primarily focused on distinguishing between shallow and deep features in learning. Shallow features, also known as superficial or surface features, are those that do not contribute to correct solution pathways [11,12,28]. For example, a learner might choose to use a pie chart because the data is demographic (shallow) rather than categorical (deep) [11]. In contrast, this research investigates scenarios where learners take correct actions based on a relevant yet incomplete set of features. Importantly, unlike shallow features, all the features used by learners exhibiting deceptive overgeneralization are part of the correct solution pathways, making their understanding appear deceptively correct.

3 Theoretical Model: Extending ACT-R and KLI to Model Deceptive Overgeneralization

3.1 Adaptive Control of Thought – Rational (ACT-R)

ACT-R, a cognitive architecture for understanding and modeling human cognitive processes, posits that cognitive behaviors are orchestrated by productions [7,8]. A production can be represented as a condition-action pair [6, p. 5], with the *condition* part specifying the circumstances under which the production can apply, and the *action* part specifying what should be done when production applies [5, p. 3]. Empirical studies underpinning ACT-R have led to a proliferation of ITS that successfully enhance learning outcomes across diverse educational settings [2,31,33].

3.2 The Knowledge-Learning-Instruction (KLI) Framework

Learning is typically characterized by a gradual and continuous process rather than sudden transformative insights [9]. The KLI framework views learning as the acquisition of Knowledge Components (KCs), which are acquired units of cognitive functions or structures [22]. The KLI framework identifies *induction and refinement* as one primary type of learning processes, particularly for acquiring KCs associated with variable conditions: for KCs with conditions that can vary in form or value, learners must induce and refine KCs so that the acquired KCs are "accurate, appropriately general, and discriminating" [22]. As we consider the induction and subsequent refinement of a KC as a continuous learning progression, learners may initially acquire an inaccurately generalized version of the target KC. This initial misunderstanding may either be refined into an accurate KC through further practice, or it may persist as inaccurate due to a lack of practice opportunities that support the refinement process.

3.3 Modeling of Deceptive Overgeneralization

According to KLI, a KC links problem features to a corresponding response [22]. A KC is considered accurate, or has "high feature validity", if it accounts for all relevant features while excluding irrelevant ones [23]. Otherwise, the acquired KC is inaccurate and requires further refinement. Inaccurate generalization can take the form of overgeneralization, undergeneralization, or a nuanced mix of both. Among these, deceptive overgeneralization is the specific phenomenon we investigate in this study.

To model the schema of deceptive overgeneralization, we build upon how production rules are represented in ITSs. In ITSs, particularly those developed using CTAT, each production's condition-action pair is structured as an IF-THEN statement [18]: `IF <condition(s)> THEN <action>`. Overgeneralization occurs when a learner acquires a production rule with an overly broad IF condition. We identify a schema of production rules prone to deceptive overgeneralization:

```
IF all required conditions are met THEN perform action
```

A learner exhibiting deceptive overgeneralization may omit part of the necessary constraints and instead acquire the following:

```
IF a subset of required conditions are met THEN perform
action
```

For example, consider a production rule requiring two conditions to be met simultaneously to warrant an action:

```
IF condition1 AND condition2 are both met THEN perform action
```

A learner exhibiting deceptive overgeneralization may instead acquire:

```
IF condition1 is met THEN perform action
```

This modeling reveals a critical issue: when instructional designs present only scenarios where the action is warranted and assess learners solely on their ability to perform it, they risk leaving deceptive overgeneralization unaddressed. Adaptive systems risk exacerbating this by inferring mastery from correct performance, potentially halting practice prematurely.

3.4 Knowledge Compilation and Deceptive Overgeneralization

A natural question arises: why not treat the verification of each condition as a separate KC? The answer lies in the expectation of task efficiency as learners develop expertise. As learners advance, they must handle increasingly complex tasks with greater fluency, necessitating compiled knowledge structures rather than independently verifying each condition. According to the KLI framework [22], KCs describe mental processes at approximately the unit task level within Newell's time scales of human action [27], typically taking about 10 s. If each condition were treated as an independent KC, decision-making would become fragmented, disrupting fluency and reducing efficiency in complex tasks.

Knowledge compilation, a core mechanism in ACT-R, improves cognitive efficiency by eliminating multiple production rule firings [7, p. 169]. A primary compilation process, known as *composition*, merges a chain of production rules into a single "macro-production," eliminating intermediate cognitive actions while maintaining the same final output [6, p. 235]. Although composition increases overall efficiency, the composed "macro-productions" tend to grow larger, particularly with an increase in the size of the condition sides [6, p. 239]. With an increasingly complex and composite condition side, it becomes more likely that some conditions will be overlooked, leading to deceptive overgeneralization. Because knowledge compilation is a fundamental process in expertise development, deceptive overgeneralization is likely just as prevalent.

4 A Procedure to Systematically Detect and Remedy Deceptive Overgeneralization

Addressing deceptive overgeneralization requires designing tailored activities that test whether students have generalized their learning appropriately. Grounded in our theoretical modeling, we propose the following procedure:

1. **Represent skills as production rules** – Model skills in the format of production rules (i.e., condition-action pairs).
2. **Identify production rules with composite conditions and singular actions** – Focus on skills where learners must evaluate multiple conditions but produce a single observable action, as these are particularly susceptible to deceptive overgeneralization.
3. **Prioritize skills where misapplication is particularly problematic** – Identify rules where overgeneralization could lead to serious errors.

4. **Create practice where learned actions should *not* be taken** – Design problems that intentionally violate some necessary conditions to detect deceptive overgeneralization. Provide targeted feedback that directly addresses the missing constraint to help learners refine their understanding.

5 Research Questions

We formulate the following research questions: **RQ1:** Do ITSs effectively improve learning outcomes in teaching complex skills? **RQ2:** Does deceptive overgeneralization occur when learning complex skills with composite conditions? **RQ3:** Does adaptive learning risk prematurely stopping practice, leaving deceptive overgeneralization unaddressed? **RQ4:** Can tailored practice designed via our proposed procedure effectively address deceptive overgeneralization?

6 Method

6.1 Task Domain

To investigate this phenomenon in a controlled yet ecologically valid setting, we require a task domain that inherently presents challenges conducive to deceptive overgeneralization. Specifically, the ideal domain should involve production rules with complex conditions but a singular observable action, as we hypothesize that this structure is particularly susceptible to deceptive overgeneralization. We selected Riichi Mahjong because it naturally exhibits these characteristics.

Riichi Mahjong, also known as Japanese Mahjong, is an incomplete-information intellectual game that requires complex cognitive processes. Its strategic depth has attracted considerable interest from AI researchers, leading to models that outperform most human players [24,26]. However, these AI models are optimized for gameplay rather than learning, lacking explanatory features to support skill acquisition. This gap highlights the need for alternative approaches to help human players develop expertise. In addition, learning Riichi Mahjong presents unique challenges: optimal moves may yield unfavorable outcomes due to randomness, while incorrect moves can sometimes succeed. This inconsistency between action and outcome disrupts natural learning, as players cannot rely on in-game outcome as accurate feedback, and players may misattribute the quality of their decisions based on results rather than the decision-making process [10]. Furthermore, since each game begins with a randomized hand and evolves through the dynamic interactions of four independent players, structured repeated practice is difficult to achieve. Given these challenges, we hypothesize that ITSs are particularly beneficial in this domain, as they can create controlled yet realistic scenarios, integrating targeted practice, immediate feedback, and adaptive problem sequencing to support learning. Meanwhile, as this domain features production rules with composite conditions and singular actions, it is particularly suitable for investigating deceptive overgeneralization.

6.2 Participants

We conducted multiple in-vivo experiments in a Riichi Mahjong course at Carnegie Mellon University, where students enrolled solely out of interest and were free from Grade Point Average (GPA) pressure. The number of students who consented to participate and completed the activities were as follows: 32 in Experiment 1, 19 in Experiment 2, 11 in Experiment 3, 13 in Experiment 4, 14 in Experiment 5, and 13 in Experiment 6.

6.3 Materials and Procedure

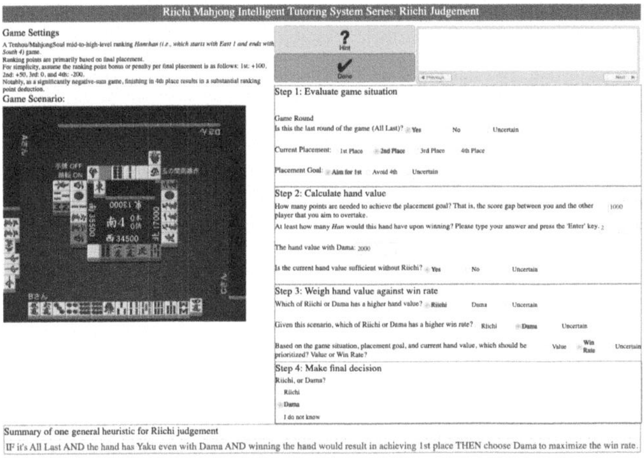

Fig. 1. The Riichi Judgement ITS. It aids students in acquiring a complex production rule formed via knowledge compilation. While it provides detailed steps to help learners understand how production rules are compiled into the final macro-production, the macro-production only produces a single observable action (as shown in the *Make Final Decision* section of the ITS interface, where the action is either *Riichi* or *Dama*).

As exemplified in Fig. 1, we developed a series of ITSs for Riichi Mahjong using CTAT. These ITSs incorporate key features that provide learners with favorable learning conditions, as synthesized by Koedinger et al. [20]. These features include immediate feedback, context-specific instruction on demand, enforcement of correct responses, tailored tasks designed through cognitive task analysis [29], and repeated practice opportunities to ensure mastery.

An important consideration in studies that aim to observe learner mistakes is whether the observed phenomenon reflects authentic learning processes or merely results from experimental "traps". In our design, we made cautious efforts to maintain ecological validity by grounding all problem scenarios in *real* gameplay. All the skills involved in these experiments—such as score calculation, Pinfu, Kabe, and Riichi judgment—are commonly taught skills featured in Mahjong textbooks [13]. The macro-productions and their commonly overgeneralized variants were not arbitrarily invented but derived through cognitive task analysis involving both experts and novices.

Experiment 1. To evaluate the efficacy of ITSs in teaching complex skills (**RQ1**), we employed a single-group pretest-posttest design. Two distinct but equivalent 10-question quizzes were used for the pre- and post-tests, with no feedback provided during the pre-test. This design aimed to mitigate biases, ensuring differences in learning outcomes stemmed from the ITS intervention rather than practice effects from the pre-test.

Experiment 2. Experiment 2 investigates whether learners form inaccurate macro-productions through knowledge compilation. Therefore, the problem set in Experiment 2 was designed to target a macro-production compiled from detailed steps covered in Experiment 1. We designed a 15-problem set: Problems 1–9 guide learners in inducing the targeted macro-production without distinguishing between accurate learning and overgeneralization, while Problems 10–15 require learners to discern whether the conditions warrant the acquired action, detecting whether overgeneralization has occurred. To establish a comparison point for Experiments 3 and 4, which employed adaptive learning, Experiment 2 disabled it so that all participants completed the same sequence of practice.

To test whether learners exhibit deceptive overgeneralization (**RQ2**), we assess two comparisons:

First Comparison: Does Performance Align with Bayesian Knowledge Tracing (BKT)'s Binary Learning State Assumption? Bayesian Knowledge Tracing (BKT) [15] is a knowledge-tracing algorithm that dynamically updates its estimate of a learner's skill mastery based on observed learner performance in real time. BKT models learning under a two-state assumption, meaning learners are either in an *Unlearned* or *Learned* state for a given KC [15, p. 260]. If the error rate on Problem 10 aligns with BKT predictions, it suggests that as learners transition from the *Unlearned* state during Problems 1–9, they accurately generalize the KC without exhibiting overgeneralization. However, if errors significantly exceed BKT predictions, it suggests a violation of this assumption, indicating that either Problem 10 introduces a new KC or that learners are systematically misapplying an overgeneralized rule. The hypotheses are as follows: **Null Hypothesis (H_0):** The error rate on Problem 10 matches the rate predicted by BKT based on the performance of Problems 1–9. **Alternative Hypothesis (H_1):** The error rate on Problem 10 exceeds BKT predictions, suggesting a violation of BKT's two-state assumption, either due to a new KC or an overgeneralized rule.

Second Comparison: Does Performance Indicate Deceptive Overgeneralization or a New KC? To differentiate between these possibilities, we compare the error rate on Problem 10 with the expected error rate for a completely new KC. If the error rate matches the new-KC baseline, errors may be attributed to encountering a novel KC. If the error rate is significantly higher, it indicates that learners are confidently misapplying an overgeneralized rule from previous problems rather than guessing. The hypotheses are as follows: **Null Hypothesis (H_0):** The error rate matches the expected rate for a new KC, indicating unfamiliarity rather than overgeneralization. **Alternative Hypothesis (H_1):** The error rate exceeds the new-KC baseline, suggesting that learners are confidently applying a flawed macro-production, indicative of deceptive overgeneralization.

Experiment 3 and Experiment 4. Experiments 3 and 4 replicated the observations from Experiment 2 while further investigating whether adaptive learning exacerbates deceptive overgeneralization by prematurely ceasing practice. To examine this, the ITSs used BKT to dynamically update mastery estimates and determine the need for further practice. Once the system reached a predefined 95% mastery threshold—a common value in CTAT-based tutors [21, p. 144]—it assumed mastery and stopped providing practice.

To evaluate whether adaptive learning prematurely ceased necessary practice, we employed a within-subjects design. Each participant completed two rounds of practice using the ITS on the same problem set: **First round (adaptive learning enabled):** The ITS stopped providing practice once it deemed the skill mastered. **Second round (full exposure):** Participants completed all problems, ensuring they encountered cases where previously learned actions were no longer applicable. If a skill was truly mastered, practice in the second round should be unnecessary—learners should correctly discern when an action should or should not be taken. However, we hypothesize that after adaptive learning ceases practice in the first round, learners will incorrectly apply the acquired action in the second round when exposed to scenarios where that action is inappropriate—revealing deceptive overgeneralization.

For each of Experiments 3 and 4, we designed an ITS that teaches a macro-production hypothesized to be particularly susceptible to deceptive overgeneralization, following the schema discussed in Sect. 3.3. Below, we present the KC from Experiment 3 as an illustrative example, as it contains relatively little Mahjong-specific jargon and partially resembles a mathematical problem.

To provide necessary context for readers unfamiliar with Mahjong, we briefly outline the logic behind this KC before presenting its formal structure. This KC pertains to defensive play, where the goal is to determine whether discarding a tile carries minimal risk of helping an opponent complete their hand. In Mahjong, players form hands using pairs (two identical tiles), triplets (three identical tiles), and sequences (three consecutive tiles, e.g., 2-3-4). Since opponents' hands are hidden, players infer safer discards based on visible tiles. A tile is considered safer if it contributes to fewer possible patterns. For example, if all copies of 3 are visible and thus cannot be in an opponent's concealed hand, then an opponent cannot be waiting to complete a 1-2-3 or 2-3-4 sequence, making 2 safer. In contrast, a tile like 8 remains risky, as it could still complete multiple patterns (6-7-8, 7-8-9, a pair, or a triplet of 8 s). Formally, the KC is structured as follows:

> **IF** [Current Goal] The goal is to determine whether a numeric tile N is relatively safer to discard
> **AND [Application Constraint] The opponent in question could be waiting to form a 3-tile sequence**
> **AND** [Mathematical] All copies of tiles K_1 and K_2 ($K_1 < K_2$) are visible, meaning they cannot be in an opponent's concealed hand. (For boundary cases, K_1 can be treated as 0 and K_2 as 10, representing the conceptual "outer limits" of the tile range)
> **AND** [Mathematical] $K_2 - K_1 \leq 3$, preventing a 3-tile sequence from forming using tiles in between
> **AND** [Mathematical] $K_1 < N < K_2$,
> **THEN** [Single Action] Discard the tile N

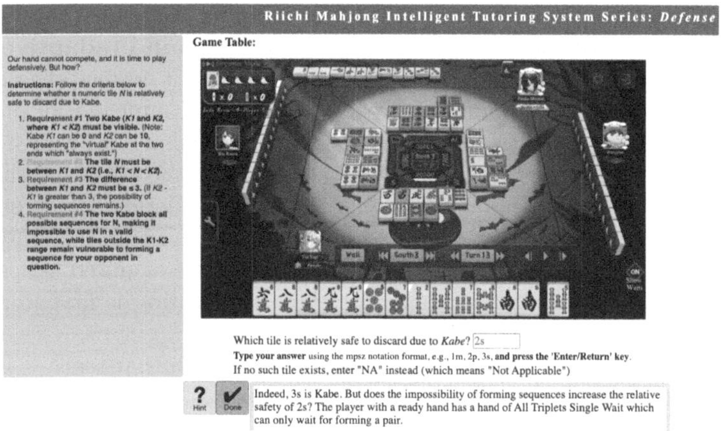

Fig. 2. Interface of the Kabe ITS. The provided scenario, based on an anonymized real game, does NOT warrant applying the KC. Learners who misapply the KC due to deceptive overgeneralization receive targeted feedback designed to refine understanding.

In this case, the application constraint—the "why"—is critical for determining whether the action is appropriate. The rule is based on the idea that a tile is safer if it cannot complete a sequence due to nearby tiles already being visible. However, learners may overgeneralize this rule by focusing solely on the "how"—discarding a tile so long as nearby tiles are visible—without fully understanding the "why." This could lead them to misapply the action even in cases where the impossibility of forming sequences does not make a tile relatively safer, such as the problem illustrated in Fig. 2.

To replicate the tests conducted for **RQ2**, a similar comparison was applied in Experiments 3 and 4. Unlike Experiment 2, where BKT was used post-experiment to predict the expected error rate on Problem 10, Experiments 3 and 4 already employed BKT dynamically to determine when to stop providing practice. Given this setup, we calculate the expected error rate based on the mastery threshold of 95%. However, if deceptive overgeneralization is present, there will be a significant deviation from this prediction, as learners may confidently misapply an overgeneralized rule when exposed to scenarios that do not warrant the learned action in the second round.

To investigate **RQ3**, we examine whether adaptive learning prematurely stops necessary practice before learners encounter scenarios where the learned action is inappropriate. If learners exhibit high error rates when faced with these scenarios in the second round, yet BKT stopped practice in the first round before they had any opportunity to encounter such cases, this would suggest that adaptive learning risks amplifying the issue of deceptive overgeneralization by prematurely terminating practice.

Experiment 5 and Experiment 6. To investigate **RQ4**, Experiments 5–6 both replicated and extended Experiments 3–4 by introducing a sequence of tailored practice problems immediately upon detecting deceptive overgeneralization. These practice problems were designed in strict accordance with our proposed procedure described in Sect. 4.

7 Results

Effectiveness of ITS in Learning Complex Skills (RQ1). We analyzed the pre-test and post-test scores in Experiment 1. A Shapiro-Wilk test confirmed that the assumption of normality was met ($W = 0.945$, $p = 0.102$). As normality was satisfied, a paired t-test was conducted, revealing a significant improvement in scores ($t(31) = 5.505$, $p < 0.001$, Cohen's $d = 0.97$), indicating a large effect size. These results support the effectiveness of ITS in learning complex skills.

Observation of Deceptive Overgeneralization (RQ2). In Experiment 2, on Problem 10—the first scenario where the acquired action should not be taken—14 of 19 participants (73.7%) misapplied the action. To evaluate whether these errors stemmed from systematic overgeneralization, we simulated Bayesian Knowledge Tracing (BKT) based on performance in Problems 1–9. The following values were used for the BKT parameters: $P_{\text{learned}} = 0.25$ (initial mastery), $P_{\text{transfer}} = 0.2$ (learning rate), and $P_{\text{slip}} = 0.1$, as these are the default and commonly used values in CTAT. We set $P_{\text{guess}} = 0.5$ because the ITS provided three options: perform the action, refrain from the action, or select "I don't know." Since selecting "I don't know" does not contribute to correctness, a learner making an intentional guess would randomly choose between performing or refraining from the action, each with an equal probability. Thus, the probability of guessing correctly is 50%. Under these conditions, the expected collective errors on Problem 10, if learners only acquired the accurate rule, were 2.95. However, the actual 14 errors significantly exceeded this expectation ($p < 0.001$), indicating a systematic deviation from the BKT two-state assumption. Next, we compared the observed errors to the expected error rate for a completely new knowledge component (KC). For a new KC under BKT assumptions: $P_{\text{error}} = P_{\text{learned}} \times P_{\text{slip}} + (1 - P_{\text{learned}}) \times (1 - P_{\text{guess}})$, with $P_{\text{learned}} = 0.25$, $P_{\text{slip}} = 0.1$, and $P_{\text{guess}} = 0.5$, the expected error rate $P_{\text{error}} = 0.4$. With 19 participants, the expected collective errors for a new KC were 7.6. The actual errors (14) significantly exceeded this estimate ($p = 0.003$), suggesting that participants were not merely encountering a new KC but were confidently misapplying an overgeneralized macro-production. This distinction highlights that learners had acquired a systematic but flawed rule from Problems 1–9, which they applied inappropriately rather than making random guesses.

A similar pattern was observed in Experiments 3–6, where learners initially demonstrated seemingly good performance when performing actions, followed by starkly high error rates in overgeneralization detector problems, manifesting as confidently misapplying previously learned actions. Specifically, in Experiment 3, an astonishing error rate of 100% was observed upon the first exposure to a scenario where the action should not have been taken. In Experiment 4, 11 of 13 participants (84.6%) misapplied the action. Experiment 5, designed as a replication of Experiment 3, also yielded an error rate of 100%; similarly, Experiment 6 as a replication of Experiment 4 yielded an error rate of 84.6%. The BKT two-state assumption predicted a 12% error rate with a 95% mastery threshold when accounting for slips [15], yet every observed error rate significantly deviated from the prediction ($p < 0.001$ for each individual experiment in Experiments 3–6). Additionally, these error rates significantly exceeded the expected error rate for a completely new KC baseline ($p < 0.001$ for Experiment 3 and 5; $p = 0.0013$ for Experiment 4 and 6). In summary, the finding in Experiment 2 was replicated in Experiments 3–6, confirming the presence of deceptive overgeneralization.

Evidence that Adaptive Learning Risks Prematurely Stop Providing Practice With Deceptive Overgeneralization (RQ3). As deceptive overgeneralization was observed in RQ2, we examined whether BKT prematurely terminated practice before learners encountered practice designed to detect it. In Experiment 3, across 11 students, none reached a problem instance assessing deceptive overgeneralization during the first round of practice with adaptive learning enabled, as BKT deemed mastery achieved beforehand. A similar pattern was observed in Experiment 4, where none of the 13 students encountered such practice opportunities. Experiments 5 and 6 replicated these findings. This consistent pattern across multiple experiments suggests adaptive learning may inadvertently amplify deceptive overgeneralization by relying on observed correctness to infer mastery, potentially halting practice before learners are able to refine their understanding of critical application constraints.

Effectiveness of Our Proposed Procedure in Addressing Deceptive Overgeneralization (RQ4). In Experiment 5 and 6, we conducted *learning curve* analysis using DataShop to identify trends of improvement or stagnation in learners' performance as they completed an increasing number of these tailored practice opportunities [19]. As shown in Fig. 3, the learning curves for both Experiment 5 (N = 14) and Experiment 6 (N = 13) exhibit a smoothly decreasing error rate, indicative of effective student learning [30]. Quantitatively, in Experiment 5, after several instances of tailored practice, the error rate dropped from 100% (14/14) to 7.14% (1/14), yielding a Cohen's $h = 2.6$—an extremely large effect. Similarly, in Experiment 6, the error rate decreased from 84.6% (11/13) to 7.69% (1/13), yielding a Cohen's $h = 1.773$. These post-remediation error rates fall below the 12% threshold predicted by BKT for accurately mastered skills, indicating that the tailored practice implemented via our proposed procedure effectively addresses deceptive overgeneralization.

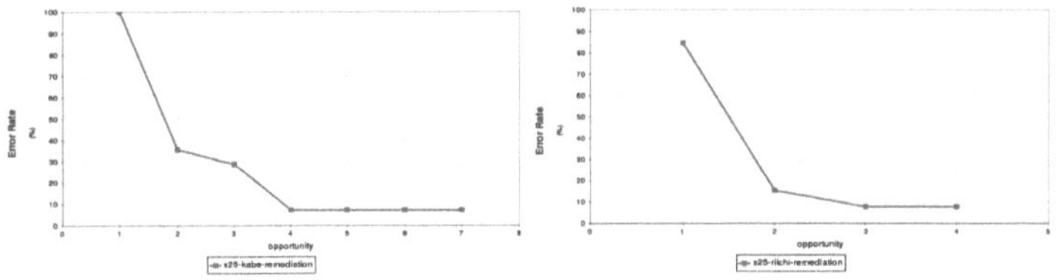

Fig. 3. Learning curves of the overgeneralization detector problem followed by tailored remediation practice in Experiment 5 (Left) and Experiment 6 (Right).

8 Discussion and Implications

Our findings provide strong evidence that deceptive overgeneralization differs fundamentally from encountering new skills. In Experiments 2–6, learners confidently misapplied acquired actions under inappropriate conditions, with error rates exceeding new-KC baselines, indicating that learners were not merely guessing but systematically applying an overgeneralized rule. Supported by the results of Experiments 5–6, our proposed procedure enables instructional designers to systematically detect and remediate deceptive overgeneralization, ensuring that learners acquire not only the ability to execute an action but also a precise understanding of its application constraints.

Several limitations of our work should be noted. First, although Riichi Mahjong provides a rich domain for studying composite-condition skills, future research should investigate whether deceptive overgeneralization manifests similarly in traditional academic subjects (e.g., mathematics). Second, although our findings have been replicated across multiple experiments, each individual experiment involved a relatively small sample size; future research should validate these findings with larger samples. Third, because our experiments intentionally structured practice sequences to observe the phenomenon, it is important to examine the extent to which similar effects occur under more natural learning trajectories. Fourth, our experiments were conducted in a course that does not affect GPA, which may limit the generalizability of our findings to educational settings with different motivational dynamics.

Despite the limitations, the implications of our work extend beyond ITSs to broader adaptive learning technologies. Many adaptive learning systems infer mastery based on observed correctness, yet our results suggest that this approach alone is insufficient for detecting deceptive overgeneralization. We believe these findings contribute to enhancing the precision of adaptive learning, enabling more accurate mastery assessments and improved learning outcomes.

Acknowledgments. We specifically thank Professor Bruce M. McLaren for sharing his insightful perspective on how we refine the approach to the research questions.

References

1. Aleven, V., McLaren, B.M., Sewall, J., Koedinger, K.R.: The cognitive tutor authoring tools (CTAT): preliminary evaluation of efficiency gains. In: Ikeda, M., Ashley, K.D., Chan, T.-W. (eds.) ITS 2006. LNCS, vol. 4053, pp. 61–70. Springer, Heidelberg (2006). https://doi.org/10.1007/11774303_7
2. Aleven, V., et al.: Example-tracing tutors: intelligent tutor development for non-programmers. Int. J. Artif. Intell. Educ. **26**, 224–269 (2016)
3. Aleven, V., McLaughlin, E.A., Glenn, R.A., Koedinger, K.R.: Instruction based on adaptive learning technologies. Handb. Res. Learn. Instruct. **2**, 522–560 (2016)
4. An, M., Stamper, J.: Deceptive overgeneralization in adaptive learning. In: International Conference on Artificial Intelligence in Education. Springer (2025). (in press)
5. Anderson, J.R.: Acquisition of cognitive skill. Psychol. Rev. **89**(4), 369 (1982)
6. Anderson, J.R.: The Architecture of Cognition. Harvard University Press, USA (1983)
7. Anderson, J.R.: Automaticity and the ACT theory. Am. J. Psychol. 165–180 (1992)
8. Anderson, J.R.: ACT: a simple theory of complex cognition. Am. Psychol. **51**(4), 355 (1996)
9. Anderson, J.R., Schunn, C.D.: Implications of the ACT-R learning theory: no magic bullets. In: Advances in instructional Psychology, vol. 5, pp. 1–33. Routledge (2013)
10. Baron, J., Hershey, J.C.: Outcome bias in decision evaluation. J. Pers. Soc. Psychol. **54**(4), 569 (1988)
11. Chang, N.M.: Learning to discriminate and generalize through problem comparisons. Ph.D. thesis, Carnegie Mellon University (2006)
12. Chi, M.T., Feltovich, P.J., Glaser, R.: Categorization and representation of physics problems by experts and novices. Cogn. Sci. **5**(2), 121–152 (1981)
13. Chiba, D.: Riichi book I: a mahjong strategy primer for European players (2019). https://dainachiba.github.io/RiichiBooks/. Version 13. Accessed 26 Mar 2019
14. Collins, A., Brown, J.S., Holum, A., et al.: Cognitive apprenticeship: making thinking visible. Am. Educ. **15**(3), 6–11 (1991)
15. Corbett, A.T., Anderson, J.R.: Knowledge tracing: modeling the acquisition of procedural knowledge. User Model. User-Adap. Inter. **4**, 253–278 (1994)

16. Kalyuga, S.: The expertise reversal effect. In: Managing Cognitive Load in Adaptive Multimedia Learning, pp. 58–80. IGI Global (2009)
17. Koedinger, K.R., Aleven, V.: Exploring the assistance dilemma in experiments with cognitive tutors. Educ. Psychol. Rev. **19**, 239–264 (2007)
18. Koedinger, K.R., Anderson, J.R., Hadley, W.H., Mark, M.A.: Intelligent tutoring goes to school in the big city. Int. J. Artif. Intell. Educ. **8**, 30–43 (1997)
19. Koedinger, K.R., Baker, R.S., Cunningham, K., Skogsholm, A., Leber, B., Stamper, J.: A data repository for the EDM community: the PSLC DataShop. Handb. Educ. Data Min. **43**, 43–56 (2010)
20. Koedinger, K.R., Carvalho, P.F., Liu, R., McLaughlin, E.A.: An astonishing regularity in student learning rate. Proc. Natl. Acad. Sci. **120**(13), e2221311120 (2023)
21. Koedinger, K.R., Corbett, A., et al.: Cognitive tutors: technology bringing learning sciences to the classroom. Na (2006)
22. Koedinger, K.R., Corbett, A.T., Perfetti, C.: The knowledge-learning-instruction framework: bridging the science-practice chasm to enhance robust student learning. Cogn. Sci. **36**(5), 757–798 (2012)
23. LearnLab: Feature validity (2011). https://learnlab.org/wiki/index.php?title=Feature_validity. Acessed 29 May 2024
24. Li, J., et al.: Suphx: mastering mahjong with deep reinforcement learning. arXiv preprint arXiv:2003.13590 (2020)
25. McLaren, B.M.: Decimal point: a decade of learning science findings with a digital learning game. In: Ilic, P., Casebourne, I., Wegerif, R. (eds.) Artificial Intelligence in Education: The Intersection of Technology and Pedagogy. Intelligent Systems Reference Library, vol. 261, pp. 145–203. Springer, Cham (2024). https://doi.org/10.1007/978-3-031-71232-6_9
26. Mizukami, N., Tsuruoka, Y.: Building a computer mahjong player based on Monte Carlo simulation and opponent models. In: 2015 IEEE Conference on Computational Intelligence and Games (CIG), pp. 275–283. IEEE (2015)
27. Newell, A.: Unified Theories of Cognition. Harvard University Press (1994)
28. Ross, B.H.: Remindings and their effects in learning a cognitive skill. Cogn. Psychol. **16**(3), 371–416 (1984)
29. Schraagen, J.M., Chipman, S.F., Shalin, V.L.: Cognitive Task Analysis. Psychology Press (2000)
30. Stamper, J.C., Koedinger, K.R.: Human-machine student model discovery and improvement using DataShop. In: Biswas, G., Bull, S., Kay, J., Mitrovic, A. (eds.) AIED 2011. LNCS (LNAI), vol. 6738, pp. 353–360. Springer, Heidelberg (2011). https://doi.org/10.1007/978-3-642-21869-9_46
31. VanLehn, K.: The behavior of tutoring systems. Int. J. Artif. Intell. Educ. **16**(3), 227–265 (2006)
32. Vygotsky, L.S., Cole, M.: Mind in Society: Development of Higher Psychological Processes. Harvard University Press (1978)
33. Woolf, B.P.: Building Intelligent Interactive Tutors: Student-centered Strategies for Revolutionizing E-learning. Morgan Kaufmann (2010)

Leveraging AI to Support Virtual Students in Intelligent Tutoring Systems

Miguel Arevalillo-Herráez[1,2](✉), Aladdin Ayesh[3], Houman Dario Rezakhanlou-Alarte[1], Pablo Arnau-González[1], Sergi Solera-Monforte[1], and Naeem Ramzan[4]

[1] Departament d'Informàtica, Universitat de València, Valencia, Spain
hourea@alumni.uv.es, {pablo.arnau,sergi.solera}@uv.es
[2] Valencian Graduate School and Research Network of Artificial Intelligence (ValgrAI), Valencia, Spain
miguel.arevalillo@uv.es
[3] School of Natural and Computing Sciences, University of Aberdeen, Aberdeen, Scotland, UK
aladdin.ayesh@abdn.ac.uk
[4] School of Computing, Engineering and Physical Sciences, University of the West of Scotland, Paisley, Scotland, UK
naeem.ramzan@uws.ac.uk

Abstract. Recently presented Large Language Models (LLM) exhibit problem-solving capabilities that can be exploited in educational settings. This paper explores the utilization of LLMs in constructing virtual agents capable of emulating student behavior and engaging with learning platforms. The results obtained by using a modest-sized LLM on an Intelligent Tutoring System for the teaching and learning of word problem-solving validate the feasibility of the approach and its potential applicability to other systems with limited computational resources. In our particular case, the efficacy of the implemented agent in solving word problems varied according to the complexity level of the task, as happens with human users. Success rates ranged from 92% for single-step problems to 14% for relatively complex problems. The potential applications of the presented approach are diverse. They extend from crafting collaborative learning settings in which individual students engage with other synthetic counterparts, to serving as invaluable tools for enhancing teacher training programs.

Keywords: NLU · Conversational Tutoring Systems · Large Language Models

1 Introduction

In a conventional Intelligent Tutoring System (ITS), the system takes the role of a teacher and attempts to provide adaptive instruction to learners, emulating a one-to-one teaching situation. To this end, most ITS include ad-hoc mechanisms

K. Tammets et al. (Eds.): EC-TEL 2025, LNCS 16063, pp. 18–30, 2026.
https://doi.org/10.1007/978-3-032-03870-8_2

that are able to validate the student's input and provide automated feedback [11].

Recent progress in Large Language Models (LLMs) has led to the development of conversational agents capable not only of engaging in natural language interactions but also of applying reasoning to offer solutions to relatively complex and previously unseen problems [17]. These abilities provide the required support to build LLM-based agents that simulate the behaviour of human students.

The potential applications of these agents in the field of computerised learning are manifold. In general, they provide invaluable support in scenarios where access to human students is limited. One practical application relates to the implementation of virtual students that can be integrated into collaborative learning environments to exploit the benefits of this learning method [8]. This approach presents numerous advantages compared to a conventional collaborative setting where multiple human students collaborate to solve a sequence of exercises. First, it eliminates the need to have several students synchronously connected. Second, it enables the system to focus on a single student model to make decisions such as selecting the next activity or determining the optimum level of scaffolding. Third, the agent is one more adaptive component and its behaviour can also be tailored to align with the needs and preferences of the learner.

Another relevant use is to support automated testing, evaluation, and fine-tuning of ITSs. One primary challenge in the design of Intelligent Tutoring Systems (ITS) is the need for thorough testing involving real students. This testing is generally time-consuming and resource-intensive. Additionally, logistical challenges such as coordinating schedules and obtaining consent from participants add further complexity. Mass testing using virtual students can produce valuable metrics that relate to the effectiveness of the instruction. Typical usage examples include comparing the effectiveness of alternative scaffolding strategies or determining the most suitable method for selecting the next activity.

Finally, LLM-based virtual students can be a valuable resource for teacher training. They enable the simulation of diverse classroom scenarios, allowing practicing teachers to refine their instructional techniques, classroom management skills, and ability to address individual student needs.

In this paper, we study and discuss the potential of using LLMs to construct virtual students who are able to seamlessly interact in a computerized environment. To perform this study, we used an already existing ITS to teach arithmetic and algebraic word problem-solving [2]. The results showed that the virtual students were capable of simulating realistic interactions and engaging in dialogues aimed at solving a series of pre-defined exercises.

While this research represents a valuable initial step toward the integration of virtual students in educational systems, its scope remains limited in several key areas. Primarily, the study focuses exclusively on the content of the virtual students' messages, overlooking other critical dimensions of interaction. For instance, it does not address when or under what conditions the virtual student should intervene during the learning process, which is an essential factor for ensuring meaningful and timely support. Additionally, the study does not explore how such interventions might be adapted to different learning contexts or aligned with scaffolding strategies aimed at enhancing student learning outcomes. Consequently, this work should be viewed as a foundational contribution that opens new avenues for future exploration, rather than a comprehensive solution for embedding virtual students into learning environments.

2 Background

Recently proposed Large Language Models (LLM) present new opportunities in education. The largest ones, with several tens of billions of parameters, exhibit surprising capabilities or behaviors that were not specifically programmed, which are generally known as emergent skills [18]. These include the ability to perform specific tasks such as understanding linguistic nuances, making logical inferences, and even generating creative content unexpectedly. Such skills, especially those related to task decomposition into simpler steps, can be leveraged to generate AI-based virtual agents that simulate student behavior. Furthermore, generative models are currently capable of adapting their responses according to specified cues provided as part of the prompt, and this adaptability allows them to simulate specific personality traits [10].

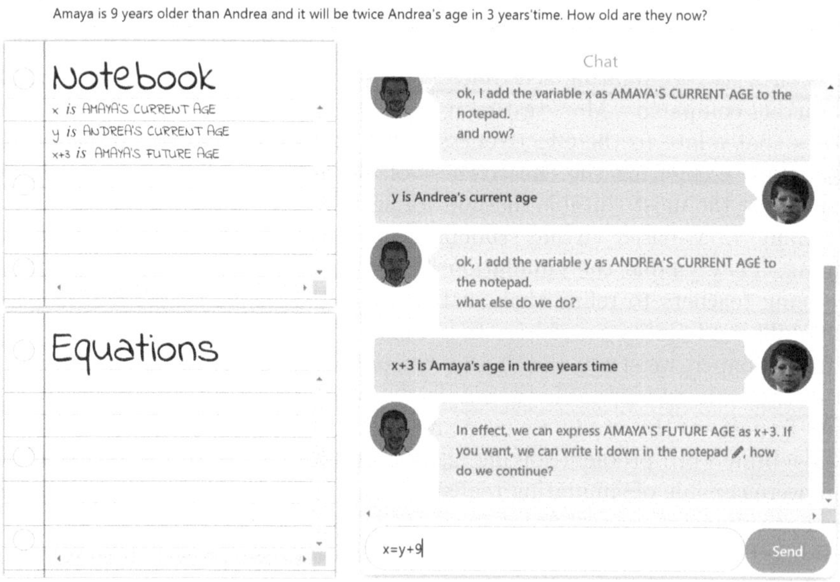

Fig. 1. GUI of HINTS.

In the context of arithmetic problem solving, recent research has shown that even relatively small LLMs with 7 and 13 billion parameters outperform children at solving single-step exercises [4]. Nevertheless, there are important differences between solving a problem and interacting with the machine and possibly other participants. In particular, new abilities get involved. For example, students are expected to interact with the computerized platform by providing consistent next steps, rather than a full solution to the exercise. This implies that success in solving word problems may not always align with the model's capability to behave as a synthetic student.

In this paper, we look at this question by using the conversational version of HINTS (Hypegraph-based Intelligent Tutoring System) [1], an ITS that focuses on the translation stage of the problems statement to a set of equations and is able to supervise students while solving arithmetic and algebraic word problems. Figure 1 shows a screenshot of HINTS' Graphical User Interface (GUI). It contains the problem statement, a notebook section for annotating definitions, an area for annotating pre-set equations, and a conversation-based chat panel. HINTS offers students complete freedom in choosing their solution path, which is composed of a sequence of the 3 different actions they can perform: assign a letter to a quantity, define an unknown quantity based on known ones, or build an equation linking different already known quantities. In addition, the student can ask for help at any time, and the system responds by describing one valid next action aligned with the user's preceding steps.

3 Methodology

3.1 Virtual Student Design

The virtual student module was programmed in python using the Selenium library[1] to automate interaction with the Web browser. Its design is structured around two components (*prompt design* and *response filtering*), which are illustrated in Fig. 2.

The first component builds the prompt by integrating information from the user interface. The data contained in the notebook and equations area is combined with the last system response in the chat area to build the input to the LLM, which is used as a service to provide a next step for the problem currently on the screen. After exhaustive testing, the prompt design that led to the best results was a simple composition as follows. The first line contains the instructions string "Given a problem, variables, and equations, define an equation that has not been defined. Do not solve the problem. Your output must only be an equation. Use '*' as the multiplication operator. Follow the suggestion.". The second line contains the string "The problem:", followed by the problem statement. The third line contains the string "Variables:", followed by the annotations in the notebook, separated by commas. The fourth line contains the string "Equations:", followed by the entries on the equations area of the GUI, also separated by commas. The final line includes the phrase "Suggestion:", followed by previous content suggested by the system. This content reflects the most recent response

[1] https://github.com/robotframework/SeleniumLibrary.

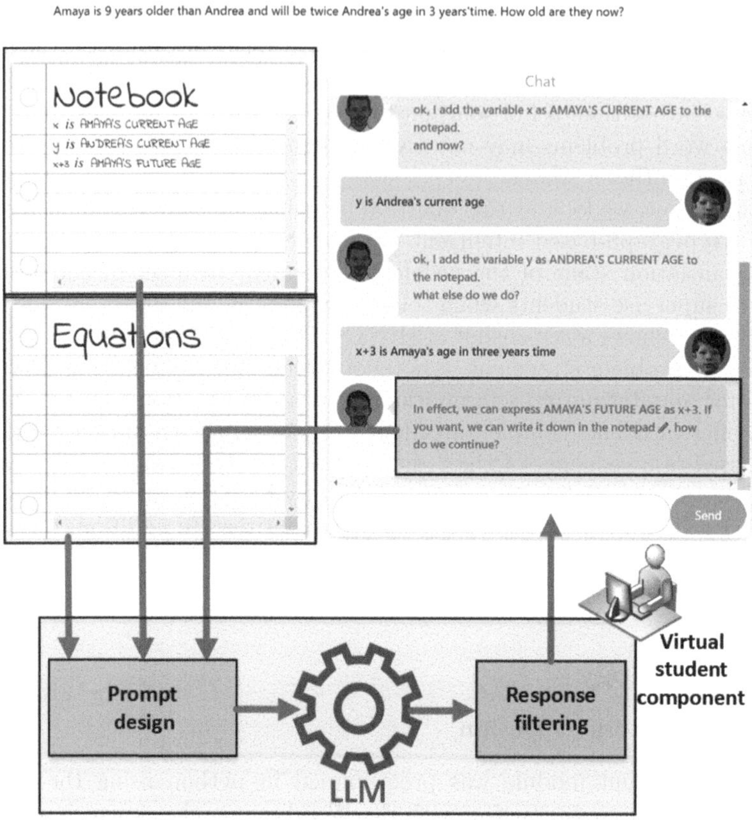

Fig. 2. General structure of the virtual student component.

to a help request and is left blank if a correct action was submitted after. As an example, the prompt generated for the screenshot shown in Fig. 1 would be:

```
Given a problem, variables and equations, define anequation that has not
been defined. Do not solve the problem. Your output must only be an
equation. Use '*' as the multiplication  operator. Follow the suggestion.
The problem: Amaya is 9 years older than Andrea and will be twice
Andrea's age in 3 years' time. How old are they now?
Variables: x is AMAYA'S CURRENT AGE, y is ANDREA'S CURRENT
AGE, x+3 is AMAYA'S FUTURE AGE
Equations:
Suggestion:
```

The resulting prompt is submitted to an instance of the instruct fine-tuned 7 billion-parameter version of Mistral [9]. The selection of this model was based on its open-source nature, deployment simplicity, computational efficiency, and compatibility with our available hardware constraints. Mistral 7B has been reported to outperform Llama2 13B and Llama1 34B on multiple benchmarks [9] and it is readily accessible from Ollama[2], facilitating experimental replication.

The LLM's response format is variable and, in its raw form, usually contains more than one action. The *response filtering* component processes the response provided by LLM to choose a single next step that aligns with the format required by the ITS. This is done by using a pipeline of filters and regular expressions. The first step is converting the answer to unicode, removing formatting and unwanted characters, trimming whitespaces, and transforming it to lowercase. Then, the resulting text is split into a list of lines. Each of these lines is classified as a quantity definition or as a mathematical expression, removing entries that do not adhere to the format of either. Afterward, if the list of quantity definitions is not empty, a random entry from that list is selected. Otherwise, an entry is chosen from the list of mathematical expressions. Was this list also empty, a request for help is made. Selenium is then used to place the filtered answer within the designated chat area and press the "Send" button.

Finally, the system checks whether the problem has been solved. If not, it triggers the *prompt design* component to initiate the process again, iterating until the problem is solved, 10 consecutive help requests are made, or 100 interactions are completed. In the latter two scenarios, the resolution process is terminated and we consider that the virtual student was not able to solve the problem.

Below, we show an illustrative full conversation between the system and a virtual student while solving the word problem "There are 200 m of fabric to make 20 suits that require 3 m of fabric each. How many coats can be produced with the remaining fabric, considering each coat requires 4 m of fabric?"

```
HINTS: Hello, my name is Clippy and I will be your virtual teacher during
       the resolution of this problem.
       Some of the things you can do are:
          - Define a variable in the system, indicating its name and
            description (It must be made up of a single letter)
          - Define an equation
       What do we do now?

VIRTUAL STUDENT: x is the number of coats that can be made

HINTS: Very good! I will add the variable x as NUMBER OF COATS to the
       notepad. And now?

VIRTUAL STUDENT: 200*3 - 20*3 + 4*x = 200*3 - 60 + 4x

HINTS: I don't understand where the number 60 comes from. Don't try to
       calculate, if it is the result of an operation, I prefer that you
       put the operation rather than its result

VIRTUAL STUDENT: I need help
```

[2] https://ollama.ai.

```
HINTS: You can try to define METERS OF FABRIC FOR ALL THE SUITS as a
       function of
           - METERS OF FABRIC PER SUIT (3)
           - NUMBER OF SUITS (20)

VIRTUAL STUDENT: n es meters of fabric for all the suits

HINTS: Very good! I will add the variable n as METERS OF FABRIC FOR ALL
       THE SUITS to the notepad. And now?

VIRTUAL STUDENT: x = (200 - n) / 4

HINTS: Very good, the equation x = (200-n)/4 is correct. I will add it
       to the equations panel.

VIRTUAL STUDENT: n = 3*20

HINTS: Perfect! You have been able to solve the problem by using the
       set of equations
           x = (200 - n) / 4
           n = 3 * 20
```

3.2 Dataset

To evaluate the performance of different LLMs considering different problem complexity, we used a collection of 25 word problems organized in 5 different levels of complexity (5 problems for each level). The problem complexity was measured as a function of the number of unknown quantities required to compute the final solution, which is the same as the minimum number of equations required in an algebraic solution if each unknown quantity was assigned a different letter. Table 1 contains one representative example per complexity level considered.

3.3 Experimental Setting

Our experiments were run on a system equipped with a single NVIDIA RTX 4090 GPU, with 24 GB of memory. To obtain a more reliable evaluation, each of the 25 word problems in the dataset was attempted 10 times. As a result, we had a total of 250 runs. For each attempt, we stored the following information:

- *Result.* Whether the virtual student was able to solve the problem successfully. It may take one of the following three values: *"Successful"*, *"Max number of steps exceeded"* (if the problem remains unsolved after 100 steps), or *"max number of consecutive help requests exceded"* (if there were 10 consecutive help requests). The last two values are considered an abandonment.

Table 1. Representative examples of problem statements for different complexity levels.

complexity level	Word problem statement
1	Peter has 127 books. Anne has 49 less than Peter. How many books does Anne have?
2	Antonio has bought 180 oranges in two bags. One bag has 30 more oranges than the other. How many oranges are there in each bag?
3	John is 15 years old. Tania is 40 years old. How long must it take for Tania's age to be twice John's age?
4	Abigail is four years older than Jonathan. Six years ago, she was twice as old as him. How old is Abigail now?
5	A shopkeeper mixes a bag of premium coffee costing 10e/kg with a bag of lower quality coffee costing 8e/kg. This results in 20 kg of mixed coffee which, in order not to lose money, must be sold at 9.5e/kg. How many kilograms of each type of coffee did he use?

- *Number of iterations.* This number is always less than or equal to 100, as the solving process is aborted when it reaches this value.
- *Number of help requests.* The number of times the virtual agent asked for help along the problem-solving process.

3.4 Evaluation Metrics

The data recorded has been analysed to produce a diversity of performance indicators for the virtual student, namely:

- The proportion of successfully solved problems.
- The number of iterations required in successfully solved problems.
- The average number of help requests for successfully solved problems.

In all cases, performance has been measured relative to the complexity of the problem, to provide data across varied levels of difficulty.

4 Results

Regarding the overall effectiveness of the virtual agent at word problem solving, Fig. 3 illustrates the proportion of successfully solved problems across different complexity levels. As it can be observed, the virtual student was able to solve over 90% of the simplest problems. However, the virtual student's performance decreases rapidly with the problem's complexity. For the most complex category, it only reached a successful result in 7 of the 50 solutions attempted.

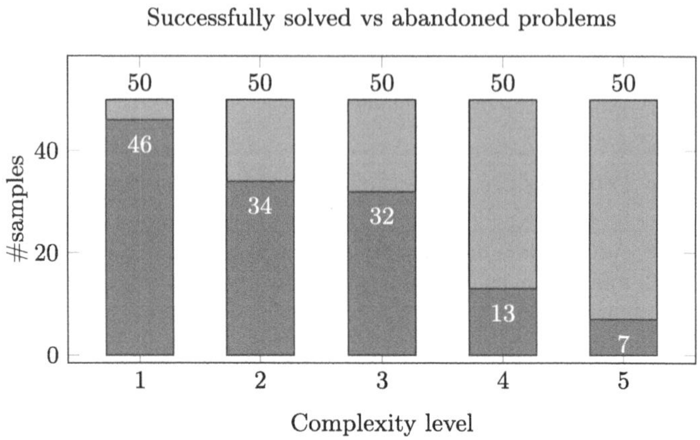

Fig. 3. Successfully solved problems (green bar) vs abandoned problems (red bar), as a function of the complexity level. Green bars represent the number of attempts that ended in a successful solution. Red bars represent the number of failed attempts. (Color figure online)

Focusing on the successfully solved problems, a deeper understanding is achieved by looking at the number of iterations that were required. Figure 4 presents this information in a boxplot. As can be observed, the number of interactions grows exponentially with the problem's complexity, showing a considerably lower performance of the virtual student when solving more complex word problems. This increase is connected to the higher challenge posed by multi-step word problems, which require higher-level thinking skills such as problem decomposition and reasoning.

The majority of problems at complexity level 1 were solved in 1 to 3 inputs from the virtual agent, a result that is aligned with the performance observed for first- to sixth-grade children at solving single-step problems in several well-established previous studies [6,7,12–14,16]. Yet, the number of steps grew fast with the complexity of the problems, and most problems at complexity level 5 required more than 30 interactions to be solved.

Another aspect that needs analysis relates to the number of aids used to solve each problem. HINTS is able to provide adaptive help, and the virtual student makes use of this functionality when no suggestion is returned by the LLM. However, this feature could potentially be exploited to solve problems by gaming the system [3], persistently asking for help and submitting the system's suggestions as inputs. To show that the virtual student does not exhibit such behaviour, Fig. 5 shows the average number of help requests for each complexity level.

By examining this data in conjunction with the information presented in Fig. 4, it can be observed that the number of help requests represents a small fraction of the total inputs. Notably, they exhibit a proportional relationship, with a consistent ratio maintained across all complexity levels, roughly equating to one help request for every five actions.

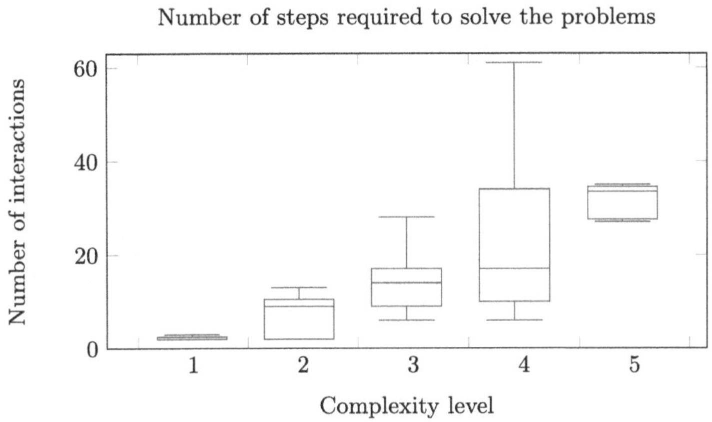

Fig. 4. Boxplots showing the number of steps required in successfully solved problems, as a function of the complexity level. Each box represents the results for the 50 different runs (10 runs × 5 problems). The lower and upper quartile accuracy values are marked by the edges of the box, and the horizontal line that splits the box in two represents the median. The whiskers extend outward from the box, but no further than 1.5 times the interquartile range, to the smallest and largest values.

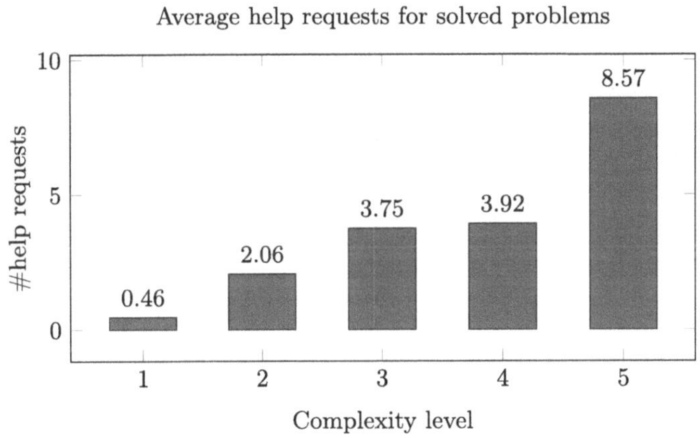

Fig. 5. Barplot showing the average number of help requests in successfully solved problems, as a function of the complexity level.

As a last analysis, we have examined the reasons for abandonment in unsolved problems. On most occasions, the solution process reached a stage where the virtual student could not suggest additional actions, leading to ongoing and unproductive requests for assistance. In a few other cases, the virtual student proposed further actions, but they were incorrect and failed to advance the problem-solving process, exceeding the fixed threshold of 100 maximum iterations. This data is shown in Fig. 6.

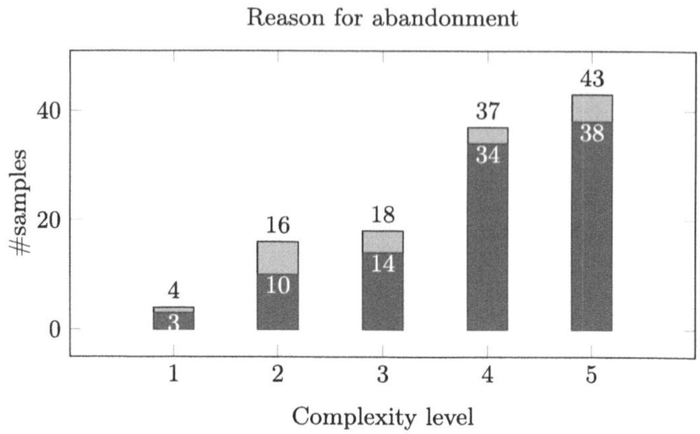

Fig. 6. Reason for abandonment in unsolved problems, as a function of the complexity level. Blue bars represent samples that fell in a help loop. The brown bar represents samples that exceeded 100 iterations. (Color figure online)

5 Discussion and Conclusions

In this paper, we have analyzed the feasibility of using virtual students in a real educational setting. To validate the approach, we have integrated an agent-based implementation into an existing ITS, demonstrating that even LLMs with relatively few parameters exhibit satisfactory performance.

Despite the positive results, our research has focused on systems that do not require expensive specialised hardware, and hence we have used relatively small LLMs. However, the difficulty children experience in solving word problems can vary depending on factors such as their age, cognitive development, mathematical proficiency, and the complexity of the problem itself. Similarly, it is expected that the performance of LLMs varies with the model size, its architecture, and whether domain-specific training or fine-tuning has been applied. Undoubtedly, there is still room for improvement by using larger models and using in-context learning [5] to better fit their particular strengths, as emergent abilities are more prominent in the largest models [19]. With regard to prompt customization, an approach that deserves further exploration relates to the application of few-shot learning strategies [5], including in the prompt a few demonstrations of the task at inference time. About larger models, we find the transformer-based Megatron-Turing Natural Language Generation (MT-NLG) model in between recent developments, with 530 billion parameters [15]. Although the practical applicability of such models within educational systems is often limited because of the hardware needs, a performance analysis is required to clarify the potential of the best-performing LLMs for the proposed task. In this direction, the analysis of the overall performance as the model size grows may be of particular interest, as well as a comparison of smaller models vs quantized versions of larger models.

We should also remark on the additional benefits of using virtual students in some specific contexts. Our experience with LLMs indicates that some of them are prone to errors typically made by students when solving word problems. This aspect is a desirable behavior as it emulates human conduct, and can be exploited in collaborative settings by searching for complementary abilities to those of the student. Additionally, generative models are currently capable of adapting their responses according to specified cues provided as part of the prompt, and this adaptability allows them to simulate personalities. Some features such as politeness, conciseness, or verbosity level, can be assigned according to the student's preferred mode of interaction. In this way, the potential use of virtual students who act as companions gives rise to a new paradigm of collaborative learning in a controlled environment, where agents may even be endowed with socio-affective characteristics that give them distinct personalities. Under this new paradigm, some of the major challenges regarding collaborative environments could be alleviated. In between major benefits, we find that adaptation depends on a single-user model, eliminating the need to build a technological environment that supports synchronous collaboration between users or to coordinate the simultaneous participation of multiple students. Instead, they can interact individually with virtual agents that can be fully customized according to the student's traits.

Acknowledgements. This research has been supported by project PID2023-150960NB-I00, funded by the Spanish Ministry of Science, Innovation and Universities and the European Union; project TED2021-129485B-C42, funded by MCIN/AEI/10.13039/501100011033 and the European Union "NextGenerationEU"/PRTR; project 12215, funded by UK Research and Innovation (UK RI) as a KTP action; project AICO/2023/065, funded by Valencian Regional Government (Spain); and grant CIACIF/2023/344, funded by the Conselleria de Educación, Universidades y Empleo de la Generalitat Valenciana.

References

1. Albornoz-De Luise, R.S., Arevalillo-Herráez, M., Arnau, D.: On using conversational frameworks to support natural language interaction in intelligent tutoring systems. IEEE Trans. Learn. Technol. **16**(5), 722–735 (2023)
2. Arevalillo-Herráez, M., Arnau, D., Marco-Giménez, L.: Domain-specific knowledge representation and inference engine for an intelligent tutoring system. Knowl.-Based Syst. **49**, 97–105 (2013)
3. Arnau, D., Antonio González-Calero, J., Arevalillo-Herráez, M.: Gaming the system: an opportunity to analyse difficulties in arithmetical problem solving. In: Krainer, K., Vondrová, N. (eds.) CERME 9 - Ninth Congress of the European Society for Research in Mathematics Education, pp. 2446–2452. Charles University in Prague, Faculty of Education and ERME, Prague (2015)
4. Arnau-Blasco, J., Arevalillo-Herráez, M., Solera-Monforte, S., Wu, Y.: Using large language models to support teaching and learning of word problem solving in tutoring systems. In: Sifaleras, A., Lin, F. (eds.) ITS 2024. LNCS, vol. 14798, pp. 3–13. Springer, Cham (2024). https://doi.org/10.1007/978-3-031-63028-6_1

5. Brown, T., et al.: Language models are few-shot learners. Adv. Neural. Inf. Process. Syst. **33**, 1877–1901 (2020)
6. Carpenter, T.P., Moser, J.M., Hiebert, J.: Problem structure and first-grade children's initial solution processes for simple addition and subtraction problems. J. Res. Math. Educ. **12**(1), 27–39 (1981)
7. Fischer, J.P.: L'enfant et le comptage. IREM, Strasbourg, a paraitre (1979)
8. Haq, I.U., Anwar, A., Basharat, I., Sultan, K.: Intelligent tutoring supported collaborative learning (ITSCL): a hybrid framework. Int. J. Adv. Comput. Sci. Appl. **11**(8) (2020)
9. Jiang, A.Q., et al.: Mistral 7B (2023)
10. Jiang, G., Xu, M., Zhu, S.C., Han, W., Zhang, C., Zhu, Y.: Evaluating and inducing personality in pre-trained language models. Adv. Neural Inf. Process. Syst. **36** (2024)
11. Mousavinasab, E., Zarifsanaiey, N., Niakan Kalhori, S.R., Rakhshan, M., Keikha, L., Ghazi Saeedi, M.: Intelligent tutoring systems: a systematic review of characteristics, applications, and evaluation methods. Interact. Learn. Environ. **29**(1), 142–163 (2021)
12. Nesher, P.: Levels of description in the analysis of addition and subtraction word problems. In: Carpenter, T.P., Moser, J.M., Romberg, T. (eds.) Addition and Subtraction: Developmental Perspective. Lawrence Erlbaum Associates, Hiilsdale (1981)
13. Nesher, P., Katriel, T.: Two cognitive modes in arithmetic word problem solving. In: Second Annual Meeting of the International Group for the Psychology of Mathematics Education, Osnabruck, West Germany (1978)
14. Nesher, P., Teubal, E.: Verbal cues as an interfering factor in verbal problem solving. Educ. Stud. Math. 41–51 (1975)
15. Smith, S., et al.: Using deepspeed and megatron to train megatron-turing NLG 530b, A large-scale generative language model. CoRR abs/2201.11990 (2022)
16. Steffe, L.P., Johnson, D.C.: Problem-solving performances of first-grade children. J. Res. Math. Educ. **2**(1), 50–64 (1971)
17. Webb, T., Holyoak, K.J., Lu, H.: Emergent analogical reasoning in large language models. Nat. Hum. Behav. **7**(9), 1526–1541 (2023)
18. Wei, J., et al.: Emergent abilities of large language models. Trans. Mach. Learn. Res. **2022** (2022)
19. Zhao, W.X., et al.: A survey of large language models. arXiv preprint arXiv:2303.18223 (2023)

AI-Based Multimodal Biometrics for Detecting Smartphone Distractions: Application to Online Learning

Alvaro Becerra[1](✉), Roberto Daza[1], Ruth Cobos[1], Aythami Morales[1], Mutlu Cukurova[2], and Julian Fierrez[1]

[1] Universidad Autónoma de Madrid, Madrid, Spain
{alvaro.becerra, roberto.daza, ruth.cobos, aythami.morales, julian.fierrez}@uam.es
[2] University College London, London, UK
m.cukurova@ucl.ac.uk

Abstract. This work investigates the use of multimodal biometrics to detect distractions caused by smartphone use during tasks that require sustained attention, with a focus on computer-based online learning. Although the methods are applicable to various domains, such as autonomous driving, we focus on the challenges learners face in maintaining engagement amid internal (e.g. motivation), system-related (e.g., course design) and contextual (e.g., smartphone use) factors. Traditional learning platforms often lack detailed behavioral data, but Multimodal Learning Analytics (MMLA) and biosensors provide new insights into learner attention. We propose an AI-based approach that leverages physiological signals and head pose data to detect phone use. Our results show that single biometric signals, such as brain waves or heart rate, offer limited accuracy, while head pose alone achieves 87%. A multimodal model that combines all signals reaches accuracy 91%, highlighting the benefits of integration. We conclude by discussing the implications and limitations of deploying these models for real-time support in online learning environments.

Keywords: Artificial Intelligence · Biometrics · Biosensors · Learning Analytics · Machine Learning · Multimodal Learning Analytics · Online Learning · Phone

1 Introduction

In recent years, the popularity of online courses has increased exponentially, especially during and after the COVID-19 pandemic [44]. This shift to online education has provided learners with greater flexibility and access to resources. However, it has also introduced several unique challenges. One of the primary difficulties facing learners in these online environments is the lack of direct interaction with instructors [32]. The absence of this personal connection in virtual classrooms can negatively impact the motivation of learners, contributing to a sense of isolation and, in many cases, resulting in higher dropout rates [49].

K. Tammets et al. (Eds.): EC-TEL 2025, LNCS 16063, pp. 31–46, 2026.
https://doi.org/10.1007/978-3-032-03870-8_3

In addition, online learners are particularly vulnerable to distractions that significantly impact their focus and overall learning outcomes. As demonstrated by research, momentary interruptions, even as brief as a few seconds, can significantly increase error rates by disrupting the cognitive processes required to maintain task sequence and continuity [4]. Distractions during online learning sessions are often caused by both external and internal factors, such as environmental disturbances and low levels of engagement, which can reduce concentration and hinder the absorption of valuable information [13].

These distractions may include constant phone notifications, emails, and other external interruptions that are less prevalent in traditional classroom settings. Such distractions are particularly pervasive in online learning environments, where the boundary between academic and non-academic tasks often blurs. Multitasking, such as responding to emails or participating in social networks during learning sessions, significantly reduces cognitive efficiency and impairs information retention, leading to measurable declines in academic performance [14,51]. In addition, passive distractions, such as background noise or household chores, can consume attentional resources and further detract from the learning process [14]. Furthermore, many factors that emanate from the physical learning space, such as the presence of others, the light, or the spatial comfort, also affect online learning [15]. As a result, maintaining concentration and staying on task becomes a major challenge for learners in online education, further complicating the learning process and affecting academic performance.

Understanding, detecting, and predicting when learners become distracted during online learning could be very beneficial, as it would allow to provide personalized feedback to guide them in reviewing content when distractions occur. Several articles have shown that giving general feedback to learners, using only data from their interactions with an online course, improves their performance [12,16,48]. However, relying solely on interactions data has several limitations, so biometric data, biosensors [3], and new online learning platforms [21,38], which incorporate biometrics and behavioral analysis, have emerged, offering a deeper understanding of learners' cognitive, emotional states, and overall behavior. This technology enables the detection of user distraction events more effectively.

Physiological and biometric signals have proven to be highly valuable in understanding the state of the learner, such as cognitive load [19], blinking of the eyes [20], facial expression [22], and pose of the learner [29], among others. These signals are especially valuable in online learning platforms, and when integrated with data from learners' interactions in an online course, they offer significant potential for enhancing predictive models. Ultimately, when these technologies are integrated with the MMLA tools, a more comprehensive insight into the behavior of the learner can be obtained [35].

In this article, our aim is to better understand distractions, particularly distractions from the mobile phone. The main contributions of this paper are:

- The development of various unimodal machine learning approaches for predicting mobile phone usage, using global features within a 40-second window. Each model uses a single signal, such as heart rate, attention, meditation,

EEG waves, or head pose. The results are analyzed to determine which signal provides the highest prediction accuracy.
- The proposal of two new multimodal systems for the detection of phone usage, one of which achieves the accuracy 91%, surpassing unimodal systems.

2 Related Works

AI-based approaches have become essential tools in MMLA, enabling the detection of complex student behaviors. By integrating multimodal data, machine learning algorithms can uncover hidden patterns that can lead to the identification of behaviors such as moments of distraction.

2.1 Multimodal Learning Analytics

Advances in Multimodal Learning Analytics (MMLA) have enabled a deeper understanding of learner behavior by combining data from multiple biosensors and interaction sources. These approaches integrate biometric signals, behavioral tracking, and machine learning models to improve learning outcome predictions, detect attention levels, and identify different events [28].

Biometric and multimodal data collected from various sensors [41] have proven to be highly valuable in gaining deeper insights into learners' interactions and success. [45] demonstrated that the integration of multimodal data streams, such as facial tracking, hand movements, and sensor inputs in real-time, enables the application of supervised machine learning techniques to predict learner outcomes in project-based learning environments. Recent research, for example, [52] showed how data from multiple sensors, such as position trackers, microphones, and heart rate monitors, can be combined to identify clear patterns of learner behavior while students interact and collaborate during learning tasks. Similarly, in [7], data from webcams, microphones, eye trackers, and wearable sensors are used to generate personalized data-based feedback on students' oral presentation skills.

The variables of the students studied the most in MMLA include performance outcomes, attention levels, and behavior detection. For example, in [39], eye tracking data, specifically fixations and saccades, are analyzed to assess the visual attention of learners and predict the tasks they are engaged in. Other studies target specific behavioral events, for example, [33] used videos from front and back webcams, combined with speech analysis, to detect cheating behaviors during online exams using a deep convolutional neural network. Recent studies have also examined the development of MMLA dashboards to visualize and synchronize multimodal data, as well as their integration with Generative AI technologies [8,10].

2.2 Detection of Distraction in Digital Learning Environments

Recent studies have focused on detecting distractions in online learning through the use of biosensors and interaction data [3]. In [42], mouse dynamics [1], including clicks, movements, and idle times, are analyzed to detect moments of distraction in students who interact with online learning platforms. Using techniques such as the DBSCAN clustering algorithm and PrefixSpan sequential pattern mining, the study identifies frequent interaction patterns that precede distraction events, such as browsing social networks instead of focusing on educational material. The results demonstrate an effective segmentation of the students into distinct groups. [13] utilized machine learning to detect student distraction during online learning sessions by extracting facial feature points and postural data from webcam recordings. Their method incorporated OpenFace and GAST-Net to track eye movements, head posture, and skeletal coordinates, achieving greater 90% recall in binary classification tasks. In this classification, the states of the students were classified into "distracted" and "concentration" states. The labeling of distraction events was determined using skin conductance responses (SCRs) obtained from wristband sensors, where distraction was defined as periods in which SCR occurred four or more times per minute. This physiological approach enabled an objective labeling mechanism that eliminates the dependency on self-reported surveys.

Other studies have focused on predicting learner attention levels [18,19,29, 40], as low attention levels can be associated with distractions. For example, [19] proposed a method for estimating attention levels (cognitive load) through an ensemble of facial analysis techniques applied to webcam videos using machine learning. This model used features such as facial expressions, blinking of the eyes, and posture to predict whether the learner's attention was high or low.

Expanding on distraction detection in immersive environments, [6] focused on detecting when learners became distracted while using Virtual Reality for education. They used eye gaze tracking to measure attention shifts in response to external distractions, such as social media notifications, mobile ringtones, and background conversations. Their approach used a CNN-LSTM deep learning model, achieving 89.8% accuracy in classifying distraction into three levels (low, medium, high). Furthermore, they demonstrated that Random Forest models achieved even higher accuracy (98.88%) when incorporating gaze angles and head-tracking data.

2.3 Detection of Phone Usage Events

The detection of phone usage events has been studied, primarily in the context of driver distraction detection. An example is the work by Artan et al. [5], which proposes a computer vision-based method to detect the usage of driver cell phones using a near-infrared (NIR) camera system directed at the front windshield of the vehicle. Their approach consists of two main stages: (1) face localization using a deformable parts model (DPM) and (2) phone usage classification through image classification techniques, such as Fisher vectors, combined with a linear Support Vector Machine (SVM). Their system was tested on a dataset of 1,500 front-view vehicle images, achieving 86.19% accuracy with the best model.

Another relevant study is the work of Seshadri et al. [43], which presents a computer vision-based system to detect driver phone usage using face-view videos. Their method employs the Supervised Descent Method to track 49 facial landmarks and extract regions of interest around the driver's ear and hand. These regions are then classified using the Histogram of Oriented Gradients features combined with the Real AdaBoost, SVM, and Random Forest classifiers. Their system was tested on 13,023 video frames, achieving 93.86% accuracy, outperforming previous approaches.

In addition to computer vision-based systems, Mendez et al. [37], proposed a mobile application that detects phone usage while driving by analyzing accelerometer and GPS data collected directly from the smartphone. Although mobile phone usage detection has been extensively explored in driving safety research, its application in online learning environments has received little attention. One of the few existing studies is that of Becerra et al. [11]. Their work focuses on detecting phone usage events by analyzing head pose deviations captured from webcam images during online learning. Using a semi-supervised approach, the system flags potential phone usage events for further human review and found that head posture changes significantly when learners engage with their phones, deviating from typical online learning behavior.

These findings highlight the growing need for automated phone usage detection in online learning, as mobile phones are a significant source of distraction in digital education settings [50].

3 MultiModal Data Description

For this study, the IMPROVE database was used [17], which provides multimodal and biometric data from learners participating in an online course. This database was selected because of its focus on studying the effects of mobile phone usage on learner performance in online courses.

In this article, out of the 120 IMPROVE learners, we focused on the 40 who use mobile phones and the 40 who do not (phone removed), since the remaining 40 learners belong to a third different experimental condition. Furthermore, of those 80 learners, those whose EEG band data showed more than 5 min of data loss were also excluded (7 from mobile phone users and 7 from nonusers). The 5-minute threshold was chosen because the sessions lasted between 25 and 30 min, which means that such a loss would represent approximately 15% to 20% of the total duration of the session. So, in total, we used 33 learners who used their phones during the learning session (LS) and 33 learners who did not have access to their phones. The learners who used their phones were required to keep them visible during the LS and were instructed to use them upon receiving notifications from messaging or email applications. Each learner received two messages from the researchers, and the periods during which they responded were labeled as phone events. The data used in this study from the IMPROVE database include:

- **Head pose (°):** Roll, yaw, and pitch angles estimated per frame using a head pose detector applied to video captured by a front-facing webcam.
- **Heart rate (bpm):** Heart rate data were collected at a frequency of 1 Hz using a Huawei Watch 2 pulsometer.

- **Attention (0–100), meditation (0–100), and brain waves (dB):** Signals were recorded using a NeuroSky EEG band at a frequency of 1 Hz, which provided five frequency bands: δ (<4 Hz), θ (4–8 Hz), α (8–13 Hz), β (13–30 Hz), and γ (>30 Hz). Using the official NeuroSky SDK, attention (focus level) and meditation (mental calmness) were also obtained.
- **Events data:** Information related to the activities the students performed during the LS, including using the phone, was collected.

Other IMPROVE data, such as keystroke activity [2,46] or eye tracking information, were not included in this study, as students using a mobile phone do not type on the computer or focus on the screen. Furthermore, thanks to the M2LADS system [9,10], all data were processed, synchronized, and labeled according to the activity the learner was doing. These activities include watching videos, reading content, solving assignments, or using a phone.

4 Methods

4.1 Phone Event Detection Models

We propose an AI-based approach to detect phone usage in learners using different physiological signals (attention, meditation, heart rate, and brain waves: alpha, beta, gamma, delta, and theta) and head pose data (roll, yaw, and pitch angles). This approach aims to identify whether a learner used the phone in the last 20 s (W_{phone}) of a 40-second window (W_{all}). A 20-second window was chosen because shorter windows may miss relevant phone usage patterns, while approximately 25% of phone usage events lasted less than 20 s. Therefore, using longer windows would require including post-usage data, which may dilute the physiological signals directly related to the phone interaction. A binary classification is proposed to distinguish between phone use and non-use for each W_{all}. To obtain the datasets, the following protocol was followed:

1. For learners who used the phone, the W_{all} windows contained 20 s before phone use (W_{pre}) and the first 20 s (W_{phone}) during phone use. In cases where the phone use lasted less than 20 s, W_{phone} included post-usage data. The pre-event window W_{pre} was considered useful for detecting changes in physiological signals triggered by phone usage.
2. For learners who did not use the phone, W_{all} were selected during the same activities as those who used the phone, specifically during the second video and while reading code. In this case, W_{all} consists of two 20-second segments (W_{nophone}) representing periods of no phone use.

In total, we obtained 66 samples for mobile phone usage and 66 samples for no mobile phone usage. To predict events of mobile phone usage, we proposed an approach based on global characteristics, which have demonstrated effectiveness in other classification tasks [19,24,36].

Table 1. Description of the global features where velocity is the first derivative of the signal, acceleration is the second, and jerk is the third. The 33 global features are calculated for all input signals $n \in \{1, 2, \ldots, S\}$, with $S = 11$ (see Fig. 1 top).

#	Feature Description	#	Feature Description
g_n^1	Total positive velocity $\sum(v > 0)$	g_n^{18}	Maximum jerk $j_{\max}$
g_n^2	Total negative velocity $\sum(v < 0)$	g_n^{19}	RMS of jerk j_{RMS}
g_n^3	(Location of the first maximum)	g_n^{20}	Location of the maximum absolute jerk
g_n^4	(Location of the second maximum)	g_n^{21}	Location of the maximum jerk
g_n^5	(Location of the third maximum)	g_n^{22}	Number of sign changes in velocity
g_n^6	(Average velocity $v)/\lvert v\rvert_{\max}$	g_n^{23}	$\sum(v > 0)\lvert v\rvert / \sum(v < 0)\lvert v\rvert$
g_n^7	(Average velocity $v)/v_{\max}$	g_n^{24}	$\sum(v > 0) / \sum(v < 0)$
g_n^8	(RMS of velocity $v_{\mathrm{RMS}})/\lvert v\rvert_{\max}$	g_n^{25}	$x_{\max} - x_{\min}$
g_n^9	(Mean of the segment $\overline{x}$)	g_n^{26}	$\overline{v}/(x_{\max} - x_{\min})$
g_n^{10}	(Standard deviation of the segment σ)	g_n^{27}	(Local maxima in segment x)
g_n^{11}	(RMS of acceleration $a_{\mathrm{RMS}})/\lvert a\rvert_{\max}$	g_n^{28}	(Average acceleration $\overline{\lvert a\rvert}$)
g_n^{12}	Median of the segment	g_n^{29}	Maximum of the segment
g_n^{13}	Standard deviation of velocity σ_v	g_n^{30}	Minimum of the segment
g_n^{14}	Standard deviation of acceleration σ_a	g_n^{31}	Skewness of x
g_n^{15}	Jerk $\lvert j\rvert$	g_n^{32}	Kurtosis of x
g_n^{16}	Average jerk	g_n^{33}	Learner's gender
g_n^{17}	Absolute value of the maximum jerk $\lvert j\rvert_{\max}$		

Each W_{all} window was divided into two segments of 20 s. For each 20-second segment and each input signal $n \in \{1, 2, \ldots, S\}$ we calculate a global vector $\mathbf{g}_n$ that includes 33 global features, as indicated in Table 1. The features of the two windows (either $\{\mathbf{g}_n^{\mathrm{pre}}, \mathbf{g}_n^{\mathrm{phone}}\}$ or $\{\mathbf{g}_n^{\mathrm{nophone}}, \mathbf{g}_n^{\mathrm{nophone}}\}$) are combined into a single vector [27], $\mathbf{f}_{\mathrm{cmb}}^{\mathrm{g}} \in \mathbb{R}^{65}$ (the learner's gender was only included once) , which is normalized to $\tilde{\mathbf{f}}_{\mathrm{cmb}}^{\mathrm{g}}$ using the z-score technique [25].

As shown in Fig. 1, we developed one model for each of the input biometric signals. For models using EEG signals and heart rate, two approaches were tested to obtain training data due to the noise present in the signals: using the raw data provided by the devices and using the same data but applying a smoothing window. If the smoothing window was size N, the value at time t was calculated as the average of the previous values N, including the one at t. In this way, different sizes of smoothing windows were compared to determine their impact on signal quality.

Finally, we developed two additional models: one using data from all EEG signals and heart rate, and the other incorporating all multimodal data. For these models, an early concatenation of the individual global features was used to obtain the training vector. Different smoothing window sizes were also compared.

For each model developed, we evaluated two classification algorithms: Random Forest (RF) and Support Vector Machine (SVM), both of which have been widely used and validated in the literature for physiological signal classification tasks [19, 47]. SVMs were trained using linear and Gaussian kernels with a regularization hyperparameter $C = 1$. RFs were trained with 250 trees after testing between 100 and 500 trees and observing no further improvement in performance

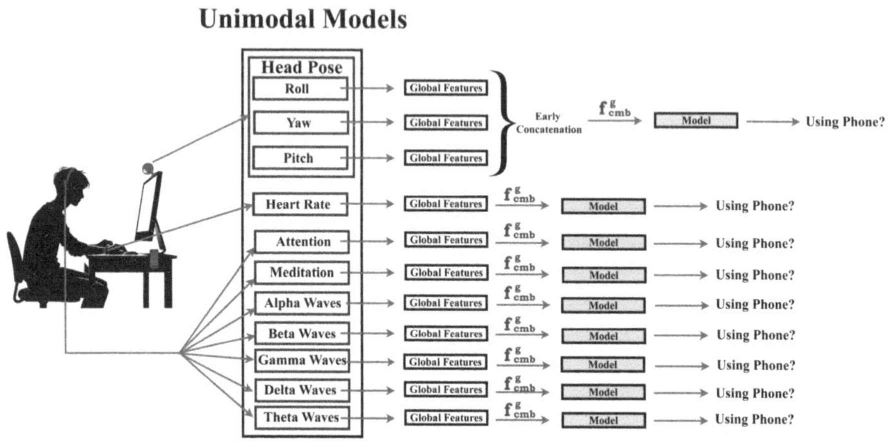

Fig. 1. Outline of the unimodal models. For the EEG signals and heart rate we developed unimodal models using global features (Table 1). For the model that use head pose angles, global features are extracted from roll, yaw and pitch and they are concatenated into a single vector. We also developed two multimodal models: one combining all EEG signals and Heart Rate and another combining all multimodal data.

beyond 250 trees. We applied two techniques for feature selection and dimensionality reduction: SelectKBest and PCA. Thus, we tested RF, SVM with a linear kernel, and SVM with a Gaussian kernel using all features, a subset of features selected with SelectKBest, and PCA with the number of components required to explain 95% of the variance. Furthermore, algorithms were tested with smoothed and unsmoothed data using window sizes (W_{smooth}) of 5, 10, 15, 20, 25, and 30 s.

As the data for each variable consisted of 132 periods - 66 with mobile phone use and 66 without - Leave-One-Out cross-validation was selected at the participant level to maximize the amount of data used for modeling training. In each fold, data from a single learner (comprising two samples) was used as the test set, while the remaining 65 learners (130 samples) were used for training. This strategy ensures that no data from the test subject appear in the training set, avoiding data leakage and providing a more realistic evaluation of model generalization.

5 Results and Discussion

5.1 Performance for Phone Detection Models

Table 2 displays the results for the different models developed. Accuracy was selected as the primary evaluation metric due to the balanced nature of the dataset and the objective of binary classification to detect mobile phone usage. The findings suggest that the use of a single physiological signal leads to poorer model performance. In particular, models based on attention, meditation, alpha

Table 2. Accuracy results and the best models for phone usage detection

Biometric Variable	Best Model	Accuracy (%)
Attention	SVM (linear kernel) with PCA and smoothing window of size 20	64%
Heart Rate (HR)	SVM (Gaussian kernel) with a subset of 40 features and smoothing window of size 5	70%
Meditation	Random Forest with PCA and smoothing window of size 20	61%
Alpha	SVM (Gaussian kernel) with all features and smoothing window of size 20	64%
Beta	Random Forest with all features and without smoothing window	68%
Gamma	Random Forest with all features and smoothing window of size 20	70%
Theta	SVM (linear kernel) with all features and smoothing window of size 30	61%
Delta	SVM (linear kernel) with PCA and smoothing window of size 25	64%
All EEG signals and heart rate (EEG+HR)	Random Forest with all features and smoothing window of size 15	76%
Head Pose (HP)	Random Forest with a subset of 120 features	87%
All EEG signals, heart rate, and head pose (EEG+HR+HP)	Random Forest with a subset of 250 features and smoothing window of size 30	91%

waves, theta waves, and delta waves exhibit the lowest accuracy. In contrast, models that incorporate heart rate, beta waves, and gamma waves perform slightly better, achieving around 70% accuracy. These results indicate that mobile phone usage has a stronger impact on certain physiological signals than others.

However, individual signals were not highly effective in detecting phone usage. By combining all EEG signals with heart rate data (EEG + HR), the model performance improved significantly by 8.57% (McNemar's test, $\chi^2 = 24.45, p < 0.001$), reaching an accuracy of 76%. This highlights that integrating multiple physiological signals offers a more comprehensive and reliable approach to detecting phone usage.

The head pose model (HP) achieved an accuracy of 87%, improved on the best unimodal models by 24.29% (McNemar's test, $\chi^2 = 31.58, p < 0.001$) and outperformed the model combining all EEG signals and heart rate by 14.47% (McNemar's test, $\chi^2 = 21.02, p < 0.001$). This result highlights the importance of head pose data, which often reveal notable changes in posture when interacting with a phone, compared to typical online learning behavior on a computer, making it particularly effective in detecting phone usage [11].

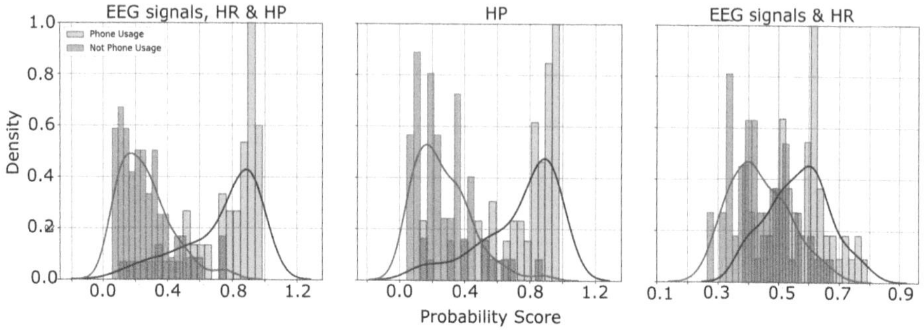

Fig. 2. Probability density distributions of the probability scores obtained with the 3 best models indicated in Table 2.

However, the most effective model was the one that combined all signals (EEG + HR + HP), achieving an accuracy of 91%. This model improved on the head pose model by 4.60% (McNemar's test, $\chi^2 = 7.61, p = 0.0058$), further confirming that integrating signals from multiple sources leads to better predictive outcomes.

It should be noted that most models achieve the best results by smoothing the signals captured from the biosensors. This smoothing helps reduce the noise in the data and utilizes information from a larger set of data, making global features more relevant [19].

Figure 2 illustrates the probability density distributions of the probability scores generated by the three best models: one that combines all EEG signals, heart rate, and head pose (EEG+HR+HP); another using only head pose data (HP); and the third combining all EEG signals with heart rate (EEG+HR). To assess the separation between the two classes, Phone usage and Not Phone usage, we calculated the Kullback-Leibler (KL) divergence. The results showed a KL divergence of 0.22 for the EEG+HR+HP model, a divergence of 0.24 for the HP model and a divergence of 0.04 for the EEG+HR model. These results indicated that the head pose-only model achieved promising class separation performance, even when compared to a multimodal model.

However, the fact that the distributions are somewhat more separated does not necessarily mean that the performance is significantly better or worse (in fact, in terms of accuracy, combining all multimodal data achieves higher performance). In Fig. 3, the ROC curves are displayed for the three models, showing that depending on the threshold, combining all multimodal data or using only the head pose may be the best option. In terms of Area Under the Curve (AUC), combining all multimodal data is slightly better than using only the head pose, but both models performed well overall.

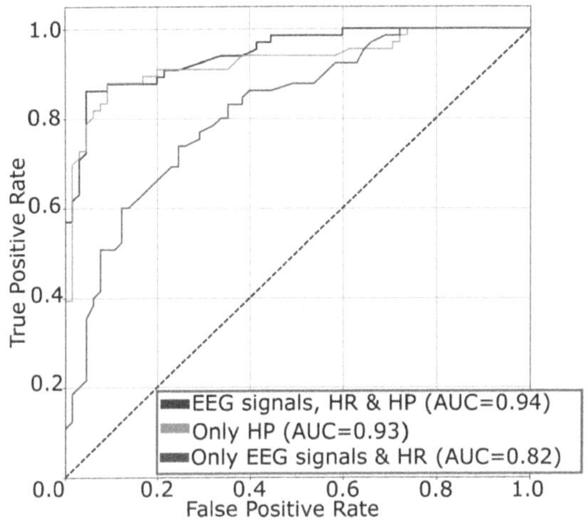

Fig. 3. ROC obtained for the most accurate models indicated in Table 2.

5.2 Practical Implications and Limitations

Although the multimodal model integrating EEG signals, heart rate, and head pose achieved the highest accuracy (91%), it is important to note that the head pose-based model also demonstrated strong performance. This suggests that movement patterns alone provide meaningful insight into phone usage detection.

A key advantage of the head pose model is its practicality for real-world applications. Unlike EEG or heart rate monitoring, which may require specialized and intrusive biosensors [30], estimation of head posture can be performed using standard webcams, making it a more accessible and scalable solution. This opens the door to integration into on-line learning platforms that already track head movements or engagement levels. By incorporating head pose analysis, these platforms could provide real-time feedback to learners, helping them stay focused and minimizing phone-induced distractions.

Given the application limitations of the model that combines all biometric signals, future work could explore estimating these variables through the webcam. If these estimations are reliable, it would be possible to integrate a proxy version of the multimodal model without requiring additional wearable sensors. This approach would not only maintain ease of implementation and user comfort, but would also enhance the generalizability of the models by enabling data collection through more accessible and cost-effective methods. By eliminating the need for expensive biosensors, this solution could facilitate the widespread adoption of distraction detection systems in online learning environments, making advanced analytics available to a broader range of users.

Although the number of samples in the IMPROVE dataset is not exceptionally large (132 instances), it is still considered a relatively substantial dataset within the MMLA field. This study has shown that it is feasible to develop accurate models to detect smartphone usage using multimodal data. As a result, this work provides an empirical basis for future research efforts to scale and refine these models. Subsequent studies may focus on increasing the number of participants to improve the generalizability of the model, potentially relying solely on more accessible modalities such as the estimation of the head pose.

6 Conclusion and Future Work

This article explores the potential of MMLA to enhance the detection of phone usage among learners by using various biometric variables. Several AI-based models were proposed and evaluated to predict when learners use their phones and become distracted during an online course. Specifically, both unimodal models (using individual biometric variables) and multimodal models (combining multiple variables) were developed.

After comparing several algorithms, the results indicate that unimodal models relying on a single EEG signal or heart rate performed significantly worse than the model that integrated all EEG signals and heart rate. The second-best model used head pose data, suggesting that movement patterns provide valuable information about phone usage. However, the highest-performing model incorporated all multimodal data (EEG signals, heart rate, and head pose), achieving an accuracy of 91%. This supports the idea that using multiple biosensors to capture different biometric signals leads to more accurate prediction models. These findings align with previous MMLA research, which highlights the value of multimodality [25, 41] in improving the performance of prediction models on various learning tasks [28, 45].

In future work, we will focus on other distractions, such as browsing or checking emails, and we will aim to develop models that can detect a wider variety of learning events. In addition, we will investigate other indicators that have proven valuable for detecting learner behaviors, such as eyeblink [20], pupil dilation [34], eye gaze patterns [39], typing [2, 46], mouse [1] and touchscreen dynamics [23, 26], among others. Furthermore, we will examine the integration of both local and global features [19] and will attempt to extend this research to face-to-face learning with multiple students in order to develop more general models.

Finally, we plan to explore real-time interventions that notify learners when they are becoming distracted, helping them stay focused, and to evaluate the impact of such interventions on students' learning outcomes. In addition, we will evaluate the effectiveness of these interventions by examining their impact on learners' learning outcomes, including engagement, comprehension, and overall performance. Through this research, we hope to gain a deeper understanding of how personalized feedback can enhance the learning experience in online courses.

Furthermore, the methods developed here are useful in estimating distractions that arise from the undesirable use of smartphones in any monitorable task that requires concentration, not only computer-based online learning. In our future work, we will also explore how our methods apply to areas such as autonomous driving (in which the driver must pay full attention to the road sometimes [31]) or traditional book-and-paper study.

Acknowledgments. Support by projects: Cátedra ENIA UAM-VERIDAS en IA Responsable (NextGenerationEU PRTR TSI-100927-2023-2), HumanCAIC (TED2021-131787B-I00 MICINN) and SNOLA (RED2022-134284-T).

References

1. Acien, A., Morales, A., et al.: BeCAPTCHA-mouse: synthetic mouse trajectories and improved bot detection. Pattern Recogn. **127**, 108643 (2022)
2. Acien, A., Morales, A., et al.: TypeNet: Deep learning keystroke biometrics. IEEE Trans. Biomet. Behav. Identity Sci. **4**(1), 57–70 (2022)
3. Acien, A., et al.: Smartphone sensors for modeling HCI: general outlook and research datasets for user authentication. In: Proceedings of the IEEE COMPSAC (2020)
4. Altmann, E.M., Trafton, J.G., Hambrick, D.Z.: Momentary interruptions can derail the train of thought. J. Exp. Psychol.: Gener. **143**(1), 215 (2014)
5. Artan, Y., Bulan, O., Loce, R.P., Paul, P.: Driver cell phone usage detection from HOV/HOT NIR images. In: Proceedings of the IEEE Conference on Computer Vision and Pattern Recognition Workshops, pp. 225–230 (2014)
6. Asish, S.M., Kulshreshth, A.K., Borst, C.W.: Detecting distracted students in educational VR environments using machine learning on eye gaze data. Comput. Graph. **109**, 75–87 (2022)
7. Becerra, A., Andres, D., Villegas, P., Daza, R., Cobos, R.: MOSAIC-F: a framework for enhancing students' oral presentation skills through personalized feedback. arXiv preprint arXiv:2506.08634 (2025)
8. Becerra, A., Cobos, R.: Enhancing the professional development of engineering students through an AI-Based Collaborative Feedback System. In: 2025 IEEE Global Engineering Education Conference (EDUCON), pp. 1–9. IEEE (2025)
9. Becerra, A., Daza, R., Cobos, R., Morales, A., Cukurova, M., Fierrez, J.: M2LADS: a system for generating multimodal learning analytics dashboards. In: Proceedings of the COMPSAC, pp. 1564–1569. IEEE (2023)
10. Becerra, A., Daza, R., Cobos, R., et al.: M2LADS demo: a system for generating multimodal learning analytics dashboards. In: Proceedings of AAAI Workshop on Innovation and Responsibility for AI-Supported Education (iRAISE) (2025)
11. Becerra, A., Irigoyen, J., Daza, R., Cobos, R., et al.: Biometrics and behavior analysis for detecting distractions in E-learning. In: Proceedings of the SIIE. IEEE (2024)
12. Becerra, A., Mohseni, Z., Sanz, J., Cobos, R.: A generative AI-based personalized guidance tool for enhancing the feedback to MOOC learners. In: 2024 IEEE Global Engineering Education Conference (EDUCON), pp. 1–8. IEEE (2024)
13. Betto, I., Hatano, R., Nishiyama, H.: Distraction detection of lectures in E-learning using machine learning based on human facial features and postural information. Artif. Life Robot. **28**(1), 166–174 (2023)
14. Blasiman, R.N., Larabee, D., Fabry, D.: Distracted students: a comparison of multiple types of distractions on learning in online lectures. Scholarsh. Teach. Learn. Psychol. **4**(4), 222 (2018)
15. Ciordas-Hertel, G.P., Rödling, S., Schneider, J., Di Mitri, D., Weidlich, J., Drachsler, H.: Mobile sensing with smart wearables of the physical context of distance learning students to consider its effects on learning. Sensors **21**(19), 6649 (2021)

16. Cobos, R.: Self-regulated learning and active feedback of MOOC learners supported by the intervention strategy of a learning analytics system. Electronics **12**, 3368 (2023)
17. Daza, R., Becerra, A., Cobos, R., Fierrez, J., Morales, A.: A multimodal dataset for understanding the impact of mobile phones on remote online virtual education. Sci. Data 12, 1332 (2025). https://doi.org/10.1038/s41597-025-05681-7
18. Daza, R., DeAlcala, D., Morales, A., Tolosana, R., Cobos, R., Fierrez, J.: ALEBk: feasibility study of attention level estimation via blink detection applied to E-learning. In: Proceedings of the AAAI Workshop on Artificial Intelligence for Education (2022)
19. Daza, R., Gomez, L.F., Fierrez, J., Morales, A., Tolosana, R., Ortega-Garcia, J.: DeepFace-attention: multimodal face biometrics for attention estimation with application to E-learning. IEEE Access **12**, 111343–111359 (2024)
20. Daza, R., Morales, A., Fierrez, J., Tolosana, R., Vera-Rodriguez, R.: mEBAL2 database and benchmark: image-based multispectral eyeblink detection. Pattern Recogn. Lett. **182**, 83–89 (2024)
21. Daza, R., Morales, A., Tolosana, R., Gomez, L.F., Fierrez, J., Ortega-Garcia, J.: edBB-demo: biometrics and behavior analysis for online educational platforms. In: Proceedings of the AAAI Conference on Artificial Intelligence, pp. 16422–16424 (2023)
22. Daza, R., Shengkai, L., Morales, A., Fierrez, J., Nagao, K.: SMARTe-VR: student monitoring and adaptive response technology for e-learning in virtual reality. In: Proceedings of the AAAI Workshop on Artificial Intelligence for Education (2025)
23. Delgado-Santos, P., Tolosana, R., et al.: SwipeFormer: transformers for mobile touchscreen biometrics. Expert Syst. Appl. **237**, 121537 (2024)
24. Fierrez-Aguilar, J., Nanni, L., Lopez-Peñalba, J., Ortega-Garcia, J., Maltoni, D.: An on-line signature verification system based on fusion of local and global information. In: Kanade, T., Jain, A., Ratha, N.K. (eds.) AVBPA 2005. LNCS, vol. 3546, pp. 523–532. Springer, Heidelberg (2005). https://doi.org/10.1007/11527923_54
25. Fierrez, J., et al.: Target dependent score normalization techniques and their application to signature verification. IEEE Trans. SMC-C **35**(3), 418–425 (2005)
26. Fierrez, J., et al.: Benchmarking touchscreen biometrics for mobile authentication. IEEE Trans. Inf. Forensics Secur. **13**(11), 2720–2733 (2018)
27. Fierrez, J., Morales, A., et al.: Multiple classifiers in biometrics. Part 1: fundamentals and review. Inf. Fusion **44**, 57–64 (2018)
28. Giannakos, M.N., Sharma, K., Pappas, I.O., Kostakos, V., Velloso, E.: Multimodal Data as a Means to Understand the Learning Experience. Int. J. Inf. Manage. **48**, 108–119 (2019)
29. Goldberg, P., et al.: Attentive or not? Toward a machine learning approach to assessing students visible engagement in classroom instruction. Educ. Psychol. Rev. **33**, 27–49 (2021)
30. Hernandez-Ortega, J., Fierrez, J., et al.: A comparative evaluation of heart rate estimation methods using face videos. In: Proceedings of IEEE COMPSAC (2020)
31. Hernandez-Ortega, J., Nagae, S., Fierrez, J., Morales, A.: Quality-based pulse estimation from NIR face video with application to driver monitoring. In: Morales, A., Fierrez, J., Sánchez, J.S., Ribeiro, B. (eds.) IbPRIA 2019. LNCS, vol. 11868, pp. 108–119. Springer, Cham (2019). https://doi.org/10.1007/978-3-030-31321-0_10
32. Iraj, H., Fudge, A., Faulkner, M., Pardo, A., Kovanović, V.: Understanding students engagement with personalised feedback messages. In: LAK 2020 Proceedings, pp. 438–447. ACM (2020)

33. Kaddoura, S., Gumaei, A.: Towards effective and efficient online exam systems using deep learning-based cheating detection approach. Intelli. Syst. Appl. **16**, 200153 (2022)
34. Krejtz, K., Duchowski, A.T., Niedzielska, A., Biele, C., Krejtz, I.: Eye tracking cognitive load using pupil diameter and microsaccades with fixed gaze. PLoS ONE **13**, 1–23 (2018)
35. Mangaroska, K., Martinez-Maldonado, R., Vesin, B., Gašević, D.: Challenges and opportunities of multimodal data in human learning: the computer science students' perspective. J. Comput. Assist. Learn. **37**(4), 1030–1047 (2021)
36. Martinez-Diaz, M., Fierrez, J., Krish, R.P., Galbally, J.: Mobile signature verification: feature robustness and performance comparison. IET Biomet. **3**(4), 267–277 (2014)
37. Mendez, E., Ortiz, A., Ponce, P., et al.: Mobile phone usage detection by ANN trained with a metaheuristic algorithm. Sensors **19**(14), 3110 (2019)
38. Morales, A., Fierrez, J.: Keystroke biometrics for student authentication: a case study. In: Proceedings of 20th Annual Conf. on Innovation and Technology in Computer Science Education, ITiCSE. ACM (2015)
39. Navarro, M., Becerra, A., Daza, R., Cobos, R., et al.: VAAD: visual attention analysis dashboard applied to e-learning. In: Proceedings of the SIIE. IEEE (2024)
40. Peng, S., Chen, L., Gao, C., Tong, R.J.: Predicting students' attention level with interpretable facial and head dynamic features in an online tutoring system. In: Proceedings of the AAAI Conference on Artificial Intelligence, pp. 13895–13896 (2020)
41. Pena, A., et al.: Human-centric multimodal machine learning: Recent advances and testbed on AI-based recruitment. SN Comput. Sci. **4**(5), 434 (2023)
42. Rodríguez, A.O., Riaño, M.A., García, P.A., Marín, C.E.: Application of learning analytics for sequential patterns detection associated with moments of distraction in students in E-learning platforms. Comput. Appl. Eng. Educ. **32**(1), e22682 (2024)
43. Seshadri, K., Juefei-Xu, F., Pal, D.K., Savvides, M., Thor, C.P.: Driver cell phone usage detection on strategic highway research program (SHRP2) face view videos. In: Proceedings of the CVPR Workshops, pp. 35–43 (2015)
44. Sharin, A.N.: E-learning during COVID-19: a review of literature. J. Pengajian Media Malay. **23**(1), 15–28 (2021)
45. Spikol, D., Ruffaldi, E., Dabisias, G., Cukurova, M.: Supervised machine learning in multimodal learning analytics for estimating success in project-based learning. J. Comput. Assist. Learn. **34**(4), 366–377 (2018)
46. Stragapede, G., Vera-Rodriguez, R., et al.: KVC-onGoing: keystroke verification challenge. Pattern Recogn. **161**, 111287 (2025)
47. Tatar, A.B.: Biometric identification system using EEG signals. Neural Comput. Appl. **35**(1), 1009–1023 (2023)
48. Topali, P., Cobos, R., Agirre-Uribarren, U., Martínez-Monés, A., Villagrá-Sobrino, S.: Instructor in action: co-design and evaluation of human-centred LA-informed feedback in MOOCs. J. Comput. Assist. Learn. (2024)
49. Topali, P., Ortega-Arranz, A., Er, E., Martínez-Monés, A., Villagrá-Sobrino, S.L., Dimitriadis, Y.: Exploring the problems experienced by learners in a mooc implementing active learning pedagogies. In: Calise, M., Delgado Kloos, C., Reich, J., Ruiperez-Valiente, J., Wirsing, M. (eds.) EMOOCs 2019. LNCS, vol. 11475, pp. 81–90. Springer, Cham (2019). https://doi.org/10.1007/978-3-030-19875-6_10

50. Wang, C.: Comprehensively summarizing what distracts students from online learning: a literature review. Hum. Behav. Emerg. Technol. **2022**(1), 1483531 (2022)
51. Winter, J., Cotton, D., Gavin, J., Yorke, J.D.: Effective E-learning? Multi-tasking, distractions and boundary management by graduate students in an online environment. ALT-J **18**(1), 71–83 (2010)
52. Yan, L., Gasevic, D., Echeverria, V., Jin, Y., Zhao, L., Martinez-Maldonado, R.: From complexity to parsimony: integrating latent class analysis to uncover multimodal learning patterns in collaborative learning. In: Proceedings of the 15th International Learning Analytics and Knowledge Conference, pp. 70–81 (2025)

Detecting LLM-Generated Short Answers and Effects on Learner Performance

Shambhavi Bhushan[1(✉)], Danielle R. Thomas[1(✉)], Conrad Borchers[1(✉)], Isha Raghuvanshi[1], Ralph Abboud[2], Erin Gatz[1], Shivang Gupta[1], and Kenneth R. Koedinger[1]

[1] Carnegie Mellon University, Pittsburgh, USA
{shambhab,drthomas,cborchers,iraghuva}@cmu.edu,
{egatz,shivangg,koedinger}@andrew.cmu.edu
[2] Learning Engineering Virtual Institute, Oxford, UK
rabboud@levimath.org

Abstract. The increasing availability of large language models (LLMs) has raised concerns about their potential misuse in online learning. While tools for detecting LLM-generated text exist and are widely used by researchers and educators, their reliability varies. Few studies have compared the accuracy of detection methods, defined criteria to identify content generated by LLM, or evaluated the effect on learner performance from LLM misuse within learning. In this study, we define LLM-generated text within open responses as those produced by any LLM without paraphrasing or refinement, as evaluated by human coders. We then fine-tune GPT-4o to detect LLM-generated responses and assess the impact on learning from LLM misuse. We find that our fine-tuned LLM outperforms the existing AI detection tool GPTZero, achieving an accuracy of 80% and an F1 score of 0.78, compared to GPTZero's accuracy of 70% and macro F1 score of 0.50, demonstrating superior performance in detecting LLM-generated responses. We also find that learners suspected of LLM misuse in the open response question were more than twice as likely to correctly answer the corresponding posttest MCQ, suggesting potential misuse across both question types and indicating a bypass of the learning process. We pave the way for future work by demonstrating a structured, code-based approach to improve LLM-generated response detection and propose using auxiliary statistical indicators such as unusually high assessment scores on related tasks, readability scores, and response duration. In support of open science, we contribute data and code to support the fine-tuning of similar models for similar use cases.

Keywords: Large language models · AI detection · Online learning

1 Introduction and Related Work

Recent advancements in generative AI, particularly large language models (LLMs), have shown exceptional performance on tasks such as answering questions and writing [16,21]. However, their impressive capability to generate

K. Tammets et al. (Eds.): EC-TEL 2025, LNCS 16063, pp. 47–60, 2026.
https://doi.org/10.1007/978-3-032-03870-8_4

human-like text raises concerns about misuse and academic integrity, especially in online and self-paced learning environments where supervision is limited [29,32]. Existing detection tools struggle to reliably distinguish between human-authored and LLM-generated responses [7]. In addition, little work exists on the pedagogical ramifications of LLM misuse, such as bypassing cognition or cheating in online assessments [35]. In contrast, misuse of instructional support in traditional technology-enhanced learning contexts, such as tutoring systems, has been reliably linked to lower learning outcomes [23,25].

In response to the ongoing challenge of distinguishing LLM-generated content, researchers have developed various detection strategies and models. Previous studies highlight that ChatGPT-generated responses often follow stylized, formulaic patterns, similar to listicles or PowerPoint-style structures with brief statements supported by one to three sentences [2,15]. Tools like GPTZero analyze linguistic patterns, perplexity, and burstiness to identify LLM-generated text [31]. However, these models, designed in controlled settings, often exhibit inconsistencies and high false positive rates in real-world applications [11]. An additional challenge also arises from the use of humanizing or paraphrasing tools, which can alter LLM-generated content to make it more human-like, effectively bypassing traditional detection methods [1,10]. While this remains a significant concern in high-stakes assessments, in the context of this study, low-stakes, online training with non-evaluative, self-paced micro-lessons, there is minimal incentive for participants to invest the effort or resources needed to use paraphrasing tools, as these lessons do not involve formal assessments or performance consequences.

This study proposes a structured codebook-based annotation process to systematically identify LLM-generated content in educational settings, generating human-verified training data to fine-tune LLM detection models. Unlike existing classifiers such as GPTZero, OpenAI's AI Text Classifier, and non-causal models like RoBERTa, which struggle with short responses (less than 100 words) [20,31], our fine-tuned model incorporates domain-specific datasets to enhance accuracy. While previous research explores model fine-tuning for specialized applications [3], limited work focuses on educational contexts, particularly short-answer responses in online learning. Additionally, there is limited research on simpler, transparent techniques based on stylometry, which can serve as a crucial baseline [24].

Building on this approach, this study introduces several key contributions to LLM-generated text detection in educational settings. First, it provides a direct comparison between GPTZero and a fine-tuned GPT model, quantifying the performance gap and demonstrating the advantages of human-verified training data. It also compares these models against a stylometric approach open-source, based logistic regression model. Second, this study extends the detection of LLM-generated content to adult tutors in low-stakes self-paced training contexts, an underexplored domain. For purposes of this work, tutor is synonymous with learner. Third, it examines how LLM-generated responses affect learning outcomes, addressing concerns about LLM reliance fostering "metacognitive laziness" [12] and reducing learner engagement [35]. By focusing on both detection and learning effects, this study aims to enhance LLM text detection reliability while providing insights into the broader impact of AI-assisted learning. To achieve this, we address the following research questions:

RQ1: Can fine-tuned models be an effective solution for LLM-generated text detection of short-form responses in online lessons?
RQ2: How does learner performance compare between learners who have authentically produced their own responses and those who are identified of using LLM tools?

The remainder of this paper includes Sect. 2 which details our methodology, including the participants and lesson context, the development of our annotation rubric for LLM-generated text, and the fine-tuning process for our GPT-4o model and the baseline models used for comparison. Section 3 presents the results, directly addressing the research questions by comparing the detection performance of the models and analyzing the differences in learning outcomes. Finally, Sect. 4 discusses the implications of our findings, acknowledges the study's limitations, and proposes directions for future work.

2 Method

2.1 Participants, Setting and Lesson

This study analyzed responses from 534 college students employed as tutors who completed the *Using Motivational Strategies* lesson. The lesson was delivered through an online platform where learners entered their responses in an open-text box or selected an MCQ option based on the condition assigned. The lesson was developed in collaboration with tutor supervisors and a university research team specializing in learning sciences and required the learners to analyze student interactions, predict the best response, and justify their reasoning.

While typical responses in such micro-lessons are relatively short, this lesson, *Using Motivational Strategies lesson* exhibited a noticeable trend: responses were often longer, well-structured, and stylistically uniform, raising concerns about the use of LLMs. To investigate this, two experienced researchers manually coded 1400+ responses to identify LLM-generated versus human-authored responses, creating a labeled dataset for fine-tuning and evaluating the GPT-4o model. The dataset, codes, annotation rubric, and lesson content are located in the GitHub.[1]

2.2 LLM-Generated and Human-Authored Response Rubric

To establish a reliable dataset, two researchers manually coded 1,635 responses using an annotation rubric based on learner sourced data and prior research on LLM-generated text detection research. Responses were labeled as LLM-generated (1) or human-authored (0). Responses in which there was no consensus between the two coders were labeled as uncertain (0.5). The inter-rater

[1] https://github.com/shambhavib20/AI-Detection.

reliability (IRR) was 0.64 and 0.68 for LLM-generated and human-authored responses, respectively. This moderate agreement is due to the intentional inclusion of ambiguous cases. These cases helped assess the model's ability to handle edge cases rather than artificially inflate accuracy by limiting the dataset to clear-cut examples.

The lessons analyzed in this study are designed to be short (5–6 minutes) and low-stakes. Since paraphrasing tools are typically used to avoid plagiarism, improve clarity, or substitute synonyms and simpler sentences [8], none of which are required in these lessons, the likelihood of learners using such tools is minimal. We hypothesize that if paraphrasing tools were used, these instances would likely manifest as uncertain or edge cases as the human-authored and LLM-generated responses showed clear evidence of authorship, as elaborated in the annotation rubric.

The lesson content involves open-ended, scenario-based learning rather than objective math problems. Basing the ground truth on human judgment allows contextual understanding of tone and intent that automated tools may miss. Research has also found that uncertainty in human decisions leads to better generalizability and error handling in models trained on human-labeled data [26]. To tackle variation in judgments, a comprehensive annotation rubric was developed and applied consistently. Table 2 displays learner-sourced examples of open responses and coding rationale to determine what constitutes LLM-generated or human-authored [2,13,17,22] (Table 1).

Table 1. Sample size (N) and inter-rater reliability for labels, as measured in Cohen's κ.

Label	Description	N	IRR
0	Human-authored	506	0.678
0.5	Uncertain	230	–[a]
1	LLM-generated	899	0.636

[a] The 0.5 label has no IRR value because it was assigned to responses where raters disagreed, indicating no consistent agreement.

2.3 Finetuning OpenAI's GPT-4o

Fine-tuning was conducted via OpenAI's API, training GPT-4o on labeled learner responses to distinguish LLM-generated and human-authored content based on patterns in structure, length, and tone. The dataset was split 80:20 for training and testing, with the split conducted at the learner level rather than the response level to avoid data leakage. Responses from 434 out of 543 students

Table 2. Learner-sourced examples of LLM-generated and human-authored open responses with coding rationale.

Learner-Sourced Open Response Examples	Coding Rationale
LLM-Generated Content	
"The article emphasizes the significance of adjusting task difficulty to improve student learning and engagement. It suggests that tasks should be tailored to students' skill levels, providing clear instructions, visual aids, and personalized support... [continues for 80 more words]"	Lengthy response that is unrelated to the lesson theme, very well-written and punctuated
"Positive Reinforcement: Explicitly acknowledges and praises Kevin's achievement, which is crucial for motivation. Creates a positive association... Builds Relationship: It opens a space for a casual conversation about a topic Kevin enjoys. Strengthens the teacher-student bond, fostering a more positive..."	Lengthy and formatted response with bullets
"Carla, let's work together to complete the rest of your assignment. Once completed, you can explain to me how you make your scarves like we discussed earlier"	Inverted commas ("") at start or end of response
"Hey Carla, I know math can be tough...", "Carla, I know math can be tough...", "Carla, I know math can be challenging...", "Carla, I know math can be overwhelming..."	Similarly structured responses
Human-Authored Content	
"The approach leverages Kevin's passion for baseball to create a compelling connection between his math work and his interests. Personal Connection Goal Setting Positive Reinforcement Encouragement and Support Overall, this approach ties the task to something Kevin values..."	Improper capitalization
"It makes the stdnut want to work in order to receive the reward"	Word misspelling
"Depending on the topic, I may change the initial practice problems we work on to fit her interests"	Humanized response using 'I'
"Will motivate him by encouraging that you can do this math lesson also"	Incomplete sentences and casual tone
Uncertain	
"This message connects his love for sports to his math work, making the learning process more engaging and motivating by framing it as a form of practice and improvement, just like baseball"	Formal but not complex
"The approach I chose works best because it praises Kevin for his hard work and connects to his love for baseball. By rewarding him with a chat about baseball, it makes him feel good and keeps him motivated to do well in math"	Use of'I' but structured similar to typical LLM-generated responses
"Hey Carla, how is your day going? Did you come up with a new design for your scarves? All your previous designs are beautiful, can I look at the new one? We can work on the assignment and then you can show me your scarf ideas"	Structured and formal response, but conversational

were allocated to the training set (1,302 responses), while the remaining 109 students formed the test set (333 responses).

To assess generalizability, the fine-tuned model was evaluated on two separate test sets: (1) the in-domain test set of 333 responses from the same lesson (*Using Motivational Strategies*) and (2) an out-of-domain test set comprising 150 responses from six additional lessons on the platform. This out-of-domain test set on novel lessons aims at testing the generalizability of our procedure to different content in the same instructional context. For classification of these responses, the fine-tuned model was queried using a prompt aligned with the human annotation rubric. Model predictions were then compared against ground truth labels to assess effectiveness in detecting LLM-generated content.

We chose to fine-tune GPT-4o for several key reasons. First, fine-tuning allows the model to learn from the specific lesson context, helping the model distinguish authentic from LLM-generated responses within the scope of the lesson or subject area [18]. Second, by fine-tuning the model on data from similar educational contexts, meaning our learner population, it gains insights into what is expected in real student responses, whereas generic AI detectors may not be trained on such domain-specific data. Finally, fine-tuning provides flexibility: if the model makes mistakes or if additional context is required, we can adjust and retrain the model to improve its performance, which is crucial in the educational domain where accuracy is essential.

2.4 Baseline Models for Comparison

To evaluate the performance of our fine-tuned GPT-4o model, we compared it against two distinct models: GPTZero and a traditional open-source stylometric classifier.

Leveraging GPTZero, a widely used commercial AI detection tool we evaluated its performance on our in-domain test set through the GPTZero API and recorded its classifications (AI, Human, or Mixed) for comparison. For transparency and a reproducible baseline, we developed a stylometric classifier using scikit-learn and writing style features based on the annotation rubric (Table 2). This writing style included a set of 13 features, including, average word length, sentence length, readability scores, punctuation, text formatting, and common human and LLM text markers. We tested the standard classifiers, Logistic Regression and Random Forest, and reported the best cross-validated performance.

2.5 Differences in Learning Performance

While knowing suspected LLM use is insightful, we aimed to investigate what differentiated students flagged as LLM misusers from those who were not. To examine the relationship between suspected LLM use and posttest performance, we estimated a mixed-effects logistic regression model [6]. Each open-response predict question in the lesson was followed by a multiple-choice question (MCQ), allowing for an analysis of item correspondence. The model estimated the likelihood of answering the MCQ correctly when the corresponding open-response question was flagged as LLM-generated by our detection model. A disproportionate increase in MCQ accuracy following LLM-generated responses would suggest reliance on LLMs for both answers, raising concerns about assessment validity and learning. The model included suspected LLM use as a fixed effect and students as a random intercept to account for student-level variation in performance and repeated observations per student [6]. Odds ratios and 95% confidence intervals were estimated using the lme4 package in R [5], with marginal R^2 used to assess the variance explained by fixed effects.

3 Results and Discussion

3.1 RQ1: Can Fine-Tuned Models Effectively Detect LLM-Generated Responses?

The fine-tuned model demonstrated strong performance in detecting LLM-generated responses within the *Using Motivational Strategies* lesson, achieving an F1 score of 86% and an overall accuracy of 80%, outperforming GPTZero, which had an accuracy of 70%. The F1 average score for the fine-tuned model on the in-domain test set was 0.78 (weighted), indicating strong performance, particularly for detecting LLM-generated and human-authored responses. In comparison, GPTZero's macro average F1 score of 0.50 and weighted average of 0.64 revealed significant performance gaps, especially in handling ambiguous responses. Both models struggled with uncertain cases, but GPTZero's F1 score of 0.00 for these cases highlights its difficulty in handling edge cases, misclassifying all instances[2]. Table 3 and Table 5 presents the performance metrics, while Fig. 1 displays the confusion matrices for both models, illustrating GPTZero's difficulty with ambiguous cases. This highlights the limitations of general-purpose AI detectors like GPTZero which are sensitive to identifying both, LLM-generated and human-authored content with similar accuracies [19]. An analysis of the confusion matrices for the 'Uncertain' class reveals a similar pattern of overestimating LLM-generation of content. The fine-tuned model misclassified 'Uncertain' responses as LLM-generated in 28 instances and human-authored in 10 cases, while GPTZero, misclassified 86 'Uncertain' responses as LLM-generated. This suggests that both systems suspect LLM-authorship for content when the content or signals are ambiguous.

To account for generalizability across other lessons, we found that our fine-tuned model achieved an overall accuracy of 77% and performed similarly to the out-of-domain test set.

Comparing GPTZero and our fine-tuned model's performance against our stylometric open-source baseline, we observed that this baseline significantly outperformed GPTZero, achieving 77% accuracy, highlighting that in AI detection of short responses, stylistic features are an accurate predictor (Table 4).

[2] GPTZero classifies responses as AI, Human, or Mixed. The numeric values of 1, 0, and 0.5 are then assigned to these classifications, respectively.

Table 3. Performance of the fine-tuned model on in-domain and out-of-domain test sets.

	In-Domain Test Set				Out-of-Domain Test Set			
	Precision	Recall	F1 Score	Support	Precision	Recall	F1 Score	Cases
Human-authored (0)	0.86	0.88	0.87	116	0.73	0.92	0.82	65
Uncertain (0.5)	0.52	0.25	0.34	51	0.25	0.17	0.20	18
LLM-generated (1)	0.81	0.92	0.86	166	0.93	0.78	0.85	67
Accuracy			0.80	333			0.77	150
Macro avg.	0.73	0.69	0.69	333	0.64	0.62	0.62	150
Weighted avg.	0.78	0.80	0.78	333	0.76	0.77	0.76	150

Table 4. Performance of GPTZero on the in-domain test set.

Label	Precision	Recall	F1 Score	Cases
Human-authored (0)	0.75	0.70	0.72	116
Uncertain (0.5)	0.00	0.00	0.00	51
LLM-generated (1)	0.67	0.91	0.77	166
Accuracy			0.70	333
Macro avg.	0.47	0.54	0.50	333
Weighted avg.	0.60	0.70	0.64	333

Table 5. Performance of open source stylometric baseline on the in-domain test set.

Label	Precision	Recall	F1 Score	Cases
Human-authored (0)	0.79	0.82	0.81	116
Uncertain (0.5)	0.47	0.18	0.26	51
LLM-generated (1)	0.79	0.93	0.86	166
Accuracy			0.77	333
Macro avg.	0.69	0.64	0.64	333
Weighted avg.	0.74	0.77	0.75	333

The improvement in accuracy achieved by the fine-tuned model over GPTZero highlights the need for human-verified training data and how general-purpose AI detectors that are verified in controlled environments are not the most accurate for specialized cases [11]. This discrepancy becomes evident when analyzing several misclassifications made by GPTZero. However, due to the closed-source nature of GPTZero, the reasoning behind its classifications remains unknown, making it challenging to understand the factors influencing the model's decision-making process. A few examples of these misclassifications are presented in Table 6.

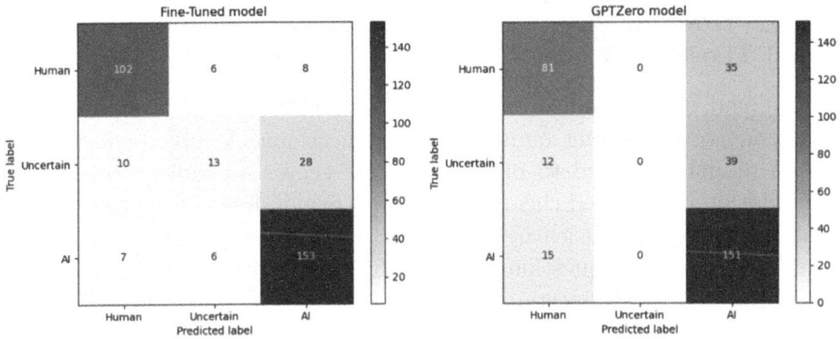

Fig. 1. Confusion matrices for the fine-tuned model (left) and GPTZero (right).

Table 6. Learner Response Classification Examples

Learner Response	True Label	GPTZero Label	Fine-tuned Label
"This approach will provide future extrinsic motivation for him to work hard and complete lessons earlier"	0	1	0
"Positive Reinforcement and encouragement can boost his self-esteem and motivation to continue working hard in the future"	0	1	0
"Collaborative Support: Working together can reduce her frustration and make the task more manageable. Encouragement: Reassuring her that she can complete the assignment boosts her confidence. Interest Connection: Linking the completion of the math assignment to your interest in scarves not only makes the task more engaging, but also more relevant to your personal interests"	1	0	1
"Carla, let's work together to complete the rest of your assignment. You can do this, I know you can. Once we're done, I'd love to hear more about how you design your scarves and your process"	1	0	1

In addition, ethical concerns surrounding AI detection tools, particularly the risk of false accusations, are critical in educational settings, where misclassifications can have serious consequences [9]. The higher false-positive rate observed in GPTZero further highlights the limitations of generic detectors. By incorporating annotated examples specific to educational contexts, fine-tuned models can better capture domain-specific linguistic patterns, making them a more reliable tool for AI detection in online learning environments [34]. This has direct implications for online learning, as it suggests that adopting domain-specific fine-tuning could enhance academic integrity monitoring while minimizing false accusations against students.

3.2 RQ2: How Do Posttest Scores Differ Between LLM Misusers and Those Who Are Not?

RQ2 examined whether LLM misuse in open-ended responses influenced performance on corresponding multiple-choice questions. A mixed-effects logistic regression model was used to predict posttest scores on multiple-choice questions in relation to detected cheating on the corresponding open-ended response. The analysis revealed that learners who used LLM-generated responses in corresponding open-response questions had significantly higher odds of answering the posttest multiple-choice question correctly (OR = 2.37, $p < .001$). This effect size was substantial, corresponding to more than doubling (~137% increase) in the odds of getting the multiple-choice question correct when LLM use was detected, compared to not. On the raw percent-correct scale, learners who did not use LLM had an estimated probability of 0.863 of answering correctly (95% CI: [0.780, 0.918]), while those suspected of LLM use had a probability of 0.937 (95% CI: [0.904, 0.960]).

Given prior research on learning gains from scenario-based training which are considerably lower than the observed doubling of performance [30], it is unlikely that this performance difference represents genuine learning. Instead the strong association between suspected LLM use and higher multiple choice scores could suggest cheating or LLM use across questions. This interpretation further aligns with Fan et al. [12], who found that LLM tools increase learner dependence and reduce knowledge gains due to "metacognitive laziness" where learners rely on LLM-generated outputs rather than actively engaging in the learning process. In educational settings, particularly in self-paced training environments with limited human supervision, LLM-generated responses may allow learners to bypass meaningful engagement with instructional material, and our findings add another piece of evidence to this growing hypothesis in the field of AI use in educational settings [12].

4 Limitations and Future Work

While this study demonstrates the effectiveness of fine-tuning LLMs for detecting LLM-generated responses in short-answer online learning environments, key limitations need to be addressed in future work. The study relies on human judgment as the ground truth, which may not always be correct and introduce bias or inconsistencies [14]. Human annotators may vary in their interpretation of responses, especially in cases where content is ambiguous [27], highlighting the need for further refinement in the annotation process to ensure fairness and accuracy, particularly across diverse student populations and writing styles.

Future work should also explore benchmarking the model's performance against multiple AI detection tools and evaluating its robustness across different instructional contexts and subject areas. This will help assess its reliability in real-world educational settings. To support practical application, detection models could also be paired with deterrence strategies that discourage the use of LLMs or aid identification [28]. Such strategies include embedding white text in scenarios with specific instructions for the LLM (e.g., "make each sentence exactly seven words long"), employing audio-visual formats to prevent copying, or disabling the ability to copy and paste content altogether. These strategies not only reduce AI misuse but also make detection easier. While this study does not focus on paraphrasing tools, they remain a significant concern, and these proposed measures could help mitigate the use of these tools too. To further strengthen future models, paraphrased responses should be included in the training dataset and detection strategies should be refined to identify such content. Augmenting training data with paraphrased LLM responses would improve detection accuracy by allowing the model to learn the nuanced differences between human-authored, LLM-generated, and paraphrased content.

Additionally, our findings show that learners suspected of LLM misuse perform better at posttest, raising concerns about genuine learning. This underscores the need for more advanced detection methods and pedagogical strategies to address AI-assisted learning, or statistical strategies to control learning gain estimates for suspected AI misuse. In particular, a promising direction for future work is to advance interventions that discourage learners from relying on LLM-generated answers that may undermine their learning. This future research may draw from interventions to mitigate students misusing scaffolding in tutoring systems (i.e., gaming the system), for instance, which have shown some success by repeating gamed exercise types [4] or displaying learning analytics to students that spur reflection [33].

5 Conclusion

This study presents a structured approach for detecting LLM-generated short answers in online learning environments, demonstrating the superior performance of a fine-tuned GPT-4o model over existing, general-purpose AI detection tools such as GPTZero, and addressing both the technical challenge of accurate detection and the pedagogical implications of AI misuse in low-stakes, self-paced lessons. Our results indicate that LLM misuse is associated with substantially higher performance on posttest questions, suggesting that learners may bypass the cognitive effort required in learning by relying on AI tools. These findings underscore the importance of integrating detection systems that are both accurate and attuned to the educational context, minimizing the risk of false positives while promoting academic integrity. Institutions must integrate ethical AI education, real-time feedback, and adaptive assessments to prevent misuse while supporting meaningful learning. By aligning detection and pedagogy, AI-assisted learning can enhance rather than undermine educational integrity and effectiveness in online training.

Acknowledgments. This work was made possible with the support of the Learning Engineering Virtual Institute. The opinions, findings and conclusions expressed in this material are those of the authors.

References

1. Aktay, S.: Analysis of ChatGPT GPTs in education. In: Proceedings of the International Texas Congress on Advanced Scientific Research and Innovation, Houston, TX, pp. 49–55 (2024)
2. Andrews, E.: Comparing AI detection tools: one instructor's experience. Academic Honesty and Integrity (2023)
3. Anisuzzaman, D., Malins, J.G., Friedman, P.A., Attia, Z.I.: Fine-Tuning LLMs for specialized use cases. Mayo Clin. Proc. Digit. Health **3**(1), 100184 (2024). https://doi.org/10.1016/j.mcpdig.2024.11.005
4. Baker, R.S.J., Corbett, A.T., Koedinger, K.R., Evenson, S., Roll, I., Wagner, A.Z., Naim, M., Raspat, J., Baker, D.J., Beck, J.E.: Adapting to when students game an intelligent tutoring system. In: Ikeda, M., Ashley, K.D., Chan, T.-W. (eds.) ITS 2006. LNCS, vol. 4053, pp. 392–401. Springer, Heidelberg (2006). https://doi.org/10.1007/11774303_39
5. Bates, D., Mächler, M., Bolker, B., Walker, S.: Package lme4: linear mixed-effects models using eigen and S4 (2014)
6. Bolker, B.M.: Linear and generalized linear mixed models. In: Ecological Statistics: Contemporary Theory and Application, pp. 309–333 (2015)
7. Chaka, C.: Detecting AI content in responses generated by ChatGPT, YouChat, and Chatsonic: the case of five AI content detection tools. J. Appl. Learn. Teach. **6**(2) (2023). https://doi.org/10.37074/jalt.2023.6.2.12
8. Chanpradit, T., Samran, P., Saengpinit, S., Subkasin, P.: Paraphrasing strategies and levels of proficiency of an AI-generated QuillBot and paraphrasing tool: case study of scientific research abstracts. J. Engl. Teach. (2024). https://ejournal.uki.ac.id/index.php/jet/article/view/5619
9. Dalalah, D., Dalalah, O.M.: The false positives and false negatives of generative AI detection tools in education and academic research: the case of ChatGPT. Int. J. Manage. Educ. **21**(2), 100822 (2023). https://doi.org/10.1016/j.ijme.2023.100822
10. Elkhatat, A.M.: Evaluating the authenticity of ChatGPT responses: a study on text-matching capabilities. Int. J. Educ. Integr. **19**(1), 15 (2023). https://doi.org/10.1007/s40979-023-00137-0
11. Elkhatat, A.M., Elsaid, K., Almeer, S.: Evaluating the efficacy of AI content detection tools in differentiating between human and AI-generated text. Int. J. Educ. Integr. **19**(1) (2023). https://doi.org/10.1007/s40979-023-00140-5
12. Fan, Y., Tang, L., Le, H., Shen, K., Tan, S., Zhao, Y., Shen, Y., Li, X., Gašević, D.: Beware of metacognitive laziness: effects of generative artificial intelligence on learning motivation, processes, and performance. Br. J. Edu. Technol. (2024). https://doi.org/10.1111/bjet.13544
13. Fisk, G.D.: AI or human? Finding and responding to artificial intelligence in student work. Teach. Psychol. (2024). https://doi.org/10.1177/00986283241251855
14. Fleckenstein, J., Meyer, J., Jansen, T., Keller, S.D., Köller, O., Möller, J.: Do teachers spot AI? Evaluating the detectability of AI-generated texts among student essays. Comput. Educ. Artif. Intell. **6**, 100209 (2024). https://doi.org/10.1016/j.caeai.2024.100209
15. Gao, C.A., et al.: Comparing scientific abstracts generated by ChatGPT to real abstracts with detectors and blinded human reviewers. NPJ Digit. Med. **6**(1), 75 (2023)
16. Hadi, M.U., et al.: A survey on large language models: applications, challenges, limitations, and practical usage. Authorea Preprints **3** (2023)

17. Herbold, S., Hautli-Janisz, A., Heuer, U., Kikteva, Z., Trautsch, A.: A large-scale comparison of human-written versus ChatGPT-generated essays. Sci. Rep. **13**(1) (2023). https://doi.org/10.1038/s41598-023-45644-9
18. Jia, L., Qi, C., Wei, Y., Sun, H., Yang, X.: Fine-tuning large language models for educational support: leveraging Gagne's nine events of instruction for lesson planning (2025). https://arxiv.org/abs/2503.09276
19. Kar, S.K., Bansal, T., Modi, S., Singh, A.: How sensitive are the free AI-detector tools in detecting AI-generated texts? A comparison of popular AI-detector tools. Indian J. Psychol. Med. (2024). https://doi.org/10.1177/02537176241247934
20. Kirchner, J.H., Ahmad, L., Aaronson, S., Leike, J.: New ai classifier for indicating AI-written text (2024). https://openai.com/index/new-ai-classifier-for-indicating-ai-written-text/
21. Menon, D., Shilpa, K.: "chatting with ChatGPT": analyzing the factors influencing users' intention to Use the Open AI's ChatGPT using the UTAUT model. Heliyon **9**(11), e20962 (2023). https://doi.org/10.1016/j.heliyon.2023.e20962
22. Mitrović, S., Andreoletti, D., Ayoub, O.: ChatGPT or human? Detect and explain. Explaining decisions of machine learning model for detecting short ChatGPT-generated text (2023). https://arxiv.org/abs/2301.13852
23. Mogessie, M., Elizabeth Richey, J., McLaren, B.M., Andres-Bray, J.M.L., Baker, R.S.: Confrustion and gaming while learning with erroneous examples in a decimals game. In: Bittencourt, I.I., Cukurova, M., Muldner, K., Luckin, R., Millán, E. (eds.) AIED 2020, Part II. LNCS (LNAI), vol. 12164, pp. 208–213. Springer, Cham (2020). https://doi.org/10.1007/978-3-030-52240-7_38
24. Opara, C.: StyloAI: distinguishing AI-generated content with stylometric analysis (2024). https://arxiv.org/abs/2405.10129
25. Pardos, Z.A., Baker, R.S., San Pedro, M.O., Gowda, S.M., Gowda, S.M.: Affective states and state tests: Investigating how affect throughout the school year predicts end of year learning outcomes. In: Proceedings of the Third International Conference on Learning Analytics and Knowledge, pp. 117–124 (2013)
26. Peterson, J.C., Battleday, R.M., Griffiths, T.L., Russakovsky, O.: Human uncertainty makes classification more robust. In: IEEE International Conference on Computer Vision (2019). https://arxiv.org/abs/1908.07086
27. Plank, B.: The "Problem" of human label variation: on ground truth in data, modeling and evaluation. In: Proceedings of the 2022 Conference on Empirical Methods in Natural Language Processing, pp. 10671–10682 (2022). https://aclanthology.org/2022.emnlp-main.731.pdf
28. Shi, Z., Wang, Y., Yin, F., Chen, X., Chang, K.W., Hsieh, C.J.: Red teaming language model detectors with language models. Trans. Assoc. Comput. Linguist. **12**, 174–189 (2024). https://doi.org/10.1162/tacl_a_00639
29. Tang, R., Chuang, Y.N., Hu, X.: The science of detecting LLM-generated text. Commun. ACM **67**(4), 50–59 (2024)
30. Thomas, D.R., et al.: Do tutors learn from equity training and can generative AI assess it? arXiv preprint arXiv:2412.11255 (2024)
31. Tian, E., Cui, A.: GPTZero: towards detection of AI-generated text using zero-shot and supervised methods (2023). https://gptzero.me
32. Wu, J., Yang, S., Zhan, R., Yuan, Y., Chao, L.S., Wong, D.F.: A survey on LLM-generated text detection: necessity, methods, and future directions. Comput. Linguist. 1–66 (2025)
33. Xia, M., Asano, Y., Williams, J.J., Qu, H., Ma, X.: Using information visualization to promote students' reflection on "gaming the system" in online learning. In: Proceedings of the Seventh ACM Conference on Learning@ Scale, pp. 37–49 (2020)

34. Yamtinah, S., Wiyarsi, A., Widarti, H.R., Shidiq, A.S., Ramadhani, D.G.: Fine-tuning AI models for enhanced consistency and precision in chemistry educational assessments. Comput. Educ. Artif. Intell. 100399 (2025). https://doi.org/10.1016/j.caeai.2025.100399
35. Zhai, C., Wibowo, S., Li, L.D.: The effects of over-reliance on AI dialogue systems on students' cognitive abilities: a systematic review. Smart Learn. Environ. **11**(1) (2024). https://doi.org/10.1186/s40561-024-00316-7

Goal Setting Engages More Caregivers in Online Math Homework than Instructional Support

Conrad Borchers[1(✉)], Ha Tien Nguyen[2], Paulo F. Carvalho[1], Kenneth R. Koedinger[1], and Vincent Aleven[1]

[1] Carnegie Mellon University, Pittsburgh, PA, USA
{cborcher,pcarvalh,krk,aleven}@cs.cmu.edu
[2] University of Washington, Seattle, WA, USA
han3@uw.edu

Abstract. Parent and caregiver involvement in homework can be critical to student success, yet many families face barriers such as limited time and content knowledge. We examine two approaches to involving caregivers in homework that students complete with tutoring systems for middle school mathematics. The first, an intelligent caregiver support module, provided real-time, step-level tutoring guidance and SMS notifications to caregivers. The second, a goal-setting contract based on prior non-digital homework interventions, facilitated structured agreements between caregivers and students to set homework goals and rewards. We conducted two four-week studies in American middle schools with diverse student populations, totaling 75 students, to determine which approach engages more households. After low initial adoption of the tutoring support module, the goal-setting contract was introduced at the second study site. While only 12% of the families enrolled in the tutoring feature, 55% engaged with the goal-setting contract when given the opportunity, a significant increase. Short interviews with students and teachers further emphasized the role of household participation—extending beyond parent-child dyads—as siblings frequently assumed homework support roles, contributing to higher engagement with goal-setting. We contribute novel evidence that caregivers were more likely to engage with tools enhancing motivational roles than with real-time instructional guidance in technology-supported homework. Specifically, goal setting emerges as a low-friction strategy to enhance student engagement while mitigating barriers that limit direct instructional support.

Keywords: technology probes · K-12 · tutoring systems · goal setting

1 Introduction and Related Work

Caregiver (i.e., a parent or member of a child's caring community) involvement can be critical for academic achievement, contributing motivational and instructional homework support. Caregiver involvement has been linked to higher grades

K. Tammets et al. (Eds.): EC-TEL 2025, LNCS 16063, pp. 61–75, 2026.
https://doi.org/10.1007/978-3-032-03870-8_5

and better test performance [17]. However, many caregivers face barriers, such as limited time, resources, and content knowledge, hindering homework support [28], and exacerbating opportunity gaps.

What motivates caregivers to support their students with homework? Seminal work [15] identifies three key factors: (a) perceptions of responsibility, (b) beliefs that their help is effective, and (c) perceptions of whether their student and school expect their involvement. However, since this framework was established nearly three decades ago, the homework environment has become increasingly digital [24], potentially altering caregiver roles. Recent research highlights new opportunities for caregiver involvement brought by the increasing availability of educational technologies in K-12 education, such as improving teacher-student communication through instant messaging and supporting student self-regulation during online homework through learning analytics [11,26,29].

Yet, these studies do not fully explore how novel technologies and interventions can encourage caregiver involvement in ways aligned with [15]'s model. For instance, technology could enhance caregivers' perceived efficacy by helping them better understand their student's homework, particularly in challenging subjects like mathematics [26]. Alternatively, it could strengthen motivational support as another key caregiver homework role [29]. While promising, the adoption rates of such interventions remain unclear. This study addresses this gap by comparing two novel interventions designed to support caregiver involvement in digital math homework and their adoption rates, including for known-to-be effective interventions such as goal setting [1,5]. As a secondary contribution, we study the obstacles to caregiver support in students' tutoring system practice that technology may introduce or solve.

1.1 Instructional vs. Motivational Caregiver Tools and Roles

The current study examines the feasibility and affordances of two distinct approaches to caregiver involvement in helping students engage in tutoring system practice. The first approach, a "hands-on" design, encourages caregivers to collaborate with students and bridge knowledge gaps, argued to address curricular challenges caregivers often report [26,28]. The second approach, a "hands-off" goal-setting model, leverages caregiver-student goal setting, which has been found effective in past research but has not been studied in tutoring systems [1].

As an instructional, hands-on tool, we study intelligent tutoring systems (ITS) that enhance student learning across K–12 and early college settings [21]. While ITS have shown promise in digital homework [10], their potential to help caregivers support their students in ITS practice remains underexplored. Caregivers often excel at providing emotional and motivational encouragement but often lack confidence in instructional roles [13]. This raises the following key questions: How can an ITS, suitably enhanced, complement caregivers' strengths? Can these systems enhance caregivers' instructional capabilities [15]? Research has highlighted caregivers' need for tools that help bridge content knowledge gaps [26]. Nguyen et al. [26] found that caregivers favor conversational support systems that offer step-level guidance during homework when integrated with ITS, underscoring the importance of integrating instructional aids into ITS.

In contrast, as a motivational, hands-off tool, we study a goal-setting approach that draws from research on homework behavioral contracts [27]. Cooper [8] defines contingency contracts as written agreements between two parties that specify roles, assigned tasks, designated rewards for the student, and the conditions required to earn rewards. Lab studies indicate that student practice time increases when parents and students jointly establish goals [18]. More recent literature reviews further support the effectiveness of contingency contracting in fostering cognitive and non-cognitive skill development in students [1].

While tutoring systems can help address instructional barriers faced by caregivers, goal-setting contracts may be more accessible due to requiring less active engagement. We conducted technology probe studies in two middle schools with distinct student populations. This setting allowed us to examine differences in the feasibility, adoption, and perceived effectiveness of these tools. We ask:

RQ1: To what extent do caregivers engage with (hands-on) intelligent tutoring and (hands-off) goal-setting probes for homework support?
RQ2: What are strategies to overcome common obstacles to caregiver engagement in computer-supported homework?

2 Methods

This study investigates the feasibility and desirability of novel designs for middle school caregiver homework support in mathematics ITS. Technology probes allow us to (1) collect information about real-world use and users, (2) field-test the novel caregiver tool, and (3) generate design insights into homework support tools in middle school math supported by learning technologies [16].

2.1 Participants and Recruitment

The study involved two American middle schools: East School, a suburban school in the Northeastern US, and West School, a suburban school in the Pacific Northwest. Both schools were recruited through previously established research partnerships with schools and school districts. Permission to conduct research was obtained from both schools following the approved IRB protocol.

We initiated contact with participating mathematics teachers by obtaining research permissions from school administrators. Collaborative discussions with administrators and teachers helped determine the classes involved in the study and set adequate data collection time frames and mathematics content.

Students of the East School participated in the study across two eighth-grade classes taught by the same teacher totaling 44 students. One class, Class 1, consisting of 24 students, was taught a standard eighth-grade math curriculum, while the other class, Class 2, with 20 students, followed an advanced math track based on state test scores. The student population of East School is predominantly Caucasian (90%) and 45% of the student population was classified as low-income based on Free/Reduced Lunch (FRL) statistics available. Less than 5% of the students are English Language Learners (ELL). Overall, 35% of the total school-wide student population met state math standards, representing curricular proficiency expectations for students of that grade level.

At West School, a classroom of 31 students participated. The classroom comprised standard eighth-grade math students, special education students, and English language learners (ELL). One teacher acted as the primary instructor. A second teacher provided additional support, particularly for the special education students. Based on national statistics, the student population at West School is 20% Caucasian and 75% of the students were classified as low-income based on Free/Reduced Lunch (FRL) and official state government resources, and 25% were ELL. Overall, 30% of the total school-wide student population met math standards assessed by the Smarter Balanced Assessments. All school demographics are rounded to 5 percentage points to preserve anonymity.

2.2 Tutoring System Probe

Recruitment Process. Student-caregiver pairs in both schools were recruited to receive access to the caregiver support probe, which involved caregivers using the tutoring system "hands-on". First, a study strategy was determined with the participating teachers. After securing approval from the school and the teacher, the participating mathematics teacher distributed an email to all caregivers containing information about the study and its objectives. These details were provided as an email attachment containing an official letter about ten days before the study was to start. This letter explained that caregivers had the opportunity to participate in a study trialing a novel homework support tool designed for caregivers, emphasizing that participation was voluntary and detailing the data collection process. Based on teacher discussions, translated study materials were provided to multilingual households at West School so that no household was excluded from participating in the study.

In addition to the letter, caregivers completed an informal, 30-minute onboarding Zoom session, which walked them through the tool's functionalities. One research team member walked participants through the system using a slideshow, as well as live demos of the tool. Participants were given an opportunity to have any questions answered and to test the system live through test accounts during the session. Across both schools, students and caregivers could sign up for the study and continue to do so until the last day. Caregiver consent and student assent were obtained for tool access. One caregiver per household could participate. Caregivers signed up for the study by filling out an online consent form in Qualtrics, followed by a brief survey on their household's demographics. Finally, all caregivers received a third letter that allowed them to opt out of having their student's practice log data retained for research purposes. No caregiver, however, opted out of that option.

Tutoring System Technology Probe Design. The first technology probe in this study is an *intelligent caregiver support module* embedded in the Lynnette tutoring system for linear equation-solving [23]. Lynnette offers immediate feedback, hints, an open learner model for skill proficiency, and a struggle detector that flags students who repeatedly fail to master targeted skills [3]. This probe examined if the detector could encourage students to seek caregiver help.[1]

The caregiver support module was informed by research on effective human tutoring [31] and computer-supported homework, which used low-fidelity prototyping through the Wizard-of-Oz method with middle school caregivers [26]. The tool built on prior research in two key ways. First, it provided caregivers with insights into students' problem-solving accuracy and suggested next steps, addressing their preference for content-level support in math homework. Second, it featured an SMS module allowing students to notify caregivers during points of struggle, aligning with caregivers' desire to offer targeted support while minimizing time commitment [26]. To further enable brief, need-based interactions, the prototype facilitated remote conversational support (Fig. 1).

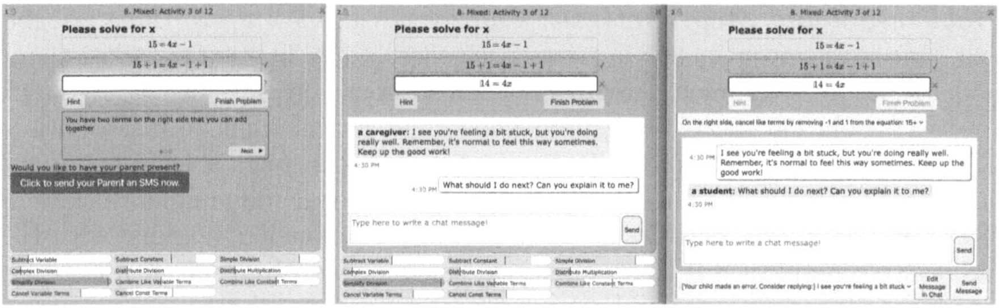

Fig. 1. Caregiver support tool with (left) student view during individual practice and caregiver SMS notification button (middle) student view during caregiver-student interaction (right) caregiver view including next-step and conversational recommendations.

The intelligent caregiver support module facilitated student and caregiver interaction during two stages of math practice. In the first stage, students practiced solving equations independently, with the system prompting them to notify caregivers via SMS when help was needed. In the second stage, caregivers could join by clicking a URL in the SMS or logging into the system on their computer, activating "coach mode". Both student and caregiver were notified of each other's presence via an icon in the top-left corner (see Fig. 1). Once connected, a chat panel appeared, enabling real-time interaction. The system supported caregivers in helping their students in three principal ways: live problem-solving broadcasting, adaptive message recommendations, and problem-solving step previews.

Problem-Solving Broadcast: This feature allows caregivers to observe their child's problem-solving process (e.g., hints, feedback) in real time.

[1] At the first school, student feedback revealed they felt "called out" by the system for struggling. Hence, students had continuous SMS button access at the second school.

Adaptive Message Recommendations: Caregivers receive tailored conversation prompts based on the student's step accuracy and hint usage, updated after each attempt. Messages are drawn from 25 pre-designed options created by two researchers using an expert tutoring model, emphasizing effort-based praise, indirect error feedback, and assessments of understanding [31]. Grounded in caregiver design research, the recommendations focus on (1) conceptual explanations, (2) effective use of the tutoring system (e.g., encouraging hint use), and (3) acknowledgment of emotions from errors. At each update, the system suggests three messages based on hint usage and recent correctness, including general advice like encouraging self-explanation, a proven strategy for enhancing learning outcomes [4]. For example, after a correct step, a caregiver might see: *"You're really tackling this problem well"*. If the student has not used hints, the prompt might be: *"How about you request a hint and walk me through it?"* And after an error, the caregiver could be prompted to say: *"Can you explain to me what you did here?"* During interactions between student and caregiver, the caregiver can select from these three recommendations, edit and adjust them in the chat panel, or send them directly to the student.

Problem-Solving Step Previews: Caregivers can view up to three possible next steps in the problem-solving sequence generated by Lynnette's instructional model to address common caregiver concerns about content support. Lynnette constructs solution paths using predefined rules for allowable transformations [23]. Steps are ranked by proximity to the final solution (e.g., solving for x) and shared with caregivers alongside brief explanations (e.g., "dividing both sides by three: $3x/3 = 9/3$"). This design discourages direct copying, aligning with Hill and Tyson's findings [14] that emphasize balancing involvement with fostering autonomy to support self-regulation and problem-solving skills.

Students without enrolled caregivers practiced independently with the tutoring system. During points of struggle, they were prompted to self-explain [4] through conversational messages randomly selected from 10 pre-generated options. Students submitted responses before proceeding and received acknowledgments such as, "Thank you. Let's move forward together! Remember, hints can help". This approach minimized differences between supported and unsupported students, preserving a naturalistic environment for the probes [16].

2.3 Homework Contract Probe

A second design probe was introduced at West School only, focusing on caregiver accountability beyond problem-solving support. This probe, and the decision to only trial it at West School, emerged from preliminary thematic analyses of interviews at East School, which revealed caregivers' inability to provide accountability support through the tool. The probe aimed to assess caregivers' perceived usefulness and response rates, aligning with the broader research goal of developing an intervention accessible to diverse caregivers. To that end, this probe did not require a formal signup process but was handed out to students similar to a homework assignment requiring caregiver sign-off at home, as detailed below.

The decision to implement a goal-setting contract was also informed by design research indicating that students prefer goal-setting support over other evidence-based, offline homework interventions when using tutoring systems [29]. Adapted from recommendations in [27], the homework contract was performed on paper and encouraged caregivers and students to negotiate practice goals and, optionally, rewards. Caregivers could also commit to providing tutoring or other forms of support. Figure 2 shows a contract example. To ensure accessibility, the contract was translated into multiple languages for non-English-speaking caregivers.

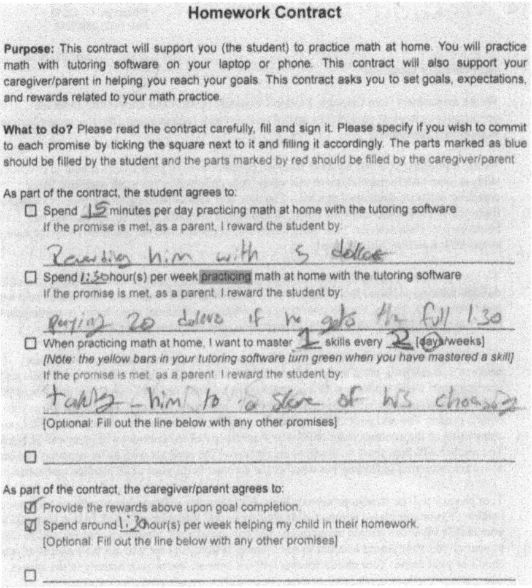

Homework Contract

Purpose: This contract will support you (the student) to practice math at home. You will practice math with tutoring software on your laptop or phone. This contract will also support your caregiver/parent in helping you reach your goals. This contract asks you to set goals, expectations, and rewards related to your math practice.

What to do? Please read the contract carefully, fill and sign it. Please specify if you wish to commit to each promise by ticking the square next to it and filling it accordingly. The parts marked as blue should be filled by the student and the parts marked by red should be filled by the caregiver/parent.

As part of the contract, the student agrees to:

☐ Spend 15 minutes per day practicing math at home with the tutoring software
If the promise is met, as a parent, I reward the student by:
Rewarding him with 5 dollar

☐ Spend 1:30 hour(s) per week practicing math at home with the tutoring software
If the promise is met, as a parent, I reward the student by:
paying 20 dolers if he gets the full 1:30

☐ When practicing math at home, I want to master 1 skills every 2 [days/weeks]
[Note: the yellow bars in your tutoring software turn green when you have mastered a skill]
If the promise is met, as a parent, I reward the student by:
taking him to a store of his choosing

[Optional: Fill out the line below with any other promises]

☐ ______

As part of the contract, the caregiver/parent agrees to:

☑ Provide the rewards above upon goal completion.
☑ Spend around 1:30 hour(s) per week helping my child in their homework.
[Optional: Fill out the line below with any other promises]

☐ ______

Fig. 2. Example redacted homework contract.

On the first day of the study at West School, a researcher introduced and passed out homework contracts for students to complete at home. A participating teacher reminded the students to complete and submit the contracts to the researcher in class daily. Twelve students returned homework contracts in the first week, and five students returned homework contracts in the second week, with 17 out of 31 (54.8%) homework contracts returned by the end of the study.

2.4 Procedure

The study took place over four-week periods. The first two weeks involved classroom practice without caregiver involvement, followed by two weeks with the intelligent caregiver support module probe to support caregiver engagement. Students practiced linear equations using the Lynnette ITS [23] for about 30 min daily in class. Lynnette offers immediate feedback and step-level hints. Daily assignments included 12 problems, with unfinished problems completed at home. For students who finished early, Lynnette integrated additional units on graph interpretation. Log data captured student practice, caregiver engagement, and tool interactions, including system usage time, hint requests, problem completion rates, and caregiver notifications. These metrics were used to assess engagement and identify usage patterns, logged in the standard DataShop format for tutoring systems [20]. A researcher was present in the classroom throughout the study to address technical issues, observe student engagement, and document factors influencing tool use. Teachers maintained their regular classroom routines, offering occasional support during student practice.

2.5 Data Analysis Methods

Engagement Rates (RQ1). We defined engagement rates by the extent of caregiver and student interaction with the probes. Caregiver engagement was measured through: **Caregiver Tool Signup and Usage:** Caregivers were considered engaged if they signed up and recorded at least one session in the tutoring system's support module based on log data. **Caregiver Tool Signup but No Usage:** Dropout rates reflected caregivers who signed up but did not use the system, based on the absence of logs. **Homework Contract Return:** Engagement with the homework contract probe was measured by the return of a signed contract, whether signed by a caregiver or another household member acting in a caregiver role.

For an exploratory analysis featuring 31 West School students, we measured engagement through average weekly math practice time based on session start and end timestamps in log data. To compare engagement between students who completed the contract and those who did not, we conducted a *t*-test, with students as the analysis unit. We replicated the *t*-test for in-class and out-of-class usage as separate outcomes, as we predicted that out-of-school student engagement might be more sensitive to caregiver support differences. For robustness, we also report Wilcoxon rank-sum tests as we observed skew in our data.

Observation Notes (RQ2). Analyses related to RQ2 derived strategies to overcome common obstacles to caregiver involvement in digital homework. Specifically, researchers observed students during homework practice sessions in classrooms, noting factors that influenced engagement or lack of participation—such as barriers, challenges, or personal preferences—through brief informal discussions with students (and, at times, with participating teachers). Some student responses reflected caregivers' perspectives on tutoring system support and reasons for non-participation or probe signups. These observations were triangulated with pre- and post-interview data and log data analyses to provide a comprehensive understanding of caregiver involvement challenges.

We used an open-ended thematic approach and consensus-based analysis [9, 12]. Two researchers reviewed class observation notes and separately developed themes related to RQ2. Themes were grouped according to forms of caregiver engagement, involvement styles, and household obstacles. The researchers then discussed the generated themes iteratively until they reached a consensus.

3 Results

3.1 RQ1 Engagement Rates

We analyzed system log data to gain quantitative insight into caregiver signup rates. Signup rates were generally low (12%). The dropout rate, defined as signing up to use the tool but not using it, was 20% in East School and 50% in West School. While caregiver engagement with the caregiver support module was comparatively low at West School, households were relatively receptive to the homework goal-setting contract probe. All households were sent the contract, and 54.8% returned a signed homework contract. Among those, 34.5% agreed to provide help with homework, and 27.6% agreed to combine help with offering rewards. Overall, adoption rates of the hands-on instructional tool (12.0%, N = 75) and hands-off, goal-setting tool (54.8%, N = 31) were significantly different based on a two-sample test for equality of proportions, $\chi^2(1) = 19.49$, $p < .001$ (Table 1).

Table 1. Comparison of Caregiver Signup Rates for the Instructional, Hands-On Tool between East and West Schools.

	East School	West School	Overall
# Students (Periods)	44 (2)	31 (1)	75 (3)
# Signups (Dropouts)	5 (1)	4 (2)	9 (3)
Signup Rate	11.4%	12.9%	12.0%
Dropout Rate	20.0%	50.0%	33.3%

Engagement with Tutoring System After Goal Contract Completion. An exploratory, associational analysis using a sample of 31 West School students was conducted. Completing the homework contract was strongly associated with increased practice in and out of school settings. System log data indicated that students who returned the homework contract practiced more than twice as much per week with the computer-based tutoring system (M = 67.65 min, SD = 62.83 min) compared to those who did not (M = 34.33 min, SD = 28.07 min), $t(29) = 2.03$, $p = .052$. Due to apparent skew in the data, we confirmed that this difference was also marginally significant using a Wilcoxon rank-sum test, $U = 162.00$, $p = .054$. The difference was even more pronounced when filtering data outside of regular classroom hours, where students who returned a contract practiced three times as much (M = 34.32 min, SD = 95.14 min) compared to those who did not (M = 11.54 min, SD = 57.46 min), $t(26) = 1.91$, $p = .067$. A similar trend was observed for in-class practice (M = 13.76 min, SD = 4.81 min for contract returners vs. M = 10.25 min, SD = 6.45 min for non-returners), $t(29) = 1.62$, $p = .117$. Both differences were similarly marginal when tested using a Wilcoxon rank-sum test (p's $> .054$).

3.2 RQ2: Obstacles to Caregiver Involvement

Student Perspectives on Non-participation. Based on informal interviews with students during classroom practice at West School (Sect. 2.5), several students (25.8%) mentioned language barriers as a significant obstacle; five students (16.1%) reported that their non-English-speaking caregivers could not understand the study requirements or interact with the tool. Caregiver availability and resources also played a role, as three students (9.7%) cited busy caregivers who "worked both day and night shifts". Notably, three West School students independently came forward to say that their caregiver was not available to sign contracts; two of them then asked if another family member could sign the contract and one later returned a contract signed by another family member.

At East School, students might have declined to participate because of the prospect of getting notified about their struggling with a skill and asking their caregiver for help (which the participating teacher communicated to students before the study). This mechanism was changed between Studies I and II so that students could always ask for caregiver help through the system, independent of struggle. The East School teacher phrased it the following way:

TeacherEast: *"[Other students] were a little turned off about their parent being notified when they got work wrong/what content they struggle with while doing the parent study. I told them not to fear that!"*

This perspective was also echoed by an East School student, sharing a preference for requesting help from their caregiver at any point in time, instead of that option being open only after the system detected that they were struggling:

Stu3East: *"I guess I was a little I mean, cause once you like you do it, cause you have to do it like a certain amount of times to get the option. So it's kind of So at that point it was a little frustrating, I guess, because you'd have to like, you know, you've already gotten it wrong so many times".* **Stu3East:** *"I wish it would have been like an option with like the hint thing"*

Teacher Perspectives on Non-participation. Some caregivers perceived the signup process and probe as "extra work", with the East School teacher remarking that broad caregiver engagement has been challenging for the district:

TeacherEast: *"I had a few students tell me that their parents didn't want them doing the study due to it "being extra work"."* and *"Parent involvement at a middle school level is quite difficult. Our district especially has this struggle as it has a wide range of socioeconomic status".*

A similar insight emerged from one of the West School teachers, who highlighted that caregiver engagement for additional education-related activities is challenging for them, in part due to language barriers. Even though translated documents explaining the study procedure and goal contract translations were provided, they were likely insufficient for participation:

Teacher1West: *"[West School] is a unique place...I think doing it earlier would have gotten more people because students check out more after Christmas in 8th* *grade. So if they aren't engaged, then the parents are much less likely to be engaged. The diversity we had brings issues with trust of unknowns and the translation doesn't always get the message through in the way we want. And it being a core 8 special education and Multi-language learner class usually has more apathy towards school and extra work. Like I said, in my [geometry] class we would have probably had almost 100% involvement just for bonus points. But that isn't the reality of school".*

In summary, language barriers and caregiver availability impacted participation, particularly at West School, where students struggled to engage. At East School, while students were more engaged, some were initially hesitant about notifying caregivers when struggling with content. Teacher feedback from both schools highlighted that caregiver involvement was an ongoing challenge.

4 Discussion

Caregiver involvement is crucial for student success, yet factors like time constraints and limited content knowledge often hinder support [28]. Tutoring systems present opportunities to enhance caregiver homework support, but effective technology designs are needed [11,26]. We examined two caregiver engagement modes—a real-time intelligent support module and a goal-setting contract—in middle school math classrooms. Findings illustrate how both approaches relate to participation and engagement, offering insights for future designs.

4.1 RQ1: How Much Did Caregivers Engage with Each Probe?

Lowering Barriers to Active Caregiver Participation. Across schools, the proportion of caregivers who signed up for the tutoring system support was similar (12.9% at West vs. 11.4% at East School), but dropouts were notably higher at West School (50% vs. 20%). Observations and informal student comments suggest that some families found the formal signup and login process burdensome; dropout after enrollment could signify that some students were able to navigate the tutoring system well on their own (or because no opportune moment to help live through the system arose). In contrast, the caregiver homework contract provided less friction, as it was completed on paper and handed out to students, similar to regular homework assignments.

Future research could systematically explore technology access and competing family responsibilities in contexts where caregivers speak multiple languages or hold multiple jobs [26,28]. Automated and multimodal translation assistance may be explored to improve inclusivity in future tool design iterations [32].

Aligning Support Tools with Household Routines. Caregivers often engage in motivational support through encouragement and accountability, yet many lack confidence in tutoring [15,26]. Accordingly, significantly more households engaged with the goal-setting contract (55%) compared to the tutoring system involvement tool (12%). Caregivers were more willing to engage in accountability mechanisms than real-time instructional guidance. Such accountability benefits students based on past research on contingency contracts in education, which have been shown to improve student persistence and practice [1,27]. Integrating such motivational support into ITS—potentially through digital contracts or automated progress reminders—could enhance student engagement without overburdening caregivers [6]. A limitation of our study is that we cannot gauge how much caregivers engaged with the homework contract beyond completing or signing off on it, which is subject to future research. Our log data analysis showed that students who completed the contract with their caregiver or household member practiced significantly more out of class than those who did not. This associational analysis, based on 31 West School students, could be explained by a selection effect (whereby more motivated students are more likely to complete a practice contract with their caregiver) or by the previously documented effectiveness of goal setting in non-digital homework [1,27]. Yet, from response rates in this study alone, it is evident that these contracts are likely to be adopted by a broader range of caregivers and households than directly involving caregivers into tutoring system instruction. Recent evidence offers quasi-experimental support for the effectiveness of practice contracts on learning and engagement in educational technology [5].

4.2 RQ2: Opportunities to Overcome Involvement Obstacles

Recognizing the Broader Household Support Network. Observations at West School revealed a need to design for peer and broad household support beyond the student-caregiver dyad. Three students at West School asked if family members other than their caregivers could complete the homework contract with them. These students requested to involve their older siblings. Bronfenbrenner's Ecological Systems Theory emphasizes that multiple layers of environmental resources (e.g., families and schools) influence a student's development [7]. The theory has been successfully used to understand student developmental outcomes [25]. Accordingly, tool design should integrate the student's broader family context and other surrounding mesosystems, such as extended school and community, that connect the family microsystem to other student experiences.

Integrating Goal Setting into Tutoring Systems. Our current goal-setting intervention presents a low-friction, low-resource tool for caregiver involvement in digital homework. It is possible, though subject to future research, that better integration of the goal-setting contract with the tutoring system could lead to better student learning. For instance, systems could integrate lightweight progress notifications in relationship to goals, which has shown promise in past research [2]. Further, goal-setting tools for tutoring systems [29] could be merged with data-driven insights for caregivers and students on goal completion based on log data. Such analytics have been previously successfully used in teacher-facing dashboards [22]. Integration with other household rituals and media for exercising accountability (e.g., through calendar applications or reminders) may further increase the ease with which caregivers can exercise accountable support.

4.3 Limitations

The design recommendations we offered assume that caregivers and students will have access to learning technologies, digital devices running them, and the internet, which is not always the case [19]. It is important to note that fundamental needs in caregiver-student relationships are prerequisites for effective relationships between educational institutions and caregivers, such as trust [30]. The technology designed here is not intended to displace these needs.

Our study was conducted in two schools with unique institutional contexts, demographics, and resources. Although these sites provided valuable contrasts in socioeconomic and linguistic diversity, the findings may not be generalizable to all K–12 settings, given differences in technology adoption and school-home communication, including rural, charter, or private schools.

Moreover, while we captured student practice time based on log data and qualitative indicators of caregiver involvement, we did not measure actual academic improvements. Our focus was on feasibility and adoption rather than learning gains. Log data and our interviews are also limited in telling the story of how exactly students and caregivers engaged with goal setting and technology at home. Analyses of different caregiver use strategies, which could be studied through at-home observations or richer diary logs and experience sampling, could further enhance the design and effectiveness of the tools studied here.

5 Conclusion

We studied two design probes that allow caregivers to support their students in practicing with tutoring systems. We contrasted motivational and instructional aids that aim to overcome time, knowledge, and resource constraints. While caregiver access to a conversational support module in a tutoring system for live interactions saw low signup and usage rates (12% overall), significantly more households chose to engage with a goal-setting probe (55%).

These findings contribute novel evidence that tools enhancing motivational caregiver roles may be more widely adopted than tools focused on enhancing instructional support that caregivers provide to students. Even when caregivers lack content knowledge or have limited availability, goal-setting, and flexible accountability supports may foster meaningful increases in student practice. Observational data further highlight the broader "caring community" that surrounds the student—siblings, other relatives, and trusted adults—who may step in where a traditional parent–child homework partnership is difficult to establish. Future research may focus on improving the integration between goal-setting contracts and tutoring systems, which can track goal progress through log data.

Acknowledgments. This research was funded by the Institute of Education Sciences (IES) of the U.S. Department of Education (Award #R305A220386). We thank Sina Shahmoradi for contributions to early data analyses and literature review.

References

1. Alwahbi, A.: The use of contingency contracting in educational settings: a review of the literature. Educ. Res. Rev. **15**(6), 327–335 (2020)
2. Aurino, E., Tsinigo, E., Wolf, S.: Nudges to improve learning and gender parity: preliminary findings on supporting parent-child educational engagement during Covid-19 using mobile phones. Technical report, EdTech Hub (2022)
3. Beck, J.E., Gong, Y.: Wheel-spinning: students who fail to master a skill. In: Lane, H.C., Yacef, K., Mostow, J., Pavlik, P. (eds.) AIED 2013. LNCS (LNAI), vol. 7926, pp. 431–440. Springer, Heidelberg (2013). https://doi.org/10.1007/978-3-642-39112-5_44
4. Bisra, K., Liu, Q., Nesbit, J.C., Salimi, F., Winne, P.H.: Inducing self-explanation: a meta-analysis. Educ. Psychol. Rev. **30**, 703–725 (2018)
5. Borchers, C., Houk, A., Aleven, V., Koedinger, K.R.: Engagement and learning benefits of goal setting with rewards in Human-AI tutoring. In: Proceedings of the 26th International Conference on Artificial Intelligence in Education (2025)
6. Borchers, C., Peng, C., Lyu, Q., Carvalho, P.F., Koedinger, K.R., Aleven, V.: Student perceptions of adaptive goal setting recommendations: a design prototyping study. In: Proceedings of the 26th International Conference on Artificial Intelligence in Education (2025)
7. Bronfenbrenner, U.: Ecological Systems Theory. American Psychological Association (2000)
8. Cooper, J.: Applied Behavior Analysis. Pearson/Merrill-Prentice Hall (2007)
9. Corbin, J.M., Strauss, A.: Grounded theory research: procedures, canons, and evaluative criteria. Qual. Sociol. **13**(1), 3–21 (1990)
10. Feng, M., Huang, C., Collins, K.: Promising long term effects of ASSISTments online math homework support. In: Wang, N., Rebolledo-Mendez, G., Dimitrova, V., Matsuda, N., Santos, O.C. (eds.) AIED 2023. CCIS, vol 1831, pp. 212–217. Springer, Cham (2023). https://doi.org/10.1007/978-3-031-36336-8_32
11. Gonzalez-DeHass, A.R., Willems, P.P.: Middle-school students and digital homework: the evolving role of family engagement. Middle Sch. J. **55**(4), 25–34 (2024)
12. Hammer, D., Berland, L.K.: Confusing claims for data: a critique of common practices for presenting qualitative research on learning. J. Learn. Sci. **23**(1), 37–46 (2014)
13. Hasan, M.A., Noor, N.F.M., Rahman, S.S.B.A., Rahman, M.M.: The transition from intelligent to affective tutoring system: a review and open issues. IEEE Access **8**, 204612–204638 (2020)
14. Hill, N.E., Tyson, D.F.: Parental involvement in middle school: a meta-analytic assessment of the strategies that promote achievement. Dev. Psychol. **45**(3), 740 (2009)
15. Hoover-Dempsey, K.V., Sandler, H.M.: Why do parents become involved in their children's education? Rev. Educ. Res. **67**(1), 3–42 (1997)
16. Hutchinson, H., et al.: Technology probes: inspiring design for and with families. In: Proceedings of the SIGCHI Conference on Human Factors in Computing Systems, pp. 17–24 (2003)
17. Jeynes, W.H.: The relationship between parental involvement and urban secondary school student academic achievement: a meta-analysis. Urban Educ. **42**(1), 82–110 (2007)
18. Kahle, A.L., Kelley, M.L.: Children's homework problems: a comparison of goal setting and parent training. Behav. Ther. **25**(2), 275–290 (1994)

19. Kamenetz, A.: It's a smartphone life: more than half of us children now have one. Natl. Public Radio **31** (2019)
20. Koedinger, K.R., Baker, R.S., Cunningham, K., Skogsholm, A., Leber, B., Stamper, J.: A data repository for the EDM community: the PSLC datashop. Handb. Educ. Data Min. **43**, 43–56 (2010)
21. Kulik, J.A., Fletcher, J.D.: Effectiveness of intelligent tutoring systems: a meta-analytic review. Rev. Educ. Res. **86**(1), 42–78 (2016)
22. van Leeuwen, A., Knoop-van Campen, C.A., Molenaar, I., Rummel, N.: How teacher characteristics relate to how teachers use dashboards: results from two case studies in K-12. J. Learn. Anal. **8**(2), 6–21 (2021)
23. Long, Y., Holstein, K., Aleven, V.: What exactly do students learn when they practice equation solving? Refining knowledge components with the additive factors model. In: Proceedings of the 8th International Conference on Learning Analytics and Knowledge, pp. 399–408 (2018)
24. Mrazek, A.J., et al.: Teenagers' smartphone use during homework: an analysis of beliefs and behaviors around digital multitasking. Educ. Sci. **11**(11), 713 (2021)
25. Newland, L.A.: Family well-being, parenting, and child well-being: pathways to healthy adjustment. Clin. Psychol. **19**(1), 3–14 (2015)
26. Nguyen, H.T., Borchers, C., Xia, M., Aleven, V.: Designing tools for caregiver involvement in intelligent tutoring systems for middle school mathematics. In: Proceedings of the 18th International Conference of the Learning Sciences-ICLS 2024, pp. 865-872. International Society of the Learning Sciences (2024)
27. Peacock, G.G., Ervin, R.A., Daly, E.J., Merrell, K.W.: Practical Handbook of School Psychology: Effective Practices for the 21st Century. Guilford Press (2009)
28. Pelemo, P.E.K.: Parental involvement: investigating the roles, barriers, and strategies of effective parent-teacher relationships in middle school math. Ph.D. thesis, Southeastern University (2022)
29. Peng, C., Borchers, C., Aleven, V.: Designing homework support tools for middle school mathematics using intelligent tutoring systems. In: Proceedings of the 18th International Conference of the Learning Sciences-ICLS 2024, pp. 1730–1733. International Society of the Learning Sciences (2024)
30. Schweizer, A., Niedlich, S., Adamczyk, J., Bormann, I.: Approaching trust and control in parental relationships with educational institutions. Stud. Paedag. **22**(2), 97–115 (2017)
31. Thomas, D., Yang, X., Gupta, S., Adeniran, A., Mclaughlin, E., Koedinger, K.: When the tutor becomes the student: design and evaluation of efficient scenario-based lessons for tutors. In: LAK23: 13th International Learning Analytics and Knowledge Conference, pp. 250–261 (2023)
32. Yang, J., et al.: M3P: towards multimodal multilingual translation with multimodal prompt. arXiv preprint arXiv:2403.17556 (2024)

Is More Gamification Better? Evaluating Playful Interactions and Narratives for Algebra Learning

Conrad Borchers[1(✉)], Tomohiro Nagashima[2], Pinyang Liu[3], Martha W. Alibali[4], and Vincent Aleven[1]

[1] Carnegie Mellon University, Pittsburgh, PA 15213, USA
{cborcher,aleven}@cs.cmu.edu
[2] Saarland University, Saarbrücken, Germany
nagashima@cs.uni-saarland.de
[3] Stanford University, Stanford, CA 94305, USA
pinyangl@stanford.edu
[4] University of Wisconsin-Madison, Madison, WI 53706, USA
martha.alibali@wisc.edu

Abstract. Gamification can enhance learning with technology, but can too much gamification diminish learning? Both (1) playful problem-solving interactions and (2) narrative elements outside of practice can enhance playfulness. However, prior research reporting benefits of playful design has often conflated these two factors. We conducted a 2×2 classroom experiment ($n = 105$) with sixth- to eighth-grade students in the US, varying the interaction style (a more playful drag-and-drop style vs. a standard type-in style) and including playful narrative (a space travel theme with mission-based achievements and dashboards vs. no theme) in a math tutoring system. We tested whether each element independently enhances engagement and learning. Results revealed a significant interaction effect such that the inclusion of narrative elements had no effect on conceptual learning in standard type-in equation solving but a *negative* effect in playful (drag-and-drop) equation solving. Drag-and-drop interaction marginally improved conceptual learning. Each playful element—drag-and-drop interaction or narrative—independently significantly increased engagement. Notably, out-of-class usage of the system was highest in the dual-playfulness condition, though about 20% of students engaged with the system outside of class. These results suggest that while combining playful components can increase out-of-class engagement for some students, it may lead to less productive in-class practice and reduced learning gains for most. These findings highlight the potential drawbacks of overloading systems with playful features, showing that "more play" is not always better.

Keywords: tutoring systems · K-12 · mathematics education · algebra · gamification

K. Tammets et al. (Eds.): EC-TEL 2025, LNCS 16063, pp. 76–90, 2026.
https://doi.org/10.1007/978-3-032-03870-8_6

1 Introduction and Related Work

Digital learning needs engaged students to be effective [3]. However, sustaining student engagement in learning activities, such as tutored practice, poses a significant challenge because active learning demands substantial cognitive effort. This challenge is particularly pronounced in subjects requiring conceptual reasoning and the practice of procedural skills, such as algebra, where prior studies have documented both a lack of student engagement [4] and persistent conceptual difficulties [5].

Recent research introduced playful system designs to enhance engagement. These playful designs can be broadly classified into two categories: (1) *narratives* outside of problem solving and (2) *playful interactions* during problem solving. First, narratives are often created through game-like elements such as storylines or achievements; for example, the completion of learning activities may align with characters traversing missions [14]. Narratives may also influence the selection of learning tasks by learners [13]. A meta-analysis reveals small positive effects of narrative design on conceptual, motivational, and procedural learning [15]. Building on this extensive research, the present study uses narrative design with achievement badges as an established and effective element of gamification, while contributing novel evidence of its impact in the context of serious practice supported by tutoring systems, an area of comparatively little prior research in the field of gamification [7, 15].

Second, playful interactions refer to designs that make problem-solving operations more enjoyable, including sounds, interaction modes (e.g., dragging as opposed to typing), and interface designs that resemble games but require rigorous practice of cognitive skills, for instance, through drag-and-drop operations that reinforce algebraic principles [5, 19]. Empirical studies on the effectiveness of playful interactions are rare; however, existing work suggests benefits of playful interactions for learning. These benefits are grounded in empirical evidence that perceptual learning through dynamic, active manipulation of algebraic expression improves conceptual understanding beyond hints and correctness feedback [17]. For instance, in one study, students using an algebra tutoring system with playful drag-and-drop interactions achieved greater learning gains and exhibited doubled engagement compared to those using a traditional type-in interface [7]. Another study reported conceptual learning gains from practicing drag-and-drop interactions to teach algebraic expressions [16]. One study, however, reported diminished posttest performance in DragonBox, a gamified app designed to teach algebra through puzzles, compared to a conventional tutoring system [15].

One challenge of these studies is that they typically evaluate alternative systems with different forms of scaffolding and assistance, preventing an unconfounded investigation of the impacts of playful interactions on learning [17]. For example, in a recent study closely comparing type-in tutoring systems for equation solving with a gamified drag-and-drop redesign [7], the comparison was confounded with playful narratives in a two-condition experiment. An exception is a study [28] that compared gamification of extrinsic compared to intrinsic, content-related aspects in a learning game, finding the latter to be more effective for learning. Given the known positive effects of playful narratives on learning and the mixed evidence for benefits of playful interactions, the present study aims to disentangle the effects of both design choices.

We predicted that playful interactions and narratives would each motivate students to engage for longer [7]. This extended practice time is expected to improve learning outcomes [2, 3]. However, it is also possible that each design feature may have distinct effects. While narratives may lead to more engagement, playful interactions in algebra may not only lead to more engagement but may also yield better conceptual learning. Playful drag-and-drop interactions require learners to actively manipulate algebraic expressions, reinforcing mathematical principles, such as needing to apply transformations to both sides of the equation [5, 19]. In traditional type-in interaction designs, these principles are less salient and might go unnoticed.

Finally, it is possible that narratives and playful interactions may lead to *complementary synergies* that enhance both engagement and learning beyond their individual, additive effects. For instance, playful narratives might increase learning through more engagement, in line with past research on gamification [7], but also make the effect of drag-and-drop interactions on learning stronger, as gamification may motivate students to engage in more effortful practice. This effect would represent a condition interaction: through more engagement caused by narratives, the isolated instructional effect of drag-and-drop designs becomes stronger. Yet, other theoretical foundations may also predict a negative interaction between narratives and playful drag-and-drop interactions. For instance, narratives may inadvertently dilute the instructional effectiveness of playful drag-and-drop designs by distracting students from algebraic principles through extensive focus on achievements; a prediction supported by the extensive literature on seductive details [18]. These competing theories warrant an analysis of the interaction effect of playful narratives and playful interactions. Therefore, we analyze engagement, procedural, and conceptual learning gains as separate dependent variables in a 2×2 randomized classroom experiment in the context of algebra learning supported by an intelligent tutoring system. We ask:

- **RQ1:** Do narratives and playful interactions, separately or in combination, lead to enhanced learning outcomes in conceptual and procedural knowledge of algebra?
- **RQ2:** Do narratives and playful interactions, separately or in combination, lead to increased engagement?

Our research contributes to a better understanding of how playful design affects student learning and engagement. These findings inform the development of more effective algebra tutoring systems, enabling educators and designers to create technology-enhanced learning systems that maximize learning gains and engagement.

2 Methods

2.1 Sample and Study Design

Participants ($N = 105$) were recruited from seven classes across two American school districts: one in a suburban area with 44.2% racial minority enrollment and the other in a rural area with 74.7% racial minority enrollment. The sample included 11 6th-, 80 7th-, and 14 8th-grade students. Students participated in classrooms during a 4-day period in May 2023, using a laptop or tablet computer. The school districts were recruited through prior project contacts. Discussions with the two participating teachers were held to ensure the practiced content was relevant and adequate. The math content focused on solving linear one-step, two-step, and multi-step equations.

The experiment implemented a 2×2 design with two factors: playful vs. traditional practice interactions for solving equations and narratives vs. no narrative (i.e., a standard learning management system design). Students in each class were randomly assigned to one of four conditions: (1) Playful interaction with narrative elements and achievement badges ($n = 27$), (2) Traditional interaction with narrative elements and achievement badges ($n = 30$), (3) Playful interaction with no narratives ($n = 21$), and (4) Traditional interaction with no narratives ($n = 27$). Students were encouraged to use the software outside of class, yielding a measure of voluntary engagement.

2.2 Materials

Playful Interaction. The drag-and-drop feature introduces a playful and interactive way for learners to practice equation transformations through hands-on practice (Fig. 1, left). With this interaction, learners can: (a) drag operators (e.g., the "+" sign) from the operators toolkit to the practice equation to transform its state, and (b) drag constant terms (numbers) or variable terms (e.g., "2x") onto like terms to simplify equations [7]. The system requires learners to drag the same operator to both sides of the equation once they apply it to one side, and learners must add a square box to each side of the equation before typing a number into the box. These interactions are deliberately designed to help learners develop and reinforce "conceptual knowledge that underlies procedures" [5], such as applying transformations to both sides [19]. By promoting conceptual understanding by requiring conceptually challenging transformation steps only (but not simplification steps with arithmetic calculations) [16], the drag-and-drop interaction allows learners to focus their cognitive effort toward algebraic thinking and reduces errors [19]. If learners make a mistake, they receive feedback and an "Undo" button appears and allows them to revert to the previous state and try again. The tutoring system provides hints upon request.

Traditional Interaction. The traditional interaction, known to benefit learning [16], asks learners to input problem-solving steps directly into the designated fields (Fig. 1, right). After entering a step, learners press "return" to receive immediate feedback on its correctness. If correct, a new input box appears below, enabling learners to proceed with the next step. If incorrect, learners can revise their input before continuing. Unlike the drag-and-drop interaction, the type-in interaction allows learners to skip intermediate steps. All other features remain consistent.

Narratives. The playful narrative version introduced mission-oriented storylines centered around planets to enhance learner motivation and engagement [7, 20]. Each storyline corresponded to a planet and algebra equation type. The story begins with the learner traveling alongside the alien character and solving math problems to complete missions. First-time users are introduced to the storyline through a seven-page illustrated guide lasting 1–2 min. Each planet's storyline is presented in a three-page illustration (Fig. 2) shown at the beginning of each assignment.

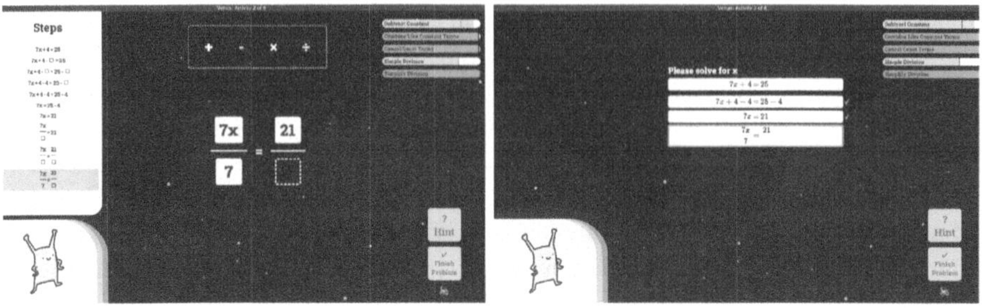

Fig 1. Playful (drag-and-drop) interaction (left) where learners drag operators and numbers to solve equations. Traditional (type-in) interaction (right) that learners type out solution steps.

As learners progress, they earn achievements for every one-third of the math problems completed on a planet, with three achievements available per planet (for completing 5, 10 problems, and 70% mastery of skills). These achievements can be tracked on the "My Achievements" page, providing motivation and a sense of accomplishment [21]. Upon finishing all problems on a planet, learners are presented with a concluding illustration that marks the successful completion of the mission.

Fig 2. Illustrations of Neptune's storyline. Learners first (left) get introduced to the planet and mission, followed by (middle) traveling to the planet, and (right) setting the mission context.

No Narratives. The no narratives condition had the same algebra content and tutoring functions as the narratives condition, but excluded themes and achievements.

Dashboard Page. The playful narrative system included a dashboard page named "My Planetary Journey," providing learners with Open Learner Models (OLMs) of their skill mastery (Fig. 3a). OLMs support learners' self-assessment, thereby enhancing their learning outcomes [23–25]. The dashboard was iteratively user-tested with secondary school students to ensure the use of student-friendly visual representations of their mastery status [31]. The dashboard in this playful narrative system was divided into three sections: "My Destinations," "My Skill Mastery," and "My Skill History." Both My Skill Mastery and My Skill History feature OLMs that reflect the skill status of the equation type associated with the planet selected in My Destinations. In addition, learners could access the "My Achievements" page via a clickable link in the upper-right corner.

My Destinations: This section (Fig. 3a, top) displayed eight planets, each corresponding to an algebra equation type learners practice in the system. For each planet, learners could see the equation type targeted within that planet, two example equations, and their progress percentage in completing the problems on that planet. They could begin practicing algebra problems by clicking on planets.

My Skill Mastery: This section (Fig. 3a, bottom left) had an OLM that listed skills required for solving each planet's equation types. These skills were based on the standard skill model of algebra tutors deployed in other tutoring systems [16]. Mastery % and the number of times each skill has been practiced was displayed.

My Skill History: This section (Fig. 3a, bottom right) displayed an OLM that had mastery percentage on the y-axis and the number of times skills had been practiced on the x-axis, to show the trajectory of the student's learning of skills.

The no-narrative system featured a dashboard design with minimal information on learners' progress and skill mastery (Fig. 3b), common in algebra tutors [29].

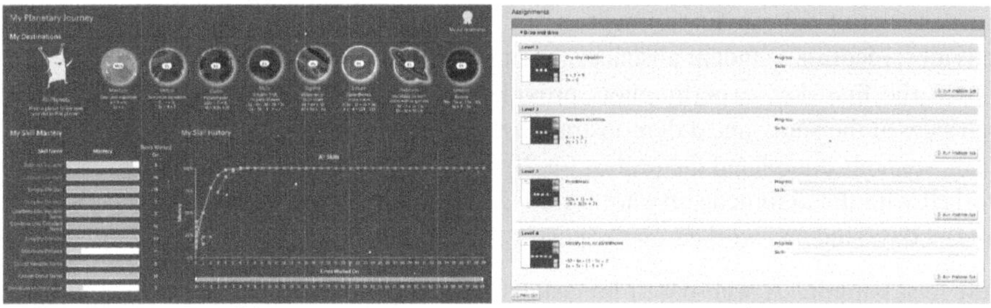

(a) (b)

Fig 3. Dashboard page of playful narrative system (a) and no-narrative system (b).

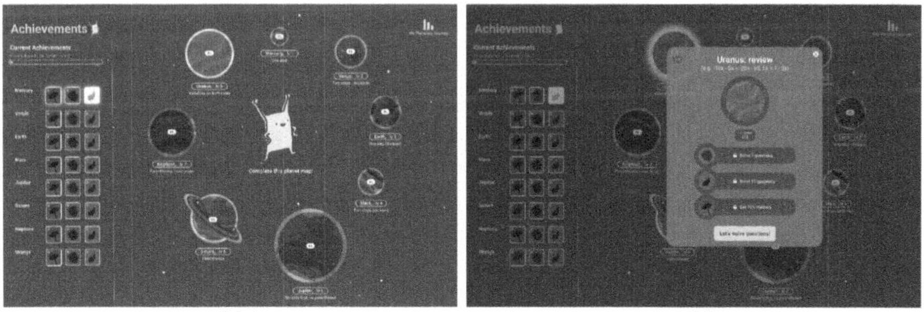

(a) (b)

Fig 4. Main achievement page (left). Interface when a planet is selected (right).

Achievement Page. This page was designed to visually represent learners' accomplishments in solving math problems, aiming to enhance their motivation (Fig. 4). This page had two sections: "My Achievements" and "My Destinations."

My Achievements: This section (Fig. 4a) tracked the total number out of 24 achievements unlocked from eight planets (unlocked by mastering target skills). Achievements were categorized by planet, with locked achievements shown as empty boxes to encourage learners to continue solving math problems and unlock them.

My Destinations: This section mapped the planetary journey displayed on the dashboard page. Learners could click on any planet to view its three associated achievements (Fig. 4b). Achievements were locked or unlocked, depending on progress, followed by a "Start Practice" button to directly access the practice session.

2.3 Procedure

The study was conducted during four mathematics class periods over four days. Experimenters facilitated the sessions remotely via a video conferencing system, working with the classroom teachers. Experimenters' roles included tracking start and end times of activities, recording student absences, and providing technical support.

On the first day, experimenters provided a 10-minute introduction, including an overview of the study and a demonstration video on how to use both software versions. Then, students completed the pretest for 20 min. On the second and third days, students worked with the assigned software for 20–25 min during their mathematics period. On the last day, students worked on the posttest for 20 min.

Test Assessment. A web-based pretest and posttest were designed to assess students' learning of domain knowledge and skills in early algebra, using items drawn from prior research [22]. These tests have been successfully used in prior research with samples in the same age range as ours (i.e., grades 6–8) [22]. Each test comprised thirteen conceptual knowledge items and five procedural knowledge items. Conceptual items evaluated students' conceptual reasoning in solving algebra problems through judgments of the correctness of provided equations (example: *If* $4x + 10 = 54$ *is true, state whether each of the following must also be true/valid:* $4x + 10 - 3 = 54 - 3$), and these items were scored as correct (1) or incorrect (0) based on the selected judgment. Procedural items asked students to solve equations in an open-ended format, typing solutions into a blank box (example: *Solve for x. Please show your steps:* $4x + 3 = 19$), and were scored as correct (1) or incorrect (0) based on the final solution. Two isomorphic versions of the test were counterbalanced across pretest and posttest. The full assessment is available via the study's supplementary repository: https://github.com/conradborchers/more-play-learning.

Measuring Engagement. Interaction data from the tutoring system and dashboard were used to compute engagement metrics. Interactions were logged to DataShop, following best practices for tutoring systems [2]. Logs captured all student-system interactions (e.g., hint requests, drag actions, dashboard element views) with timestamps. To provide nuanced insights into **different types of engagement**, we aggregated time spent on practice problems, time spent on dashboard interactions (for the playful narrative conditions), and number of problems solved. Engagement time was defined as the sum of the individual action time spent on each interaction, with interaction times being capped at 60 seconds in line with DataShop's transaction data format [2] to account for idle time.

All metrics were aggregated for each participant and then averaged by condition. Further, timestamps were aligned to the study schedule to distinguish between in-class and out-of-class interactions, though both interaction times were summed for the primary analysis of engagement.

2.4 Data Analysis

To address RQ1 (whether playful interactions and narratives resulted in improved learning), we analyzed students' conceptual and procedural learning gains. We calculated percent correct on the procedural ($n = 5$) and conceptual items ($n = 13$) for each participant. Following Nagashima et al. [7], we used linear regressions modeling posttest scores as the dependent variable, with playful narrative (yes/no) and playful interactions (yes/no) and their interaction as predictors, and pretest score as covariate. Separate models were fit for each knowledge type (procedural vs. conceptual).

To address RQ2 on the impact of playful interactions and narratives on engagement, we analyzed time spent practicing and the number of problems solved. To account for positive skew in engagement times, we employed linear regression models using log-transformed time as the dependent variable, with playful narrative (yes/no) and playful interactions (yes/no) and their interaction as predictors. The number of problems solved was analyzed as count data using Poisson regression. An exploratory analysis of engagement during class and voluntary engagement outside of class (with a binary outcome and logistic regression) was conducted, too.

For all models and statistical tests performed, we confirmed that distributional and modeling assumptions were met via visual inspection of standard diagnostic plots. These included Q-Q plots for normality of residuals, residuals vs. fitted values plots for homoscedasticity and linearity, scale-location plots for heteroscedasticity patterns, and residuals vs. leverage plots to identify influential observations (Cook's distance).

3 Results

First, we report descriptive statistics on learning gains, pretest and posttest scores by condition. **Procedural gains** varied, with the **Traditional Interaction with Narratives** condition showing the highest increase ($M = 13.3\%$), followed by the Playful Interaction with Narratives condition ($M = 7.4\%$). The Traditional Interaction with No Narratives and Playful Interaction with No Narratives conditions showed smaller improvements ($M = 4.1\%$ and $M = 2.7\%$, respectively). Across conditions, these gains were significant ($t(104) = 2.64$, $p = .010$) and averaged 7.3% across the full sample, corresponding to a small effect size of $d = .27$. Considering each condition separately, only the Traditional Interaction with Narratives condition achieved significant procedural learning gains ($t(29) = 2.18$, $p = .037$), and other conditions did not (p's $> .246$). However, we note that sample sizes for each condition were small. Further, as a manipulation check, regressing study conditions onto procedural (p's $> .188$) and conceptual (p's $> .194$) pretest scores revealed no significant variation in prior knowledge across conditions.

For **conceptual gains**, the **Playful Interaction with No Narratives** condition had the largest gain ($M = 4.4\%$) followed by the **Traditional Interaction with Narratives** condition ($M = 1.8\%$). The other two conditions showed no positive learning gains. Conceptual learning gains were not significantly different from zero, either across the whole sample, $t(104) = -0.13$, $p = .906$, $d = 0.01$, or when considering individual conditions (p's > .166). An overview of all test scores is presented in Table 1.

Table 1. Mean Conceptual and Procedural Scores for Pretest and Posttest across Conditions.

Condition	Conceptual Scores		Procedural Scores	
Measurement	*Pre*	*Post*	*Pre*	*Post*
Traditional Interactions - No Narratives	71.3%	68.9%	28.9%	33.0%
Traditional Interactions - Narratives	74.1%	75.9%	30.0%	43.3%
Playful Interactions - No Narratives	76.0%	80.4%	36.2%	38.9%
Playful Interactions - Narratives	70.5%	66.7%	25.9%	33.3%

3.1 Do Learning Outcomes Differ for Playful Interactions, Narratives? (RQ1)

For conceptual knowledge scores, the interaction between narratives (present or not) and interaction type (playful or traditional) was significant, $\beta = -0.16$ (*95% CI*: $-0.29 - -0.02$, $p = .023$). Playful interaction (i.e., drag-and-drop equation solving) was beneficial for conceptual learning when no narrative was present, but *decreased* conceptual learning compared to traditional interaction (i.e., type-in equation solving) when narratives were present (Fig. 5). There was also a marginal main effect of the interaction condition, with those in the playful (drag-and-drop) interaction conditions outperforming those in the traditional (type-in) interaction conditions, $\beta = 0.09$ (*95% CI*: $-0.01 - 0.19$, $p = .084$). The main effect of the narratives condition was not significant. For procedural knowledge scores, no effects were significant.

Across procedural and conceptual tests, the type-in interface, but not the drag-and-drop interface, exhibited relatively high learning gains when paired with a playful story. Given this pattern, we conducted an exploratory post-hoc multivariate ANOVA jointly predicting conceptual and procedural posttest scores, adjusting for pretest scores. The analysis confirmed a marginally significant interaction between interaction type and narrative presence, $F(2, 98) = 2.69$ ($df = 2, 98$), $p = .073$.

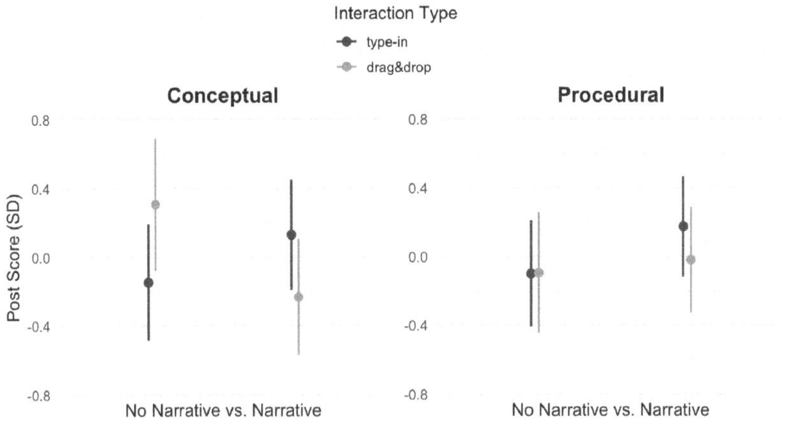

Fig 5. Posttest scores in SD for conceptual (left panel) and procedural (right panel) outcomes across no narratives and narratives conditions, differentiated by interaction type (traditional vs. playful). Error bars represent 95% confidence intervals.

3.2 Learner Engagement for Playful Interactions and Narratives (RQ2)

RQ2 examined the effects of playful interaction and narratives on engagement with learning algebra. We investigated total practice time and the number of problems solved, an engagement measure validated in past research [27]. Median engagement times (which are less prone to skew distributions than means) with all aspects of the learning environment varied by condition: traditional interaction with no narratives (68.5 minutes), traditional interaction with narrative elements and achievement badges (84.8 min), playful interaction with no narratives (73.6 min), and playful interaction with narratives (85.3 min). However, based on a linear regression with log-transformed minutes as the outcome, only the narrative effect was statistically significant ($\beta = 1.95$, $p = .048$), while the interaction type effect was not ($\beta = 1.15$, $p = .699$). There was no significant interaction on the number of minutes spent practicing.

Students also solved significantly more problems in the narratives condition, with an *IRR* of 1.25 (*95% CI*: 1.13–1.37, $p < .001$). However, this main effect was qualified by a significant interaction of interaction type and narrative presence (*IRR* = 0.78, *95% CI*: 0.67–0.90, $p = .001$), indicating that the narrative effect was reduced when combined with playful interaction, in line with the learning gain findings. Narratives increased the number of completed problems by 24.3% in the traditional interaction condition (26.3 to 32.7) but *decreased* it in the playful interaction condition by 3% (26.7 to 25.9). There was no main effect of interaction type (traditional vs. playful) on how many problems were solved ($p = 0.785$).

One explanation for why students solved fewer problems when *both* narratives and playful interactions were present even though time spent was increased is that students spent more time with the enhanced dashboard in the narratives condition as opposed to practicing algebra. However, log data showed students spent little time with their home screen (no narratives) or dashboard (narratives condition): traditional interaction with no narratives (2.5 min), traditional interaction with narrative elements and achievement badges (4.6 min), playful interaction with no narratives (3.8 min), and playful interaction with narratives (5.4 min). Participants spent significantly more time on the narrative dashboard than on the home screen ($\beta = 1.49$, $p = .024$).

Nagashima et al. [7] found a notable doubling of engagement during pandemic-time remote instruction when playful interaction was combined with narratives. One interpretation of this effect included students' increased self-initiated engagement outside of regular instruction. In our sample, notably and despite encouragement, only 24 out of 105 students accessed the system outside of class time (22.9%), with no significant differences between conditions (p's $> .414$). However, if students *did access* the software outside of regular school hours, in line with Nagashima et al. [7], we found significant engagement benefits of playful interactions *and* narratives and no significant interactions between the two. Outside regular class hours, playful interactions were associated with more solved problems (*IRR* = 2.53, *95% CI*: 1.63–4.00, $p < .001$). For context, using unadjusted descriptive means, this condition showed +325.7% more problems solved (approximately tripling). Narratives also showed higher engagement in terms of the number of problems solved (*IRR* = 1.64, *95% CI*: 1.05–2.62, $p = .031$); descriptively, the mean was +216.8% higher (approximately doubling). This pattern is consistent with Nagashima et al. [7]. This suggests differential effects of narratives and interaction on students who voluntarily engage with the software outside of class hours.

4 Discussion

This work explores how playful interactions (e.g., drag-and-drop) and narratives in tutoring systems impact algebra learning and engagement. By experimentally isolating gamification design elements, we provide new evidence on which features drive the established benefits of gamification—a gap highlighted in a seminal meta-analysis on gamified learning [15]. We conducted a 2 × 2 experiment using a tutoring system for middle school equation solving. We argue that combining certain gamification elements may inadvertently diminish their individual effects, stressing the need for confirmatory design experiments in educational gamification research.

Our results highlight a complex and counter-intuitive interaction: while playful drag-and-drop equation-solving improved conceptual learning *without* narratives (i.e., storylines and achievements), it *decreased* conceptual learning when narratives were present, relative to the standard type-in equation solving interface. The conceptual benefits of playful drag-and-drop manipulation have been argued to teach learners to actively manipulate algebra expressions, reinforcing conceptual principles [5, 19]. Past research has also argued that gamification (akin to our narratives condition) can be detrimental when it fosters off-task behavior [26], though we could partially rule out that explanation by investigating student time spent with the dashboard. We suspect a third factor may explain the obtained interaction: the students being more idle during practice and distracted by task-irrelevant details [29] when they are exposed to a learning environment that is thoroughly playful, and, in the case of the narrative dashboard, encourages paying attention to such details and managing practice time independently. This idleness was reflected in fewer problems solved. In addition to fewer practice opportunities, we also suspect that these seductive details could have had negative motivational impacts on students, leading to less effort in the posttest, which was reflected in negative conceptual learning gains in the dual-playfulness condition. This motivational explanation is directly supported by recent experimental evidence showing that the detrimental effect of seductive details on learning is especially pronounced when the presence of extrinsic motivators is strong [30]–in our case badges and other motivators in the narrative condition. Our findings directly align with that evidence, which also featured a 2 × 2 experiment [30].

The significant interaction between narratives and playful interactions diverges from Nagashima et al. [7], who reported tangible learning and engagement benefits in an intervention combining narratives and playful interactions. One reason for this difference may lie in the patterns of engagement. Nagashima et al. [7] was situated in *pandemic remote instruction*. In contrast, students in this study were encouraged to practice during *and* outside of regular class hours. Consequently, when students chose to access the system voluntarily outside of school hours, both narratives and playful drag-and-drop interfaces were effective in boosting engagement in our sample, mirroring the pattern observed by Nagashima et al. [7]. We suspect that this minority of students (about 20%) who accessed the system outside of regular school hours was especially motivated, benefiting from gamification. Our sample size did not allow us to scrutinize what differences exist between these student groups. One possible difference in students' self-regulation skills (helping proactively set and execute practice goals) could explain this benefit whereby students with more developed self-regulation used the dashboard strategically in the narrative conditions (e.g., to identify which skills they would need to practice and focus on those skills [13]).

An important implication for future work is that encouraging students to use the system outside of class through gamification may enhance engagement beyond what is achieved through standard in-class use of tutoring systems. Most students in our sample (about 80%) did not solve a single problem outside of their school hours. Future research studying how out-of-class use could be fostered merits future research. Meta-analyses on goal setting suggest that several psychological factors can contribute to not even starting intended practice behavior, among which are forgetting the intention to practice, not recognizing opportunities to practice, or feeling reluctant to start practicing [8]. None of the pre-actional phases are supported in our current design, though these could potentially be realized through reminder systems or at-home practice recommendations delivered through phones or laptops.

Overall, procedural learning gains were significant but small. One possible explanation for small gains is transfer-appropriate processing [9]. If students practice solving equations only through structured or playful tasks, they may not develop the capacity to generalize those procedural skills to more open-ended, free-form equation solving (such as the text entry box in our assessment). Similar transfer issues in tutoring system practice have been noted in comparisons of tutor-based and paper-based tests [10]. Future instructional design may incorporate practice opportunities that more closely reflect real-world or freeform conditions.

Notably, traditional type-in interactions without narratives did not facilitate meaningful learning (unlike prior studies using the Lynnette tutor [11]), and in some cases, average learning gains were negative, suggesting a possible loss of motivation during the posttest assessment. It is possible that the learning gains reported here underestimate the effectiveness of the tutoring system conditions.

4.1 Limitations and Future Work

The current study has several limitations. First, our sample size limited detection of subgroup differences (e.g., based on prior knowledge) in the effectiveness of the playful elements. The finding that productive use of a fully gamified system was present for a minority of students (i.e., those who elected to use the system outside of class) merits future research into which students benefit most from playful design. Second, the binary grading of procedural items into correct and incorrect final solutions provided only coarse-grained measures of learning. It is possible that a more fine-grained grading would lead to more sensitive measures of learning gains. Third, the study was conducted in two US schools and recruited through an established research partnership, limiting generalizability as students in other geographic regions may exhibit different use patterns with tutoring systems [1].

5 Conclusion

Technology-enhanced learning systems often integrate playful features to make practice engaging. We conducted a 2 × 2 classroom experiment that manipulated interaction style (drag-and-drop vs. type-in) and the presence of a narrative storyline. Contrary to expectations, playful problem-solving (drag-and-drop) interactions were more beneficial for conceptual learning when narratives were absent. A similar interaction was found for the overall number of problems solved. For students who voluntarily engaged with the system outside of class, however, engagement was highest in the "fully gamified" condition. Our findings underscore the importance of selectively integrating playful elements in algebra software in a way sensitive to the context of use (home or school), as "more play" can inadvertently undermine learning for some students, while benefiting those who are more self-motivated. We suspect that students used their practice time less productively due to seductive details present in the practice interface when narrative dashboards encouraged paying attention to such elements. Our findings suggest that researchers and practitioners must carefully design and identify the conditions under which playful features enhance learning and consider that extensive gamification can invite unproductive use of practice time.

Acknowledgements. This material is based upon work supported by the National Science Foundation under Grant No. 1760922. Any opinions, findings, and conclusions or recommendations expressed in this material are those of the author(s) and do not necessarily reflect the views of the National Science Foundation.

References

1. Nye, B.D.: Intelligent tutoring systems by and for the developing world: a review of trends and approaches for educational technology in a global context. Int. J. Artif. Intell. Educ. **25**, 177–203 (2015)
2. Koedinger, K.R., Stamper, J., Leber, B., Skogsholm, A., Cunningham, K., Baker, R.S.J.: A data repository for the EDM community: the PSLC datashop. In: Handbook of Educational Data Mining, pp. 43–56 (2010)

3. Koedinger, K.R., Carvalho, P.F., Liu, R., McLaughlin, E.A.: An astonishing regularity in student learning rate. Proc. Natl. Acad. Sci. **120**(13), (2023)
4. Norton, S., Irvin, J.: Developing positive attitudes towards algebra. Math. Essential Res. Essential Pract. 561–570 (2007)
5. Crooks, N.M., Alibali, M.W.: Defining and measuring conceptual knowledge in mathematics. Dev. Rev. **34**, 344–377 (2014)
6. Nagashima, T., et al.: Designing playful intelligent tutoring software to support engaging and effective algebra learning. In: Lecture Notes in Computer Science, pp. 258–271 (2022)
7. Gollwitzer, P.M., Sheeran, P.: Implementation intentions and goal achievement: a meta-analysis of effects and processes. In: Advances in Experimental Social Psychology, pp. 69–119 (2006)
8. Veltre, M.T., Cho, K.W., Neely, J.H.: Transfer-appropriate processing in the testing effect. Memory **23**, 1229–1237 (2015)
9. Borchers, C., Carvalho, P.F., Xia, M., Liu, P., Koedinger, K.R., Aleven, V.: What makes problem-solving practice effective? Comparing paper and AI tutoring. In: European Conference on Technology Enhanced Learning, pp. 44–59 (2023)
10. Long, Y., Aleven, V.: Gamification of Joint Student/system control over problem selection in a linear equation tutor. In: Lecture Notes in Computer Science, pp. 378–387 (2014)
11. Borchers, C., Ooge, J., Peng, C., Aleven, V.: How learner control and explainable learning analytics on skill mastery shape student desires to finish and avoid loss in tutored practice. In: Proceedings of the 15th International Learning Analytics and Knowledge Conference, pp. 810–816 (2025)
12. Mystakidis, S., Filippousis, G., Tolis, D., Tseregkouni, E.: Playful metaphors for narrative-driven e-learning. Appl. Sci. **11**, 11682 (2021)
13. Sailer, M., Homner, L.: The gamification of learning: a meta-analysis. Educ. Psychol. Rev. **32**, 77–112 (2020)
14. Long, Y., Aleven, V.: Educational game and intelligent tutoring system. ACM Trans. Comput.-Hum. Interact. **24**, 1–27 (2017)
15. Chan, J.Y.-C., Lee, J.-E., Mason, C.A., Sawrey, K., Ottmar, E.: From here to there! A dynamic algebraic notation system improves understanding of equivalence in middle-school students. J. Educ. Psychol. **114**, 56–71 (2022)
16. Koedinger, K.R., Aleven, V.: Exploring the assistance dilemma in experiments with cognitive tutors. Educ. Psychol. Rev. **19**, 239–264 (2007)
17. Nagashima, T., Bartel, A.N., Silla, E.M., Vest, N.A., Alibali, M.W., Aleven, V.: Enhancing Conceptual knowledge in early algebra through scaffolding diagrammatic self-explanation. Int. Soc. Learn. Sci. (ISLS). **1**, 35–42 (2020)
18. Kusuma, G.P., Wigati, E.K., Utomo, Y., Putera Suryapranata, L.K.: Analysis of gamification models in education using MDA framework. Procedia Comput. Sci. **135**, 385–392 (2018)
19. da Rocha Seixas, L., Gomes, A.S., de Melo Filho, I.J.: Effectiveness of gamification in the engagement of students. Comput. Hum. Behav. **58**, 48–63 (2016)
20. Booth, J.L., Lange, K.E., Koedinger, K.R., Newton, K.J.: Using example problems to improve student learning in algebra: differentiating between correct and incorrect examples. Learn. Instr. **25**, 24–34 (2013)
21. Mitrovic, A., Martin, B.: Evaluating the effect of open student models on self-assessment. Int. J. Artif. Intell. Educ. **17**, 121–144 (2007)
22. Long, Y., Aleven, V.: Supporting students' self-regulated learning with an open learner model in a linear equation tutor. In: Lecture Notes in Computer Science, pp. 219–228 (2013)
23. Long, Y., Aleven, V.: Enhancing learning outcomes through self-regulated learning support with an open learner model. User Model. User-Adap. Inter. **27**, 55–88 (2016)
24. Andrade, F.R., Mizoguchi, R., Isotani, S.: The bright and dark sides of Gamification. In: Intelligent Tutoring Systems: 13th International Conference, pp. 176–186 (2016)

25. Marwan, S., Price, T.W., Chi, M., Barnes, T.: Immediate data-driven positive feedback increases engagement on programming homework for novices. In: CSEDM@ EDM (2020)
26. Habgood, M.P., Ainsworth, S.E.: Motivating children to learn effectively: exploring the value of intrinsic integration in educational games. J. Learn. Sci.. Learn. Sci. **20**, 169–206 (2011)
27. Aleven, V., et al.: An integrated platform for studying learning with intelligent tutoring systems: CTAT+TutorShop. In: Fifth Annual Workshop on Learning@Scale 2024: A/B Testing and Platform-Enabled Learning Research (2024)
28. Wesenberg, L., Jansen, S., Krieglstein, F., Schneider, S., Rey, G.D.: The influence of seductive details in learning environments with low and high extrinsic motivation. Learn. Instr. **96**, 102054 (2025)
29. Hou, X., Nagashima, T., Aleven, V.: Design a dashboard for secondary school learners to support mastery learning in a gamified learning environment. In: European Conference on Technology Enhanced Learning, pp. 542–549 (2022).

Structured Prompts, Better Outcomes? Exploring the Effects of a Structured Interface with ChatGPT in a Graduate Robotics Course

Jérôme Brender[1,2(✉)], Laila El-Hamamsy[2], Kim Uittenhove[1], Francesco Mondada[1], and Engin Bumbacher[2]

[1] MOBOTS & LEARN, EPFL, Lausanne, Switzerland
{jerome.brender,kim.uittenhove,francesco.mondada}@epfl.ch
[2] University of Teacher Education (Haute École Pédagogique) Vaud, Lausanne, Switzerland
{laila.elhamamsy,engin.bumbacher}@hepl.ch

Abstract. Prior research shows that how students engage with Large Language Models (LLMs) influences their problem-solving and understanding, reinforcing the need to support productive LLM-uses that promote learning. This study evaluates the impact of a structured GPT platform designed to promote "good" prompting behavior with data from 58 students in a graduate-level robotics course. The students were assigned to either an intervention group using the structured platform or a control group using ChatGPT freely for two practice lab sessions, before a third session where all students could freely use ChatGPT. We analyzed student perception (pre-post surveys), prompting behavior (logs), performance (task scores), and learning (pre-post tests). Although we found no differences in performance or learning between groups, we identified prompting behaviors - such as having clear prompts focused on understanding code - that were linked with higher learning gains and were more prominent when students used the structured platform. However, such behaviors did not transfer once students were no longer constrained to use the structured platform. Qualitative survey data showed mixed perceptions: some students perceived the value of the structured platform, but most did not perceive its relevance and resisted changing their habits. These findings contribute to ongoing efforts to identify effective strategies for integrating LLMs into learning and question the effectiveness of bottom-up approaches that temporarily alter user interfaces to influence students' interaction. Future research could instead explore top-down strategies that address students' motivations and explicitly demonstrate how certain interaction patterns support learning.

Keywords: ChatGPT · Computing Education · Behaviors · Performance · Learning · Effectiveness

---

We thank our colleagues (N.A., J.W., A.B., R.B., C.C., C.L., P.M., S.A.) for their support, and the students who generously volunteered to participate in the study.

K. Tammets et al. (Eds.): EC-TEL 2025, LNCS 16063, pp. 91–106, 2026.
https://doi.org/10.1007/978-3-032-03870-8_7

1 Introduction and Related Work

Since the public release of ChatGPT in late 2022, large language models (LLMs) have gained rapid adoption for a wide range of tasks and fields [17,22,24]. Early studies show that access to such tools can significantly improve productivity in knowledge-intensive work [22,24]. Although a recent meta-analysis of 51 experimental studies across multiple disciplines found ChatGPT use to generally enhances academic performance [10], other work has found that students can use ChatGPT in ways detrimental for learning [7], that use of ChatGPT can lead to procrastination [26] or laziness [30], to increased memory retention issues [1], and to reduced academic performance [1]. Such findings demonstrate that many questions remain about the impact of LLMs on learning.

1.1 Over-Reliance on ChatGPT in Computing Education Contexts

In computing education, understanding the impact of LLMs, such as ChatGPT, is critical as AI-based code generation tools are increasingly adopted by students and teachers [3]. On the one hand, LLMs can scale the benefits of one-on-one tutoring [6], aid conceptual understanding, and expand topic coverage in programming contexts [18]. On the other hand, concerns remain that LLMs may inhibit learning by reducing cognitive effort, especially in domains requiring active problem-solving, such as programming. For example, in mathematics, Bastani et al. [5] show that overreliance on LLMs leads to a decline in performance when LLM support is removed, highlighting the need for LLM-interfaces that support learning and "ensure that humans continue to learn critical skills" [5] and prevent "metacognitive laziness" [12].

More recent studies suggest a nuanced picture: when students substitute their learning activities with LLMs (e.g., by generating complete solutions to exercises), they can cover a larger breadth of topics but understand them less deeply [16]. In contrast, students who complement their learning with LLMs—using them to reflect or clarify rather than replace their work—show improved conceptual understanding without necessarily expanding topic coverage [16]. Finally, another study demonstrated that while students may improve their performance while using ChatGPT, this does not necessarily translate into improved conceptual understanding [7], with the question of how ChatGPT is used being of the utmost importance. These findings thus highlight the importance of understanding the impact of how students use LLMs and how specific types of LLM use impact learning [7]. Indeed, while thoughtful engagement with LLMs can foster learning gains, excessive reliance on these tools, especially for solving practice exercises, may impair learning outcomes [16].

These findings underline the importance of both examining how students use LLMs and teaching them how to use LLMs effectively.

1.2 The Importance of Establishing Guidelines for Effective LLM Use

Crafting effective prompts remains challenging, particularly for users without LLM expertise [2]. Prompt engineering has therefore emerged as a strategy to improve interactions with LLMs, alongside efforts to formalize prompting with guidelines [11,20,25]. Yet these guidelines often lack empirical grounding and rarely address how prompting supports understanding and transfer to other environments with LLMs. To foster LLM literacy, especially among students, there is a need to translate such guidelines into accessible, evidence-informed formats [29] and ensure that changes in practices persist after guidance is removed (i.e., transfer). Some interventions have introduced AI tutors [5,13] that personalize student interactions with LLMs, but these approaches raise even more concerns about dependency on LLMs. One study found that once scaffolded support provided by an AI tutor is removed, students struggle to engage meaningfully with the AI on their own, potentially impairing long-term skill development [5]. It therefore appears that the transfer of productive prompting strategies from guided to unguided AI environments remains poorly understood.

1.3 Motivation

To address this gap, we designed a structured, form-based interface to structure students' prompting of ChatGPT during programming labs at the university level (see Sect. 2). The interface decomposed prompt construction into blank-based fields, encouraging more reflective and deliberate AI use. Unlike Socratic bots [13] that aim to simulate pedagogical dialogue, our goal was to empower students to develop their own prompting strategies. With this structured interface, we sought to answer the following research question: How does exposure to a structured prompting interface impact good prompting practices, student learning and performance during practice labs? To answer this question and investigate (i) whether guided prompting habits persist once support is withdrawn (i.e., transfer), and (ii) whether such structuring contributes to improved learning and performance, we conducted an intervention over three lab sessions. During the first two sessions the students were divided into two groups: those with access to ChatGPT, and those with access to the structured interface. In the third session, the structured interface was removed, and students were allowed to interact freely (i.e., without constraint) with ChatGPT. For the purpose of the present article, we focused our analysis on the data from the second practice lab session, where half the students were required to use the structured interface, and the third practice lab session, where both groups could freely use ChatGPT.

2 The Structured Interface with ChatGPT API

Drawing from research on metacognitive scaffolding and reflective learning [8,23], we developed a structured interface (see Fig. 1) that acts as a reflective layer, encouraging students to clarify their intent before submitting a prompt. A similar approach has previously demonstrated effectiveness in promoting metacognitive awareness among novice programmers [19]. Concretely, the structured interface was designed to help students decompose their prompts on GPT-based tools. Students must first select a prompt category drawing from prior research on prompt classification in similar educational contexts [7] (*Understanding*, *Implementing*, or *Debugging*, see item 2 in Fig. 1). This categorization aimed to raise students' awareness of their goals and reasoning when engaging with the system.

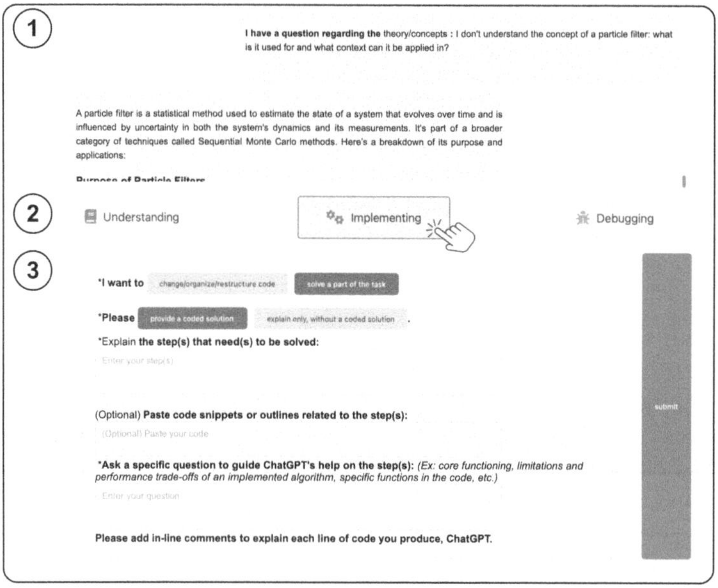

Fig. 1. Structured interface with integrated GPT API comprising of (1) an interactive interface, (2) prompt type category selection (understanding, implementing, or debugging), and (3) a structured format for prompt composition.

Once students select the prompt category, a corresponding structured form appears (see Fig. 1 item 3) to have students elaborate on their query. These forms were informed by research on effective questioning in ill-structured problem-solving [8] and programming [19,23] to encourage metacognitive engagement, prompting learners to reflect on and refine their own prompts. Once completed, the structured fields are compiled into a single prompt and sent to the ChatGPT API (GPT-o-mini, free access at the time of the study). The interface did not alter or constrain the underlying knowledge base of the GPT model.

3 Methodology

3.1 Study Context and Design

A mixed-methods classroom intervention was conducted at the university level[1] to address our RQs and understand how engaging first with a structured GPT platform, and subsequently with GPT alone, affects students' performance, learning outcomes, and perceptions during a practical lab session.

Participants. The study took place during the practice lab sessions of a graduate-level mobile robotics course at EPFL and involved 58 (39 male, 18 female, 1 undisclosed) of 143 students. These students volunteered and consented to participate in the study, in exchange for monetary compensation.

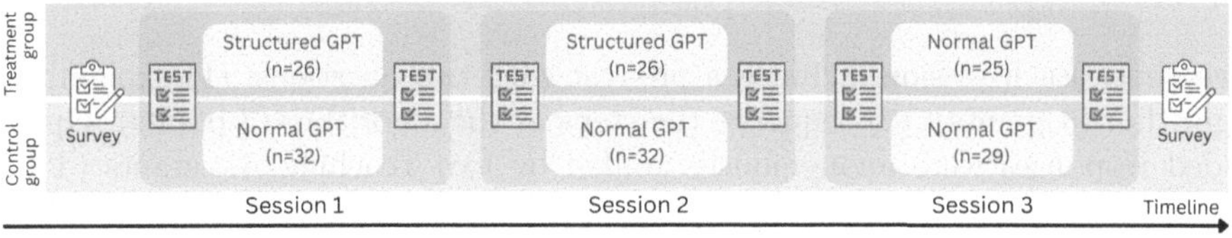

Fig. 2. Overview of study design with participants allocated to structured GPT and normal GPT interfaces. A pre-survey was conducted before practice lab session 1 and a post-survey after session 3. Learning assessments (pre/post-tests), prompt logs, and task performance logs were collected each session.

Study Design. The study outline is reported in Fig. 2. Before the first session, a preliminary survey on students' prior LLM perception and use was administered.

The 58 students were then randomly assigned into two groups: an intervention group using the structured interface (n = 26) and a control group using ChatGPT freely (n = 32). Please note that we ensured that both groups were equivalent in terms of (i) prior usage and perception based on the first perception survey (Mann Whitney U test, $p > 0.05$ on all questions) (ii) prior knowledge based on each session's pre-test (Mann-Whitney, session 2: $U = 454.0, p = .55, M = 60 \pm 26\%$, session 3: $U = 387.0, p = .87, M = 44.1 \pm 27.7\%$).

During the first two sessions the students were divided into two groups: those with access to ChatGPT and those with access to the structured interface. In the third session, all the students interacted freely with ChatGPT.

Finally, the students responded to a post-survey to establish whether the intervention led to changes in LLM perception and use.

[1] The study was approved by EPFL's Ethics Committee (HREC000560/12.08.2024) and students' informed consent was obtained prior to participation.

Practice Lab Session. Each practice lab session was structured as follows:

(i) A 15 min briefing on the study objectives, including a 10 min pre-test assessing prior knowledge of the course material.
(ii) 75 min of hands-on tasks[2] that are decomposed into subtasks (5 in Session 2 and 8 in Session 3) graded on a 0, 0.5, or 1 scale. The complexity of the tasks made the use of ChatGPT pedagogically meaningful.
(iii) A 10 min post-test with in-depth questions on the same content.

3.2 Data Collection and Reliability Measures

Perception Surveys. The pre and post intervention surveys were adapted from the Technology Acceptance Model (TAM) developed for educational contexts [28], and encompasses five dimensions: utility, ease of use, attitude/interest, self-efficacy, and intent to employ in future teaching activities[3].

Pre-test. Each session included a pre-test with two questions: (1) explain the algorithm (3 points); (2) sequence the steps of the algorithm (3 points). Open-ended responses were anonymously graded by two Teaching Assistants (TAs) who reached substantial inter-rater reliability on the 20% of the data (IRR, $\kappa_{S2} = 0.71$, $\kappa_{S3} = 0.75$) before coding the full dataset ($\kappa_{S2} = 0.69$, $\kappa_{S3} = 0.71$).

Practice Lab Tasks (Performance). The codes produced for each task (5 in session 2, 8 in session 3) were graded by three TAs using a 3-point scale: 0 for incomplete, 0.5 for over 70% correct, and 1 for fully correct solutions. We randomly selected 20% of the codes of each task and had the three TAs grade them and achieved substantial agreement on each task (Fleiss' κ_{S2} in $[0.71; 0.77]$; and κ_{S3} in $[0.7, 0.78]$). The remaining data was distributed between the three TAs and coded individually. The total practice lab score is computed as the standardized sum of the individual tasks' scores.

ChatGPT Prompts (Usage). We analyzed 291 prompts from session 2, and 411 from session 3[4] from 58 students (32 control, 26 intervention) who consented to share them ($M_{S2} = 4.84 \pm 3.97$ $M_{S3} = 7.61 \pm 4.23$ per student). Two researchers first analyzed a subset to define a prompt categorization based on observed uses of ChatGPT in computing education [7,15], resulting in three main prompt types (as in [7]): (i) *Development*, i.e. generating code or solutions; (ii) *Conceptual*, i.e. explaining task elements or computing concepts; (iii) *Debugging*, i.e. identifying or resolving coding errors. Three TAs obtained substantial agreement ($\kappa = .71$) on 20% of the dataset, before coding the full dataset.

[2] The hands-on tasks are part of a robotics course and focused on the Dijkstra and A-star algorithms in session 2, and particle filters in session 3. All tasks were computer-based: students coded robotics algorithms without using physical robots.
[3] The complete survey is accessible here.
[4] Excluding 16 and 18 off-task prompts (e.g., "hello", jokes) from sessions 2 and 3.

To provide more insight into students' prompts, three additional binary attributes were annotated per prompt (Table 1) whether the student was seeking to increase their understanding (*Understanding*, e.g., "explain this code [...]"), whether student was specific and provided details in their prompt (*Granularity*, e.g., referring to variables or lines of code rather than general tasks), whether the student had clear, well-structured, unambiguous phrasing (*Clarity*). Three TAs obtained substantial agreement on 20% of the data ($\kappa_{understanding} = .76$, $\kappa_{granularity} = .74$, $\kappa_{clarity} = .68$), before coding the remaining prompts individually.

Finally, to quantify the proportion of personal input within each prompt, two teaching assistants (TAs) collaboratively worked on identifying where the student's original contribution began and ended. Based on these annotations, we computed the percentage of each prompt that consisted of personally written input relative to the total prompt length.

Post-test (Learning). The post-tests were in MCQ format and consisted of 8 advanced questions in session 2 and 5 in session 3, targeting conceptual understanding of the practice lab session's subject. One point was attributed per question, and then summed and standardized to compute the overall post-test score per session ($M_{S2} = 66 \pm 18\%$; $M_{S3} = 55 \pm 20\%$).

Table 1. Prompt coding explanations, examples and counter-examples

Dimension	Explanation	Example included	Counter example not included
Understanding	Clarifies or seeks to understand concepts explicitly	"“explain me this code [...])"	"Here's my code"
Granularity	Specificity of the prompt regarding a part of the task or code (fine-grained)	"Could you explain line 4, specifically why the index is set to zero initially?"	"What does this function do?"
Clarity	Clear and explicit request structure	"I started coding the algo and need help debug this error:[...], explain me the bug"	"Here my bug:"

3.3 Data Analysis

Effect of the Structured Intervention on Learning and Performance. For sessions 2 and 3, we used multiple linear regressions and continuous variables so that the resulting standardized regression coefficients β provide effect size estimates. Each model includes (1) the group (control, treatment) and (2) the interaction between the group and pre-test score to see how prior knowledge might modify the intervention's effect. In addition, we computed a normalized learning gain $\frac{\text{post}-\text{pre}}{100\%-\text{pre}}$ to capture individual learning improvement [21], with the exclusion of two students with full scores in the pre-test. To evaluate whether certain prompting behaviors were associated with higher performance, we conducted a forward stepwise regression and then a multiple linear regression on performance (post-test and practice lab), with prompt types as predictors.

Effect of the Structured Intervention on ChatGPT Usage. For sessions 2 and 3, we compared the prompt types, attributes and amount generated by the students in both conditions using t-tests, χ^2 tests, and Mann-Whitney U tests.

Students' Perception of ChatGPT Usage. Having established that there were no pre-existing differences between students' perceptions of ChatGPT useage prior to the intervention, we used non-parametric Mann-Whitney U tests to determine whether there were differences between conditions after the intervention, and provide Cohen's d effect size when the difference is significant.

4 Results

4.1 Effect of the Structured Intervention on Learning and Performance

For sessions 2 and 3, we implemented multiple linear regression models with (i) post-test scores (learning), and (ii) practice lab scores (performance) as dependent variables and (a) pre-test scores, (b) group (control vs. intervention) and (c) their interaction as independent variables. None of the models revealed a significant main effect of the group, nor a significant interaction effect between group and pre-test scores on either performance or learning. The only significant predictor of learning was pre-test scores in session 3 ($\beta = 0.521$; p=.007).

An additional analysis of task completion rates during the practice labs indicates that there is no difference between groups in terms of (i) the number of completed tasks (t-test, session 2: $t(57) = 0.23$, $p = .81$, session 3: $t(53) = 0.74$, $p = .46$), and (ii) the number of attempted tasks (t-test, session 2: $t(57) = 0.02$, $p = .97$, session 3: $t(53) = 0.68$, $p = .50$).

Therefore, it appears that there is no direct impact of the intervention on learning or performance. To understand this finding, we investigated whether certain prompting behaviors were more conducive to learning, and whether using the structured interface could have promoted such behaviors, but maybe not enough as to be reflected in learning or performance differences.

The Influence of Specific Prompting Patterns on Learning: As will be explained in the next sub-section, we did not find significant differences between conditions in the use of prompt types ("Conceptual", "Debugging", "Development"), nor in the characteristics of prompts when examined separately ("Understanding", "Clarity", "Granularity"). Thus, we decided that for this analysis we could aggregate the two conditions into one dataset and examine whether overall behaviors emerged that seemed productive for learning.

As *Conceptual* prompts and *Debugging* prompts account for less than 15% of all prompts, we focused on *Development* prompts (>70% of prompts) in order to examine the relationship between prompting behaviors and learning.

A stepwise forward regression was conducted using *Development*, *Clarity*, *Understanding*, and *Granularity*, and their interaction as predictors of learning gain. For the session 2, the final model retained only *Clarity*; however, the overall model was not statistically significant, $F(1, 56) = 2.06$, $p = .15$, explaining only 3.6% of the variance in *learning_gain* ($R^2 = .036$). However, for the session 3, the final model retained all the variables. The model explains approximately 45% of the variance in learning gains ($R^2 = .45$; adjusted $R^2 = .35$) and the overall model was statistically significant ($F(8, 45) = 2.06$, $p < 0.01$).

The results show that a larger proportion of *Understanding* prompts is a significant positive predictor ($\beta = 0.23$, $p = 0.017$, $p < 0.05$) of learning gain. Although the main effect of having clear prompts is not significant (*Clarity* $\beta = 0.05$, $p = .58$), having development prompts that are clear (interaction between *Clarity* and *Development*, $\beta = 0.77$, $p < .001$) and clear prompts that seek to improve students' understanding (interaction effect between *Clarity* and *Understanding*, $\beta = 0.75$, $p < .001$) contribute to learning. These findings suggest that higher *Clarity* amplifies the positive relationships of *Development* and *Understanding* with learning gains. A significant negative interaction between *Understanding* and *Granularity* ($\beta = -0.36$, $p = .022$) suggests that overly detailed prompts may dampen the benefits of learning. However, no significant interaction was found between *Development* and *Granularity* ($\beta = -0.29$, $p = .29$).

In summary, *Understanding* enhances learning, and its effects are substantially strengthened when *Clarity* is high, and when Clarity is associated to *Development* prompts. When *Clarity* is low, their positive influences are comparatively

Table 2. Regression model for the impact of specific development-related prompting patterns on learning

Predictors	Learning Gain		
	Estimate	CI	p
(Intercept)	0.19**	0.06–0.31	0.005
development	0.13	−0.06–0.32	0.189
clarity	0.05	−0.13–0.23	0.590
understanding	0.23*	0.05–0.43	0.017
granularity	−0.04	−0.22–0.14	0.685
development:clarity	0.77***	0.48–1.06	5e−06
clarity:understanding	0.75***	0.45–1.05	1e−05
development:granularity	−0.29†	−0.58–0.01	0.065
understanding:granularity	−0.36*	−0.66 – −0.06	0.022
Observations 54	R^2/R^2 adjusted 0.45/0.35		

†$p \leq 0.1$ *$p \leq 0.05$ **$p \leq 0.01$ ***$p \leq 0.001$

weaker. To understand why there were no significant learning or performance differences between conditions, we looked at both groups' usage patterns.

4.2 Effect of the Structured Intervention on ChatGPT Usage

Number of Prompts. On average, students submitted 4.8 ± 4.0 prompts in session 2 and 7.6 ± 4.2 prompts in session 3, with no significant differences between conditions (t-test $t(57)_{S2} = 1.27$, $p_{S2} = 0.2$, and $t(53)_{S3} = 0.17$, $p_{S3} = 0.86$). However, the group using the structured interface tended to disengage more (46% did ≤ 3 prompts, compared to 25% in the control group).

Types of Prompts: There are no significant differences between conditions for the type of prompts (Conceptual: $U = 470$, $p = .14$; Development: $U = 386$, $p = .95$; Debugging: $U = 321$, $p = .19$). In both sessions, prompts categorized as *Development* prompts were the most frequent, accounting for over 70% of students' prompts in both sessions[5]. In contrast, *Conceptual* and *Debugging* prompts were less common, accounting for approximately 10% of students' prompts, with many students submitting no *Conceptual* or *Debugging* prompts[6]

Prompt Attributes: On average, students in both conditions had prompts with similar levels of *Understanding* (i.e., prompts with questions to improve understanding) (37.1% in session 2 and 23.3% in session 3), *Granularity* (i.e., prompts with sufficient detail provided) (21.2% in session 2 and 20.4% in session 3), and *Clarity* (i.e., prompts with a clear and explicit request) (37.5% in session 2 and 16.5% in session 3). There were no significant differences between conditions.

We extend our analysis by focusing on *Development* prompts and their interaction with attributes, in light of the learning effects identified in Sect. 4.1 for both session 2 and 3. It appears that students in the intervention group had a higher proportion of clear development prompts (prompts coded as *Development* and *Clarity*), $\chi^2(3) = 8.57$, $p = .036$, in session 2, when using the structured interface, but there was no significant difference in session 3 when all students could use the normal ChatGPT interface. As a reminder (see Table 2), a higher proportion of such types of prompts are significant positive predictors of learning. No other associations between *Development* prompts and quality dimensions were statistically significant between groups (see Table 3). We also examined condition differences for both sessions for the other combinations of other prompt categories and attributes, but found no significant differences.

This finding indicates that the structured interface seems to have been conducive to the increased use of Clear *Development* prompts, which are associated

[5] Average proportion of prompts: Development session 2: $70.0 \pm 31.5\%$, session 3: $72.7 \pm 26.2\%$; Conceptual session 2: $11.1 \pm 24.6\%$, session 3: $14.2 \pm 23.5\%$; Debugging session2: $12.5 \pm 22.8\%$, session 3: $9.4 \pm 15.2\%$.

[6] 44 students in session 2 and 31 in session 3 submitted no conceptual prompts. 38 students in session 2 and 34 in session 3 submitted no debugging prompts.

with higher learning gains, but that this effect was short-lived: When the structured interface was removed (session 3), students' use of Clear Development prompts was not different from the comparison group.

Table 3. Chi-square test comparing the joint distribution of prompt types and metrics between conditions for sessions 2 and 3.

Category	Attributes	Session 2			Session 3		
		χ^2	p-value	dof	χ^2	p-value	dof
Development	Understanding	0.92	0.820	3	0.96	0.812	3
Development	Granularity	2.26	0.521	3	3.21	0.360	3
Development	Clarity	8.57	0.036	3	4.69	0.196	3

Proportion of Student-Generated Input in Prompts: We also examined whether writing more of the prompt oneself and copy-pasting less was associated with learning gains, and whether there were differences between conditions.

In Session 2, students wrote on average 71 ± 57 characters themselves per prompt and 457 ± 564 copy-pasted characters per prompt. In Session 3, these values were 64 ± 45 typed characters and 280 ± 401 copy-pasted characters.

We implemented multiple regression models with learning as dependent variables, and the interaction between proportion of student-generated text in prompts as the independent variables on the session 3 data. We found a marginally significant positive effect of proportion of student-generated input on learning gain, $\beta = 0.43, p = .075$, 95% $CI[-0.05, 0.91]$[7].

We found that students using the structured interface in session 2 had a significantly higher average of self-written text in prompts, $t(56) = 2.07$, $p = .048$. However, no difference was found in session 3, $t(53) = 0.48$, $p = .69$, when the normal ChatGPT interface was being used.

4.3 Students' Perception of ChatGPT Between Conditions

The previous analysis shows that despite the lack of significant differences in learning gains or practice lab performance between conditions, students in the intervention group were more likely to engage in productive prompting behaviors while using the structured interface, but not when the structured interface was removed. To better understand why no transfer in behavior occurred, we examined the post-intervention perception survey data.

When asked about their overall perception of ChatGPT use, independent of the learning tasks, students in the intervention group were more likely to consider the use of ChatGPT to be effective for solving tasks, $U = 345$, $p = .01$, Cohen's $d = 0.63$, to generate high quality code, $U = 387$, $p = .046$, Cohen's $d = 0.52$, to be easy to use, $U = 324$, $p = .0042$, Cohen's $d = 0.76$, to be enjoyable, $U = 334$,

[7] The model accounts for a small portion of the variance (adj $R^2 = .041, p = .075$).

0.006, Cohen's $d = 0.62$, and to continue to use ChatGPT in future practice lab sessions, $U = 392$, $p = .049$, Cohen's $d = 0.46$.

However, when asked about the future use of the structured interface, 60% of the students in the intervention group wanted to continue to use ChatGPT exclusively, compared to only 12% who wanted to use the structured interface only, 20% who were willing to use both, and 8% who did not want to use any type of LLM. Students who expressed interest in using the structured interface indicated that it was "more effective and more efficient in answering [their] questions" (student a), with some having even (wrongly) thought that the model was "pretrained on elements of the course" (student b), with results that were "more focused on the course content [thus providing] information and explanations that are more accurate" (student c), which in turn was thought to have helped "speed up the task completion" (student d). One student did nevertheless mention that they learned to improve the quality of their prompts through the structured interface and would apply what they learned when using ChatGPT.

However, of the 40 justifications given for why students preferred to use ChatGPT only, we found the following reasons : (A) Preference for ChatGPT's interface (11/40). (B) Disliking being forced to fill out multiple sections in the structured interface (2/40). (C) Did not see the added value of the structured interface compared to using ChatGPT directly (14/40). (D) Were used to using ChatGPT (9/40) or had a subscription (1/40), had access to more advanced models (3/40) or used GitHub Copilot (5/40).

In total, about 75% of these students preferred ChatGPT only because of already having established working patterns with it, preferring its user interface and not seeing the added value of using the more constrained interface. These findings might partially explain why students who interacted with the structured interface during the interventions had a more positive perception of ChatGPT after the intervention, and also why some of the positive behaviors found in the use of the structured interface did not transfer.

Limitations. Given the relatively small sample size of students who ended up participating across sessions 2 and 3 (n = 58), the statistical power of our analyses is limited. To strengthen our claims, we supplemented the quantitative results with qualitative analyses. Nonetheless, further research with larger samples and across diverse contexts is needed to replicate and extend these results.

5 Discussion and Conclusion

LLMs are increasingly being used by teachers and students alike, but research has indicated that not all LLM use is equivalent, with some types of behavior even being detrimental to learning. It is therefore relevant to understand how to support students to use LLMs in a way that supports learning and to help them develop good prompting behaviors for using such systems in general. We addressed this question with a mixed-methods experimental study to investigate (i) whether using a structured interface to guide prompting behaviors during a multi-session intervention contributes to improved prompting behaviors, performance, and learning, and (ii) whether potential improvements in prompting behaviors and their impact on learning transferred to subsequent ChatGPT use. Students engaged in three practice labs. In the first two practice labs, 58 students either used ChatGPT with the normal interface (control group with 32 students), or ChatGPT with the structured interface (intervention group with 26 students). In the third session, all students used the normal ChatGPT interface. The structured interface was designed based on research on effective questioning strategies in ill-structured problem-solving contexts and required that students think about the type of prompt, and structure the prompts' content before submitting to the LLM. We used pre- and post-measures of learning, process and performance data, and perception questionnaires.

5.1 Structured Interfaces Can Promote Productive Prompting Behaviors, but These Do Not Transfer to Unstructured Interfaces

A first analysis of performance and learning revealed no significant differences between the conditions. To understand why, we investigated whether specific types of prompting patterns were overall more conducive to learning. Specifically, when considering the interaction between prompt type and prompt attributes, we found a positive interaction effect on learning gains between the proportion of "Development" prompts (prompts focused on developing code) with "Clarity" (proportion of prompts with clear and explicit requests), and between overall proportions of "Clarity" and "Understanding" (prompts focused on understanding-related questions). These findings align with prior work on student-generated questions that shows that students' learning improves when they articulate their ideas and questions more clearly [8].

We found no differences between conditions in either prompt attributes or types when examining them separately. But we found that students in the intervention group had a higher proportion of prompts of type "Development" with the attribute "Clarity", i.e. a higher proportion of prompts that were found to be productive for learning, while using the structured interface.

This aligns with Kumar et al. [14] who observed that pedagogically informed guidance, such as metacognitive questioning, reduced superficial interactions and encouraged deeper engagement with learning content. These exploratory results support the view that the impact of LLMs on learning outcomes depends on *how* they are used [16]. Unfortunately, and as found in another recent study [5], the changes in prompting behavior did not extend beyond the intervention: once the students were free to use ChatGPT, they tended to have the same prompting behaviors to those in the control group.

Similarly, we observed a trend where the proportion of student-generated text in prompts (in contrast to the proportion of copy-pasted prompts) correlated with better outcomes. While additional data is required to substantiate this effect, the pattern aligns with the hypothesis that personalized, self-generated text in interaction with AI tools can support learning [14]. Students using the structured interface tended to have higher proportion of self-generated input in their prompts, but as before, this effect disappeared once guidance was removed.

5.2 Why Don't "Good" Prompting Practices Persist When Scaffolding is Removed?

A final analysis of the student survey data revealed that participants using the structured interface perceived the use of ChatGPT overall (independent of the structured interface) as significantly more positive than students in the control group. While this might seem surprising, it appears to be a reaction to the structured interface, which many students considered to be overly constraining: less than 20% of students in the intervention group appreciated the added value of the structured interface. In contrast, about 75% of the students in the intervention group did not see an added value in this interface compared to the normal user interface, with habit of use of ChatGPT and the more appealing user interface indicated as reasons.

This indicates that when trying to teach good prompting behaviors through the use of novel pedagogical LLM tools, or "pedagogy-fied" interfaces for existing LLMs, we need to consider students' prior experiences and habits with LLMs. Even if ChatGPT has been in broad use for only about 2 years by now, a majority of students have already had significant experiences with this tool, and thus developed their own habits and expectations that might increase the resistance to adopting novel other tools. Thus, if we are to design effective pedagogical approaches to help students develop good prompting behaviors, we need to take their history with LLM tools into consideration, as well as their expectations of such tools. Two intervention sessions were not sufficient for the students to adopt new behaviors. Effective interventions likely need a longer duration, and the integration of more explicit approaches, such as elaborating productive prompting behaviors or addressing possible contrasts between pre-existing tools and these more "pedagogical" tools [9].

5.3 Conclusion and Future Work

Overall the findings confirm "the complexities of designing learner–LLM interactions" [14] to support learning, and to develop productive prompting behaviors. This work underscores the challenge of transfer also in this context [4]: one-off scaffolding or training often fails to translate into long-term skill adoption. Learners frequently abandon strategies when external support vanishes [5], especially if those strategies require extra effort [27]. Future research should therefore explore strategies to maintain effective AI interaction behaviors in educational contexts beyond structured interventions. For instance, structured interfaces could integrate more personalization, such as adaptive scaffolding or reflective follow-up questions, may further engage the user and support metacognitive reflection. Moreover, combining interface support with explicit instruction and classroom dialogue around effective LLM use could help learners better understand and retain productive strategies. Ultimately, fostering lasting changes in students' interactions with LLMs may require not only interface-level nudges, but also sustained pedagogical and motivational support that aligns with learners' goals to promote durable learning outcomes.

References

1. Abbas, M., Jam, F.A., Khan, T.I.: Is it harmful or helpful? Examining the causes and consequences of generative AI usage among university students. Int. J. Educ. Technol. High. Educ. **21**(1), 10 (2024)
2. Abdellatif, A., Costa, D., Badran, K., Abdalkareem, R., Shihab, E.: Challenges in chatbot development: a study of stack overflow posts. In: Proceedings of the 17th International Conference on Mining Software Repositories, pp. 174–185 (2020)
3. Bahroun, Z., Anane, C., Ahmed, V., Zacca, A.: Transforming education: a comprehensive review of generative artificial intelligence in educational settings through bibliometric and content analysis. Sustainability **15**(17), 12983 (2023)
4. Barnett, S.M., Ceci, S.J.: When and where do we apply what we learn?: A taxonomy for far transfer. Psychol. Bull. **128**(4), 612 (2002)
5. Bastani, H., Bastani, O., Sungu, A., Ge, H., Kabakcı, O., Mariman, R.: Generative AI can harm learning. Available at SSRN 4895486 (2024)
6. Bowman-Perrott, L., Davis, H., Vannest, K., Williams, L., Greenwood, C., Parker, R.: Academic benefits of peer tutoring: a meta-analytic review of single-case research. Sch. Psychol. Rev. **42**(1), 39–55 (2013)
7. Brender, J., El-Hamamsy, L., Mondada, F., Bumbacher, E.: Who's helping who? when students use chatGPT to engage in practice lab sessions. In: Olney, A.M., Chounta, IA., Liu, Z., Santos, O.C., Bittencourt, I.I. (eds.) AIED 2024. LNCS, vol. 14829, pp. 235–249. Springer, Cham (2024). https://doi.org/10.1007/978-3-031-64302-6_17
8. Byun, H., Lee, J., Cerreto, F.A.: Relative effects of three questioning strategies in ill-structured, small group problem solving. Instr. Sci. **42**, 229–250 (2014)
9. Choi, W.C., Chang, C.I.: A survey of techniques, key components, strategies, challenges, and student perspectives on prompt engineering for large language models (LLMs) in education (2025)
10. Deng, R., Jiang, M., Yu, X., Lu, Y., Liu, S.: Does chatGPT enhance student learning? A systematic review and meta-analysis of experimental studies. Comput. Educ. 105224 (2024)
11. Denny, P., et al.: Promptly: using prompt problems to teach learners how to effectively utilize AI code generators. arXiv preprint arXiv:2307.16364 (2023)
12. Fan, Y., et al.: Beware of metacognitive laziness: effects of generative artificial intelligence on learning motivation, processes, and performance. BJET **56**(2), 489–530 (2025)
13. Favero, L., Pérez-Ortiz, J.A., Käser, T., Oliver, N.: Enhancing critical thinking in education by means of a socratic chatbot. arXiv preprint arXiv:2409.05511 (2024)
14. Kumar, H., et al.: Impact of guidance and interaction strategies for LLM use on learner performance and perception. arXiv preprint arXiv:2310.13712 (2023)
15. Lau, S., Guo, P.: From "Ban it till we understand it" to "resistance is futile": how university programming instructors plan to adapt as more students use AI code generation and explanation tools such as ChatGPT and GitHub copilot. In: ICER 2023, vol. 1, pp. 106–121. ACM (2023)

16. Lehmann, M., Cornelius, P.B., Sting, F.J.: AI meets the classroom: when do large language models harm learning? (2025). https://arxiv.org/abs/2409.09047
17. Li, Y., et al.: Competition-level code generation with alphacode. Science **378**(6624), 1092–1097 (2022)
18. Liu, R., Zenke, C., Liu, C., Holmes, A., Thornton, P., Malan, D.J.: Teaching cs50 with AI: leveraging generative artificial intelligence in computer science education. In: Proceedings of the 55th ACM SIGCSE TS, pp. 750–756 (2024)
19. Loksa, D., Ko, A.J., Jernigan, W., Oleson, A., Mendez, C.J., Burnett, M.M.: Programming, problem solving, and self-awareness: effects of explicit guidance. In: 2016 CHI Conference on Human Factors in Computing Systems, pp. 1449–1461 (2016)
20. Mollick, E.R., Mollick, L.: New modes of learning enabled by AI chatbots: three methods and assignments. Available at SSRN 4300783 (2022)
21. Nissen, J.M., Talbot, R.M., Nasim Thompson, A., Van Dusen, B.: Comparison of normalized gain and Cohen'sd for analyzing gains on concept inventories. Phys. Rev. Phys. Educ. Res. **14**(1), 010115 (2018)
22. Noy, S., Zhang, W.: Experimental evidence on the productivity effects of generative artificial intelligence. Science **381**(6654), 187–192 (2023)
23. Prather, J., et al.: First things first: providing metacognitive scaffolding for interpreting problem prompts. In: Proceedings of the 50th ACM SIGCSE TS (2019)
24. Singhal, K., et al.: Large language models encode clinical knowledge. Nature **620**(7972), 172–180 (2023)
25. Stokel-Walker, C., Van Noorden, R.: What chatGPT and generative AI mean for science. Nature **614**(7947), 214–216 (2023)
26. Swargiary, K.: The impact of ChatGPT on student learning outcomes: a comparative study of cognitive engagement, procrastination, and academic performance (2024). https://doi.org/10.2139/ssrn.4914743
27. Sweller, J., Van Merrienboer, J.J., Paas, F.G.: Cognitive architecture and instructional design. Educ. Psychol. Rev. **10**, 251–296 (1998)
28. Teo, T.: Modelling technology acceptance in education: a study of pre-service teachers. Comput. Educ. **52**(2), 302–312 (2009)
29. Yang, H.: How i use chatGPT responsibly in my teaching. Nature **10** (2023)
30. Yilmaz, R., Yilmaz, F.G.K.: Augmented intelligence in programming learning: examining student views on the use of chatGPT for programming learning. Comput. Hum. Behav.: Artif. Hum. **1**(2), 100005 (2023)

Toward Realistic AI-Generated Student Questions to Support Instructor Training

Francesco Cardia[1], Viviana Pentangelo[2], Stefano Lambiase[2], Carmine Gravino[2], Fabio Palomba[2], and Mirko Marras[1](✉)

[1] University of Cagliari, Cagliari, Italy
f.cardia32@studenti.unica.it, mirko.marras@acm.org
[2] University of Salerno, Salerno, Italy
{vpentangelo,slambiase,gravino,fpalomba}@unisa.it

Abstract. Instructor effectiveness is fundamental to student learning, with the ability to manage student inquiries serving as a critical component of effective teaching. Student questions represent a valuable training resource for instructors to strengthen their teaching strategies, yet interactions with students are often constrained by several factors. In this paper, we investigate how instructors perceive machine- and student-generated questions, considering the potential for the former to complement the latter in a cost-effective manner. Our study involved 121 undergraduate students and an equivalent number of simulated students modeled using a state-of-the-art large language model, generating over 360 questions in total based on video lectures given by seven university instructors. We assessed whether instructors could distinguish between human- and machine-generated questions and how they evaluated their relevance, clarity, answerability, challenge level, and cognitive depth. Results show that instructors struggle to differentiate between the two sets of questions, with accuracy close to random chance. Instructors tended to (i) rate machine-generated questions slightly higher in relevance, clarity, answerability, and challenge—though only relevance and answerability showed significant differences—and (ii) associate them marginally more often with higher-order cognitive skills. This confirms the potential of machine-generated questions as tools for instructor training. **Repository**: https://github.com/tail-unica/realistic-ai-generated-questions.

Keywords: Generative AI · Instructor Training · Student Simulation · Student Questioning · Question Generation · Large Language Models

1 Introduction

Motivation. Instructors can influence student learning and achievement, with some instructors showing greater effectiveness in fostering positive educational outcomes for students than others [1]. Teaching effectiveness encompasses actions

F. Cardia and V. Pentangelo—These authors contributed equally to this work.

K. Tammets et al. (Eds.): EC-TEL 2025, LNCS 16063, pp. 107–122, 2026.
https://doi.org/10.1007/978-3-032-03870-8_8

that enhance or facilitate learning [26]. Improving this effectiveness requires identifying strategies that support instructors in optimizing their practices [17]. In this regard, a key aspect is answering students' questions and doubts during a lesson, which may represent a challenging situation for the instructors, demanding them to refine and reflect on their communication and content delivery.

In recent years, this challenge has been amplified by the spreading adoption of remote learning environments—such as Massive Open Online Courses (MOOCs) [7]. On the one hand, students are adopting this modality for its flexibility and availability, which are increasing access to educational resources, overcoming constraints such as class size, limited time, and student availability [11,24]. On the other hand, they limit the instructor's ability to interact with students in real-time: student questions often arrive asynchronously, and instructors must find effective ways to respond post-hoc without immediate feedback or classroom cues [23]. As this model becomes increasingly common, supporting instructors in anticipating and handling student inquiries becomes essential.

Open Issues. In traditional settings, instructors may progressively improve their responses to student questions through direct interaction. However, in asynchronous online contexts, opportunities for such practice are scarce. In this way, many instructors are not regularly exposed to dynamic, question-driven teaching environments, which limits their ability to innovate or adjust methods based on immediate feedback [12,31]. Critically, instructors have no way to predict what questions will be asked nor rehearse answering them, which could reduce their potential to improve student learning outcomes [30,32]. From a constructivist view, this lack of questioning inhibits the reflective practice essential for instructor learning. Questions serve not only as indicators of student thinking but also as stimuli for instructors to construct pedagogical responses [10,25].

To address these limitations, simulations have increasingly been introduced in educational contexts [15]. However, these efforts are generally directed at the instructor side of the educational interaction. They simulate how an instructor might respond to a student's input, such as through teaching assistants who offer feedback [19]. Rarely, though, do these simulations replicate students [3]. Most studies using learner simulations focus on method-related goals, e.g., benchmarking [22,27] and validating techniques [29]. Some focus on optimizing student models via parameter learning [8]. However, no study has examined simulated student-generated questions nor instructor perceptions of them.

Contributions. In this paper, we want to take a foundational step toward using machine-generated student questions as a support mechanism for instructor training. The goal is to investigate whether it is feasible to simulate realistic student inquiries in view of their possible future usage for instructor training and continuous teaching improvement—particularly in asynchronous contexts such as MOOCs[1]. To this end, we recruited seven university instructors who recorded

[1] It should be noted that machine-generated questions should not be seen as a replacement for real student input, but as a complementary resource in settings where direct student interaction is sparse or delayed as well as for pre-class training.

video lectures on topics they regularly teach at the university. These lectures were then presented to real students, who formulated their questions, and a large language model generated inquiries based on student personas. Instructors then reviewed both sets of questions, attempting to distinguish between machine- and human-generated questions (**RQ$_1$**), while also assessing their clarity, relevance, answerability, challenge level, and cognitive depth (**RQ$_2$**).

The rest of this paper is organized as follows: Sect. 2 details the study design. Section 3 presents the findings, while Sect. 4 interprets them. Finally, Sect. 5 summarizes key insights and points to future research.

2 Methodology

In this section, we present the methodology designed to investigate the potential of machine-generated questions as a source that can complement real student inquiries in instructional settings where additional support is needed (Fig. 1). Our methodological choices are informed by constructivist learning studies, which emphasize the importance of engaging instructors in interactions with learner-generated content [10,25]. In this context, student questions—whether real or simulated—act as cognitive artifacts that challenge instructors to analyze, interpret, and respond in ways that foster their growth. With this in mind, we followed a three-step approach: (1) preparing teaching materials by collecting and curating lectures from university instructors; (2) generating student questions through two parallel processes—real students submitting inquiries and a large language model producing machine-generated questions using few-shot prompting with student personas; and (3) assessing instructor perceptions by evaluating their ability to distinguish between human- and machine-generated questions (**RQ$_1$**) and rating questions based on key quality dimensions (**RQ$_2$**).

2.1 Lectures Collection

When designing the study, we considered various instructional formats, including face-to-face lectures, live interactive sessions, and pre-recorded video lessons. While traditional and live lectures offer spontaneous interactions, they introduce substantial variability, such as unscripted peer discussions and real-time instructor adaptations, that complicate systematic comparisons across participants. In contrast, short, structured video lectures ensure that both real and simulated students engage with consistent instructional content, thereby enabling controlled and replicable evaluation of question-generation phenomena [21]. Importantly, this design choice is not a simplification but a deliberate alignment with the realities of modern MOOC and online learning platforms, where asynchronous video content is the norm and one of the key challenges is the lack of real-time student feedback [28]. With this educational setting as a target, we could enable, for instance, the use of machine-generated questions by instructors to anticipate common points of confusion, refine instructional content, and prepare for potential student inquiries in asynchronous environments (e.g., forums).

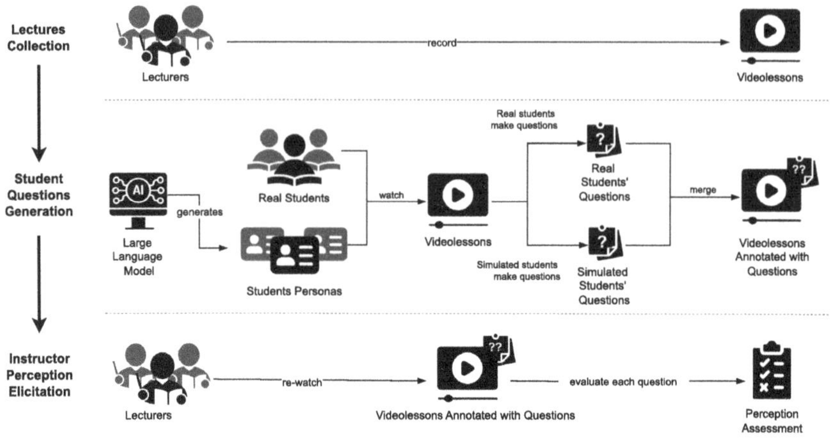

Fig. 1. Method. Overview of our method, including video lecture collection, question generation by real and simulated students, and instructor perceptions collection.

Table 1. Collected Lectures. Lectures, recorded by university instructors and covering distinct topics, served for generating human- and machine-generated questions.

ID	Topic	Complexity	Duration	Transcript	Frequency
SVM	Support Vector Machines	Beginner	9:45	1,469 words	151 words/min
NNE	Neural Networks	Beginner	11:14	1,588 words	141 words/min
FAI	Fairness in AI	Intermediate	12:01	1,718 words	143 words/min
IMC	Image Classification	Intermediate	12:18	1,796 words	146 words/min
TSC	Time Series Classification	Intermediate	8:36	1,087 words	126 words/min
TAR	Transformer Architecture	Advanced	8:17	1,300 words	157 words/min
AIC	AI and Code Smells	Advanced	9:55	1,195 words	120 words/min

In a first stage, we therefore curated a set of video lectures[2] that simulate real-world instructional scenarios typically part of online learning platforms. Specifically, we collected seven distinct lectures from as many instructors, each covering a unique topic relevant to a Computer Science Bachelor's degree program with a focus on Artificial Intelligence[3]. The instructors were not provided with a structured template or predefined slides, allowing them to maintain their own teaching styles and delivery. The cohort of instructors consisted of two females (28.6%) and five males (71.4%), ensuring a degree of perspectives diversity.

The collected lectures exhibit notable variability in duration, transcript length, and complexity (Table 1). The shortest lecture lasted just over 8 min (`TAR`, 8:17 min), while the longest exceeded 12 min (`IMC`, 12:18 min), reflecting different

[2] Once recorded, the lectures were uploaded to `YouTube` under private access settings, ensuring that they could only be accessed via direct links, for the subsequent steps.

[3] This choice enabled the analysis of question-generation patterns across diverse subtopics while minimizing confounding factors from disciplinary differences. Future work can extend this study to other domains to assess generalizability.

depths of topic coverage. Transcript lengths also varied, from 1,087 words (TSC) to 1,796 words (IMC), showing differences in speaking pace and content density. The words per minute (WPM) further indicates a spectrum of instructional styles, with some instructors delivering fast-paced explanations (TAR, 157 WPM), while others adopt a slower approach (AIC, 120 WPM). In terms of topic complexity, the collected lectures include beginner (SVM, NNE), intermediate (FAI, IMC, TSC), and advanced (TAR, AIC) lectures. This diversity in content and delivery allows for a robust evaluation of real and simulated student questions.

2.2 Student Questions Generation

As a second step, we employed a dual, parallel approach: real students formulated their own questions while engaging with instructional content, while a large language model generated questions following structured student personas.

Human Questions Generation. The question-generation process was conducted asynchronously, allowing students to engage with the assigned videos at their own pace. This setting ensured that students interacted with the lectures in a flexible manner, similar to modern online course platforms. Participants were recruited through a voluntary survey, with a total of 121 students enrolled in the third year of the same Computer Science Bachelor's degree program from which the instructors and lecture recordings originated. This consistency in academic background facilitated a controlled analysis, ensuring that all participants had comparable foundational knowledge and were accustomed to the instructional style of their institution. The sample included 40% female students.

To ensure that student-generated questions were meaningful and reflective of genuine knowledge gaps, the recruitment survey asked participants to self-report their familiarity with each lecture topic. Based on these self-assessments, students were assigned to two lectures where they had the least prior knowledge. This assignment strategy balanced the distribution of participants across all lectures, ensuring that question-generation was not biased toward topics where students already had expertise and so possibly were less likely to make questions.

Following this assignment, students received an email with experimental instructions and access to a custom web-based platform we developed[4]. This platform facilitated structured question submission while ensuring precise tracking. Specifically, once submitted, each question was appended to a unique CSV file, recording (i) the date and time of the submission, (ii) the anonymized participant identifier, (iii) the lecture from which the question comes, (iv) the lecture time when the question was asked, and (v) the question text. For example, one entry might indicate that on June 12, 2024, at 11:35:16, participant 87 submitted a question for the lecture TRA at the 1:17 mark, asking: "Does this type of architecture form the basis of the most well-known translation applications?".

In the instructions, students were encouraged to submit questions whenever they encountered confusion or curiosity, mimicking the natural inquiry process

[4] First, students enter their anonymized ID, assigned video IDs, and perform a self-assessment on key student profiling dimensions. Subsequent pages display each video with an embedded player and an interface component for question submission.

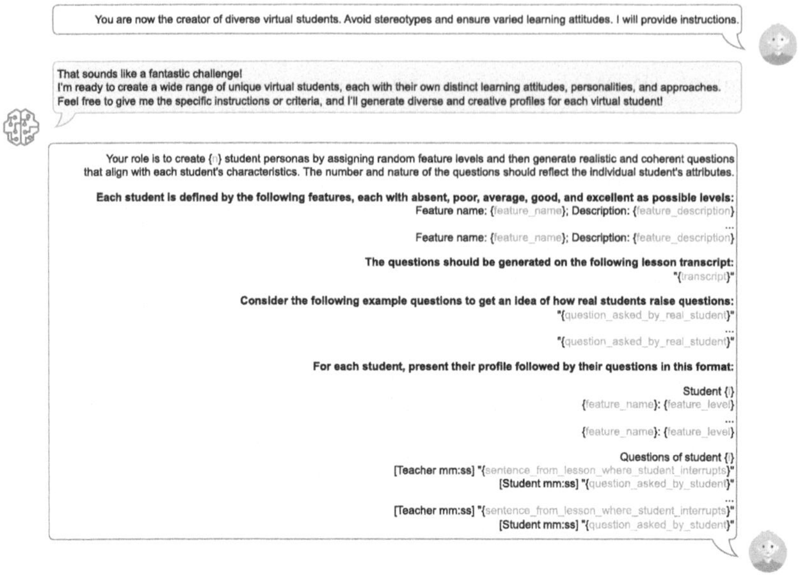

Fig. 2. Prompt Template. Simplified schema of the prompt for simulating university student personas and generating realistic questions based on randomized characteristics. These templates structure student features, their levels, and questioning moments.

that occurs in real learning environments. To further promote active engagement and prevent passive participation, at the end of the session, they were also required to provide a short summary of each lecture they watched. These summaries, typically five to six sentences long, not only served as a means of verifying their comprehension but also reinforced content retention by encouraging students to synthesize and reflect on the key points presented in the lecture.

Machine Questions Generation. The first step involved extracting lecture transcripts, which were automatically generated by `YouTube`. These transcripts captured the content of each lecture from a machine perspective, differing from human students who had access to both audio and visual cues. This decision was made for three key reasons. First, it eliminates multimodal confounders such as intonation and gestures, ensuring that differences between machine- and human-generated questions stem from textual comprehension rather than extraneous factors. Second, it aligns with computational constraints, as most state-of-the-art models are trained primarily on text and lack robust multimodal reasoning. Third, prior research confirms that textual data alone captures essential semantic content for meaningful question generation [6]. While future work may explore multimodal approaches, arranging them goes beyond the scope of this study.

The generation process was grounded in two key pillars: (1) modern role-play prompting [18] to guide the language model's behavior, and (2) relevant student profiling dimensions to create diverse and realistic student personas [2,9,13].

For each lecture, we employed a two-stage framework leveraging a role-playing prompting technique [18], adapted specifically to the educational domain and the student questioning task. The selection of this technique builds on prior findings showing that role-playing enhances large language models' zero-shot reasoning [18]. Specifically, we used GPT-4o as the language model, since the same prior work showed its superiority. The prompt we designed (see Fig. 2) provided structured instructions, including persona's attributes, the lecture transcript, example questions from other contexts, and the expected output format.

Within the prompt, we asked to characterize each student persona by twelve dimensions grounded in findings from prior research in student modeling [2]. Such dimensions included prior knowledge, interest, motivation, concentration, critical thinking, ability to learn, and memory [9], as well as intuition, creativity, logical reasoning, emotionality, and language proficiency [13]. In GPT-4, simulated students were internally modeled by randomly assigning a level to each dimension on a discrete scale from 1 (absent) to 5 (excellent), with unit increments[5]. Such choice facilitated different questioning patterns. For instance, motivated and knowledgeable personas might produce in-depth inquiries, while less engaged personas might generate simpler or fewer questions.

The model instantiated each student persona and processed the lecture transcript in a sequential manner, identifying points at which questions would naturally emerge. The number of questions generated per persona remained unconstrained to allow for natural variation in questioning behavior. All generated questions were systematically recorded in a structured dataset formatted identically to the human-generated corpus, enabling direct comparability. Each entry was annotated with a timestamp reflecting the date and time of submission, an anonymized participant identifier, the corresponding lecture video, and the precise temporal location within the lecture when the question was raised. Additionally, the dataset preserved the textual content of each generated question.

2.3 Instructor Perception Elicitation

With the collected questions, we implemented a structured assessment protocol to determine whether instructors could reliably distinguish between human- and machine-generated questions and to analyze their perceptions regarding relevance, clarity, answerability, level of challenge, and cognitive depth.

To ensure an unbiased evaluation, instructors conducted their assessments[6] independently, without access to other raters' evaluations. Each instructor received a spreadsheet containing a set of fields about questions of their own

[5] While these attributes exist on a continuum in real learners, categorizing them into discrete levels aligns with widely used educational frameworks, such as Bloom's taxonomy, which structure cognitive and affective traits into distinct stages.

[6] We acknowledge that evaluating questions in isolation does not fully reflect the complexity of classroom instruction, where instructors consider interpersonal cues, prior discussion threads, and the evolving classroom atmosphere. However, our goal at this stage was to establish whether machine-generated questions are perceived as realistic, i.e., a prerequisite before integrating them into high-variance environments.

lecture[7], including the timestamp the question was posed in the lecture, the text of the question, and a source field where they were asked to indicate whether they believed the question was human- or machine-generated. The spreadsheet also incorporated four numerical evaluation criteria (relevance, clarity, answerability, and level of challenge for instructors) aligned with established frameworks on the quality of student-generated questions [12,31]. Instructors rated each criterion on a 1 to 10 scale, with higher values indicating stronger alignment with the respective property. Each question was also classified in terms of perceived cognitive depth according to Bloom's Taxonomy by the instructor [5], selecting among remembering, understanding, applying, analyzing, evaluating, or creating.

To maintain a balanced assessment, we selected an equal number of human- and machine-generated questions to be added into the evaluation spreadsheet for a given lecture. The total number of questions per lecture was determined by the smaller of the two available sets (human- or machine-generated questions) for that specific lecture (i.e., down-sampling the larger set), to prevent imbalances and potential biases. The selected questions were randomly shuffled to eliminate any patterns that could indicate their origin in the spreadsheet. The inclusion of timestamps allowed instructors to evaluate each question in its proper lecture context. It should be noted that instructors were not informed that the machine-generated questions were produced solely from textual transcripts of the lectures.

3 Experimental Results

We analyzed the students' questions to determine whether instructors can reliably distinguish between human- and machine-generated inquiries ($\mathbf{RQ_1}$). Additionally, we examined how instructors perceive the questions in terms of relevance, clarity, answerability, challenge level, and cognitive depth ($\mathbf{RQ_2}$).

3.1 Turing Test for Question Source Classification [$\mathbf{RQ_1}$]

In this analysis, we were interested in evaluating whether instructors could reliably distinguish between machine-generated (MQ) and human-generated (HQ) questions. Specifically, we examined the extent to which instructors correctly classified MQ as machine-generated or misclassified them as human-generated, and similarly, whether HQ were correctly identified as human-generated or misclassified as machine-generated. Results are summarized in Table 2, which reports the percentage of (in)correctly classified questions across different lectures. The final row presents the averaged results across all lectures, providing a general measure of the instructors' ability in differentiating between the two sources.

[7] To strengthen the evidence and improve generalizability, future work will incorporate cross-instructor rating conditions and extend the study to instructors from other disciplines and with varying levels of experience with technology.

Table 2. [RQ$_1$] Question Source Classification. The proportion of machine- (MQ) and human-generated questions (HQ) that were either correctly classified or misclassified. The Accuracy column represents the sum of correctly classified MQ and HQ per lecture. Bold values indicate the highest percentage per column.

Lecture	# Questions	Instructor Accuracy	MQ predicted as		HQ predicted as	
			MQ	HQ	MQ	HQ
SVM	44× 2	40.9%	22.7%	27.3%	31.8%	18.2%
NNE	64× 2	45.3%	29.7%	20.3%	**34.4%**	15.6%
FAI	54× 2	42.6%	16.7%	33.3%	24.1%	25.9%
IMC	52× 2	**69.2%**	**32.7%**	17.3%	13.5%	**36.5%**
TSC	76× 2	39.5%	13.2%	**36.8%**	23.7%	26.3%
TAR	34× 2	61.8%	26.5%	23.5%	14.7%	35.3%
AIC	36× 2	50.0%	19.4%	30.6%	19.4%	30.6%
Average	52× 2	49.9%	23.0%	27.0%	23.1%	26.9%

The average classification accuracy of 49.9% suggests that instructors struggled to distinguish between machine- and human-generated questions, performing basically as a random guesser. Specifically, on average, instructors correctly identified 23.0% of MQ, while 27.0% of MQ were misclassified as HQ. Conversely, 23.1% of HQ were incorrectly labeled as MQ, while 26.9% were correctly identified as HQ. The fact that more MQ were misclassified as HQ than correctly identified implies that machine-generated questions often appeared natural enough to be perceived as human-authored. Likewise, the relatively high proportion of HQ misclassified as MQ indicates that certain student-generated questions may have exhibited features resembling algorithmically structured questions.

Accuracy varied significantly across different lectures, ranging from 39.5% (TSC) to 69.2% (IMC), revealing considerable disparities in instructors' ability to classify questions depending on the topic. In some cases, such as IMC and TSC, instructors exhibited higher accuracy in recognizing MQ, with 32.7% and 36.8% correctly classified as machine, respectively. Meanwhile, for RNN, the highest misclassification of HQ as MQ was recorded at 34.4%, suggesting that human-generated questions in this lecture may have shared stylistic or structural features with machine-generated ones. The highest overall accuracy in IMC (69.2%) suggests that the questions in this lecture may have had clearer distinguishing characteristics between human and machine origins. On the other hand, TSC (39.5%) and FAI (42.6%) had notably lower accuracy, indicating that MQ and HQ in these topics were more ambiguous, making classification more difficult. When examining patterns across lectures with similar characteristics (Table 1), we observed that beginner and intermediate topics consistently led to the lowest classification accuracy, often with reversed judgments, except for IMC. This may be due to the straightforward nature of simpler topics, leading both machine- and human-generated questions to converge toward generic, surface-level inquiries.

RQ$_1$. ***Instructors substantially struggled to distinguish machine from human questions, particularly in lectures with lower instructional levels. This finding suggests machine-generated questions as credible real learner-like inquiries.***

Table 3. [RQ_2] Evaluation of Relevance, Clarity, Answerability, Challenge. The average ratings of machine- (MQ) and human-generated (HQ) questions across the four numerical dimensions. The final row reports the average score per column. Bold values indicate the highest score in each lecture for each dimension. Statistical significance analyses between MQ and HQ in each lecture for each dimension are based on Mann-Whitney U tests with Bonferroni correction (* $p < 0.01$, ** $p < 0.05$).

Lecture	Relevance		Clarity		Answerability		Challenge	
	MQ	HQ	MQ	HQ	MQ	HQ	MQ	HQ
SVM	**4.41**	3.59	**6.14**	4.95	**6.23**	5.27	3.18	**3.55**
NNE	**7.41**	7.12	**7.78**	7.47	**6.94**	6.69	**3.50**	3.22
FAI	**8.70***	7.37	**8.48***	7.04	**8.52***	7.11	**5.93**	4.89
IMC	6.96	**7.00**	**6.69**	6.65	**7.27**	7.04	**6.08**	5.73
TSC	**5.89**	5.79	6.32	**6.61**	**6.50**	6.13	5.08	**5.34**
TAR	**8.06****	5.88	**9.29**	8.24	**9.06**	8.29	**6.18***	2.82
AIC	**9.33**	8.50	**8.89**	8.67	**7.89**	6.83	5.44	**6.06**
Average	**7.11****	6.45	**7.47**	6.98	**7.34***	6.67	**4.97**	4.56

3.2 Multi-dimensional Question Quality Perception [RQ_2]

In a second analysis, we examined how instructors perceived machine- (MQ) and human-generated (HQ) questions across relevance, clarity, answerability, challenge level, and cognitive level. To address this, we analyzed the average ratings[8] of instructors for the first four dimensions (Table 3) as well as the cognitive classification of questions according to Bloom's taxonomy (Table 4).

On average, MQs received higher scores than HQs across all four evaluated numerical dimensions (relevance, clarity, answerability, and challenge level). Statistically significant differences emerged in relevance ($p < 0.05$) and answerability ($p < 0.01$), with MQs rated as more relevant (7.11 vs. 6.45) and easier to answer (7.34 vs. 6.67). The higher relevance may emerge from LLMs generating questions instantly, anchoring them closely to the target part of the lecture. In contrast, students often take longer to process information and submit questions later—unless pausing the video—leading to prompts less tied to the specific part. The gain in answerability likely reflects the LLMs' intrinsic knowledge base, enabling them to generate questions with a sense of the expected answer, unlike students who naturally ask questions without knowing the answer. While MQs also scored higher in clarity (7.47 vs. 6.98) and challenge (4.97 vs. 4.56), these differences were not statistically significant, indicating less consistent patterns.

Examining individual lectures reveals notable similarities between MQs and HQs. In most cases, ratings were closely matched—though MQs often scored slightly higher—indicating a comparable perceived quality. Significant differences were rare exceptions. In FAI, MQs significantly outperformed HQs in rel-

[8] We also explored the nested structure of our data - questions within lectures, lectures within instructors - by fitting mixed-effects models that included random intercepts for instructors and lectures. We also computed rank-biserial correlations to estimate effect sizes. These analyses yielded patterns consistent with the primary results.

Table 4. [RQ$_2$] Evaluation of Cognitive Levels. The percentage of machine- (MQ) and human-generated (HQ) questions classified into each Bloom's category, namely *Rem* for *Remembering*, *Und* for *Understanding*, *App* for *Applying*, *Anl* for *Analyzing*, *Evl* for *Evaluating*, and *Crt* for *Creating*. The last row shows the average scores across all lectures. Bold values indicate the highest score in each lecture for MQ and HQ.

Lecture	MQ						HQ					
	Rem	Und	App	Anl	Evl	Crt	Rem	Und	App	Anl	Evl	Crt
SVM	**36.36%**	9.09%	4.55%	31.82%	18.18%	0.00%	**40.91%**	22.73%	9.09%	9.09%	9.09%	9.09%
NNE	6.25%	**34.38%**	21.88%	15.62%	21.88%	0.00%	15.62%	**31.25%**	28.12%	18.75%	6.25%	0.00%
FAI	14.81%	**29.63%**	11.11%	7.41%	14.81%	22.22%	18.52%	**25.93%**	7.41%	7.41%	25.93%	14.81%
IMC	**42.31%**	11.54%	7.69%	15.38%	7.69%	15.38%	**23.08%**	**23.08%**	0.00%	19.23%	19.23%	11.54%
TSC	**31.58%**	5.26%	26.32%	7.89%	18.42%	10.53%	**57.89%**	2.63%	10.53%	7.89%	5.26%	15.79%
TAR	**23.53%**	11.76%	**23.53%**	**23.53%**	11.76%	5.88%	**58.82%**	29.41%	5.88%	5.88%	0.00%	0.00%
AIC	0.00%	**55.56%**	11.11%	11.11%	16.67%	5.56%	0.00%	**61.11%**	0.00%	0.00%	38.89%	0.00%
Average	22.12%	**22.46%**	15.17%	16.11%	15.63%	8.51%	**30.69%**	28.02%	8.72%	9.75%	14.95%	7.32%

evance ($p < 0.01$), clarity ($p < 0.01$), and answerability ($p < 0.01$). This could be attributed to the longer transcript compared to other lectures, providing the LLM with more context to generate well-aligned and coherent questions. Similarly, in TAR, MQs showed significant gains in relevance ($p < 0.05$) and challenge ($p < 0.01$). The higher WPM rate might have contributed, as the denser information flow could make it harder for students to formulate immediate, well-targeted questions. In contrast, the LLM's ability to process the entire transcript at once likely enabled it to generate more relevant and complex questions.

In terms of cognitive skill classification, MQs were more frequently associated with higher-order cognitive levels compared to HQs. MQs were often categorized under Analyzing (16.11%) and Evaluating (15.63%), while HQs were predominantly assigned to lower-order categories such as Remembering (30.69%) and Understanding (28.02%). This suggests that MQs typically required deeper engagement and critical thinking. However, this pattern varied across lectures. For example, in NNE, both MQs and HQs were mostly categorized under Understanding (34.38% and 31.25%, respectively), indicating similar cognitive demands. In contrast, SVM showed a clear distinction, with 31.82% (9.09%) of MQs (HQs) classified as Analyzing, reinforcing the cognitive strength of MQs in this lecture.

RQ$_2$. ***Instructors rated machine-generated questions higher than human-generated ones in relevance, clarity, answerability, and challenge level, but with statistically significant gains only in relevance and answerability. The former were also more frequently associated with higher-order cognitive skills.***

4 Discussion and Implications

Our findings reveal how instructors distinguish between machine-generated (MQ) and human-generated (HQ) questions and perceive their quality. This section explores the implications of and contextualize these results within prior works.

One notable outcome of this study is that instructors struggled to reliably distinguish between MQs and HQs (**RQ₁**). Misclassification rates were balanced in both directions, indicating that MQs were frequently mistaken for authentic student contributions, while HQs were often confused for machine-generated content. This result aligns with prior studies on the effectiveness of machine-generated content in educational settings, which have shown that well-designed machine-generated questions can mimic human inquiry patterns and pass as plausible student-generated contributions [14,29,31]. For instructor training, this finding has significant implications. Since instructors exhibited no systematic accuracy in classifying MQs versus HQs, their perception of student engagement may not be significantly altered by the presence of machine-generated questions. This suggests that MQs could be incorporated into professional development programs without disrupting instructors' natural assessment of student inquiry. By simulation, MQs can help instructors practice adaptive teaching. For example, the metaverse can enhance training with simulated student avatars raising dynamic questions, exposing instructors to diverse questioning behaviors and refining responses to spontaneous inquiries [4,20]. Importantly, we view machine-generated questions not merely as content artifacts but as pedagogical prompts designed to support instructor reflection. This aligns with constructivist views of teaching as a form of learning, where engaging with student inquiries helps instructors refine their mental models of effective instruction [10,25].

Our findings also highlight how instructors perceive machine-generated questions (MQs) in terms of relevance, clarity, answerability, and challenge (**RQ₂**). While MQs generally received higher ratings than HQs across these dimensions, statistically significant differences were observed only in select cases. This suggests that although MQs are often perceived as well-structured, content-aligned, and easy to answer based on the available instructional materials, these advantages are not consistently significant. Nonetheless, these findings align with prior work showing that machine-generated questions can show strong structural coherence and relevance [16,24]. Our results also indicate that MQs were more frequently associated with higher-order thinking skills, such as analyzing and evaluating, aligning with previous studies suggesting that machine-generated questions tend to emphasize structured reasoning and analytical depth [30,32]. This is a promising opportunity: since MQs are perceived as of comparable quality, they could serve as scaffolding tools to support instructor training.

While real student questions undoubtedly carry unique qualities, such as informal phrasing or misconceptions, that reflect authentic cognitive processes, our goal was to examine the extent to which MQs can approximate the overall quality of student questioning. Rather than replacing authentic interactions, MQs should be viewed as valuable complements that enhance instructor preparedness, especially in contexts where direct student input may be limited, delayed, or inconsistent, such as in asynchronous or large-scale online learning environments. Far from narrowing pedagogical awareness, exposure to a spectrum of MQs (including also higher-order and reflective prompts) can enrich instructors' repertoire of responses and promote anticipatory thinking. At the same time, incorporating a balance of question types by playing with the simulated student personas in MQ design can help maintain sensitivity to the full range of student learning needs. More importantly, MQs offer a low-risk, high-availability resource for rehearsal and reflection, empowering instructors to refine their pedagogical strategies and better support students across varying levels of understanding.

5 Conclusion and Future Work

In this paper, we examined instructors' ability to distinguish between machine- and human-generated questions and their perceptions of question quality. To this end, we introduced a novel protocol for comparing real and machine-generated student inquiries, a novel method for generating student-like questions using structured personas, and an novel annotated dataset including human- and machine-generated questions to video lectures we collected as well. Results show that instructors struggled to differentiate between the two, indicating that artificially generated questions closely resemble authentic student inquiries. Moreover, machine-generated questions were consistently rated higher in relevance, clarity, and answerability and were more frequently classified under higher-order cognitive skills. These findings show their potential in instructor training to refine questioning strategies, improve assessment design, and foster critical thinking.

While our findings show the potential of machine-generated questions in instructor training, several limitations suggest avenues for future research. The sample of instructors and curricula leaves space for investigating the generalizability of our results. However, our study serves as a foundational step in exploring the role of machine-generated questions in instructional settings. We prioritized internal validity by selecting a coherent curricular context. This allowed us to control for domain-specific variables and establish a clear methodological framework. In future work, we will extend this analysis to other disciplines—especially those with distinct characteristics from computer science—but we view our contribution as a necessary step toward broader interdisciplinary validation. In future work, we also plan to systematically compare question outputs across diverse personas, e.g., varying in prior knowledge, confidence, or motivation, and analyze how these factors shape the style, complexity, and pedagogical relevance of generated questions. Furthermore, while the machine-generated questions were based solely on textual transcripts, students engaged with the full audiovisual content of the lectures. This intentional design choice allowed us to isolate and assess the capabilities of text-based models in simulating student-like questioning. In future work we will explore multimodal approaches that incorporate visual and auditory information to more closely mirror the full context available to students. Our current findings thus provide a necessary baseline for evaluating the added value of such multimodal integration. To enhance realism, future studies will also consider sampling simulated student personas from survey data rather than uniform random draws, better aligning with authentic student diversity.

Beyond dataset representativeness, instructor evaluations may have been influenced by covariates, such as the tendency to rate more polished questions higher regardless of their pedagogical depth. Implementing explicit controls for such covariates and collecting instructors beliefs on machine-generated questions could provide a more comprehensive assessment. Moreover, our findings show that machine-generated questions can closely resemble those posed by students, that is an important step in validating their potential role in educational settings. In future iterations, we aim to move beyond isolated evaluation by embedding machine-generated student questions within real instruction contexts, e.g., with controlled A/B tests that compare instructor responses, reflection level, and improvements across conditions involving no questions, student questions, and machine-generated questions. Our current design thus represents a foundational, low-risk step to validate realism and instructional plausibility before advancing to this deployment in the wild. Finally, evaluating multiple large language models would offer a deeper understanding of how different generative architectures, training data, and decoding strategies influence the formulation and quality of machine-generated questions. Such a comparative analysis could reveal important nuances in how models represent student thinking, generate various cognitive levels of inquiry, or reflect domain-specific patterns. This technical direction will be also actively pursued in future steps to enhance robustness and generalizability of machine-generated questions across educational settings.

References

1. Bardach, L., Klassen, R.M.: Smart teachers, successful students? A systematic review of the literature on teachers' cognitive abilities and teacher effectiveness. Educ. Res. Rev. **30**, 100312 (2020)
2. Batool, S., Rashid, J., Nisar, M.W., Kim, J., Kwon, H.Y., Hussain, A.: Educational data mining to predict students' academic performance: a survey study. Educ. Inf. Technol. **28**(1), 905–971 (2023)
3. Bhowmik, S., et al.: Evaluation of an LLM-powered student agent for teacher training. In: In: Ferreira Mello, R., Rummel, N., Jivet, I., Pishtari, G., Ruipérez Valiente, J.A. (eds.) EC-TEL 2024. LNCS, vol 15160, pp. 68–74. Springer, Cham (2024). https://doi.org/10.1007/978-3-031-72312-4_7
4. Bilotti, U., Di Dario, D., Palomba, F., Gravino, C., Sibilio, M.: Machine learning for educational metaverse: how far are we? In: Proceedings of ICCE 2023, pp. 01–02. IEEE (2023)
5. Bloom, B.S., Engelhart, M.D., Furst, E.J., Hill, W.H., Krathwohl, D.R., et al.: Taxonomy of Educational Objectives: The Classification of Educational Goals. Handbook 1: Cognitive Domain. Longman, New York (1956)
6. Blšták, M., Rozinajová, V.: Automatic question generation based on sentence structure analysis using machine learning approach. Nat. Lang. Eng. **28**(4), 487–517 (2022)
7. Calvo, S., Lyon, F., Morales, A., Wade, J.: Educating at scale for sustainable development and social enterprise growth: the impact of online learning and a massive open online course (mooc). Sustainability **12**(8), 3247 (2020)

8. Chen, H., Wang, J.: Awaking the slides: a tuning-free and knowledge-regulated AI tutoring system via language model coordination. arXiv preprint arXiv:2409.07372 (2024)
9. Chrysafiadi, K., Virvou, M.: Student modeling approaches: a literature review for the last decade. Expert Syst. Appl. **40**(11), 4715–4729 (2013)
10. Clarke, D., Hollingsworth, H.: Elaborating a model of teacher professional growth. Teach. Teach. Educ. **18**(8), 947–967 (2002)
11. Graesser, A.C., Person, N.K., Magliano, J.P.: Question asking during tutoring. Am. Educ. Res. J. **31**(1), 104–137 (1994)
12. Griffith, J., Vercellotti, M.L., Folkers, H.: What's in a question? A comparison of student questions in two learning spaces. Teach. Learn. Commun. Sci. Disord. **3**(1), 7 (2019)
13. Hamim, T., Benabbou, F., Sael, N.: Student profile modeling: an overview model. In: Proceedings of ICSCA 2019, pp. 1–9 (2019)
14. Huang, Y., Wang, L.: A case study on chatGPT question generation. IEEE Trans. Learn. Technol. (2023)
15. Käser, T., Alexandron, G.: Simulated learners in educational technology: a systematic literature review and a turing-like test. Int. J. Artif. Intell. Educ. **34**(2), 545–585 (2024)
16. Kaya, S., Temiz, M.: Improving the quality of student questions in primary science classrooms. J. Balt. Sci. Educ. **17**(5), 800–811 (2018)
17. Klassen, R.M., Kim, L.E., Rushby, J.V., Bardach, L.: Can we improve how we screen applicants for initial teacher education? Teach. Teach. Educ. **87**, 102949 (2020)
18. Kong, A., et al.: Better zero-shot reasoning with role-play prompting. In: Proceedings of NAACL 2024, pp. 4099–4113 (2024)
19. Nazaretsky, T., Mejia-Domenzain, P., Swamy, V., Frej, J., Käser, T.: AI or human? Evaluating student feedback perceptions in higher education. In: In: Ferreira Mello, R., Rummel, N., Jivet, I., Pishtari, G., Ruipérez Valiente, J.A. (eds) EC-TEL 2024. LNCS, vol. 15159, pp. 284–298. Springer, Cham (2024). https://doi.org/10.1007/978-3-031-72315-5_20
20. Pentangelo, V., Di Dario, D., Lambiase, S., Ferrucci, F., Gravino, C., Palomba, F.: SENEM: a software engineering-enabled educational metaverse. Info. Softw. Technol. 107512 (2024)
21. Poehner, M.E.: Dynamic assessment in the classroom. In: The Concise Companion to Language Assessment, p. 55 (2024)
22. Shao, Y., Li, L., Dai, J., Qiu, X.: Character-LLM: a trainable agent for role-playing. In: Proceedings of EMNLP 2023, pp. 13153–13187 (2023)
23. Sher, A.: Assessing the relationship of student-instructor and student-student interaction to student learning and satisfaction in web-based online learning environment. J. Interact. Online Learn. **8**(2) (2009)
24. Song, D.: Student-generated questioning and quality questions: A literature review. Res. J. Educ. Stud. Rev. **2**(5), 58–70 (2016)
25. Van Es, E.A., Sherin, M.G.: Learning to notice: scaffolding new teachers' interpretations of classroom interactions. JTTE **10**(4), 571–596 (2002)
26. Vieluf, S., Klieme, E.: Teaching effectiveness revisited through the lens of practice theories. In: Praetorius, AK., Charalambous, C.Y. (eds) Theorizing Teaching, pp. 57–95. Springer, Cham (2023). https://doi.org/10.1007/978-3-031-25613-4_3
27. Wang, N., et al.: RoleLLM: benchmarking, eliciting, and enhancing role-playing abilities of large language models. In: Findings of the Association for Computational Linguistics ACL 2024, pp. 14743–14777 (2024)

28. Wang, R., Cao, J., Xu, Y., Li, Y.: Learning engagement in massive open online courses: a systematic review. In: Frontiers in Education, vol. 7, p. 1074435 (2022)
29. Wu, L., Kim, S.: Generative students: using LLM-simulated student profiles to support question item evaluation. In: Proceedings of the ACM L@S 2024 (2024)
30. Xiang, W., Liu, X., Wu, Y., Chen, Y.: KHANQ: a dataset for generating deep questions in education. In: Proceedings of COLING 2022 (2022)
31. Xu, Y., Zhao, M., Liu, X., Sun, X., Zhang, H.: Can autograding of student-generated questions quality by chatGPT match human experts? IEEE Trans. Learn. Technol. (2024)
32. Yang, L., Chen, X., Liu, B., Gao, J.: LearninGQ: a large-scale dataset for educational question generation. In: Proceedings of ICWSM 2018 (2018)

The Effect of Unplugged and Plugged-In Programming with Influencing Factor of Collaborative Versus Individual Work Regarding the Impact on Computational Thinking in Preschoolers

Connie Claerhout[1](✉) and Nardie Fanchamps[2]

[1] Connie Claerhout, Canteclaerstraat 6, 8560 Moorsele, Belgium
connie.claerhout@gmail.com
[2] Open University, Valkenburgerweg 177, 6419 AT Heerlen, The Netherlands

Abstract. Integrating computational thinking (CT) into curricula challenges educators and researchers to reflect on effective pedagogy for successful classroom implementation. This identifies the importance for developing CT in young children but also the remaining knowledge gap in this respect. In particular, how to organize the provision regarding CT development and what infant school children can learn with and from each other in the process is still little explored. Moreover, to what extent such orientation when applying either plugged-in or unplugged programming environments can generate differences in yields. Therefore, a quasi-experimental comparative intervention study was conducted among one hundred and forty-seven preschoolers aged four to six years originating from Belgium to examine the effect of a plugged-in versus unplugged programming approach on CT development, and to what extent the conditions of collaborative versus individual work are an influencing factor. To assess development on CT, a pre-test-post-test design was adopted, using the validated Beginners Computational Thinking test (BCTt). The study included eight interventions of 30-min each spread over six weeks. Unplugged interventions were conducted by applying SmartGames through board games, and plugged-in interventions by applying Bee-Bot-robotics programming tasks. Our results indicate that both programming interventions in preschoolers significantly improved CT development. Unplugged programming activities in general seem to be more effective in promoting CT development. The impact of collaborative or individual work within both intervention conditions depended on CT (sub)skills to be developed. To more accurately identify the impact of collaborative programming in preschoolers, a long-term follow-up study with more participants is recommended.

Keywords: Computational Thinking · Preschoolers · Unplugged versus Plugged-in · Collaboration versus Individual Work

K. Tammets et al. (Eds.): EC-TEL 2025, LNCS 16063, pp. 123–137, 2026.
https://doi.org/10.1007/978-3-032-03870-8_9

1 Introduction

As many aspects of our current society are subject to far-reaching technological implementation, change and digitization, it is important to prepare children from an early age and align education accordingly [1, 2]. Providing education that focuses on developing thinking, subject-specific and basic skills, including digital literacy [2] seems to be fundamental for later coping with complex issues and challenges related to required 21st century skills [1, 3]. Computational thinking (CT), an essential component of digital literacy [3], has become indispensable in education and is gradually being integrated into all curricula of Flemish and Dutch primary and secondary education [3, 4]. The term CT refers not only to the thought processes needed to reformulate a problem and generate solutions in a way that can be performed by both a computer and a human [2]. It also includes the thinking and reasoning processes to understand, explain and interpret the world, in terms of information processes [5]. These thinking processes can be promoted by offering children developmentally appropriate interventions through plugged-in (using technology) and unplugged (without technological intervention) programming approaches [6, 7].

The integration of CT into early childhood curricula and the wide influx of software and developmentally appropriate materials challenges educators and researchers to think critically not only about various computational approaches, but also about appropriate learning and developmental opportunities [8–10]. Teachers can, for instance, choose to offer CT-based activities individually that can stimulate autonomy, benefiting children's thinking and solution processes. Applied in such a way, children learn to solve problems independently and discover their own solution strategies [10]. In addition to individual work, collaboration is receiving increasing attention during CT interventions.

Research shows that a peer-based collaborative environment is not only beneficial for socio-emotional development and motivation [3, 11] but also leads to more effective and efficient work, thus stimulating and enriching the impact and efficiency of educational programs [10, 11]. Collaborative learning can therefore offer interesting opportunities for the development of CT. In addition to the various forms of organization and implementation to be adopted, there is increasing recognition of the importance of offering CT-based activities also to very young children and integrating them into curricula. Developing CT at a very young age and in different contexts promotes computational skills that children will later need to tackle complex problems, and to manifest themselves in our mostly digitally oriented society [11, 12]. Noting that supporting scientific research concerning CT development among preschoolers as an early age group is still limited [3, 7, 13, 14] and rather focused on regular primary, secondary and higher education [3, 15]. As a result, more research is needed based on the gap in knowledge about effective conditions that ensure successful development of CT skills in very young children.

2 Related Work

In this study, the focus is on developing CT in young children. Back in 1980, Papert [16] laid a foundation for the concept of CT. Building on Piaget's constructivist ideas, Papert believed that the best way to build knowledge in children is by actively constructing something shareable, such as a story, a computer program or a musical composition [15, 16]. Together with colleagues at MIT, he developed the programming language LOGO and the accompanying application Turtle to offer children, through simple programming activities, meaningful learning experiences in which their procedural thinking was activated and developed [15, 16]. Jeanette Wing [2] further fleshed out the concept, defining CT as the thinking processes required to formulate and solve complex problems using the concepts fundamental to computer science.

Although CT has been defined several times over the years, no consensus on the definition of CT has been reached to date. The International Society for Technology in Education (ISTE) and the Computer Science Teachers Association (CSTA) define CT as a problem-solving process that involves skills, such as logically organizing and analyzing data, automating solutions through algorithmic thinking, and identifying efficient solutions to various problems [17]. This with the aim of not only developing problem-solving ability but also to apply them in different contexts [18]. Relkin et al. [15] define CT as a set of heuristic reasoning skills divided into specific subdomains relevant to problem solving in both computer science and other disciplines.

Nevertheless, to approach CT in a structured way and thus to understand and integrate the different dimensions of CT into educational practice, Brennan et al. [19] developed a 3D-framework. This framework focuses on three core components of CT: (1) computational concepts, the concepts used in programming; (2) computational practices, the thinking practices that emerge during programming such as debugging or remixing; and (3) computational perspectives, insights about oneself, about one's relationships with others and about the technical world, which emerge during programming. This framework also provides an opportunity to assess the development of CT in young children [11, 19].

Although the definition of CT is a subject of debate, many experts and researchers are convinced that CT contains a set of core components that should be taught from an early age [3, 20]. Research indicates that developmental effects of interventions that start at an early age are often associated with sustained effects, than interventions that start later [5]. Developing CT is often linked to programming [19, 20]. Programming requires the ability to (1) think logically, (2) analyze problems, (3) decompose tasks into smaller steps, (4) recognize patterns and (5) apply abstract concepts - all core aspects of CT [9]. Recent scientific research indicates that offering programming interventions to young children is an appropriate way to practice computational skills and generate a positive effect on their CT development [3, 8].

The to-be-developed computational skills can be acquired in plugged-in programming environments. In this approach, computer-based tools and/or programming environments are used and include a distinction between graphical programming interfaces and tangible technologies [21]. By using analog robots, children can create and program a series of instructions by pressing various buttons or by scanning barcodes from physical programming blocks [20, 21]. Tangible programming of introductory robot systems, such as a Bee-Bot-robot, can facilitate young children to think logically and requires them to apply more basic programming concepts such as sequences, loops and patterns [3, 22]. By using such tangible approaches this can also encourage collaboration, increase children's learning interest and engagement [14, 21].

In addition, associated CT-skills in young children can be also developed and encouraged in an unplugged programming approach without the use of digital technology or ICT. Research shows that unplugged programming has the potential to develop CT in an approachable and practical way with a lower cognitive load [3, 23], focusing on understanding CT concepts rather than mastering (new) digital technologies or practical coding skills associated with most programming languages [24, 25]. In addition, research shows that physical, kinesthetic experiences, or playing board games, for example, SmartGames is an effective unplugged approach to develop CT in children [23, 25]. Such approaches stimulate memory, language development and visual perception in addition to problem-solving and flexible thinking, developing spatial awareness and planning, and can be played individually, in pairs, or in groups.

Although researchers suggest that unplugged activities in young children are a powerful way to promote and generate positive effects on CT-development in young children contrasted against plugged-in approaches [23, 25, 26], however, comparative experimental research in young children aged between four and six years is limited to generalize general decisions around effective programming approaches [27].

It is known from the field of psychology that young children develop strongly in motor, cognitive and socio-emotional areas. Speech-language development and the growing ability to think, opens up a new world of reasoning and communication [26], with social interaction, cooperation and the role of language in young children being crucial to the development of their cognitive skills [27]. Developing such cognitive skills happens best in learning contexts that are just a little more complex than the learner can handle. In this zone of near development, the learning tutee strives to solve problems with the help of a tutor, e.g. another child. In this form of collaboration, peer tutoring, learners help each other and both the tutee and the tutor achieve a higher cognitive level [28]. Same-age tutoring ensures that peer interactions provide more opportunities exchange ideas and problems in a more spontaneous and critical way [29]. Although research [30] also shows that young children are able to take on the role of tutor during a construction task, one should be critical of this teaching approach. It is argued that children can learn more while working together than individually, and that learning gains depend on the child's developmental state and intellectual capabilities [29, 31]. This encompasses the situation that some children do all the work and other children just "tag along" [29]. However, individual work and learning remain important in children's development and it allows children to work at their own level and pace. This promotes their autonomy and challenges children to discover their own solution strategies. Remarkably, to date, very little scientific research has been done on which approach, collaborative or individual work, while practicing CT leads to better skill development.

3 Method

The aim of our quantitative study was to identify the difference in the effect of a plugged-in versus unplugged programming approach on the development of CT in four- to six-year-old preschoolers. This involved examining the impact of collaborative versus individual work to understand whether collaboration in preschoolers has a significant impact on CT development. With the results of this study, we aim to provide educators with additional tools that will enable effective CT implementation in young children. Directing the research, four sub-questions were formulated: 1) to what extent does programming affect the development of CT-skills in preschoolers, 2) to what extent can a difference between an unplugged or plugged-in programming approach establish a growth in the development of CT- skills in preschoolers, 3) does collaborative or individual work during programming influence the development of CT-skills in preschoolers', 4) to what extent does the type of programming approach and the impact of collaborative versus individual work influence the development of CT- skills in preschoolers.

In order to obtain indications, the following hypotheses were tested: a) programming leads to a significant impact on the development of CT- skills in preschoolers, b) an unplugged programming approach generates a more substantial impact on the development of CT- skills in preschoolers than plugged-in programming, c) collaborative programming has a more extensive impact on the development of CT-skills in preschoolers than working individually, d) a plugged-in programming approach that incorporates collaboration generates the greatest impact on the development of computational thinking skills in preschoolers.

3.1 Procedure

To test hypotheses and to find an answer to the sub-questions to be able to answer the main research question, a quantitative quasi-experimental research design (Fig. 1) was conducted.

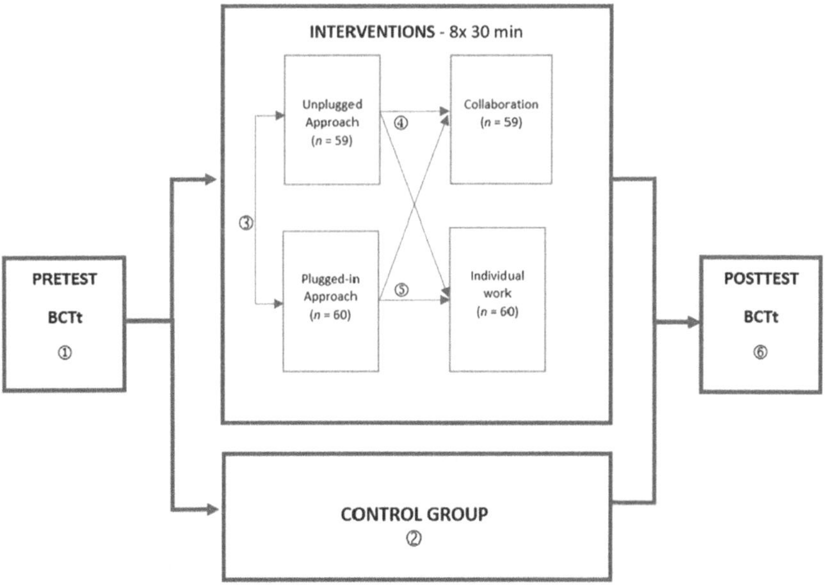

Fig. 1. Schematic representation of the research design.

3.2 Participants

Two Flemish schools from Belgium participated in this study. The study involved 147 participating preschool children who were assigned to either one of four experimental conditions or to the control group (Fig. 1). Given the practical aspect (including enough participants) and the ethical aspect (excluding preschoolers who are too old within the same class group) of the study, only the age range between 4 and 6 years was considered beforehand. However, after test collection, it was checked whether the mean age of the group working together (M_age = 4.96 years) had the same values as the mean age of the group working individually (M_age = 5.07 years). In addition, the mean age of the control group (M_age = 4.89 years) versus the participating preschoolers (M_age = 5.07 years) was calculated for which we also found similar values. Considering they followed the same school curriculum and were randomly distributed over the different conditions, the generic starting level differences were therefore negligible. In this regard, CT and programming were not a standard part of the regular curriculum. A pre-test (1) was administered to all participating preschoolers at the start of the experiment. Preschoolers from the control group ($n = 28$) only took the pre-test and post-test and followed the regular curriculum (2) during the experimental phase. Preschoolers in the intervention group ($n = 119$) were subjected to eight 30-min interventions over six weeks. Each intervention group was assigned a programming approach (3). The intervention group was then randomly divided into two groups, preschoolers who worked together and preschoolers who worked individually (4 and 5). To measure the effect of the interventions, a post-test was conducted on all participating preschoolers (6).

3.3 Materials

To assess the level of CT development of the participating preschoolers, the validated Beginners Computational Thinking test (BCTt) was administered [11]. The BCTt assesses six computational concepts and practices from the Brennan et al. framework [19], namely "basic directions and sequences," "loops-repeat times"; "loops-repeat until", "if-simple conditionals", "if-else-complex conditionals" and "while conditionals".

To answer the research questions, two different types of interventions were used divided into two different conditions: a plugged-in approach via programmable robotics technology via individual work or collaboration, and an unplugged approach with tangible materials via individual work or collaboration. Interventions in the plugged-in approach were realized by manipulating the robot Bee-Bot. A Bee-Bot is a tangible programmable robot designed to teach young children how to program in a simple way (Fig. 2). On the back of the Bee-Bot are several function arrow keys, namely: forward, backward, rotate 90° left or right, pause and an erase command, which are used to enter or undo a command sequence. The GO-button activates the Bee-Bot-robot where it traverses the entered course in a step size of 15 cm each time. This motion distance is fixed and cannot be manipulated. The X-button clears the preprogrammed route and the pause button allows the Bee-Bot to pause briefly during the route. Each movement of 15 cm occurs at a speed of 65 mm/sec. The complexity of programming is determined by the commands on the different command mats. In this study, three farm-themed mission mats were used for this purpose (Fig. 2) with corresponding programming commands of increasing difficulty. The assignments were designed to practise and develop computational concepts: (1) sequence, (2) simple-loop, (3) nested-loop, (4) if-then, (5) if-then-else and (6) while. Figure 2 shows an example of a simple-loop exercise.

Fig. 2. The Bee-Bot-robot with one of the 3 mats used and an example of a command card.

Six different SmartGames, operationalized by applying board games, were offered during the interventions in the unplugged environment. The SmartGames selected were (1) Five Little Birds, (2) Sleeping Beauty, (3) Three Little Pigs, (4) Dress Code, (5) Little Red Riding Hood, and (6) Smart Farmer (Fig. 3). These games are suitable for four- to six-year-old preschoolers, can be played individually or with multiple children as collaborative games, and have increasing levels of difficulty and abstraction. All SmartGames encourage problem-solving thinking and emphasize logical thinking, spatial awareness, planning, concentration, visual perception and flexible thinking. These cognitive skills were defined and benchmarked for each game prior to the study by a group of game experts and developers from SmartGames themselves and were included in the study based on these selection criteria. The teacher explained each SmartGame. Subsequently, preschoolers started with simple tasks and were encouraged to solve increasingly difficult

Fig. 3. The SmartGames offered during the interventions. Games top row: Five Little Birds, Sleeping Beauty and Three Little Pigs. Games bottom row: Dress Code, Little Red Riding Hood and Smart Farmer.

ones. Furthermore, preschoolers were allowed to ask for additional game explanations from the supervisor.

4 Results

4.1 Impact of Programming on Computational Thinking Skills

To examine whether programming had an impact on CT-skills among preschoolers, the differences between pre-test and post-test values of both the interventions groups and the control group were compared. From the data analysed (Table 1), it can be inferred that for both intervention groups the mean scores of all (sub)categories as examined by administering the BCTt increased compared to the pre-test. For the control group, only the categories "sequence", "simple-loop" and "if-then-else" indicated higher values.

A paired samples T-test illustrated that there is a significant measurable effect on the overall mean of the BCTt comparing the post- and premeasurement for both experimental groups, $t(119) = 10.293$, $p < .001$, 95% CI [.072,.106], $d = .94$. In addition, there appeared to be a mean significant measurable effect for the (sub)categories (a) "sequence" $t(119) = 5.928$, $p < .001$, 95% CI [.060,.120], $d = .54$, (b) "simple-loop" $t(119) = 4.819$, $p < .001$, 95% CI [.060,.142], $d =. 44$, (c) "nested-loop" $t(119) = 4.928$, $p < .001$, 95% CI [.048,.113], $d = .45$, (d) "loops-overall" $t(119) = 6.906$, $p < .001$, 95% CI [.065,.117], $d = .63$ and (e) "while" $t(119) = 5.586$, $p < .001$, 95% CI [.101,.212], $d = .51$. No significant effects could be identified for the sub-categories "if-then" and "if-then-else". The sub-category "conditionals-overall" reveals a small significant measurable effect, $t(119) = 3.786$, $p < .001$, 95% CI [.036,.116], $d = .35$. The first hypothesis, namely that programming in preschoolers leads to a positive significant effect in the development of overall computational thinking skills, can be confirmed.

4.2 Impact Programming Condition on Computational Thinking Skills

For both intervention conditions, unplugged and plugged-in programming, preschoolers were divided into two groups who either worked collaboratively or individually.

The analysis of pre- and post-test averages shows that the unplugged condition indicates higher values for all (sub)categories by administering the BCTt. This increase is also observed for the plugged-in condition except for subcategories "if-then" and "if-then-else". The analyses for both individual and collaborative conditions show higher percentage calculations in the post-assessment, except for subcategory "if-then-else".

An ANOVA analyses was conducted to examine whether differences in the development of CT-skills among preschoolers' CT-skills are significant comparing an unplugged or plugged-in programming approach. Levene's test indicated that the homogeneity of variances was not violated ($p > .05$), except for the subcategories "simple-loop" and "loops-overall". For these two (sub)categories, Games-Howell post hoc-test was performed. The ANOVA-analyses showed a significant difference ($p < .05$) on all CT-subcategories comparing all unplugged and plugged-in groups, except for the subcategory "if-then-else". As a remark, the control group was not adopted from the statistical analysis due to its irrelevance within the hypothesis associated. Further post-hoc-analysis

Table 1. Paired Samples T-Test between post- and premeasurement in condition programming.

	M	*SD*	*t*	*p*	*d*
AverageTotal_post-test-Average Total_pretest	.089	.094	10.293	< .001	.944
AverageSequence_post-test-AverageSequence_pretest	.089	.165	5.928	< .001	.543
AverageSimpleloop_post-test-AverageSimpleloop_pretest	.101	.228	4.819	< .001	.442
AverageNestedLoop_post-test-AverageNestedLoop_pretest	.080	.178	4.928	< .001	.452
AverageLoopsOverAll_post-test-AverageLoopsOverAll_pretest	.090	.143	6.906	< .001	.633
AverageIfThen_post-test-AverageIfThen_pretest	.059	.413	1.555	.061	.143
AverageIfThenElse_post-test-AverageIfThenElse_pretest	.013	.388	.355	.362	.033
AverageWhile_post-test-AverageWhile_pretest	.157	.306	5.586	< .001	.512
AverageConditionalsOverAll_post-test-AverageConditionalsOverAll_ pretest	.076	.219	3.786	< .001	.347

Note. M = mean, *SD* = standard deviation, *t* = *t*-value; *p* = *p*-value; *d* = effect size

regarding the "total" of the BCTt indicates that an unplugged approach entailed a positively significant effect compared to a plugged-in approach. Positively significant effects within (sub)categories found concerns (a) "nested-loop", (b) "loops-overall", (c) "if-then", (d) "while" and (e) "conditionals-overall". Differences between unplugged and plugged-in programming within other (sub)categories are not significant. The second hypothesis stating that an unplugged programming approach provides a greater impact on the development of computational thinking skills in preschoolers than plugged-in programming can be partially confirmed.

By performing an ANOVA-analysis it was explored whether working together has a greater impact on the development of CT-skills in preschoolers than working individually contrasted with the control group. Based on examining a Shapiro-Wilk test, by bootstrapping and a Bonferroni post-hoc test, we indicated significant differences between the conditions individual work and collaborative work regarding (sub)categories combined: (a) "total", $F(2,144) = 16.411$; $p < .001$, (b) "sequence", $F(2,144) = 11.950$; $p < .001$, (c) "simple-loop", $F(2,144) = 11.311$; $p < .001$, (d) "nested-loop", $F(2,144) = 12.598$; $p < .001$ and (e) "loops-overall", $F(2,144) = 16.184$; $p < .001$. However, the post-hoc test also shows that no significant difference can be found between collaborative and individual work in any (sub)category. Therefore, the third hypothesis was rejected.

4.3 Impact Collaboration and Individual Work on Plugged-In Versus Unplugged Programming

In order to understand the impact of the interventions based on the unplugged and plugged-in programming condition and the collaborative modality and whether this actually led to higher levels of CT-skills, a contrast analysis was conducted comparing five groups, excluding the control group due to irrelevance.

The contrast analysis regarding the total correctly solved CT tasks (MeanTotal) indicates a significant difference, with a medium effect comparing working individually and collaborating in an unplugged programming approach, $t(142) = 2.042, p = .043, g =$ .531. Working individually versus collaborating in a plugged-in programming approach yields a significant negative difference, with a medium effect, $t(142) = -2.276$, $p =$ .024, $g = -.586$. In addition, the contrast analysis shows a significant difference with a large effect, comparing working individually unplugged and (a) working individually plugged-in, $t(142) = 5.417$, $p < .001$, $g = 1.394$ and (b) collaborating in a plugged-in programming approach, $t(142) = 3.251, p = .001, g = .809$. A significant difference was identified regarding collaborating unplugged and working individually in a plugged-in programming approach, with a large effect, $t(142) = 3.219$, $p = .002$, g = .864.

Although the contrast analysis of the total number of correctly solved CT tasks shows a significant difference between working individually versus collaboratively in an unplugged programming approach, significant differences were found for (sub)categories (a) "simple-loop" $t(142) = 2.\ 247$, $p = .026$, $g = .584$, (b) "nested-loop" $t(142) = 2.154$, $p = .033$, $g = .560$ and (c) "loops-overall" $t(142) = 2.629$, $p =$ .009, $g = .683$.

The contrast analysis shows that there is a significant difference, with a large measurable effect, when working individually in an unplugged versus plugged-in programming approach for the categories combined (a) "sequence" $t(142) = 3.475, p < .001, g = .894$, (b) "loops-overall" $t(142) = 4.643$, $p < .001$, $g = 1.195$ and (c) "conditionals-overall" $t(142) = 3.285, p = .001, g = .846$. Significant differences, with a large measurable effect are found in the subcategories "simple-loop", "nested-loop" and "while". Furthermore, working individually in an unplugged programming approach compared to collaborating in a plugged-in programming approach, indicates significant differences, with large effects, for the categories combined "loops-overall" $t(142) = 2.431, p = .016, g = .605$ and "conditionals-overall" $t(142) = 5.590$, $p < .001$, $g = .893$. For the subcategories "nested-loop", "if-then", "if-then-else" and "while", significant differences were found with an average effect.

Comparing collaborating in an unplugged programming approach and working individually in a plugged-in approach shows significant differences, with moderate to large effect, for the categories combined "sequence" $t(142) = 2.119, p = .036$, $g = .568$ and "conditionals-overall" $t(142) = 3.048$, $p = .003$, $g = .818$. For the category combined "loops-overall", there appeared to be no significant difference ($p = .059$). The following subcategories indicated significant differences: (a) "nested-loop" t(142) = 2.192, $p =$ .030, $g = .588$, (b) 'if-then' $t(142) = 2.312$, $p = .022$, $g = .620$ and (c) 'while' $t(142)$ $= 3.295, p = .001, g = .884$.

In the contrast analysis, no significant differences were found within the total number of correctly solved CT exercises between the group of preschoolers who worked together in an unplugged versus a plugged-in programming approach. However, the contrast analysis shows that significant differences, with medium to large effect, were found for the (sub)categories (a) "if-then" $t(142) = 2.710, p = .008, g = .704$, (b) "while" $t(142) = 2.562$, p = .011, $g = .666$ and (c) "conditionals-overall" $t(142) = 3.327, p = .001, g = .865$.

The contrast analysis comparing working individually with collaborating in a plugged-in programming approach shows negative significant differences, with an average effect, for the categories combined "sequence" $t(142) = -2.329, p = .021, g = -.600$ and "loops-overall" $t(142) = -2.294, p = .023, g = -.590$. Only the subcategory "nested-loop" $t(142) = -2.167, p = .032, g = -.558$, indicated significant differences.

The fourth hypothesis stating that collaborative plugged-in programming approaches have the most impact regarding CT development in preschoolers can be partially rejected.

5 Discussion

This study investigated whether unplugged or plugged-in programming applied through either individual working or collaboration would lead to significant effects on CT-development in preschoolers.

An interpretation from the results for the control group reveals that a regular curriculum in kindergarten promotes CT-skills "sequence", "simple-loop" and "if-then-else", although the impact is rather limited. Almost all CT-(sub)categories assessed by administering the BCTt increased in comparison with both groups that either applied an unplugged or plugged-in programming approach. These findings are consistent with previous research findings concluding that offering programming interventions to young children is an appropriate way to practice computational skills [3, 8]. Only for (sub)categories "if-then" and "if-then-else", no significant differences were noticeable. This conclusion is confirmed in the study conducted by Zapata-Cáceres & Fanchamps [11], which indicate that these (sub)categories may not be attainable concepts for preschoolers.

The analyses of the programming conditions applied, unplugged and plugged-in, showed that both approaches contributed to a growth in CT-skills. However, on generic level regarding the BCTt administered, unplugged programming indicated a significantly greater positive impact. This supports the second hypothesis, which stated that unplugged programming has a bigger impact than plugged-in programming. However, significant differences regarding both approaches assessed varied per (sub)category, suggesting that the effectiveness of the different programming approaches applied depends on specific skills being evoked and developed.

Furthermore, our study indicates that no significant differences could be established comparing unplugged and plugged-in programming in preschoolers for (sub)categories "sequence", "simple loops" and conditionals "if-then-else". These indications can be attributed to the developmental level of preschoolers. According to Piaget [4, 5], preschoolers are in a pre-operational stage where imagination and symbolic thinking take precedence. For unplugged materials provided, this stimulates preschoolers' perception and thinking skills by, for instance, using fairy tales and other fantasy scenarios. Moreover, the application of SmartGames encourages the development of computational skills as preschoolers play and act concretely. These results also reinforce the research by Fanchamps et al. [23] which states that playing SmartGames, for example, is an effective unplugged approach to develop CT by detecting significant results in a younger target group. On the contrary, the usage of the plugged-in material provided requires a higher level of abstract thinking in which assignments are presented schematically, and programming commands need to be entered via push buttons [21]. The associated tasks which require a higher level of abstraction might not be in preschoolers' zone of near development and thus be too difficult, affecting learning and development [24, 30].

It is interesting to note for consideration that during the study, it was found that certain groups of preschoolers found it difficult to work together because of different character traits and developmental levels. This led to conflict and frustration among some preschoolers. Therefore, it is important to recognize that differences in developmental level and/or heterogeneous or homogeneous group composition may be indicative of preschoolers' CT skills.

6 Conclusion

Although the research results show that both individual work and collaboration led to an improvement of CT-skills in preschoolers, post-hoc tests show that no significant differences could be identified between both approaches. A possible explanation for this could be attributed to the different developmental level or out of school experiences of preschoolers, or that they still find both individual work and cooperation difficult without clear teacher guidance.

The results of the contrast analysis conducted show that the type of programming approach, either unplugged programming by applying SmartGames or plugged-in programming by applying Bee-Bot-robots, and the level of individual work or collaboration can lead to significant effects on overall CT-development and/or on the development of multiple (sub)categories of CT. The interpretation of the contrast analyses concerning the total number of correctly solved CT tasks, indicates that collaboration in a plugged-in programming approach has a greater effect on CT than working individually. In an unplugged environment, the impact of working individually is significantly higher than for collaboration. This implies that working together in a higher level of abstraction has more effect on preschoolers' thinking development than working individually, and/or preschoolers are less motivated to share knowledge or collaborate if they have to complete less complex tasks. These findings are consistent with the research of Lin et al. [14] who reported on the same effects measured.

In general, our study was able to identify that (a) programming interventions in preschoolers provide significant improvements in CT development, (b) unplugged programming activities in general have been found to be more effective in promoting CT development in preschoolers than plugged-in programming activities (with the exception of identified (sub)categories regarding the BCTt administered), (c) collaborative versus individual work for this age group shows no significance, and (d) the combination of collaborative or individual work in an unplugged or plugged-in programming approach can lead to several significant improvements within overall CT development or within various (sub)categories. The effectiveness of the collaborative and programming approach thus depends on CT-subskills to be developed.

7 Limitations and Future Research

The research conducted has some limitations to which the results presented should be considered with some caution. First, considering this research was framed within the context of a master's thesis, the decision was made to just focus on one aspect of social learning. Because the study was conducted with very young children (preschoolers), the choice was made to focus on only the aspect of collaboration. Underlying motivation for this was because in education with such young children, there is a clear appeal for the power of collaborative learning, but there is still little knowledge of what impact this can have in CT learning. Second, the study was executed in two primary schools from the same school community, which limits the generalizability of the results to preschool children in primary schools in other regions. Future research with a more geographically dispersed sample may significantly improve the generalizability of the findings presented. A third limitation concerns preschoolers' task span. Both teachers and researchers observed during test-taking by administering the BCTt, that concentration levels of the youngest preschoolers decreased significantly which encouraged random answering questions. Future research could reconcile to divide the BCTt into several short fill-in moments to obtain more reliable data. A fourth limitation is the limited intervention period. More time-on-task would facilitate effects established regarding both programming approaches and the long-term impact of collaboration. A final limitation is the selection of materials used. Unplugged programming was executed by applying a selection of available SmartGames. Plugged-in programming was executed by applying Bee-Bot-robots. Consequently, and based on these only applied materials, it is not feasible to generalize to other materials similar in characteristics. Follow-up research should include different types of intervention materials to reinforce the results presented.

Acknowledgements. The authors would like to thank primary school BaMo and Wijnberg, Belgium, for their participation. In addition, they would like to thank the SmartGame company for donating the requested SmartGames.

Disclosure of Interests. All authors declare they have no competing interests.

References

1. Voogt, J., Erstad, O., Dede, C., Mishra, P.: Challenges to learning and schooling in the digital networked world of the 21st century. J. Comput. Assist. Learn. **29**(5), 403–413 (2013). https://doi.org/10.1111/jcal.12029
2. Wing, J.M.: Computational thinking and thinking about computing. Philos. Trans. Royal Soc. Math. Phys. Eng. Sci. **366**(1881), 3717–3725 (2008). https://doi.org/10.1098/rsta.2008.0118
3. Bers, M., Strawhacker, S., Sullivan, A.: The state of the field of computational thinking in early childhood education. In: OECD Education Working Papers, No. 274, OECD Publishing, Paris (2022). https://doi.org/10.1787/3354387a-en
4. Wing, J.M.: Computational thinking. Commun. ACM **49**(3), 33–35 (2006). https://doi.org/10.1145/1118178.1118215

5. Denning, P. J., Tedre, M.: Computational thinking: a disciplinary perspective. Inf. Educ. (2021). https://doi.org/10.15388/infedu.2021.21
6. Caeli, E.N., Yadav, A.: Unplugged approaches to computational thinking: a historical perspective. TechTrends **64**(1), 29–36 (2020). https://doi.org/10.1007/s11528-019-00410-5
7. Li, W., Yang, W.: Promoting children's computational thinking: a quasi experimental study of web-mediated parent education. J. Comput. Assist. Learn. **39**(5), 1564–1575 (2023). https://doi.org/10.1111/jcal.12818
8. Fessakis, G., Gouli, E., Mavroudi, E.: Problem solving by 5–6 years old kindergarten children in a computer programming environment: a case study. Comput. Educ. **63**, 87–97 (2013). https://doi.org/10.1016/j.compedu.2012.11.016
9. Lee, J., Joswick, C., Pole, K.: Classroom play and activities to support computational thinking development in early childhood. Early Childhood Educ. J. **51**(3), 457–468 (2023). https://doi.org/10.1007/s10643-022-01319-0
10. Manches, A., Plowman, L.: Computing education in children's early years: a call for debate. Br. J. Edu. Technol. **48**(1), 191–201 (2017). https://doi.org/10.1111/bjet.12355
11. Zapata-Cáceres, M., Fanchamps, N.: Using the beginners computational thinking test to measure development on computational concepts among preschoolers. In: Proceedings of the 5th APSCE International Computational Thinking and STEM in Education Conference 2021 pp. 32–37. Asia-Pacific Society for Computers in Education (2021)
12. Lavigne, H., Lewis Presser, A., Rosenfeld, D., Wolsky, M., Andrews, J.: Creating a preschool computational-thinking learning blueprint to guide the development of learning resources for young children. Connected Sci. Learn. **2**(2), 12318732 (2020). https://doi.org/10.1080/24758779.2020.12318732
13. Hamidi, A., Zerega, R., Tavajoh, S., Milrad, M., Masiello, I.: Digital competence & computational thinking for preschool pre-service teachers: from lab to practice. In: CTE-STEM 2022 Conference (2022). https://doi.org/10.34641/ctestem.2022.464
14. Lin, S.-Y., Chien, S.-Y., Hsiao, C.-L., Hsia, C.-H., Chao, K.-M.: Enhancing computational thinking capability of preschool children by game-based smart toys. Electronic Commerce Research and Applications, 44, 101011 (2020)
15. Relkin, E., De Ruiter, L.E., Bers, M.U.: Learning to code and the acquisition of computational thinking by young children. Comput. Educ. **169**, 104222 (2021). https://doi.org/10.1016/j.compedu.2021.104222
16. Papert, S.: Mindstorms: Children, Computers, and Powerful Ideas. Basic Books, New York (1980)
17. ISTE Operational Definition of Computational Thinking for K-12 Education. Retrieved from: https://ap.lc/OLMXK Last accessed 2025–06–19
18. Shute, V.J., Sun, C., Asbell-Clarke, J.: Demystifying computational thinking. Educ. Res. Rev. **22**, 142–158 (2017). https://doi.org/10.1016/j.edurev.2017.09.003
19. Brennan, K., Resnick, M., MIT Media Lab.: New frameworks for studying and assessing the development of computational thinking. In: Proceedings of the 2012 Annual Meeting of the American Educational Research Association, Vancouver, Canada, vol. 1, p. 25 (2012)
20. Angeli, C., Georgiou, K.: Investigating the effects of gender and scaffolding in developing preschool children's computational thinking during problem-solving with Bee-Bots. Front. Educ. **7**, 757627 (2023). https://doi.org/10.3389/feduc.2022.757627
21. Pugnali, A., Sullivan, A., Umashi Bers, M.: The impact of user interface on young children's computational thinking. J. Inf. Technol. Educ. Innov. Pract. **16**, 171–193 (2017). https://doi.org/10.28945/3768
22. Seckel, M.J., Salinas, C., Font, V., Sala-Sebastià, G.: Guidelines to develop com-putational thinking using the bee-bot robot from the literature. Educ. Inf. Technol. **28**(12), 16127–16151 (2023). https://doi.org/10.1007/s10639-023-11843-0

23. Fanchamps, N., Van Gool, E., Slangen, L., Hennissen, P.: The effect on computational thinking and identified learning aspects: comparing unplugged SmartGames with SRA-programming with tangible or on-screen output. Educ. Inf. Tech. (2024). https://doi.org/10.1007/s10639-023-11956-6
24. Kotsopoulos, D., et al.: A pedagogical framework for computational thinking. Digit. Exp. Math. Educ. **3**(2), 154–171 (2017). https://doi.org/10.1007/s40751-017-0031-2
25. Tsarava, K., Moeller, K., Ninaus, M.: Training computational thinking through board games: the case of crabs & turtles. Int. J. Ser. Games **5**(2), 25–44 (2018). https://doi.org/10.17083/ijsg.v5i2.248
26. Bers, M.U., Flannery, L., Kazakoff, E.R., Sullivan, A.: Computational thinking and tinkering: exploration of an early childhood robotics curriculum. Comput. Educ. **72**, 145–157 (2014). https://doi.org/10.1016/j.compedu.2013.10.020
27. Sigayret, K., Tricot, A., Blanc, N.: Unplugged or plugged-in programming learning: a comparative experimental study. Comput. Educ. **184**, 104505 (2022). https://doi.org/10.1016/j.compedu.2022.104505
28. Topping, K., Duran, D., Van, K.: Using Peer Tutoring to Improve Reading Skills. A Practical Guide for Teachers. Routledge, New York/Londen (2016). https://doi.org/10.4324/9781315731032
29. Daiute, C., Campbell, C.H., Griffin, T.M., Reddy, M., Tivnan, T.: Young authors' interactions with peers and a teacher: toward a developmentally sensitive sociocultural literacy theory. New Dir. Child Adolesc. Dev. **1993**(61), 41–63 (1993). https://doi.org/10.1002/cd.23219936105
30. Verba, M.: Tutoring interactions between young children: how symmetry can modify asymmetrical interactions. Int. J. Behav. Dev. **22**(1), 195–216 (1998). https://doi.org/10.1080/016502598384577
31. Zapata-Cáceres, M., Martín-Barroso, E., Román-González, M.: Computational thinking test for beginners: design and content validation. In: 2020 IEEE Global Engineering Education Conference (EDUCON), pp. 1905–1914. IEEE (2020). https://doi.org/10.1109/EDUCON45650.2020.9125368

Knowledge Scaffolding Recommendation System for Supervising Term Papers

Nghia Duong-Trung[1,2(✉)], Xia Wang[1], Rahul Rajkumar Bhoyar[1], Angelin Mary Jose[1], Silke Elisabeth Wrede[3], Lars van Rijn[3], Theresa Panse[3], Claudia de Witt[3], and Niels Pinkwart[1,4]

[1] German Research Center for Artificial Intelligence (DFKI), Alt-Moabit 91 C, 10559 Berlin, Germany
{nghia_trung.duong,xia.wang,rahul_rajkumar.bhoyar,angelin_mary.jose, niels.pinkwart}@dfki.de

[2] IU International University of Applied Sciences, Frankfurter Allee 73A, 10247 Berlin, Germany

[3] FernUniversität in Hagen, Universitätsstraße 11, 58097 Hagen, Germany
{silke.wrede,lars.vanrijn,claudia.dewitt}@fernuni-hagen.de

[4] Humboldt-Universität zu Berlin, Unter den Linden 6, 10117 Berlin, Germany

Abstract. Generative AI is increasingly used to enhance educational support in higher education, particularly for distance learning. This paper introduces the Term Paper Recommendation System (TPRS), an AI-powered scaffolding tool designed to assist students in selecting and refining research topics for academic writing. TPRS integrates generative language models with knowledge-based and expert-driven recommendation strategies, dynamically adapting feedback based on the student's confidence level. The system leverages structured validation, multi-shot prompting with historical supervision data, and semantic similarity for literature recommendations. Deployed within a Bachelor of Arts program in Culture and Social Sciences at FernUniversität in Hagen, TPRS was evaluated using the CRS-Que framework and expert grading of student submissions. Results show statistically significant improvements in topic formulation quality, enhanced engagement, and reduced instructor workload. However, user feedback highlighted the need for improved transparency and control. TPRS offers a novel hybrid architecture that positions AI as a learning scaffold rather than an automation tool. This work contributes to responsible AI integration in higher education by demonstrating how generative systems can support inquiry-based learning while preserving student agency.

Keywords: AI Recommendation · Intelligent Tutoring · Generative AI · Distance Learning · Knowledge Scaffolding · CRS-Que

1 Introduction

Integrating AI technologies into teaching and learning has become a key strategy for addressing pedagogical challenges and improving instructional efficiency

K. Tammets et al. (Eds.): EC-TEL 2025, LNCS 16063, pp. 138–152, 2026.
https://doi.org/10.1007/978-3-032-03870-8_10

in higher education [2]. AI-driven tools have been widely explored in various domains, including personalized education [14], intelligent tutoring [17], and automated feedback [30]. This study focuses on a specific use case: developing and evaluating a TPRS designed to support German-speaking students in a Bachelor of Arts distance learning program in Culture and Social Sciences. A core challenge in our distance learning programs is the cognitive complexity of research topic selection and question formulation. Students are expected to independently propose research topics and refine their questions, usually submitting them through the Moodle platform for instructor feedback. However, this process is time-intensive, prone to delays, and results in inconsistent guidance across students. From the cognitive perspective, distilling complex academic materials into a focused research idea can be overwhelming, leading to cognitive overload and fragmented workflows. Delayed feedback further demotivates students, reducing engagement and academic persistence.

To mitigate these issues, we propose AI-powered knowledge scaffolding as a pedagogical framework for enhancing student support. Scaffolding, a well-established concept in educational psychology, refers to providing structured, adaptive guidance gradually reduced as learners develop competence [9,37]. Unlike AI systems that provide fully automated answers, TPRS is a scaffolded learning assistant [15,23], supporting students in refining research topics while preserving independent inquiry and critical thinking. The system employs large language models (LLMs) alongside traditional knowledge-based and expert-based recommendation mechanisms to (i) *Analyze student inputs and suggest structured and relevant research topics*; (ii) *Provide instant, formative feedback on the clarity and feasibility of research questions*; and (iii) *Recommend domain-specific literature to guide further academic exploration.* Unlike purely generative AI approaches, which may encourage overreliance on automated outputs, TPRS is explicitly designed to foster student autonomy by offering personalized, inquiry-driven support. Its recommendations act as cognitive scaffolds, helping students construct their ideas without replacing the need for academic reasoning and decision-making. To evaluate the effectiveness of TPRS, we apply the CRS-Que framework [13] to assess system usability and pedagogical impact. This framework examines key dimensions such as accuracy, explainability, user control, trust, and transparency. Our findings highlight that TPRS recommendations: (i) Enhance student engagement by reducing cognitive barriers in topic selection; (ii) Improve efficiency in feedback loops, allowing students to refine ideas more quickly; and (iii) Alleviate instructor workload, enabling educators to focus on higher-order feedback.

2 Related Work

The integration of AI into education has been extensively studied, focusing on enhancing student learning, personalizing feedback, and streamlining administrative processes. Pérez-Ortiz *et al.* summarized the concept of AI-based personal learning companions, emphasizing their potential to provide adaptive support tailored to the personalization of learning [27]. Many systematic reviews of AI applications in higher education have been conducted, highlighting the growing role of AI-powered tools in facilitating self-directed learning and academic support [6,26,36]. The UNESCO AI Competency Frameworks for Teachers and Students highlight the urgent need to equip educators and learners with AI-related knowledge, skills, and ethical awareness, emphasizing AI's transformative impact on education. The teacher framework underscores AI pedagogy, ethical considerations, and professional learning, ensuring educators can effectively integrate AI into teaching [20]. Meanwhile, the student framework focuses on AI literacy, ethical responsibility, and system design, preparing learners for an AI-driven world [21]. Together, these frameworks motivate research on AI-driven educational systems, advocating for adaptive learning, personalized AI tutors, and responsible AI development to enhance educational equity, inclusivity, and sustainability.

In the context of higher education, the integration of a literature recommender system has the potential to enhance the learning experience and to support students in their academic journey, such as course selection and planning [34], provision of personalized feedback and guidance [19] in an online learning environment [1,25]. Recommender systems are crucial in supporting students and researchers in selecting relevant literature, refining research topics, and structuring their academic writing [10,11,24]. Beel *et al.* reviewed research-paper recommender systems, identifying challenges in optimizing relevance, novelty, and personalization [4]. Similarly, Knoth & Herrmannova explored recommendation mechanisms that assist researchers in identifying pertinent literature by measuring the semantic similarity of publications connected in a citation network [16]. Haruna *et al.* addressed the challenge of efficiently guiding researchers to pertinent publications amid an overwhelming volume of information [12]. In that paper, the authors used a public dataset to demonstrate personalized recommendations regardless of the research field and regardless of the user's expertise. Similarly, Chen & Lee tackled the challenge of information overload in academia by developing a recommender system tailored to assist scholars in discovering pertinent research papers. The system leverages big scholarly data to enhance the relevance and accuracy of its recommendations, thereby facilitating more efficient literature exploration for researchers [7]. Recent surveys on scientific paper recommender systems highlight significant challenges, including cold start, trust, transparency, privacy, and the lack of unified scholarly data standards [3,29].

3 TPRS System Design and Development

3.1 Challenges in the Research-Oriented Term Paper Process

In the final semester of a Bachelor of Arts program, students must write a term paper synthesizing knowledge from previous courses, particularly in Media Education and Media Pedagogy. This research-oriented semester follows a structured three-phase process but presents several challenges for students and teachers. The Term Paper Preparation phase requires students to engage with course materials independently, reflect on their thematic interests, and formulate a research topic with corresponding questions. However, this process can be overwhelming. The intention to distill broad and complex learning materials into a specific research focus often leads to cognitive overload. Many students struggle to articulate straightforward, well-defined research topics and questions without substantial guidance, resulting in frustration and delays.

The Student-Teacher Interaction phase, conducted via a Moodle discussion forum, adds another layer of difficulty. Students must submit their preliminary research ideas for review, but feedback is not immediate. The long wait times for responses disrupt their workflow and motivation. Additionally, the quality of initial proposals varies significantly, often requiring multiple rounds of revision. While necessary for refining research ideas, this iterative process extends the timeline and can make students feel stuck in a cycle of revisions rather than progressing toward their final paper. Once the research topic is approved, students move into the Term Paper Writing phase, where they develop their final submission. However, delays from the earlier phases can compress the time available for actual writing, potentially affecting the quality of their work.

From the teachers' perspective, the process is equally challenging. The individual nature of the feedback required in the Moodle forum creates a substantial workload. Reviewing and refining numerous proposals within tight academic timelines is labor-intensive, especially for large cohorts. Additionally, ensuring consistency and depth of feedback across students with varying abilities and research topics is difficult. Some students require extensive guidance, while others need minimal intervention, leading to an uneven distribution of effort. The administrative burden of tracking revisions across multiple iterations further consumes valuable time that could otherwise be spent on enhancing the learning experience.

3.2 System Architecture and Workflow

TPRS aims to encourage students to reflect more deeply and effectively on their term paper topics and research questions through AI-generated feedback and recommendations. This eventually helps them identify the subject and relevant content for their term papers. Our TPRS system combines generative AI with traditional recommendation techniques, including knowledge-based [32] and expert-based methods [5], to provide reliable and contextually relevant suggestions. The overall workflow of TPRS is illustrated in Fig. 1.

The process begins when a student submits a short initial term paper proposal, which consists of a research topic (RT) and a set of research questions (RQ_i, where $i \geq 0$). A sentiment analysis (SA) module assesses the student's confidence level in their submission. Based on this evaluation, TPRS selects either the knowledge-based engine (KE) or the expert-based engine (EE) to generate feedback. If the student's confidence is high, the knowledge-based engine is activated, offering literature-based recommendations that provide further relevant academic reading resources. However, if the student's confidence is low, which means that he or she might need more professional help in specifying a research topic, the expert-based engine provides more fundamental guidance, such as

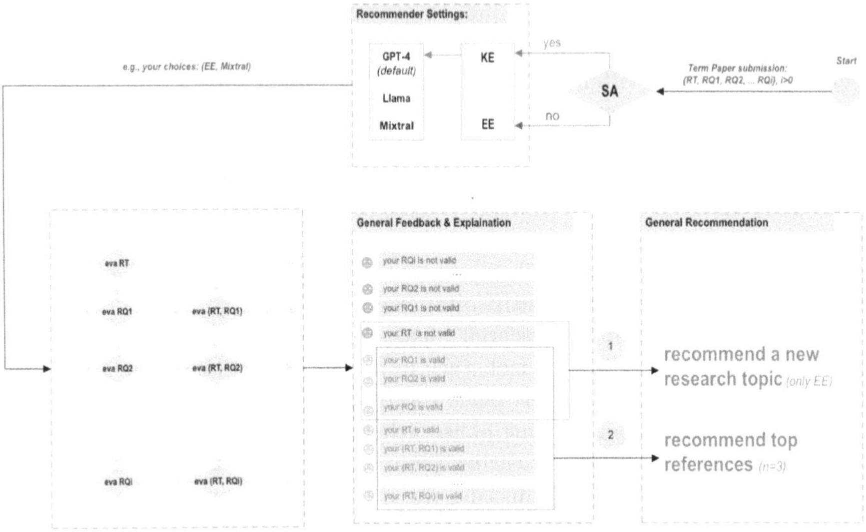

Fig. 1. TPRS v2.0 System Workflow.

refining the research topic or restructuring the research questions. Students also have the flexibility to override the system's choice and manually select a recommender engine and LLMs, such as ChatGPT-4o, Mixtral-8x7B-Instruct-v0.1, and Llama-3-8B.

Following the initial analysis, the system evaluates the research topic and questions through structured validation. A set of evaluation modules (Eva_X) have been designed to assess the validity of these submitted research statements. More specifically, these validators analyze coherence and feasibility by evaluating the research topic ($\mathrm{Eva}_{\mathrm{RT}}$), each research question ($\mathrm{Eva}_{\mathrm{RQ1}}, \mathrm{Eva}_{\mathrm{RQ2}}, ..., \mathrm{Eva}_{\mathrm{RQ}_i}$), and the pair of the research topic and a research question ($\mathrm{Eva}_{\mathrm{RT,\ RQ}_i}$). Currently, the validation module is simply implemented through structured prompting techniques using ChatGPT-4o.

Once the validation process is complete, the general feedback module can provide positive or negative feedback based on the results with a brief explanation (for system transparency and trustworthiness). Furthermore, the current TPRS only generates general recommendation information for two situations: 1) when the research topic is invalid but the research questions are valid, the expert-based engine suggests a new research topic aligned with the valid research questions. 2) When the research topic and questions are all valid, the knowledge-based engine recommends up to three most relevant academic literature for students' further reading. Such a general recommendation module ensures that students receive contextually appropriate and academically rigorous suggestions that help them refine their submissions effectively.

TPRS employs an expert-based multi-shot prompting approach to enhance accuracy, leveraging historical interactions from previous Moodle-based supervision. It has been trained on a dataset of approximately 70 students, each engaging in an average of 13∼15 interactions with teachers, allowing it to simulate high-fidelity teacher feedback. The dataset and those interactions were collected from the same bachelor program during 2023 and the winter semester of 2023/2024. The multi-shot prompting technique incorporates historical exchanges into AI-generated responses, ensuring the system provides detailed and pedagogically relevant recommendations. Those pairs of interactions were fed into ChatGPT-4o to create a master prompt [18], acting as a teacher or an expert. Additionally, TPRS uses Chain-of-Thought (CoT) reasoning to decompose complex queries into logical steps, improving interpretability and the overall coherence of feedback.

Generally, the feedback generation process follows a structured algorithm (see Algorithm 1). First, the system constructs a feedback prompt by integrating historical interactions into a structured format. A prompt template is generated, instructing the model to produce feedback that closely mimics teacher responses. This template combines the student's initial submission to form the final input prompt. The selected LLM, whether ChatGPT- 4o, Mixtral-8x7B-Instruct-v0.1, or Llama-3-8B, processes the input and generates structured feedback. The feedback output aims to provide actionable insights that guide students in refining their research topics and formulating more precise research questions.

Algorithm 1. Feedback Generation via Multi-shot Prompting

Require: Student submission $\mathbf{T}$, historical interactions $\mathcal{C} = \{C_1, C_2, \ldots, C_n\}$, number of top relevant interactions k, LLMs $\text{LLM}_1, \text{LLM}_2, \text{LLM}_3$

1: Generate a feedback prompt template P: $P \leftarrow \text{Generate\_Prompt}(\mathcal{C})$
2: Integrate student submission Q into the prompt: $P' \leftarrow [P, \mathbf{T}]$
3: Select $\text{LLM}_j \in \{\text{LLM}_1, \text{LLM}_2, \text{LLM}_3\}$
4: Generate feedback F_j using the LLM_j: $F_j \leftarrow \text{LLM}_j(P')$
5: **return** Feedback F_j

4 Evaluation

4.1 Demographic Insights

In the evaluation, we asked for voluntary in one cohort in the Bachelor of Arts program. Eighteen students participated, covering six age groups. Figure 2 presents a detailed analysis of participant demographics and behavioral characteristics across different age groups. The study included 18 students, spanning six age groups. Female participants accounted for the majority, representing 77.78% of the total, with 14 participants. Male and miscellaneous gender participants made up 16.67% and 5.55%, with 4 and 1 participants, respectively. The largest age group was 35–44 years, which included 7 participants, followed by the 25–34 and 45–54 years groups with 3 participants.

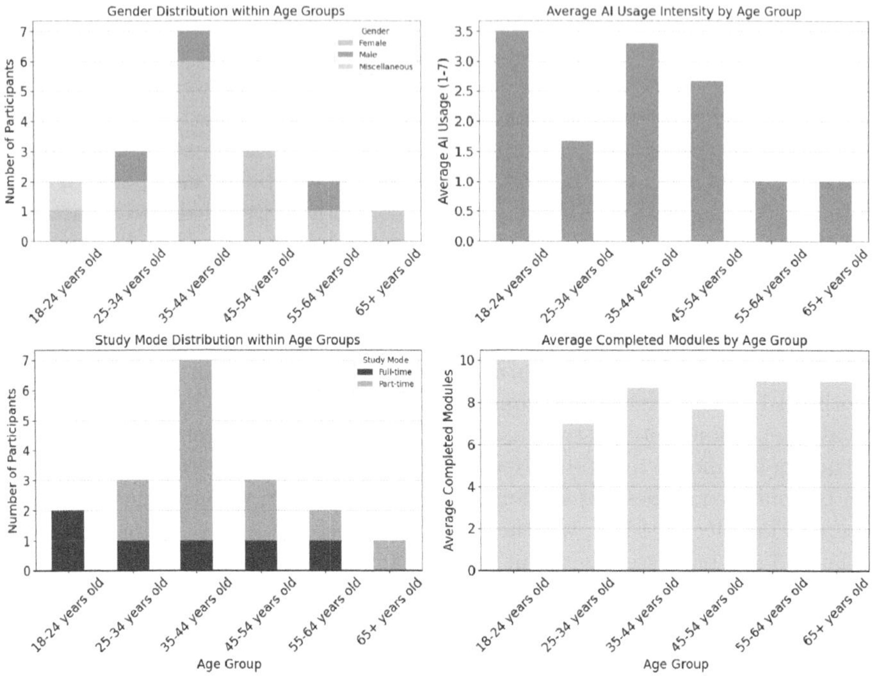

Fig. 2. Summary of Demographic Data.

AI usage intensity varied significantly across age groups. The highest engagement was reported by younger participants in the 18–24 years group, with a mean score of 3.5, and mid-career participants in the 35–44 years group, with a mean score of 3.3. In contrast, older participants in the 55–64 years and 65+ years groups reported lower AI adoption, with mean scores of 0.8 and 1.0, respectively. The overall average AI usage across all participants was 2.1. Study mode preferences also differed by age. Among all participants, 33.33%, corresponding to 6 individuals, were full-time students, while 66.67%, corresponding to 12 individuals, studied part-time. Despite these differences, academic progress remained relatively stable across age groups. On average, participants completed 8.5 modules, with the highest completion rate observed among participants in the 18–24 years group, who completed an average of 9.5 modules. The lowest completion rate was recorded in the 25–34 years group, with an average of 6.8 modules. These findings highlight the need for flexible and accessible educational technologies to support students with diverse learning needs. The higher AI engagement among younger participants suggests opportunities to integrate AI-driven tools into academic workflows, potentially enhancing learning experiences and improving study efficiency.

4.2 System Assessment Using the CRS-Que Framework

The authors conducted the pilot evaluation for the Bachelor of Arts program in Culture and Social Sciences at FernUniversität in Hagen from 01.11.2024 to 20.12.2024. We apply the CRS-Que: A User-centric Evaluation Framework for Conversational Recommender Systems [13] to evaluate our system. We believe this framework could help researchers conduct standardized user-centric research for conversational recommender systems and provide practitioners with insights into designing and evaluating a CRS from users' perspectives. The CRS-Que framework assessed multiple dimensions of user experience, including **Perceived Qualities**, **User Beliefs**, **User Attitudes**, and **Behavioral Intentions**. Below, we summarize the key findings from the evaluation results.

The **Perceived Qualities** dimension included metrics such as *Accuracy*, *Novelty*, and *Explainability*. The participants rated the system for:

- *Accuracy*: Users found the recommendations to be well-chosen, relevant, and interesting.
- *Novelty*: Participants noted that the system helped them discover new aspects or ideas. Unexpected and positive recommendations were frequently highlighted as a key strength.
- *Explainability*: The system effectively communicated the reasons behind its recommendations, enhancing transparency and trust.

The **User Beliefs** dimension measured constructs such as *Perceived Ease of Use*, *Perceived Usefulness*, and *User Control*. The participants rated the system for:

- *Ease of Use*: Participants reported that the system was intuitive and easy to use for obtaining recommendations related to their academic tasks.
- *Usefulness*: TPRS was highly effective in supporting users to complete core tasks, including identifying topics and relevant resources.
- *Control*: Users appreciated the ability to tailor recommendations and felt in control of modifying outputs based on their preferences.

The **User Attitudes** dimension evaluates *Trust and Confidence* and *Satisfaction*; specifically:

- Users trusted the system's recommendations and expressed confidence in its ability to assist with planning homework.
- Satisfaction scores reflected overall happiness with the system's performance, highlighting its role in improving task outcomes.

The **Behavioral Intentions**, including *Intention to Use*, revealed strong user loyalty and advocacy. Participants expressed their willingness to continue using the system for academic planning and recommend it to peers.

Besides the CRS-Que framework, the authors added **Judgment on Quality of Work** dimension by asking the students: How would you rate the quality of your work on the three main tasks for finding a topic for your homework in the module? Please rate individually in the case study, theoretical references, selected topic, and central question. We present the details of those dimensions in Table 1.

Table 1. Evaluation Metrics are defined in the CRS-Que and our department's evaluation frameworks. 7-point Likert scale: Do not agree at all, Disagree, Rather disagree, Neither agree nor disagree, Agree more, Agree, I completely agree.

Dimension	Code	Item
Perceived Qualities		
Accuracy	Acc1	The recommendations were well chosen
	Acc2	The recommendations were relevant
	Acc3	The recommendations were interesting
Novelty	Nov1	TPRS helped me discover new aspects/ideas
	Nov2	I received unexpected recommendations, pointing out new aspects that I would not have thought of
	Nov3	TPRS gave me recommendations that I would not have considered at first, but which turned out to be a positive and unexpected discovery
	Nov4	They were welcome recommendations, some aspects of which I would not have discovered elsewhere
Explainability	Expl1	RS explained to me why I received the recommendations and related information
	Expl2	The logic of the information received in the recommendations was explained to me by TPRS
	Expl3	The reason why I received the recommendations was given to me by TPRS
User Beliefs		
Perceived Ease of Use	PEU1	I was able to easily use TPRS to get recommendations related to my research interest
	PEU2	With TPRS, it was easy to find the recommendations that would help me plan my homework
	PEU4	It was easy to get recommendations that I found helpful
Perceived Usefulness	PU1	TPRS helped me to find the ideal recommendations for my solutions to the three leading tasks from the module
	PU2	It is easy to use TPRS to help me complete the three tasks
	PU3	TPRS gave me helpful recommendations for solving the three main tasks
User Control	UC1	I felt like I had control over changing the recommendation output in TPRS
	UC2	I was able to control the issue of recommendations well
	UC3	I had control over tailoring the recommendations to my interests
User Attitudes		
Trust & Confidence	TC1	TPRS's recommendations can be trusted
	TC2	I can rely on TPRS when I want to receive recommendations on how to plan my homework
	TC4	The recommendations convinced me
	TC5	I was confident that the recommendations would help me in planning my homework
Satisfaction	Sat1	I was satisfied with the recommendations
	Sat4	I was happy with TPRS
Behavioral Intentions		
Intention of Use	IU1	I would use TPRS again
	IU2	I would use TPRS more often while planning my homework
	IU3	I will tell fellow students about TPRS
Quality of Work (Extracted from our department's evaluation framework)		
Case study	QF	Evaluative criteria
Theoretical References	QTB	Evaluative criteria
Selected Topic	QGT	Evaluative criteria
Central question	QZF	Evaluative criteria

4.3 Measuring System Effectiveness

We analyzed user ratings across multiple evaluation dimensions to evaluate the effectiveness of the TPRS. Figure 3 presents the average scores and standard deviations. The system performed well in several key dimensions, though some areas require improvement. As shown in Fig. 3, the highest-scoring criteria were *Accuracy* (*Acc1*, *Acc2*, *Acc3*) and *Perceived Usefulness* (*PU1*, *PU2*, *PU3*), all of which had mean scores above 5. It indicates that participants generally found TPRS useful and effective in providing relevant recommendations. However, *Satisfaction* (*Sat1*, *Sat4*) received mean scores below 5, suggesting that while students acknowledged the system's utility, they were not entirely satisfied with its overall performance. Similarly, *Trust and Confidence* (*TC1*, *TC2*) received moderate ratings, indicating that users found the system somewhat reliable but still had reservations. The criteria related to *Explainability* (*Expl1*, *Expl2*, *Expl3*) received moderate ratings, indicating that while users generally understood the rationale behind the recommendations, there is room for improvement in making the system's decision-making process more transparent. Given that trust (*TC1*, *TC2*) was also rated moderately, enhancing explainability could help strengthen user confidence in the system.

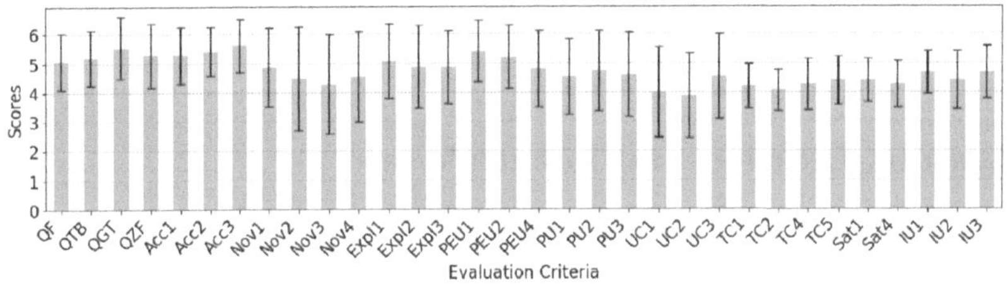

Fig. 3. Average Scores with Standard Deviations Across Evaluation Dimensions.

4.4 Impact Assessment on Student Submissions

To systematically evaluate the impact of TPRS on students' academic writing, domain experts conducted a structured assessment of submission quality. Drawing on the benefits of personalized recommendations in supporting the scientific writing process, we hypothesized that the system would contribute to an improvement in submission quality over time. To test this hypothesis, the research team collaborated with course lecturers to develop a coding scheme that ensures consistency and objectivity in evaluation. The scheme was applied to assess both the initial and final submissions recorded in the system log, as well as submissions made in the tutoring forum. A two-stage analysis was conducted using an 11-point scale, measuring four key academic criteria: use case description (3 points), theoretical background (3 points), topic of term paper (2 points), and research question formulation (3 points).

Two domain experts independently rated each submission, ensuring inter-rater reliability. To quantify agreement among raters, we calculated quadratic weighted Cohen's k, which revealed substantial agreement ($k = .675$, $p < .001$). Discrepancies in coding were resolved through discussion to establish consensus. Additionally, to account for potential covariate effects, we collected demographic information, including age, gender, study mode (full-time or part-time), and academic progress (measured through completed credit points). However, subsequent analysis showed no significant correlations between these variables and submission quality, confirming that covariates did not influence the observed trends.

The results indicate a modest but statistically significant improvement in submission quality following the use of TPRS ($\mathbf{M}_{t1} = 6.79$, $\mathbf{sd}_{t1} = 2.07$; $\mathbf{M}_{t2} = 7.53$, $\mathbf{sd}_{t2} = 1.74$). Given the absence of significant covariate effects, a directional paired t-test was deemed appropriate to assess the significance of this change. A Shapiro-Wilk test revealed that the $t1$ data was not normally distributed ($p < .05$). Further examination identified a single outlier; however, upon reviewing the corresponding submission, it was determined to be a valid data point and retained in the analysis. As directional t-tests are generally robust to minor deviations from normality and the presence of outliers, we proceeded with the analysis. Hedge's g was used to estimate effect size, yielding a small to moderate effect ($g = .44$, $p < .05$), indicating that TPRS significantly enhanced student submissions' quality.

5 Lessons Learned and Future Work

5.1 Addressing the Challenge of Missing Labeled Data

In scenarios like ours, where structured feedback data was unavailable, we faced significant hurdles in developing a retrieval system capable of generating high-quality prompts, denoted as $P = \text{Generate\_Prompt}(\mathcal{C})$. To address this challenge, we directly involved teachers in annotating their reasoning and judgment criteria for providing feedback on students' term papers. Teachers were asked to reflect on their past interactions and respond to strucHowed questionnaires such as: "Does the term paper contain practical examples?", "How many topics are covered in the term paper?", "Is the problem well formulated?", "Are appropriate theories or theoretical concepts provided?", "Do the listed theories align with the Bachelor Module Handbook?", "Does the term paper contextualize its findings within an educational framework?" This approach revealed a critical insight: teachers inherently apply their judgment criteria, honed through years of experience, to evaluate and provide feedback on term papers [22]. Although consistent, these criteria are typically applied implicitly rather than explicitly. Therefore, the central question became: how can we fine-tune LLMs to replicate these well-established, experience-driven judgment criteria? [8]. We believe this challenge is not unique to our project. Many educators and developers face similar difficulties in creating robust AI models without access to comprehensive, labeled datasets. To address this issue, we devised a forward-looking strategy:

leveraging the outputs generated by LLMs during the pilot phase and engaging teachers to refine and annotate these outputs. By asking educators to correct and expand upon the model's suggestions, we aim to build a high-quality labeled dataset iteratively. This dataset will not only support the future development of TPRS but also serve as a valuable resource for other academic AI systems.

5.2 Effectiveness of Small Language Models (SLMs)

The experimental results revealed an intriguing trend: students engaged more frequently with Mixtral-8x7B-Instruct-v0.1, regarding the number of interactions and the diversity of term paper content explored. This increased interaction suggests that Mixtral-8x7B-Instruct-v0.1, with its tailored instruction tuning, aligned more closely with the student's needs and expectations. Moreover, the outputs of Mixtral-8x7B-Instruct-v0.1 demonstrated greater consistency, as evidenced by the smallest variation in output token counts across all models. This consistency hints at its potential to deliver predictable, reliable feedback under varied conditions, a critical factor in building trust and usability for educational AI tools. These findings underscore a pivotal opportunity: With carefully designed prompts and well-labeled datasets, SLMs can serve as viable alternatives to larger models. They offer scalable and cost-effective solutions without compromising on quality, which is particularly relevant for educational institutions and researchers operating under limited computational resources or budget constraints [28,31].

5.3 Applying AI to Support Learning, Not Replace It

From the outset, we recognized the potential risks associated with generative AI in academic contexts [33,35]. If students were to rely on AI to perform the core tasks of researching, writing, and analyzing, the educational value of the learning process would be lost. Instead of fostering deep learning and critical thinking, such misuse could lead to superficial engagement with the subject matter. To mitigate this risk, we deliberately chose to hard-code safeguards into TPRS. For example, when prompted with questions such as "Can you write the term paper for me?", TPRS is programmed to respond in ways that redirect the student toward active participation in the learning process, offering guidance, feedback, and suggestions rather than performing the task. This design philosophy ensures that TPRS is a supportive tool that encourages inquiry-based learning. By guiding students through the iterative process of refining their ideas and addressing weaknesses in their term papers, TPRS maintains the integrity of the learning experience while leveraging AI's strengths to enhance accessibility and efficiency.

6 Conclusion

This study introduced the TPRS, a hybrid AI-powered platform designed to scaffold students through the cognitively demanding process of academic inquiry in distance learning. By integrating generative language models with knowledge- and expert-based recommender strategies, TPRS supports learners in formulating, refining, and validating research topics while alleviating instructor workload and feedback bottlenecks.

A key technical contribution of this work is the hybrid recommendation architecture, which integrates LLMs with structured knowledge repositories to ensure pedagogically sound and domain-relevant recommendations. Unlike traditional AI-assisted writing tools, TPRS dynamically selects recommendation strategies based on user confidence levels, employing knowledge-based retrieval for experienced users and expert-driven scaffolding for those needing additional guidance. The multi-shot prompting mechanism, informed by historical teacher interactions, enhances feedback accuracy while preserving adaptability. Furthermore, the evaluation framework and logging infrastructure provide a scalable foundation for future iterations and deployment across diverse educational settings. Through a systematic evaluation, we analyzed the effectiveness of TPRS using system logs and expert assessments, comparing students' initial and final submissions. The findings indicate a statistically significant improvement in submission quality, suggesting that AI-driven formative feedback enhances students' ability to structure their academic work. Additionally, the CRS-Que framework confirmed that students perceived the system as accurate, transparent, and pedagogically useful, though challenges related to user control and explainability remain areas for improvement. More broadly, this study contributes to the ongoing development of AI-driven educational tools, offering a scalable, modular framework that balances automation with domain expertise. By demonstrating the feasibility of hybrid recommendation architectures in academic writing support, TPRS serves as a blueprint for future AI-assisted research guidance systems, paving the way for larger-scale deployments in distance learning and beyond.

Acknowledgment. The authors kindly appreciate the support of CATALPA—Center of Advanced Technology for Assisted Learning and Predictive Analytics, FernUniversität in Hagen—through the Project "AI.EDU Research Lab 2.0".

References

1. Abel, M., Germain, W., Mahatody, T.: Pedagogical alignment of large language models (LLM) for personalized learning: a survey, trends and challenges (2024)
2. Al-Zahrani, A.M., Alasmari, T.M.: Exploring the impact of artificial intelligence on higher education: the dynamics of ethical, social, and educational implications. Humanit. Soc. Sci. Commun. **11**(1), 1–12 (2024)
3. Bai, X., Wang, M., Lee, I., Yang, Z., Kong, X., Xia, F.: Scientific paper recommendation: a survey. IEEE Access **7**, 9324–9339 (2019)
4. Beel, J., Gipp, B., Langer, S., Breitinger, C.: Paper recommender systems: a literature survey. Int. J. Digit. Libr. **17**, 305–338 (2016)
5. Bhoyar, R.R., Wang, X., Duong-Trung, N.: KaggleGPT: prompt-based recommender system for efficient dataset discovery. In: Proceedings of DELFI Workshops 2024, pp. 10–18420. Gesellschaft für Informatik eV (2024)

6. Castillo-Martínez, I.M., Flores-Bueno, D., Gómez-Puente, S.M., Vite-León, V.O.: AI in higher education: a systematic literature review. In: Frontiers in Education, vol. 9, p. 1391485. Frontiers Media SA (2024)
7. Chen, T.T., Lee, M.: Research paper recommender systems on big scholarly data. In: Yoshida, K., Lee, M. (eds.) PKAW 2018. LNCS (LNAI), vol. 11016, pp. 251–260. Springer, Cham (2018). https://doi.org/10.1007/978-3-319-97289-3_20
8. Duong-Trung, N., Wang, X., Kravčík, M.: BloomLLM: large language models based question generation combining supervised fine-tuning and bloom's taxonomy. In: Ferreira Mello, R., Rummel, N., Jivet, I., Pishtari, G., Ruipérez Valiente, J.A. (eds.) EC-TEL 2024. LNCS, vol. 15160, pp. 93–98. Springer, Cham (2024). https://doi.org/10.1007/978-3-031-72312-4_11
9. Ertugruloglu, E., Mearns, T., Admiraal, W.: Scaffolding what, why and how? A critical thematic review study of descriptions, goals, and means of language scaffolding in bilingual education contexts. Educ. Res. Rev. 100550 (2023)
10. Fathi, J., Rahimi, M.: Utilising artificial intelligence-enhanced writing mediation to develop academic writing skills in EFL learners: a qualitative study. Comput. Assist. Lang. Learn. (2024)
11. Fleckenstein, J., Liebenow, L.W., Meyer, J.: Automated feedback and writing: a multi-level meta-analysis of effects on students' performance. J. Educ. Manag. Instr. **6**, 1162454 (2023)
12. Haruna, K., Akmar Ismail, M., Damiasih, D., Sutopo, J., Herawan, T.: A collaborative approach for research paper recommender system. PLoS One **12**(10), e0184516 (2017)
13. Jin, Y., Chen, L., Cai, W., Zhao, X.: CRS-QUE: a user-centric evaluation framework for conversational recommender systems. ACM Trans. Recommender Syst. **2**(1), 1–34 (2024)
14. Kaswan, K.S., Dhatterwal, J.S., Ojha, R.P.: AI in personalized learning. In: Advances in Technological Innovations in Higher Education, pp. 103–117. CRC Press (2024)
15. Kim, J., Lee, H., Cho, Y.H.: Learning design to support student-AI collaboration: perspectives of leading teachers for AI in education. Educ. Inf. Technol. **27**(5), 6069–6104 (2022)
16. Knoth, P., Herrmannova, D.: Towards semantometrics: a new semantic similarity based measure for assessing a research publication's contribution. D-Lib Mag. **20**(11), 8 (2014)
17. Lin, C.C., Huang, A.Y., Lu, O.H.: Artificial intelligence in intelligent tutoring systems toward sustainable education: a systematic review. Smart Learn. Environ. **10**(1), 41 (2023)
18. Lo, L.S.: The art and science of prompt engineering: a new literacy in the information age. Internet Ref. Serv. Q. **27**(4), 203–210 (2023)
19. Maier, U., Klotz, C.: Personalized feedback in digital learning environments: classification framework and literature review. Comput. Educ.: Artif. Intell. **3**, 100080 (2022)
20. Miao, F., Cukurova, M.: AI competency framework for teachers (2024)
21. Miao, F., Shiohira, K.: AI competency framework for students (2024)
22. Monarch, R.M.: Human-in-the-Loop Machine Learning: Active learning and annotation for human-centered AI. Simon and Schuster (2021)
23. Munshi, A., Biswas, G., Baker, R., Ocumpaugh, J., Hutt, S., Paquette, L.: Analysing adaptive scaffolds that help students develop self-regulated learning behaviours. J. Comput. Assist. Learn. **39**(2), 351–368 (2023)

24. Muslimin, I.: The use of chatgpt to improve scientific article productivity of postgraduate students. J. Educ. Manag. Instr. **3**, 63–71 (2023)
25. Ng, C., Fung, Y.: Educational personalized learning path planning with large language models (2024)
26. Ouyang, F., Zheng, L., Jiao, P.: Artificial intelligence in online higher education: a systematic review of empirical research from 2011 to 2020. Educ. Inf. Technol. **27**(6), 7893–7925 (2022)
27. Perez-Ortiz, M., Novak, E., Bulathwela, S., Shawe-Taylor, J.: An AI-based learning companion promoting lifelong learning opportunities for all. arXiv preprint arXiv:2112.01242 (2021)
28. Shan, R.: Language artificial intelligence at a crossroads: deciphering the future of small and large language models. Computer **57**(8), 26–35 (2024)
29. Sharma, R., Gopalani, D., Meena, Y.: An anatomization of research paper recommender system: overview, approaches and challenges. Eng. Appl. Artif. Intell. **118**, 105641 (2023)
30. Shi, H., Aryadoust, V.: A systematic review of AI-based automated written feedback research. ReCALL, pp. 1–23 (2024)
31. Sterbini, A., Temperini, M.: An exploration of open source small language models for automated assessment. In: 2024 28th International Conference Information Visualisation (IV), pp. 1–6. IEEE (2024)
32. Uta, M., et al.: Knowledge-based recommender systems: overview and research directions. Front. Big Data **7** (2024)
33. Vázquez-Madrigal, C., García-Rubio, N., Triguero, Á.: Generative artificial intelligence in education: risks and opportunities. In: Valls Martínez, M.D.C., Montero, J. (eds.) Teaching Innovations in Economics, pp. 233–254. Springer, Cham (2024). https://doi.org/10.1007/978-3-031-72549-4_11
34. Yu, J., et al.: From MOOC to MAIC: reshaping online teaching and learning through LLM-driven agents (2024)
35. Yusuf, A., Pervin, N., Román-González, M.: Generative AI and the future of higher education: a threat to academic integrity or reformation? Evidence from multicultural perspectives. Int. J. Educ. Technol. High. Educ. **21**(1), 21 (2024)
36. Zawacki-Richter, O., Marín, V.I., Bond, M., Gouverneur, F.: Systematic review of research on artificial intelligence applications in higher education-where are the educators? Int. J. Educ. Technol. High. Educ. **16**(1), 1–27 (2019)
37. Zeng, J., Zhang, P., Zhou, J., Shang, J., Black, J.B.: The impact of embodied scaffolding sequences on stem conceptual learning. Educ. Technol. Res. Dev. 1–26 (2024)

CRAFT: A Course Recommendation Advisor for Future Talent

Fatemeh Fathi(✉), Tao Wu, and Stefan Decker

Chair of Computer Science 5, RWTH Aachen University, Aachen, Germany
{fathi,decker}@dbis.rwth-aachen.de, tao.wu@rwth-aachen.de

Abstract. Rapidly changing job markets highlight the growing need for continuous and targeted skill development aligned with individual career goals. Existing course recommender systems in higher education predominantly rely on collaborative filtering or content-based techniques, and these systems struggle to match online courses with the targeted job skill demands due to their reliance on historical behavior data, resulting in issues such as the cold-start problem and limited adaptability to evolving career goals. To address these limitations, we introduce CRAFT as a course Recommender System (RS) for the German career context that integrates educational ontologies as a comprehensive domain knowledge and Large Language Models (LLMs) to provide personalized, career-oriented course recommendations along with clear explanations. In this way, CRAFT helps users continuously enhance their skills and make informed learning decisions. Experimental evaluations demonstrate CRAFT's effectiveness in analyzing the skill gap and providing relevant recommendations supported by detailed explanations, increasing user satisfaction. This research contributes to personalized learning frameworks in education by providing personalized, continuous learning opportunities through effectively linking online courses with evolving occupational competencies.

Keywords: Lifelong learning · Skills and labor market · Course recommender system · Large language models · Prompt engineering

1 Introduction

According to the rapidly evolving job market, continuous upskilling and reskilling have become more essential nowadays [13]. Meanwhile, technological advances and economic shifts are constantly redefining skills required by employers for different occupations, which has led to widespread agreement that education needs to become a lifelong and personalized process [2]. In Europe, for example, policy initiatives under the European Year of Skills 2023 emphasize that individuals must engage in ongoing learning to remain employable [2,14]. Recent results indicate that by 2027, 44% of workers' core skills will be disrupted, mostly due to Artificial Intelligence (AI) and automation, necessitating fast adaptations through training [4].

K. Tammets et al. (Eds.): EC-TEL 2025, LNCS 16063, pp. 153–167, 2026.
https://doi.org/10.1007/978-3-032-03870-8_11

Traditional recommender systems often fall short, particularly due to the cold-start problem [3] and a lack of transparent, comprehensible justifications behind their suggestions [9]. Within the specific context of Germany, an additional complexity arises from the mismatch between national occupational classifications (e.g., the German Federal Employment Agency's KldB system) and broader European standards like ESCO (European Skills, Competences, Qualifications, and Occupations) and the German Federal Employment Agency (BA), complicating the task of aligning course recommendations effectively [8]. Such resources enable semantic matching of learner goals to course content, and improve relevance and alignment with job demands. Moreover, recent advances in Large Language Models (LLMs), further enhance the capability of recommender systems by enabling many opportunities such as contextual ranking of recommendation candidates or generating detailed and reasonable explanations. Such features offer generalization ability in sparse data scenarios and support transparency in automated decisions [18].

To overcome these limitations, we present CRAFT as a **C**ourse **R**ecommendation **A**dvisor for **F**uture **T**alent. CRAFT's architecture is ontology-driven; it employs a hybrid architecture composed of a BERT-based retrieval module for efficient filtering of courses and a LoRA-fine-tuned LLM that reranks course recommendations and generates clear and personalized explanations for each recommended course. Central to this idea is a custom-trained Named Entity Recognition (NER) module and the annotated German courses dataset with ESCO skills, capable of automatically extracting relevant skills from German-language course descriptions, thereby dynamically connecting authoritative occupational frameworks with educational content. To investigate the effectiveness and transparency of CRAFT in supporting career-oriented lifelong learning, we explore three main research questions:

- **RQ1:** How can domain knowledge from ESCO and BA be effectively utilized to align course recommendations with job requirements?
- **RQ2:** What is the contribution of different modules within our system to the overall performance of the recommendation system?
- **RQ3:** How effective are the generated explanations in providing users with clear, understandable, and useful justifications for each course recommendation?

In the following sections, we detail the design of CRAFT's architecture, the implementation of its components, and the results of our experiments, which together demonstrate the system's potential to support lifelong learning through personalized and career-aligned learning recommendations[1].

2 State-of-the-Art

Recent research in educational recommender systems has moved towards knowledge-grounded recommendations. This approach uses external knowledge

[1] Source code is available at https://github.com/FatemeFathii/CRAFT.

sources, like Knowledge Graphs (KGs), to improve the recommendation process. By representing courses, skills, and occupations as parts of a graph, these systems can find complex relationships that are not visible in simple user data. For instance, [16] showed how a KG framework could be used to recommend learning paths, proving that structured knowledge helps create more logical course sequences. Although this is a powerful method, the success of these systems fully depends on the quality of the KG used [12]. Moreover, many available KGs are too general or are built from data sources that are not official enough for important career planning [5].

At the same time, recent progress in LLMs has created new possibilities for recommender systems. There are different ways to use LLMs. One way is to use an LLM as the entire recommender system. For instance, TALLREC [1] shows how to use tuning frameworks to make LLMs work for recommendation tasks. This method shows that LLMs are very capable, but it can also be like a *black-box* that is expensive, difficult to manage, and may not base its recommendations on verifiable, domain-specific facts. In contrast, CRAFT has a modular *retrieval-then-ranking* pipeline. In CRAFT, a fine-tuned BERT model first retrieves a set of relevant candidates, which are then re-ranked by LLM. This hybrid approach is designed for scalability and allows for more direct control over the recommendation logic, avoiding a black-box scenario where the LLM is the sole recommender.

A second, more common approach is to use LLMs in hybrid systems, where they perform specific sub-tasks using their strong language understanding skills. Many systems now use pre-trained models like BERT to better represent text. The original work on Sentence-BERT [15], for example, introduces a good method for creating meaningful embeddings of course descriptions to improve content analysis. Following this idea, newer works use LLMs in more complex recommendation pipelines. [17] created GLRec, which uses a fine-tuned LLM to understand graph data for job recommendations. This is a promising idea, but its knowledge comes from user behavior graphs, which might not always be available or reliable, especially for a specific country's job market. Another system, Chat-REC [11], uses conversation to give interactive and explainable recommendations. However, because it does not use a formal knowledge base, its analysis of skill gaps might be less accurate. CRAFT, alternatively, grounds its recommendations in formal, authoritative ontologies—specifically ESCO and German BA frameworks—to build a stable Occupation-Skill Knowledge Base (OSKB). By extracting skills from unstructured course text and mapping them to this knowledge base, CRAFT employs an approach to provide a strong domain-specificity and consistency, which is crucial for the high-stakes domain of career development. This knowledge-driven foundation is also CRAFT's primary strategy for mitigating the cold-start problem, as recommendations depend on a user's stated career goals rather than their interaction history.

3 Methodology

CRAFT is implemented as a web application, specifically designed to address the skill gaps between users' current capabilities and their desired career goals through personalized and explainable course recommendations. This section details the methodology we used to address the challenges of generating personalized, and career-oriented course recommendations.

3.1 System Design

Key Features. The course recommendation workflow consists of three main stages: 1) *Candidate course retrieval*, 2) *LLM-based re-ranking*, and 3) *Generating explanations*.

1) Candidate Course Retrieval: The process begins when the user visits the CRAFT web application and the system collects user inputs on their target occupation and current skill set. Using an occupation-skill knowledge base, the system identifies the skills gap required for the target occupation. This skill gap, combined with the specified target occupation, triggers a BERT-based course recommendation. The BERT retriever, fine-tuned on Sentence BERT, processes the input to map courses related to the occupation and skills into a vector space. This allows for a swift retrieval of courses pertinent to the user's needs. The output from this stage is a set of top N candidate courses believed to effectively address the user's skills gap.

2) LLM-Based Re-ranking: In the second stage, we re-rank candidate courses from the initial retrieval using an LLM. A prompt constructor creates structured prompts for the LLM, including specific instructions detailing the task, information about the target occupation, the identified skill gaps, and pairs of candidate courses. The LLM then performs pairwise evaluations to determine the most relevant course based on how well each addresses the user's skill gaps. Through iterative pairwise comparisons, this stage finalizes a refined ranking, resulting in a curated list of top K most relevant courses to the user's career goals.

3) Generating Explanations: The final stage involves generating explanations for each recommended course. Using a structured prompt containing the target occupation and recommended courses ranked by the LLM, the system generates explanations that articulate the rationale behind each recommendation. These explanations explicitly link the recommended courses to the user's skill gaps and career goals.

System Architecture. The CRAFT system follows a modern client-server model designed for scalability and efficiency. As depicted in Fig. 1, the system consists of several key components including the frontend for user interface(UI), a set of backend services, databases as data storages, and LLMs module.

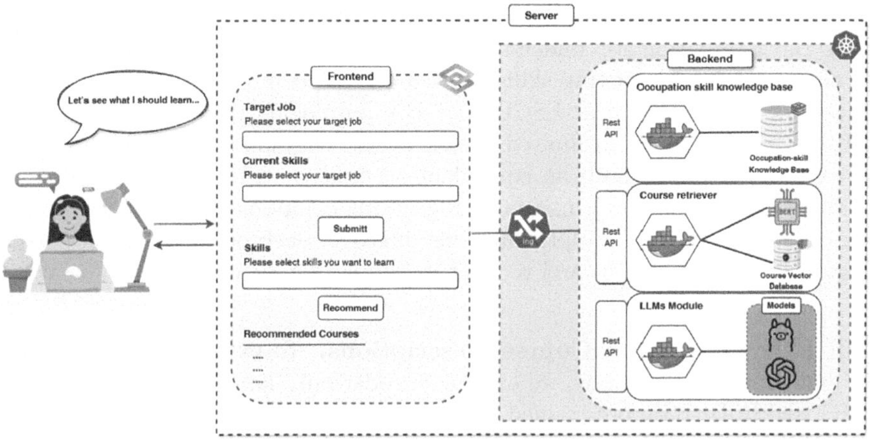

Fig. 1. The architectural overview of the CRAFT system.

Frontend is built with Gradio, providing a browser-accessible platform for users to enter their target occupation and current skills, and receive course recommendations along with explanations. The application routes user requests via a Kubernetes Ingress Controller to the designated services in the backend.

Backend Services are implemented as independent microservices orchestrated via Kubernetes as Docker containers, exposed through a central Ingress Controller, and communicate over RESTful APIs. The main backend services include *Occupation Skill Knowledge Base*, which efficiently processes requests from the frontend and retrieves relevant skills based on the user's occupation, *Course Retriever*, that identifies relevant courses from a course vector base, and *LLMs Module* to re-rank and generate explainable recommendation list of course recommendations.

Databases. Redis is used to store skill data to ensure low-latency access during searching for skills. A course vector database, which stores the context of courses along with their metadata, including course name, link, and description, supports similarity-based retrieval in the Course Retriever module.

Large Language Models (LLMs) module is responsible to perform inference tasks. These tasks include ranking course recommendations provided by the Course Retriever and generating explanations for each recommendation, ensuring that the final recommendations are comprehensively and effectively presented to the user.

3.2 Implementation Details

The following subsections provide technical details about the implementation of each component.

Occupation-Skill Knowledge Base. The occupation-skill knowledge base forms the foundation for understanding user context, focusing on users' target occupations and existing skills. It is constructed by aggregating structured educational data from the ESCO and BA ontologies via their official APIs and data portals. Due to limited access to the German Labor Market Ontology (GLMO) [10], we built an equivalent occupation-skill mapping inspired by GLMO to ensure comprehensive coverage. This component enables the extraction of both essential and optional skills linked to each occupation, supporting accurate skill gap analysis and recommendation alignment.

Skill Extraction from Course Descriptions. To extract skills from both job and course descriptions, we employ encoder-only language models, such as BERT and RoBERTa, pre-trained for this task using the Masked Language Modeling (MLM) technique. To choose a model with a good performance, we pre-trained two deepset/gbert-large[2] and FacebookAI/xlm-roberta-large[3] models on the German educational corpus and developed ***EduGBERT***[4] and ***EduXLMR*** models respectively. Additionally, to ensure the model accurately identifies and classifies skills, we fine-tune BERT model for the NER task[5]. Since course descriptions often exceed the input constraints of many models, we consider identified skills of each course as course's learning outcomes. Hence, we represent each course by its name and related learning outcomes.

Initial Course Retrieval: The BERT-based course retriever module[6] is responsible for efficiently filtering relevant courses from a large course database, based on user's current skills and target job role. The system employs SBERT [15] in a Siamese network structure, which conducts contrastive learning. The input includes occupation-related content (such as occupation names, descriptions, and identified skill gaps) on one side, and course-related content (such as course names and learning outcomes) on the other side.

Both the occupation and skill context, as well as course content are encoded into hidden states by SBERT:

$$\mathbf{H} = \{\mathbf{h}_{[CLS]}, \mathbf{h}_1, \mathbf{h}_2, \ldots, \mathbf{h}_m, \mathbf{h}_{[SEQ]}\} \quad (1)$$

where [CLS] token represents the contexts.

The relation between the user and course contexts is also computed using cosine similarity.

Then, we consider pairs of related occupations and course contexts as positive examples and pairs with unrelated courses as negative examples. We used the occupation-course dataset to train the BERT-based model with negative

[2] https://huggingface.co/deepset/gbert-large.
[3] https://huggingface.co/FacebookAI/xlm-roberta-large.
[4] https://huggingface.co/wt3639/EduGBERT.
[5] https://huggingface.co/wt3639/NER_skill_extractor.
[6] https://huggingface.co/wt3639/EduGBERT_CourseRec.

Instruction Input	
Task Instruction	As an education expert, you have been provided with a target occupation, a skill gap, and information on two candidate courses. Your task is to determine which course better matches the target occupation and skills gap. Please respond with "*First*" or "*Second*" to indicate your recommendation.
Input	**Target occupation:** Name: {occupation name} Description: {occupation description} **Skills gap:** {skills gap} **Candidate courses:** First: {course name 1}, Learning Outcomes: ... Second: {course name 2}, Learning Outcomes: ...
Instruction Output	
Output	First (or Second)

Fig. 2. Pairwise Recommendation Tuning Prompt Template.

sampling (14 irrelevant courses from the training set as negative samples per pair). To effectively map related occupations and courses into proximate vector spaces, we use the InfoNCE loss to fine-tune the model, which is designed to maximize the occupation-course pairs' similarity while minimizing unrelated pairs' similarity:

$$\mathcal{L} = -\log \frac{\exp(s_{\text{pos}})}{\exp(s_{\text{pos}}) + \sum_{i=1}^{N} \exp(s_{\text{neg}_i})} \tag{2}$$

S_{pos} is the similarity score for related pairs, and s_{neg_i} are the scores for unrelated pairs. Finally, the top k courses with the highest scores will be considered as the initial candidate set.

LLM-Based Re-ranking: After the BERT-based course retriever filters relevant courses, the LLM Ranker[7] re-ranks the list of retrieved courses based on their relevance to the user's skills gap and target occupation to finalize the top k recommendations.

To enable the LLM to compare two course candidates simultaneously and choose the one that better aligns with the user's needs, we use the LoRA Pairwise Recommendation Fine-tuning method [17]. We combine each positive occupation-course candidate with 14 negative pairs to create 14 prompts. Each prompt consists of one positive and one negative candidate and we randomly assign whether each candidate is positioned as First or Second, and the output always selects the positive pair. Figure 2 illustrates the tuning process utilizing structured prompts to guide the LLM's decision-making process.

In addition, to efficiently fine-tune our LLM for this task, we utilize LoRA, training it to act as a comparator within our course recommendation system.

[7] https://huggingface.co/wt3639/Llama-3-8B-Instruct_CourseRec_lora.

The adapted model's function is expressed using the following loss function:

$$\mathcal{L}_{REC} = -\sum_{(X,y)\in D} \log(P_{\Theta_0+\Delta\Theta}(y|X)) \tag{3}$$

where X represents the tokens in the Instruction Input, y is the expected token in the Instruction Output (either 'First' or 'Second'), and D is the training dataset consisting of (X, y) pairs. Here, $P_{\Theta_0+\Delta\Theta}(y|X)$ denotes the probability of token y given the input X and the model parameters $\Theta_0 + \Delta\Theta$, with Θ_0 representing the pre-existing LLM parameters and $\Delta\Theta$ the parameters of the LoRA adapter.

Finally, the LLM evaluates the relevance of courses based on their alignment with the user's skill gap and their career goals. The model iterates over the N candidate courses, and ranks them by their relevance and effectiveness in filling the skills gap. We utilize a custom sorting algorithm, that incorporates the LLM's output to order the courses from most to least suitable. The algorithm is outlined in Algorithm 1.

Algorithm 1. Compare courses using LLM

```
procedure LLMComparator(course_a, course_b)
    courses ← "First: name: " + course_a['course_name'] + ", skills: " +
    course_a['course_skills'] + " Second: name: " + course_b['course_name']
    + ", skills: " + course_b['course_skills']
    target_occupation ← "name: " + occupation['occupation_name'] + ",
    description: " + occupation['occupation_dsp']
    skill_gap ← occupation['occupation_skills']
    prompt ← GeneratePrompt(target_occupation, skill_gap, courses)
    result ← LLM([prompt])
    if result['logit'][0]['First_id'] > result['logit'][0]['Second_id']
    then
        return 1                                  ▷ LLM prefers course_a
    else if result['logit'][0]['First_id'] <
    result['logit'][0]['Second_id'] then
        return -1                                 ▷ LLM prefers course_b
    else
        return 0                                  ▷ They are equal or unclear
    end if
end procedure
```

Explanation Generation: In the final stage, we generate detailed explanations for each recommended course using an LLM fine-tuned specifically for this task[8] to enhance transparency and user trust. To ensure the generated explanations are both context-aware and technically precise, we use the synthetic recommendation

[8] https://huggingface.co/wt3639/Llama-3-8B-instruct-exp-adapter.

Instruction Input	
Task Instruction	As an education expert, you have been provided with a target occupation, a skills gap, and recommended course information. Your task is to explain the recommendation.
Input	**Target occupation:** Name: {occupation name} Description: {occupation description} **Skills gap:** {skills gap} **Recommended courses:** Name: {course name} Learning outcomes: { learning outcomes}
Instruction Output	
Output	Recommendation Explanation

Fig. 3. Explanation Generation Tuning Prompt Template.

explanation dataset to train the model. The process involves constructing a detailed prompt that includes the target occupation, the identified skills gap, and the ranked list of recommended courses with their key details, as shown in Fig. 3.

Furthermore, we apply LoRA to fine-tune the LLM efficiently for explanation generation. The loss function used in this context differs from that used in pairwise recommendation tuning, as it deals with generating text sequences rather than binary decisions, making the model to generate fluent and relevant justifications:

$$\mathcal{L}_{EXP} = -\sum_{(X,E)\in D}\sum_{t=1}^{|E|}\log(P_{\Theta_0+\Delta\Theta}(e_t|X, e_{<t})) \tag{4}$$

4 Evaluation

To evaluate the effectiveness and usability of CRAFT, we conducted detailed experiments across multiple datasets, ablation studies to isolate the contribution of each component, and a systematic user study that we discuss each in detail in the following.

4.1 Datasets and Pre-processing

We conducted our experiments on multiple datasets for training and evaluation:

- *Course Dataset:* Collected from Udemy[9] and Federal Employment Agency (Arbeitsagentur) APIs and portals[10], including course title, course description, URL, and removed HTML tags. In total, it includes 16,176 courses

[9] https://www.udemy.com/.
[10] https://www.arbeitsagentur.de/.

from Arbeitsagentur and 4,683 from Udemy. We employed the BeautifulSoup library to clean and convert the HTML to plain text.
- *Skill Annotation* Dataset[11]: 500 German courses from the course dataset (80% from BA, 20% from Udemy) annotated by the Prodigy annotation tool[12]. To annotate the dataset, we trained the NER model from the skill extractor module, iteratively and provided 22,520 annotated sentences.
- *Occupation-Skill Knowledge Base:* Occupation-to-skill mappings from ESCO (containing 3,008 occupations and 13,890 skills) and BA (containing 2,148 occupations and 47,670 skills) APIs to analyze the skill gaps. We formatted the ontology of the data by referencing ESCO and GLMO ontologies.
- *Ground Truth Occupation-Course Dataset:* We employed the web mining method based on the approach in [10] to collect courses identified as relevant to specific occupations. For each BA occupation, we retrieved courses using Weiterbildungssuche API, including 4,479 records of occupation-course pairs.
- *Synthetic Recommendation Explanation Dataset:* To generate explanations, we used occupation-course pairs from the Ground Truth Occupation-Course Dataset and generated prompts to guide GPT-4o in generating explanations. It includes 4,479 explanation pairs, each containing approximately 295 tokens.
- *German Education Corpora:* A dataset of all collected German course content from Arbeitsagentur, Udemy, ESCO, and BA for model pre-training.

4.2 Experiment Setup

Ablation Study. To isolate the contributions of each key component, we conducted a series of ablation experiments. We compare our model with and without each system's component. Results are shown in Table 1.

Results demonstrate that by removing the skill extractor, the performance of the system decreases across all metrics. This demonstrates that the skill extractor plays a crucial role in identifying relevant skills from the course description and the skills are bridging the gap between occupations and courses. While domain-specific pretraining of the BERT retriever offered slight improvements, the gains were minimal, indicating limited impact on recommendation quality. Also, in comparing LLM backbones, both LLaMA3-8B-Instruct (LoRA fine-tuned) and GPT-3.5 Turbo showed strengths on different metrics; notably, LLaMA3-8B-Instruct achieved competitive performance despite its smaller size, which shows its efficiency and effectiveness for scalable recommendation systems.

Model Training. For the German-based BERT model, both *EduGBERT* and *EduXLMR* models were trained with AdamW $(\beta_1, \beta_2) = (0.9, 0.999)$, a learning rate of 2e-5, batch size of 16, sequence length of 512 tokens, over 5 epochs and 3,000 steps. To fine-tune the BERT model for skill extraction, each model was

[11] https://huggingface.co/datasets/wt3639/Skill_Annotation_Dataset.
[12] https://prodi.gy/.

Table 1. Ablation study results across different components. Bold values indicate the best performance for each comparison.

Ablation Study	Model	HR@1	HR@3	HR@5	NDCG@3	NDCG@5
Skill Extractor	w/ skill extractor	**0.4162**	**0.6091**	**0.6802**	**0.5073**	**0.5338**
	w/o skill extractor	0.3376	0.5355	0.6320	0.4329	0.4677
Domain Pre-training	w/ domain pretrain	**0.4162**	**0.6091**	0.6802	**0.5073**	**0.5338**
	w/o domain pretrain	0.4060	0.5990	**0.6827**	0.4996	0.5308
LLM Backbone	llama3-8B-Instruct	**0.4162**	0.6091	0.6802	**0.5073**	**0.5338**
	gpt-3.5-turbo	0.3832	**0.6218**	**0.6954**	0.4995	0.5278

trained for 10 epochs with a batch size of 32, a learning rate of 2e-5, and AdamW optimizer. We divided the dataset into training, validation, and test sets with the 8:1:1 distribution ratio. For the retriever model, data was divided into 8:1:1, and trained over 100 epochs with a batch size of 4, a learning rate of 1e-5, and AdamW optimizer with $(\beta_1, \beta_2) = (0.9, 0.999)$. For pairwise recommendation, we adopted the LLaMa-3-8B-instruct model and use the ground truth occupation-course dataset for training. LoRA reduced training parameters to 0.52% of the full model parameters (41,943,040 from 8,072,204,288 parameters) with a learning rate of 1e-4, batch size of 8, and 200 epochs with LoRA rank and LoRA α 16, and 0.05 dropout. For the explanation generation, we fine-tuned the model with the same parameter configurations as the pairwise recommendation model. The only difference is the dataset; we use the synthetic recommendation explanation dataset to train the model. We initially considered using public datasets such as CoCo and MOOCube. However, their characteristics do not align well with our application scenario. Our system focuses on recommending courses based on users' professions and required skills, and both MOOCube and COCO lack detailed information about professions and skills. This makes them less suitable for effectively validating our approach. Therefore, we chose to use data provided by the Federal Employment Agency in Germany, which contains rich information on professions and skills that is essential for training and evaluating our system. Data was split into training and validation with an 8:2 ratio, and generated explanations were evaluated in a user study phase.

4.3 User Study

We conducted a three-week user study involving participants with a balanced distribution of age and gender. In this study, participants were first asked to select their target occupation, current skill set, and desired skills from the provided list of skill gaps. Based on the user's input, CRAFT recommends five actually offered online courses along with concise, LLM-generated explanations linked to the identified skills gap. Participants then completed a structured questionnaire (overall 10 questions with 3 demographic and 7 statements rated on a 1–5 Likert scale), designed to capture their evaluation of three key aspects: *domain knowledge coverage*, *recommendation relevance*, and *explanation clarity*.

Participants Demographics. The study involved 50 participants with diverse demographics. Approximately 45.5% identified as male, 50% as female, and 4.5% as non-binary. In terms of professional backgrounds, 18% were from IT and Technology, 16% from Engineering, 12% from Health and Medicine, while 10% each came from Legal and Humanitarian fields and Business and Management, with an additional 8% representing the Environment sector; 26% of the participants identified with other fields. The age distribution ranged from the early twenties to the late fifties, with a notable concentration in the mid-twenties, reflecting a balanced mix of early-career and experienced professionals.

4.4 Results

The user study results shown in Fig. 4 demonstrate that CRAFT performs well across multiple dimensions of system quality. Regarding *domain knowledge coverage and quality (Q4–Q6)*, explained below, most participants rated the system highly in terms of occupation coverage, skill relevance, and skill coverage. This indicates that the system effectively covers the domain knowledge required for career and skills development. However, in comparison to occupation coverage, participants were less satisfied with the skill coverage provided by the system. This suggests that there is room for improvement in the skill coverage of domain knowledge from ESCO and BA. The relationship between occupations and related skills evolves with the labor market, and as technology advances, some occupations require newly emerging skills. Users are highly attuned to these shifts. However, due to its large scale, domain knowledge is not updated frequently, which can also result in a decline in user satisfaction of skills coverage.

- Q4: The occupation provided by the system covers all my professional needs.
- Q5: The skills provided by the system are related to the target occupation I selected.
- Q6: The skills provided by the system cover all my needs for professional development.

In terms of *recommendation quality (Q7–Q8)*, the majority of participants rated the system favorably, highlighting the relevance of recommended courses to their target occupations and their effectiveness in addressing skill gaps. This suggests that the system successfully recommends courses that are well-aligned with users' professional objectives and skill requirements. However, satisfaction levels were somewhat lower regarding the system's ability to address skill gaps compared to its relevance to target occupations. This discrepancy may arise because the skills that can be acquired from a course are inherently limited. Although the system is designed to identify courses that cover most of the skills listed in the skills gap, there are inevitably some skills that may not be addressed by the recommended courses.

- Q7: The recommended courses are relevant to the target occupation I provided.
- Q8: The recommended courses address the skills gaps I provided.

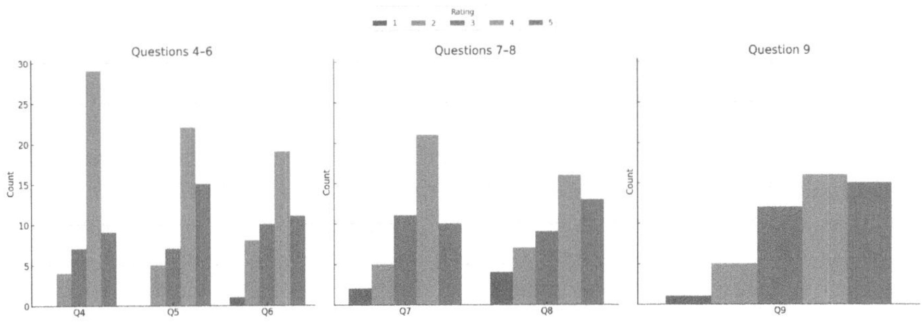

Fig. 4. Distribution of participants' ratings to the questionnaire questions.

Lastly, for *explanation quality (Q9)*, the majority of users found the system's explanations and justifications for course recommendations to be helpful in selecting suitable learning options. This indicates that the explanations are clear, informative, and relevant, providing users with valuable insights into the recommended courses. The explanations are generated based on the skills extracted from the course descriptions and the user's target occupation and skills gap. By linking the course content to the specific skills required for various careers, the system enhances the precision of course recommendations and provides detailed explanations for its suggestions. This feature is particularly important for users who may not be familiar with the course content or the skills required for their target occupation.

- Q9: The explanations about the recommended courses helped me in choosing the course for my needs.

5 Conclusion and Future Work

In this study, we presented CRAFT—a course recommendation system that integrates structured domain knowledge from educational ontologies such as ESCO and BA with advanced LLM capabilities in the German labor market to recommend courses aligned with the user's targeted job. By integrating a BERT-based retriever with a LoRA fine-tuned LLM for re-ranking course candidates and explanation generation, CRAFT effectively analyzes the skill gap based on standard educational ontologies, job target requirements, and the learning outcomes of online courses. The skill-annotated course dataset, with the custom-trained NER model for automated skill extraction, provides courses recommended based on standard educational ontologies and a robust solution to the cold-start problem.

In addressing **RQ1**, our experimental evaluations demonstrated that structured domain knowledge from ESCO and BA provides highly relevant, career-aligned suggestions. The ablation studies for **RQ2** confirmed the effectiveness of each system component. We learned that the LLM-based re-ranking and explanation generation modules significantly enhanced both the relevance and interpretability of the recommended courses, indicating their crucial role in the overall performance and user satisfaction. We also learned that domain-specific pre-training of language models is essential for specific tasks like skill extraction in German, and that resource-efficient fine-tuning with LoRA allows smaller LLMs to achieve competitive performance. Finally, regarding **RQ3**, user studies confirmed the effectiveness of generated explanations and that clear and detailed explanations behind course suggestions notably increased user trust and comprehension. User study results explicitly valued explanations linking course content directly to their identified skill gaps and career objectives.

The broader impacts of this work are threefold. For lifelong learners, it provides personalized and explainable course recommendations to enhance learning and employability in a dynamic job market. For educators, it can offer detailed and more concise insights to align curricula with labor market needs. For the labor market, it contributes to a better-skilled workforce by connecting education directly to occupational competencies.

For future work, we could refine the UI of the system or incorporate the user feedback into the loop to enhance user engagement, as well as enhance the system's adaptability to a broader array of job roles and occupations by integrating additional occupational datasets and ontologies. Furthermore, to address the static nature of educational ontologies, we will explore methods for incorporating more dynamic data sources, and real-time labor market information. Another promising direction is refining the skill extraction techniques, possibly through the application of more advanced and fine-tuned NER models or leveraging more extensive domain-specific training datasets. Furthermore, by integrating the recommendation logic and the explanation generation process through a unified ranking and explanation generation module, the resulting explanations could be more meaningful and faithful.

Acknowledgments. This work was supported by the German Federal Ministry of Education and Research for the project "MyEduLife– The blockchain as a tool for decentralised storage of individual continuing education biographies" under grant No. 21INVI02.

References

1. Bao, K., Zhang, J., Zhang, Y., Wang, W., Feng, F., He, X.: TALLRec: an effective and efficient tuning framework to align large language model with recommendation. In: Proceedings of the 17th ACM Conference on Recommender Systems. ACM (2023). https://doi.org/10.1145/3604915.3608857
2. Bayly-Castaneda, K., Ramirez-Montoya, M.S., Morita-Alexander, A.: Crafting personalized learning paths with AI for lifelong learning: a systematic literature review. In: Frontiers in Education, vol. 9, p. 1424386. Frontiers Media SA (2024)

3. Beutling, N., Spahic-Bogdanovic, M.: Personalised course recommender: linking learning objectives and career goals through competencies. In: Proceedings of the AAAI Symposium Series, vol. 3, pp. 72–81 (2024)
4. Bouwmans, M., Lub, X., Orlowski, M., Nguyen, T.V.: Developing the digital transformation skills framework: a systematic literature review approach. PLoS ONE **19**(7), e0304127 (2024)
5. Buongiorno, S., Clark, C.: A framework for leveraging human computation gaming to enhance knowledge graphs for accuracy critical generative AI applications. arXiv preprint arXiv:2404.19729 (2024)
6. Chan, B., Schweter, S., Möller, T.: German's next language model. In: Scott, D., Bel, N., Zong, C. (eds.) Proceedings of the 28th International Conference on Computational Linguistics, pp. 6788–6796. International Committee on Computational Linguistics, Stroudsburg, PA, USA (2020). https://doi.org/10.18653/v1/2020.coling-main.598
7. Conneau, A., et al.: Unsupervised cross-lingual representation learning at scale. arXiv preprint arXiv:1911.02116 (2019)
8. Dörpinghaus, J., Samray, D., Helmrich, R.: Rule-based detection of access to education and training in Germany. arXiv preprint arXiv:2304.06307 (2023)
9. Fan, W., et al.: A comprehensive survey on trustworthy recommender systems. arXiv preprint arXiv:2209.10117 (2022)
10. Fischer, A., Dörpinghaus, J.: Web mining of online resources for German labor market research and education: finding the ground truth? Knowledge **4**(1), 51–67 (2024). https://doi.org/10.3390/knowledge4010003
11. Gao, Y., Sheng, T., Xiang, Y., Xiong, Y., Wang, H., Zhang, J.: Chat-rec: towards interactive and explainable LLMs-augmented recommender system (2023). http://arxiv.org/pdf/2303.14524v2
12. Kumar, R., Kumar, H., Shalini, K.: Detecting and mitigating bias in LLMs through knowledge graph-augmented training. In: 2025 International Conference on Artificial Intelligence and Data Engineering (AIDE), pp. 608–613 (2025). https://doi.org/10.1109/AIDE64228.2025.10987418
13. Laal, M., Salamati, P.: Lifelong learning; why do we need it? Procedia - Soc. Behav. Sci. **31**, 399–403 (2012). https://doi.org/10.1016/j.sbspro.2011.12.073
14. Milana, M., Brandi, U., Hodge, S., Hoggan-Kloubert, T., Morris, T.H.: Skills, skills, skills! the European commission's endorsement of a skills-first approach and the future of adult education and lifelong learning (2025)
15. Reimers, N., Gurevych, I.: Sentence-BERT: sentence embeddings using Siamese BERT-networks. arXiv preprint arXiv:1908.10084 (2019)
16. Shi, D., Wang, T., Xing, H., Xu, H.: A learning path recommendation model based on a multidimensional knowledge graph framework for e-learning. Knowl.-Based Syst. **195**, 105618 (2020). https://doi.org/10.1016/j.knosys.2020.105618
17. Wu, L., Qiu, Z., Zheng, Z., Zhu, H., Chen, E.: Exploring large language model for graph data understanding in online job recommendations. In: Proceedings of the AAAI Conference on Artificial Intelligence, vol. 38, pp. 9178–9186 (2024)
18. Wu, L., et al.: A survey on large language models for recommendation. World Wide Web **27**(5), 60 (2024)

Reframing Computational Thinking for AI Education

Valentina Ferraioli[1,2](✉), Francesco Mondada[1], and Victoria Abou-Khalil[1]

[1] EPFL, Lausanne, Switzerland
{valentina.ferraioli,francesco.mondada,victoria.aboukhalil}@epfl.ch
[2] ETH Zurich, Zurich, Switzerland

Abstract. While Computational Thinking (CT) has long been a foundational concept in computer science education, the increasing prominence of AI in modern curricula requires exploring if and how AI concepts can be incorporated into CT-based curricula. This study systematically examines the relationship between AI concepts and CT principles by analyzing five widely recognized AI educational frameworks. Key AI concepts are identified, categorized into thematic groups, and if possible mapped to CT elements. The findings reveal areas of convergence where AI concepts align with CT principles and areas where AI provides new dimensions to CT-based curricula. Based on this mapping, we present a case study analyzing a CT-based primary school informatics curriculum and showcase how it can be expanded to integrate AI concepts. The results provide insights into how educators can integrate AI into existing curricula traditionally rooted in classical CT, addressing both the technical and ethical dimensions of AI education. This paper contributes to the ongoing discourse on how AI can enhance and expand the scope of CT, offering a practical approach to the gradual integration of AI concepts within existing educational paradigms.

Keywords: computational thinking · AI literacy · K-12 education

1 Introduction

There has been ongoing debate about how to incorporate AI concepts into existing educational frameworks based on Computational Thinking (CT). Some scholars, such as Van Brummelen [24], have proposed ways to extend CT by integrating AI-related concepts. Similarly, Zerenga [27] and colleagues argue that CT and AI are not entirely distinct paradigms, but rather share overlapping principles like abstraction, generalization and algorithmic thinking. Their analysis of the *5 Big Ideas of AI* developed by Touretzsky et al. [22] shows that many AI concepts are embedded within CT education, supporting the idea that CT can provide deeper insights into AI computational techniques. On the other hand, scholars like Tedre et al. [20] challenge this view, arguing that AI and CT represent fundamentally different paradigms. CT 1.0 enables students to solve computational

K. Tammets et al. (Eds.): EC-TEL 2025, LNCS 16063, pp. 168–182, 2026.
https://doi.org/10.1007/978-3-032-03870-8_12

problems by defining explicit computational steps, whereas CT 2.0 adds computational thinking for machine learning that introduces new perspectives proper of data-driven reasoning.

While it is clear that a paradigm shift is required to integrate AI concepts with CT principles, we argue that CT remains fundamentally flexible and adaptable to multiple programming paradigms. Rather than requiring a disruptive shift towards AI, CT can evolve by incorporating data-driven reasoning. This approach maintains continuity in computational education while expanding problem-solving strategies to include AI methodologies.

Building on this perspective, this paper proposes a mapping of AI concepts to CT principles, using definitions and frameworks derived from existing literature. This mapping illustrates how AI education can build on CT's foundations, while identifying points of convergence and divergence between the two. Accordingly, this paper aims to address the following research questions:

- **RQ1**: To what extent do the principles of Computational Thinking align with AI concepts proposed in the literature?
- **RQ2:** How can the alignment between computational thinking and artificial intelligence inform the integration of AI concepts into CT-based educational frameworks?

To illustrate practical application, this paper analyzes the Swiss *Plan d'Études Romand* (PER) curriculum and propose an expanded version incorporating AI concepts based on the mapping. This practical example demonstrates how educators and curriculum designers can bridge CT and AI. Thus, this paper offers two primary contributions within a broader research agenda grounded in design-based research (DBR). First, it introduces a theoretical mapping of the relationships between AI and CT, serving as a groundwork for future expert validation and refinement. Second, it proposes a practical approach to embedding AI into CT curricula, which is ready for planned classroom implementation and iterative evaluation in the next phase of the DBR process.

2 Background

This section presents an overview of traditional CT frameworks and examines the current landscape of AI literacy in K-12 education. Together, these perspectives establish a basis for understanding how existing CT frameworks may support the integration of AI concepts.

2.1 Computational Thinking

The concept of computational thinking was first popularized by Seymour Papert [17] in *Mindstorms* and later brought to greater attention by Jeannette Wing in 2006 [25]. Wing defined CT as: 'the thought processes involved in formulating problems and their solutions so that the solutions are represented in a form that can be effectively carried out by an **information-processing agent**', framing it as a generalizable approach to computational problem-solving, not restricted to specific programming languages or paradigms.

Since then, scholars and educational organizations have proposed new definitions of CT and identified its core skills and practices [1,5,9]. In a synthesis of these definitions, Lodi [11] confirmed a shared understanding of CT as a way of thinking focused on computational problem-solving, in which both the formulation of the problem and the design of its solution are intended to be executed by an external agent (either human or machine). Lodi further summarized the proposed definitions into four dimensions that structure computational problem-solving: *mental process*, which involves cognitive strategies to solve problems, *methods*, which refer to operational approaches used, *practices* used to solve problems, and *transversal skills* which extend beyond computing to foster general problem-solving and critical thinking. These categories, summarized in Table 1, provide a broad classification of CT principles found across multiple frameworks.

Table 1. Overview of CT Components

Category	CT Components	Description
Mental Process	Algorithmic Thinking	Use algorithmic/procedural thinking
	Logical Thinking	Use logical thinking and reasoning to make sense of things, establish and check facts
	Problem Decomposition	Split a complex problem into simpler subproblems to solve it more easily
	Abstraction	Get rid of useless details to focus on relevant information or ideas
	Pattern Recognition	Discover and use regularities in data and problems
	Generalization	Use discovered similarities to make predictions or to solve more general problems
Methods	Automation	Use a computer or machine to do repetitive tasks
	Parallelization	Carry out tasks simultaneously to reach a common goal
	Programming	Use common concepts in programming (e.g. loops, events, conditionals)
	Modeling and Simulation	Represent data and real-world processes through models
	Data Collection, Analysis, Representation	Use discovered similarities to make predictions or solve more general problems
	Analysis and Evaluation	Implement and analyze solutions in terms of effectiveness and efficiency (time and resources)
Practices	Experimenting, Tinkering, Iterating	In iterative and incremental software development
	Testing and Debugging	Verify that solutions work by trying them out
	Reusing and Remixing	Build solutions on existing code, projects, ideas
Transversal Skills	Designing and Creating	
	Communicating and Collaborating	
	Reflecting, Learning, Meta-reflecting, and Understanding the World Computationally	
	Ambiguity Tolerance	
	Persisting Through Complex Problems	

However, despite being defined as paradigm-agnostic, CT has historically been tied to imperative programming, especially in educational contexts. In imperative programming, solutions are expressed as sequences of instructions that guide a machine through steps to solve a problem. This approach aligns with particular notional machines, that represent a simplified model of the underlying computational process [7]. For instance, an imperative notional machine includes memory storage, control flow, and execution rules [7]. In contrast, AI systems rely on different notional machines, such as those based on probabilistic operations, which makes it difficult to trace the precise computational steps that lead to a given output [14].

2.2 AI Literacy in Education and New View on CT

Historically, AI education has been offered primarily at the university level, targeting students in computing and ICT-related disciplines [2,18]. However, in recent years, growing efforts have been made to introduce artificial intelligence into K-12 education [15,18]. For instance, several frameworks have been proposed that list the core ideas and skills students should learn [13,16,22,26]. Building on these frameworks, current research now focuses on translating these guidelines into practical curricula.

Meanwhile, authors have suggested aligning CT with the current technological need [6,8,24,26,27]. For instance, Van Brummelen [24] proposed expanding the definition of CT to include concepts such as *classification, prediction,* and *generation*, practices like *training, validating and testing* and the perspective of *evaluation*. In contrast, Tedre et al. [20] argue that AI and CT represent fundamentally different paradigms. While traditional CT emphasizes step-by-step problem solving, CT for machine learning (referred to as CT 2.0) focuses on data-driven approaches.

In this context, Zerega et al. [27] examined the alignment between the *Five Big Ideas of AI* [22] and Brennan & Resnick's [1] framework for CT. Their analysis identified overlaps between the idea of *perception* and CT principles of algorithms, automation, and data, as well as between *representation & reasoning* and the CT concepts of abstraction, generalization, and algorithmic thinking. Similarly, *learning* from data aligns with pattern recognition, while *AI's interaction with humans* relates to algorithms, abstraction, and pattern recognition. However, *AI's societal impact* did not correspond to any traditional CT concept, highlighting a gap in addressing the ethical, societal, and human-centered dimensions of AI. The authors also acknowledge the differences between systems that explicitly control their flow and those shaped by data. Thus, the challenge lies in bridging this gap, ensuring that students understand how AI systems operate and also their broader implications.

3 Methodology

This study employs a mapping methodology to analyze the integration of AI concepts into CT, using the definition proposed by Lodi [12] as a reference point.

This definition, summarized in Table 1, was selected because it is the result of a comprehensive analysis of CT frameworks proposed between 2006 and 2019. Moreover, Lodi's definition employs a union approach rather than an intersectional one, thus offering a broad classification of CT principles that expands across multiple frameworks. In this study, the definition is used as a classification framework to evaluate the alignment between CT principles and AI concepts.

To ensure a comprehensive analysis, several AI frameworks proposed in the literature were selected. These frameworks were chosen for their prominence in educational literature and detailed representation of foundational AI concepts. By examining them, the study captures the broad spectrum of AI-related principles, from technical to ethical and societal considerations. A summary of the selected frameworks is provided below:

- *Five Big Ideas od AI* [22]: Developed by AI education experts, this framework introduces key AI concepts for K-12 education,
- *Competencies and design considerations for AI literacy* [13]: Based on an extensive review, this framework outlines essential competencies for AI literacy in educational settings.
- *The holistic approach to the design of AI education for k12 schools* [3,4]: Provides a curriculum developed in collaboration with teachers, covering four dimensions: content, product (teaching as instrumental to student competencies), process (teacher-student interaction), and praxis (application in the real world).
- *Unesco report, mapping of endorsed curricula* [23]: Provides global insights and recommendations for integrating AI into K–12 curricula.
- *Artificial Intelligence and Computer Science in Education: from Kindergarten to University* [10]: Presents a framework centered on technical AI knowledge derived drawing on foundational AI textbooks such as those by Russell and Norvig [19].

The mapping began by identifying building blocks proposed by the different AI frameworks. Blocks that overlapped with the established CT definition were excluded to prevent redundancy. Also basic application usage, the history of AI, and general AI awareness, were removed as they do not directly contribute to CT. The remaining elements were then grouped into thematic clusters based on their conceptual similarities. Below is an overview of the identified clusters, with Table 2 detailing the corresponding building blocks.

- **Classical AI**: focuses on traditional AI methods such as rule-based systems, symbolic reasoning, and expert systems. Key techniques include search, planning, and sorting, emphasizing structured knowledge and logical reasoning.
- **Data Understanding**: explores how data is represented, structured, and processed within digital and AI systems. It covers fundamental topics such as data representation and data structures and extends to include features, feature extraction, and big data.
- **Ethics and Societal Impact**: examines ethical considerations and societal implications of AI, including fairness, transparency, accountability, and bias

Table 2. Mapping of AI Building Blocks to Thematic Clusters

Clusters	AI Building Blocks
Classical AI	Ambiguity, intelligent system, automation, logic, reasoning algorithms, classic planning, planning, sorting, programming search, decision making, domain knowledge, pattern recognition
Data Understanding	Abstract representation, abstraction, symbolic representations, big data, generalization, cloud computing, programming, data literacy, data collection, analysis, representation, critically interpreting data, data structures, dataset, encoding, features, graph, experimenting, tinkering, iterating, features extraction, knowledge representation
Ethics and Societal Impact	AI for social good, digital citizenship, transparency, security, AI social benefit, accountability, biases, cybersecurity, trust, privacy, intellectual Property, AI risks, AI strengths & weaknesses, pros and cons, environmental impact, ethical decision making, ethics of AI, fairness, future of work, impact of AI on society, understanding existing conceptions, responsibility, self-reflect on their AI knowledge
Learning	AI models, abstraction, classification, generalization, language, pattern recognition, learning, analysis and evaluation, learning from data, automation, learning from experience, machine learning, neural network, understanding intelligence, Testing
Perception and Interaction	Action and reaction, perception, communication with AI: prompt engineering, automation, computer recognition, modeling and simulation, human sensing, sensors, language recognition

in decision-making. It also explores broader impacts, such as AI's influence on the future of work, intellectual property, and global challenges.

- **Learning**: focuses on machine learning and deep learning, showing how AI models learn from data and experience. Key concepts include training, testing, evaluation, and learning approaches.
- **Perception and Interaction:** examines how AI systems perceive and interact with their environment through sensory inputs and actions. Topics include human perception, as well as AI's ability to replicate processes like computer vision and speech recognition.

These clusters were then analyzed to assess their alignment with the principles of CT as defined by Lodi et al. [12]. Table 3 visually summarizes this process, illustrating the connections between AI clusters and CT principles, along with the justifications for their alignment.

4 Findings

The analysis revealed that the six thematic clusters identified during the mapping process capture a broad spectrum of AI literacy content. These clusters generally align with the Five Big Ideas proposed by Touretzky et al. [22], though with some distinctions. Notably, the explicit treatment of Classical AI as a separate domain, rather than embedding it under Knowledge Representation and Reasoning. When assessed against Lodi et al.'s CT principles, the findings point to both opportunities and challenges in integrating AI into existing curricula. The following sections explore these in greater detail.

Table 3. Alignment of CT principles with thematic clusters and their rationale.

Clusters	CT Components	Alignment Rationale
Classical AI	Logical Thinking	Involves formal logic and rule-based systems for reasoning in classical AI
	Problem Decomposition	Uses systematic breaking of tasks into smaller subproblems
	Automation	Enables automated processes for decision-making
	Programming	Uses programming for implementation.
	Testing and Debugging	Uses verification and validation processes to identify logical flaws
Data Understanding	Algorithmic Thinking	Uses structured pipelines requiring algorithmic planning for data manipulation
	Abstraction	Involves filtering out irrelevant information to focus on key features
	Generalization	Supports reusable code and drawing conclusions from data
	Data Collection, Analysis, Representation	Involves gathering, analyzing, and representing data to extract meaningful insights
	Programming	Uses programming skills necessary for manipulating data
	Experimenting, Tinkering, Iterating	Requires multiple iterations to preprocessing data effectively.
	Testing and Debugging	Ensure data models are accurate and reliable.
Ethics and Societal Impact	Ambiguity Tolerance	Requires tolerance for uncertainty, as AI models often produce outcomes without clear explanations.
	Reflect, Learn, Meta-reflect, Understand the World Computationally	Uses critical reflection on AI's societal impact and implications.
Learning	Algorithmic Thinking	Involves designing algorithms that enable systems to learn and improve from data.
	Abstraction	Helps models focus on relevant features, enabling generalization to unseen data.
	Generalization	Enables machine learning models to perform well on new data.
	Pattern Recognition	Enables AI to detect trends and learn from examples.
	Analysis and Evaluation	Uses continuous performance evaluation and assessment for AI systems.
	Automation	Enables automated processes for decision-making
	Programming	Involves using programming to implement and train learning algorithms
	Experimenting, Tinkering, Iterating	Uses continuous experimentation to improve AI model performance
	Reuse and Remix	Involves adapting existing models or code for new tasks or applications
	Testing and Debugging	Involves testing and debugging to ensure models are accurate, reliable, and functioning as intended
Perception and Interaction	Algorithmic Thinking	R Involves computational steps to process raw data (e.g., image filtering)
	Abstraction	Involves understanding and simplifying data representations to make sense of complex information.
	Automation	Enables processes like visual recognition and response to input.
	Modeling and Simulation	Uses computational modeling for tasks like computer vision and speech recognition.
	Data Collection, Analysis, Representation	Involves real-time data acquisition and processing capabilities.
	Communication and Collaboration	Facilitates human–AI and system–system interaction

4.1 The Intersection of AI and CT

The mapping reveals that many AI literacy concepts naturally align with existing CT principles. One clear area of alignment is *data understanding*, fundamental to both CT and AI. It relies on abstraction to represent knowledge digitally and involves collecting, organizing, and processing data. These processes introduce structured pipelines that are rooted in algorithmic thinking. Important CT blocks, like data structures and knowledge representation, play a critical role in the AI field as well, as it enables efficient data manipulation. Other core CT methods, such as programming, remain crucial, even in the context of data-driven models of modern AI. Indeed, traditional programming concepts such as loops, conditions and functions, are still essential for implementing such models and the workflow around them.

Similarly, *perception and interaction* rely on a strong data understanding to transform sensory inputs, such as images, audio, or environmental data, into meaningful representations that machines can process in a way similar to humans. AI systems must not only interpret raw data but also abstract and structure it in a format that enables automated reasoning and decision-making. This cluster integrates abstraction, modeling and simulation, as well as automation for real-time responses. It includes techniques like computer vision and natural language processing, which enable systems to see, hear and respond intelligently, improving the interaction between machines and humans.

Classical AI places a strong emphasis on logical reasoning through rule-based logic, symbolic reasoning, and search-based problem-solving, which makes it fully deterministic and more interpretable compared to data-driven learning. Examples of *Classical AI* include expert systems, constraint satisfaction problems, and planning algorithms, all of which allow systems to infer solutions without direct instruction. These processes leverage abstraction to generalize knowledge into structured rules, enabling machines to infer conclusions, make decisions, and automate problem-solving. Furthermore, Classical AI's use of sorting, search, and planning algorithms aligns with CT and remains highly relevant in fields that prioritize explainability and structured reasoning. The domain of *learning*, instead, introduces pattern recognition, and generalization from data. Models here rely on abstraction to model real-world complexity into computational representation and on algorithmic thinking to structure and optimize the learning processes.

Finally, the *Ethics and Social Impact* cluster moves beyond technical principles to focus on societal implications, such as fairness, accountability, and transparency. Societal concerns are not proper to AI, but AI's scale and complexity have amplified their importance, requiring a deeper critical and ethical awareness. This encourages the development of transversal skills, like a mindset of reflection and meta-learning or tolerance to ambiguity to continuously reassess their understanding of AI's decision-making processes.

Together, these clusters demonstrate how AI literacy incorporates core CT principles in the full spectrum. Educators and learners can recognize how foundational CT skills form the backbone of AI systems. By building on familiar concepts, they can use this understanding as a stepping stone to explore more advanced topics, particularly the machine learning paradigm, which further expands computational thinking into data-driven and adaptive problem-solving approaches [27].

4.2 The Distinctions Between CT and AI

While CT and AI share common ground, several points need to be expanded to accommodate AI peculiar aspects. Some scholars argue that AI requires a not negligible paradigm shift from traditional programming to data-driven computing [21]. This shift requires both the introduction of new topics and the expansion of existing CT concepts to accommodate AI-driven methodologies.

Data understanding has always been fundamental to CT and AI, but AI has dramatically expanded its scope to include large, often unstructured and dynamic datasets. Modern AI systems work with high-dimensional data such as images, text, and time series, which require new data structures to efficiently store, represent, and process them. AI introduces feature engineering, big data processing, and dataset curation as essential components. In AI-driven learning, data is not just input, it shapes the model itself. Therefore, students must understand how to evaluate data quality, considering factors like bias and completeness to ensure that the model is reliable and fair in the decision-making.

The most significant expansion of CT principles occurs in *learning*. CT in education has traditionally emphasized explicit programming and deterministic algorithms, where a defined algorithm always returns the same output. While probabilistic approaches (e.g. bayesian inference or Monte Carlo methods) have long existed, they were historically peripheral in mainstream CT education. In AI-based learning, however, these elements are amplified, as programming shifts from explicitly defining rules to inferring them from data. Unlike traditional CT approaches, where students write explicit step-by-step algorithms, AI-based learning requires students to train a model by adjusting hyperparameters and refining its dataset to improve classification accuracy over time. As also pointed out by Tedre et al. [21] debugging in AI-based learning extends beyond locating logical errors in code execution. It involves evaluating the dataset for biases, analyzing feature importance, and addressing model performance risks. Similarly, AI-based evaluation extends beyond time and resource efficiency to include performance metrics such as accuracy or precision-recall trade-offs, which assess how well a model generalizes and how it balances false positives and false negatives. However, while these differences are notable, they present the opportunity to reframe existing debugging and evaluation definitions in CT, and accommodate for these new processes. Thus, by introducing both new topics (e.g., advanced data structures, model training workflows) and revising established CT concepts (e.g., the nature of debugging, the scope of evaluation criteria), AI Literacy transforms CT into a more comprehensive framework that adapts to different paradigms.

4.3 Case Study: Extending the Plan d'Études Romand (PER) with AI Literacy

This section presents a curriculum-level analysis to examine the applicability of the preceding findings and to illustrate how AI literacy can be introduced within existing educational frameworks. The curriculum under review is the *Plan d'Études Romand (PER)*, applied in the French-speaking part of Switzerland. The Plan d'Études Romand is a mandatory school curriculum expanded to include digital education. This new subject is structured around three main areas: *Computer Science*, *Media and Society*, and *Usages*, spanning over three educational cycles. In this case study, we focus on Cycle 1 (ages 4 to 7), with particular attention to the *Computer Science* and *Media & Society* modules, as they are most relevant to CT. The *Usages* module emphasizes the practical use of digital tools and is therefore excluded, as it relates primarily to ICT rather than CT or AI literacy.

In Tables 4 and 5, we present a summary of the main objectives for Cycle 1 along with the proposed instructional activities, translated from French to English. Each activity is initially mapped to one of the previously defined thematic clusters. Where applicable, we then suggest potential trajectories toward AI, highlighting opportunities for gradual integration within the curriculum. The initial mapping of activities based on the clusters reveals that most clusters are present across the two modules, with additional ICT-related elements emerging in certain areas.

In particular, the *Computer Science* module, introduces students to algorithmic thinking, starting with real-life activities that mirror computational logic. These activities help students understand how sequences of instructions form the foundation of programming. The next step extends this understanding into programming automata, robots, or virtual characters, allowing students to explore automation and logical control structures. An important expansion toward AI concepts is proposed here: instead of simply programming a robot to follow a predefined path, students start working with rule-based decision-making. The focus shifts from following a predefined set of instructions to identifying the rule that better fits every step, evaluating them, and backtracking if ineffective. This introduces conditional logic and basic AI reasoning, bridging the gap between classical programming and AI-driven decision systems. Concerning data understanding, the curriculum introduces students to knowledge representation, helping them learn how information and data types are structured for computation. This sets the ground for the concepts of features and features extraction, allowing representing data at a higher level than binary representation. By incorporating these concepts, students gain early exposure to how data are inputted into AI models. At this stage, children also engage in sorting objects based on one or more characteristics, a foundational CT skill that aligns with pattern recognition and data categorization. This process encourages reflection on why sorting is done in a particular way and what machines are trying to simulate when they classify data. This sets the stage for discussions on how AI learns, where do the errors come from, and how data influences its decisions.

Table 4. PER, Computer Science module cycle 1. Summary of the key objectives, highlighting connections with CT and proposal in the direction of AI.

Discovering Computer Science...		
Clusters	**Activities**	**AI Extensions**
1... by creating and executing algorithms and programs		
Computational Thinking	Performing daily tasks with step-by-step instructions to introduce algorithms	
	Control and programming of an automata or robot	
	Movement of an object or person based on instructions with loops and conditions	Introduce rule-based programming, where actions are chosen based on rules instead of fixed instructions
		Understand that some algorithms make decisions based on data, using predefined rules or past examples to solve problems
		Experiment with algorithms that analyze data to generate predictions or recommendations
2... by using data, their encoding, and their transmission		
Data Understanding	Using symbols to represent information	Understand how AI represents information at a higher level using features (instead of raw data)
3... by using machines and highlighting their interactions		
Perception and Interaction	Discovery through experimentation of the differences between humans, robots, and automatons	Explore how humans, robots, and automatons perceive and process information differently
		AI perceives its environment by collecting data via sensors
	Awareness that objects are interconnected and communicate with each other	
	Use appropriate terminology to identify, name, and describe key visible components: keyboard, screen, sensor, etc.	
Learning, Classical AI, Data Understanding	Classifying objects based on one or more characteristics and counting them	AI program can sort objects according to specific characteristics
		Identifying causes of classification errors

The *Media & Society* section of the curriculum integrates AI literacy, ethics, and societal awareness to help students critically understand digital tools. As AI shapes information access and decisions, students must learn how algorithms influence content, recognize bias, and consider digital ethics. Children often engage with AI-curated content without realizing it. Simple, relatable examples can help them see that online content is not random and encourage them to question how AI works, why it errs, and what ethical issues it raises. In Cycle 1, activities should be interactive and age-appropriate to foster early critical thinking.

Table 5. PER, Media and Society module cycle 1. Summary of the key objectives, highlighting connections with CT and proposal in the direction of AI.

Learn to look, be selective and critical when looking at the media...		
Clusters	**Activities**	**AI Extensions**
1...by discovering their role in society		
Ethics and Societal Impact	Awareness of the opportunities offered (access to knowledge, information, entertainment, etc.) through the use of media	Explore how AI impacts the way we access, consume, and interact with information, shaping our behaviors and choices
		Explore how our data is collected and used to tailor information
Perception and Interaction	Awareness of the relationship between image and reality	Explore how filters, deepfakes, and AI alter perceptions of reality
2...by using their knowledge and experience to justify their media consumption choices		
Ethics and Societal Impact	Compare different reactions to media messages and identify personal preference criteria	Compare different reactions to AI content and reflect on personal preferences
Data Understanding	Explore key visual elements (framing, colors, lighting, etc.) that influence image interpretation	
3...by developing simple criteria to distinguish various communication formats		
ICT	Understand the unique characteristics of different media platforms (internet, print press, television, radio, cinema, etc.)	
ICT	Identify key elements (text, static images, motion images, interactive animations, sound, etc.) that make up a media message (web page, advertisement, poster, etc.)	
Ethics and Societal Impact	Raise awareness of the communication process through media and its ethical implications	Understand how AI can inherit biases from training data, impacting recommendations and automated decisions
4...by collaborating on the creation of a media message		
ICT	Contribute to showcasing student work through exhibitions, class websites, and other media platforms	
Ethics and Societal Impact	Analyze the purpose of a message by considering its communication context	

5 Conclusion

Computational Thinking has become a key part of school curricula, offering students a foundation in algorithmic problem-solving. However, its traditional focus on imperative programming limits its relevance in today's data-driven landscape, which demands greater abstraction. This shift has led to an ongoing debate on how to effectively integrate CT and AI, particularly in bridging the gap between these two distinct approaches.

In response to this challenge, several AI-focused curricula have been developed to provide guidance on what should be taught [3,10,13,22,23]. This paper addresses the critical question of how to integrate emerging AI topics into a landscape where CT is still gaining traction—without disrupting computational education. We show that AI represents both a natural extension and a significant shift from traditional CT-based education. While it shares key problem-solving strategies with CT, it introduces new ways of reasoning, learning, and decision-making that require adaptations in pedagogy and curriculum design. Rather than viewing AI as an entirely separate field, we argue that CT in education must evolve to accomodate this new emerging paradigm. By highlighting points where CT and AI share common ground the existing CT frameworks can provide stepping stones for introducing AI concepts early in education.

The case study on the Swiss Plan d'Études Romand (PER) curriculum illustrates how AI can be progressively introduced in primary education by leveraging familiar CT concepts. By recognizing both the continuity and divergence between CT and AI, we propose a framework for integrating AI in an existing CT-based curriculum, without disrupting the current landscape.

5.1 Limitations

While these contributions are significant, it is also important to acknowledge certain limitations that may require further attention. Firstly, the study lacks external validation from AI or educational experts. While the arguments presented are grounded in existing AI literacy frameworks and CT research, they have not been reviewed or formally assessed by specialists in AI education, pedagogy, or curriculum design. Expert input would be valuable in refining the proposed integration strategies, and ensuring their practical feasibility in diverse educational settings. This validation is planned as part of the broader research agenda. Second, the scope of the case study is limited to early primary education (K2–5) within the Swiss Plan d'Études Romand (PER) curriculum, and the proposed framework has not yet been tested in classroom settings. While this focus helps demonstrate how AI concepts can be introduced from the earliest stages of education, it limits the generalizability of the proposal. Future work will involve expanding the scope through comparative analysis and empirical testing in classroom settings. These next steps, aligned with a design-based research (DBR) approach, aim to inform iterative development based on teaching practices and feedback from real-world implementations.

Acknowledgements. This work was supported by the Jacobs Foundation as part of the consortium DEEP (Digital Education for Equity in Primary Schools).

Disclosure of Interests. The authors declare that they have no conflict of interest.

References

1. Brennan, K., Resnick, M.: New frameworks for studying and assessing the development of computational thinking (2012)
2. Casal-Otero, L., Catala, A., Fernández-Morante, C., Taboada, M., Cebreiro, B., Barro, S.: AI literacy in K-12: a systematic literature review. Int. J. STEM Educ. **10**(1), 29 (2023). https://doi.org/10.1186/s40594-023-00418-7
3. Chiu, T.K.F.: A holistic approach to the design of Artificial Intelligence (AI) education for K-12 schools. TechTrends **65**(5), 796–807 (2021). https://doi.org/10.1007/s11528-021-00637-1

4. Chiu, T.K.F., Ahmad, Z., Ismailov, M., Sanusi, I.T.: What are artificial intelligence literacy and competency? A comprehensive framework to support them. Comput. Educ. Open **6**, 100171 (2024). https://doi.org/10.1016/j.caeo.2024.100171. https://www.sciencedirect.com/science/article/pii/S2666557324000120
5. Denning, P.J., Tedre, M.: Computational Thinking. MIT Press (2019). googleBooks-ID: WzyUDwAAQBAJ
6. Dohn, N.B., Kafai, Y., Mørch, A., Ragni, M.: Survey: artificial intelligence, computational thinking and learning. KI - Künstliche Intelligenz **36**(5), 1–12 (2022). https://doi.org/10.1007/s13218-021-00751-5
7. Fincher, S., et al.: Notional machines in computing education: the education of attention. In: Proceedings of the Working Group Reports on Innovation and Technology in Computer Science Education, pp. 21–50. ACM, Trondheim, Norway (2020). https://doi.org/10.1145/3437800.3439202
8. Grover, S.: Teaching AI to K-12 learners: lessons, issues, and guidance. In: Proceedings of the 55th ACM Technical Symposium on Computer Science Education, vol. 1, pp. 422–428. ACM, Portland, OR, USA (2024). https://doi.org/10.1145/3626252.3630937. https://dl.acm.org/doi/10.1145/3626252.3630937
9. Grover, S., Pea, R.: Computational thinking in K—12: a review of the state of the field. Educ. Res. **42**(1), 38–43 (2013). https://www.jstor.org/stable/23360476
10. Kandlhofer, M., Steinbauer, G., Hirschmugl-Gaisch, S., Huber, P.: Artificial intelligence and computer science in education: from kindergarten to university. In: 2016 IEEE Frontiers in Education Conference (FIE), pp. 1–9 (2016). https://doi.org/10.1109/FIE.2016.7757570. https://ieeexplore.ieee.org/abstract/document/7757570
11. Lodi, M.: Informatical thinking. Olympiads Inform. 113–132 (2020). https://doi.org/10.15388/ioi.2020.09. https://ioinformatics.org/journal/v14_2020_113_132.pdf
12. Lodi, M., Martini, S.: Computational thinking, between papert and wing. Sci. Educ. **30**(5), 1–26 (2021). https://doi.org/10.1007/s11191-021-00202-5
13. Long, D., Magerko, B.: What is AI literacy? Competencies and design considerations. In: Proceedings of the 2020 CHI Conference on Human Factors in Computing Systems, CHI 2020, pp. 1–16. Association for Computing Machinery, New York, NY, USA (2020). https://doi.org/10.1145/3313831.3376727. https://dl.acm.org/doi/10.1145/3313831.3376727
14. Munasinghe, B., Bell, T., Robins, A.: Computational thinking and notional machines: the missing link. ACM Trans. Comput. Educ. **23**(4), 1–27 (2023). https://doi.org/10.1145/3627829. https://dl.acm.org/doi/10.1145/3627829
15. Ng, D.T.K., Lee, M., Tan, R.J.Y., Hu, X., Downie, J.S., Chu, S.K.W.: A review of AI teaching and learning from 2000 to 2020. Educ. Inf. Technol. **28**(7), 8445–8501 (2023). https://doi.org/10.1007/s10639-022-11491-w
16. Ng, D.T.K., Leung, J.K.L., Chu, S.K.W., Qiao, M.S.: Conceptualizing AI literacy: an exploratory review. Comput. Educ.: Artif. Intell. **2**, 100041 (2021). https://doi.org/10.1016/j.caeai.2021.100041. https://www.sciencedirect.com/science/article/pii/S2666920X21000357
17. Papert, S.: Mindstorms: Children, Computers, and Powerful Ideas. Basic Books, New York (1980)
18. Rizvi, S., Waite, J., Sentance, S.: Artificial Intelligence teaching and learning in K-12 from 2019 to 2022: a systematic literature review. Comput. Educ.: Artif. Intell. **4**, 100145 (2023). https://doi.org/10.1016/j.caeai.2023.100145. https://www.sciencedirect.com/science/article/pii/S2666920X23000243
19. Russell, S.J., Norvig, P.: Artificial Intelligence: A Modern Approach. Pearson (2016). https://thuvienso.hoasen.edu.vn/handle/123456789/8967

20. Tedre, M., Denning, P., Toivonen, T.: CT 2.0. In: Proceedings of the 21st Koli Calling International Conference on Computing Education Research, pp. 1–8. ACM, Joensuu, Finland (2021). https://doi.org/10.1145/3488042.3488053. https://dl.acm.org/doi/10.1145/3488042.3488053
21. Tedre, M., et al.: Teaching machine learning in K-12 classroom: pedagogical and technological trajectories for artificial intelligence education. IEEE Access **9**, 110558–110572 (2021). https://doi.org/10.1109/ACCESS.2021.3097962. https://ieeexplore.ieee.org/abstract/document/9490241
22. Touretzky, D., Gardner-McCune, C., Martin, F., Seehorn, D.: Envisioning AI for K-12: what should every child know about AI? In: Proceedings of the AAAI Conference on Artificial Intelligence, vol. 33, no. 01, pp. 9795–9799 (2019). https://doi.org/10.1609/aaai.v33i01.33019795. https://ojs.aaai.org/index.php/AAAI/article/view/5053
23. UNESCO: K-12 AI Curricula: A Mapping of Government-Endorsed AI Curricula (2022). https://www.gcedclearinghouse.org/fr/resources/k-12-ai-curricula-mapping-government-endorsed-ai-curricula?language=ko
24. Van Brummelen, J.: The Popstar, the Poet, and the Grinch: Relating Artificial Intelligence to the Computational Thinking Framework with Block-Based Coding (2019)
25. Wing, J.M.: Computational thinking and thinking about computing. Philos. Trans. R. Soc. A Math. Phys. Eng. Sci. **366**(1881), 3717–3725 (2008). https://doi.org/10.1098/rsta.2008.0118. https://royalsocietypublishing.org/doi/10.1098/rsta.2008.0118
26. Wong, G.K.W., Ma, X., Dillenbourg, P., Huan, J.: Broadening artificial intelligence education in K-12: where to start? ACM Inroads **11**(1), 20–29 (2020). https://doi.org/10.1145/3381884
27. Zerega, R., Milrad, M.: Computational thinking & artificial intelligence in k-12 education: two distinct but still complementary worlds. In: Milrad, M., et al. (eds.) MIS4TEL 2023, vol. 764, pp. 207–218. Springer, Cham (2023). https://doi.org/10.1007/978-3-031-41226-4_22

Empowering Equitable Learning with LLMs: Enhancing Writing Skills in Low-Resource Contexts

Rafael Ferreira Mello[1,2], Lenon Anthony[1], Jamilla Lobo[2], Fabíola Gonçalves Coelho Ribeiro[3], Cleon Xavier[3], Newarney Torrezão da Costa[2,3], Dragan Gasevic[4], and Luiz Rodrigues[2,5](✉)

[1] Federal Rural University of Pernambuco – UFRPE, Recife, Pernambuco, Brazil
{rafael.mello,lenon.anthony}@ufrpe.br
[2] CESAR School, Recife, Pernambuco, Brazil
jsl@cesar.school
[3] Instituto Federal Goiano – IF Goiano, Goiânia, Goiás, Brazil
{fabiola.ribeiro,cleon.junior,newarney}@ifgoiano.edu.br
[4] Monash University, Melbourne, Australia
dragan.gasevic@monash.edu
[5] Federal Technological University of Paraná (UTFPR), Apucarana, Brazil
luizrodrigues@utfpr.edu.br

Abstract. Technology-Enhanced Learning powered by Artificial Intelligence in Education (AIED) systems offers substantial benefits, including automated assessments and personalized feedback. Yet, deploying these systems in resource-constrained classrooms is challenging due to limited internet connectivity and insufficient access to digital devices. The AIED Unplugged (AIEDU) paradigm addresses these issues by emphasizing offline operation, teacher-mediated proxy interactions, multi-user capabilities, and minimal digital skill requirements. However, scaling AIEDU applications remains problematic. This study investigates integrating state-of-the-art multimodal Large Language Models (LLMs) into an Automatic Essay Scoring system specifically designed for low-resource educational settings. This study uses datasets of handwritten Brazilian Portuguese essays to assess LLM effectiveness in transcription accuracy and essay evaluation according to official Brazilian educational criteria. Results highlight Gemini 1.5 Pro's superior transcription accuracy and Gemini 2.0 Flash's outstanding essay evaluation performance, with Mean Absolute Errors of approximately 110 points overall on a scale of 0–1,000.

Keywords: Automatic Essay Scoring · LLM · Equitable Access · AIED Unplugged

1 Introduction

Writing is a fundamental skill for academic, professional, and social development, enhancing students' critical thinking, communication, and language abilities [10].

K. Tammets et al. (Eds.): EC-TEL 2025, LNCS 16063, pp. 183–197, 2026.
https://doi.org/10.1007/978-3-032-03870-8_13

Among written assessments, the essay is a widely used format to evaluate writing proficiency [7]. It demands a well-defined structure and appropriate linguistic mechanisms, essential for developing writing skills. Despite the central role of essay writing in education, providing timely and high-quality feedback on students' assignments remains a significant challenge, largely due to the heavy workload faced by educators.

In this context, Technology-Enhanced Learning (TEL) systems can support instructors by improving their capacity to deliver high-quality feedback or even automate essay assessment processes [17]. For instance, Conijn et al. [4] designed a human-centered dashboard that visualizes students' revisions during writing, helping instructors understand the writing behavior of students. Similarly, Yang et al. [30] introduced Rhetor, a system that leverages Large Language Models (LLMs) to provide feedback on students' argumentative essays.

However, implementing TEL systems in classrooms with limited technological infrastructure presents significant challenges [28]. These issues are particularly pressing in resource-constrained regions, where stable connectivity and well-established infrastructure are often lacking [9]. In response to these challenges, the AIED Unplugged (AIEDU) paradigm has been proposed [13]. AIEDU seeks to enable students in underserved areas to benefit from AIED, even in the absence of reliable internet connectivity or advanced technological resources.

Although the AIEDU approach has gained attention in recent research, most studies remain mostly theoretical [27], or are limited to early-stage prototypes [5,22]. Furthermore, they often lack detailed technical discussions on the practical feasibility and integration of the multiple AI components required for a fully functional AIEDU system [14]. In this context, the continuous advancements in LLMs have positioned them as strong candidates to support the effective implementation of AIEDU in real-world scenarios. LLMs have shown great promise in both transcribing texts from images [11] and analyzing student-generated textual content [8], making them particularly valuable for educational applications in low-resource settings.

This study aims to demonstrate how to build a scalable AIEDU application that effectively supports the development of writing skills by incorporating LLMs in the pipeline of an existing named *Escreva Mais*. Specifically, it explores the use of LLMs to (i) support the transcription of handwritten texts produced by Brazilian Portuguese-speaking students and (ii) evaluate essays based on the main criteria used by the Brazilian government to assess high school students. As such, this paper contributes to the TEL field by demonstrating how LLMs can be integrated with commonly available hardware—such as mobile phones—to provide AI-powered writing support for students in underserved contexts.

2 Background

2.1 Evaluation of Writing Tasks

Essay assessment plays an important role in developing and measuring students' written skills. However, teachers face substantial challenges when evaluating large volumes of essays, such as limited time for individualized assessment [16] and the labor-intensive nature of grading [1]. This burden is exacerbated by teacher shortages, a situation projected to worsen in the coming years[1].

Automatic Essay Scoring (AES) systems have emerged as a promising solution to the challenges in the evaluation of writing. By automating the evaluation of student writing, AES systems aim to facilitate the assessment process, improve feedback consistency, and reduce teachers' workload [7]. These systems are designed to evaluate essays based on various dimensions—such as content, coherence, grammar, and argumentation—often aligning with human scoring rubrics.

Various techniques have been explored for AES, ranging from traditional machine learning to transformer-based architectures. For instance, [29] explored Support Vector Machines for AES through regression models, whereas [1] introduces a model combining a RoBERTa encoder with a Bi-LSTM to overcome input length limitations. Moreover, recent studies evaluated competencies like cohesion and formal language proficiency, which are widely considered in context-specific assessments like ENEM (Brazilian National High School Exam) [2,26].

Although recent research has shown promising results in evaluating essays [7], these studies remain dependent on having training data and technical knowledge for model development. In contrast, recent studies have highlighted LLMs' potential in assessing textual productions [24]. For instance, an AI language model for AES is proposed in [19] to evaluate the reliability and accuracy of GPT-3. The model was applied to the evaluation of 12,100 essays and demonstrated a reasonable level of accuracy. However, further improvements are still necessary, particularly in refining prompts and applying task-specific fine-tuning. In [8], the authors performed prompt engineering to assess GPT-4's performance in Automated Short Answer Grading for both English and Brazilian Portuguese questions. It found consistent results supporting that LLMs' valuable performance towards increased generalization. [20] presents an approach to automatically predict textual cohesion in essays using regression-based models. In a complementary line of research, [16] proposes five independent AES models based on feature engineering, word embeddings, and Recurrent Neural Networks (RNNs) to assess essays according to the competencies defined by the ENEM. The study provides a set of features aligned with each ENEM competency and shows that the first two competencies are better evaluated through feature engineering, whereas the last three benefit from RNN-based models.

A broader perspective on AI in Brazilian higher education is provided by [6], who analyze 18 graduate programs and 63 academic works—including master's theses and doctoral dissertations—focused on AI applications in distance learning environments. This study provides an overview of current technological implementations, solution development, and evaluation practices involving AI in educational settings. Among its key contributions, the study identifies ongoing difficulties faced by the adoption of AIED in Brazil, such as the need for robust

[1] https://unesdoc.unesco.org/ark:/48223/pf0000388832.

and reliable datasets, limited data privacy policies, the demand for stakeholder training, and the lack of equitable access to AI tools and infrastructure.

These advances exemplify the growing relevance of AES systems in enhancing students' writing development. Nevertheless, challenges remain—particularly in ensuring the equitable deployment of such technologies [9]. Barriers such as the digital divide, limited access to devices, and reliable internet connectivity reduce the potential use of AES in diverse educational contexts [13].

2.2 AIED Unplugged

In response to these challenges, recent research has introduced innovative strategies to broaden the inclusivity of AIED. One such initiative is the AIEDU paradigm [13]. According to Isotani et al. [13], AIEDU solutions *conform* to current educational practices rather than demanding radical changes, allowing seamless integration into classrooms with limited technology. Additionally, these systems operate *offline* but can utilize internet connectivity opportunistically, such as to update models and collect data. Since many students lack personal devices or digital literacy in resource-constrained settings, AIEDU introduces *proxy* mechanisms, enabling intermediaries such as teachers to facilitate student-AI interactions. Furthermore, *multi-user* functionality ensures that shared devices accommodate multiple learners without requiring individual logins. Lastly, by focusing on *minimal digital skills*, AIEDU provides an inclusive approach, ensuring AI-driven educational benefits extend to underserved communities without technological disruption [13]. Thanks to its five principles, AIEDU can make adaptive learning more inclusive and accessible, motivating recent studies that present valuable research efforts toward implementing it.

To exemplify, consider the solution presented by Isotani et al., which focused on supporting Brazilian students' development of writing skills. They developed an application for mobile devices, widely available nowadays, to digitalize, assess, and diagnose handwritten essays in Brazilian Portuguese (*conformity*). The system captures student essays written on paper sheets with QR codes and specific markings, which facilitates transcribing them to be assessed by an AIED system and enables addressing the *multi-user* perspective. By doing so, teachers act as intermediaries (*proxy*), using the mobile application to photograph the essays, which are stored on the device and later uploaded to a server when an internet connection is available (*offline*). Upon upload, Computer Vision techniques segment the handwritten text into Portuguese words, whereas Natural Language Processing (NLP) assesses the essays based on a predefined rubric. To facilitate feedback delivery and instructional support, the researchers designed paper-based dashboards that can be printed for classroom use, facilitating their adoption by users with *minimal digital skills* [13].

The literature demonstrates that AIEDU has been explored in several research efforts. In the math domain, previous research has proposed frameworks towards more equitable AIED systems that support the adoption of these systems, including both theoretical [27] as well as more targeted settings like homework [5]. Additionally, recent research contributed prototypes [22] and case studies [23] on how Brazilian math teachers perceive these tools. Similarly, past research explored how AIEDU systems support German students from a rural school [14].

In the writing domain, besides the one presented along with the AIEDU paradigm [13], subsequent research contributed case studies discussing how such an AIED system supports Brazilian learners depending on whether they live in urban or rural areas [21].

In summary, past research has demonstrated increasing interest in addressing the AIEDU paradigm. While they explore various AI techniques, they are consistent in reporting limited performance from the AI systems, specially those that transcribe handwritten content. Therefore, there is a need to investigate other AI techniques, such as LLMs, that can potentially address that gap.

2.3 Research Questions

One key limitation of the AIEDU approach lies in the difficulty of scaling its transcription and assessment phases. Generally, existing solutions depend on creating large datasets that pair images with transcriptions, as they have relied on neural network-based models like Yolo [3,23], and require the evaluation of specific activity criteria, as they relied on AI models based on supervised learning [13,21]. Against this backdrop, our study investigates to what extent LLMs can simplify and broaden the implementation of AIEDU principles. Accordingly, both research questions (RQs) in this study assess the effectiveness of using LLMs for targeted tasks within the AIEDU workflow. As such, the proposed RQs are:

Research Question 1 (RQ1):
To what extent can LLMs accurately transcribe Brazilian Portuguese essays written by high school students?

Research Question 2 (RQ2):
How effectively do LLMs assess essays according to the Brazilian government guidelines, which encompass multiple criteria?

No prior data or training modifications (not even few-shot learning) were introduced into the evaluated LLMs for both RQs. In contrast, past research is widely based on supervised learning models, such as Support Vector Machine [29], BiLSTM [1], and BERT [2,26], which demand substantial effort for data collection and annotation as well as model development. Thus, our approach ensures that no annotated dataset is required for deploying a new AIEDU application, emphasizing the feasibility of rapid, on-demand solutions in diverse educational contexts.

3 Context: *Escreva Mais* Usage Flow

Escreva Mais[2] is a mobile application that enables teachers to explore AI-based support in resource-constrained classrooms to enhance students' writing skills.

[2] *Escreva Mais*'s website: https://escreva-mais-812386266414.us-east1.run.app.

Figure 1 presents how *Escreva Mais* interacts with a traditional classroom to address the need for an AIEDU system, which includes capturing a student's essay through a picture, then transcribing (RQ1) and forwarding it to an AES system (RQ2). Particularly, *Escreva Mais* runs as follows.

1. According to its goal of supporting the development of writing skills, *Escreva Mais* usage starts once students have produced an essay. According to the principle of *conformity*, students might use a pen or a pencil to write their essays on any paper sheet. Once students are done, the teacher collects the essays for assessment.
2. The teacher uses *Escreva Mais* to take a picture of each essay when it is time to grade students' assignments. By enabling the teacher to capture each student's essay, *Escreva Mais* offers a solution that corroborates AIEDU's principle of *multi-user*, avoiding the need for each student to log in and register its solution. Moreover, no internet connection is needed for this task, as the tool relies on a local database and only uses internet in its next step, hence complying to AIEDU's principle of *disconnect*.
3. *Escreva Mais* processes the automatic scoring of the writing activity for each student and generates the final grades.
4. The teacher can access students' performances, with a general mark overall as well as specific grades for different aspects of the text. *Escreva Mais* presents outcomes from two perspectives. The *on-device* perspective presents summarized analytics compatible with a mobile device's screen, which is aimed to provide an overview of the teacher's class. The *external* perspective presents detailed analytics through a PDF report sent to the teacher's e-mail, which is aimed to offer a comprehensive visualization including both class and student-level insights. By providing the outcome from different perspectives, *Escreva Mais* acknowledges teachers may have different needs and abilities. Hence, not only depending on the desired level of detail, a teacher with less digital skills might benefit more from the printable PDF version compared to a more digitally skilled one. As a result, *Escreva Mais* complies with AIEDU's principle of *minimal digital skills*.
5. The teacher can rely on *Escreva Mais* analytics to provide feedback to students, which they can do by explaining abilities in which they excel and need to work more. Therefore, *Escreva Mais* adheres to AIEDU's principle of *proxy* by providing AI-powered insights that reach students through their teachers.

Fig. 1. *Escreva Mais* usage flow.

4 Method

4.1 Dataset

As outlined in the RQs, this paper presents two main analyses: (1) transcribing the text from images, and (2) evaluating the extracted content based on the criteria of the Brazilian National High School Exam (ENEM). The following subsections describe the data used in each of these steps.

Image Dataset. It consists of a collection of high-resolution images of handwritten essays captured through a smartphone. The essays were written in Brazilian Portuguese by high school students aged between 15 and 17 years old, with a range of handwriting styles, including cursive, print, and mixed styles, with varying levels of legibility. The dataset captures differences in stroke quality, spacing, and alignment, reflecting the diverse writing patterns of the students. Each essay was annotated by two independent annotators, fluent in Brazilian Portuguese and familiar with the challenges of transcribing handwritten text. To ensure the reliability of the annotations, the transcriptions were compared, and any discrepancies were resolved through discussion, leading to a final consensus transcription. The inter-annotator agreement for the dataset was high (Cohen's Kappa = 0.85), supporting the reliability and robustness of the annotations. The final dataset consisted of 1,199 images of students' essays, enabling the evaluation of the performance of optical character recognition (OCR) algorithms for handwritten text transcription in educational contexts, providing a comprehensive benchmark for addressing RQ1.

Textual Dataset. For this, we used the **Extended Essay-BR** dataset [15], which has been extensively used by AES research in Brazilian Portuguese [16, 26]. Extended EssayBR features 6,579 argumentative essays written in Brazilian Portuguese by Brazilian high school students through an online platform, where students received a contextually relevant issue as the topic to be addressed in their essays. As a result, Extended EssayBR essays concern 151 different topics, including fake news, deforestation, and healthcare, among others [16].

The essays were evaluated according to five competencies: (C1) Demonstrating proficiency in the formal written form of the Portuguese language; (C2) Understanding the essay objectives and applying concepts from various fields of knowledge to develop the topic, while respecting the structural boundaries of the discursive-argumentative essay in prose; (C3) Selecting, relating, organizing, and interpreting information, facts, opinions, and arguments to support a point of view; (C4) Demonstrating knowledge of the linguistic mechanisms necessary for building a coherent argument; (C5) Developing an essay regarding the problem addressed, while respecting human rights. According to ENEM, human experts scored each of the Extended EssayBR's competencies within a 40-point categorical interval ranging from 0 to 200. Whereas C1 to C5 range from 0 to 200, resulting the total score ranges from 0 to 1000.

Similar to past research using LLMs for AES and similar tasks [8], we limit our study to 15% of the whole dataset (see Table 1). The goal is to simulate testing trained models' performances on a test set as well as coping with the time and monetary costs involved in experimenting with these models.

Table 1. Class distribution for Extended EssayBR, the dataset used to address RQ2.

Score	C1	C2	C3	C4	C5
0	19 (01.93%)	18 (01.82%)	28 (02.84%)	32 (03.24%)	79 (08.00%)
40	6 (00.61%)	17 (01.72%)	30 (03.04%)	11 (01.11%)	46 (04.66%)
80	93 (09.42%)	144 (14.59%)	249 (25.23%)	138 (13.98%)	210 (21.28%)
120	446 (45.19%)	386 (39.11%)	455 (46.10%)	369 (37.39%)	329 (33.33%)
160	387 (39.21%)	344 (34.85%)	198 (20.06%)	275 (27.86%)	231 (23.40%)
200	36 (03.65%)	78 (07.90%)	27 (02.74%)	162 (16.41%)	92 (09.32%)

4.2 LLM Models and Prompts

Text Transcription. Given that RQ1 focuses on essay transcription, this study evaluated two distinct approaches: (i) transcribing the entire essay in a single step, and (ii) transcribing the essay line by line. To explore these strategies, we assessed the performance of several state-of-the-art LLMs in transcribing handwritten essays in Brazilian Portuguese, including GPT-4o, Gemini (1.5 Pro and 2.0 Flash), and Claude (Sonnet 3.7). We chose those LLMs as they were the most recent models available during the time of writing, including models from different companies (e.g., Google, OpenAI and Anthropic).

Hence, our study encompassed a representative set of multimodal models. Despite that, to ensure a fair comparison among models, we used the same prompt for all models, as shown below.

- **Essay extraction prompt:** *Transcribe the text from this image considering it is written in Portuguese language.*

This prompt, which we selected after preliminary empirical explorations, is based on related work highlighting the potential for achieving reliable results with similar prompts [25]. Nevertheless, we understand that prompt engineering plays a prominent role in LLMs' outputs and discuss this threat to our study validity in Sect. 6. Note that, to prevent the LLMs from answering differently for the analysis of similar images, we set the temperature to 0 for all of them.

Essay Scoring. To address RQ2, we employed the same set of LLMs used in RQ1, as they demonstrated strong performance in previous work on AES tasks [8, 24]. However, we designed a more sophisticated prompting strategy, drawing on findings from prior research in automated assessment [8]. This enhanced prompt incorporates key elements such as a detailed task description, explicit reasoning steps, a step-by-step thinking approach, and the assignment of a specific role to the model, all of which have been shown to improve the reliability and quality of AI-generated evaluations. Table 2 presents the detailed prompt. Note that the instructional prompt was written in Brazilian Portuguese, ensuring alignment with the language of the student essays.

Table 2. Prompt Elements for the Assessment Task Translated to English

Element	English text
Instruction	Assess the input essay according to the five established criteria, assigning a score between 0 and 200 for each competence, totaling a maximum of 1000 points. The score should be given in intervals of 40 points, and the distribution should approximate the official corrections of similar essays
Criteria	Consider the following criteria: Competence 1: Demonstrate mastery of the formal written form of the Portuguese language. Competence 2: Understand the essay proposal and apply concepts from various areas of knowledge to develop the theme, within the structural limits of the argumentative-discursive text in prose. Competence 3: Select, relate, organize and interpret information, facts, opinions and arguments in defense of a point of view. Competence 4: Demonstrate knowledge of the linguistic mechanisms necessary for the construction of the argument. Competence 5: Prepare a proposal for intervention for the problem addressed, respecting human rights
Role	You are an essay evaluator for the Brazilian National High School Exam (ENEM)
Think	Think step by step
Justification	Reasoning about the justification for your response by explaining why you made the choices you actually made
Output	Your final score should be one of these grades for each competency: "0", "40", "80", "120", "160" or "200". Evaluate the essay: *essay_text*; Essay topic: *prompt_text*

4.3 Evaluation Methodology

To address RQ1, we evaluated the performance of the models using the following metrics: **Exact Match**, defined as the percentage of words transcribed perfectly by the model; **Average Word Error Rate (WER)**, which measures the average proportion of incorrect words per essay relative to the ground truth; **Average Character Error Rate (CER)**, indicating the average proportion of incorrect characters per essay; and **precision, recall, and F1-score**, all computed at the character level to provide a more fine-grained assessment of transcription accuracy.

To address RQ2, we adopted evaluation metrics commonly used in previous research, specifically Mean Absolute Error (MAE) and Root Mean Squared Error (RMSE) [8]. Although the LLMs were prompted to produce categorical scores, the use of MAE and RMSE enables a detailed analysis that goes beyond simple exact match accuracy. These metrics assess how closely the predicted scores align with the ground truth, offering a more precise understanding of the models' performance by capturing proximity and neighborhood-level accuracy [26]. This approach allowed us to answer RQ2 from a more comprehensive perspective, facilitating comparisons with related studies while providing insights that are aligned with the assessment practices of the Brazilian educational system.

5 Results

5.1 RQ1: LLMs for Brazilian Portuguese Essay Transcription

Table 3 presents the results concerning RQ1. For the line-based input, GPT-4o reached better results than the other models in all metrics but recall, perfectly matching almost 66%. In that perspective, the second best model was Claude SOonnet 3.7, which yielded an exact match of almost 62%. For the full essay-based input, Gemini 1.5 pro obtained the highest exact match (79.10%), CER (10.20%) and recall (89.36%). Claude and GPT-4o achieved the second best performance, achieving roughly 73% of exact match with between 13% and 18% of CER. Notably, GPT-4o presented the best WER among all models (30.21%), whereas Gemini 2.0 flash resulted in the best precision (88.31%) and F1 (87.11%). These findings demonstrate that providing the full essay led to better results compared to the line-based perspective, where Gemini 1.5 pro reached better performance.

Table 3. LLMs' performance in transcribing Brazilian Portuguese essays by lines and full essays.

Input	Model	Prec	Recall	F1	CER	WER	Ex Match
Line	Gemini 2.0 flash	82.97%	82.68%	81.93%	26.82%	45.56%	57.08%
Line	Gemini 1.5 pro	69.36%	65.56%	66.78%	43.93%	69.38%	33.46%
Line	Claude Sonnet 3.7	85.55%	**88.01%**	86.13%	33.40%	40.91%	61.63%
Line	GPT-4o	**87.17%**	86.07%	**86.17%**	**22.90%**	**36.09%**	**65.79%**
Essay	Gemini 2.0 flash	**88.31%**	86.20%	**87.11%**	13.73%	33.64%	69.59%
Essay	Gemini 1.5 pro	79.47%	**89.36%**	83.71%	**10.20%**	40.17%	**79.10%**
Essay	Claude Sonnet 3.7	71.04%	82.64%	76.15%	18.88%	41.51%	73.87%
Essay	GPT-4o	87.05%	86.97%	86.88%	13.71%	**30.21%**	73.10%

5.2 RQ2: LLMs for Brazilian Portuguese Essays Grading

Table 4 presents the results concerning RQ2. Overall, Gemini 2.0 flash outperformed the other LLMs in all metrics but C5. Particularly, Gemini 2.0 flash reached MAE values between 21 and 28 for C1 to C5 on a scale that ranges from 0 to 200 in 40-point intervals. Even for C5, which Gemini 2.0 flash's MAE was 39.76, its average error did not surpass the 40-point interval and was close to the best model in that competence (i.e., Claude Sonnet 3.7; MAE = 37). Notably, all models fit within that context for most competences, with only Gemini 1.5 pro performing above the 40-point error threshold. Concerning the overall score, Gemini 2.0 flash MAE was about 110 on a scale that ranges from 0 to 1000, similarly highlighting its strong performance. These findings demonstrate that the LLMs yielded promising results in assessing Brazilian Portuguese essays, both overall and by competence, where Gemini 2.0 flash's performance stood out compared to GPT-4o, Claude Sonnet 3.7, and Gemini 1.5 pro.

Table 4. LLMs' performance in assessing Brazilian Portuguese essays by competence (C1 to C5) and total score (overall).

Metric	Models	C1	C2	C3	C4	C5	Overall
MAE	Gemini 2.0 flash	**21.18**	**24.14**	26.15	**28.42**	39.76	**109.94**
MAE	Gemini 1.5 Pro	30.04	38.93	38.05	49.75	67.49	208.94
MAE	Claude Sonnet 3.7	24.42	26.69	**24.58**	36.71	**37.00**	118.34
MAE	GPT-4o	22.37	26.23	30.97	29.70	37.30	123.53
RMSE	Gemini 2.0 flash	**32.83**	**36.01**	**34.41**	**39.52**	53.27	**145.15**
RMSE	Gemini 1.5 Pro	41.61	51.02	49.43	61.42	79.95	249.61
RMSE	Claude Sonnet 3.7	36.08	38.85	37.05	48.25	50.35	154.33
RMSE	GPT-4o	33.76	37.97	42.14	41.03	**49.88**	158.96

6 Discussion and Practical Implications

By implementing the AIEDU paradigm, *Escreva Mais* provides AI-powered classroom support, even in settings with limited technological infrastructure. Teachers only need a smartphone to use *Escreva Mais*, which enables them to capture and automatically assess handwritten essays. This allows teachers in resource-constrained environments to benefit from AES, a proven tool for enhancing learning [7]. The primary objective of this study was to demonstrate that integrating LLMs into the *Escreva Mais* pipeline can further broaden the scope of AIEDU, ensuring more inclusive and scalable applications.

Thus, we demonstrate how state-of-the-art LLMs perform in transcribing handwritten essays in Brazilian Portuguese (**RQ1**). From the perspective of complete essay-based transcription, we demonstrate Gemini 1.5 pro reached the best performance, compared to Gemini 2.0 flash, Claude Sonnet 3.7, and GPT-4o, in terms of exact matches and CER. In terms of WER, however, GPT-4 stood out compared to the remaining models, following Gemini 1.5 flash closely regarding exact match (73% vs 79%). Moreover, these performances are superior to those reported in related work [25] even though we relied on a simple prompt and did not use previously annotated data. Considering these results will likely be improved with prompt engineering [12], this paper informs practitioners that they might achieve state-of-the-art results in transcribing Brazilian Portuguese essays with a small prompt engineering effort, especially with Gemini 2.0 flash.

Additionally, we demonstrate how state-of-the-art LLMs perform in automatically grading essays written in Brazilian Portuguese (**RQ2**). Gemini 2.0 flash reached the best results in our experiments, outperforming GPT-4o, Claude Sonnet 3.7, and Gemini 1.5. Specifically, Gemini 2.0 flash MAE was below 29 (out of 200) in all aspects analyzed, but it still needs further improvements with the analysis of subjective criteria (e.g., C5), which is similar to that of recent research [2,26]. While previous research relied on specialist models (e.g., fine-tuned BERT), which demand significant efforts for data collection and model training, exploring LLMs alleviates these needs. Moreover, whereas we used a literature-informed prompt, our experiments did not include prompt engineering, which has proven to increase LLMs' performance in similar tasks [18]. Hence, our findings corroborate recent research highlighting LLMs' generalizability potential compared to specialist models on Automatic Short Answer Grading [8], expanding this understanding to AES.

Furthermore, our findings contribute to deploying *Escreva Mais* AES system in authentic learning settings. In Brazil, Brazilian National High School Exam essays are scored independently by two evaluators based on five competencies, each worth up to 200 points (totaling 1000). A significant discrepancy is flagged if the total score difference exceeds 100 points or if there is more than an 80-point difference in any single competency. In such cases, a third evaluator is assigned. If disagreement remains, a panel of senior evaluators determines the final score[3]. In this context, no MAE lower than 40 points was observed for individual competencies, and the overall MAE for the total score reached 109.94 when using Gemini 2.0 Flash. Thereby, as a practical implication, this paper demonstrates the validity of the *Escreva Mais* AES system, which not only supports the tool's adoption in practice but suggests the potential of expanding and employing its AES system for other contexts.

In light of these implications, this paper expands the literature as follows:

- While past research presents small and focused AIEDU solutions [13,21] or backgrounding it on interventions tailored for writing skills development [5, 27], this paper presents a scalable solution to integrating AI-based writing support into low-resource classrooms.
- Whereas handwriting recognition remains a substantial challenge in AIEDU research [25], we evaluate state-of-the-art LLMs in transcribing handwritten Brazilian Portuguese essays.

[3] Assessment guidelines available in this link.

- Given that NLP has been dominated by studies in English [7], limited to traditional techniques or neural networks [26], or focused on scoring particular competencies independently [2], this paper assesses state-of-the-art LLMs' in scoring Brazilian Portuguese essays across multiple competencies at once.

7 Limitation and Future Directions

Despite its contributions, this study has limitations that should be acknowledged. Despite the experiments relying on comprehensive datasets, they might fail to fully capture the diversity of Brazilian students' writing. Future research should expand dataset coverage to ensure better generalizability. Additionally, although we evaluated state-of-the-art LLMs, the rapid evolution of these models necessitates continuous assessment to keep findings up to date. Future studies should also investigate prompt engineering strategies, as our study used a single prompt for consistency. Exploring adaptive or optimized prompts could improve LLM performance in essay transcription and scoring.

Acknowledgments. This research was partially supported by the Google Academic Research Award Program.

References

1. Beseiso, M., Alzubi, O.A., Rashaideh, H.: A novel automated essay scoring approach for reliable higher educational assessments. J. Comput. High. Educ. **33**(3), 727–746 (2021). https://doi.org/10.1007/s12528-021-09283-1
2. Carvalho, R., et al.: Exploring NLP and embedding for automatic essay scoring in the Portuguese. In: Olney, A.M., Chounta, I.A., Liu, Z., Santos, O.C., Bittencourt, I.I. (eds.) AIED 2024. CCIS, vol. 2150, pp. 228–233. Springer, Cham (2024). https://doi.org/10.1007/978-3-031-64315-6_18
3. Chevtchenko, S.F., et al.: An optimization approach for elementary school handwritten mathematical expression recognition. In: Olney, A.M., Chounta, I.A., Liu, Z., Santos, O.C., Bittencourt, I.I. (eds.) AIED 2024. CCIS, vol. 2151, pp. 234–241. Springer, Cham (2024). https://doi.org/10.1007/978-3-031-64312-5_28
4. Conijn, R., Van Waes, L., van Zaanen, M.: Human-centered design of a dashboard on students' revisions during writing. In: Alario-Hoyos, C., Rodríguez-Triana, M.J., Scheffel, M., Arnedillo-Sánchez, I., Dennerlein, S.M. (eds.) EC-TEL 2020. LNCS, vol. 12315, pp. 30–44. Springer, Cham (2020). https://doi.org/10.1007/978-3-030-57717-9_3
5. Davis, S.R., DeCapito, C., Nelson, E., Sharma, K., Hand, E.M.: Homework helper: providing valuable feedback on math mistakes. In: Bebis, G., et al. (eds.) ISVC 2020. LNCS, vol. 12510, pp. 533–544. Springer, Cham (2020). https://doi.org/10.1007/978-3-030-64559-5_42
6. Durso, S., Arruda, E.: Artificial intelligence in distance education: a systematic literature review of Brazilian studies. Probl. Educ. 21st Century **80**, 679 (2022). https://doi.org/10.33225/pec/22.80.679

7. Ferreira, R., et al.: Words of wisdom: a journey through the realm of NLP for learning analytics-a systematic literature review. J. Learn. Anal. 1–24 (2024)
8. Ferreira Mello, R., et al.: Automatic short answer grading in the LLM era: does GPT-4 with prompt engineering beat traditional models? In: Proceedings of the 15th International Learning Analytics and Knowledge Conference, LAK 2025, pp. 93–103. Association for Computing Machinery, New York (2025). https://doi.org/10.1145/3706468.3706481
9. Gasevic, D., et al.: Learning Analytics for the Global South. Foundation for Information Technology Education and Development, Quezon City, Philippines, published edn. (2018)
10. Graham, S.: Changing how writing is taught. Rev. Res. Educ. **43**(1), 277–303 (2019)
11. Guo, R., et al.: A survey on advancements in image-text multimodal models: from general techniques to biomedical implementations. Comput. Biol. Med. 108709 (2024)
12. Hu, Y., et al.: Improving large language models for clinical named entity recognition via prompt engineering. J. Am. Med. Inform. Assoc. **31**(9), 1812–1820 (2024)
13. Isotani, S., Bittencourt, I.I., Challco, G.C., Dermeval, D., Mello, R.F.: AIED unplugged: leapfrogging the digital divide to reach the underserved. In: Wang, N., Rebolledo-Mendez, G., Dimitrova, V., Matsuda, N., Santos, O.C. (eds.) AIED 2023. CCIS, vol. 1831, pp. 772–779. Springer, Cham (2023). https://doi.org/10.1007/978-3-031-36336-8_118
14. Khazanchi, R., Di Mitri, D., Drachsler, H.: The effect of AI-based systems on mathematics achievement in rural context: a quantitative study. J. Comput. Assist. Learn. **41**(1), e13098 (2025)
15. Marinho, J.C., Anchiêta, R.T., Moura, R.S.: Essay-BR: a Brazilian corpus to automatic essay scoring task. J. Inf. Data Manage. **13**(1) (2022)
16. Marinho, J.C., Cordeiro, F., Anchiêta, R.T., Moura, R.S.: Automated essay scoring: an approach based on ENEM competencies. In: Anais do XIX Encontro Nacional de Inteligência Artificial e Computacional, pp. 49–60. SBC (2022)
17. Mello, R.F., et al.: Enhancing instructors' capability to assess open-response using natural language processing and learning analytics. In: Hilliger, I., Muñoz-Merino, P.J., De Laet, T., Ortega-Arranz, A., Farrell, T. (eds.) EC-TEL 2022. LNCS, vol. 13450, pp. 102–115. Springer, Cham (2022). https://doi.org/10.1007/978-3-031-16290-9_8
18. Mello, R.F., et al.: Prompt engineering for automatic short answer grading in Brazilian Portuguese. In: Simpósio Brasileiro de Informática na Educação (SBIE), pp. 1730–1743. SBC (2024)
19. Mizumoto, A., Eguchi, M.: Exploring the potential of using an AI language model for automated essay scoring. SSRN Electron. J. (2023). https://doi.org/10.2139/ssrn.4373111
20. Oliveira, H., et al.: Towards explainable prediction of essay cohesion in Portuguese and English, pp. 509–519 (2023). https://doi.org/10.1145/3576050.3576152
21. Portela, C., et al.: AI in education unplugged support equity between rural and urban areas in Brazil. In: Proceedings of the 13th International Conference on Information & Communication Technologies and Development, pp. 143–154 (2024)
22. Rodrigues, L., et al.: Mathaide: a qualitative study of teachers' perceptions of an its unplugged for underserved regions. Int. J. Artif. Intell. Educ. 1–29 (2024)
23. Rodrigues, L., et al.: Mathaide in the classroom: a qualitative analysis of teachers' perspectives of intelligent tutoring systems unplugged. In: Simpósio Brasileiro de Informática na Educação (SBIE), pp. 1515–1528. SBC (2024)

24. Seßler, K., Fürstenberg, M., Bühler, B., Kasneci, E.: Can AI grade your essays? A comparative analysis of large language models and teacher ratings in multidimensional essay scoring. In: Proceedings of the 15th International Learning Analytics and Knowledge Conference, pp. 462–472 (2025)
25. e Silva, L.C., et al.: Assessing students' handwritten text productions: a two-decades literature review. Expert Syst. Appl. 123780 (2024)
26. Tavares, J., Rodrigues, L., Dermeval, D.: Clarice: Uma abordagem neural para a correção automática de redações. In: Simpósio Brasileiro de Informática na Educação (SBIE), pp. 1824–1836. SBC (2024)
27. Veloso, T.E., et al.: Its unplugged: leapfrogging the digital divide for teaching numeracy skills in underserved populations. In: Towards the Future of AI-augmented Human Tutoring in Math Learning 2023 - Proceedings of the Workshop on International Conference of Artificial Intelligence in Education co-located with the 24th International Conference on Artificial Intelligence in Education (AIED 2023). Springer, Cham (2023)
28. Vinuesa, R., et al.: The role of artificial intelligence in achieving the sustainable development goals. Nat. Commun. **11**(1), 233 (2020)
29. Wang, Y., Wei, Z., Zhou, Y., Huang, X.: Automatic essay scoring incorporating rating schema via reinforcement learning, pp. 791–797 (2018). https://doi.org/10.18653/v1/D18-1090
30. Yang, K.B., Nam, S., Huang, Y., Wood, S.: Rhetor: providing LLM-based feedback for students' argumentative essays. In: Ferreira Mello, R., Rummel, N., Jivet, I., Pishtari, G., Ruipérez Valiente, J.A. (eds.) EC-TEL 2024. LNCS, vol. 15160, pp. 201–205. Springer, Cham (2024). https://doi.org/10.1007/978-3-031-72312-4_28

Does Feedback Based on Gaze and Stress Indicators Help Novice Programmers?

Anahita Golrang(✉) and Kshitij Sharma(✉)

Department of Computer Science, Norwegian University of Science and Technology, 7034 Trondheim, Norway
{anahita.m.golrang,kshitij.sharma}@ntnu.no

Abstract. Multimodal learning analytics have significantly improved our understanding of learning processes. One of the most discussed advantages of multimodality is the holistic view of the learning processes. In this contribution, we explore whether giving feedback based on multimodal analytics benefits learners. We designed and developed a novel system that collects learners' eye-tracking and heart rate variability data while they debug a given code. The system computes the cognitive load from the eye-tracking data and physiological stress from the heart rate variability data. If the cognitive load and/or physiological stress were more than a threshold, the system would provide feedback on the problem. We conducted a controlled study involving 120 students, with one control condition and three experimental feedback conditions (cognitive load only, stress only, and both cognitive load and stress). The results show that the debugging performance was improved with the feedback. More importantly, we found that the feedback also positively affected students' cognitive load and physiological stress. We discuss the implications of these results in the view of scalability and impact.

Keywords: Multimodal learning analytics · MMLA · eye-tracking · heart rate variability · cognitive load · physiological stress · feedback · programming · debugging

1 Introduction

Programming is like solving puzzles—programmers constantly analyse, plan, debug, and design [9]. If the brain is concerned with too many unrelated tasks at once (e.g., remembering syntax, keeping track of variable names, switching between tabs, or trying to decipher unclear code), it becomes harder to focus on the actual problem they are trying to solve [5]. If a developer is trying to debug a performance issue but also has to mentally track how different modules interact (with no clear documentation), their cognitive load increases rapidly [5]. Higher cognitive load leads to slower progress and less effective solutions. By managing cognitive load, through appropriate support, of the developers we can enable them to think more clearly and work more efficiently [42,53].

K. Tammets et al. (Eds.): EC-TEL 2025, LNCS 16063, pp. 198–213, 2026.
https://doi.org/10.1007/978-3-032-03870-8_14

When a programmer is experiencing high cognitive load, small details often get ignored. This can lead to bugs in logic, incorrect assumptions, or missed edge cases. The higher is the cognitive load, the more likely it is that the programmer will make mistakes [5]. For example, if a function or the structure of the code is complex, a developer might accidentally misuse it or introduce a bug—even if the actual code looks fine at first glance. Therefore, it is important to provide support when situations with higher cognitive load arise. Such a support can lead to fewer bugs and smoother debugging but can also keep programmer's cognitive load to a manageable level [50].

Cognitive load is a major factor in how well people learn and retain new knowledge. If a programmer is learning a new framework or language, and the environment or documentation is complex, they will spend more cognitive processing trying to understand the basics to actually applying them [57]. Reducing cognitive load leads to clear learning paths, good tooling, and minimal distractions—makes it easier to absorb new concepts and apply them effectively [50].

Eye-tracking is a powerful tool for assessing cognitive load and code complexity because it reveals how developers process and interact with code. Longer fixations (more time spent looking at a single point) indicate increased cognitive load, meaning the code is harder to understand [20]. Short fixations suggest quick recognition, likely due to familiarity or simpler syntax [23]. Eye-tracking can also help identify which code structures (e.g., recursion, deep nesting, unfamiliar APIs) demand the most cognitive load [1]. Frequent saccades (rapid eye movements) between different parts of the code suggest that the developer is trying to establish connections (e.g., variable dependencies, function calls) [45]. Increased pupil dilation is a strong indicator of higher cognitive load [14]. When working with complex or unfamiliar code, the brain exerts more effort, which causes dilation. Researchers use this to measure the difficulty of programming languages, paradigms (e.g., functional vs. imperative), and specific code constructs [17,38,48].

Another important aspect of programming and learning is physiological stress. Programming is mentally intensive. Physiological stress affects memory, concentration, and problem-solving ability, the core functions of writing, debugging, and understanding code. Physiological stress can lead to mental fatigue, making it harder to focus or retain new information [26]. Stressed programmers are more prone to make mistakes. These could be simple syntax errors or more critical logic flaws that take significant time to track down and fix [28]. Reducing stress improves accuracy and reduces rework. Short-term stress might lead to bursts of productivity (e.g., crunch time), but long-term stress results in burnout. Burned-out developers are likely to disengage, become less creative, or even leave their job entirely—hurting team continuity and morale [43].

Physiological stress measurements (e.g., heart rate variability – HRV, skin conductance – EDA, and cortisol levels) can provide valuable insights into the cognitive and emotional challenges of debugging. Stress measurements can provide valuable insights into cognitive load and code complexity during debugging by tracking physiological responses [15]. Lower HRV indicates higher cognitive load and stress [47], suggesting a developer is struggling with complex code [8]; while increased sweating (captured by EDA) signals cognitive load, frustration, or difficulty understanding logic [29]. Increased physiological stress responses pinpoint areas in the code that require more cognitive load. Loops, recursion, concurrency, and poorly structured functions tend to trigger higher stress levels [35]. Frequent re-reading of certain lines (linked with stress spikes) suggests ambiguity or confusion in the logic. Stress levels are also related to the error detection and task complexity. Simple syntax errors may cause brief stress spikes, while logical errors and hidden bugs lead to prolonged stress responses. Higher cognitive load when debugging suggests that the code requires deep problem-solving, not just surface-level fixes. These stress measurements can indicate mental fatigue and debugging efficiency [22]. Sustained high stress levels over time indicate mental fatigue, which can lead to reduced focus, slower debugging, and increased errors. Stress measurements can help determine the optimal length for debugging sessions before performance declines [33].

Debugging is a cognitively demanding and ill-structured task that combines technical knowledge with higher-order reasoning skills. It involves ambiguity, hidden issues, and trial-and-error, placing heavy strain on working memory. According to Cognitive Load Theory, debugging generates high intrinsic and germane load, often worsened by external challenges like unclear error messages. Additionally, stress impairs key cognitive functions and serves as a major barrier to learning, with physiological signals like increased heart rate and skin conductance indicating moments of mental strain during the process. [2,51,55]. Minor bugs may trigger brief stress spikes, while logical and structural errors lead to prolonged stress and fatigue [13,18,24,30,44]. These fluctuations, such as sharp drops during moments of insight, highlight the trial-and-error nature of debugging. As a result, programming education should address both cognitive load and physiological stress through real-time, supportive instructional designs that help regulate learners' mental effort and stress.

In this contribution, we designed a feedback tool, using eye-tracking and HRV, to support and manage cognitive load and physiological stress of the programmers. We created three different versions of the system. First provides the feedback when the physiological stress was above a threshold. Second provides the feedback when the cognitive load was above a threshold. Finally, the third combine the first two. Our working hypothesis is that such a tool can help the programmers in maintaining a manageable levels of cognitive load and physiological stress. Specifically, we address the following research questions:

RQ1: What is the effect of feedback on immediate cognitive load?
RQ2: What is the effect of the feedback on immediate physiological stress?
RQ3: What is the effect of feedback on the long-term cognitive load?
RQ4: What is the effect of feedback on long-term physiological stress?

2 Related Work

Feedback plays a crucial role in effective teaching, with its impact hinging on delivery. As emphasized by Wisniewski et al. [56] and Hattie and Timperley [19], the most effective feedback is timely, specific, and informative, making it actionable and supportive of learners' progress. Wearable technologies like eye trackers and physiological sensors offer new ways to enhance feedback by monitoring learners' cognitive and emotional states in real time [27,34,54]. Intelligent Tutoring Systems such as GazeTutor [11] and GIFT [49] demonstrate how this data can inform adaptive instructional strategies by detecting attention lapses and mental effort. Despite advances, most systems still use sensor data for retrospective analysis rather than real-time feedback. However, studies by Rimolsrønning & Plassen [41] and Larsen & Romskaug [31] show that real-time feedback based on pupillary metrics can improve learner performance and reduce cognitive load during programming tasks.

Reliable measurement of cognitive load is key to effective real-time feedback. While subjective measurement methods like self-reports are common, they lack reliability [6]. Objective methods such as fMRI and EEG offer more accurate data [46], but are impractical in dynamic tasks like programming. Eye-tracking, as an indirect and scalable objective method, has proven effective through metrics like pupil dilation and fixation duration [4,7,21,39] and is reinforced by multi-indicator studies [16,25,40].

In parallel, physiological stress, measured through heart rate variability (HRV), is a validated indicator of cognitive effort and emotional stress [3,10,36]. HRV's reliability is supported by its correlation with other physiological markers and systematic reviews [37]. However, its instructional application remains underexplored.

To address this, our study integrates eye-tracking and HRV for delivering immediate, adaptive feedback using wearable technologies, advancing real-time multimodal learning analytics in practical educational contexts.

3 Methodology

To investigate the impact of real-time physiological and cognitive feedback on debugging performance, we designed a controlled laboratory experiment using a between-subjects design. The study involved 120 participants and compared the effects of three feedback conditions: cognitive load-based, stress-based, and combined feedback, against a control group without feedback. Our goal was to evaluate whether such multimodal feedback could enhance task performance and reduce completion time during debugging.

3.1 Participants

The study involved 120 participants (including 28 females), all recruited from a European university's computer science department. Eligibility required prior completion of a basic programming course to ensure familiarity with debugging and Python syntax. Participants came from diverse academic backgrounds but shared a foundational knowledge of programming. To assess their skill level, participants completed a Python pretest prior to the main task, resulting in a programming expertise score ranging from 0 (novice) to 10 (expert). This metric was used as a covariant in subsequent analysis.

3.2 Experimental Setup

The debugging task took place in a quiet, controlled environment, with only the participant and an experimenter present. Each participant was equipped with two wearable sensors: Tobii Pro Glasses 2 for eye-tracking, and an Empatica E4 wristband for physiological stress monitoring via heart rate variability (HRV). Participants used a desktop computer running Visual Studio Code to perform the debugging task. The experiment was designed to be non-intrusive, with feedback delivered through an integrated notification bubble within the IDE.

3.3 Task Design

The debugging task consisted of identifying and correcting five logical bugs in a medium-sized (200–250 lines) Python program implementing a simplified version of the Tetris game using the PyGame library. The program was syntactically correct, but contained semantic issues that affected functionality, for example, misbehaving arrow keys, score miscalculations, and incorrect physics for Tetris block interactions. The duration of the task was fixed at 25 min for all participants, to ensure consistency between conditions and to avoid time-based performance bias.

3.4 Feedback Conditions

Participants were randomly assigned to one of four conditions ($N = 30$ per condition) as follows:

Control Group (No Feedback): Participants debugged the program without receiving any feedback during the task.
Cognitive Load-Based Feedback (T1): Feedback was triggered based on elevated cognitive load, detected via changes in pupil dilation using the Index of Pupillary Activity (IPA) [12]. The trigger threshold was defined as exceeding two standard deviations above the baseline measured during a resting state.
Stress-Based Feedback (T2): Feedback was triggered based on increased physiological stress, computed via HRV as proposed in [32]. Stress levels were computed based on the decreasing slope of heart rate, where steeper negative slopes indicated higher stress [52]. Similar to T1, feedback was activated when stress passed two standard deviations from the baseline.

Combined Feedback (T3): In this condition, feedback was triggered if either the cognitive load or stress metric exceeded its respective threshold. This ensured comprehensive monitoring and timely intervention based on either input channel.

Feedback Mechanism: Across all conditions, feedback content and format remained consistent, only the triggering mechanism differed. Hints were context-specific, drawn from a database of bug-related suggestions tied to the participant's current code view. While participants could disable feedback via a "Help" toggle in the IDE, none chose to do so. This option was clearly explained at the start of the session. As shown in Fig. 1, the system initiated with a prompt ("Hey! Do you need help?"), and upon acceptance, provided a targeted suggestion. Each pop-up included interactive buttons and was labeled by its feedback source (e.g., Stress- or Cognitive-Aware).

Fig. 1. Examples of real-time feedback pop-ups shown in the Visual Studio Code IDE.

3.5 Measurement and Instrumentation

For both cognitive load and stress, we used a rest state measurement to normalize the subsequent data to have a more stable measurement of the two quantities from each participant and have them comparable to each other. This was accomplished by telling participants to wear the devices and calibrating them before the experiment started and then letting them sit for two minutes before giving instructions. The data from these two minutes to remove all the subjective biases from the subsequent data.

Cognitive Load Measurement: Cognitive load was assessed using Tobii Pro Glasses 2, which tracked pupil diameter at 250 Hz. We applied the Index of Pupillary Activity (IPA), a wavelet-based signal processing method that quantifies microscale pupil oscillations indicative of mental effort [12]. Data were preprocessed to account for lighting changes and blink artifacts, followed by segment-wise computation of pupil variability. Feedback was triggered when these fluctuations surpassed the defined threshold.

Stress Measurement: Physiological stress was quantified using Empatica E4 wristbands. We focused on Heart Rate Variability (HRV), calculated through frequency domain analysis. The Low Frequency (LF) and High Frequency (HF) power bands were extracted, and the LF/HF ratio was used as the main stress indicator. A high LF/HF ratio reflects elevated sympathetic nervous system activity, commonly associated with stress. We implemented a sliding time window approach to capture continuous changes in stress, and feedback was triggered upon sustained high-stress states.

Performance Metrics: Debugging Performance was measured by the number of correctly resolved bugs (maximum score = 5). Each fix was automatically logged by the system upon saving the code.

3.6 Procedure

The experiment followed a structured timeline: 1) Introduction (5 min): Consent forms were signed, and participants were briefed about the study. 2) Calibration (5 min): Eye-tracker and wristband were calibrated to ensure reliable data collection. 3) Baseline Recording (2–3 min): A short resting phase was conducted to establish individual baseline metrics for pupil dilation and HRV. 4) Pretest (10 min): Participants completed a Python quiz to assess their programming skills. 5) Debugging Task (25 min): Participants attempted to fix the bugs, during which physiological and eye-tracking data were collected continuously. Real-time feedback was delivered based on the participant's assigned condition. Throughout the task, the system monitored which bugs were fixed and ensured that feedback only addressed unresolved issues. This dynamic hint system maintained relevance while avoiding redundancy.

3.7 Data Analysis

First, we present the results for the manipulation test, that is, whether the feedback was effective. For this we conduct an ANOVA with debugging performance as the dependent and the feedback conditions as the independent variables. Furthermore, we perform pairwise tests to distinguish between the different conditions. To answer RQ1, we conducted an ANOVA with the stress after the feedback was provided (one each for every 10 s) as the dependent variable and the feedback conditions as the independent variable. To answer RQ2, we conducted an ANOVA with the cognitive load after the feedback was provided (one each for every 10 s) as the dependent variable and the feedback conditions as the independent variable. To answer RQ3, we conducted an ANOVA with the stress after the feedback was provided (one each for every five minutes) as the dependent variable and the feedback conditions as the independent variable. To answer RQ4, we conducted an ANOVA with the cognitive load after the feedback was provided (one each for every five minutes) as the dependent variable and the feedback conditions as the independent variable. For all the ANOVAs, in the control condition, we knew when the feedback should have been provided. Therefore, we counted 10 s or 5 min after that moment. The posthoc tests for all the ANOVAs to answer the RQ1-4 was the Tukey-HSD (honestly significant differences). Prior to conducting any ANOVA, we made sure that the conditions were satisfied. We tested the normality with the Sahpiro-Wilk tests and the homoskedasticity was tested with the Breusch-Pegan Tests. All the p-values were corrected using the Bonferroni corrections for the multiple tests. We would like to point out here that we are interested in the individual effect of the interventions on cognitive load and stress (even though the two quantities can be related to each other); therefore, we are using ANOVA instead of MANOVA. This will enable us to design more ecologically valid and scaled-up interventions in the future.

4 Results

First, as a manipulation check, we analysed the impact of the feedback types on the debugging success. An ANOVA with the feedback type as the independent variable and the debugging performance as the dependent variable shows a significant difference in performance across the four conditions ($F[3,116] = 109.98$, $p < .05$). Furthermore, pairwise tests showed that Control condition corresponded with the lowest performance (Stress-based: $F[1,58] = 43.74$, $p < .05$; Cognitive load-based: $F[1,58] = 69.13$, $p < .05$; Both: $F[1,58] = 116.08$, $p < .05$, $CD = 2.83$), followed by only stress based feedback (Cognitive load-based: $F[1,58] = 7.66$, $p < .05$; Both: $F[1,58] = 29.92$, $p < .05$), followed by cognitive load based feedback (Both: $F[1,58] = 5.12$, $p < .05$), and finally the performance was the highest when both types of feedbacks were provided.

4.1 Short Term Effect

Next, we examined the short term impact of feedback on stress and cognitive load. Figures 2a and 2b show the evolution of stress and cognitive load 10 s before and 10 s after feedback was provided. It is evident from both the Fig. 2a and Table 1 that there is a significant difference between the control condition and the three feedback conditions. The stress (Fig. 2a) decreases significantly after the feedback is provided (Table 1) in all the feedback conditions. Moreover, stress decreases significantly more in the stress-only and combined conditions compared to the cognitive load-only condition. Furthermore, for most of the time in the 10 s after the feedback was shown, we do not see any difference between the stress and combined conditions.

We can also observe from both the Fig. 2b and Table 2 that there is a significant difference between the control condition and the three feedback conditions. The cognitive load (Fig. 2b) decreases significantly after the feedback is provided (Table 2) in all the feedback conditions. Moreover, the cognitive load decreases significantly more with the cognitive load and combined conditions than the stress condition. Furhtermore, for most of the times in the 10 s after the feedback was shown, we do not see any difference between the cognitive load and combined conditions.

4.2 Long Term Effect

Finally, we examined the long term impact of feedback on stress and cognitive load. Figures 3a and 3b show the evolution of stress and cognitive load five

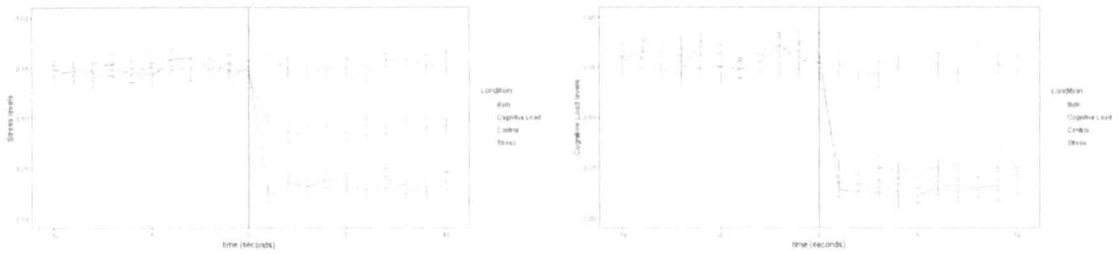

(a) Short term impact of the different feedback on the physiological stress values.

(b) Short term impact of the different feedback on the cognitive load values.

Fig. 2. Short-term effects of feedback on physiological stress and cognitive load. The bars depict the 95% confidence interval. For the control condition the feedback was not provided but we can compute when it "should have been provided".

Table 1. Short term impact on stress for the different feedback types (F-values from ANOVA and tukey-HSD values). The red values are non-significant.

Seconds after feedback	F value (3, 116)	Control V Cognitive load	Control V Stress	Control V Both	Cognitive load V Stress	Cognitive load V Both	Stress V Both
1	2506	−0.31	0.67	−0.67	−0.36	−0.36	0
2	1066	−0.31	−0.57	−0.56	−0.26	−0.25	0.01
3	1365	−0.33	−0.58	−0.58	−0.25	−0.25	0
4	1177	−0.29	−0.55	−0.56	−0.26	−0.27	0.01
5	1392	−0.33	−0.57	−0.59	−0.24	−0.26	−0.02
6	964	−0.25	−0.59	−0.56	−0.34	−0.31	0.03
7	1380	−0.34	−0.59	−0.64	−0.25	−0.3	−0.05
8	1909	−0.3	−0.65	−0.67	−0.35	−0.37	−0.02
9	1289	−0.3	−0.65	−0.6	−0.35	−0.3	0.05
10	1281	−0.32	−0.59	−0.59	−0.27	−0.27	0

minutes after feedback was provided. It is evident from both the Fig. 3a and Table 3 that there is a significant difference between the control condition and the three feedback conditions. The stress (Fig. 3a) decreases significantly after the feedback is provided (Table 3) in all the feedback conditions. Moreover, the stress decreases significantly more with the stress and combined conditions than the cognitive load condition. Furhtermore, for most of the times in the five minutes after the feedback was shown, we do not see any difference between the stress and combined conditions.

We can also observe from both Fig. 3b and Table 4 that there is a significant difference between the control condition and the three feedback conditions. The cognitive load (Fig. 3b) decreases significantly after feedback is provided (Table 4) under all feedback conditions. Moreover, the cognitive load decreases significantly more with the cognitive load and combined conditions than the

Table 2. Short term impact on cognitive load for the different feedback types (F-values from ANOVA and tukey-HSD values). The red values are non-significant.

Seconds after feedback	F value (3,116)	Control V Cognitive load	Control V Stress	Control V Both	Cognitive load V Stress	Cognitive load V Both	Stress V Both
1	1204	−0.63	−0.53	−0.62	0.1	0.01	−0.09
2	1153	−0.6	−0.52	−0.6	0.08	0	−0.08
3	718	−0.53	−0.46	−0.6	0.07	−0.07	−0.14
4	1547	−0.67	−0.54	−0.61	0.13	0.06	−0.07
5	2133	−0.71	−0.56	−0.7	0.15	0.01	−0.14
6	1433	−0.64	−0.52	−0.61	0.1	0.01	−0.09
7	1009	−0.58	−0.45	−0.55	0.13	0.03	−0.1
8	1277	−0.72	−0.67	−0.73	0.05	−0.01	0.06
9	872	−0.61	−0.47	−0.58	0.14	0.03	−0.11
10	602	−0.54	−0.46	−0.56	0.08	−0.02	−0.1

Table 3. Long term impact on stress for the different feedback types (F-values from ANOVA and tukey-HSD values). The red values are non-significant.

	F value (3, 116)	Control V Cognitive load	Control V Stress	Control V Both	Cognitive load V Stress	Cognitive Load V Both	Stress V Both
Minute 1	238	−0.18	−0.25	−0.30	−0.07	−0.12	−0.05
Minute 2	228	−0.19	−0.26	−0.33	−0.07	−0.14	−0.07
Minute 3	261	−0.22	−0.28	−0.27	−0.06	−0.05	0.01
Minute 4	215	0.20	−0.27	−0.26	−0.07	−0.06	0.01
Minute 5	209	−0.21	−0.28	−0.31	−0.07	−0.1	−0.03

stress condition. Furhtermore, for most of the times in the five minutes after the feedback was shown, we do not see any difference between the cognitive load and combined conditions.

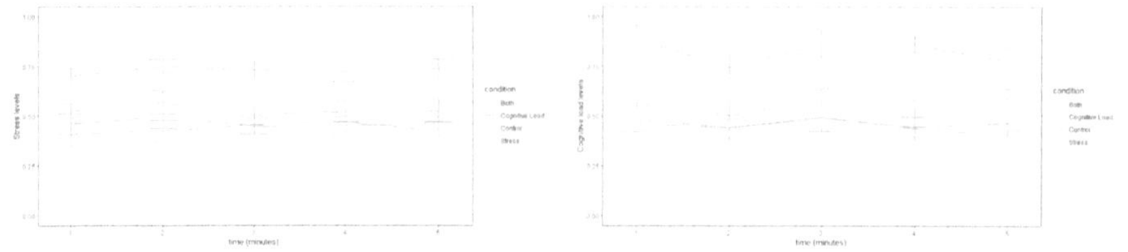

(a) Long term impact of the different feedback on the physiological stress values.

(b) Long term impact of the different feedback on the cognitive load values.

Fig. 3. Long-term effects of feedback on physiological stress and cognitive load. The bars depict the 95% confidence interval. For the control condition the feedback was not provided but we can compute when it "should have been provided".

Table 4. Long term impact on cognitive load for the different feedback types (F-values from ANOVA and tukey-HSD values). The red values are non-significant.

	F value (3, 116)	Control V Cognitive load	Control V Stress	Control V Both	Cognitive load V Stress	Cognitive Load V Both	Stress V Both
Minute 1	389	−0.40	−0.32	−0.42	−0.08	−0.02	−0.10
Minute 2	179	−0.30	−0.24	−0.31	0.06	−0.01	−0.07
Minute 3	226	−0.37	−0.28	−0.38	0.09	−0.01	−0.1
Minute 4	413	−0.43	−0.35	−0.42	0.08	0.01	−0.07
Minute 5	268	−0.37	−0.18	−0.31	0.19	0.05	−0.13

5 Discussion and Conclusion

This study investigates the effects of feedback based on cognitive load and physiological stress on programmers. The results demonstrate that such feedback not only enhances debugging performance but also reduces cognitive load and stress in both the short and long term. In particular, although participants could disable feedback at any time, none chose to do so, suggesting that they found it helpful. The improvement in performance further indicates that the feedback was well-designed and effectively supported the debugging process.

The fact that feedback about how to solve the bugs did not only improved the performance but also reduced the short term physiological stress and cognitive load of the participants identifies the importance of real-time feedback as it is also pointed out in the literature [19,56]. It is also important to point out another aspect of the feedback in our contribution. The results show that the stress based feedback reduces the stress (Fig. 2a), as it was intended, but at the same time it also reduces the cognitive load (Fig. 2b). The decrement in stress is from an average of 0.75 to an average of 0.20 (on a scale of 0 to 1) and the decrement in cognitive load is from an average of 0.8 to an average of 0.25 (on a scale of 0 to 1). On the other hand the cognitive load based feedback reduces the cognitive load (Fig. 2b), as intended, but also reduces the physiological stress (Fig. 2a). The decrement in cognitive load is from an average of 0.80 to an average of 0.12 (scale 0–1) and the decrement in stress is from an average of 0.75 to an average of 0.45 (scale 0–1). Thus, we can see that the decrement in cognitive load due to the stress based feedback is higher then the decrement in the stress due to the cognitive load based feedback. This indicates that on the process level stress based feedback is more effective in managing the learning process. These results are similar (with different decrement levels) when it comes to the long term changes in stress and cognitive load (Figs. 3a and 3b). However, when we see the manipulation check results, we observe that cognitive load is more effective in the terms of the learning outcome. Therefore, the implications for instruction design are different from our results. If we want to optimise the use of devices, for example in the case where we have to decide between using eye-tracking and wristband and at the same time we would want to optimise the learning performance, we will select eye-tracking. But, in the case when we want to optimise device usage and learning processes, we will select the wristband.

The feedback tool as an intervention serves another purpose towards a better understanding of the learning processes. One of the methods to establish causal relationships between two variables is to design interventions and measure the impact. In our case, in the long term, we are interested in the causal relationship between the multimodal measurements (physiological stress and cognitive load) and the learning outcomes (debugging performance). With the current intervention focusing on the multimodal measurements and evaluating the impact of managing them on the learning outcome moves us one step further in the direction of showing a potential causal relationship between them. We already know that correlation-based relationship between learning performance and the multimodal measurements [17,29,35,38,47,48]. This study enacts as the first instance to show that it is actually the cognitive load and physiological stress that might cause the learning performance. However, more similar studies are required to reach to a consensus about generalizability of this causal relationship.

Furthermore, we have mentioned before that most of the feedback tools using real time tracking of cognitive [27,34,54] and physiological states [11,49] detect lapses in attention or increased mental effort, allowing instructional strategies to adapt dynamically to individual needs. However, most existing systems rely on sensor data primarily for retrospective analysis or learner awareness rather than for delivering immediate instructional interventions. In our contribution, we propose real-time feedback using reliable measurements from eye-tracking and HRV and show that they are effective in both improving learning performance and managing learning processes. Moreover, most of the studies are limited by the use of non-wearable equipment whereas, both the eye-tracker and the wristband used in our study were wearables. With the current advents in technology and consistent reduction in the prices of such devices the implications from our results can be used at scale. However, there is a requirement for further research if the findings will generalize in a more ecologically valid setting, such as a classroom. Based on the current findings, there is potential to develop a physio-cognitive theory of scaffolding. However, further data analysis is needed—for instance, to understand why cognitive load–based feedback enhances performance, while stress-based feedback better supports the learning process (cognitive load and physiological stress). Additionally, we plan to replicate these results in other learning environments to explore how context influences these effects.

References

1. Abbad-Andaloussi, A., Sorg, T., Weber, B.: Estimating developers' cognitive load at a fine-grained level using eye-tracking measures. In: Proceedings of the 30th IEEE/ACM International Conference on Program Comprehension, pp. 111–121 (2022)
2. Ahlawat, S., Khurana, D.D.: A proposed framework for enhancing software bug severity prediction using smote to handle data imbalance. Available at SSRN 5148763
3. Ahmad, M.I., Keller, I., Robb, D.A., Lohan, K.S.: A framework to estimate cognitive load using physiological data. Pers. Ubiquit. Comput. 1–15 (2023)
4. Backs, R.W., Walrath, L.C.: Eye movement and pupillary response indices of mental workload during visual search of symbolic displays. Appl. Ergon. **23**(4), 243–254 (1992)
5. Berssanette, J.H., de Francisco, A.C.: Cognitive load theory in the context of teaching and learning computer programming: a systematic literature review. IEEE Trans. Educ. **65**(3), 440–449 (2021)
6. Brunken, R., Plass, J.L., Leutner, D.: Direct measurement of cognitive load in multimedia learning. Educ. Psychol. **38**(1), 53–61 (2003)
7. Buettner, R.: Cognitive workload of humans using artificial intelligence systems: towards objective measurement applying eye-tracking technology. In: Timm, I.J., Thimm, M. (eds.) KI 2013. LNCS (LNAI), vol. 8077, pp. 37–48. Springer, Heidelberg (2013). https://doi.org/10.1007/978-3-642-40942-4_4
8. Chandrasekaran, A., Bielicke, L., Shah, D., Janakiraman, H., Mauriello, M.L.: "I spent 14 hours debugging just one assignment": toward computer-mediated personal informatics for computer science student mental health (2025)
9. Christakis, M., Bird, C.: What developers want and need from program analysis: an empirical study. In: Proceedings of the 31st IEEE/ACM International Conference on Automated Software Engineering, pp. 332–343 (2016)
10. Cranford, K.N., et al.: Measuring load on working memory: the use of heart rate as a means of measuring chemistry students' cognitive load. J. Chem. Educ. **91**(5), 641–647 (2014)
11. D'Mello, S., Olney, A., Williams, C., Hays, P.: Gaze tutor: a gaze-reactive intelligent tutoring system. Int. J. Hum.-Comput. Stud. **70**(5), 377–398 (2012)
12. Duchowski, A.T., et al.: The index of pupillary activity: measuring cognitive load vis-à-vis task difficulty with pupil oscillation. In: Proceedings of the 2018 CHI Conference on Human Factors in Computing Systems, pp. 1–13 (2018)
13. Fritz, T., Begel, A., Müller, S.C., Yigit-Elliott, S., Züger, M.: Using psycho-physiological measures to assess task difficulty in software development. In: Proceedings of the 36th International Conference on Software Engineering, pp. 402–413 (2014)
14. Gavas, R., Chatterjee, D., Sinha, A.: Estimation of cognitive load based on the pupil size dilation. In: 2017 IEEE International Conference on Systems, Man, and Cybernetics (SMC), pp. 1499–1504. IEEE (2017)

15. Girardi, D., Novielli, N., Fucci, D., Lanubile, F.: Recognizing developers' emotions while programming. In: Proceedings of the ACM/IEEE 42nd International Conference on Software Engineering, pp. 666–677 (2020)
16. Gollan, B., Haslgrübler, M., Ferscha, A.: Demonstrator for extracting cognitive load from pupil dilation for attention management services. In: Proceedings of the 2016 ACM International Joint Conference on Pervasive and Ubiquitous Computing, pp. 1566–1571 (2016)
17. Gonçales, L.J., Farias, K., da Silva, B.C.: Measuring the cognitive load of software developers: an extended systematic mapping study. Inf. Softw. Technol. **136**, 106563 (2021)
18. Graziotin, D., Wang, X., Abrahamsson, P.: Understanding the affect of developers: theoretical background and guidelines for psychoempirical software engineering. In: Proceedings of the 7th International Workshop on Social Software Engineering, pp. 25–32 (2015)
19. Hattie, J., Timperley, H.: The power of feedback. Rev. Educ. Res. **77**(1), 81–112 (2007)
20. Hung, J.C., Wang, C.C.: The influence of cognitive styles and gender on visual behavior during program debugging: a virtual reality eye tracker study. HCIS **11**(22), 1–21 (2021)
21. Hyönä, J., Tommola, J., Alaja, A.M.: Pupil dilation as a measure of processing load in simultaneous interpretation and other language tasks. Q. J. Exp. Psychol. **48**(3), 598–612 (1995)
22. Issever, D., Catalbas, M.C., Duran, F.: Examining factors influencing cognitive load of computer programmers. Brain Sci. **13**(8), 1132 (2023)
23. Jessup, S., Willis, S.M., Alarcon, G., Lee, M.: Using eye-tracking data to compare differences in code comprehension and code perceptions between expert and novice programmers (2021)
24. Khan, I.A., Brinkman, W.P., Hierons, R.M.: Do moods affect programmers' debug performance? Cogn. Technol. Work **13**, 245–258 (2011)
25. Klingner, J., Kumar, R., Hanrahan, P.: Measuring the task-evoked pupillary response with a remote eye tracker. In: Proceedings of the 2008 Symposium on Eye Tracking Research & Applications, pp. 69–72 (2008)
26. Kock, N., Moqbel, M., Jung, Y., Syn, T.: Do older programmers perform as well as young ones? Exploring the intermediate effects of stress and programming experience. Cogn. Technol. Work **20**, 489–504 (2018)
27. Korbach, A., Brünken, R., Park, B.: Measurement of cognitive load in multimedia learning: a comparison of different objective measures. Instr. Sci. **45**(4), 515–536 (2017). https://doi.org/10.1007/s11251-017-9413-5
28. Krizsan, T., Lambic, D.: Examining the impact of pair programming on efficiency, motivation, and stress among students of different skills and abilities in lower grades in elementary schools. Educ. Inf. Technol. 1–24 (2024)
29. Krogstie, J., Sharma, K.: Towards neuro-adaptive modelling environments: report from a study on prediction of business process model comprehension performance using biometric data (2024)
30. Kurian, R.M., Thomas, S.: Perceived stress and fatigue in software developers: examining the benefits of gratitude. Pers. Individ. Differ. **201**, 111923 (2023)
31. Larsen, E.S., Romskaug, T.: Real time stress-aware feedback system for programming. Master's thesis, NTNU (2022)
32. Lee-Cultura, S., Sharma, K., Cosentino, G., Papavlasopoulou, S., Giannakos, M.: Children's play and problem solving in motion-based educational games: Synergies

between human annotations and multi-modal data. In: Proceedings of the 20th Annual ACM Interaction Design and Children Conference, pp. 408–420 (2021)
33. Migliaccio, G.M., et al.: Effects of mental fatigue on reaction time in sportsmen. Int. J. Environ. Res. Public Health **19**(21), 14360 (2022)
34. Mills, C., Fridman, I., Soussou, W., Waghray, D., Olney, A.M., D'Mello, S.K.: Put your thinking cap on: detecting cognitive load using EEG during learning. In: Proceedings of the Seventh International Learning Analytics & Knowledge Conference, pp. 80–89 (2017)
35. Minas, R.K., Kazman, R., Tempero, E.: Neurophysiological impact of software design processes on software developers. In: Schmorrow, D.D., Fidopiastis, C.M. (eds.) AC 2017. LNCS (LNAI), vol. 10285, pp. 56–64. Springer, Cham (2017). https://doi.org/10.1007/978-3-319-58625-0_4
36. Mukherjee, S., Yadav, R., Yung, I., Zajdel, D.P., Oken, B.S.: Sensitivity to mental effort and test-retest reliability of heart rate variability measures in healthy seniors. Clin. Neurophysiol. **122**(10), 2059–2066 (2011)
37. Peabody, J.E., Ryznar, R., Ziesmann, M.T., Gillman, L., Ryznar, R.J., Gillman, L.M.: A systematic review of heart rate variability as a measure of stress in medical professionals. Cureus **15**(1) (2023)
38. Peitek, N., et al.: Correlates of programmer efficacy and their link to experience: a combined EEG and eye-tracking study. In: Proceedings of the 30th ACM Joint European Software Engineering Conference and Symposium on the Foundations of Software Engineering, pp. 120–131 (2022)
39. Poole, A., Ball, L.J.: Eye tracking in HCI and usability research. In: Encyclopedia of Human Computer Interaction, pp. 211–219. IGI Global (2006)
40. Prieto, L.P., Sharma, K., Kidzinski, Ł, Dillenbourg, P.: Orchestration load indicators and patterns: in-the-wild studies using mobile eye-tracking. IEEE Trans. Learn. Technol. **11**(2), 216–229 (2017)
41. Rimolsrønning, A., Plassen, O.: Eye tracking studio–designing and evaluating a feedback system utilizing eye-tracking to improve remote collaboration between pair programmers. Master's thesis, NTNU (2022)
42. Sands, P.: Addressing cognitive load in the computer science classroom. ACM Inroads **10**(1), 44–51 (2019)
43. Schubert, C., Lambertz, M., Nelesen, R., Bardwell, W., Choi, J.B., Dimsdale, J.: Effects of stress on heart rate complexity–a comparison between short-term and chronic stress. Biol. Psychol. **80**(3), 325–332 (2009)
44. Siitonen, V., Ritonummi, S., Salo, M., Pirkkalainen, H.: The emergence of technostress in software development work: technostressors and underlying factors. In: Socio-Technical Perspective in Information Systems Development, pp. 265–286. CEUR Workshop Proceedings (2022)
45. Silva Da Costa, J.A., Gheyi, R.: Evaluating the code comprehension of novices with eye tracking. In: Proceedings of the XXII Brazilian Symposium on Software Quality, pp. 332–341 (2023)
46. Smith, E.E., Jonides, J.: Working memory: a view from neuroimaging. Cogn. Psychol. **33**(1), 5–42 (1997)
47. Solhjoo, S., et al.: Heart rate and heart rate variability correlate with clinical reasoning performance and self-reported measures of cognitive load. Sci. Rep. **9**(1), 14668 (2019)
48. Sorg, T., Abbad-Andaloussi, A., Weber, B.: Towards a fine-grained analysis of cognitive load during program comprehension. In: 2022 IEEE International Conference on Software Analysis, Evolution and Reengineering (SANER), pp. 748–752. IEEE (2022)

49. Sottilare, R.A., Graesser, A., Hu, X., Goldberg, B.: Design Recommendations for Intelligent Tutoring Systems: Instructional Management, vol. 2. US Army Research Laboratory (2014)
50. Stachel, J., Marghitu, D., Brahim, T.B., Sims, R., Reynolds, L., Czelusniak, V.: Managing cognitive load in introductory programming courses: a cognitive aware scaffolding tool. J. Integr. Des. Process. Sci. **17**(1), 37–54 (2013)
51. Stepp, M., Simon, B.: Introductory computing students' conceptions of illegal student-student collaboration. In: Proceedings of the 41st ACM Technical Symposium on Computer Science Education, pp. 295–299 (2010)
52. Taelman, J., Vandeput, S., Spaepen, A., Van Huffel, S.: Influence of mental stress on heart rate and heart rate variability. In: Vander Sloten, J., Verdonck, P., Nyssen, M., Haueisen, J. (eds.) ECIFMBE 2008. IFMBE Proceedings, vol. 22, pp. 1366–1369. Springer, Heidelberg (2009). https://doi.org/10.1007/978-3-540-89208-3_324
53. Unal, A., Topu, F.B.: Effects of teaching a computer programming language via hybrid interface on anxiety, cognitive load level and achievement of high school students. Educ. Inf. Technol. **26**(5), 5291–5309 (2021). https://doi.org/10.1007/s10639-021-10536-w
54. Vanneste, P., et al.: Towards measuring cognitive load through multimodal physiological data. Cogn. Technol. Work **23**, 567–585 (2021)
55. Weidemann, A., Russwinkel, N.: Investigation of frustration. In: Proceedings of the Mensch and Computer, pp. 819–824 (2019)
56. Wisniewski, B., Zierer, K., Hattie, J.: The power of feedback revisited: a meta-analysis of educational feedback research. Front. Psychol. **10** (2020)
57. Yousoof, M., Sapiyan, M., Kamaluddin, K.: Reducing cognitive load in learning computer programming. Trans. Eng. Comput. Technol. **12**, 259–262 (2006)

Accessible Design in Integrated Development Environments: A Think Aloud Study Exploring the Experiences of Students with ADHD

Luke Halpin(✉), Phillip Benachour, Tracy Hall, Ann-Marie Houghton, and Emily Winter

Lancaster University, Lancaster, UK
{l.halpin,p.benachour,tracy.hall,a.houghton,e.winter}@lancaster.ac.uk

Abstract. Coding forms a key part of computer science education in universities. As part of this education, Integrated Development Environments (IDEs) are essential tools for coding. However, it is currently unknown how the design of an IDE's interface impacts on students with Attention Deficit Hyperactivity Disorder (ADHD).

In this study we investigated the use of IDEs by students with ADHD. We conducted a think aloud study with nine university computing students, followed by qualitative observational interviews to analyse their learning and engagement with the Visual Studio Code IDE. The paper reports on these experiences and seeks to understand the role IDEs play in the educational setting.

Our work also examines how digital accessibility and usability are considered in the current design of IDEs. We analysed the qualitative data using a thematic analysis and identified three primary themes: self-confidence, interaction, and learning as well as various sub-themes.

The themes and their sub-themes illustrate key areas of consideration when designing IDEs for students with ADHD. The primary findings highlight experiences of frustration and barriers in the current design and layout of IDEs.

Through our participatory approach we provide a rare insight into ADHD user experiences around usability and accessibility, and describe the need for better design of development environments to ensure a positive learning experience for the students.

Keywords: ADHD · Integrated Development Environment · Usability · Digital Accessibility · Computer Science Education

1 Introduction

Integrated Development Environments (IDEs) are a valuable tool for software developers, allowing them to use various integrated tools to improve the process of development. Yet IDE's design and poor usability, as demonstrated by

K. Tammets et al. (Eds.): EC-TEL 2025, LNCS 16063, pp. 214–228, 2026.
https://doi.org/10.1007/978-3-032-03870-8_15

Dillon & Thompson [8], can often be disconcerting to those at the early stages of learning the various skills associated with development and computer science [24].

Investigating the experience of students with Attention Deficit Hyperactivity Disorder (ADHD) in computing education is especially important considering Kirdani-Ryan & Ko's discussions around neurodivergent students being more likely to study computing [13]. In addition to this fact, Leow et al. [17] found ADHD to have a strong correlation with students discontinuing their studies, which is already more prevalent in computing than other subjects [11]. ADHD is a developmental condition which impacts the regulation of executive functions and is often first noticed in childhood but is usually a lifelong condition [1].

In this exploratory study we invited undergraduate computer science students with ADHD to take part in a think aloud activity. Charters [6] describes think aloud as a research method involving a participant vocalising their thought process while completing an activity to give insight into their interaction experience. The study activity in this paper consisted of students using an IDE to complete coding tasks then discussing their experiences using the IDE. This approach will address a current gap in the literature around the impact of IDE design on students with ADHD.

Our study was exploratory in nature, with the goal of developing an understanding of the experience of students with ADHD when using an IDE to complete coding tasks. The following research questions were formed to accomplish this goal:

RQ1. How does the design of the IDE user interface (UI) impact the usability for a student with ADHD?
RQ2. What are the experiences of students with ADHD when using an IDE?

RQ1 will allow aspects of current design to be identified that have an impact on students, while RQ2 will give insight into how students experience the overall interaction. These questions will be answered through a thematic analysis of the data collected during the think aloud activity and short interviews.

The contributions of this paper provide important insight on key challenges to making IDEs more accessible to students with ADHD and supporting them in their learning such as:

- Supporting issues with self-confidence
- Managing a sense of overwhelm
- Improving communication between the IDE and the learner

The structure of this paper is as follows: Sect. 2 covers the background and related work giving an overview of current research around IDE usability and ADHD digital accessibility. Section 3 lays out the overall methodology including the design of the study and analysis of data. Section 4 breaks down the results of the analysis, explaining and evidencing the findings. Section 5 presents a discussion of the results and their implications while also addressing limitations. Section 6 contains the conclusion of our paper.

2 Background and Related Work

2.1 IDEs and Usability

While IDEs are a frequently utilised tool in software development [16], the current research around their usability is limited. The work of Kline et al. [14] evaluates the usability of IDEs through interviews and heuristics evaluation and discusses how these tools are often centred on being designed for functionality rather than usability by developers. This design mentality can also lead to educational environments instead using slimmed down IDE variants such as BlueJ [15]. While slimmed down variants may be beneficial to learning environments through being simplified and easier to use, this can lead to skill gaps between what is expected at university level and what is expected in industry itself [2].

Few of these studies on IDE usability focus on accessibility, with only a limited amount of research on ADHD and IDEs. Kasatskii et al. [12], for example, explored the role of perceptual load in the efficiency of software developers. They used a plugin to create different levels of perceptual load in the IDE to compare the performance of developers working in the differing environments, finding a positive impact of adaptability and need for individualised support and design.

This paper however differs from existing work like that of Kasatskii et al. by examining the overall experience of using IDEs rather than just perceptual load and by examining an educational context rather than one in industry.

2.2 ADHD and Digital Accessibility Research

Spiel et al. [23] discuss the current body of work through a critical systematic literature review of ADHD and technology research. The review highlighted a lack of research with ADHD users as primary participants, and a significant focus on tech to mitigate ADHD symptoms rather than support ADHD in context. The existing body of research focuses heavily on the current diagnostic criteria for ADHD, which has been criticised by researchers [1], and often implements a medical model approach. The medical model of disability is one which focuses on the disability being the condition and having a need to reduce the impact of the condition [9]. An alternative and less explored model in ADHD research is the social model of disability where the barriers arising from an inaccessible environment are the problem that leads to the person with ADHD being disabled [9]. The work of this paper addresses the gap in research by providing a social model perspective and considering the environmental barriers created by the IDE, in line with calls for such work by the likes of Spiel et al. [23]. By taking this approach participants give a full and detailed account of their holistic experience and how interfaces disable them, rather than focusing on specific aspects of their disabilities. This will identify the features of design which detriment the usability of the IDEs, and hence the obstacles that currently impact someone with ADHD.

3 Methodology

3.1 Study Design

A retrospective think aloud protocol was followed. As part of the protocol, participants completed a coding task consisting of debugging and contributing original code to a provided code base. A retrospective protocol was chosen as it has been previously reported to provide more explanations and design information compared to a concurrent approach [4]. A retrospective protocol also allows participants to have more focus on the coding task and the think aloud activity individually. The code and materials used can be found in the replication package [10].

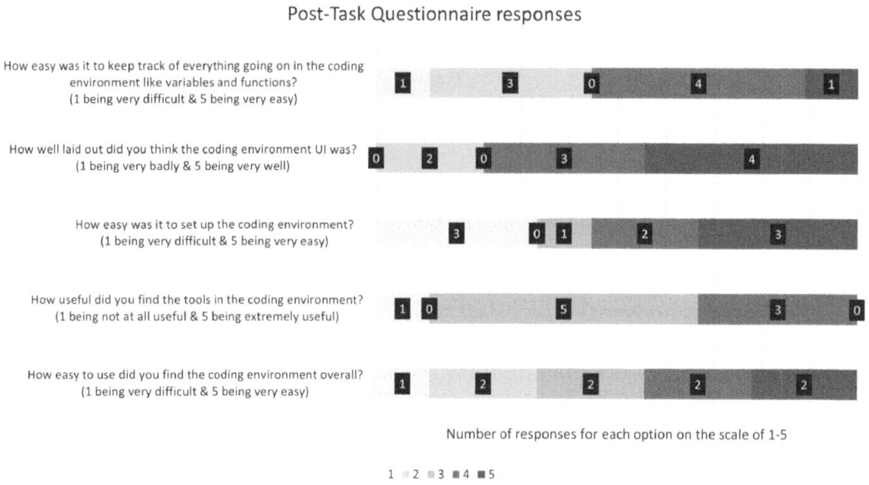

Fig. 1. Participant responses to post-task questionnaire using Likert scales with 1 being a negative response and 5 being a positive response.

When designing the study, data triangulation was kept in mind to address some of the methods limitations [6]. Firstly, by using the retrospective method, a lot of information that is sometimes lost in the concurrent variant is included with a lower cognitive load and gives more time for the participant to consider their thoughts. Secondly, the participants filled out a short questionnaire rating the five questions in Fig. 1 on Likert scales to provide some quantitative values and understand the general feeling of participants about the activity. Finally, the use of short informal interviews, which allowed us to discuss both the activity and questionnaire with the participants, and some of their wider experiences.

3.2 Participants

The participants recruited were undergraduates studying computer science related subjects. Participants ranged in age from 19 to 23 years old (19:1, 20:3,

21:3, 22:1, 23:1) with a majority female participants (male:3, female:6) and varying ethnic backgrounds (white:5, Black/African/Caribbean:1, Asian:3).

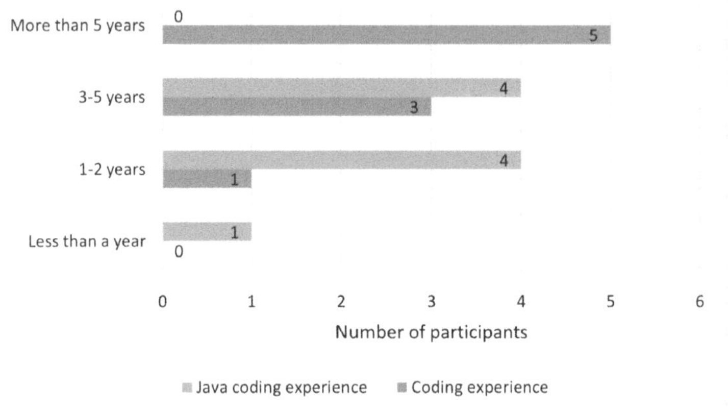

Fig. 2. A bar chart showing the coding experience of participants.

Participants were asked which IDEs they use most frequently, with the vast majority using VS Code (VS Code:7, Visual Studio:1, Jetbrains:1) and their experience coding was documented as shown in Fig. 2.

For the study we required ADHD as an eligibility requirement. Self-diagnosis was accepted due to the work of Rutter et al. [20] who found self-diagnosis as a reasonable indicator of an internalised condition and to fall in line with similar works [12].

3.3 Data Gathering

The data collection took place between June and July 2024 following ethics approval from the Faculty of Science and Technology Ethics Committee at Lancaster University in May. Participants were given detailed instructions on what would take place from a script used by the researcher. Participants were given chance to ask any questions they might have before beginning the session. They then completed a coding task involving debugging and generating original code while the screen activity was being recorded. Once the coding activity was complete, the participant would watch the recording while narrating their thought process. They would then take a short break before filling out a Likert scale survey and then taking part in a short interview. The interviews discussed the coding activity and the students' interaction with the IDE. The session was recorded and automatically transcribed.

3.4 Data Analysis

Thematic analysis was used as described by Braun & Clarke [5]. The transcripts were reviewed for accuracy of the auto transcription and prepared for analysis by marking when participants or the researcher were speaking. Multiple read-throughs were then conducted of the full corpus of nine transcripts, which contained 37965 words in total. Notes were made on observations of potential codes throughout until saturation was reached. The notes made were then reviewed and compiled into a list of open codes and axial codes to form a code book. Two researchers then independently coded a sample transcript. The transcript was selected at random from any of the transcripts which constituted at least 10% of the total corpus using the code book [19]. Once the sample was coded the two coders met and reviewed the coded transcripts to reach negotiated agreement on the code book before coding the remaining transcripts.

Following the coding phase, we identified a number of themes as shown in Fig. 3 in line with the methods of Braun and Clark [5].

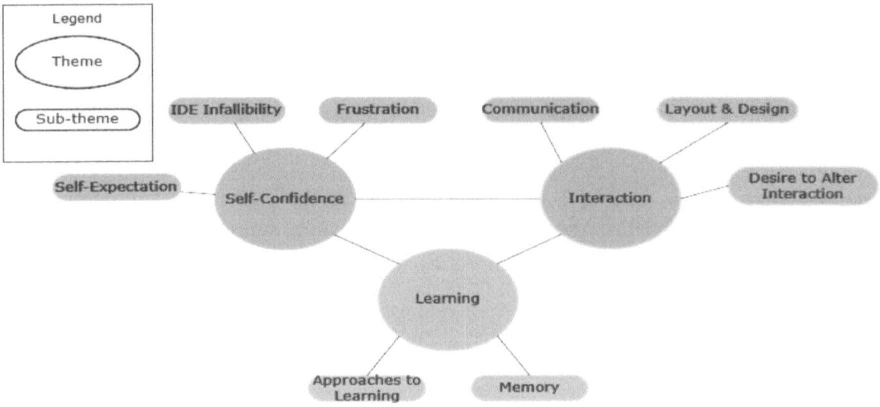

Fig. 3. Diagram representing themes identified through thematic analysis

4 Results

4.1 Main Themes Descriptions

The theme of self-confidence demonstrates the difficulties students experienced when completing the coding task as part of the study and how their perceptions impacted their ability to complete it.

The interaction theme highlighted aspects of the IDE which impacted students' ability to complete the task.

The learning theme demonstrated the ways students engaged with learning in relation to the IDE and also barriers they faced to fully understanding and utilising the tool.

4.2 Self-confidence Sub-themes

Self Expectation. One of the major factors that was identified was the high level of self expectation participants placed on themselves. Participants in the study often seemed stressed or disheartened and harsh on themselves when they failed to meet their high standards.

> *"And now I look like an idiot."* (P04 Interview, describing how long it took them to get the code to run).

The balance of self expectation and difficulty experienced was also visible when participants provided justifications for not meeting their desired standard. This need to clarify why they didn't perform as they would have liked was often self focused rather than allowing consideration for other factors such as usability.

> *"But I basically just expected better of myself really. I should know this stuff. If I'd been doing a bunch more Java development in the last week or so, I probably would've been better at this, but I think that's just me being a bit rusty and feeling it should be a bit better than that.*
> ...
> *If this was python we would have been gone 20 minutes ago"* (P08 Interview, describing their disappointment in themselves for not being able to complete the task quicker).

This sub-theme also lead to participants focusing the blame on themselves for their mistakes rather than the IDE, even in situations where the IDE had been unclear or had not functioned as expected.

> *"The coding environment was easy enough, myself is the problem."* (P07 Interview, describing their belief that they were the reason they struggled in the task).

IDE Infallibility. An assumption present throughout this study was students assuming the IDE must be working correctly and the fault was on them for how they were using the tool. The IDE infallibility could also be clearly seen in the Likert scale responses from Fig. 1, with participants giving the IDE positive scores, despite qualitative statements in both the think aloud and interview contradicting those scores, such as Participant 3 who gave the design and layout of the IDE a high Likert score despite struggling with the layout.

> *"So sometimes if I'm just trying to use a terminal and then I see on the side there's 10 terminals or something or there's just so many buttons that you can press. But I'm just trying to do something simple."* (P03 Interview, describing being overwhelmed by the UI of the IDE).

This theme was consistent and present throughout the study, with participants taking longer to solve issues due to being focused on their own work rather than potential issues with the IDE set up.

"Yeah, I think I was more inclined to think it was probably me." (P03 Interview, describing how they assumed they were doing something wrong rather than the IDE not being set up correctly).

Frustration. Frustration was evident throughout most of the activities, with participants being visibly frustrated and annoyed with both their own performance and the IDE failing to behave as expected. It was notable that participants frustrations would often grow rapidly and make it harder for them to focus, especially when not meeting their own standards.

"It almost feels frustrating that it took you so long to figure something out that was such a simple fix and I was overthinking it in a way and I was ignoring certain details." (P01 Think aloud activity, describing how installing an extension fixed all the issues they had been having getting the IDE to run the code).

"And I don't think it's an error with my coding anymore and I'm trying to find the solution online but not being able to quickly locate the correct information to change what I'm doing and it becomes very frustrating quite quickly." (P07 Interview, describing trying to look up information on how to run the code in the IDE).

Even participants who found the task simple recounted how outside of the study there were occasions where the IDE would cause frustration, despite the participant considering themselves skilled at using the tool.

"Sometimes that can be more annoying if it's only got part of the validation rules right. Or if it's not set up properly." (P09 Interview, describing the experience of using an IDE when it is not working as expected).

4.3 Interaction Sub-themes

Communication. The interaction between the participants and the IDE was often limited and restricted by how well the IDE communicated with the participant. Its ability to communicate if it was running or not, or if it was set up correctly to compile the code was limited and often caused confusion for the participant.

"And then yeah, I tried to start running and then nothing happened." (P03 Think aloud activity, describing trying to use the IDE to run the code).

"It just downloads a random folder for you and then I wasn't sure if you are meant to open the folder or if you are meant to move that folder elsewhere. (P02 Interview, describing how the IDE downloaded a file to run the code without information on using the file).

The communication of errors also caused confusion for participants, with it often being unclear how serious the warning was.

> *"Yeah, I think I got stuck on that warning for a while. Although I think it's a bit confusing when it has that light bulb next to it. I know that it does the light bulb when it's something that Visual Studio could help resolve, whereas the other warnings are things that it can't find an easy fix for, but I think it was slightly confusing if that's an error or a warning."* (P01 Think aloud activity, describing the similarity between warnings and other indications in the IDE).

Layout and Design. It was frequently observed that the design and layout of the IDE had an impact on the experience of participants. This varied between participants with some finding the amount on the screen overwhelming, while some felt the IDE was not displaying enough information. The first aspect of design was how the pop ups and amount of activity on screen created a frequent susceptibility to overwhelm.

> *"It's like you open it up and a bunch of stuff just pops up on the screen and it's really a little bit overwhelming."* (P05 Think aloud activity, describing the how the IDE appears when first turned on).

It was also highlighted that this sense of overwhelm discouraged participants from making use of helpful and sometimes essential tools for completing the task.

> *"I get overwhelmed by a lot of information quite easily and I feel like the extensions, to me, feel very overwhelming and over stimulating. So I don't go to them so it never crossed my mind that the problem was with the extension rather than anything else."* (P01 Think aloud activity, describing how they avoided the extensions needed to run the code due to finding them overwhelming).

The difficulty of managing overwhelm while trying to find tools could be amplified by the difficulty of knowing what to look for. Participants described the interface as busy and cluttered, which made it difficult to notice when the IDE was trying to give useful information.

> *"And a lot of tools that are available while they're supposed to be very useful aren't necessarily very clear, and it can become very easy to click on a button and think why has nothing happened and you've missed the little pop up window at the top that does everything because so many functions in Visual Studio lead to that pop up window where you then not only may miss it, but you also may already need to know what you need to type to get the next thing to happen."* (P07 Interview, describing the issues with keeping track of important pop ups in the IDE).

Desire to Alter the Interaction. This sub-theme highlights the consistent desire to alter the design or layout of the IDE. This could be seen with the participants wanting to change what was on screen at different times and again there was not one standard desire with variations of participants wanting more or less on screen or only specific things. This sub-theme was most prevalent in how participants wanted information to be shown, such as the position on the screen or being able to see multiple aspects of code at once.

> *"I split the my code into the other bit so I could process it."* (P06 Think aloud activity, describing using the split screen function in the IDE to look at different code files at the same time).

There was also a prevalent feeling of wanting to change or reduce what information was visible and to have it limited to things useful at the time.

> *"Because if you minimise everything and if you neaten it just because it looks nicer. But if you minimise everything then you can go to the important classes and if you do your find the methods it'll take you straight to the methods."* (P02 Interview, describing how they like to minimise the amount of things on screen at once while coding).

4.4 Learning Sub-themes

Approaches to Learning. The approaches displayed by participants highlighted the different ways users might try and solve problems they could be faced with in an IDE. The sub-theme of approaches to learning was put prominently upfront by the study. This prominence was partially due to the frequent feeling that there was a knowledge barrier to using the tool, which could not be overcome by the guidance the tool provided. These barriers often required peer support or independent research when other help was unavailable.

> *"At first I found there was a lot that you had to do to get it ready to go and if you didn't have someone there to explain some of it to you, you do have to Google it to discover the information."* (P07 Interview, describing the difficulty of getting the IDE set up).

When conducting this research participants had to overcome other aspects of difficulty, such as navigating information which was outdated due to updates and changes to the IDE tool, and would sometimes seek visual confirmation to help in their research to identify relevant information.

> *"So something that you find online that's talking about a certain UI might be different to the UI that you have currently. I usually try and find images to make sure that there are similarities."* (P01 Think aloud activity, describing trying to find solutions to get the IDE working while navigating solutions online which are different versions of the IDE).

Participants would struggle with navigating dense sources of information which were difficult to parse or would be challenging for the participant to quickly review for useful information. This difficulty in navigating the information would result in the participant missing useful information.

> *"Albeit when I do my research I kind of skip over a lot of stuff that may be helpful to me."* (P01 Think aloud activity, describing how they tend to skip over big pieces of text trying to find a quick solution).

Memory. This sub-theme is perhaps most relevant to the area of learning for people with ADHD as they often struggle with memory [1]. The sub-theme highlights the difficulty of balancing learning multiple coding languages and remembering how to navigate a complex interface. One aspect of memory that appeared as difficult for participants was balancing negative interaction experiences with the tool and keeping track of the different variables and functions as part of the coding task.

> *"I think with ones that don't suit my style of work and don't conform to how I read and interact with things, it can be very difficult. And because I have to bounce around and re-remember where everything is every couple of seconds."* (P05 Interview, describing how different interfaces can make it more difficult to keep track of things when coding).

The most prevalent impact on memory was remembering specifics of Java when they potentially hadn't used it recently, which is common when learning how to programme and completing different courseworks in different coding languages.

> *"And I'm used to that whereas well mainly because I haven't used Java in a while so that happened."* (P04 Interview, describing how they are used to the run button being different in different IDEs and being out of practice with the way to run Java code).

The above also amplified some of the earlier aspects of self-confidence that have been discussed with struggling to remember leading to participants blaming themselves for not being able to get the tool to work.

> *"I think I just assumed I didn't know how to run it. I'd just forgotten everything with coding."* (P02 Interview, describing their confusion over the code not running before the IDE was set up correctly but assuming they had done something wrong).

5 Discussion

5.1 Self-confidence

The presence of self-confidence as a major theme of a study involving ADHD is not surprising. Existing literature discusses how people with ADHD often have issues with self-esteem [18]. Bodalski et al. [3] also discuss the relationship between self-esteem and procrastination in students with ADHD. Self-confidence was found to play a considerable role in how students interacted with the IDE and their experience while using it. Issues such as self-deprecation, self-doubt and worrying about or losing track of time were some of the prominent observations. The presence of the observations in line with the established understanding from literature highlights the weight that should be given to supporting students with ADHD and their difficulties with self-confidence. However, insights from this study show that while the theme of self-confidence was present, the design of the IDE seemed to amplify this phenomenon.

Instances of the IDE not being clear on its state of readiness lead to students being untrusting of the code they had generated rather than considering other factors at play. The implications of the impacts from the current design leads to the potential aggravation of difficulties already faced by students with ADHD. The findings around the interaction of self-confidence and the current design of IDEs would indicate the need for further research in how we can design tools to support this prevalent factor.

5.2 Interaction

The nature of interaction was a prevalent theme throughout the study. The various preferences and feelings regarding aspects of the design and use of the IDE appeared in both the think aloud exercise and the interview. A common occurrence was participants feeling there was too much happening on screen, a phenomenon also observed more generally by Seery et al. [21] for users with ADHD. Understanding the accessibility impact of IDE design is especially important due to the negative impact that can be had on disabled people's ability to engage when technology is not equally usable for them [22].

Adaptability and being able to personalise the interaction were major factors. This falls in line with the work of Kasatskii et al. [12] who discuss the importance of control over perceptual load for individual software engineers. Making it easier for students to influence their interaction with the IDE could improve their overall learning experience.

5.3 Learning

The theme of learning was evident through students' varied approaches to solving a coding problem, including how and to what extent prior experience was utilised. This theme interacted heavily with the themes of self-confidence and interaction, which has been documented in other literature. Di Lonardo Burr & LeFevre for example, discuss the impact of self-confidence on learning [7] and highlight the importance of trying to mitigate detrimental factors to self-confidence by creating a positive learning environment.

How participants approach the learning aspect of problem solving was closely linked to how they used the IDE. Some participants were heavily dependent on search tools or trial and error, while others focused on making notes in the comments and using those to "rubber duck" the problem. Some participants also discussed how they might find alterations to the IDE or extra features beneficial towards their approaches to learning.

In the previous theme of interaction, adaptability was identified as a factor which could support accessibility. The learning theme endorses this concept, displaying adaptability as an avenue to better integrate the IDE in students' approaches to learning. The desire of participants to personalise the IDE to their approaches to learning highlights a key consideration for making IDEs digitally accessible, and a positive learning environment.

5.4 Limitations and Opportunities

The primary limitation of this work would be that the sample size for the study conducted is relatively small. While the sample size is somewhat standard for a study of this nature, it still leaves opportunities for future work to build on these findings with larger groups of participants.

Another potential area of development for this work would be comparing the experiences of those with and without ADHD. The reason for this not being included in this study was due to focusing on presenting the experiences of students with ADHD rather than aiming to contrast those experiences against those without, though this would be an important contribution for future work.

6 Conclusion

We set out the following research questions which drove our research:

RQ1. Does the UI design and tools within an IDE have an impact on ease of use for a student with ADHD?
RQ2. What are the experiences of students with ADHD when using an IDE?

Our findings show that the answer to RQ1 would be that yes, the design and tools within an IDE have an impact on students with ADHD. The impact being that layout and usability can be a barrier for the students and impact their ability to complete tasks and build confidence in coding.

Further, we identified various experiences when using an IDE but primarily identified frustration and that students had difficulty making full use of the tool leading to an overall negative experience for the students.

Finally the identified themes provide insight into the user experience of computing students with ADHD and helpful information for those who design digital tools for them. In future work we anticipate building on these findings to guide a design process addressing and understanding the best way to support students with ADHD in their coding education. We believe by using these themes in further participatory research, researchers will be able to understand how to create accessible and usable IDEs for students with ADHD in a learning setting.

Acknowledgements. Thanks to Professor Joe Finney for providing the initial code base for the coding task and George Limbert for assistance in the open coding process.

References

1. Barkley, R.A.: Attention-Deficit Hyperactivity Disorder: A Handbook for Diagnosis and Treatment, 4th edn, paperback The Guilford Press, New York (2018)
2. Birillo, A., et al.: Bridging education and development: ides as interactive learning platforms. In: Proceedings of the 1st ACM/IEEE Workshop on Integrated Development Environments, IDE 2024, pp. 53–58. Association for Computing Machinery, New York (2024). https://doi.org/10.1145/3643796.3648454
3. Bodalski, E.A., Flory, K., Canu, W.H., Willcutt, E.G., Hartung, C.M.: Adhd symptoms and procrastination in college students: the roles of emotion dysregulation and self-esteem. J. Psychopathol. Behav. Assess. **45**(1), 48–57 (2023). https://doi.org/10.1007/s10862-022-09996-2
4. Bowers, V.A., Snyder, H.L.: Concurrent versus retrospective verbal protocol for comparing window usability. In: Proceedings of the Human Factors Society Annual Meeting, vol. 34, pp. 1270–1274. SAGE Publications, Los Angeles (1990). https://journals.sagepub.com/doi/10.1177/154193129003401720
5. Braun, V., Clarke, V.: Toward good practice in thematic analysis: avoiding common problems and be (com) ing a knowing researcher. Int. J. Transgender Health **24**(1), 1–6 (2023). https://www.tandfonline.com/doi/full/10.1080/26895269.2022.2129597
6. Charters, E.: The use of think-aloud methods in qualitative research an introduction to think-aloud methods. Brock Educ. J. **12**(2) (2003). https://journals.library.brocku.ca/brocked/index.php/home/article/view/38
7. Di Lonardo Burr, S.M., LeFevre, J.A.: Confidence is key: unlocking the relations between adhd symptoms and math performance. Learn. Individ. Differ. **77**, 101808 (2020). https://doi.org/10.1016/j.lindif.2019.101808
8. Dillon, B., Thompson, R.: Software development and tool usability. In: 2016 IEEE 24th International Conference on Program Comprehension (ICPC), pp. 1–4 (2016). https://doi.org/10.1109/ICPC.2016.7503730
9. Haegele, J.A., Hodge, S.: Disability discourse: overview and critiques of the medical and social models. Quest **68**(2), 193–206 (2016). https://www.tandfonline.com/doi/full/10.1080/00336297.2016.1143849
10. Halpin, L., Benachour, P., Hall, T., Winter, E., Finney, J.: Example code and materials for an adhd thinkaloud study (2025). https://doi.org/10.5281/zenodo.15640668
11. Higher Education Statistics Agency: Non-continuation: Uk performance indicators (2022). https://www.hesa.ac.uk/data-and-analysis/performance-indicators/non-continuation
12. Kasatskii, V., Sergeyuk, A., Serova, A., Titov, S., Bryksin, T.: The effect of perceptual load on performance within ide in people with adhd symptoms. In: International Conference on Human-Computer Interaction, pp. 122–141. Springer (2023). https://arxiv.org/abs/2302.06376
13. Kirdani-Ryan, M., Ko, A.J.: Neurodivergent legitimacy in computing spaces. ACM Trans. Comput. Educ. **24**(4) (2024). https://doi.org/10.1145/3690651
14. Kline, R.B., Seffah, A.: Evaluation of integrated software development environments: challenges and results from three empirical studies. Int. J. Hum.-Comput. Stud. **63**(6), 607–627 (2005). https://www.sciencedirect.com/science/article/pii/S1071581905001102
15. Kölling, M., Quig, B., Patterson, A., Rosenberg, J.: The bluej system and its pedagogy. Comput. Sci. Educ. **13**(4), 249–268 (2003). https://www.tandfonline.com/doi/abs/10.1076/csed.13.4.249.17496

16. LaToza, T.D., Venolia, G., DeLine, R.: Maintaining mental models: a study of developer work habits. In: Proceedings of the 28th International Conference on Software Engineering, ICSE 2006, pp. 492–501. Association for Computing Machinery, New York (2006). https://doi.org/10.1145/1134285.1134355
17. Leow, T., Li, W.W., Miller, D.J., McDermott, B.: Prevalence of university non-continuation and mental health conditions, and effect of mental health conditions on non-continuation: a systematic review and meta-analysis. J. Mental Health 1–16 (2024). https://www.tandfonline.com/doi/full/10.1080/09638237.2024.2332812
18. Newark, P.E., Elsässer, M., Stieglitz, R.D.: Self-esteem, self-efficacy, and resources in adults with adhd. J. Attention Disorders **20**(3), 279–290 (2016). https://journals.sagepub.com/doi/10.1177/1087054712459561
19. O'Connor, C., Joffe, H.: Intercoder reliability in qualitative research: debates and practical guidelines. Int J Qual Methods **19**, 1609406919899220 (2020). https://doi.org/10.1177/1609406919899220
20. Rutter, L.A., Howard, J., Lakhan, P., Valdez, D., Bollen, J., Lorenzo-Luaces, L.: "I haven't been diagnosed, but I should be"—insight into self-diagnoses of common mental health disorders: cross-sectional study. JMIR Formative Res. **7**(1), e39206 (2023). https://formative.jmir.org/2023/1/e39206/
21. Seery, C., Cochrane, R.H., Mulcahy, M., Kilbride, K., Wrigley, M., Bramham, J.: "A one-stop shop": real-world use and app-users' experiences of a psychoeducational smartphone app for adults with adhd. Internet Interventions 100807 (2025). https://pubmed.ncbi.nlm.nih.gov/39996148/
22. Shaheen, N.L., Lohnes Watulak, S.: Bringing disability into the discussion: examining technology accessibility as an equity concern in the field of instructional technology. J. Res. Technol. Educ. **51**(2), 187–201 (2019). https://www.tandfonline.com/doi/full/10.1080/15391523.2019.1566037
23. Spiel, K., Hornecker, E., Williams, R.M., Good, J.: Adhd and technology research – investigated by neurodivergent readers. In: Proceedings of the 2022 CHI Conference on Human Factors in Computing Systems, CHI 2022. Association for Computing Machinery, New York (2022). https://doi.org/10.1145/3491102.3517592
24. Valez, M., Yen, M., Le, M., Su, Z., Alipour, M.A.: Student adoption and perceptions of a web integrated development environment: an experience report. In: Proceedings of the 51st ACM Technical Symposium on Computer Science Education, SIGCSE 2020, pp. 1172–1178. Association for Computing Machinery, New York (2020). https://doi.org/10.1145/3328778.3366949

Enhancing Engagement and Social Capital Through an AI-Generated Summary-Driven Learning Design in Online Discussion Forums

Xinyuan Hao(✉) and Mutlu Cukurova

University College London, London, UK
xinyuan.hao.21@ucl.ac.uk

Abstract. Providing discussion summaries and examples has long been recognised as an effective way to enhance learners' online learning activities. Previous research has primarily focused on human-written summaries and examples as well as their impact on students' behaviours. However, recent developments in large language models have demonstrated the potential for generating accurate discussion summaries and example posts at human levels. Despite this, limited research has explored the educational impacts of such AI-generated learning support and how it might affect the social capital students receive from their peers. This paper proposes an AI-generated summary-driven learning design (ASLD) to facilitate peer interactions in online discussion forums. A total of 128 students participated in a design-based research study to examine the influence of the ASLD on students' viewing breadth, temporal changes in viewing activities, and the social capital students gained over 8 weeks. The results indicate that ASLD significantly improves viewing breadth, as well as the overall connectedness of the cohort and individuals' bridging social capital. However, ASLD did not prevent the decrease in viewing activities towards the end of the intervention. The implications of the findings, along with the future directions for research of AI-generated support in online learning environments, are discussed.

Keywords: AI-generated text summarisation · AI-generated learning content · Online discussion forum · Online engagement

1 Introduction

Well-designed online asynchronous discussion forums have long been used to promote online collaborative learning [1]. Previous research has explored strategies to encourage students' engagement in online discussion forums, such as implementing more structured forums [2] and setting up participation deadlines [3]. However, many of these studies primarily targeted encouraging online posting and replying activities [4]. While there is no doubt that expressing ideas in discussions is more valuable than lurking [5], it is important to recognise that the quantity and quality of students' posts and replies are closely linked to the attention they pay to their peers [6]. Learners are more likely to produce high-quality posts and replies with greater critical understanding and innovative

K. Tammets et al. (Eds.): EC-TEL 2025, LNCS 16063, pp. 229–243, 2026.
https://doi.org/10.1007/978-3-032-03870-8_16

arguments if they attend to peers' contributions in depth and breadth [7, 8]. Therefore, providing support to facilitate online viewing activities, while also encouraging students to post and reply more, is vital to creating valuable online dialogues and boosting peer collaboration.

Many scholars advocate asking students to summarise the discussions [9] as a way to motivate both online posting and viewing activities. However, the heavy workload associated with creating a discussion summary might demotivate students in the long term [9]. Recent advancements in artificial intelligence (AI) offer some alternatives. Since large language models (LLMs) such as GPT-4 have demonstrated strong performance in generating academic summaries and argumentation [10], it is worth considering the utilisation of AI to provide summary-driven learning support.

Despite this promising potential, few empirical studies have investigated the educational impact of AI-generated learning support in online discussion forums. To address this gap, this paper proposes an integrated AI-generated summary-driven learning design (ASLD) to promote learners' online engagement in discussion forums and examines the impact of ASLD on online viewing activities and bridging social capital.

2 Theoretical Considerations and Related Work

2.1 Social Capital and Online Interactions

The concept of social capital is frequently mentioned in research on online discussion forums. Social capital refers to the social networks and resources that individuals gain through their memberships and interactions within a community [11]. Online discussion forums, as spaces for groups of students to interact, have the potential to facilitate the building of social capital. There are various types of social capital, in this study, we adopted the category provided by Zhang and Kaufman [12] and focused especially on bridging social capital. Bridging social capital refers to the weak ties between individuals with diverse backgrounds who can bring new perspectives. Although previous research has reported mixed results regarding the relationship between online interactions and students' bridging social capital [13], more recent studies suggest that in blended learning environments, increased online interactions can boost a learner's bridging social capital, which in turn can predict higher-quality contributions [11, 12]. Additionally, as most scholars have focused on online posting and replying as the primary form of interaction, further research into online viewing and bridging social capital is needed.

2.2 The Importance of Online Viewing Activities and the Need for Improved Solutions

Even though many previous studies have considered viewing others' posts as a form of passive engagement, online viewing is in fact a core element of active conversation because it is the prerequisite for creating replies to peers' contributions and learning from them [7]. Scholars who have focused on understanding online viewing behaviours have found that students' viewing activities can predict the quality of their own posts [6]. Moreover, when students pay attention to peers' posts in breadth, they are more likely to achieve better academic performance [14].

Despite these benefits, the common situation in a typical discussion forum is that learners hardly attend to others' posts or interact with them shallowly by skimming randomly [15]. One reason for this low viewing engagement is that locating specific information or obtaining an overview of the discussion from the overwhelming number of ill-named threads on the forum is difficult and time-consuming [16]. Although adding sorting and filtering functions to discussion forums has indeed accelerated the process of searching for relevant information [17, 18], these measures have not helped learners quickly grasp the overview of the discussion or resolve the redundancy issue caused by many posts with similar ideas. Similarly, while a querying function may quickly locate interesting threads, real-world students often do not use accurate and specific queries, making the relevance of the search results and their impacts on supporting viewing activities questionable [19]. Including a post recommendation system might tackle the information overload problem and encourage viewing engagement [20], but it might also risk promoting passive viewing activities and narrow viewing breadth, which are less likely to lead to robust peer interactions. Thus, improved support for online viewing activities shall be implemented in online discussion forums.

2.3 Summary-driven Learning Design for Online Discussion Forums

Given that refining the technical design of asynchronous discussion forums alone might not be enough to facilitate more active online engagement, it is necessary to implement appropriate teaching and learning strategies to support learners. Allowing students to choose their preferred topics could be an approach to boost participation [21], but intrinsic motivation tends to decrease over time, especially when students' academic pressures (e.g. draft assignment or presentation preparation) increase. Hence, this approach might be more effective when combined with other strategies to encourage students in the long term. Some scholars encourage learners to pay more attention to the forum discussions by providing more instructor's inputs, such as feedback and comments. However, this strategy risks promoting teacher-centred discussions and prioritising attention to the instructor's replies over peer interactions [2]. Because learners' viewing breadth is closely associated with the number of peers' posts are available on the forum, encouraging more students to participate in the online discussions earlier can be seen as an indirect way of supporting viewing activities. Woods and Bliss [3] argued that establishing a deadline for participation might motivate students to begin earlier, indirectly encouraging more viewing activities as students have more time to read their peers' contributions. Previous studies also found that if instructors provide some guidelines and examples, more students might participate in discussions [22]. Even though some scholars criticised that instructor-provided examples might set the tone for the discussion [2, 23], it is worth exploring whether including an example from non-experts might influence learners' posting and viewing activities. In general, although the abovementioned strategies can indirectly support learners' online viewing under certain circumstances, more direct encouragement for viewing is needed.

Discussion summary can be an effective approach to support viewing activities directly. An online discussion summary can be provided by the course instructors or generated by students individually or collaboratively. For an instructor-provided summary, scholars [2] reckoned that providing summary at the end of each discussion session is an essential instructional input to help highlight the key points. Although instructor-provided summaries can be helpful, it is demanding for instructors to extract helpful information from the numerous posts, even with the help of forum reporting tools [24]. Thus, some prior research attempted to ask students to summarise the forum posts. Naturally, when performing the summarising role, learners would engage with others' posts more broadly and comprehensively [9]. Promisingly, summaries can be beneficial to enhancing the viewing activities of the students without the summarising role as well [25], as they would help reduce the redundancy issue [18] that usually negatively impacts students' engagement with and benefit from peers' threads. Moreover, student-written summaries might motivate learners without summarising roles to initiate a new round of discussions based on the overall conclusions reached in the summaries [25]. However, it is important to note that summarising is a time-consuming task, it would be impractical and unfair to ask a single student to handle all the work [26]. Yet, when the summarising role is rotated, students' viewing engagement tended to drop after they have been assigned with the role [9]. Thus, while rotating the summarising roles solves the workload problem, it comes at the cost of demotivating students to pay consistent attention to peers' posts in the long term [9]. Nevertheless, if discussion summaries can be produced through some alternative methods as a learning strategy that can support both viewing and posting activities, they have great potential to become an integral part of learning design to support online discussion engagement.

2.4 An ASLD for Online Discussion Forums

Thanks to the recent developments in LLMs, discussion summaries and examples can be generated with AI [10] without burdening students and instructors. Recent studies have demonstrated that ChatGPT's recent models can produce good academic summaries [27]. However, it is essential to note that the majority of prior research has focused on single-authored long documents. Since limited attention has been paid to multi-authored forum discussion threads with high content redundancy and built-in hierarchical relationships [28], more research is needed.

Existing studies have also highlighted the feasibility of AI-generated learning content and support. For instance, Denny et al. [29] compared student-written and AI-generated (Codex model) explanations and resources in terms of correctness, helpfulness, and quality, and they reported no significant difference. Shin et al. [30] also demonstrated that AI is capable of generating helpful feedback for formative assessments. Despite the technical readiness, research examining the educational value of such AI-generated support for online discussions remains scarce [26]. To fill this research gap, this paper reports the results of design-based research evaluating the impact of the ASLD on learners' online viewing activities and bridging social capital. Specifically, we aim to answer the following research questions:

- **RQ1.** To what extent does the proposed ASLD impact learners' viewing breadth in online discussion forums?
- **RQ2.** To what extent does the proposed ASLD impact the temporal changes in learners' viewing activities?
- **RQ3.** To what extent does the proposed ASLD impact learners' bridging social capital gained from viewing activities?

3 Methodology

A design-based research (DBR) methodology [31] was adopted because it allows for iterative development and refinement of interventions in real-world educational settings. Students who enrolled in a 10-week postgraduate-level elective module about designing and deploying technology in educational settings were invited to participate. From Week 2 (W2) to W9 of the module, weekly cohort-level online discussions featuring carefully designed open-ended discussion topics were held to help students gain a deeper understanding of the weekly key concepts[1]. Each week, the online discussion functioned as a pre-class activity, and the in-person lecture began with a short reflection on the key points raised in the discussion. Learners were suggested to create one post and at least two replies every week, with the suggested deadline for finishing the initial post being Tuesday before the in-person lecture. However, the weekly discussion forums were kept open until the end of the academic year so that students could access them at any time. Log data from the learning management system (Moodle) was collected over three years. Students who enrolled in the academic year of 2021–2022 are considered as the baseline group participants (BG, n = 49), those in 2022–2023 form the pilot study group (PSG, n = 40), and those in 2023–2024 are the main study group participants (MSG, n = 39). Approximately 80% of the students came from social science backgrounds, and 75% of them were non-native speakers.

3.1 First Cycle with the BG

In the first cycle of DBR, BG learners received no additional support for their forum discussions. The instructor explained the aims and the expectations of students' forum contributions verbally to the BG group at the beginning of the course.

3.2 Second Cycle with the PSG – A Wizard of Oz (WoZ) Study

A WoZ design was employed in the second cycle of DBR. PSG students were provided with discussion summaries that were made by human researchers but they were told that the summaries were AI-generated. This design was intended to better understand how students might interact with the AI-generated summaries in this specific context [32]. This method helped us to detect potential biases students may have against AI. The same verbal explanation was provided by the same instructor to the PSG students.

The "AI-generated" summaries were written by imitating the way AI does when conducting summarising tasks. The length of the summaries was maintained between 10% to 30% of the original threads, following the recommendation from previous literature [33]. Because topic-based summary was rated as the most popular by students [34], we chose to adopt this design. The summaries were presented in a bullet-point style with embedded links that directed students back to the original threads, including the summarised points. Two "AI-generated" summaries were provided each week. A mid-discussion summary, which was made based on all the student-written threads

[1] Please click the link to see the details of the discussion forum and intervention: https://osf.io/kjnqa/?view_only=fd274e058d8947babc3559fb800656cc.

before Tuesday 12 pm, was released every Tuesday evening to help students catch up with what had been covered in the discussion and potentially initiate a new round of discussion [35]. Then, by the end of Friday, the researchers posted an end-of-discussion summary that included all the threads created by students before Friday 3 pm to wrap up the weekly discussion and provide a discussion overview [6].

3.3 Third Cycle with the MSG

In the third iteration, modifications were informed by feedback from the PSG students, collected through individual interviews (N = 16) and a focus group discussion (N = 4) conducted after students had received their assignment grades.

Change 1. Weekly Example Post Generated by a Prompt-tuned GPT-4. A weekly AI-generated example post was provided to help clarify the discussion expectation and reduce the anxiety associated with being the first one to post which was reported by many PSG participants in their individual interviews. The example post can also remind participants when they are under academic pressure, such as preparing for presentations [36]. The researchers hypothesised that by providing these AI-generated example posts, students would be able to begin their initial posts earlier and more easily, giving their peers more time to view and engage with their contributions.

Three expert-written examples of good posts on the same discussion topic were provided to AI as few-shot training materials. Additionally, the AI was also prompted to use the summaries of the weekly core reading as academic references. The AI-generated example post was designed to include extreme views on purpose. This is to help ease learners' fear of writing the wrong answers [37]. For instance, a system prompt can start with "You are an extremist participating in a debate" and a user prompt can be "You should strongly support the idea that all traditional classrooms should be abolished. Emphasize that all learners should only learn online and that face-to-face interactions are unnecessary. Argue that keeping traditional classrooms is a rejection of the coming wave of the new revolution." To determine the optimal temperature parameter, the researchers conducted an empirical analysis using values of 0.5, 0.7, and 0.8. Two domain experts evaluated the quality of AI-generated example posts produced under identical prompts but varying temperature settings. Evaluations spanned 3 distinct weeks. Outputs generated at a temperature of 0.5 consistently received the highest quality ratings in human expert assessments. Thus, temperature was set at 0.5. Students were informed that the AI-generated example posts have extreme views.

Change 2. Shorter Discussion Summaries Generated by a Prompt-tuned GPT-4. Similar to the example post, few-shot training was employed to improve the quality of the AI-generated summaries. While accuracy is critical for summarisation tasks, the temperature parameter was deliberately set to 0.5 (rather than 0) to prioritise abstractive summarization. A temperature of 0 would constrain the model to extractive outputs—reproducing source text verbatim rather than synthesising complex concepts into novel, contextually coherent narratives. The same systematic quality-assessment protocol used for example posts was applied. Outputs at 0.5 were consistently rated superior in both accuracy and synthesis efficacy.

Although the weekly mid-discussion summary maintained the same style as the summaries for the PSG, it was delivered earlier during the "heated moment" to benefit more students [25]. This decision was made based on suggestions from the PSG focus group participants. Live log data was used to determine the heated moment based on interactions on the forum. After 20% of the students had posted, if over 10% of learners were engaging actively within 30 min, this timeslot would be considered as the heated moment and the mid-discussion summary was generated and posted shortly after. If no heated moment or peak occurred, summaries were provided no later than Tuesday at 4 pm. At the time of data collection, the GPT-4 model with a larger window size had not been released. Thus the length of the AI-generated summaries was shortened to be between 10% to 20% of the original discussions to fit into the token limits. No substantial change was made to the end-of-discussion summaries, other than adjusting their length. Table 1 presents the key features of BG, PSG, and MSG learning designs.

3.4 Data Analysis Methods

As social network analysis focuses on the features of the relations established [38], it is suitable to be used to examine the viewing interaction patterns among students across the three groups. We constructed directed networks for each subset of the viewing log data, where nodes represented students and edges showed the interaction between the nodes. An interaction in this paper is defined as a student viewing others' discussion threads by actively clicking on them within the forum. To answer the first research question about viewing breadth, the analysis focused on out-degree centrality, which indicates the number of connections an individual initiates [38]. Additionally, the density of a network, which represents the ratio of the actual relations made to the number of all possible relations [39], is taken into account. Weekly density trend is also visualised and analysed to investigate the temporal changes of participants' online viewing activities. To understand learners' bridging social capital, out-degree centrality, and betweenness centrality, which shows the extent to which a node serves as the connecting point between others in the network [39], were examined. Recognising that viewing interactions can be reciprocal, in-degree centrality was also included to provide additional context, even though this paper does not address the individual popularity aspect.

Mixed-effects models were used to assess the difference in centrality measures across groups and discussion topics over time. These models accounted for the repeated structure of the data, with random intercepts specified at the student level to account for individual variation. Although the researchers tried to use a model with random slopes for week nested within students, convergence issues appeared due to the sparsity of the data. Because there were many students did not consistently participate in all 8 weeks. Therefore, the researchers opted for a simpler structure (random intercept only), balancing model complexity and stability. To ensure comparability and improve interpretability, all centrality measures were standardised (z-scored) before modelling.

An ordinary least squares (OLS) regression was conducted to investigate changes in network density across groups and over time. To account for attrition and elements not attributable to student behaviour (e.g., AI-generated summaries and example posts), the researchers computed an adjusted network density metric. This adjustment excluded interactions involving these non-student nodes, ensuring that the density reflects only peer-to-peer engagement. This approach helps isolate temporal trends in student interaction from declines in density that may arise due to fewer active participants or AI outputs. While a mixed-effects model was initially considered, it was not used due to the limited number of groups (N = 3), which restricted the ability to model group-level variance robustly.

Table 1. Key Features of the BG, PSG, MSG Learning Designs

	BG	PSG	MSG
Example Post/Guideline	Verbal guideline	Verbal guideline	Verbal guideline + AI-generated example post with an extreme view
Mid-discussion Summary Scope	Not provided	Every student-written thread (created before Tue 12 pm)	Every student-written threads (created by the "heated moment" or Tue 4 pm)
Mid-discussion Summary Provision Time	NA	Every Tue at 7 pm	Every Tuesday shortly after the "heated moment" or before 4 pm
End-of-discussion Summary Scope	Not provided	Every student-written thread (created before Fri 3 pm)	Every student-written threads (created before Fri 5 pm)
End-of-discussion Provision Time	NA	Every Fri before 7 pm	Every Fri before 7 pm
Summary Generation Methods	NA	Human-written	AI-generated
Summary Length	NA	10%-30% of the original text	10%-20% of the original text

4 Results

To contextualise the viewing activity findings, we first looked at students' participation in weekly discussion postings. Since students typically view posts in conjunction with their own contributions, participation patterns can reflect overall engagement. Descriptive statistics revealed that the MSG group maintained relatively consistent on-time participation across most weeks, while PSG showed more fluctuation, particularly in W6 and W7. Significant group differences emerged from W3 onwards. Across all groups, posting activity declined notably over time. For instance, the number of active students in the PSG group dropped from 34 in W2 to just 21 by W9.

4.1 ASLD's Impact on Viewing Breadth

From Table 2, we can observe that, compared to BG, participants in the PSG ($\beta = 0.547$, $p < 0.001$) and MSG ($\beta = 0.438$, $p < 0.001$) exhibited significantly higher standardised out-degree centrality which indicates that they interacted with more peers. And the large effect sizes indicate that both PSG and MSG interventions had large positive effects on out-degree centrality. Additional analyses using PSG as the reference group showed no statistically significant differences between MSG and PSG in out-degree centrality, suggesting that both interventions had similar effects in enhancing students' viewing breadth. Regarding different discussion topics, for the majority of the weeks, no significant difference was observed. However, it is important to note that in W7 and W9, the topic was significantly associated with lower out-degree centrality.

While out-degree centrality is indeed the primary measure for viewing breadth, network density can provide additional context for understanding the differences observed. As presented in Fig. 1, the three groups seem to have quite different network densities in W7 and W9. These results suggest that while the ASLD might boost individuals' viewing breadth, certain topics might have negative impacts on viewing activities.

Table 2. Mixed Linear Model Regression Results of Out-degree Centrality

Predictor	Coefficient	Standard error	z value	p value
Intercept	−0.516	0.136	−3.787	<0.001*
C(Group) [T.PSG]	0.547	0.069	7.972	<0.001*
C(Group) [T.MSG]	0.438	0.071	6.145	<0.001*
C(Topic) [T.W2]	−0.084	0.116	−0.726	0.468
C(Topic) [T.W3]	−0.008	0.166	−0.048	0.962
C(Topic) [T.W4]	−0.102	0.117	−0.872	0.383
C(Topic) [T.W5]	−0.107	0.119	−0.897	0.370
C(Topic) [T.W6]	−0.064	0.119	−0.540	0.589
C(Topic) [T.W7]	−0.291	0.118	−2.469	0.014*
C(Topic) [T.W8]	−0.097	0.119	−0.817	0.414
C(Topic) [T.W9]	−0.251	0.120	−2.089	0.037*

4.2 ASLD's Impact on Temporal Changes of Viewing Activities

The OLS model explained 91.7% of the variance in network density ($R^2 = 0.917$, $p < 0.001$). This high R^2 shows that the combined effects of the different group learning designs and time are strong indicators of the level of network connectivity. As shown in Table 3, both the PSG ($p = 0.006$) and MSG ($p = 0.007$) have significantly higher adjusted network density compared to the BG. In terms of the change over time, for all the groups, density decreased significantly as weeks progressed. However, the rate of decline in density was significantly slower in the PSG. Interestingly, no significant difference was observed for MSG. As a robustness check, we also ran an OLS regression using raw density (including AI-generated summaries and example posts). This time, only MSG ($p = 0.045$) shows significantly higher density than BG. No significant interaction with time was found for either PSG ($p = 0.142$) or MSG ($p = 0.094$), indicating that neither intervention significantly altered the trajectory of density decline.

Table 3. Ordinary Least Squares Regression Results of Adjusted Density

Predictor	Coefficient	Standard error	t	p value
Intercept	0.3959	0.044	9.002	<0.001*
C(Group) [T.PSG]	0.1595	0.051	3.128	0.006*
C(Group) [T.MSG]	0.1322	0.043	3.096	0.007*
Week_Num	−0.0205	0.007	−2.923	0.009*
C(Group) [T.PSG]:Week_Num	−0.0180	0.008	−2.252	0.038*
C(Group) [T.MSG]:Week_Num	−0.0132	0.008	−1.660	0.115
Num_Posters_z	−0.0571	0.021	−2.734	0.014*

4.3 ASLD's Impact on Bridging Social Capital

In addition to out-degree centrality, betweenness centrality is another measure related to an individual's bridging social capital. Table 4 shows that compared to the students in BG, participants in both PSG ($p = 0.024$) and MSG ($p = 0.001$) obtained significantly lower betweenness centrality. Topics did not appear to have any significant impact on learners' betweenness centrality. Additional analyses using PSG as the reference group showed no statistically significant differences between MSG and PSG in betweenness centrality, indicating comparable levels of network position across both groups.

When examining in-degree centrality, the results also show that PSG ($p < 0.001$) and MSG ($p = 0.008$) students exhibited significantly higher in-degree centrality than BG participants. By combining the results of out-degree, betweenness, and in-degree centrality, it is sensible to argue that ASLD might influence students' bridging social capital but its impact might not be strong enough to help learners achieve a central position.

Table 4. Mixed Linear Model Regression Results of Betweenness Centrality

Predictor	Coefficient	Standard error	z value	p value
Intercept	0.013	0.118	0.109	0.913
C(Group) [T.PSG]	−0.175	0.077	−2.261	0.024*
C(Group) [T.MSG]	−0.277	0.080	−3.458	0.001*

(continued)

Table 4. (*continued*)

Predictor	Coefficient	Standard error	z value	p value
C(Topic) [T.W2]	−0.046	0.135	−0.345	0.730
C(Topic) [T.W3]	0.010	0.192	0.051	0.960
C(Topic) [T.W4]	0.079	0.137	0.577	0.564
C(Topic) [T.W5]	0.177	0.138	1.282	0.200
C(Topic) [T.W6]	0.160	0.139	1.158	0.247
C(Topic) [T.W7]	0.094	0.137	0.689	0.491
C(Topic) [T.W8]	0.145	0.138	1.056	0.291
C(Topic) [T.W9]	0.223	0.139	1.600	0.110

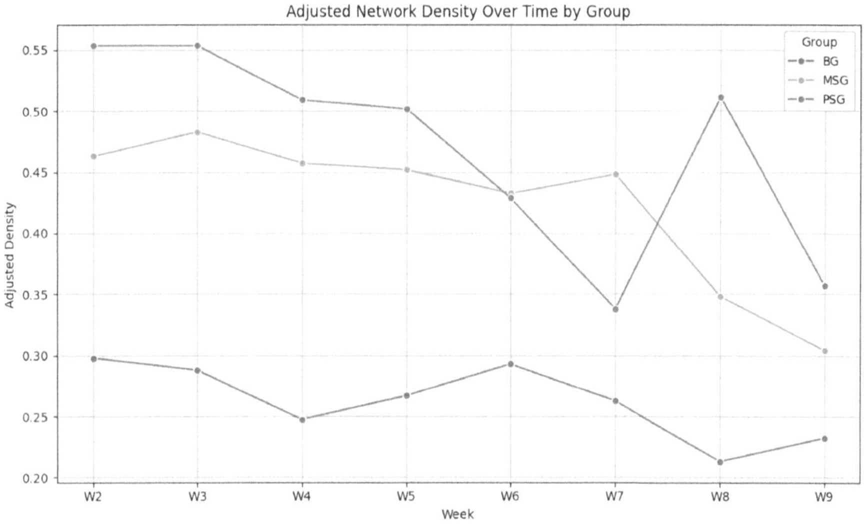

Fig. 1. Three Groups' Adjusted Network Density Trend Over Time

5 Discussion

Regarding the first research question concerning the impact of ASLD on participants' viewing breadth, our findings align with previous literature, which highlights that providing a discussion summary can enhance viewing interactions, especially in terms of breadth [9]. However, as most scholars have exclusively focused on human-written discussion summaries [8, 9], this study makes an important contribution by demonstrating that AI-generated discussion summaries can also facilitate broader viewing. Moreover, further analysis using PSG as the reference group revealed no significant difference in out-degree centrality between PSG and MSG. This indicates that the AI-generated summaries in MSG, when released during the heated moments, can be equally effective in fostering broader viewing behaviours as the human-written summaries framed as AI-generated in PSG. This finding is particularly notable as it suggests that AI summaries can serve as a viable alternative to human-written ones in motivating students to engage more broadly with peers' forum contributions.

Interestingly, we found that the discussion topic might mediate the impact of ASLD on viewing. W7's discussion topic was particularly relatable to students' past experiences. Thus, the significant difference observed in W7 might indicate that, with the support of summaries, when students encounter a familiar topic, they might choose to pay less attention to peers' contributions. Although previous literature on encouraging online posting and replying activities often suggests that choosing familiar topics facilitates more interaction [40], our finding contrasts with this view and highlights that while familiarity might encourage initial posting, it does not necessarily translate into a broader exploration of peers' contributions.

In terms of the second research question, our findings suggest that ASLD can facilitate increased viewing activities and help form a more connected network overall. However, while ASLD appears to enhance network density early in the intervention, it did not prevent the viewing engagement drop in the later weeks.

Notably, when adjusting for network density, the rate of decline in viewing activity was slower for PSG group compared to both the MSG and BG. This suggests that the PSG intervention might have had a more sustained impact on fostering engagement throughout the course. In contrast, when examining the unadjusted density, no significant differences were observed between PSG and MSG, which could imply that MSG students may have paid more attention to the AI-generated summaries and example posts. As the weeks progressed, MSG students might have shifted their attention more towards the summaries as an efficient overview of the discussion, rather than engaging in more individual post interactions. This shift could be due to increased academic pressure towards the end of the semester, with students choosing to focus on summarising content rather than engaging with every post in detail. If this is the case, it could suggest that the decline in density is not necessarily a negative outcome. It might reflect a more targeted way of engaging with the discussions. However, this remains speculative, and further qualitative insights, such as student interviews, would be needed to fully understand the underlying causes. Additionally, it is important to note that students' participation in online discussion forums tends to decrease over time [41], which might need more significant interventions than the one proposed in this paper. Since viewing is closely related to posting and replying activities, the decrease in active participation may inevitably result in a drop in viewing engagement as well. Further analysis, such as Simulation Investigation for Empirical Network Analysis, is needed to understand the evolution of the network while considering the influence of individual behaviours [42].

The third research question examines the influence of ASLD on individuals' bridging social capital. Because ASLD can indeed help broaden viewing breadth, it shows the potential in increasing bridging social capital. However, the impact of ASLD might not be sufficient to enhance students' central positions within the network. This finding should be interpreted with caution, as lower betweenness centrality might not necessarily be negative. Some scholars have pointed out the potential negative impact of having a few "superposters" who dominate the discussion [43]. In that case, a well-connected but not overly centralised network might be the ideal structure for this research context. However, further analysis of the bonding social capital is needed.

6 Conclusion and Future Directions

This paper proposes an AI-generated summary-driven learning design (ASLD) approach to encourage more peer viewing in online discussion forums. The results suggest that ASLD significantly affects students' viewing breadth, the overall connectedness of the cohort, and individuals' bridging social capital. However, ASLD did not prevent the decrease in viewing activity toward the end of the intervention. These initial insights highlight the potential of LLMs to be integrated into online learning design to improve the learning experience and outcomes of students engaged in online discussion activities. It also highlights the limitations in addressing some of the challenges such as the engagement drop towards the end. If ASLD is adopted, it should be complemented with additional socio-pedagogical strategies to sustain online engagement over time.

Researchers should replicate this research in other disciplines to see whether participants' openness to technology impacts their engagement Although the focus of this work was on bridging social capital, future work should also examine the influence of ASLD on other theoretical considerations (e.g. the quality of viewing activities).

Disclosure of Interests. The authors have no competing interests to declare that are relevant to the content of this article.

References

1. Xu, B., Chen, N.-S., Chen, G.: Effects of teacher role on student engagement in WeChat-based online discussion learning. Comput. Educ. **157**, 103956 (2020)
2. Xie, J., Correia, A.-P.: The effects of instructor participation in asynchronous online discussions on student performance: a systematic review. Br. J. Edu. Technol. **55**, 71–89 (2024). https://doi.org/10.1111/bjet.13350
3. Woods, K., Bliss, K.: Facilitating successful online discussions. J. Effect. Teach. **16**, 76–92 (2016)
4. Salter, N.P., Conneely, M.R.: Structured and unstructured discussion forums as tools for student engagement. Comput. Hum. Behav. **46**, 18–25 (2015)
5. Laurillard, D.: Teaching as a Design Science: Building Pedagogical Patterns for Learning and Technology. Routledge, New York (2013). https://doi.org/10.4324/9780203125083
6. Wise, A.F., Hausknecht, S.N., Zhao, Y.: Attending to others' posts in asynchronous discussions: learners' online "listening" and its relationship to speaking. Intern. J. Comput.-Support. Collab. Learn. **9**, 185–209 (2014). https://doi.org/10.1007/s11412-014-9192-9
7. Wise, A., Marbouti, F., Speer, J., Hsiao, Y.-T.: Towards an understanding of "listening" in online discussions: a cluster analysis of learners' interaction patterns. In: Proceedings of International Conference on Computer Supported Learning, pp. 88–95. China (2011)
8. Peterson, A.T., Roseth, C.J.: Effects of four CSCL strategies for enhancing online discussion forums: Social interdependence, summarizing, scripts, and synchronicity. Int. J. Educ. Res. **76**, 147–161 (2016)

9. Wise, A.F., Chiu, M.M.: The impact of rotating summarizing roles in online discussions: effects on learners' listening behaviors during and subsequent to role assignment. Comput. Hum. Behav. **38**, 261–271 (2014). https://doi.org/10.1016/j.chb.2014.05.033
10. Liu, Y., et al.: Summary of ChatGPT-related research and perspective towards the future of large language models. Meta-Radiol. **1**, 100017 (2023). https://doi.org/10.1016/j.metrad.2023.100017
11. Diep, N.A., Cocquyt, C., Zhu, C., Vanwing, T., de Greef, M.: Effects of core self-evaluation and online interaction quality on adults' learning performance and bonding and bridging social capital. Internet High. Educ. **34**, 41–55 (2017)
12. Zhang, F., Kaufman, D.: The impacts of social interactions in MMORPGs on older adults' social capital. Comput. Hum. Behav. **51**, 495–503 (2015)
13. Williams, D.: On and off the 'Net: scales for social capital in an online era. J. Comput.-Mediat. Commun. **11**, 593–628 (2006)
14. Chiu, T.K.F., Hew, T.K.F.: Factors influencing peer learning and performance in MOOC asynchronous online discussion forum. Australas. J. Educ. Technol. **34** (2018). https://doi.org/10.14742/ajet.3240
15. Wise, A., Hsiao, Y.-T., Marbouti, F., Speer, J., Perera, N.: Initial validation of "listening" behavior typologies for online discussions using microanalytic case studies. In: 10th International Conference of the Learning Sciences. Proceedings, vol. 1 (2012)
16. Tarnpradab, S., Liu, F., Hua, K.: Toward extractive summarization of online forum discussions via hierarchical attention networks. In: Proceedings of the Thirtieth International Florida Artificial Intelligence Research Society Conference, pp. 288–292 (2018)
17. Wang, P.-Y., Yang, H.-C.: Using collaborative filtering to support college students' use of online forum for English learning. Comput. Educ. **59**, 628–637 (2012)
18. Zhang, A.X., Verou, L., Karger, D.: Wikum: Bridging discussion forums and wikis using recursive summarization. In: Proceedings of the 2017 ACM Conference on Computer Supported Cooperative Work and Social Computing, pp. 2082–2096. ACM, USA (2017)
19. Verberne, S., Krahmer, E., Wubben, S., van den Bosch, A.: Query-based summarization of discussion threads. Nat. Lang. Eng. **26**, 3–29 (2020)
20. Irish, I., Chatterjee, S., Tailor, C., Finkelberg, R., Arriaga, R., Starner, T.: Post recommendation system impact on student participation and performance in an online AI graduate course. In: Proceedings of the Ninth ACM Conference on Learning @ Scale, pp. 24–34. USA (2022)
21. Chan, K., Lai, S., Leung, H., Wan, K.: Engagement in online asynchronous discussions: roles of students' interests and preferences. In: International Conference on e-Learning, pp. 32–36 (2016)
22. Aderibigbe, S.A.: Online discussions as an intervention for strengthening students' engagement in general education. J. Open Innov. Technol. Market Complex. **6**, 98 (2020). https://doi.org/10.3390/joitmc6040098
23. Zhao, H., Sullivan, K.P.H.: Teaching presence in computer conferencing learning environments: effects on interaction, cognition and learning uptake. Br. J. Edu. Technol. **48**, 538–551 (2017). https://doi.org/10.1111/bjet.12383
24. Carbonaro, A.: Towards an automatic forum summarization to support tutoring. In: Technology Enhanced Learning. Quality of Teaching and Educational Reform, pp. 141–147 (2010). https://doi.org/10.1007/978-3-642-13166-0_21
25. Wise, A., Chiu, M.M.: Analyzing temporal patterns of knowledge construction in a role-based online discussion. Comput. Support. Learn. **6**, 445–470 (2011)
26. Hao, X., Cukurova, M.: Exploring the effects of "AI-Generated" discussion summaries on learners' engagement in online discussions. In: Wang, N., Rebolledo-Mendez, G., Dimitrova, V., Matsuda, N., and Santos, O.C. (eds.) Artificial Intelligence in Education. Posters and Late Breaking Results, Workshops and Tutorials, Industry and Innovation Tracks, Practitioners, Doctoral Consortium and Blue Sky, pp. 155–161. Springer, Cham (2023)

27. Chen, Y., Eger, S.: Transformers go for the LOLs: generating (Humourous) titles from scientific abstracts end-to-end. In: Deutsch, D., et al. (eds.) Proceedings of the 4th Workshop on Evaluation and Comparison of NLP Systems, pp. 62–84. ACL, Indonesia (2023)
28. Ma, C., Zhang, W.E., Guo, M., Wang, H., Sheng, Q.Z.: Multi-document Summarization via deep learning techniques: a survey. ACM Comput. Surv. **55**, 102:1–102:37 (2022)
29. Denny, P., Khosravi, H., Hellas, A., Leinonen, J., Sarsa, S.: Can we trust AI-generated educational content? Comparative analysis of human and AI-generated learning resources (2023). http://arxiv.org/abs/2306.10509
30. Shin, I., Hwang, S.B., Yoo, Y.J., Bae, S., Kim, R.Y.: Comparing student preferences for AI-generated and peer-generated feedback in AI-driven formative peer assessment. In: Proceedings of the 15th International Learning Analytics and Knowledge Conference, pp. 159–169. ACM, USA (2025)
31. Philippakos, Z.A., Howell, E., Pellegrino, A.: Design-Based Research in Education: Theory and Applications. Guilford Press (2021)
32. Riek, L.D.: Wizard of Oz studies in HRI: a systematic review and new reporting guidelines. J. Hum.-Robot Interact. **1**, 119–136 (2012). https://doi.org/10.5898/JHRI.1.1.Riek
33. Botarleanu, R.-M., Dascalu, M., Allen, L.K., Crossley, S.A., McNamara, D.S.: Multitask summary scoring with Longformers. In: Rodrigo, M.M., Matsuda, N., Cristea, A.I., and Dimitrova, V. (eds.) Artificial Intelligence in Education, pp. 756–761. Springer, (2022)
34. Uddin, G., Baysal, O., Guerrouj, L., Khomh, F.: Understanding how and why developers seek and analyze API-related opinions. IEEE Trans. Software Eng. **47**, 694–735 (2021). https://doi.org/10.1109/TSE.2019.2903039
35. Wise, A.F., Chiu, M.M.: Statistical discourse analysis of a role-based online discussion forum: patterns of knowledge construction. In: 2012 45th Hawaii International Conference on System Sciences, pp. 3378–3386 (2012). https://doi.org/10.1109/HICSS.2012.546
36. Wandler, J., Imbriale, W.J.: Promoting college student self-regulation in online learning environments. OLJ. **21**, (2017). https://doi.org/10.24059/olj.v21i2.881
37. Symeonides, R., Childs, C.: The personal experience of online learning: An interpretative phenomenological analysis. Comput. Hum. Behav. **51**, 539–545 (2015)
38. Carceller, C., Dawson, S., Lockyer, L.: Social capital from online discussion forums: differences between online and blended modes of delivery. Australas. J. Educ. Technol. **31** (2015). https://doi.org/10.14742/ajet.1448
39. Ouyang, F., Scharber, C.: The influences of an experienced instructor's discussion design and facilitation on an online learning community development: a social network analysis study. Internet High. Educ. **35**, 34–47 (2017)
40. Dennen, V.P.: From message posting to learning dialogues: factors affecting learner participation in asynchronous discussion. Distance Educ. **26**, 127–148 (2005)
41. Giesbers, B., Rienties, B., Tempelaar, D., Gijselaers, W.: A dynamic analysis of the interplay between asynchronous and synchronous communication in online learning: the impact of motivation. J. Comput. Assist. Learn. **30**, 30–50 (2014)
42. Xiang, M., Zhang, J., Saqr, M., Jiang, H., Liu, W.: Capturing the temporal dynamics of learner interactions in moocs: a comprehensive approach with longitudinal and inferential network analysis. In: Proceedings of the 15th International Learning Analytics and Knowledge Conference, pp. 851–857. ACM, USA (2025)
43. Hew, K.F., Cheung, W.S., Ng, C.S.L.: Student contribution in asynchronous online discussion: a review of the research and empirical exploration. Instr. Sci. **38**, 571–606 (2010)

Prompt vs. Supervise: A Case of Using Language Models to Assess Students' Science Explanations

Shamya Karumbaiah[1(✉)], Ananya Ganesh[2], Shanglin Yang[1], and Nora Tseng[1]

[1] University of Wisconsin-Madison, Madison, WI 53706, USA
{shamya.karumbaiah,syang662,ntseng}@wisc.edu
[2] University of Colorado Boulder, Boulder, CO 80309, USA
ananya.ganesh@colorado.edu

Abstract. General-purpose Language Models (LMs) open up new possibilities for automated assessment through simple textual prompts and little to no supervised data. However, there are significant tradeoffs in using prompt-based approaches compared to predictive modeling (e.g., flexibility in model training v. limitations with model evaluation). With a case study assessing middle school students' written science explanations, we empirically investigate the differences in prompting LMs versus using annotated data to train supervised models. Our results across six scientific concepts show that finetuning LMs with supervised data leads to notable improvements model performance. The best performing model across all the content units was the fully supervised RoBERTa finetuned models, with AUCs above 0.90 in most cases. With access to only a few examples, the Llama 3 few-shot models with no supervision also perform consistently well with AUCs above 0.77. However, it is unclear if the flexibility in task redefinition without annotated data and model training outweighs the drop in performance. We conclude by presenting a discussion on these design tradeoffs.

Keywords: Language models · Prompting · Finetuning · Assessment · Science explanations

1 Introduction

Student work such as math solutions [5], science essays [8], and short answers [17] is often assessed to infer where the student is in their learning. In most cases, such inference is formative i.e., assessment for supporting student learning by adapting instructions, providing feedback for revision, or identifying noteworthy ideas in their thinking to build on [8]. Predictive models have been powerful in automating the often laborious task of continuous assessment, especially in real-world classrooms where teachers' time could be freed up to focus on students who need them the most [15].

K. Tammets et al. (Eds.): EC-TEL 2025, LNCS 16063, pp. 244–258, 2026.
https://doi.org/10.1007/978-3-032-03870-8_17

Supervised learning has traditionally been the popular approach in machine learning to build predictive models for automated assessment. Here, supervision refers to expert knowledge embedded in the data used to train a predictive model (e.g., pairs of student responses and human assessment). The annotated dataset needs to be large and diverse enough to learn a reliable model.

In contrast, general-purpose Language Models (LMs) bypass the need for supervised data and training by allowing textual prompts to specify a downstream task such as assessment in a format familiar to LMs from their training [18]. For example, we can assess a student's response, "Energy can't be created or destroyed" by prompting the LM to fill in the blank in a continuing sentence "This explanation is ___" with an evaluative adjective (e.g., correct, incorrect). Instead of using supervised data, general-purpose LMs are trained on large datasets to learn general-purpose features of the language it is modeling.

Such enticing prospects often come with significant tradeoffs. For instance, when neural network models were introduced in education for their ability to learn latent features on their own, we had to assess the tradeoff in the loss of interpretability and explainability as compared to expert-engineered features [14]. Now, as we embrace advances in language modeling for automated assessment with little to no supervised data and training, we need to similarly assess the tradeoffs between prompting and supervised learning. In other words, when taking advantage of general-purpose LMs, should we use it as-is with prompting or still consider collecting annotated data for supervised training?

Hence, in this paper, we evaluate the affordances and constraints of prompting and supervised training of LMs in the automated assessment of students' scientific explanations from their inquiry-based learning of energy concepts. We empirically examine the performance of two pre-trained LMs: 1) Llama 3, a popular open-source LM that can be prompted to perform classification, and 2) RoBERTa, an LM that can be extended architecturally to perform text classification with supervised data. By investigating how prompt-based classification with Llama 3 without supervised training compares to a supervised classifier with RoBERTa, we ask the following research question: *How effective are general-purpose LMs in assessing students' inquiry-based learning of scientific explanations with and without supervised data?*

2 Learning Context

2.1 Inquiry-Based Learning Of Scientific Explanations

Research has identified that engaging students in inquiry-based investigations where they deeply explore phenomena by asking questions, collecting and analyzing data, and identifying and using evidence to support explanations can enhance students' understanding of science [23]. These kinds of investigations, where students explore the cause and effect mechanisms of phenomena to write scientific explanations using appropriate evidence to convince others of an explanation's merit are core aspects of engaging in the scientific enterprise [3]. Helping students engage in core science practices, such as constructing explanations, is essential for helping them learn about and understand science. The construction of scientific explanations from this perspective highlights that "writing provides members of a community with a tool for learning that can be used in a goal-directed fashion to foster thinking, meaning-making, and action" [9]. Thus, when students construct and justify scientific explanations, they are required to think deeply about scientific ideas and evidence as well as engage in multiple science practices, such as planning and carrying out investigations and analyzing and interpreting data; this helps them not only learn about science ideas and relationships but also about how scientific knowledge is constructed and how to justify their ideas [20].

2.2 The Virtual Learning Environment

We created a design-based roller coaster unit to help students learn about motion, forces, and energy. Each student was provided with a paper and pencil scientist's journal, which provided them with instructions and prompts to support their inquiries and learning about how, for example, changing the height of the roller coaster or mass of the roller coaster car would affect the amount of energy and speed the roller coaster car would have for the ride. One of the features of our virtual learning environment is called CoMPASS (Fig. 1; left); it is an e-textbook with navigable concept maps where students read about important science ideas and relationships to learn background information to help them make hypotheses and set up their experiments. Throughout the unit, students conducted their investigations using an online roller coaster simulation (Fig. 1; right) where they performed experiments and collected data, which they could use as evidence in their scientific explanations for their final roller coaster designs.

2.3 Research Design

The roller coaster curriculum is a design-based unit where students are challenged to work in teams of three to four students to design a fun and safe roller coaster for an amusement park that has experienced a reduction in attendance. The unit occurred over approximately 12 weeks (50 min per day) as a part of a regular science class. We engaged students in multiple activities during the unit to help them learn about the physics of roller coasters and write a final essay that explained their roller coaster design. Students took a pretest, were introduced to the roller coaster challenge, conducted background research, and conducted multiple simulated experiments using the roller coaster simulation before writing their final design essay. The final design essay required students to explain their roller coaster design based on the physics of roller coasters, using data to justify their ideas. We gave students the following instructions for writing their design essays after completing their investigations: "Explain the science behind why your team's current roller coaster design will be exciting and make it to the end of the ride without stopping. Include data from your trials to justify your ideas. Make sure you write in clear and complete sentences". The teachers introduced the writing activity and provided students with prompts about: a) general tips for writing clear and concise essays and b) the science relationships they should include in their essays. Students were asked to revised their essays after receiving feedback.

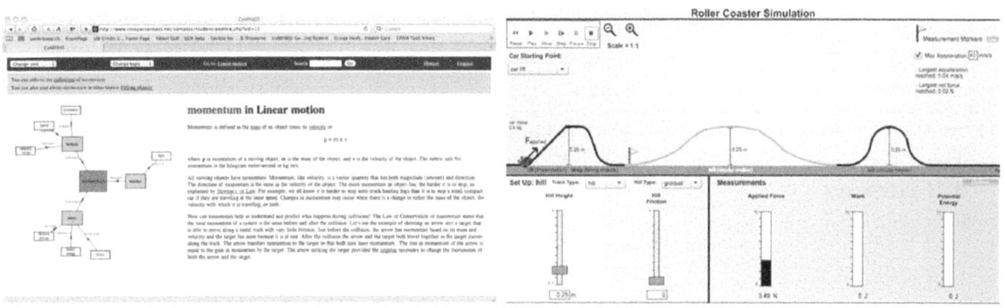

Fig. 1. (left) Screenshot of CoMPASS showing text students can read as well as concept maps that show how concepts are related. (right) Screenshot of roller coaster simulation showing inputs and outputs from one trial in an experiment.

3 Data

3.1 Participants

This study involved three 8th-grade science teachers and 238 students who gave their consent to participate, from two semi-rural public-school districts in the Midwest region of the United States. Teacher 1 taught 96 students in one district, while Teachers 2 and 3 worked in another district, instructing 80 and 62 students, respectively. Both schools served 7th and 8th graders, with a predominantly white student population (around 80–85% white). All middle school students took science classes, including those with disabilities and those who were non-native English speakers. The students in each class demonstrated a wide range of academic abilities and writing skills. Among the 238 students, only 175 students submitted both the initial and revised essays, giving us a total of 350 essays to analyze.

3.2 Human Annotation

In this paper, we are interested in identifying six highly weighted ideas or content units (CUs) that students should have learned and explained in their essays during the roller coaster unit. Descriptions and examples of each CU can be found in Table 1. Two coders independently read and coded 10% of the essays. The first coder is a domain expert who was a science teacher for a decade and is currently a science education researcher. The second coder is an undergraduate student, who was trained by the first coder. To ensure consistency between

Table 1. Illustrative Examples of Conservation of Energy Concepts

CU#	Description	Illustrative Examples
CU0	The greater the height the greater the PE	"This is because the more height an object has, the more potential energy it has" "height and Energy are directly related. In other words, when the drop height is greater the total energy will be greater" "When I decreased the height to 4 m the PE deceased to 1564 J"
CU1	as the car moves down the track the PE decreases as the KE increases	"As the car goes down the track the PE transforms its energy into KE. It always starts with all PE but at the bottom, the PE transforms all its energy into KE" "PE and KE are inversely related. This means that as PE goes up, KE goes down" "As the car goes down the initial drop, the potential energy decreases while the kinetic energy increases, causing the roller coaster to move"
CU2	Total energy remains the same. PE and KE at any point on the track adds up to the total energy	"The total energy that we have at the top of the hill is the same through out the entire ride, it never changes" "TE is always the same as the starting PE, and it doesn't change either at the end of the ride. The TE is always the amount of KE and PE when there's no friction" "The total energy will never change during this time"
CU3	The Law of Conservation of Energy States that energy cannot be created or destroyed, only transformed	"The law of Conservation of Energy says that energy is not created nor destroyed but can transfer between energy types, when we lose energy to friction the energy transfers to non useful energy" "This is because the Law of Conservation of Energy states that energy cannot be created or destroyed. Instead it is just transferred between energy"
CU4	Hill should be lower than the initial drop	"The hill height cannot be higher than the drop height" "We wanted to have the highest possible drop height because, to make it all the way, your hills and loops have to be smaller" "When the hill height was the same as the car made it over the hill but when the height was increased to 5 m the car could not make it over the hill"
CU5	Greater mass equals greater (any kind of) energy	"Lastly when it comes to mass the greater the mass the greater the PE and KE" "the more mass an object has, the more PE it has" "The more mass, the more total energy for the cart to use" "The cart will also have more TE if it is heavier"

coders, Cohen's Kappa statistic was calculated, revealing substantial agreement (Kappa = .768) (Stemler, 2001). Any discrepancies between coders were resolved through discussion, after which one of the authors coded the remaining data, highlighting the sentence in each essay that corresponds to a given CU.

3.3 Data Curation

Using the highlights provided by the coders, we extract individual sentences in each essay that contain an acceptable definition for a given CU, yielding a dataset of 200 *acceptable* definitions alone for each CU. From the remaining sentences in all essays, we sampled 800 sentences to serve as *unacceptable* definitions in our classification dataset. Since many of the unrelated sentences across essays may be repetitive, we ensured that the sampled sentences were unique using an additional clustering step: we first computed a vector representation of each sentence using the BERT model [6], and then used the k-means algorithm to cluster all the sentence representations by similarity. This results in k clusters (where k $\leq$ 10) such that all the sentences within a cluster are highly similar to each other. We then sampled sentences from each cluster to maximize the diversity of *unacceptable* sentences. We thus have a dataset of 1000 sentences for each CU, where the ratio of acceptable to unacceptable sentences is 20:80.

Given the small size of the dataset, we perform 5-fold cross-validation to train and evaluate our models. The same 5 folds are used in all our subsequent experiments across all models.

4 Models

4.1 Prompting

The prominent paradigm for interacting with LLMs is the mechanism of prompting, where a user can construct a textual input describing a request or instruction for the LLM, such as a question for which an answer needs to be provided. The LLM then generates a textual response conditioned on the input. While their ability to generate plausible text has led to their wide adoption as response generation tools [21,28], they can also be prompted to solve classification tasks. The prompt must contain an instruction describing the classification task, the input text to be classified, and the desired output, i.e., the labels that the model is required to output. We experiment with two prompting techniques, namely zero and few shot prompting. We first describe Llama 3, the LLM that we use for all our experiments, and then discuss the details of our prompting strategies.

Model: For all our prompting experiments, we use the Llama 3 open source model with 8 billion parameters (*Meta-Llama-3-8B-Instruct*) from Meta AI [10]. Its architecture is based on the Transformer model [26], and it has been pre-trained on a multilingual corpus of 15 trillion tokens. Improvements from its predecessor include: pre-training and finetuning on significantly more data, and the additional use of RLHF (Reinforcement Learning with Human Feedback) to align model behavior with human instruction using reward function of safety and helpfulness. This process, known as instruction tuning, improves the skills of the Llama model at downstream tasks such as reasoning or question answering, and thus makes it suitable for our purposes as well, i.e., for identifying whether a concept unit is defined correctly in student statements. The Llama 3 model is considered a state-of-the-art model and outperforms contemporaneous models such as Gemma [1] and Mistral [13] on benchmarks measuring a wide range of reasoning skills [4,11]. Moreover, we choose the Llama 3 model over closed-source variants such as GPT-4 because they can be run locally on GPUs, which i) prevents the need to share sensitive student data with the servers where the models are hosted ii) saves on cost, since the closed-source models charge for usage based on the number of tokens in the input and output.

Experimental Setup: We use the 8 billion parameter of Llama 3 which we run on a single Nvidia A40 GPU. As the inherent stochasticity of the language modeling process can lead to inconsistent outputs, we perform three different runs with each prompt, and select the prediction that is generated a majority of the times: i.e., if on prompting the model three times, the outputs were *acceptable, unacceptable, unacceptable*, we record the final output as *unacceptable.*

Zero-Shot Prompting: We prompt the model to classify a given sentence by providing the definition of the relevant concept unit as described in the grading rubric. An example prompt for CU0 is:

Does the following sentence contain the physics concept:
'Greater height means greater Potential Energy.'
If yes, return acceptable. Otherwise, return unacceptable:

Each sentence in the dataset is then appended to this prompt before querying the model. The model then outputs either the label "Acceptable" or the label "Unacceptable".

Few-Shot Prompting: The few-shot prompting approach additionally includes a few examples in the prompt, intended to guide the model to perform the task more effectively. We include one example that is considered acceptable, and one that is considered unacceptable. An example of the prompt for CU0 is:

Task: Check if the Answer describes the given Concept.
1. Concept: What is the key idea you are looking for.
2. Answer: Does the answer mention or relate to the concept?
3. Classification: Acceptable: if the answer contains or clearly relates to the concept. Unacceptable: If the concept is missing or referenced wrong.

Example 1: Concept: Greater Height means greater Potential energy. Answer: The more mass an object has, the more Potential Energy it has. Decision: Unacceptable

Example 2: Concept: Greater Height means greater Potential energy. Answer: The total energy will never change. Decision: Unacceptable

Chain-of-Thought Prompting: The chain-of-thought prompting approach additionally includes a few examples of reasoning in the prompt, intended to guide the model to reason as it performs the task more effectively. We include one example that is considered acceptable, and one that is considered unacceptable. An example of the prompt for CU0 is:

Task: Check if the Answer describes the given Concept.
1. Concept: What is the key idea you are looking for.
2. Answer: Does the answer mention or relate to the concept?
3. Classification: Acceptable: if the answer contains or clearly relates to the concept. Unacceptable: If the concept is missing or referenced wrong. Explain your reasoning first, then make your decision.

Example 1: Concept: Greater Height means greater Potential energy. Answer: This is because the more height an object has, the more potential energy it has. Explanation: The student correctly links height with potential energy, reflecting the core idea of gravitational potential energy. Decision: Acceptable

Example 2: Concept: Greater Height means greater Potential energy. Answer: The total energy will never change. Explanation: The response mentions energy but not potential energy or height, and does not address the specific concept. Decision: Unacceptable

4.2 Supervised Learning

Supervised learning typically involves training a machine learning model on a large dataset of labeled examples for solving a specific task. In recent years, pre-trained models such as BERT [6] or RoBERTa [19] have emerged as the models of choice for classification tasks where labeled examples are available. These models have been trained on massive text corpora to learn rich, contextualized representations of language, and can subsequently be adapted to solve specific tasks using additional data, as described below.

Model: RoBERTa (Robustly Optimized BERT Pretraining Approach) is an improvement upon the BERT (Bidirectional Encoder Representations from Transformers) model, which marked a significant breakthrough in NLP by showing how contextual representations of language could be learned through masked language modeling, a training objective where the model has to predict a masked token in a sentence, given access to context in both directions. It implements dynamic masking during pretraining and removes the Next Sentence Prediction (NSP) objective, concentrating solely on masked language modeling. These alterations, along with the utilization of larger datasets and increased batch sizes during training, have notably improved its performance across various NLP benchmarks [27]. RoBERTa's high performance combined with its accessible training and use has led to its wide use for classification tasks in the educational domain among others [2,7,24], and also makes it suitable for our assessment task.

Finetuning (Full Supervision): Finetuning is a process through which models such as RoBERTa and Llama 3 which have already gone through the pre-training stage are then provided domain and task-specific signals. For classification tasks, this is typically done by taking a pre-trained model and training it on a labeled dataset. During this process, all the parameters of the model are typically updated when the model sees the labeled data during training.

For finetuning the RoBERTa model, we start with the "roberta-large" trained open-source model. We add a classification head to the pre-trained model that maps from the internal representations of the pre-trained model to our label space, followed by a softmax layer that produces probabilities that we can use for prediction. We train the model on our sentence level labeled data using a cross-entropy loss function, for a maximum of 20 epochs. We use early stopping with a patience of 8 to avoid overfitting – if the loss on the validation set does not decrease for 8 consecutive steps, then training terminates. Since each of the 6 CUs represents different *tasks*, we train 6 different models as described above.

For fine-tuning the Llama 3 model, we used Unsloth's open-source library [25] to accelerate training with LoRA (Low-Rank Adaptation) [12] and reduce memory usage. We fine-tuned the model for 3 epochs with a learning rate of 2e-4.

Indirect Supervision: The finetuning process is most effective when labeled training data for the task of interest is available. However, collecting task-specific labeled data can be a cost and labor intensive process, and this shortcoming is where the no supervision approach with LLMs is seen as most promising. We explore an alternate approach used for zero-shot text classification that requires finetuning a model such as RoBERTa, but does not require any task-specific labeled data [22,29]. This approach requires re-framing the classification task as a *textual entailment* problem, with the latter providing supervision for the former task. The textual entailment problem, commonly termed the Recognizing Textual Entailment (RTE) task requires models to reason about the relationship between two statements, and identify whether one can be inferred from the other. The first statement is called the premise, and the second is called the hypothesis. Given a premise such as *"The boy was playing the guitar"*, and a hypothesis such as *"The boy was awake"*, the correct relationship is *entails*, since the second statement is a natural conclusion from the first. We reformat our data such that a student's definition about a concept unit is given as the premise, and a statement of the form "This example suggests that as height increases, potential energy also increases" is given as the hypothesis. A prediction of entailment would mean that the model believes that given the essay or sentence, it can be deduced that the science concept is defined in an acceptable manner. We use a pre-trained RoBERTa model that has been finetuned for the RTE task as a zero-shot classification model for all six CUs, varying the hypothesis appropriately in each case.

5 Results

Table 2 presents the results for the four models in three conditions: 1) no supervision (Llama 3 zero-shot and few-shot), 2) indirect supervision (RoBERTa RTE), and 3) full supervision (Llama 3 and RoBERTa finetuned).

Table 2. Model performances measured in AUC for no (Llama 3), indirect (RoBERTa RTE), or full (RoBERTa and Llama 3 FT) supervision conditions. ZS = Zero-Shot, FS = Few-Shot, CoT = Chain-of-Thought, RTE = Recognizing Textual Entailment, FT = Finetuned.

Model	Supervision	CU0	CU1	CU2	CU3	CU4	CU5
Llama 3 ZS	No	0.719	0.550	0.790	0.774	0.788	0.589
Llama 3 FS	No	0.786	0.823	0.789	0.768	0.777	0.847
Llama 3 CoT	No	0.789	0.862	0.774	0.705	0.717	0.834
RoBERTa RTE	Indirect	0.749	0.531	0.588	0.853	0.788	0.861
Llama 3 FT	Full	0.640	0.636	0.793	0.818	0.848	0.751
RoBERTa FT	Full	0.946	0.904	0.915	0.966	0.902	0.958

Table 3. Illustrative examples of errors committed by the best performing RoBERTa finetuned model. FP = False Positive, FN = False Negative.

CU	Sentence	Error	Hypothesis
CU0	We needed to find the **best height** to provide the greatest amount of energy to be able to insure a fast ride.	FP	Model error
CU0	The hill has to be the highest possible because **the higher the hill is, the more energy the car will have.**	FP	Human error
CU1	The one decreasing is going to be the PE, while the one increasing is going to be KE.	FN	Context missing
CU2	When the cart is all the way at the bottom of the initial drop, then the PE and KE should be completely flipped around(Start: PE = 2443 J, KE = 0 J/End: PE = 0–1 J, KE = 2443-2442 J (**PE + KE = TE(Total Energy)**)).	FN	Model error
CU3	However, because energy can't be created or destroyed, the TE will remain the same throughout the ride.	FP	Human error
CU5	In this experiment we discovered that our highest mass of 60 kg with the same height of the initial drop it provided a potential energy of 2938.	FN	Context missing

Full Supervision with RoBERTa is a Clear Winner. The best performing model across all the six CUs is the RoBERTa finetuned model (AUC ranging 0.902-0.966), a model trained on the annotated data. The high performance of 0.966 AUC on CU3 is not surprising as it is a more straightforward concept of the Law of Conservation of Energy (see Table 1) that students often write with a consistent language. The CUs for which the RoBERTa finetuned model performs relatively poorly are CU1 and CU4, while still at a considerably high AUC of 0.904 and 0.902 respectively. One potential explanation for reduced performance could be that both these CUs are task-specific. That is, they are defined with a particular emphasis on the specifics of the roller coaster design (e.g., car moving down the track in CU1 and hill higher than the initial drop in CU4) as compared to the generic physics concepts in the other CUs. In contrast to RoBERTa, Llama 3 finetuning only improves its performance for half the CUs.

Seeing a Few Examples Significantly Improves No Supervision. Although not trained on annotated essay data, the Llama 3 few-shot model appears to have benefited significantly from having seen a few examples of the downstream task and its expected outcome. All the Llama 3 few-shot models across the six CUs perform considerably well with AUCs ranging from 0.768 to 0.847. In three out of six CUs, Llama 3 few-shot model clearly outperforms its zero-shot counterpart with improvements in AUC ranging from 0.07 to 0.27 (CU0 = 0.786 v. 0.719; CU1 = 0.823 v. 0.550; CU5 = 0.847 v. 0.589), while their performances are comparable in the other three CUs (CU2 = 0.799 v. 0.792, CU3 = 0.768 v. 0.774, CU4 = 0.777 v. 0.788).

Zero-Shot is Comparable to Indirect Supervision. Even without any supervision, the Llama 3 zero shot model performs at a level comparable to the RoBERTa RTE model with indirect supervision on the downstream task. In both cases, there are two CUs for which the model performance is somewhat close to chance (CU1 = 0.531 and CU2 = 0.588 for RoBERTa RTE; CU1 = 0.550 and CU5 = 0.589 for Llama 3 zero-shot). The at-chance performance of both models with CU1 could be attributed to the task-specific nature of the prediction involving the roller coaster design. The two models have comparable performances for CU0 (0.719 v. 0.749) and CU4 (0.788).

Few-Shot Surpasses Indirect Supervision. While RoBERTa RTE significantly outperforms the at-chance performance of Llama 3 in the zero-shot for CU5 (0.861 v. 0.589), the performance of LLama 3 model improves notably with an increase in AUC of 0.26 in the few-shot setting. We observe a similar pattern in CU1, where the at-chance performance of Llama 3 zero-shot model (0.55) improves to 0.823 with few-shot prompting. Indeed, including two CUs where RoBERTa RTE performs somewhat close to chance despite indirect supervision (CU1 = 0.531 v. 0.823, CU2 = 0.588 v. 0.799).

Where do the Finetuned Models Fail? A qualitative error analysis of RoBERTa finetuned models reveals that the while the model makes genuine errors in some cases, the other reasons may also include mismatch in expectations (e.g., not counting equations as acceptable), error in human annotation, and missing context in sentence-level classification (see Table 3).

6 Discussion

One of the main benefits of using a prompt-based classifier is that it circumvents the need for supervised data and training on the downstream task. In this paper, we examine how well this approach fares with the more common practice of using supervised models.

6.1 Summary of Findings

We empirically analyzed the performance of four models in assessing acceptable explanations of student ideas from an inquiry-based science learning environment. The best performing model across all the content units was the fully supervised RoBERTa finetuned models, with AUCs above 0.90 for most part. With access to only a few examples, the Llama 3 few-shot models with no supervision also perform consistently well with AUCs above 0.77. The tradeoff between the two models highlights the goal of our study. Despite having a performance that is significantly better, the fully supervised model is limited in its adaptability. Any task redefinition would require effortful re-annotation of data and retraining of the models. In contrast, the Llama 3 few-shot models could be prompted to perform assessments with a handful of examples. However, it is unclear if the flexibility outweighs the drop in performance of 0.13 AUC. Since the decision is likely to be driven by the context, we present a discussion of these design tradeoffs in the next section.

We only use local LMs such as RoBERTa and Llama 3 over proprietary models such as GPT to have full access to the backend model, maintain a stable model across updates, and protect student privacy. After assessment, if LMs are used to generate feedback, we must pay careful attention to student safety around toxicity, hallucination, and being culturally appropriate. As we noted earlier, our sample is limited in its diversity. Hence, future downstream use must conduct a thorough bias analysis with the target population to ensure that the LMs' effectiveness is fairly distributed. Other ethical considerations we would contend with before adopting LMs include the environmental impact of its training, exploitative data labor, and applicability to low-resource languages.

6.2 Prompting vs. Supervised Learning

While prompting general-purpose LMs affords flexibility in model building and task redefinition, it may be constrained in its ability to generate consistent output (e.g., "incorrect" v. "not correct"). Moreover, without large enough annotated datasets, prompting often needs to rely on general benchmarks, such as for classification tasks in other domains [27] for model evaluation.

In contrast, while supervised training affords flexibility in model updates and consistency in output, it is laborious to change the task definition (e.g., assessment of science content vs. language) as it also involves acquiring new annotated data and then retraining the model. However, as compared to prompting with general-purpose LMs, supervised models can be evaluated rigorously using the already annotated data. Lastly, if the algorithm used to train the supervised model is simple (e.g., simple regression or tree-based models), it offers significantly better transparency in understanding how the model works and how a prediction was made. See Table 4 for a summary of the affordances and constraints of using prompting and supervised learning for automated assessment.

We conclude that in a high-stakes setting like education that may contain data not represented in LM training (e.g., middle school students' science essays)

Table 4. Affordances and constraints of prompting and supervised learning.

	Prompting	Supervised Learning
Model training	✓Not necessary; pre-trained	✗Needs training or finetuning
Annotated data	✓Not necessary	✗Necessary for supervision
Model updates	✗Limited	✓As needed
Output consistency	✗Low; generates freeform text	✓High; outputs trained labels
Task redefinition	✓Easy; edit prompt	✗Effortful; reannotate, retrain
Model evaluation	✗General benchmarks; need annotated data otherwise	✓At training, cross-validation, held out testing
Transparency	✗Low; explanations may not be reliable	✓High; with simple models

and in novel assessment contexts (e.g., inquiry based learning of science explanations using roller coaster design experiments), it may be preferable in some cases to collect annotated data to test and improve the reliability of prompt-based predictions. Our findings provide evidence that finetuning LMs with supervised data leads to notable model improvements. However, supervised finetuning is only possible if the pre-trained LMs are publicly available. For a reliable use of LMs in education, future research also needs to evaluate LMs more rigorously beyond generalization estimates [16] and build approaches to improve transparency.

Acknowledgements. This work was supported by the Office of the Vice Chancellor for Research and Graduate Education at the University of WisconsinMadison, with funding from the Wisconsin Alumni Research Foundation. We thank Dana Gnesdilow and Sadhana Puntambekar for sharing the data. We also appreciate Adi Dalal, Bowen Wang, Dong Hyun Lee, Gyuho Shim, Minghao Zhou, and Nott Laoaron for their contributions to the data analysis.

References

1. Gemma Team et al.: Gemma: Open models based on Gemini research and technology (2023)
2. Alic, S., Demszky, D., Mancenido, Z., Liu, J., Hill, H., Jurafsky, D.: Computationally identifying funneling and focusing questions in classroom discourse. In: Kochmar, E., et al. (eds.) Proceedings of the 17th Workshop on Innovative Use of NLP for Building Educational Applications (BEA 2022), Seattle, Washington, pp. 224–233. Association for Computational Linguistics (2022)
3. Berland, L.K., Hammer, D.: Framing for scientific argumentation. J. Res. Sci. Teach. **49**(1), 68–94 (2012)
4. Clark, P., et al.: Think you have solved question answering? Try arc, the AI2 reasoning challenge (2018)

5. Corbett, A.T., Anderson, J.R.: Knowledge tracing: modeling the acquisition of procedural knowledge. User Model. User-Adapted Interact. **4**, 253–278 (1994)
6. Devlin, J., Chang, M.-W., Lee, K., Toutanova, K.: BERT: pre-training of deep bidirectional transformers for language understanding. In: Burstein, J., Doran, C., Solorio, T. (eds.) Proceedings of the 2019 Conference of the North American Chapter of the Association for Computational Linguistics: Human Language Technologies (Volume 1: Long and Short Papers), Minneapolis, Minnesota, pp. 4171–4186. Association for Computational Linguistics (2019)
7. Ganesh, A., et al.: Navigating wanderland: highlighting off-task discussions in classrooms. In: Wang, N., Rebolledo-Mendez, G., Matsuda, N., Santos, O.C., Dimitrova, V. (eds.) AIED 2023. LNCS, vol. 13916, pp. 727–732. Springer, Cham (2023). https://doi.org/10.1007/978-3-031-36272-9_63
8. Gerard, L.F., Linn, M.C.: Using automated scores of student essays to support teacher guidance in classroom inquiry. J. Sci. Teach. Educ. **27**(1), 111–129 (2016)
9. Graham, S., Kiuhara, S.A., MacKay, M.: The effects of writing on learning in science, social studies, and mathematics: a meta-analysis. Rev. Educ. Res. **90**(2), 179–226 (2020)
10. Grattafiori, A.: The llama 3 herd of models (2024)
11. Hendrycks, D., et al.: Measuring massive multitask language understanding (2020)
12. Hu, E.J., et al.: Lora: low-rank adaptation of large language models. ICLR **1**(2), 3 (2022)
13. Jiang, A.Q., et al. Mistral 7b (2023)
14. Jiang, Y., et al.: Expert feature-engineering vs. deep neural networks: which is better for sensor-free affect detection? In: Penstein Rosé, C., et al. (eds.) AIED 2018. LNCS (LNAI), vol. 10947, pp. 198–211. Springer, Cham (2018). https://doi.org/10.1007/978-3-319-93843-1_15
15. Karumbaiah, S., et al.: A spatiotemporal analysis of teacher practices in supporting student learning and engagement in an AI-enabled classroom. In: Wang, N., Rebolledo-Mendez, G., Matsuda, N., Santos, O.C., Dimitrova, V. (eds.) AIED 2023. LNCS, vol. 13916, pp. 450–462. Springer, Cham (2023). https://doi.org/10.1007/978-3-031-36272-9_37
16. Karumbaiah, S., Ganesh, A., Bharadwaj, A., Anderson, L.: Evaluating behaviors of general purpose language models in a pedagogical context. In: Olney, A.M., Chounta, I.A., Liu, Z., Santos, O.C., Bittencourt, I.I. (eds.) AIED 2024. LNCS, vol. 14830, pp. 47–61. Springer, Cham (2024). https://doi.org/10.1007/978-3-031-64299-9_4
17. Li, Z., Zhang, C., Jin, Y., Cang, X., Puntambekar, S., Passonneau, R.J.: Learning when to defer to humans for short answer grading. In: Wang, N., Rebolledo-Mendez, G., Matsuda, N., Santos, O.C., Dimitrova, V. (eds.) AIED 2023. LNCS, vol. 13916, pp. 414–425. Springer, Cham (2023). https://doi.org/10.1007/978-3-031-36272-9_34
18. Liu, P., Yuan, W., Fu, J., Jiang, Z., Hayashi, H., Neubig, G.: Pre-train, prompt, and predict: a systematic survey of prompting methods in natural language processing. ACM Comput. Surv. **55**(9), 1–35 (2023)
19. Liu, Y., et al.: Roberta: a robustly optimized BERT pretraining approach. arXiv preprint arXiv:1907.11692 (2019)
20. McNeill, K.L., Katsh-Singer, R., González-Howard, M., Loper, S.: Factors impacting teachers' argumentation instruction in their science classrooms. Int. J. Sci. Educ. **38**(12) (2016)

21. Chowdhury, S.P., Zouhar, V., Sachan, M.: Autotutor meets large language models: a language model tutor with rich pedagogy and guardrails. In: Proceedings of the Eleventh ACM Conference on Learning@ Scale, pp. 5–15 (2024)
22. Pàmies, M., et al.: A weakly supervised textual entailment approach to zero-shot text classification. In: Vlachos, A., Augenstein, I. (eds.) Proceedings of the 17th Conference of the European Chapter of the Association for Computational Linguistics, Dubrovnik, Croatia, pp. 286–296. Association for Computational Linguistics (2023)
23. NGSS Lead States. Next generation science standards: For states, by states. National Academies Press (2013)
24. Suresh, A., Jacobs, J., Perkoff, M., Martin, J.H., Sumner, T.: Fine-tuning transformers with additional context to classify discursive moves in mathematics classrooms. In: Proceedings of the 17th Workshop on Innovative Use of NLP for Building Educational Applications (BEA 2022), Seattle, Washington, pp. 71–81. Association for Computational Linguistics (2022)
25. Unsloth AI. Unsloth: Sloth-bot for automating tasks on the web (2023). https://github.com/unslothai/unsloth
26. Vaswani, A., et al.: Attention is all you need. In: Proceedings of the 31st International Conference on Neural Information Processing Systems, NIPS 2017, Red Hook, NY, USA, pp. 6000–6010. Curran Associates Inc. (2017)
27. Wang, A., et al.: Superglue: a stickier benchmark for general-purpose language understanding systems. In: Advances in Neural Information Processing Systems, vol. 32 (2019)
28. Wang, R.E., Demszky, D.: Is chatgpt a good teacher coach? Measuring zero-shot performance for scoring and providing actionable insights on classroom instruction. arXiv preprint arXiv:2306.03090 (2023)
29. Yin, W., Hay, J., Roth, D.: Benchmarking zero-shot text classification: datasets, evaluation and entailment approach. In: Inui, K., Jiang, J., Ng, V., Wan, X. (eds.) Proceedings of the 2019 Conference on Empirical Methods in Natural Language Processing and the 9th International Joint Conference on Natural Language Processing (EMNLP-IJCNLP), pp. 3914–3923, Hong Kong, China. Association for Computational Linguistics (2019)

Automatic Large Language Models Creation of Interactive Learning Lessons

Jionghao Lin[1,2,3](✉), Jiarui Rao[2], Sandy Yiyang Zhao[2], Yuting Wang[2], Ashish Gurung[2], Amanda Barany[4], Jaclyn Ocumpaugh[4], Ryan S. Baker[4], and Kenneth R. Koedinger[2]

[1] The University of Hong Kong, Pokfulam Rd, Hong Kong, China
jionghao@hku.hk
[2] Carnegie Mellon University, Pittsburgh, PA 15213, USA
[3] Monash University, Wellington Rd, Clayton, VIC 3800, Australia
[4] University of Pennsylvania, Philadelphia, PA 19104, USA

Abstract. We explore the automatic generation of interactive, scenario-based lessons designed to train novice human tutors who teach middle school mathematics online. Employing prompt engineering through a Retrieval-Augmented Generation approach with GPT-4o, we developed a system capable of creating structured tutor training lessons. Our study generated lessons in English for three key topics—Encouraging Students' Independence, Encouraging Help-Seeking Behavior, and Turning on Cameras—using a task decomposition prompting strategy that breaks lesson generation into sub-tasks. The generated lessons were evaluated by two human evaluators, who provided both quantitative and qualitative evaluations using a comprehensive rubric informed by lesson design research. Results demonstrate that the task decomposition strategy led to higher-rated lessons compared to single-step generation. Human evaluators identified several strengths in the LLM-generated lessons, including well-structured content and time-saving potential, while also noting limitations such as generic feedback and a lack of clarity in some instructional sections. These findings underscore the potential of hybrid human–AI approaches for generating effective lessons in tutor training. Our code is available on GitHub: https://github.com/GEMLab-HKU/ECTEL_Course_Gen_APP.

Keywords: Generative Artificial Intelligence · Large Language Models · Content Generation · Professional Development · Lesson Design

1 Introduction

One-on-one human tutoring is widely recognized as an effective strategy for enhancing student learning, with substantial evidence highlighting its positive impact on learning outcomes [18]. However, scaling human tutoring remains a significant challenge due to the scarcity of skilled tutors [18]. To address this

K. Tammets et al. (Eds.): EC-TEL 2025, LNCS 16063, pp. 259–274, 2026.
https://doi.org/10.1007/978-3-032-03870-8_18

issue, professional development programs have been developed to equip novice and nonprofessional tutors with the skills needed for effective instruction [18]. Online scenario-based training has emerged as a promising approach, simulating real-life tutoring situations to prepare novice tutors for their roles [22]. Central to scenario-based tutor training program is well-constructed lessons that offer specific instructional strategies and practical guidance for adapting human tutoring to diverse learner needs. However, developing such lessons manually requires significant time and expertise, making the lesson design process costly and difficult to scale. These challenges underscore the urgent need for artificial intelligence (AI) technologies for automatic lesson generation, which can streamline lesson development and expand access to effective tutor training programs.

Lesson generation using AI techniques has been investigated in previous research to address the challenges of the time-consuming and labor-intensive process of creating educational materials. Early approaches employed rule-based systems to generate quiz questions, providing a foundational method but lacking adaptability and depth [10,24]. Subsequent approaches introduced template-based methods and early AI models, which improved the variety and relevance of generated content [19]. However, these approaches still faced significant limitations, including inflexibility and a lack of contextual understanding [19].

Recently, large language models (LLMs) demonstrate exceptional capabilities in generating human-like text, leveraging pretraining on extensive datasets [20]. These capabilities enable LLMs to potentially address the shortcomings of earlier approaches by producing nuanced, contextually relevant, and adaptable content, making them particularly well-suited for educational purposes. However, generating comprehensive lessons for tutor training remains a complex task. A lesson typically consists of multiple interconnected segments, including well-defined learning objectives and quiz. Each segment serves a specific instructional purpose and must align with the overall pedagogical goals of the lesson. Given the complexity of lesson design, generating all components in a single step risks overwhelming the model, resulting in shallow or disjointed outputs [9].

To address this, we adopt a prompting strategy similar to [25], chaining multiple LLM steps together—where the output of one step serves as the input for the next—and has been shown to enhance the quality of task outcomes. Research highlights the benefits of such decomposition strategies for tasks requiring multi-step reasoning, as they help improve the quality of generated content [9,25]. However, it remains unknown how extensively a task should be decomposed to ensure optimal performance, since overly complex sub-goals might still overwhelm the LLM [13]. In the context of lesson generation, this challenge becomes particularly relevant, as lessons consist of multiple interdependent components that must align both structurally and pedagogically. It remains unclear how the number of segments or the level of decomposition impacts the quality, coherence, and pedagogical rigor of the generated lessons.

The demand for high-quality lesson content in tutor training programs remains substantial; however, the development of content specifically tailored for tutor training has been relatively under-explored. Our study developed a lesson content generation system that leverages prompt engineering with LLMs. The system was designed to generate scenario-based lessons for training novice tutors who teach middle school mathematics in online environments. To evaluate the effectiveness of the generated lessons, we collaborated with human instructional designers, who evaluated the lesson quality using a comprehensive rubric. This evaluation aimed to determine how effectively LLMs can generate lesson content that meets the pedagogical and practical needs of tutor training. Based on this investigation, our study proposed two **R**esearch **Q**uestions (**RQs**): **RQ1:** *How does the level of task decomposition influence the quality of tutor training lessons generated by LLMs?* **RQ2:** *How does the quality of lessons generated by LLMs compare to those created by expert human lesson designers?*

2 Related Work

2.1 Scenario-Based Lesson Development for Tutor Training

Scenario-based lessons are a key component of effective tutor training, providing a realistic context for tutors to apply their skills [4]. These lessons simulate authentic tutoring interactions, helping tutors understand and navigate common challenges they might face. By working through scenarios that mimic real-world situations, tutors develop the flexibility needed to effectively support diverse learners. Additionally, lessons focusing on advocacy, empathy, and cultural competence are important for preparing tutors to work with diverse student populations [22]. These competencies enable tutors to deliver academic content and address students' emotional well-being and equity-related challenges, fostering supportive learning environments [4].

Lessons structured around "learning by doing" methodologies, such as the modified Predict-Observe-Explain (POE) model, have shown significant success in enhancing tutor preparedness [11]. In the scenario-based lessons, tutors first engage with a scenario by predicting the best response and then explaining their rationale. This approach fosters active engagement and critical reflection, helping tutors develop a deeper understanding of effective tutoring strategies [1]. Moreover, incorporating a combination of multiple-choice questions (MCQs) and open-ended questions within these lessons has proven effective for developing both basic and advanced tutoring skills [2]. MCQs help in assessing foundational knowledge in an efficient manner, while open-ended questions encourage deeper cognitive engagement, enabling tutors to articulate their understanding [8].

2.2 Lesson Generation

Lessons designed for tutor training are essential for equipping tutors with the skills needed to support diverse learners. However, manually crafting these lessons can be both time-consuming and labor-intensive, particularly when scaling tutor training programs to meet growing demand [18,22]. Automated lesson generation approaches have emerged as a potential solution to these challenges, offering benefits such as time savings, scalability, and consistency in instructional content. Traditional methods of automated learning content generation, such as rule-based approaches or template-based approaches [6], often lack the flexibility and contextual depth. These limitations highlight the need for more advanced approaches to generating structured, pedagogically rich lessons.

The rise of LLMs has brought significant advancements to content generation in education. LLMs have demonstrated strong performance across a range of educational tasks, including generating feedback [5,17], course learning topics [14] and questions [16]. For instance, GPT models have been used to provide feedback on open-ended student responses, producing actionable suggestions that support learning [5]. Despite the growing interest in LLMs for education, their use in generating structured, scenario-based lessons tailored to tutor training remains under-explored. Given the unique requirements of tutor training, the potential for LLMs to automate high-quality lesson generation at scale presents a significant opportunity.

3 Methods

3.1 Lesson Structure from a Tutor Training Platform

To develop training lessons for novice human tutors teaching middle school mathematics online, our study builds upon an existing tutor training program structured around the SMART framework demonstrated in [4,22], which encompasses five key competencies critical for successful tutoring: **S**ocial-emotional Learning, **M**astery of Content, **A**dvocacy, **R**elationship-building, and **T**echnology. All lessons in our study were generated in English. The lessons are divided into five main sections, each designed to support specific aspects of tutor training:

- **Title Page:** This section provides a description of the lesson topic, including the key focus areas and the learning objectives the lesson aims to achieve.
- **Scenario I Section:** In this section, tutors are presented with the first tutoring scenario and are required to answer open-ended questions and multiple-choice questions (MCQ). These questions are designed to replicate real-world tutoring situations, asking tutors to respond as they would during an actual session and to justify their responses.
- **Instruction:** This section offers research-backed instruction for effective tutoring practices, helping tutors understand both desired and undesired tutoring practice. Each instruction section includes specific examples that help clarify best practices.
- **Scenario II Section:** This section follows a structure similar to the **Scenario I** section but presents a different scenario that requires tutors to apply their learned skills in a slightly altered context. This variation ensures that tutors understand the applicability of concepts beyond a single situation.
- **Conclusion:** The lesson concludes with a summary that reviews the key concepts covered throughout the lesson, reinforcing the understanding of tutoring strategies discussed. The conclusion section also includes a list of references, providing tutors with additional resources for deeper exploration

3.2 Human-Crafted Lesson

We invited two lesson designers to craft the lessons for tutor training and both lesson designers followed the structured lesson format outlined in Sect. 3.1. Each designer was tasked with creating lessons aligned with specific tutoring scenarios. The first lesson designer developed two lessons. The first lesson is *"Encouraging Students' Independence"* which focuses on fostering student autonomy by training tutors to use polite, constructive language to guide learners without undermining their independence and the second lesson is *"Turning on Cameras"*, which aims to equip novice tutors with strategies to encourage camera use in online tutoring sessions, aiming to improve student engagement and active participation. The second lesson designer developed one lesson, i.e., *"Encouraging Help-Seeking Behavior"*, which aims to train tutors in identifying and addressing barriers that prevent students from seeking help, fostering a more supportive learning environment. All three lessons underwent rigorous review and multiple iterations, ensuring they were polished and ready for publication on the tutor training platform. The topics of these three human-crafted lessons were subsequently used to prompt the LLMs, following the prompt engineering approaches detailed in Sect. 3.3. The human-crafted lessons are publicly accessible through the OSF repository.

3.3 Large Language Model-Generated Lessons

We aim to generate comprehensive tutor training lessons based on research articles related to effective tutoring practices. For generating more topic-specific content, Retrieval-Augmented Generation (RAG) has emerged as a powerful technique [7,12]. RAG-based LLM content generation combines both retrieval and generation capabilities, allowing the model to first retrieve relevant documents and then utilize the relevant information to generate content. The strength of RAG lies in its ability to produce contextually accurate content by incorporating the generated output into factual data, which is particularly advantageous when generating educational content that requires specific knowledge from reliable sources [21]. As shown in Fig. 1, we propose a two-step approach for lesson generation. Firstly, a lesson designer retrieves articles related to specific tutoring practices, providing the foundational knowledge on effective instructional strategies. Secondly, these retrieved articles are used to prompt the GPT-4o model (`gpt-4o-2024-05-13`). The GPT-4o model has been recognized for its balance of cost efficiency and strong performance in content generation tasks, making it a suitable choice for producing pedagogically sound lesson content.

An important aspect of generating tutor training lessons is determining the optimal prompting strategy for content generation. As discussed in Sect. 3.1, each lesson consists of five main sections. It is important to explore whether it is more effective to generate an entire lesson in one step or generate multiple segments of lesson section (e.g., generate each section independently). As shown in Fig. 1, the lesson structure includes five sections, and each section can be generated using different prompting strategies. Additional details about our prompting strategies can be accessed through the OSF repository.

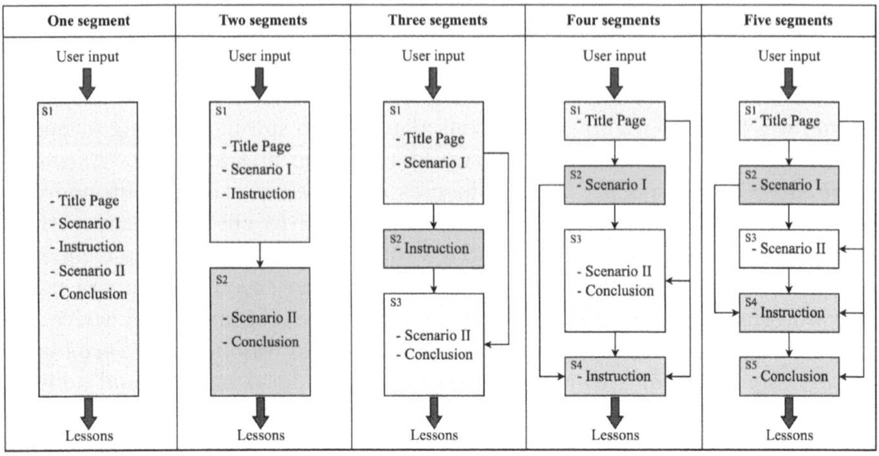

Fig. 1. Our approaches for prompting LLM to generate lessons for tutor training.

- **One Segment:** The entire lesson (all five sections) is generated at once.
- **Two Segments:** The lesson is split into two main segments for generation. The content from S1, including the title page and the description of Scenario I, is incorporated as part of the prompt for generating S2.
- **Three Segments:** The lesson was divided into three segments. The content from S1 is used to prompt the generation of the instructional content (S2), while both S1 and S2 are incorporated as inputs to generate Scenario II and the conclusion (S3).
- **Four Segments:** The lesson was split into four segments. Since the instruction section includes descriptions of research-recommended tutoring practices, generating it independently enhances clarity and depth. Scenario II and the Conclusion are generated together to streamline transitions.
- **Five Segments:** The most granular approach involves generating each of the five segments. This approach provided the highest level of detail and customization for each section, allowing the model to focus exclusively on the objectives of a single segment.

3.4 Lesson Evaluation

To evaluate the influence of different prompting strategies for lesson generation (RQ1), we hired two human coders to rate the content generated by the LLM. Both coders were experienced in tutoring middle school math subjects and had completed over ten tutor training lessons on the tutor training platform. The coders followed a detailed rating rubric, which was summarized from previous research [23] and included 17 distinct codes for evaluating lesson quality. Due to the page limit, the rating rubric is illustrated in Table A1 in Digital Appendix. To ensure rating consistency, both coders participated in multiple training sessions where they collaboratively rated a sample of LLM-generated lessons. These sessions continued until the coders achieved sufficient agreement on the application of the codes. After training, the two coders independently rated the LLM-generated lessons. The inter-rater reliability was assessed using Cohen's κ, which resulted in a score of 0.72. This score indicates substantial agreement [15]. Any discrepancies were addressed through discussion involving both coders and a third reviewer, who also had experience tutoring middle school math and had completed over ten tutor training lessons on the platform. This process ensured that the final ratings accurately reflected the quality of the generated lessons. To answer RQ2, we collected feedback from two lesson designers using a structured written questionnaire. The designers were provided with a set of open-ended questions (see Table A2 in Digital Appendix). Each designer independently provided written responses to all questions.

4 Results

4.1 Analyze the Quality of LLM-Generated Tutor Training Lessons

The results of the human rating scores (Table 1) demonstrate that the three-segment approach (**Three Seg.**) achieved the highest average rating (14.67) for lesson generation, while the one-segment approach (**One Seg.**) received the lowest average rating (10.67). These findings indicate that decomposing the lesson generation task into multiple subtasks can enhance the quality of the generated content. Interestingly, the five-segment approach (**Five Seg.**), which represents the highest level of task decomposition, performed slightly worse than the three-segment approach.

Table 1. Rating scores for LLM-generated tutor training lessons in different segments.

Lessons	One Seg.	Two Seg.	Three Seg.	Four Seg.	Five Seg.
Encouraging Students' Independence	12	11	13	13	13
Encouraging help-seeking behavior	8	11	15	15	12
Turning on Cameras	12	14	16	14	15
Average	10.67	12	14.67	14	13.33

Note: **Seg.** denotes **Segment**.

To gain a deeper understanding, we further analyzed the details of the rating scores for each section across the segment approaches. The scores in Table 2 reflect the final consensus ratings across the three generated lessons for each segmentation approach. For each criterion (e.g., *Specific* or *Clarity*), a score of 3/3 indicates that all three lessons met the standard for that code, while a score of 0/3 means that none did. In the **Title page** (see Table 2), across all segments, the code *Specific* achieved consistently high scores, indicating that the generated content effectively specified what the trainees would be able to do and under what

Table 2. Consensus ratings for each lesson section across different segmentation

Evaluation Codes	One Seg.	Two Seg.	Three Seg.	Four Seg.	Five Seg.
Title page					
Specific	3/3	3/3	3/3	3/3	3/3
Clarity	1/3	0/3	2/3	2/3	1/3
Scenario 1					
Problem Structure	3/3	3/3	3/3	3/3	3/3
Alignment with LO	2/3	3/3	3/3	2/3	2/3
Feedback	1/3	1/3	3/3	2/3	2/3
Plain Language	3/3	3/3	3/3	3/3	3/3
Instruction					
Alignment with LO	3/3	3/3	3/3	3/3	3/3
Clarity of Writing	0/3	0/3	1/3	2/3	2/3
Plain Language	1/3	2/3	3/3	3/3	3/3
Use of Examples	3/3	3/3	3/3	3/3	3/3
Pedagogy Grounded	0/3	1/3	3/3	1/3	1/3
Scenario 2					
Problem Structure	3/3	3/3	3/3	3/3	3/3
Alignment with LO	2/3	3/3	3/3	3/3	3/3
Feedback	1/3	2/3	2/3	2/3	2/3
Plain Language	3/3	3/3	3/3	3/3	3/3
Conclusion					
Alignment with LO	3/3	3/3	3/3	3/3	3/3
Authenticity of References	0/3	0/3	0/3	1/3	0/3

Note: **Seg.** denotes **Segment**. Each score (e.g., 3/3) represents the number of generated lessons (out of three) that received a positive consensus rating for the given criterion and segmentation.

conditions they would demonstrate the behavior. However, significant variability was observed in the code *Clarity*. In particular, the language used to define learning objectives often lacked clarity in certain segment configurations, such as the one-segment, two-segment, and five-segment approaches.

For **Scenario 1** and **Scenario 2**, the code *Problem Structure* consistently received high ratings across all segment prompts, highlighting the model's ability to replicate the structured format of tutor training lessons effectively. Additionally, both scenarios demonstrated strong alignment with learning objectives and employed clear, accessible language, as reflected in the high ratings for the codes *Alignment with Learning Objectives (LO)* and the *Plain Language* across all segment prompts. The provision of feedback (code *Feedback*) showed notable improvements in prompts using three or more segments compared to the one- or two-segment approaches. This improvement is likely attributed to the decomposition of content generation tasks, which enables the LLM to allocate more attention to generate feedback-related content

In the **Instruction** section, the LLM-generated lessons also demonstrated strong alignment with the learning objectives and provided practical examples. However, the code *Clarity of Writing* received lower scores for the one- and two-segment approaches. This limitation likely stems from the generation process, where the instruction section was integrated into a larger task that combined multiple components (see Fig. 1). In contrast, the instruction section was generated independently in the three-, four-, and five-segment approaches, which allowed the LLM to focus more on delivering specialized concepts with detailed explanation derived from research-based articles. The code *Pedagogy Grounded* also showed variability across segment configurations, receiving lower scores across all approaches except the three-segment setup. Pedagogical grounding, which assesses the integration of theoretical principles into practical instructional guidance, was most effective in the three-segment approach. This improvement might be attributed to the sequential generation process, where the instruction section was generated earlier in the three-segment strategy compared to the four- and five-segment approaches. Further investigation is required to better understand the underlying reasons for the lower scores in *Clarity of Writing* and *Pedagogy Grounded*, which will help refine the prompting strategies to achieve more consistent performance across all sections of the lesson.

Finally, the LLM-generated lesson section **Conclusion** consistently underperformed in generating authentic references across all segment configurations, as reflected by the low scores for the code *Authenticity of References* in Table 2. Even with the optimal segment configuration (i.e., three segments) combined with the RAG approach—which integrated academic papers containing verified references—the model still produced references that did not exist (see Table A3 in Digital Appendix). This finding highlights that while the RAG approach enhances the contextual relevance of generated content by incorporating retrieved documents, it does not inherently address the issue of citation authenticity.

4.2 Compare LLM-Generated Lessons with Human-Crafted Lessons

To answer **RQ2**, we invited two lesson designers who were asked to identify strengths and weaknesses of these generated lessons compared to their manually crafted lessons, which encouraged critical analysis rather than subjective preference. Building on the findings from RQ1, we selected lessons generated using the three-segment prompt for comparison, as it generally demonstrated optimal performance across different lessons and codes as shown in Table 1 and 2. The reflections of lesson designers revealed several positive aspects of LLM-generated lessons, highlighting the system's utility in lesson design.

Strengths of LLM-Generated Lesson Time-Saving in Creating Lesson: One of the most significant advantages of LLM-facilitated lesson generation, as

Strategy	Description	Good Example	Bad Example
Polite Request	Encourage initial engagement with polite requests.	"Could you please show me how you've tried to solve this problem so far?"	"Tell me what you've done on this problem."
Balanced Feedback	Provide polite feedback initially, then shift to direct feedback as needed.	"That's a good start, Sam. Let's see if we can fix this part together."	"That's wrong. You need to fix this part."
Assess Progress	Assess students' prior progress to tailor instructions.	"What steps have you taken so far on this problem?"	"Why haven't you made any progress on this problem yet?"

Fig. 2. LLM-generated examples of strategies for the lesson *Encouraging Students' Independence*. The chart highlights three strategies—Polite Request, Balanced Feedback, and Assess Progress—along with their descriptions, good examples of implementation, and corresponding bad examples to avoid.

highlighted by both lesson designers, is the substantial time savings in drafting scenario sections. Crafting effective scenarios is a difficult process that requires maintaining a careful balance between similarity and distinctiveness across questions. As described in Sect. 3.1, Scenario I and Scenario II in a lesson must be comparable in difficulty and context to provide consistent learning opportunities, yet distinct enough to prevent students from perceiving them as identical. Lesson designer 1 elaborated on the challenge, noting, *"...The process of authoring and adjusting is incredibly time-consuming. The AI can quickly generate variations of scenarios, allowing educators to focus more on fine-tuning and less on repetitive drafting..."* Similarly, Lesson designer 2 emphasized the benefit of LLM assistance in creating multiple-choice questions within these scenarios, stating, *"...I think the LLM-generated lessons do save a lot of time from researching and creating the multiple choice questions."* Both designers agreed that this time-saving feature significantly reduces the cognitive and logistical load associated with scenario design. Additionally, designer 1 further commend *"...the instructional charts that's generated are mostly very helpful. ..."* as shown in Fig. 2. The feedback from the two lesson designers suggests that the LLM-generated lessons can enhance the lesson creation workflow.

Generating Diverse and Real-World Scenarios: Lesson designer 1 noted, *"The AI can quickly generate variations of scenarios,"* and *"I think the scenarios are generally very-well generated. When given a strategy, GPT seems to be able to give scenarios where that strategy can be used, which I think is pretty helpful"* highlighting the model's capability to provide multiple scenarios tailored to different instructional strategies. For example, in the lesson focused on Encouraging Students' Independence, the LLM-generated content in both scenario sections:

- **Scenario I:** *"Tutor Alex is working with a student named Jamie, who often waits for direct answers rather than attempting to solve math problems inde-*

pendently. Jamie has shown some progress but still lacks confidence in tackling problems alone."

- **Scenario II:** *"Tutor Taylor is working with a student named Sam, who frequently asks for hints and confirmations before making any progress on math problems. Sam has shown the ability to solve problems but often seeks reassurance, which hinders independent problem-solving."*

The examples above demonstrate how subtle variations in the scenarios can address distinct aspects of encouraging independence—one focusing on building confidence in hesitant students (**Scenario I**) and the other on managing students' reliance on reassurance (**Scenario II**).

Unidentified Biased or Offensive Content: Ensuring unbiased and appropriate AI-facilitated learning content generation is essential for building trust among educators and learners. Lesson designer 1 highlighted this positive aspect, stating, *"I haven't seen any biased or offensive content in GPT-generated lessons."* Similarly, Lesson Designer 2 affirmed, *"I haven't seen this,... do not seem to include biased or offensive material."* The feedback from both lesson designers suggests that the LLM-generated lesson has avoided inappropriate content.

Facilitating Human-AI Collaboration: As acknowledged by both lesson designers, the AI-generated content provided a foundational draft that could be iteratively improved, significantly reducing the time and effort required to create lessons from scratch. Lesson designer 1 emphasized the value of this collaboration, noting, *"...The AI can quickly generate variations of scenarios, allowing educators to focus more on fine-tuning and less on repetitive drafting..."* and similarly, lesson designer 2 indicated, *"The quality of some LLMs generated lessons are good since they can be used after a few rounds of modification. The lessons I create also have been reviewing and polishing for several rounds..."* These observations underscore the collaborative potential of LLMs in lesson preparation and highlight a synergistic approach: AI efficiently handles repetitive and time-intensive tasks, while human expertise ensures the final output aligns with instructional best practices and meets the unique needs of learners.

Weaknesses of LLM-Generated Lessons. While the positive aspects of LLM-facilitated lesson generation highlight its potential to streamline the process, reduce repetitive tasks, and generate realistic scenarios, it also has limitations. Lesson designers identified several areas where AI-generated content falls short of the standards achieved in human-crafted lessons.

Generic Feedback Content: Unlike handcrafted lessons, which often include detailed and targeted feedback for each possible answer, the AI-generated feedback content mostly focused on explaining the correct answer. This approach overlooked the importance of addressing why specific options were incorrect, leaving gaps in the learning experience. Lesson designer 1 noted, "*...Handcrafted questions often provide targeted feedback for each possible answer, explaining why a specific choice is correct or incorrect. In contrast, LLM-generated courses tend to focus only on explaining the correct answer, neglecting the nuanced reasoning behind other options. In the cases where an explanation for a wrong answer is provided, the explanation given is generally more one-size-fits-all style, which lacks that important factor of targeted feedback...*" Lesson designer 2 indicated "*The explanation for options 2, 3, 4 is not specific enough, since it doesn't explain exactly why we don't choose them.*" and provided a specific example of LLM-generated feedback (see Table A4 in Digital Appendix). These observations highlight the necessity of incorporating more nuanced explanations for all answer options, both correct and incorrect. Lacking detailed feedback for incorrect answers diminishes the educational value of the lesson. Targeted feedback is critical for helping learners understand the rationale behind their choices and correct misconceptions. The generic explanations provided by the LLM fail to address this need, resulting in less effective learning experiences.

Clarity in the Title Page and Instruction Section: Both designers noted instances where the generated lessons inconsistently used terms like "learners", "teachers", "tutors", and "students". This inconsistency sometimes confused the intended novice tutors, as the lessons were specifically designed for training tutors on how to teach their students effectively. As shown in Table 3, the examples generated by one-segment prompt fail to maintain clarity about the intended novice tutors—confusing "learners" with "tutors"—and does not clearly address the objectives of the tutor training lesson. Such inconsistencies can hinder novice tutors' understanding of how the training content applies to their practice.

Additionally, the instruction section of the LLM-generated lessons exhibited similar issues of lack of clarity. Lesson designer 1 highlighted that "*...the generated instructions are overly long and lack a logical backbone to support the reasoning behind the strategies...*" This disorganization often made it difficult for users to follow the intended flow, as instructions were included excessive details and citations. Additionally, lesson designer 1 added "*...There are some cases where the length and citations used are too much, making it difficult to pick out the emphasis of the instruction...*" An example of this overuse of citations can be seen in Table A3 in Digital Appendix. Lesson designer 2 echoed similar concerns, emphasizing the structural and logical disconnect in the instruction sections. "*...The flow and logic can be more natural....*". This lack of cohesive structure often led to instructions that felt fragmented and harder to comprehend. "*...I find it difficult to read and understand since the logic can be a bit disconnected...*". An example of this issue can be found in the following excerpt from a generated lesson: "*...Wallace, Hand, and Prain (2004) highlighted the effectiveness of the Science Writing Heuristic (SWH) in improving conceptual understanding through student-generated questions...*" The lack of context or explanation about what the SWH framework entails makes it difficult for read-

Table 3. Examples of learning objectives generated using three-segment and one-segment prompts

Three-segment generation	One-segment generation
"Explain how polite instructional strategies can improve student engagement and problem-solving in online math tutoring" *"Develop and implement a balanced approach to using polite and direct instructions to foster student independence"*	*"Describe how learners will interpret or explain the tutoring strategy"* *"Outline how learners will generate or implement the tutoring strategy"*

ers unfamiliar with the framework to understand its relevance. This omission can leave readers, particularly novice tutors, struggling to understand how such frameworks apply to their tutoring practices.

5 Discussion and Conclusion

Our study investigated the potential of using large language models (LLMs), specifically with the retrieval-augmented generation (RAG) approach, to automate the generation of tutor training lessons for middle-school math pedagogy. Through structured evaluations, we assessed the quality, strengths, and limitations of LLM-generated lessons. Our findings underscore the importance of task decomposition in lesson generation. By decomposing the task into manageable subtasks, the LLM could maintain logical coherence across lesson components, demonstrating consistency with prior research advocating task decomposition strategies [9,25]. Conversely, the one-segment approach, which involved generating the entire lesson within a single prompt, resulted in lower-quality outputs. Interestingly, the five-segment approach, representing the highest level of decomposition, introduced challenges such as reduced clarity and weaker pedagogical grounding. These challenges highlight the need for further investigation to determine whether they stem from excessive decomposition, potentially disrupting the logical flow and consistency of the generated content, or from rating bias or manual rating inconsistencies that may have influenced the findings. Moreover, our study offers practical insights for using LLMs in educational content creation, demonstrating their ability to generate diverse and realistic lesson scenarios, establish the ethical reliability of the generated lessons, and support their value in scaling inclusive educational resources.

Despite these advantages, our investigation identified key areas where LLM-generated content requires further improvement. Feedback provided for open-ended and multiple-choice questions frequently lacked detailed explanations necessary for addressing misconceptions related to incorrect responses. Furthermore, issues with clarity were evident in the lesson content including title page (e.g., unclear descriptions of learning objectives) and instructional sections (e.g., logical disconnects, and insufficient explanation of jargon). These shortcomings highlight the need for refined prompting strategies to improve precision and coherence in generated content. Another weakness of LLM-generated lessons is the authenticity of academic references, which were often unreliable. Human lesson designers still need to manually verify and supplement references if lessons require source citations. The strengths and weaknesses of LLM-generated lessons emphasize that while LLMs hold immense potential for automating lesson generation, their effectiveness is maximized within a human-AI collaborative workflow. Educators and instructional designers play a crucial role in reviewing and refining AI-generated content to ensure it aligns with pedagogical objectives and meets the nuanced needs of learners.

Future Works. Future research should focus on designing more targeted and specific technical approaches to address limitations identified in LLM-generated lessons. For instance, a multi-agent approach could assign specialized agents to generate, evaluate, and refine lesson content, thereby improving feedback quality through iterative review [3]. Moreover, integrating multiple modalities—such as pairing AI-generated text with relevant visuals or slides—into lessons could better support diverse learning preferences in tutor training [26]. Additionally, our study's lesson evaluation rubric was primarily informed by one resource [23]. While the rubric [23] is comprehensive, future research could benefit from comparing or integrating it with established rubrics in the field to further validate and strengthen lesson evaluation. Then, enabling direct collaboration between instructional designers and the LLM during the refinement process can provide opportunities for real-time adjustments. For example, instructional designers could request immediate changes to tone, clarity, or content specificity, iteratively improving lesson quality. This interactive feedback loop would increase the quality of generated content and streamline the lesson creation process. Lastly, our study primarily focused on evaluating LLM-generated lessons based on human evaluators' judgments, serving as a foundational step in identifying high-quality lessons for further exploration. Future research should conduct experiments to evaluate the relative effectiveness of LLM-generated lessons compared to human-crafted ones, providing insights into their impact on participants' learning outcomes. The results would help clarify the extent to which LLM-generated lessons achieve comparable or complementary results to those designed by human experts.

Acknowledgment. This work was supported by the Learning Engineering Virtual Institute, (https://learning-engineering-virtual-institute.org/) and a grant from the University Research Committee (Grant No. 2401102970) at The University of Hong Kong. The opinions, findings, and conclusions expressed in this paper are solely those of the authors.

References

1. Aleven, V.A., Koedinger, K.R.: An effective metacognitive strategy: learning by doing and explaining with a computer-based cognitive tutor. Cogn. Sci. **26**(2), 147–179 (2002)

2. Butler, A.C.: Multiple-choice testing in education: are the best practices for assessment also good for learning? J. Appl. Res. Mem. Cogn. **7**(3), 323–331 (2018)
3. Cao, J., et al.: From first draft to final insight: a multi-agent approach for feedback generation. arXiv preprint arXiv:2505.04869 (2025)
4. Chhabra, P., Chine, D., Adeniran, A., Gupta, S., Koedinger, K.: An evaluation of perceptions regarding mentor competencies for technology-based personalized learning. In: Society for Information Technology & Teacher Education International Conference, pp. 1812–1817. AACE, San Diego (2022)
5. Dai, W., et al.: Assessing the proficiency of large language models in automatic feedback generation: an evaluation study. CAEAI **7**, 100299 (2024)
6. Diwan, C., Srinivasa, S., Suri, G., Agarwal, S., Ram, P.: Ai-based learning content generation and learning pathway augmentation to increase learner engagement. CAEAI **4**, 100110 (2023)
7. Gao, Y., et al.: Retrieval-augmented generation for large language models: a survey. arXiv preprint arXiv:2312.10997 (2023)
8. Gurung, A., et al.: Multiple choice vs. fill-in problems: the trade-off between scalability and learning. In: Proceedings of the 14th Learning Analytics and Knowledge Conference, pp. 507–517 (2024)
9. Khot, T., et al.: Decomposed prompting: a modular approach for solving complex tasks. arXiv preprint arXiv:2210.02406 (2022)
10. Koedinger, K.R., Corbett, A.T.: Cognitive tutors: technology bringing learning science to the classroom. In: The Cambridge Handbook of the Learning Sciences, pp. 61–77 (2006)
11. Koedinger, K.R., Kim, J., Jia, J.Z., McLaughlin, E.A., Bier, N.L.: Learning is not a spectator sport: doing is better than watching for learning from a mooc. In: Proceedings of the Second (2015) ACM Conference on L@S, pp. 111–120. ACM, Vancouver (2015)
12. Lewis, P., et al.: Retrieval-augmented generation for knowledge-intensive nlp tasks. Adv. Neural. Inf. Process. Syst. **33**, 9459–9474 (2020)
13. Li, H., Leung, J., Shen, Z.: Towards goal-oriented large language model prompting: a survey. arXiv preprint arXiv:2401.14043 (2024)
14. Moein, M., Molavi Hajiagha, M., Faraji, A., Tavakoli, M., Kismihók, G.: Beyond search engines: can large language models improve curriculum development? In: European Conference on Technology Enhanced Learning, pp. 131–136. Springer, Heidelberg (2024). https://doi.org/10.1007/978-3-031-72312-4_17
15. Neuendorf, K.A.: The Content Analysis Guidebook. SAGE Publications (2017)
16. Nguyen, H.A., Bhat, S., Moore, S., Bier, N., Stamper, J.: Towards generalized methods for automatic question generation in educational domains. In: European Conference on Technology Enhanced Learning, pp. 272–284. Springer, Heidelberg (2022). https://doi.org/10.1007/978-3-031-16290-9_20
17. Nguyen, H.A., Stec, H., Hou, X., Di, S., McLaren, B.M.: Evaluating chatgpt's decimal skills and feedback generation in a digital learning game. In: European Conference on Technology Enhanced Learning, pp. 278–293. Springer, Heidelberg (2023). https://doi.org/10.1007/978-3-031-42682-7_19
18. Nickow, A., Oreopoulos, P., Quan, V.: The impressive effects of tutoring on prek-12 learning: a systematic review and meta-analysis of the experimental evidence. Working Paper 27476, National Bureau of Economic Research (2020). https://doi.org/10.3386/w27476
19. Paladines, J., Ramirez, J.: A systematic literature review of intelligent tutoring systems with dialogue in natural language. IEEE Access **8**, 164246–164267 (2020)

20. Radford, A.: Improving language understanding by generative pre-training. OpenAI technical report (2018)
21. Rao, J., Lin, J.: Ramo: retrieval-augmented generation for enhancing moocs recommendations. arXiv preprint arXiv:2407.04925 (2024)
22. Thomas, D., Yang, X., Gupta, S., Adeniran, A., Mclaughlin, E., Koedinger, K.: When the tutor becomes the student: design and evaluation of efficient scenario-based lessons for tutors. In: LAK23, pp. 250–261. ACM, Arlington (2023)
23. Vai, M., Sosulski, K.: Essentials of Online Course Design: A Standards-Based Guide. Routledge, Abingdon (2011)
24. Wiemer-Hastings, P., Graesser, A.C., Harter, D.: The foundations and architecture of autotutor. In: Goettl, B.P., Halff, H.M., Redfield, C.L., Shute, V.J. (eds.) ITS 1998. LNCS, vol. 1452, pp. 334–343. Springer, Heidelberg (1998). https://doi.org/10.1007/3-540-68716-5_39
25. Wu, T., Terry, M., Cai, C.J.: AI chains: transparent and controllable human-ai interaction by chaining large language model prompts. In: Proceedings of the 2022 CHI, pp. 1–22 (2022)
26. Zhao, C.Q., Cao, J., Chen, E., Koedinger, K.R., Lin, J.: Slideitright: using AI to find relevant slides and provide feedback for open-ended questions. arXiv preprint arXiv:2505.04584 (2025)

Augmenting Active Learning with GenAI: Enhancement or Impairment? Evidence from a Data Visualization Course

Vladimir Macko[1], Abdessalam Ouaazki[1], Natalia Bartłomiejczyk[1], Barbara Monteiro[1], Pascal Felber[1], and Adrian Holzer[1,2](✉)

[1] University of Neuchâtel, Rue A.-L. Breguet 2, 2000 Neuchâtel, Switzerland
{vladimir.macko,abdessalam.ouaazki,natalia.bartlomiejczyk, barbara.monteiro,pascal.felber,adrian.holzer}@unine.ch
[2] TD School, University of Technology Sydney, Ultimo, NSW 2007, Australia

Abstract. As Generative Artificial Intelligence (GenAI) is becoming ubiquitous across learning domains, it is crucial to better understand how learning experiences could take advantage of its possibilities and avoid its pitfalls. In this paper, we address this issue by focusing on the context of a data visualization course. What makes this context unique is its combination of two areas where GenAI has shown notable effectiveness: writing code and storytelling. To evaluate how undergraduate students would leverage GenAI in this context, we conducted an in-class between-subjects experiment (N = 43) with a control (no GenAI) and treatment group (with GenAI). In the 60-min experiment, students from the data visualization course were asked to prepare a data story within Jupyter Notebook, including both textual story elements and data visualization. In addition to these two groups, we included AI-only group in which task instructions were given directly to a GenAI tool without further human intervention. The results of our experiment indicate that students perceive GenAI as a tool improving both their learning experience and outcomes. However, an analysis of the learning outcomes exhibits no statistically significant difference between creations of students with or without GenAI support. Interestingly, the outputs generated by GenAI alone outperformed those of both student groups.

Keywords: Generative AI · Data Visualization · Jupyter Notebooks

1 Introduction

Generative Artificial Intelligence (GenAI) has taken over the world in the short two years since the public release of ChatGPT. The fields of learning and education are no exception, with GenAI affecting everything from assessment and authorship to learning tools and tutoring.

Even before GenAI, chatbots have already been investigated for a while in the learning context, as they can help with everything from content integration and

K. Tammets et al. (Eds.): EC-TEL 2025, LNCS 16063, pp. 275–290, 2026.
https://doi.org/10.1007/978-3-032-03870-8_19

access to increasing motivation, maximizing student abilities and engagement [2], providing rapid assistance [23], and saving time overall [31]. These chatbots have become increasingly popular in education, largely because of their ability to improve the learning experience [32]. They simulate human conversation, allowing students to interact through natural language. These tools can make it easier to access learning materials, boost motivation and engagement, support large numbers of users at once, and provide instant help when needed [23]. They are also used as virtual assistants, helping with academic or administrative tasks [37], or answering common questions to create a more personalized and helpful experience [28,31,35].

With the rise of GenAI, a multitude of studies have investigated how this technology can be used in various computational thinking contexts such as Data-Oriented Programming, Python for Data Analysis, and Computational Thinking [8,17,25,26,29,46]. Other studies investigate AI's role in a variety of broad IT and programming-related courses, such as database management, text mining, computer networks and software testing [9,11,18,20,34,36,44]. GenAI allows for the creation of customized learning experiences tailored to individual students' needs, leading to improved learning outcomes [24,38]. It elevates efficiency and productivity by enabling greater task automation and fostering co-creation between humans and AI [27,39]. By handling routine tasks and content delivery, it also frees up educators to concentrate on higher-order thinking skills and provide more meaningful mentorship [6].

Data science is particularly impacted by GenAI as most coders[1] in the industry use GenAI tools as part of their workflows [14]. Some authors see the future as moving from writing code to prompting AI to write code for them [42]. Coders will focus more on quality control rather than syntactic errors [4]. As GenAI seems particularly well suited both for writing code and writing stories [4,45], it could potentially be leveraged to make it easier to craft such data stories [43] and make this task more accessible for less technically oriented individuals [1]. As such, it is crucial to better understand how learners can take advantage of the possibilities of GenAI to craft data stories and avoid their pitfalls [7]. In this paper, we tackle this issue by addressing the following question:

RQ: How can GenAI tools support learners in crafting data visualization stories?

To answer this question, this paper is structured as follows: Sect. 2 presents the related work, Sect. 3 the methodology, and Sect. 4 the results. Then Sect. 5 discusses the findings before Sect. 6 wraps up with a conlusion.

2 Related Work

Several studies specifically investigated the use of GenAI tools for data visualization in educational contexts [3,5,15,21,41].

[1] https://survey.stackoverflow.co/2023/#section-sentiment-and-usage-ai-tools-in-the-development-process.

In terms of methodology, these studies range from a prospective critical analysis of a single author ($N = 1$) [3], to interview studies of several participants ($N = 10$) [5], to multimodal studies with repeated measure experiments in class ($N = 59$ and $N = 26$) [15,41] or in the lab ($N = 39$) [21]. In these studies, the focus was generally solely on coding visualizations, rather than on the combination of storytelling with coding. Most studies did not investigate different conditions comparing a GenAI-augmented learning experience with a non-augmented one. Nonetheless, one study conducted a within-subjects experiment where students experienced several conditions with and without GenAI in the classroom [41].

In terms of findings, the studies explored how students used GenAI when they had access to it. They established that participants predominantly used it for coding assistance [15]. Reported benefits included both efficiency-related improvements, such as time savings, and enhanced learning outcomes [15,41]. Moreover, previous results suggested that GenAI could play an important role in broadening data analysis access as it was found to increase confidence [15] and lower the technical threshold for creating visualizations and conducting exploratory data analysis [3,21]. Most studies found positive user feedback [21,41]. Efficiency and lower access barriers could encourage creativity, as they allow for rapid prototyping and iterative refinement [5]. Among the identified risks, research mentions inaccuracies in GenAI outputs, difficulty in effectively prompting the tool, as well as concerns about over-reliance [3,15].

These studies provide promising preliminary findings and hint at open research gaps. First, while some studies included data narratives or storytelling in their task description, it is not clear how GenAI improves these aspects. Second, it is still unclear how a GenAI-augmented learning experience compares quantitatively with a learning experience without GenAI in terms of both students' perceived task efficiency and actual performance. This paper will aim to address these gaps by (1) setting up a task combining storytelling and data analysis and (2) conducting a between-subject experiment in the wild to better understand outcomes quantitatively.

3 Methodology

The study takes an experimental design approach in the wild. As such, we designed a controlled experiment with a treatment group in which students had access to GenAI (HAI, where H stands for humans) and a control group in which students were alone (H). This design allows for a between-group comparison. We gathered data in a multi-modal fashion, combining student surveys with learning outcomes and log data from chatbot conversations. In addition to these two groups, we also created a third group (AI) in which GenAI operated alone, based only on an initial human prompt, to investigate how it approaches the task with minimal human intervention.

3.1 Pedagogical Scenario

As part of their final assignment for an undergraduate Data Visualization course, students were asked to prepare a Jupyter Notebook file containing annotated data visualizations in the context of a charity donation request. The dataset, sourced from https://www.gapminder.org, includes yearly values (2000–2022) for four indicators–access to water, sanitation, internet, and extreme poverty–across a selection of developing countries. The selected developing countries were intentionally chosen in order to showcase the continuous improvement of the measured variables. To highlight a stark contrast, we also included a non-developing country with the highest Human Development Index in 2024, offering a benchmark against the data from developing countries. Figure 1 shows the 60-minute assignment description.

```
- Assignment -- You are a data visualization expert, and you have received a
  request from a local charity to prepare convincing support material for
  their campaign. Leaflets will be designed later on in the campaign based
  on your essential input. You should now:

- Prepare a simple but complete Jupyter Notebook file (.ipynb) that contains
  a captivating title, two commented, professionally looking Python
  visualizations using the provided data and a catchy punchline at the end.
  Limit the total text amount to 2 sentences per visualization at maximum.
  The notebook should contain all the Python code needed for their
  construction (the notebook is self-sufficient).

- Also, include a textual description of a suggestion of 1 illustrative
  photograph that should be included to enhance the impact of your
  visualizations (do not include the image, just describe how it should
  look). No other files should be prepared.

- Keep in mind that the main goal is to use storytelling to convince the
  general public that their contributions to charity make a real difference,
  and therefore, they should contribute. Only the data from the provided
  dataset (CharityDataset.csv) can be used in the visualizations, and no
  other sources should be included.

- Markdown cells can be used in the Jupyter notebook to include text
  comments. The text comments should be factually correct and should be
  related to the visualization presented. All visualizations should respect
  all the Visual design principles, and all good practices of data
  visualization should be followed.}
```

Fig. 1. Study assigmnent description

3.2 Procedure

The experiment was conducted during the final class of the Data Visualization course taught in French. The participants were bachelor students in data science, economics, and digital humanities. Out of 54 students taking this class, 46 students voluntarily participated in this study. They received a financial compensation equivalent to USD 10.

At the beginning of the class, students were randomly assigned to two groups based on the numbers they drew from an envelope. Groups were then placed in two different classrooms. All participants were presented with the same assignment description. This assignment was scored for study purposes but did not impact the students' grades for the course. The only difference between the groups was that group HAI was encouraged to use a GenAI tool such as ChatGPT or Copilot to help them to solve the task, while group H was explicitly asked not to use any AI tool and use only their knowledge and internet search engines to solve the tasks. Furthermore, group AI was generated by submitting the assignment description (in Fig. 1) to ChatGPT4-o. To ensure coherence with the student notebooks, the following sentence was added at the end of the description: *Make sure you produce a Python Jupyter notebook with content in French that can be run.* We prompted the model 50 times, resulting in 50 different Jupyter Notebook files. We removed files that did not meet the expected format (.ipynb) or those that could not be opened (24 occurrences in total). Accepted files ($N = 26$) from the AI group were then renamed for anonymity before they were scored. The study was approved by our ethics board.

3.3 Measures

We gathered data from three main sources: surveys to inquire about demographics and to measure student attitudes about the learning process, task output inspection to measure learning outcomes, and chatbot conversations to measure learning process behaviour for students in the HAI group. We also measured the level of academic performance by collecting their final course grade.

Learning outcome metrics. Two co-authors, who were not involved in the creation of AI-only group files, analyzed all anonymized notebooks from all three groups. Each notebook was evaluated along five main dimensions (Visual quality, Storytelling, Illustration Quality, Content relevance, and Notebook quality) on a scale from 1 (poor) to 5 (excellent) and combined into an average *Assignment score*. The measures relied on students adequately including visual design principles in their productions, as well as following standard storytelling approaches covered in the course [12]. The relevance of the visualization and illustration is evaluated based on how fitting it is to a leaflet showing the impact of a charitable organization. For instance, line charts showing evolution over the years are considered a suitable type of visualization. In contrast, pie-charts or bar-charts showing only the differences between measures in different countries in a single year are less relevant. Finally, notebook quality was assessed based on how effectively it was used to structure the assignment, such as organizing information clearly, grouping related content, and separating code from narrative text.

Two independent experts graded the notebooks. We measured inter-rater reliability on the total score for each notebook using the quadratic weighted Cohen κ and Pearson correlation. The results of a quadratic weighted Cohen's κ ($\kappa = 0.690$), and a Pearson correlation ($r = 0.827$, $p < 0.001$) showed acceptable agreement between experts.

Learning Process Metrics. For the learning process, we used the items of the NASA task load index (NASA TLX [10]): *Mental Demand*, which assesses how mentally demanding the students perceived the task to be, *Physical Demand*; which assesses how physically demanding the students perceived the task to be; *Temporal Demand*, which assesses how time-pressured or hurried the students felt during the task; *Perceived Performance*, which assesses how successful students believed they were in completing the task (this item is reverse in a *Failure* item to calculate the combined TLX score); *Effort*, which assesses how much effort students felt they needed to invest to complete the task; and *Frustration*, which assesses the degree to which students felt frustrated, stressed, or discouraged during the task. The items are combined to create an index from 0–100.

Usefulness Metrics. To evaluate the attitudes towards the usefulness of the GenAI tool, we developed a 4-item TAM-based questionnaire [19] with items that asked about: (1) How useful GenAI was for this task, (2) how GenAI helped improve the quality of work, (3) how effective GenAI was to reducing the time spent on the task, and (4) if the student would want to use GenAI in the future for similar tasks.

4 Results

A total of 69 Jupyter notebooks were included in the study, with 22 assigned to the H group, 21 to the HAI group, and 26 to the AI group. As illustrated in Fig. 2, the two student groups were comparable in terms of age, with a mean age of 23.55 years ($SD = 5.57$) in the H group and 21.48 years ($SD = 2.93$) in the HAI group. Gender distribution was balanced across groups, with 36% female in the H group and 33% female in the HAI group. No significant differences were found between groups in demographics, i.e., Age ($t = 1.54$, $p = .135$) and Gender ($z = 0.21$, $p = .835$) or academic achievement, i.e., Grade ($t = 1.35$, $p = .186$).

4.1 Learning Outcomes (H Vs. HAI Vs. AI)

We conducted a one-way analysis of variance (ANOVA) to compare the effects of three experimental conditions (H, HAI, and AI) on the Assignment Score. The results are visualized in boxplots with significance levels in Fig. 3 for the Assignment Score as well as for each of its five dimensions. The results show a

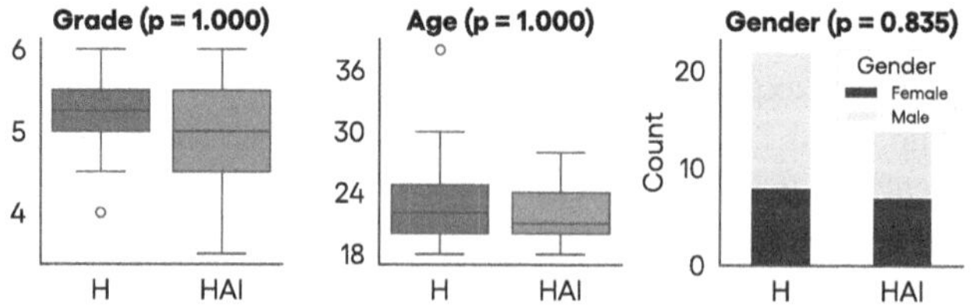

Fig. 2. Comparison of baseline characteristics between the H (N = 22) and HAI (N = 21) groups with p values.

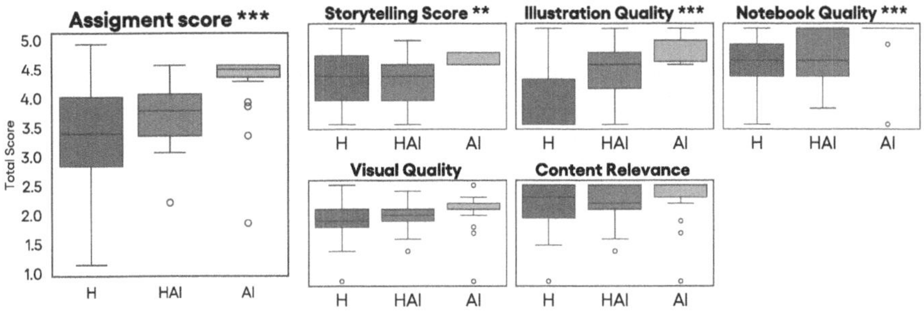

Fig. 3. Assignment scores and sub-dimension ratings for each group (H, HAI, AI). Left: overall Assignment Score; Right: breakdown across sub-dimensions. Sig. levels from ANOVA tests are indicated with asterisks: p < .05 (*), < .01 (**), < .001 (***).

significant difference between the groups for the Assignment Score ($F = 10.466$, $p = .0001$). This significant difference is also found in three out of five dimensions of the score (Storytelling, Illustration quality, and Notebook quality). Visually, it seems that for the Assignment Score, as well as for its composing dimensions, the more automated the task (moving from all humans to all AI), the better the score. To confirm this intuition, we conducted a post hoc Tukey HSD test for the Assignment Score (see Table 1).

The results show that the AI group appears to be significantly superior to the other groups with very large effect sizes (Cohen's d > 1.0). Interestingly, the results do not detect any significant differences between the AI+H and the H groups. It should be noted that when conducting this post hoc analysis on the composing dimension of the Assignment Score, a similar picture arises, AI scores significantly better than both other groups on the Storytelling score, the notebook quality and the illustrative quality. However, except for the Illustration Quality, HAI performs better. The HAI and H groups are not statistically different in 4 out of 5 dimensions. As such, students with or without GenAI performed similarly on this task.

4.2 Learning Process (H Vs. HAI)

To understand if there were differences in how students perceived the task, we conducted a series of t-tests between the two groups of students on the task loading index (TLX) scores (see Fig. 4). Overall, the TLX score was significantly higher in the group without GenAI ($M = 50.00$, $SD = 16.49$) compared to the group with GenAI assistance ($M = 31.47$, $SD = 16.91$), $t = 3.636$, $p = 0.0008$, with a very large effect size (Cohen's $d = 1.11$). As such, students who had access to GenAI found the task easier than those who did not. All dimensions of the TLX, except Physical load score, are significantly higher for students without access to GenAI. Interestingly, students with GenAI had a higher perception of their Performance (reversed Failure), even though this did not translate into actual improved performance as measured by their assignment scores.

4.3 Chatbot Perception (HAI)

To understand if students were able to adequately judge whether GenAI was an asset for their task, we conducted a linear regression with the Assignment Score as the dependent variable and GenAI usefulness as the main predictor, using data from the *HAIgroup*. The model included Gender, Age, and Grade as control variables. The regression showed a significant *negative* effect of GenAI usefulness on the Assignment Score ($\beta = -3.23$, $p = .025$). Gender, Age, and Grade were not significant. Table 2 presents the statistics, while Fig. 5 shows the results visually. The model explained 36.8% of the variance in Assignment Score ($R^2 = .368$; adjusted $R^2 = .210$; $F(4, 16) = 2.33$, $p = .100$). The standardized coefficient for GenAI usefulness was $\beta = -0.55$, and the semi-partial R^2 indicated that it uniquely explained 24% of the variance in the Assignment Score (a medium to large effect). A reason for this negative correlation could be that students who are less proficient academically might find GenAI more useful, and even if their results are worse, they could nevertheless have benefited from the help of GenAI. However, since we controlled for academic achievement by including the Grade variable as a control, this explanation seems less plausible. As such, these results seem to show that students were not only not able to see when GenAI is useful for them (an absence of correlation would have supported that claim), but they also seemed to be misled as to when GenAI is useful.

Table 1. Tukey HSD post-hoc comparisons for assignment scores between groups (H, HAI, AI). Table includes group means and standard deviations, mean differences with 95% confidence intervals, adjusted *p*-values, sig. levels, and Cohen's *d* effect sizes.

Comparison	Mean(SD)	Mean(SD)	Mean Diff	95% CI	p-adj	Sig.	Cohen's d
AI vs. H	4.29 (0.57)	3.40 (0.90)	−0.89	[−1.37, −0.42]	<.001	***	1.18
AI vs. HAI	4.29 (0.57)	3.73 (0.54)	−0.56	[−1.04, −0.08]	.018	*	1.02
H vs. HAI	3.40 (0.90)	3.73 (0.54)	+0.33	[−0.17, +0.83]	.264		–

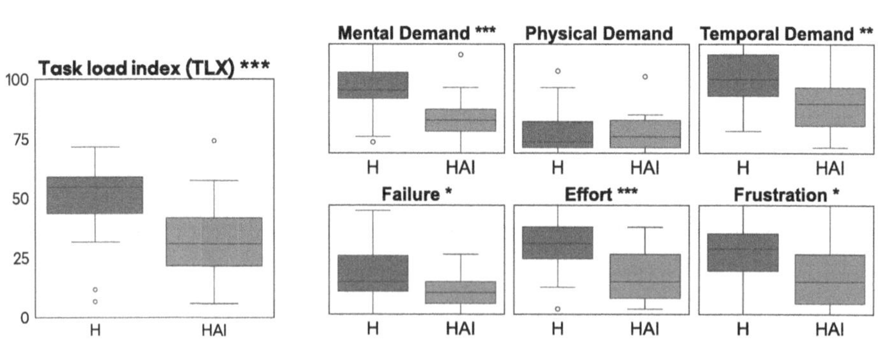

Fig. 4. Perceived workload ratings (NASA-TLX) for the H and HAI groups. Left: total score; Right: overview for each dimension of the NASA-TLX score. Significance levels from T-tests are indicated with asterisks: p < .05 (*), < .01 (**), < .001 (***).

4.4 Qualitative Insights Into GenAI User Experience (HAI)

Besides collecting quantitative data, the survey gathered qualitative feedback on user perceptions about their experience during the task.

Perceived Benefits. Reflecting the quantitative results, participants in the HAI group perceive GenAI to be generally "easy to use" (P17, M, 21y), very helpful and efficient for their project. Descriptions such as *"very efficient tool, understands almost everything you want to do"* (P35, M, 19y) and *"The time required for the task is considerably reduced"* (P27, M, 25y) were common. Several participants also reported that AI assistance reduced their cognitive load. As one explained, *"ChatGPT has helped me remember certain details that I wouldn't have thought of. It also reminded me of things I'd forgotten. Overall, it decreased my mental workload in relation to the task in hand"* (P41, F, 27y). The use of AI was described as helpful and enhanced overall productivity. As participants stated, *"It's a tool that saves time and also allows you to learn in a more practical and effective way"* (P26, M, 28y), and *"ChatGPT makes the task look easy"* (P33, M, 19y). Several participants further emphasized the pedagogical

Table 2. Linear regression predicting Assignment Score (TOTAL) from GenAI usefulness, controlling for Gender, Age, and self-reported Grade. The table includes unstandardized and standardized coefficients, and semi-partial R^2 for the main predictor.

Predictor	β (raw)	β (std)	SE	p-value	95% CI	Semi-partial R^2
Intercept	37.84	–	16.79	0.039	[2.25, 73.43]	–
GenAI usefulness	−3.23	−0.55	1.31	**0.025**	[−6.00, −0.45]	0.240
Gender	−2.58	−0.33	1.59	0.124	[−5.95, 0.79]	–
Age	0.35	0.27	0.42	0.416	[−0.53, 1.23]	–
Grade	−0.34	−0.06	1.72	0.846	[−3.99, 3.31]	–

Model fit: $R^2 = 0.368$, Adjusted $R^2 = 0.210$, $F(4, 16) = 2.33$, $p = 0.100$

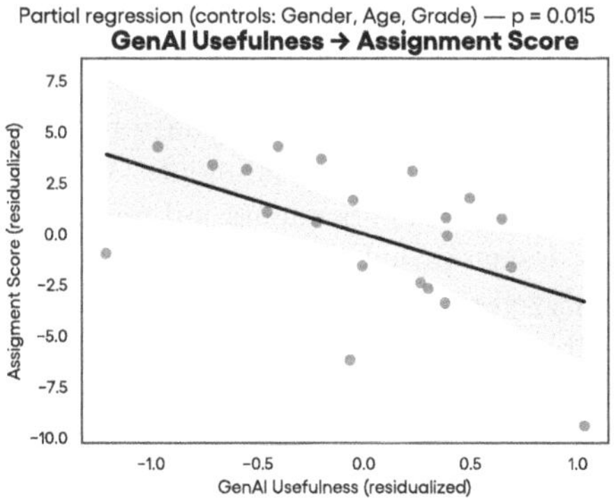

Fig. 5. Partial regression plot showing the relationship between *GenAI usefulness* and *Assignment Score*, controlling for Gender, Age, and Grade.

and motivational impact of the tool. One referred praised GenAI for assisting them in *"finding solutions to the problems people face"* (P20, F, 21y). At the same time, another described it as *"a teacher who is always available, which is very motivating"* (P25, M, 21y). Another participant reported that the tool enabled a rapid transition from ideation to execution, stating that *"ChatGPT makes it quite easy to have a good brainstorm and then come up with a solid project base quickly, which allowed me to concentrate on developing the content"* (P30, M, 25y).

Perceived Risks. In addition to the perceived benefits, some participants identified risks associated with the use of GenAI. Despite a participant explaining that *"the use is practical and allows non-completer or beginner students to succeed by understanding"* (P13, F, 20y), several others questioned how useful the technology is for beginners and how easy-to-use the solution really is. One participant noted challenges related to prompting, stating that it was *"very efficient, but the request made to ChatGPT must be precise and clear"* (P06, F, 24y). Another expressed concerns about the quality of GenAI's generated content, noting that *"the output was not qualitative"* (P37, M, 21y). Others questioned the tool's ability to understand users' requests. As P23 noted, *"Using ChatGPT was moderately helpful to me because it took a long time for it to understand exactly what I was asking. It was complicated"* (P23, F, 20y). P10 (M, 21y) also noted that *"it took several attempts to get what I wanted. I think someone with the right skills on the program [without ChatGPT] might have been quicker"*. Furthermore, one participant highlighted risks related to hindering their critical thinking, stating that *"it [ChatGPT] prevented me from relying on my ideas, even though the AI was good. The AI ideas sometimes made me forget my critical mind"* (P16, M, 19y).

These insights suggest that GenAI is perceived as an easy-to-use tool that provides an immediate sense of usefulness. However, upon closer inspection, it appears that users need more time and skill than they initially expected to get exactly what they want from the tool.

4.5 Chatbot Conversation Analysis (HAI)

Participants in the HAI group were asked to share the conversations they had with ChatGPT while completing their assignments. We received data from 86% of the participants (18 out of 21). Students submitted 288 prompts in total ($M = 16.3, SD = 17.3$). Usage varied substantially, ranging from 3 to 72 prompts per participant. We analyzed the content of each prompt and coded it into one of six categories based on how participants used GenAI: General, Analysis, Visual, Storytelling, Off-topic, and Other (see Table 3 for details and example prompts).

To gain additional insights into how students who found GenAI to be more useful than average utilized the tool, we conducted case studies of the two highest performers and the two lowest performers based on the Assignment Score.

The first low performer (P26, M, 28y, score 3.4), who has the second highest number of total interactions (45), appears to have started the assignment in an

Table 3. Prompt categories, descriptions, and example prompts

Category	Example Prompt(s)
Analysis (28.8%) Technical queries focused on programming help, troubleshooting, or debugging	*"Correct this code: [Copy-paste error message]"; "Hi, could you generate some code for me to upload .csv content to python so that I can use the content to create visualizations?"*
Storytelling (17.4%) Requests for written content, ideas, explanations, or help making sense of text	*"I have this database, and I need to find some interesting plots to do, which variables pair well?"; "Add emotion"; "'Percentage of the population with access to sanitation' What does this sentence mean?"*
Visual (11.5%) Design-related prompts, including aesthetic adjustments and visual consistency	*"Perfect, is there any way the colours can match (each country has its own colour)?"; "For the first graph I want to thicken the lines"; "Generate an illustrative photograph that can be added to reinforce the impact of your visualisations"*
General (8.7%) General questions, sometimes minimal interaction (i.e., copy-pasted task instruction)	*[copy-paste the instructions], "Show it to me directly", "Can you do the same thing with my database?"*
Off-topic (31.3%) Prompts unrelated to the task sent before the experiment began. This category is included to consider the impact of students performing the task in an old conversation threat	*[student starts the exercise on an old conversation]; "Explain to me the concept of frontiers of opportunity in economics"*
Other (2.4%) Simple interaction words	*"Perfect"; "Thank you"; "Continue"*

old conversation. In fact, 39 of them fell into the Off-topic category, all of which were generated before the assignment queries. Four of the remaining six prompts were used for analysis, mainly to help him with coding issues by copy-pasting the same error message three times in a row. This suggests that the student had difficulties correcting his code and struggled to get the answer he was looking for. The second low-performer (P10, M, 20y, score 2.2) used GenAI sparingly (9 prompts), despite finding it very useful. He also saw his own limitations, reporting that he needed several attempts to get results, and believed a skilled person might be faster without GenAI. This is reflected in his prompts, mostly related to code or debugging (5 out of 9), where he struggled to clearly express his needs. For example, after receiving several unsatisfactory responses, he ended up typing simple instructions like *"but say the code"*, reflecting a struggle to formulate effective queries.

The first high-performer (P6, F, 24y, score 4.5), understood that to be efficient, her instructions needed to be *"precise and clear"*. Her usage was minimal (4 prompts in total), consisting of two General prompts and two storytelling-related prompts. The prompts show a clear and targeted strategy: sending the assignment, uploading the necessary files, and asking for a French version of the output. This efficient use aligns with a low prompt count and a focused interaction. The second high performer (P20, F, 21y, score 4.5) took a different approach and performed iterative refinement. She performed an average number of prompts (16), mainly to improve her Storytelling (10 prompts) and visual design (4 prompts). The conversation reflects rich ideation and refinement, with repeated requests for additional alternatives such as *"another"* or *"many"*.

On one hand, these results confirm that GenAI's pontential can be unlocked by an adequate prompting strategy and by using the tool in a more creative and iterative way during exploratory processes, an aspect students seem to be aware of. On the other hand, the two low-performers repeatedly reformulated their prompts, suggesting that GenAI's potential is limited when students struggle to clearly express their needs.

5 Discussion

This research aimed to answer how GenAI tools can support learners in crafting data visualization stories (RQ). Our findings indicate that the introduction of GenAI into data visualization learning significantly decreased the perceived workload of students. As shown by the NASA-TLX results, students who used GenAI reported less mental and temporal demand to accomplish their tasks and expressed less frustration and fear of failure. The differences in these measures between groups are significant ($p < .001$) with a very large effect size (Cohen's $d = 1.11$). These results complement the existing literature that highlights the potential of GenAI to scaffold complex tasks and reduce cognitive load in learning environments [13,46]. These findings, combined with the qualitative analysis of student comments, suggest that augmenting a data visualization task with GenAI can make it much less overwhelming for students and potentially more motivating to complete. Accordingly, GenAI seems to play a positive role in lowering the entry barrier to data visualization learning by guiding users and reducing uncertainty, in line with the previous literature [5].

However, our results do not indicate an improvement in learning outcomes measured through Assignment Scores. The existing literature reported mixed results about the impact of GenAI on learning outcomes. While several studies highlight improvements [33,34], others observe declines [20,22], and some report no significant change [40]. In our context, GenAI integration did not lead to statistically significant differences in assignment performance. This suggests that while GenAI may have eased the learning process and reduced perceived workload, it did not necessarily translate into measurable gains in learning outcomes.

Based on our results, one could argue that GenAI's support improves the learning experience without reducing performance, which is a positive outcome.

However, our investigation of the link between AI's usefulness and the Assignment Scores showed that there was a significant negative association between these two variables, controlling for Age, Gender and Grade. This finding seems to indicate that there was an illusion of usefulness rather than real learning support. This finding can be viewed in light of previous work that identified the risk of overreliance as a potential danger [3,15].

Furthermore, our results show that the AI-alone group failed to produce valid outputs in terms of format in 48% of the cases. But, when it did, it outperformed the groups involving students significantly. These findings suggest that the HAI group could have achieved better results simply by submitting the assignment instructions as a prompt and using the AI's output directly. However, students did not take this approach. This underlines the lack of skills in using these tools to their full extent, a concern highlighted in the previous literature [8,29]. This could potentially be mitigated by training students in using GenAI tools and improving their prompting skills, as highlighted in prior work (e.g., [20,30]). The conversations students had with GenAI show that low performers shared a pattern of engaging with ChatGPT in long, multi-topic conversations without starting a new chat for the study task. The earlier content in those threads likely introduced noise that may have impacted the model's ability to generate relevant and coherent responses. This aligns with known limitations of large language models, which can struggle with context retention and topic relevance in extended, multi-topic conversations [16]. In contrast, high performers used several efficient strategies, from a few precise prompts to repeated iterations to refine the output. These findings show that user prompting behavior and tool literacy emerge as central factors in determining the effectiveness of GenAI in educational tasks [18]. As such, it might be important to further integrate GenAI into a learning experience by constraining its capabilities and providing more task-focused interaction. As advocated by Mezzaro et al. [20], even if restricting access to the GPT model may limit students' freedom, it can support their learning. This approach could be leveraged for more open-ended projects such as the one discussed here.

Finally, this research is not without limitations. While a blind review process was used, reviewers were often able to guess which group an output belonged to, which could have introduced bias in the evaluation. In addition, the relatively small sample size per group limited the ability to detect small effect sizes. Also, this study does not explore the long-term effects of GenAI integrations on learning outcomes; therfore, the future research is needed to understand sustained impact on students' skills and knowledge.

6 Conclusions

With the increasing need to teach students to craft convincing data stories, it is crucial to understand how GenAI can lower the entry barrier and lead to improved outcomes. To do so, we conducted a between-subject controlled experiment in a classroom setting (N = 43) with a treatment group where students have access to GenAI (HAI) and a control group where they do not (H). Our findings show that when students have access to GenAI, the task load is significantly reduced with a very large effect size. However, the results show that the actual performance scores did not improve. What is more concerning is that the more students found GenAI useful, the worse their learning outcomes were, indicating a risk of overreliance. Finally, we also included a third group (AI alone), which outperformed the other two groups significantly in most performance qualities. This final result shows that GenAI offers promising possibilities for improved outcomes, yet learning experiences should be carefully scaffolded and students guided to take full advantage of GenAI capabilities.

Acknowledgments. This research was partially supported by the Swiss National Science Foundation (SNSF) under project number IZSEZ0_225217, and by Swissuniversities PgB project *STAGE: STEM Teaching in the Age of Generative AI.*

References

1. Bhaskaran, H., Kashyap, G., Mishra, H.: Teaching data journalism: a systematic review. Journal. Pract. **18**(3), 722–743 (2024)
2. Clarizia, F., Colace, F., Lombardi, M., Pascale, F., Santaniello, D.: Chatbot: an education support system for student. In: Castiglione, A., Pop, F., Ficco, M., Palmieri, F. (eds.) CSS 2018. LNCS, vol. 11161, pp. 291–302. Springer, Cham (2018). https://doi.org/10.1007/978-3-030-01689-0_23
3. DeJeu, E.B.: Using generative ai to facilitate data analysis and visualization: a case study of olympic athletes. J. Bus. Tech. Commun. **38**(3), 225–241 (2024)
4. Denny, P., et al.: Computing education in the era of generative AI. CACM **67**(2), 56–67 (2024)
5. Ding, Z., Chan, J.: Intelligent canvas: enabling design-like exploratory visual data analysis with generative ai through rapid prototyping, iteration and curation. arXiv preprint arXiv:2402.08812 (2024)
6. Firat, M.: What chatgpt means for universities: perceptions of scholars and students. J. Appl. Learn. Teach. **6**(1) (2023)
7. Fu, Y., Stasko, J.: More than data stories: broadening the role of visualization in contemporary journalism. IEEE Trans. Visualizat. Comput. Graph. (2023)
8. Garg, A., Rajendran, R.: The impact of structured prompt-driven generative ai on learning data analysis in engineering students. In: CSEDU'24. Science and Technology publications (2024)
9. Gottipati, S., Shim, K.J., Shankararaman, V.: Ai for connectivism learning - undergraduate students' experiences of chatgpt in advanced programming courses. In: AMCIS. AIS (2023)
10. Hart, S.G., Staveland, L.E.: Development of nasa-tlx (task load index): results of empirical and theoretical research. In: Advances in Psychology, vol. 52, pp. 139–183. Elsevier (1988)
11. Hsin, W.J.: The effect of chatgpt: student perspective and performance achievement. J. Comput. Sci. Coll. **39.0** (2024)
12. Kernbach, S.: Storytelling canvas: a visual framework for developing and delivering resonating stories. In: IV'18, pp. 390–395. IEEE (2018)

13. Khatib, R., Mattalo, B.: Enhancing learning experiences with genai chatbots: a tutorial approach. In: ICIS. AIS (2024)
14. Khemka, M., Houck, B.: Toward effective AI support for developers: a survey of desires and concerns. CACM **67**(11), 42–49 (2024)
15. Kim, N.W., Ko, H.K., Myers, G., Bach, B.: Chatgpt in data visualization education: a student perspective. In: VL/HCC'24, pp. 109–120. IEEE (2024)
16. Kim, Y., Lee, J., Kim, S., Park, J., Kim, J.: Understanding users' dissatisfaction with chatgpt responses: types, resolving tactics, and the effect of knowledge level. In: IUI'24, pp. 385–404. ACM (2024)
17. Liao, J., Zhong, L., Zhe, L., Xu, H., Liu, M., Xie, T.: Scaffolding computational thinking with chatgpt. IEEE Trans. Learn. Technol. **17.0** (2024)
18. Lyu, W., Wang, Y., Chung, T., Sun, Y., Zhang, Y.: Evaluating the effectiveness of llms in introductory computer science education: a semester-long field study. In: L@S'24. ACM (2024)
19. Masrom, M.: Technology acceptance model and e-learning. Technology **21**(24), 81 (2007)
20. Mezzaro, S., Gambi, A., Fraser, G.: An empirical study on how large language models impact software testing learning. In: EASE'24. ACM (2024)
21. Ochoa, X., Huang, X., Shao, Y.: Exploring the potential of generative ai to support non-experts in learning analytics practice. J. Learn. Anal. (2025)
22. Ohm, M., Bungartz, C., Boes, F., Meier, M.: Assessing the impact of large language models on cybersecurity education: a study of chatgpt's influence on student performance. In: ARES '24. IEEE (2024)
23. Okonkwo, C.W., Ade-Ibijola, A.: Chatbots applications in education: a systematic review. Comput. Educ. **2**, 100033 (2021)
24. Ouaazki, A., Bergram, K., Farah, J.C., Gillet, D., Holzer, A.: Generative ai-enabled conversational interaction to support self-directed learning experiences in transversal computational thinking. In: CUI'24. ACM (2024)
25. Ouaazki, A., Bergram, K., Holzer, A.: Leveraging chatgpt to enhance computational thinking learning experiences. In: TALE'23. IEEE (2023)
26. Padiyath, A., et al.: Insights from social shaping theory: the appropriation of large language models in an undergraduate programming course. In: ICER'24. ACM (2024)
27. Peña-Fernández, S., Meso-Ayerdi, K., Larrondo-Ureta, A., Díaz-Noci, J.: Without journalists, there is no journalism: the social dimension of generative artificial intelligence in the media. El Profesional de la información **32**(2) (2023)
28. Peyton, K., Unnikrishnan, S.: A comparison of chatbot platforms with the state-of-the-art sentence bert for answering online student faqs. Res. Eng. **17**, 100856 (2023)
29. Qureshi, B.: Chatgpt in computer science curriculum assessment: an analysis of its successes and shortcomings. In: ICSLT '23: Proceedings of the 2023 9th International Conference on e-Society, e-Learning and e-Technologies. ACM (2023)
30. Rajala, J., Hukkanen, J., Hartikainen, M., Niemelä, P.: Call me kiran – chatgpt as a tutoring chatbot in a computer science course. In: Mindtrek '23 (2023)
31. Ranoliya, B.R., Raghuwanshi, N., Singh, S.: Chatbot for university related faqs. In: ICACCI'17, pp. 1525–1530. IEEE (2017)
32. Rodrigues, C., Reis, A., Pereira, R., Martins, P., Sousa, J., Pinto, T.: A review of conversational agents in education. In: TECH-EDU'22. Springer, Heidelberg (2022). https://doi.org/10.1007/978-3-031-22918-3_37

33. Samarakoon, P., Asanka, D., Jayalal, S., Jayalath, N.: Analyzing the learning effectiveness of generative ai for software development for undergraduates in sri lanka. In: SCSE'24, vol. 7.0. IEEE (2024)
34. Sengewald, J., Wilz, M., Lackes, R.: Ai-assisted learning feedback: should gen-ai feedback be restricted to improve learning success? A pilot study in a sql lecture. In: ECIS'24. AIS (2024)
35. Sethi, F.: FAQ (frequently asked questions) chatbot for conversation. Int. J. Comput. Sci. Eng. **8**(10), 7–10 (2020)
36. Sheese, B., Liffiton, M., Savelka, J., Denny, P.: Patterns of student help-seeking when using a large language model-powered programming assistant. In: ACE '24. ACM (2024)
37. Sinha, S., Basak, S., Dey, Y., Mondal, A.: An educational chatbot for answering queries. In: Mandal, J.K., Bhattacharya, D. (eds.) Emerging Technology in Modelling and Graphics. AISC, vol. 937, pp. 55–60. Springer, Singapore (2020). https://doi.org/10.1007/978-981-13-7403-6_7
38. Su, J., Yang, W.: Unlocking the power of chatgpt: a framework for applying generative ai in education. ECNU Rev. Educ. **6**(3), 355–366 (2023)
39. Sun, Y., Jang, E., Ma, F., Wang, T.: Generative AI in the wild: prospects, challenges, and strategies. In: CHI'24, pp. 1–16 (2024)
40. Vadaparty, A., et al.: Cs1-llm: integrating llms into cs1 instruction. In: ITiCSE'24. ACM (2024)
41. Valverde-Rebaza, J., González, A., Navarro-Hinojosa, O., Noguez, J.: Advanced large language models and visualization tools for data analytics learning. In: Frontiers in Education, vol. 9, p. 1418006. Frontiers Media SA (2024)
42. Welsh, M.: The end of programming. CACM **66**(1), 34–35 (2022)
43. Wenger, D., Hossain, M.S., Senseman, J.R.: Ai and the impact on journalism education. Journal. Mass Commun. Educ. **80**(1), 97–114 (2025)
44. Yang, A.C.M., Lin, J.Y., Lin, C.Y., Ogata, H.: Enhancing python learning with pytutor: efficacy of a chatgpt-based intelligent tutoring system in programming education. Comput. Educ. **7.0** (2024)
45. Ye, Y., et al.: Generative ai for visualization: State of the art and future directions. Visual Inf. (2024)
46. Yilmaz, R., Yilmaz, F.G.K.: The effect of generative artificial intelligence (ai)-based tool use on students' computational thinking skills, programming self-efficacy and motivation. Comput. Educ. **4.0** (2023)

Improving Text Readability to Support Student Comprehension and Learning: An LLM-Powered Approach

Guilherme Pascoal[1,4], Marlinde van den Bosch[1,6], Olga Viberg[1,5](✉), Jacqueline Wong[2,5], and Carrie Demmans Epp[3,5]

[1] KTH Royal Institute of Technology, 10044 Stockholm, Sweden
oviberg@kth.se
[2] Utrecht University, Utrecht, The Netherlands
[3] EdTekLA, University of Alberta, Edmonton, Canada
[4] Instituto Superior Técnico, Universidade de Lisboa, Lisbon, Portugal
[5] Digital Futures, Stockholm, Sweden
[6] Leiden University, Leiden, The Netherlands

Abstract. Reading proficiency is predictive of academic success, yet many students, especially those with diverse learning needs, struggle with complex academic texts. Existing support tools often fail to adequately address challenges related to the complexity of text vocabulary and grammar. However, large language models (LLMs) might be able to meet this need. We compared the effectiveness of two prompting strategies for simplifying academic texts (N = 2,000): one that used plain-text instructions and another that incorporated a readability metric. The Metric-Guided Prompt demonstrated a significant reduction in text complexity as measured by the Flesch-Kincaid Grade Level. Following this intrinsic evaluation, we conducted a between-subjects study with 37 students to determine whether there were differences in learner perceptions of the texts and their learning gains, based on the source of the information provided (i.e., the original and simplified texts). The results of both the intrinsic evaluation and the user study indicate that the Metric-Guided Prompt improves text readability without hindering learning. These findings underscore the potential for appropriately prompted LLMs to foster academic success for diverse learners by improving information access and supporting comprehension.

Keywords: Readability · Prompt Engineering · Learning · GenAI

1 Introduction

Reading is a fundamental skill that predicts student success [24]. Unfortunately, due to the complexity of academic texts, many students struggle to read and understand their course materials [26,32,37]. These difficulties are particularly common among students with diverse learning needs, including those with

K. Tammets et al. (Eds.): EC-TEL 2025, LNCS 16063, pp. 291–305, 2026.
https://doi.org/10.1007/978-3-032-03870-8_20

dyslexia or attention deficit hyperactivity disorder (ADHD), or those who participate in educational programs offered in a non-native language [12]. Difficulties in reading comprehension, word reading, and spelling can hinder learning progress and academic achievement [20], limiting students' access to higher levels of education [24] and their future job opportunities [14]. The global decline in reading proficiency among students in the last decade, especially in recent years, further emphasizes the critical need to develop support in reading for all learners [19].

Existing mechanisms to support learners with weaker reading skills, such as text-to-speech tools, provide useful assistance for specific challenges that include difficulties in decoding written text and limited reading fluency [21]. They can also support general comprehension [5]. However, these tools often fail to help learners process the complex vocabulary and grammatical structures found in academic texts [32]. An obvious solution to this would be to simplify the grammar and vocabulary used in these texts. However, traditional methods for text simplification [6] can be labor intensive and may not accurately capture the essence of the original content [22], indicating a need for effective automated text simplification approaches.

Recent advances in natural language processing (NLP) and generative artificial intelligence (genAI) present promising opportunities to improve text readability. In particular, research indicates that large language models (LLMs), such as the one used in ChatGPT, can help reduce the complexity of academic texts through text simplification, improving readability based on established metrics like LIX, ('Läsbarhetsindex' in Swedish) [11]. However, despite the potential of these technological advances, their use in educational settings remains limited, and many students and educators are unaware of their potential benefits.

The current study builds on recent advances in NLP and preliminary findings suggesting the utility of LLMs in simplifying complex texts when appropriate prompting strategies are used [11,18]. Aiming to take advantage of the improved comprehension that simplified texts provide [4], we investigated the utility of including a *measure of text readability within the prompt*. We then evaluated how much students learned when reading the original text and when reading the simplified text generated by an LLM using the best-performing prompting strategy. This two-study approach provides insight into the ability of LLMs to make text accessible to students with varied learning needs by answering the below research questions:

RQ1: Does including a readability metric in the prompt support better text simplification?
RQ2: How readable do students feel the original and simplified text are?
RQ3: How much do students learn when reading the simplified text in contrast to the original text?

To answer these questions, we examine how generative AI can be used to automate the text simplification process and identify potential implications for educational practice and student learning.

2 Background

The challenges of reading academic texts often arise from complex sentences and advanced vocabulary [20,24,30]. Traditional readability metrics, such as the Flesch-Kincaid Grade Level (FKGL) [15] and the Gunning Fog Index [10], allow evaluation of key components of text readability using proxies for syntactic complexity and vocabulary difficulty [11]. Although these metrics can provide an estimate of how readable a text is (e.g., [9,13,28,31]), they fail to capture many of the aspects of a text that affect students' comprehension and retention of information [20]. This limited representation of the factors that contribute to reading comprehension implies that readability measures cannot be relied on as the only indicator of a text's readability. They can, however, be used as an initial proxy indicator when trying to increase the readability of texts through manual or automated means.

2.1 Improving Text Readability

Text readability can be increased through modifications that improve clarity and information access [7]. One such modification is text simplification, which typically involves simplifying the vocabulary and syntax within a text to reduce cognitive load and support comprehension [8]. Although text simplification can be beneficial for reading practices, there is a risk that essential information will be lost through the simplification process. When simplified texts are used for instructional purposes and learning, preserving key information and conceptual nuance is essential to avoid disadvantaging students who rely on this form of support. In short, the nuance contained in academic texts must be preserved as much as possible. Concerns about the potential loss of important information as part of the simplification process are probably the reason why early text simplification used manual methods to shorten the length of sentences, replace complex words with simpler synonyms, and restructure paragraphs [6,16,25]. Although effective, these manual methods are resource intensive and lack scalability.

While not targeted towards supporting student learning, NLP researchers have invested considerable effort in techniques for summarizing and simplifying text. The resulting approaches include rule-based transformations [27], machine-learning models that identify and rephrase difficult sentences [1], and the use of genAI [11]. These recent genAI approaches, especially LLMs, have surpassed previous techniques in their ability to transform complex text. Unlike earlier rule-based (e.g., [27]) or statistical methods (e.g., [33]), LLMs can adapt to diverse contexts to offer contextually appropriate transformations [3]. However, given the importance of maintaining key information and nuance in simplified texts, there remains a need to explore which prompting strategies most effectively support modifications that enhance the readability of academic texts.

2.2 Strategic Prompting for Improved Readability

Previous studies have begun to explore the potential of LLMs to enhance the readability of academic texts. In their recent study, Estling and colleagues [11] examined this potential using 136 Swedish academic texts, while evaluating four prompting strategies: Standard, Meta, Roleplay, and Chain-of-Thought. The LIX readability metric [2] was included in all prompting strategies. It was also used as the target measure since the texts were in Swedish. The results showed Meta prompting best supported the task, but all prompting approaches produced more readable texts. This preliminary study only conducted an intrinsic evaluation of the simplification methods, as such, it is unclear how learners would respond to or learn from the simplified texts. This raises two questions, *What happens when a readability metric is not included in the prompt?* and *How do learners respond to LLM-simplified texts?*

Both of these questions need to be answered to determine the utility of LLMs to support student access to the information found in academic texts. Above and beyond examining the use of LLMs to improve readability from a metric perspective, the simplified texts also need to facilitate student learning. Therefore, it is necessary to evaluate this support with learners. In the present paper, we report the results of two studies. The first is the intrinsic evaluation that answers RQ1 by investigating how much the readability of the text changes using two prompting strategies: one that used plain-text instructions (Plain-Language Prompt) and another that incorporated a readability metric (Metric-Guided Prompt). Study 1's results aim to help identify which prompting strategy is more appropriate for improving text readability from a metric perspective. The second study then evaluates student learning and perceptions when they have access to either the simplified text or the original text (RQ2 & RQ3). Study 2's results aim to provide insights into how simplified text may support learners.

3 Study 1 - Intrinsic Evaluation

We conducted an intrinsic evaluation of text readability after they had been simplified using an LLM. We specifically compared the results of two prompting strategies to identify which prompting strategy should be used in the student reading study (see Sect. 4).

3.1 Methods

To enhance text readability, two prompting strategies, namely Metric-Guided Prompt and Plain-Language Prompt, were developed and tested. After simplifying the texts using these prompts, we obtained a readability measure for each of the original texts and the simplified versions that the LLM output in response to each of our two prompting strategies.

Prompting Procedures and Strategies. The GPT-3.5 Turbo LLM was used due to its affordability. This LLM employs two types of prompts. The first, a system prompt, determines what the LLM does in response to user prompts. This is the prompt we manipulated. The second type, the user prompt, provided the text that needed to be simplified.

The two system prompting strategies that we used were a *plain-language* prompt and a *metric-guided prompt* as this combination provides insight into the value of including the readability metric as part of the prompt.

Plain-Language Prompt: This approach broadly focused on text simplification by having the LLM rephrase sentences for clarity and replace complex vocabulary with simpler synonyms. It instructs the LLM to focus on improving readability while preserving the information contained in the original content. It is a flexible approach, which enables the model to simplify text without imposing rigid constraints.

The prompt used was the following: "You are a text enhancement AI. Your main goal is to make the text simpler while keeping the main idea. You will also correct any grammatical errors and improve the text. You will not change the main idea of the text. You will not add any new information to the text." This prompt is equivalent to the Standard prompt used in prior work [11] with one modification: it does not include the readability formula.

Metric-Guided Prompt: This strategy employed the FKGL measure of readability [15]. The use of this formula constrains the text simplification task so that it consistently targets the same aspects of the text. It emphasized measurable improvements in sentence structure and vocabulary complexity, with prompts explicitly instructing the model to optimize text based on predefined criteria. This prompt is equivalent to the previously-examined standard prompt strategy (see [11]). Additional information about how we refined the prompt can be seen in our repository.

The prompt used was the following: "Your task is to reduce the Flesch-Kincaid Grade Level of texts. The Flesch-Kincaid Grade Level is calculated using the formula: Grade Level = 0.39 * (Total Words/Total Sentences) + 11.8 * (Total Syllables/Total Words) - 15.59. Given a text, rewrite it to significantly reduce its complexity by focusing on: Simplifying sentence structures; Using fewer syllables per word; Reducing the average sentence length. Ensure the rewritten text maintains its original meaning while achieving a much lower grade level."

Both strategies were implemented through Python scripts[1], enabling automated processing of the texts and ensuring consistency in application.

Data. The effectiveness of the two prompts was evaluated using 2,000 academic papers from a dataset that contained 37,464 academic texts on artificial intelligence [34]. All texts were open-source academic preprints.

This dataset consists of four lists of files. We randomly sampled the employed texts from the first of the four files. We then cleaned the texts' introduction using a script that removed LaTeX artifacts. The text was retained if at least 50% of the original text remained following cleaning.

Each of the original texts that was sampled contained at least 46 words ($M = 793.2, SD = 619.36$) and four sentences ($M = 40.4, SD = 31.58$). The texts contained at most 5,813 words and 336 sentences.

[1] Repository: https://osf.io/ukcxf/?view_only=118f57f76bcd45b586ad049aed9c3393.

Readability Measure. We used the FKGL as a readability metric [15]. FKGL is commonly used in education, publishing, and software to evaluate the complexity of written material [29,31]. This measure uses information about sentence length and vocabulary complexity (number of syllables) to infer the approximate grade level associated with a text. Lower grade levels are considered to have higher readability [35].

Analysis. We used a repeated measures ANOVA to determine whether there were differences in FKGL across the three sets of texts (i.e., the original text and the two text versions that were generated using each prompting approach). Greenhouse-Geisser correction was used because the data did not meet the sphericity assumption as determined through Mauchly's tests. We applied Bonferroni correction to the post-hoc paired t-tests. The paired tests of raw scores were one-tailed because we expected the simplified text to have lower scores.

As others have done, we characterized the change in readability through an adaptation of the normalized gain score [11]. We used 22 (the ceiling of the maximum observed FKGL from our data) instead of the test score ceiling (i.e., 100) employed in the original formula. Because the gain data were not normally distributed, we used a Wilcoxon-signed rank test to determine whether there was a difference in the amount of improvement seen across prompting strategies. These pairwise tests were two-tailed because there was limited theoretical or empirical support for hypothesizing the direction of the difference.

3.2 Results

A large difference was found across versions of the texts: $F(1.76) = 241.54, p < .001, \eta^2 = .108$. The original texts had the highest grade level ($M = 13.1, SD = 2.14$), and only the *metric-guided prompting* strategy supported measurable changes in text-readability (Table 1). This prompting strategy also resulted in scores ($M = 12.1, SD = 2.38$) that were around one grade lower than those seen for the plain-language prompt ($M = 13.0, SD = 1.92$), and improvements over the original text could be as large as 13 grades for the metric-guided prompt ($M = 0.98, SD = 2.64$).

Table 1. Differences in FKGL across the original and simplified texts.

Text 1	Text 2	Statistics
Original	Metric-Guided	$t(1999) = 16.65, p < .001, d = 0.37$
Original	Plain-Language	$t(1999) = 1.04, p = .450, d = 0.23$
Plain-Language	Metric-Guided	$t(1999) = 20.12, p < .001, d = 0.45$

These differences are consistent with the changes seen in the number of sentences and words used to communicate information in the simplified texts

(Table 2). For both strategies, the median number of words is approximately one-third the median length of the original texts ($Mdn = 633$), and the number of sentences was half that of the original texts ($Mdn = 32$).

Table 2. Descriptive statistics of the simplified texts' characteristics (Mdn - median; IQR - inter-quartile range)

Strategy	Min.	Mdn	Max	IQR
Plain-Text Prompt				
Words	44	248	1440	103
Sentences	3	15	79	5
Metric-Guided Prompt				
Words	35	234	1135	117
Sentences	4	16	59	7

In addition to a difference in the FKGL scores, we found a medium difference in the amount of improvement seen when applying each prompting strategy ($Z = 17.99, p < .001, r = .40$). The apparent reductions in grade level map to negligible normalized gains ($M = 0.07, SD = 0.770$) for the plain text prompting strategy. The normalized gains for the metric-based prompting approach were three times higher ($M = 0.20, SD = 0.92$).

These results clearly indicate that the metric-based prompting strategy simplified the texts the most. We, therefore, used this strategy to simplify the texts for our follow-up study to determine whether this strategy could support student learning.

4 Study 2 – Learner Evaluation

This between-subjects study aimed to determine whether there were differences in student perceptions and learning based on the source of the information they were given. Two sources were considered: the original text and a simplified text. The simplified text was created using the best-performing approach (i.e., Metric-Guided Prompt) from Study 1.

4.1 Methods

We recruited participants through social-media groups for science, technology, engineering, and mathematics (STEM) students in November-December 2024. Participants were divided into two groups: one group read the original text ($n = 22$), while the other read the simplified text ($n = 15$). Participants were assigned to a group using a random number.

Participants. Participants ($n = 37$) were recruited based on their minimal prior knowledge of the academic topics used in the text. The STEM groups we advertised the study to were for students who did not focus on medicine or pharmaceuticals.

Of those who consented to participate, two were native-English speakers. The remaining 35 spoke English as an additional language.

Text. The original text was extracted from a paper about bacteriophage therapy [17]. The selection of this text was motivated by two factors: it was expected to be difficult to read because it had a high FKGL, and there was little overlap between its topic and expected student backgrounds. During the text selection process, we also tested the text to ensure that the FKGL for the simplified version (11.5) was markedly different from that of the original text (16.0) so that the two versions could be easily contrasted.

Procedures. Consistent with work by Bernholt and colleagues [4], all participants completed a pre- and post-test to assess their knowledge of the topic from the text. Participants read the text in between completing the two tests. There was no time limit, so they could engage with the material at their own pace to maximize comprehension.

Instruments. Both the pre- and post-test used a set of questions to assess learner knowledge of the topic (i.e., antibiotics, bacteriophage, and phage therapy). The tests included true/false items and multiple choice items, which have been shown to provide a dependable measure of reading comprehension [23]. The tests were designed to avoid priming effects so that performance on the post-test was not influenced by the pre-test. The pre-test contained five items and the post-test had ten items. Scores are reported as percentages.

To obtain learner perceptions of the provided texts, the questionnaire included items about the qualities of the text and whether there was missing information (Yes, Maybe, No). The students were asked to rate the comprehensibility of the text on a 5-point rating scale from "I did not understand it" (1) to "I understood it perfectly" (5). They were also asked to rate text readability from "It was hard to read" (1) to "It was easy to read".

Analyses. We present descriptive statistics of students' raw scores and ratings in addition to reporting descriptive statistics of their raw gain score (post-test – pre-test). We report this raw gain since several learners scored 100% on the pre-test, making the use of normalized learning gains infeasible for these learners.

We used single-tailed inferential statistics because we expected post-test scores to be higher than pre-test scores. Independent t-tests were used for between group comparisons when the ratio data met the assumptions of the test. A paired t-test was used when comparing pre-test to post-test performance. The Mann-Whitney test was used for rank-based data and the Chi square test was used for detecting differences in categorical data.

4.2 Results

Participant Assessment of Text Qualities. Overall, study participants reported that the texts were both easy to read and understand (Fig. 1). No differences were found between the text versions for participants' ratings of how understandable the text was ($U = 117.5, p = .143, r = .25$). However, moderate differences were found between groups for their perception of how readable the text was ($U = 91.0, p = .022, r = .40$), with the simplified text group providing higher readability scores.

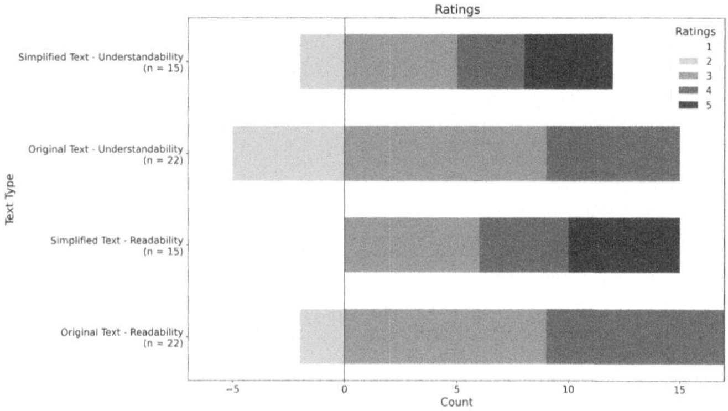

Fig. 1. Participant ratings of text comprehensibility and readability by condition

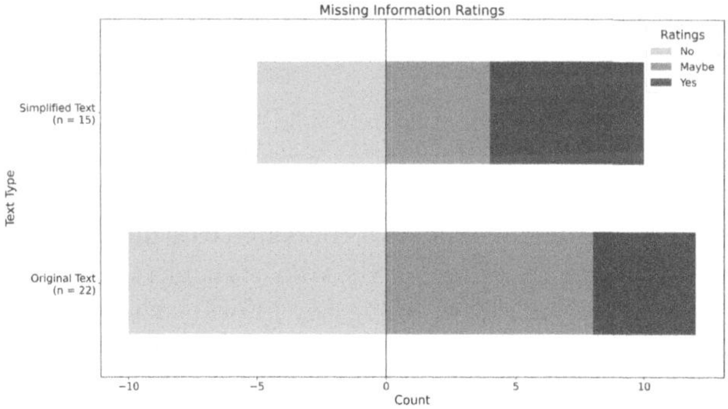

Fig. 2. Participant perceptions of whether the text was missing information they needed

There was no difference between the two conditions ($\chi^2(2) = 2.12, p = .171, \phi = .24$) for participants' assessment of whether the provided text was missing information (Fig. 2), with up to half of participants in each condition feeling that some information was missing.

Learning. A small improvement in participant scores (Fig. 3) from the pre-test ($M = 49.7, SD = 22.91$) to the post-test ($M = 57.8, SD = 16.69$) was identified across all learners: $t(36) = 1.84, p = .037, d = .31$. So those who received the simplified text learned as did those who used the original text.

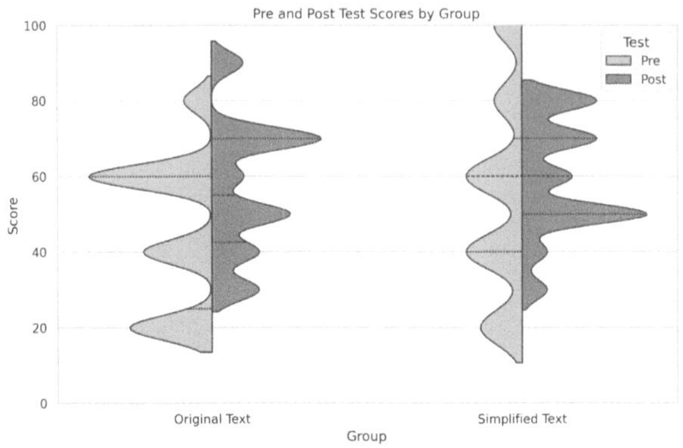

Fig. 3. Distribution of participant scores on the pre- and post-test by condition

For those in the original text condition, this meant an improvement of approximately 10% (Fig. 4) from the pre-test ($M = 46.4, SD = 19.89$) to the post-test ($M = 56.8, SD = 17.83$). For those who read the simplified texts, the observed gain from the pre-test ($M = 54.7, SD = 26.69$) to the post-test ($M = 59.3, SD = 15.34$) appeared to be smaller ($\approx 5\%$). But statistical testing found no significant differences across groups: $t(35) = 0.64, p = .263, d = .21$. It is worth noting that ceiling effects were observed on the pre-test for the simplified text group and the variability in their performance dropped from the pre- to the post-test.

5 Discussion

The complexity of academic texts poses a challenge to student success, especially for students with diverse learning needs who struggle to read. Furthermore, simplification tools carry the risk of losing key information from academic texts. So, we adopted a two-study approach to address this critique and examine the utility of LLMs in text simplification as a means of making texts more accessible to all students. Findings from both studies highlight the potential of LLMs in addressing the challenges associated with reading and comprehending academic texts.

5.1 Does Including a Readability Metric in the Prompt Support Better Text Simplification?

Study 1 demonstrated that the Metric-Guided Prompt generated academic texts with improved readability compared to those generated using the Plain-

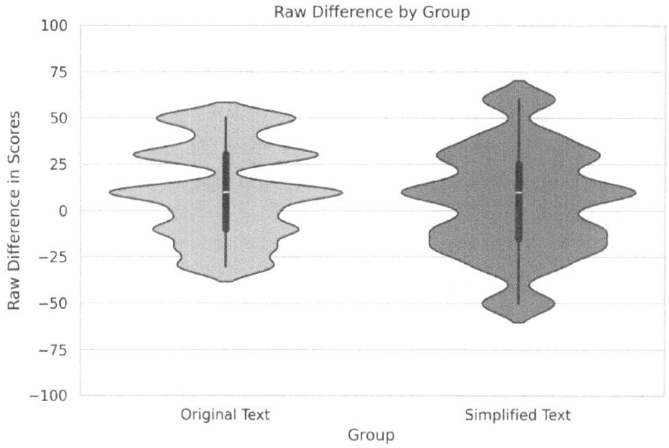

Fig. 4. Distribution of raw difference scores from the pre-test to the post-test by condition

Language Prompt. This aligns with earlier research suggesting that systematic approaches using predefined metrics can support text simplification (e.g., [11]). The guidance provided by the Metric-Guided Prompt, using the FKGL measure of readability [15], could have helped to emphasize objective readability criteria and, as such, generated simplified text that is more aligned with established standards. In contrast, the Plain-Language Prompt used a less structured approach (i.e., the LLM was prompted to rephrase sentences for clarity and replace complex vocabulary with simpler synonyms), which did not result in a change in text readability because this prompting approach preserved the variability in readability values seen in the original texts. Taken together, these results indicate the importance of including a measure of readability as part of the prompt when simplifying texts.

While the GPT-3.5 Turbo model has great capabilities, newer models with potentially better performance are being released. Further research could compare how different models influence the text simplification approach. Another limitation is the maximum token limit imposed by ChatGPT's API rules, potentially resulting in summarization instead of simplification despite the explicit prompt. Future work could address this by evaluating prompt strategies for longer academic texts outside of these constraints.

5.2 How Readable Do Students Feel the Original and Simplified Text Are?

A major criticism of readability measures (e.g., FKGL) is the focus on syllables, words, and sentence length that reflect the surface structure of a text and not its syntactic or semantic structure [36]. The findings indicate that students perceived the simplified text to be more readable than the original text. The simplified text also had a lower FKGL. Taken together, these findings from an evaluation with a single text suggest that including the readability metric when prompting an LLM to simplify complex, academic text not only improves readability from a metric perspective but also from a learner perspective.

5.3 How Much Do Students Learn When Reading the Simplified Texts in Contrast to the Original Texts?

The students' test performance did not significantly differ between those who read the simplified text and those who read the original text, with both groups improving their scores by at least 5% on average. Although these findings should be interpreted with caution, given the small sample size and the ceiling effects observed in the pre-test of those in the simplified text condition, the comparable performance between the simplified text and original text conditions is noteworthy. Moreover, there was no difference in the amount of information students felt was missing in each condition. These results suggest LLM-simplified texts may enhance readability without compromising comprehension, preserving learning outcomes.

While the learner evaluation had a relatively small sample size, we identified important distinctions in learner perceptions. Post-hoc sample size estimation indicates that we would have needed between 527 and 1,246 more participants to reliably detect the small differences that may exist in student learning and perceptions between the original and the simplified text groups. Furthermore, we only investigated the differences between the original and simplified versions of one text on one topic. Future research is needed to validate these findings on more texts across more topics. Additionally, a larger and more diverse sample of students is needed to gain deeper insights into the interaction between the reader and the text [20]. Future work can evaluate learning based on standardized reading assessment to gain a more comprehensive understanding of the impact of LLM-simplified texts, allowing for further solidification of current knowledge on whether simplified texts could increase accessibility for diverse learners by enhancing readability while preserving comprehension.

6 Conclusions

The integration of LLM-driven tools in education offers a promising opportunity to enhance students' access to complex academic content based on their individual learning needs. These tools can simplify challenging texts, often written in non-native languages, while maintaining their essential meaning, thereby promoting educational equity. Additionally, it is possible to integrate these tools into classrooms through a teacher portal to assign students with reading difficulties simplified texts, and enroll them in support classes targeted for reading. Helping them stay on track academically while meeting specific learner reading needs, showing promise, particularly for students with diverse learning challenges, including those diagnosed with common reading and other learning disorders.

This study explored the impact of incorporating readability metrics in prompt strategies when using LLMs to improve academic text readability, gauge students' perceptions of the simplified text, and assess its impact on learning. The findings indicate that the Metric-Guided prompting approach significantly enhanced text readability, resulting in clearer and more accessible academic content. Further research is needed to refine the prompting strategies, evaluate their applicability across various text types and languages, and investigate their long-term effects on learning outcomes.

The results contribute valuable insights to the growing body of research on the application of AI in educational settings. Together, they serve as a starting point for future research aimed at refining strategic prompting, for example, by incorporating readability measures in prompts, to generate academic texts that are more accessible to support reading across diverse learner populations.

Acknowledgments. This work received financial support from Digital Futures (Sweden) and Killam Trusts (Canada).

References

1. Al-Thanyyan, S.S., Azmi, A.M.: Automated text simplification: a survey. ACM Comput. Surv. (CSUR) **54**(2), 1–36 (2021)
2. Anderson, J.: Lix and Rix: variations on a little-known readability index. J. Read. **26**(6), 490–496 (1983)
3. Arbel, I., Refael, Y., Lindenbaum, O.: Transformllm: adapting large language models via llm-transformed reading comprehension text (2024). https://arxiv.org/abs/2410.21479
4. Bernholt, S., Härtig, H., Retelsdorf, J.: Reproduction rather than comprehension? Analysis of gains in students' science text comprehension. Res. Sci. Educ. **53**(3), 493–506 (2023)
5. Bonifacci, P., Colombini, E., Marzocchi, M., Tobia, V., Desideri, L.: Text-to-speech applications to reduce mind wandering in students with dyslexia. J. Comput. Assist. Learn. **38**(2), 440–454 (2022). https://doi.org/10.1111/jcal.12624
6. Chandrasekar, R., Doran, C., Bangalore, S.: Motivations and methods for text simplification. In: COLING 1996 Volume 2: The 16th International Conference on Computational Linguistics (1996)
7. Crossley, S.A., Yang, H.S., McNamara, D.S.: What's so simple about simplified texts? A computational and psycholinguistic investigation of text comprehension and text processing. Read. Fore. Lang. **26**(1), 92–113 (2014)
8. Gaies, S.J.: The investigation of language classroom processes. TESOL Q. **17**(2), 205–217 (1983). https://doi.org/10.2307/3586650
9. Goh, O.S., Fung, C.C., Depickere, A., Wong, K.W.: Using gunnnig-fog index to assess instant messages readability from ecas. In: Third International Conference on Natural Computation (ICNC 2007), vol. 5, pp. 480–486 (2007). https://doi.org/10.1109/ICNC.2007.800
10. Gunning, R.: The Technique of Clear Writing, rev. ed edn.. McGraw-Hill (1968). https://cir.nii.ac.jp/crid/1130000796418620544

11. Hedlin, E., Estling, L., Wong, J., Demmans Epp, C., Viberg, O.: Got it! prompting readability using chatgpt to enhance academic texts for diverse learning needs. In: Proceedings of the 15th International Learning Analytics and Knowledge Conference, LAK '25, pp. 115–125. Association for Computing Machinery, New York (2025). https://doi.org/10.1145/3706468.3706483
12. Hulme, C., Snowling, M.J.: Reading disorders and dyslexia. Curr. Opin. Pediatr. **28**(6), 731–735 (2016)
13. Jindal, P., MacDermid, J.C.: Assessing reading levels of health information: uses and limitations of flesch formula. Educ. Health **30**(1), 84–88 (2017)
14. Karimiabdolmaleki, M., Farias Wanderley, L., Cutumisu, M., Rezazadeh, M., Demmans Epp, C.: Negative language transfer identification in the english writing of chinese and farsi native speakers. Int. J. Artif. Intell. Educ. (2025). https://doi.org/10.1007/s40593-025-00468-8
15. Kincaid, J.P., Fishburne Jr, R.P., Rogers, R.L., Chissom, B.S.: Derivation of new readability formulas (automated readability index, fog count and flesch reading ease formula) for navy enlisted personnel (1975)
16. Kriz, R., Miltsakaki, E., Apidianaki, M., Callison-Burch, C.: Simplification using paraphrases and context-based lexical substitution. In: Walker, M., Ji, H., Stent, A. (eds.) Proceedings of the 2018 Conference of the North American Chapter of the Association for Computational Linguistics: Human Language Technologies, vol. 1, pp. 207–217. Association for Computational Linguistics, New Orleans (2018). https://doi.org/10.18653/v1/N18-1019
17. Lu, T.K., Koeris, M.S.: The next generation of bacteriophage therapy. Curr. Opin. Microbiol. **14**(5), 524–531 (2011). https://doi.org/10.1016/j.mib.2011.07.028
18. Marulli, F., Campanile, L., de Biase, M.S., Marrone, S., Verde, L., Bifulco, M.: Understanding readability of large language models output: an empirical analysis. Procedia Comput. Sci. **246**, 5273–5282 (2024)
19. National Center for Education Statistics: Fast facts: Long-term trends in reading and mathematics achievement. https://nces.ed.gov/fastfacts/display.asp?id=38. Accessed 27 Mar 2025
20. Nie, Y., Deacon, H., Fyshe, A., Demmans Epp, C.: Predicting reading comprehension scores of elementary school students. In: Proceedings of the International Conference on Educational Data Mining (EDM), pp. 158–170. International Educational Data Mining Society, Durham (2022). https://doi.org/10.5281/ZENODO.6852952
21. Olakanmi, O.A., Akcayir, G., Ishola, O.M., Demmans Epp, C.: Using technology in special education: current practices and trends. Educ. Tech. Res. Dev. **68**(4), 1711–1738 (2020). https://doi.org/10.1007/s11423-020-09795-0
22. Petersen, S.E., Ostendorf, M.: Text simplification for language learners: a corpus analysis. In: SLaTE, pp. 69–72 (2007)
23. Säuberli, A., et al.: Digital comprehensibility assessment of simplified texts among persons with intellectual disabilities. In: Proceedings of the 2024 CHI Conference on Human Factors in Computing Systems. CHI '24. Association for Computing Machinery, New York (2024). https://doi.org/10.1145/3613904.3642570
24. Savolainen, H., Ahonen, T., Aro, M., Tolvanen, A., Holopainen, L.: Reading comprehension, word reading and spelling as predictors of school achievement and choice of secondary education. Learn. Instr. **18**(2), 201–210 (2008). https://doi.org/10.1016/j.learninstruc.2007.09.017
25. Siddharthan, A.: Syntactic simplification and text cohesion. Res. Lang. Comput. **4**, 77–109 (2006)

26. Singh, M.K.M.: Challenges in academic reading and overcoming strategies in taught master programmes: a case study of international graduate students in Malaysia. High. Educ. Stud. **4**(4), 76–88 (2014)
27. Suter, J., Ebling, S., Volk, M.: Rule-based automatic text simplification for German, pp. 279–287 (2016)
28. Świeczkowski, D., Kułacz, S.: The use of the gunning fog index to evaluate the readability of Polish and English drug leaflets in the context of health literacy challenges in medical linguistics: An exploratory study. Cardiol. J. **28**(4), 627–631 (2021)
29. Tahir, M., et al.: Evaluation of quality and readability of online health information on high blood pressure using discern and flesch-kincaid tools. Appl. Sci. **10**(9) (2020). https://doi.org/10.3390/app10093214
30. Wagner, R.K., Muse, A.E., Tannenbaum, K.R. (eds.): Vocabulary Acquisition: Implications for Reading Comprehension. Guilford Press, New York (2007)
31. Williamson, J.M.L., Martin, A.G.: Analysis of patient information leaflets provided by a district general hospital by the flesch and flesch-kincaid method. Int. J. Clin. Pract. **64**(13), 1824–1831 (2010). https://doi.org/10.1111/j.1742-1241.2010.02408.x
32. Wood, S.G., Moxley, J.H., Tighe, E.L., Wagner, R.K.: Does use of text-to-speech and related read-aloud tools improve reading comprehension for students with reading disabilities? a meta-analysis. J. Learn. Disabil. **51**(1), 73–84 (2018). https://doi.org/10.1177/0022219416688170
33. Xu, W., Napoles, C., Pavlick, E., Chen, Q., Callison-Burch, C.: Optimizing statistical machine translation for text simplification. Trans. Assoc. Comput. Linguist. **4**, 401–415 (2016). https://doi.org/10.1162/tacl_a_00107
34. Yang, P., Sun, X., Li, W., Ma, S.: Automatic academic paper rating based on modularized hierarchical convolutional neural network. In: Proceedings of the 56th Annual Meeting of the Association for Computational Linguistics, ACL 2018, Melbourne, Australia, 15–20 July 2018, vol. 2: Short Papers, pp. 496–502 (2018)
35. Zainurrahman, Z., Yusuf, F.N., Sukyadi, D.: Text readability: its impact on reading comprehension and reading time. J. Educ. Learn. (EduLearn) **18**(4), 1422–1432 (2024)
36. Zamanian, M., Heydari, P.: Readability of texts: state of the art. Theory Pract. Lang. Stud. (TPLS) **2**(1) (2012)
37. Zhang, J., Wang, Q.: Reading and writing difficulties in bilingual learners. Ann. Dyslexia **73**(1), 1–5 (2023)

Assessing Computational Thinking Using Log Data: A Scoping Review

Cristiana Mergianian(✉), Ninja Hienonen, Muhterem Dindar, and Mari-Pauliina Vainikainen

Tampere University, Tampere, Finland
{cristiana.mergianian,ninja.hienonen,muhterem.dindar, mari-pauliina.vainikainen}@tuni.fi

Abstract. With the increasing presence of technology in education, foundational skills that can encourage learners' understanding of and meaningful interactions with technology should not be overlooked. Computational thinking (CT) is one such skill with applications to multiple domains. While CT assessment has traditionally focused on final outcomes, a more comprehensive perspective can emerge by also examining the process through means such as log data. The aims of this scoping review are to map how existing research has utilized log data to assess CT and to present research gaps for future studies in this area. Multiple databases from different disciplines were searched for peer-reviewed journal articles and conference papers. Relevant studies analyzed log data of individual learners from open-ended tasks to gauge CT performance. The following five areas were examined from each study: 1) form of CT, 2) education level, 3) log data process features, 4) interpretations of the features, and 5) theoretical contextualization of the features. The analysis revealed text-based programming as the most researched form of CT, followed by block-based programming. Additionally, higher education was the most studied level of education. Regarding log data features, attempts and time on task were among the most extracted. In studies justifying the choice of features, a variety of theories and empirical studies were referenced. The suggested interpretation of the features also varied, leading to inconsistent conclusions about what could be inferred from the log data. This valuable insight into existing research patterns can steer future studies towards theory-based measures in underrepresented areas of research, advancing the discussion on how technology can enhance learning. Furthermore, using log data for assessment can enable scalable personalized feedback and scaffolding. Combining a strong theoretical understanding of these topics from educational sciences with the technology-oriented approach to log data could substantially promote new ways of developing effective interventions.

Keyword: Computational Thinking · Learning Analytics · Log Data · Review

1 Introduction

Computational thinking (CT) is considered an essential skill in an increasingly digital society, with applications to problem solving in several contexts and domains [68, 74]. This generalizability stems from the definition of CT, which emphasizes the thinking

K. Tammets et al. (Eds.): EC-TEL 2025, LNCS 16063, pp. 306–320, 2026.
https://doi.org/10.1007/978-3-032-03870-8_21

processes involved in identifying problems and representing their solutions in a way that can be executed by a computer [75]. Although the concrete conceptualization of CT is still debated, the reliance on cognitive processes appears to be a recurring theme in the literature on CT [e.g., 68, 70]. The proposed focus on how computational problems are solved rather than on knowledge of particular programming languages implies that final assessment products alone may not contain enough evidence of the latent thought processes involved [68, 70].

The measurement and analysis of these underlying processes can be inferred from task behaviour as part of learning analytics and are thought to be linked to performance [45, 61]. A commonly used approach for collecting information about the process is through log data, e.g., time, keystrokes, and mouse clicks from user interactions with a task [69]. This approach offers several advantages, including the ability to gather large amounts of fine-grained information discretely, supporting the understanding of complex skills such as problem solving [69, 72].

Aligned with the aims of scoping reviews described by Arksey and O'Malley [54], this scoping review examines the state of the art by mapping existing research on the use of log data for assessing CT and presenting research gaps that can guide future studies in this area. Studies were regarded as relevant to CT if they included process measures in recognized CT contexts, such as different types of programming. Although CT is not synonymous with programming, their established close relationship and the examination of the process in the studies as part of the assessment were deemed representative of CT for the purposes of this review [52, 68].

The comprehensive assessment of CT entails more than the evaluation of the final performance product [46]. Considering the process leading to the outcome through task behaviour is important for providing learners with effective support [45]. Two learners demonstrating an identical final performance level may take substantially different paths towards achieving that performance, translating to a need for personalized support, e.g., in the form of feedback and scaffolding. These types of individualized support for learning can be enhanced and made scalable through log data that give insight into task behaviour. Therefore, developing a more holistic understanding of the information that can be gathered and inferred from log data is essential. This study aims to contribute to this goal.

2 Methodology

The systematic process of conducting this scoping review on the assessment of CT using log data consisted of five main steps [54], as outlined below.

2.1 Research Questions

First, the overall aims and research questions were set. The research questions are: 1) Which forms of CT have been examined in the studies? 2) At which level of education have the studies been implemented? 3) What process features have been extracted from the log data? 4) How have the features been interpreted? 5) How have the features been contextualized theoretically?

2.2 Search Strategy and Inclusion Criteria

Next, a search was conducted on February 20, 2025 to locate relevant publications in five databases: Scopus, EBSCO Education Research Complete (ERC), ProQuest Education Collection, ProQuest Social Science Premium Collection, and IEEE Xplore. Although the topic of assessment using log data is education-focused, it can also be considered multidisciplinary. Grey literature was excluded by default due to the theoretical and technical nature of the topic from the CT perspective. Accordingly, only academic databases covering a range of disciplines were selected.

The search term consisted of three main components that were combined using 'AND': 1) computational thinking: "computational thinking" OR CT* OR programming* OR "computer programming" OR coding OR Scratch; 2) log data: "log data*" OR "log file*" OR "log based" OR log-based OR "log record*" OR "interaction log*" OR "interaction data*" OR "trace log*" OR "trace data*" OR "process data*"; and 3) education/educational assessment: teaching* OR learning* OR education* OR student* OR assess* OR evaluat* OR measure* OR test* OR exam* OR task* OR "learning outcome*" OR perform* OR achieve*. This search term was used in each database with modifications depending on the characteristics of each database (e.g., the third component was omitted from education database searches).

Third, the search results were screened according to the established inclusion and exclusion criteria. The search was expanded to include conference papers for a more extensive overview of the limited literature [67]. In all five databases, the inclusion criteria used to screen the records and reports were the following: 1) Language: English; 2) Publication type: Peer-reviewed journal articles and conference papers; 3) Time period: 2006-present (starting when the term CT is acknowledged as being most prominent in scientific literature due to Wing [74]); 4) Empirical, quantitative studies; 5) Research on CT learners; 6) Assessment of CT skills (not necessarily the focus of the study); 7) Assessment of individual learners; 8) Log data used to analyze task behaviour/process of solving active CT-related tasks; and 9) CT form, education level and log data features were clearly identified.

The exclusion criteria used were: 1)Publication type: Conference posters or short papers; 2)Research on professionals; 3)Assessment of only something other than CT skills (e.g., engagement, motivation); 4) Assessment in a collaborative setting; 5) System-level log data unrelated to task-specific behaviour/processes or from passive tasks (e.g., interactions with general course content in Learning Management Systems or multiple choice questions).

The first author conducted all steps of the scoping review process, screening and reading every study. Records that clearly did not meet the inclusion criteria were excluded, while records for which this was uncertain or unclear were included in the next stage. In the screening of full reports, uncertain cases were discussed among authors to reach a conclusion. Two authors reviewed 11 studies and the agreement was relatively strong.

The systematic search and selection processes described above were conducted according to PRISMA guidelines [66]. The snowballing method was not implemented to prioritize the reproducible and structured nature of the search process.

After the final publications for review were identified, the relevant data from these studies were extracted. Finally, an overview of the findings was organized and is reported in the next section.

3 Results

3.1 Overview

Based on the search strategy, 5652 records were identified. Ultimately, 52 studies were included in the review. The detailed results of the search and selection process are displayed in the PRISMA diagram [66] in Fig. 1.

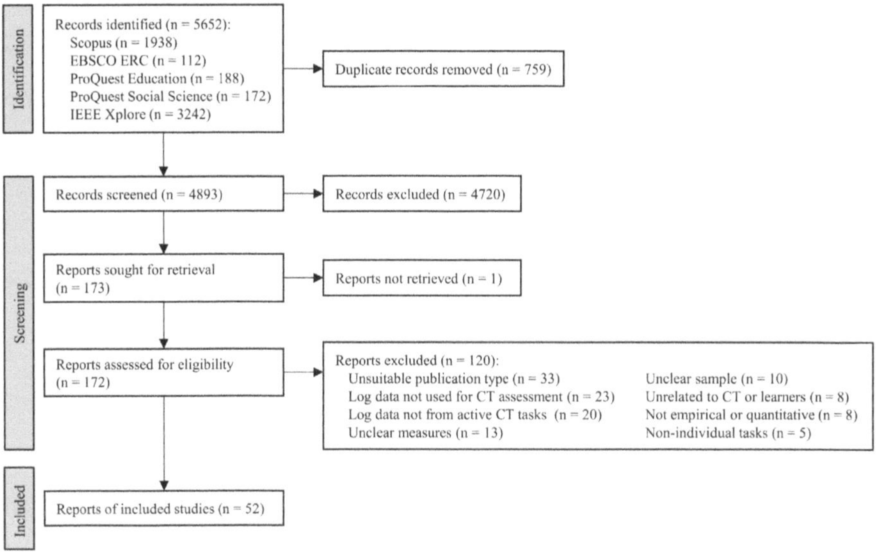

Fig. 1. PRISMA flow diagram of search and selection process.

The 52 reviewed studies were published between 2012 and 2025, with the majority from the last five years (83% since 2020). Conference papers (n = 30) outnumbered journal articles (n = 22). In terms of sample size, nearly two-thirds of studies involved hundreds (n = 27) or thousands (n = 8) of participants. Finally, less than half of studies (n = 22) included the term 'computational thinking' in the text.

3.2 Form of CT and Education Level

The first two aims of this scoping review were to map the CT form and education level of CT assessment studies based on log data. A summary of results is displayed in Table 1. The most common form of CT examined in the literature was text-based programming, followed by block-based programming. Other forms of CT included logic puzzles [41] and game design [34]. The most studied education level was higher education.

Table 1. Summary of CT form and education level of reviewed studies.

Form of CT	n	%	Studies according to reference list number
Text-based programming	28	54	[1, 2, 4, 5, 7, 8, 14, 22–24, 26–33, 36, 37, 39, 40, 42–45, 50, 52]
Block-based programming	20	38	[3, 6, 9–13, 15–21, 25, 35, 38, 48, 49, 51]
Both text-based and block-based	2	4	[46, 47]
Other	2	4	[34, 41]
Education level	n	%	Studies according to reference list number
Pre-school	1	2	[35]
Primary school	1	2	[38]
Middle/Junior high school	6	11	[18–20, 46, 47, 49]
High school	3	6	[3, 17, 48]
Primary and middle school	5	10	[10, 15, 34, 41, 51]
Primary, middle, and high school	4	8	[12, 13, 16, 21]
Higher education	32	61	[1, 2, 4–9, 11, 14, 22–33, 36, 37, 39, 40, 42–45, 50, 52]

Inspecting combinations of CT form and education level revealed that more than half of studies examined text-based programming in higher education (n = 28), while four higher education studies focused on block-based programming [6, 9, 11, 25]. Except for two studies [46, 47] on both text-based and block-based programming, the remaining studies on non-higher education examined block-based programming [3, 10, 12, 13, 15–21, 35, 38, 48, 49, 51] or other forms of CT [34, 41].

Furthermore, of the 22 studies that explicitly mentioned 'computational thinking' in the text, only three focused on text-based programming [43, 45, 52] and four were conducted in higher education [6, 43, 45, 52].

3.3 Log Data Features

The next aim of this scoping review was to identify the process features extracted from log data in studies on CT assessment. An overview of the ten most utilized log data feature categories is presented in Table 2, divided by text-based and block-based programming. Studies involving both types of programming were repeated in each column. Additionally, two studies on other CT forms extracted log data related to time between events [34, 41], and one of the studies used log data on event frequencies [34].

From Table 2, the attempts category refers to the frequency of attempts or runs, while the time between events includes, e.g., pauses or time between debugs. The event frequencies category refers to general events excluding runs such as creating blocks or file operations. Code edits include, e.g., frequency of block changes and deleting code, whereas the presence of errors category includes frequency of errors and error metrics such as the Error Quotient [63]. The keystrokes category refers to various measures including the number of keystrokes per time period or character. Finally, the code comparisons category refers to features comparing the submitted code to, e.g., the shortest correct code.

Table 2. Log data features from reviewed studies.

Feature category (# unique studies)	Text-based programming	Block-based programming
Attempts (n = 32)	n = 13: [7, 14, 27, 29–32, 36, 37, 40, 43, 45, 50]	n = 19: [3, 6, 9–13, 15–21, 25, 35, 48, 49, 51]
Time on task (n = 30)	n = 16: [5, 7, 8, 23, 24, 27, 28, 31–33, 36, 37, 40, 43–45]	n = 14: [3, 10, 11, 13, 17–21, 25, 35, 38, 48, 49]
Time between events (n = 16)	n = 14: [1, 4, 7, 22, 27, 29, 32, 36, 37, 39, 40, 42, 46, 47]	n = 4: [21, 46, 47, 49]
Event frequencies (n = 14)	n = 8: [2, 23, 29, 32, 40, 43, 46, 52]	n = 7: [6, 9–12, 25, 46]
Code edits (n = 14)	n = 9: [2, 7, 32, 36, 37, 40, 43, 46, 47]	n = 7: [11, 12, 21, 38, 46, 47, 49]
Presence of errors (n = 13)	n = 13: [1, 5, 7, 30–32, 36, 37, 39, 42, 44, 46, 47]	n = 2: [46, 47]
Sequences of events (n = 10)	n = 5: [4, 5, 22, 39, 46]	n = 6: [6, 9–12, 46]
Code size (n = 9)	n = 8: [2, 7, 27, 28, 30, 36, 37, 52]	n = 1: [6]
Keystrokes (n = 7)	n = 7: [1, 7, 8, 26, 28, 36, 37]	–
Code comparisons (n = 7)	n = 2: [36, 37]	n = 5: [10, 13, 16, 38, 49]

According to the trends in Table 2, attempts and time on task were among the most selected features overall. Text-based and block-based programming appeared to share other features such as event frequencies, code edits, and sequences of events. Conversely, more emphasis seemed to be placed on time between events and errors in text-based programming, whereas code comparisons were reported more frequently in block-based programming. In this latter form of CT, code size was often incorporated in code comparisons, leading to fewer block-based studies under the code size category.

3.4 Interpretation and Theoretical Contextualization of Features

The final aims of this scoping review were to identify how the log data features were interpreted and how they were contextualized theoretically. In terms of both aspects, there were general trends, but ultimately a variety of perspectives were presented in the reviewed studies.

Suggestions about the information that could potentially be inferred from the log data were proposed in many studies but not all. It appeared that the log data features had been associated with multiple distinct interpretations in different studies, whether it was by the authors themselves based on their own data or based on the work of other authors cited in the text. For instance, seven possible interpretations were reported for attempts in text-based programming: competence [7], effort [1, 14, 32], engagement [37], learner effectiveness [36, 37], performance quality [14, 27, 29, 36, 37, 40], resilience [36, 37], and problem-solving strategies [7, 29, 30]. In block-based programming, attempts were viewed as relating to nine possible representations: CT concepts or dimensions [17], effort [13, 16, 51], frustration [49], item difficulty [15, 17, 18, 20, 21, 51], performance quality [12, 13], persistence [16], productivity [49], solution effectiveness [6], and problem-solving approaches [6, 16, 49]. Effort, performance quality, and problem-solving approaches were interpretations common to both CT forms.

Furthermore, in the studies, certain latent processes were considered to be related to multiple features. For example, effort and engagement were each thought to be linked to the same five feature categories: attempts, time on task, time between events, event frequencies, and sequences of events. The features were also sometimes interpreted together, such as in clusters of different behaviours instead of in isolation [e.g., 9, 32].As for the theoretical contextualization, nine studies did not appear to clearly identify theory connected to their selected log data features [2, 9, 15, 18, 20, 22, 23, 46, 51]. Theories were clearly identifiable from twelve studies and appeared to be linked to the log data features. In most of these studies, the term CT was included in the text. Theories relating to the following topics were used: problem solving [6, 14, 27, 48], CT frameworks [12, 41, 52], Evidence-Centered Design [12, 41], constructionism [19], cognitive load theory and scaffolding [49], FUMA framework [34], teaching debugging and feedback [43], and program comprehension [42]. The remaining 31 studies justified the selection of features with other empirical studies based on the same design or features. Frequently cited authors included Watson and colleagues [73], Jadud [63], Pereira and colleagues [e.g., 37], Blikstein [55], Leinonen and colleagues [e.g., 24], Carter and colleagues [e.g., 5], Ahadi and colleagues [53], Estey and Coady [60], Hosseini and colleagues [62], Eguíluz and colleagues [59], and Guenaga and colleagues [13].

4 Discussion

To better understand the state of the art of log data use in CT assessment, 52 journal articles and conference papers from 2012 and 2025 were analyzed. The findings of this scoping review revealed that text-based programming and higher education were the most studied, and the term CT was used relatively rarely in this combined context. Block-based programming was examined more often in non-higher education. Further research on non-higher education or block-based programming in higher education could be beneficial.

These results are in line with previous literature indicating the same association between certain forms of CT and certain education levels [65, 71]. Other reviews on

CT assessment limited their search query to the term CT, leading to the conflicting conclusion that CT assessments concentrated on non-higher education [e.g., 57]. Those reviews examined different forms of assessment, while this scoping review focused on assessments incorporating log data as process measures. The wider perspective of CT used in this review was justified by thinking processes being a core component of the CT definition. Furthermore, challenges have been observed in how CT has been received and conceptualized in higher education [58], which might explain why the term appeared less often in higher education studies included in this review. Other possible explanations could be the assumption that CT is a skill already acquired before higher education or the CT research trend in higher education is emerging. This discussion could be worth revisiting for more cohesive research in the future.

The most utilized log data process features in the reviewed studies were attempts and time on task, along with other popular features related to frequencies and durations. The prevalence of these types of features was similar in the review by Wang and colleagues [72] on log data use in open-ended learning environments. Additionally, the differences found in the types of features from different CT forms indicated that studies on block-based programming could further explore the utility of times between events and errors as potentially relevant features. On the other hand, several similar features were used in both text-based and block-based programming studies, despite varying education levels and mentions of the CT term in the text (e.g., [7] versus [49]). A notable difference across education levels was that the number of attempts was more frequently extracted in non-higher education studies, which may imply its perceived usefulness for this population. Compulsory education is more inclusive of the population than the more selective, optional higher education level. This difference may lead to nuanced variations in, e.g., motivation and task behaviour in the latter that may not be captured as effectively by certain log data features. Therefore, the age and selection of the sample could be important considerations in the selection of features. Perhaps considering these similarities and differences in log data process features used could also help us seek further clarity on the definition and scope of CT.

The final observations of this scoping review were that the meaning of the same log data features was inferred in multiple distinct ways, and there was relatively little theoretical justification for feature selections given that more empirical articles were used as the basis for justification. Studies on block-based programming explicitly mentioning the term CT appeared to be more likely to incorporate theory, suggesting that more studies on text-based programming could consider supplementing the data-driven approach with educational or psychological theories.

The variety in interpretations and justifications necessitates a more detailed examination of the studies, accounting for differences in, for example, measures (e.g., at the level of the overall task or individual items), sample sizes, and analysis methods. This knowledge would help determine if there is enough quality evidence to warrant a systematic literature review on topics like the effectiveness of certain features in measuring learning or the usage of a particular feature.

Moreover, the extraction and interpretation of log data features could be influenced by the increasing use of artificial intelligence (AI) in CT skill development. According to Lepp and Kaimre [64], most undergraduate computer science students have utilized

AI tools for activities such as understanding and debugging code. While CT skills have traditionally been viewed as essential to solving computational problems independently, the importance of CT in certain contexts is appearing to shift towards solving computational problems by interacting efficiently and critically with AI tools [56, 64]. If such tools are incorporated into CT assessments, the relevance and application of commonly extracted log data features may require reviewing.

4.1 Limitations

While this scoping review presented important insights into log data use in CT assessment, certain limitations need to be acknowledged. First, despite efforts to perform a comprehensive systematic search, relevant studies may have been excluded, especially if the term 'computational thinking' was not included in the text to indicate other CT forms. Furthermore, given the rapid development of the field, a follow-up search that also addresses the AI aspect would reveal whether and how this aspect has been examined in the literature related to log data use. Second, the range of disciplines, study designs, and text conventions made comparisons more challenging. For instance, tasks in unsupervised environments may not have been completed individually. Third, extracting information from the studies involved interpretation, particularly regarding feature interpretations and theoretical contextualization, increasing the risk of misinterpreting authors' intentions. Finally, the search generated a limited number of similar studies due to evolving topics and conference papers progressing to journal articles, leading to a small amount of repetition in the analyzed information.

5 Conclusion

This scoping review on using log data to assess CT revealed relatively distinct categories of studies based on CT form and education level, such as those focusing on text-based programming in higher education versus block-based programming at other education levels. An examination of the log data process features demonstrated both similarities and differences across different contexts. On the surface, it might appear that the different types of programming and CT forms are disconnected due to different education levels and digital learning environments. However, a closer look at the process features used in their assessment reveal similarities that potentially could be connected by the concept of CT. Furthermore, the features used in the reviewed studies appeared to be data-driven, based on earlier empirical work, and interpreted in a variety of ways. The multidisciplinary nature of this research area is a strength that could be harnessed more effectively. By combining educational and psychological theories with the methodology typically applied in technical fields, there is great potential for increasing our understanding of learning processes and developing effective technology-enhanced interventions to support them.

Acknowledgement. This study was funded by the Research Council of Finland (EDUCA Flagship #358924) and the Ministry of Education and Culture (Doctoral school pilot #VN/3137/2024-OKM-4).

References: Reviewed Studies

1. Ahadi, A., Lister, R., Haapala, H., & Vihavainen, A.: Exploring machine learning methods to automatically identify students in need of assistance. In: Proceedings of the 11th Annual ACM Conference on International Computing Education Research, pp. 121–130. ACM, Omaha (2015). https://doi.org/10.1145/2787622.2787717
2. Ardimento, P., Bernardi, M.L., Cimitile, M., Redavid, D., Ferilli, S.: Understanding coding behavior: an incremental process mining approach. Electronics **11**(3), 389 (2022). https://doi.org/10.3390/electronics11030389
3. Avital, B., Hershkovitz, A., Israel-Fishelson, R.: Associations between computational thinking and figural, verbal creativity. Thinking Skills Creativity **50**, 101417 (2023). https://doi.org/10.1016/j.tsc.2023.101417
4. Carter, A.S., Hundhausen, C.D.: Using programming process data to detect differences in students' patterns of programming. In: Proceedings of the 48th ACM SIGCSE Technical Symposium on Computer Science Education, pp. 105–110. ACM, Seattle (2017). https://doi.org/10.1145/3017680.3017785
5. Carter, A.S., Hundhausen, C.D., Adesope, O.: The normalized programming state model: predicting student performance in computing courses based on programming behavior. In: Proceedings of the 11th Annual ACM Conference on International Computing Education Research, pp. 141–150. ACM, Omaha (2015). https://doi.org/10.1145/2787622.2787710
6. Chao, P.-Y.: Exploring students' computational practice, design and performance of problem-solving through a visual programming environment. Comput. Educ. **95**, 202–215 (2016). https://doi.org/10.1016/j.compedu.2016.01.010
7. Chuang, Y.-T., Chang, H.-Y.: Analyzing novice and competent programmers' problem-solving behaviors using an automated evaluation system. Sci. Comput. Program. **237**, 103138 (2024). https://doi.org/10.1016/j.scico.2024.103138
8. Edwards, J., Leinonen, J., Hellas, A.: A study of keystroke data in two contexts: written language and programming language influence predictability of learning outcomes. In: Proceedings of the 51st ACM Technical Symposium on Computer Science Education, pp. 413–419. ACM, Portland (2020). https://doi.org/10.1145/3328778.3366863
9. Emerson, A., et al.: Cluster-based analysis of novice coding misconceptions in block-based programming. In: Proceedings of the 51st ACM Technical Symposium on Computer Science Education, pp. 825–831. ACM, Portland (2020). https://doi.org/10.1145/3328778.3366924
10. Fu, Q., Tang, W., Zheng, Y., Ma, H., Zhong, T.: Predicting programming performance by using process behavior in a block-based programming environment. Interact. Learn. Environ. **32**(6), 1–15 (2022). https://doi.org/10.1080/10494820.2022.2146141
11. Gao, G., Marwan, S., Price, T.W.: Early performance prediction using interpretable patterns in programming process data. In: Proceedings of the 52nd ACM Technical Symposium on Computer Science Education, pp. 342–348. ACM, Virtual (2021). https://doi.org/10.1145/3408877.3432439
12. Grover, S., Basu, S., Bienkowski, M., Eagle, M., Diana, N., Stamper, J.: A framework for using hypothesis-driven approaches to support data-driven learning analytics in measuring computational thinking in block-based programming environments. ACM Trans. Comput. Educ. **17**(3), 1–25 (2017). https://doi.org/10.1145/3105910
13. Guenaga, M., Eguíluz, A., Garaizar, P., Gibaja, J.: How do students develop computational thinking? Assessing early programmers in a maze-based online game. Comput. Sci. Educ. **31**(2), 259–289 (2021). https://doi.org/10.1080/08993408.2021.1903248
14. Guo, H., Zhang, M., Ko, A. J., Li, M., Zhou, B., Lim, J., et al.: Measuring students' programming skill via online practice. In: CEUR Workshop Proceedings of the 8th Educational Data Mining in Computer Science Education Workshop. CEUR-WS, Atlanta (2024). https://ceur-ws.org/Vol-3796/CSEDM-24_paper_9417.pdf

15. Hershkovitz, A., Sitman, R., Israel-Fishelson, R., Eguíluz, A., Garaizar, P., Guenaga, M.: Creativity in the acquisition of computational thinking. Interact. Learn. Environ. **27**(5–6), 628–644 (2019). https://doi.org/10.1080/10494820.2019.1610451
16. Israel-Fishelson, R., Hershkovitz, A.: Log-based analysis of creativity in the context of computational thinking. Educ. Sci. **15**(1), 3 (2024). https://doi.org/10.3390/educsci15010003
17. Israel-Fishelson, R., Hershkovitz, A.: Log-based multidimensional measurement of CT acquisition. In: Proceedings of the 6th APSCE International Conference on Computational Thinking and STEM Education, pp. 128–133. Asia Pacific Society for Computers in Education, Delft (2022). https://doi.org/10.34641/ctestem.2022.477
18. Israel-Fishelson, R., Hershkovitz, A., Eguíluz, A., Garaizar, P., Guenaga, M.: Computational thinking and creativity: a test for interdependency. In: Proceedings of the 4th International Conference on Computational Thinking Education, pp. 15–20. The Education University of Hong Kong, Hong Kong (2020)
19. Israel-Fishelson, R., Hershkovitz, A., Eguíluz, A., Garaizar, P., Guenaga, M.: A log-based analysis of the associations between creativity and computational thinking. J. Educ. Comput. Res. **59**(5), 926–959 (2021). https://doi.org/10.1177/0735633120973429
20. Israel-Fishelson, R., Hershkovitz, A., Eguíluz, A., Garaizar, P., Guenaga, M.: The associations between computational thinking and creativity: the role of personal characteristics. J. Educ. Comput. Res. **58**(8), 1415–1447 (2021). https://doi.org/10.1177/0735633120940954
21. Kanellopoulou, I., Garaizar, P., Guenaga, M.: First steps towards automatically defining the difficulty of maze-based programming challenges. IEEE Access **9**, 64211–64223 (2021). https://doi.org/10.1109/ACCESS.2021.3075027
22. Karvelas, I., Becker, B.A.: Sympathy for the (Novice) developer: programming activity when compilation mechanism varies. In: Proceedings of the 53rd ACM Technical Symposium on Computer Science Education, pp. 962–968. ACM, Virtual (2022). https://doi.org/10.1145/3478431.3499347
23. Keuning, H., Heeren, B., Jeuring, J.: Student Refactoring behaviour in a programming tutor. In: Proceedings of the 20th Koli Calling International Conference on Computing Education Research. ACM, Virtual (2020). https://doi.org/10.1145/3428029.3428043
24. Leinonen, J., Castro, F.E.V., Hellas, A.: Time-on-task metrics for predicting performance. In: Proceedings of the 53rd ACM Technical Symposium on Computer Science Education, pp. 871–877. ACM, Virtual (2022). https://doi.org/10.1145/3478431.3499359
25. Lestari, V.A., Andoko, B.S., Abdullah, M.Z., Ikawati, D.S., Hamimudin, M.A.: Analysis of experimental log data on pseudolearn in pseudo-code algorithm learning. In: Proceedings of the 2024 International Conference on Electrical and Information Technology, pp. 213–218. IEEE, Malang (2024). https://doi.org/10.1109/IEIT64341.2024.10763144
26. Liu, D., Xu, S., Cui, Z.: Programmer's performance with the keystroke as an indicator: a further study. In: 2012 IEEE/ACIS 11th International Conference on Computer and Information Science, pp. 577–583. IEEE, Shanghai (2012). https://doi.org/10.1109/ICIS.2012.88
27. Liu, F., Zhao, L., Zhao, J., Dai, Q., Fan, C., Shen, J.: Educational process mining for discovering students' problem-solving ability in computer programming education. IEEE Trans. Learn. Technol. **15**(6), 709–719 (2022). https://doi.org/10.1109/TLT.2022.3216276
28. Liu, H., Liu, D., Xu, S.: Evaluating programming performance with keystroke characteristics: an empirical experiment. In: Proceedings of the 14th ACIS International Conference on Software Engineering, Artificial Intelligence, Networking and Parallel/Distributed Computing, pp. 329–335. IEEE, Honolulu (2013). https://doi.org/10.1109/SNPD.2013.49
29. Mangaroska, K., Sharma, K., Gašević, D., Giannakos, M.: Multimodal learning analytics to inform learning design: lessons learned from computing education. J. Learn. Anal. **7**(3), 79–97 (2020). https://doi.org/10.18608/jla.2020.73.7

30. Meier, H., Lepp, M.: Clusters of solvers' behavioral patterns based on analysis of the programming process. In: Proceedings of the 2023 IEEE Frontiers in Education Conference, pp. 1–6. IEEE, College Station (2023a). https://doi.org/10.1109/FIE58773.2023.10343479
31. Meier, H., Lepp, M.: Effectiveness of feedback based on log file analysis in introductory programming courses. J. Educ. Comput. Res. **61**(3), 696–719 (2023). https://doi.org/10.1177/07356331221132651
32. Meier, H., Tonisson, E., Lepp, M., Luik, P.: Behaviour patterns of learners while solving a programming task: an analysis of log files. In: Proceedings of the 2020 IEEE Global Engineering Education Conference, pp. 685–690. IEEE, Porto (2020). https://doi.org/10.1109/EDUCON45650.2020.9125134
33. Mi, H., Liu, Y., Meng, R., Tang, Y., Zhang, Q.: A study of learning behavior analysis and student achievement based on an online judge system. In: Proceedings of the 9th International Conference on Distance Education and Learning, pp. 278–284. ACM, Guangzhou (2024). https://doi.org/10.1145/3675812.3675817
34. Murali, R., Lallé, S., Conati, C.: An intelligent pedagogical agent for in-the-wild interaction in an open-ended learning environment for computational thinking. In: Proceedings of the 24th ACM International Conference on Intelligent Virtual Agents, pp. 1–9. ACM, Glasgow (2024). https://doi.org/10.1145/3652988.3673948
35. Ono, Y., Saito, D., Washizaki, H.: Evaluating preschoolers' block programming using complexity and personality traits. In: Proceedings of the 36th International Conference on Software Engineering Education and Training. IEEE, Wurzburg (2024). https://doi.org/10.1109/CSEET62301.2024.10663038
36. Pereira, F.D., Fonseca, S.C., Oliveira, E.H.T., Cristea, A.I., Bellhauser, H., Rodrigues, L., et al.: Explaining individual and collective programming students' behavior by interpreting a black-box predictive model. IEEE Access **9**, 117097–117119 (2021). https://doi.org/10.1109/ACCESS.2021.3105956
37. Pereira, F.D., Oliveira, E.H.T., Oliveira, D.B.F., Cristea, A.I., Carvalho, L.S.G., Fonseca, S.C., et al.: Using learning analytics in the amazonas: understanding students' behaviour in introductory programming. Br. J. Educ. Technol. **51**(4), 955–972 (2020). https://doi.org/10.1111/bjet.12953
38. Pozzan, G., Padova, C., Montuori, C., Arfé, B., Vardanega, T.: Experimental analysis of first-grade students' block-based programming problem solving processes. In: Proceedings of the 29th Conference on Innovation and Technology in Computer Science Education, pp. 143–149. ACM, Milan (2024). https://doi.org/10.1145/3649217.3653586
39. Price, T.W., Hovemeyer, D., Rivers, K., Gao, G., Bart, A.C., Kazerouni, A.M., et al.: ProgSnap2: a flexible format for programming process data. In: Proceedings of the 25th ACM Conference on Innovation and Technology in Computer Science Education, pp. 356–362. ACM, Trondheim (2020). https://doi.org/10.1145/3341525.3387373
40. Pullar-Strecker, Z., Pereira, F.D., Denny, P., Luxton-Reilly, A., Leinonen, J.: G is for Generalisation: predicting student success from keystrokes. In: Proceedings of the 54th ACM Technical Symposium on Computer Science Education, pp. 1028–1034. ACM, Toronto (2023). https://doi.org/10.1145/3545945.3569824
41. Rowe, E., Almeda, M.V., Asbell-Clarke, J., Scruggs, R., Baker, R., Bardar, E., et al.: Assessing implicit computational thinking in Zoombinis puzzle gameplay. Comput. Hum. Behav. **120**, 106707 (2021). https://doi.org/10.1016/j.chb.2021.106707
42. Shah, A., Hogan, E., Agarwal, V., Driscoll, J., Porter, L., Griswold, W.G., et al.: An empirical evaluation of live coding in CS1. In: Proceedings of the 19th Annual ACM Conference on International Computing Education Research, pp. 476–494. ACM, Chicago (2023). https://doi.org/10.1145/3568813.3600122

43. Shynkarenko, V., Zhevaho, O.: A video-based approach to learning debugging techniques. In: Proceedings of the 14th International Scientific and Practical Programming Conference, pp. 462–473. CEUR-WS, Kiev (2024). https://ceur-ws.org/Vol-3806/S_18_Shynkarenko_Zhevaho.pdf
44. Somasundaram, T.S., Kiruthika, U., Gowsalya, M., Hemalatha, A., Philips, A.: Determination of competency of programmers by classification and ranking using AHP. In: Proceedings of the 2015 IEEE International Conference on Electro/Information Technology, pp. 194–200. IEEE, Dekalb (2015). https://doi.org/10.1109/EIT.2015.7293340
45. Song, D., Hong, H., Oh, E.Y.: Applying computational analysis of novice learners' computer programming patterns to reveal self-regulated learning, computational thinking, and learning performance. Comput. Hum. Behav. **120**, 106746 (2021). https://doi.org/10.1016/j.chb.2021.106746
46. Sun, D., Ouyang, F., Li, Y., Zhu, C., Zhou, Y.: Using multimodal learning analytics to understand effects of block-based and text-based modalities on computer programming. J. Comput. Assist. Learn. **40**(3), 1123–1136 (2024). https://doi.org/10.1111/jcal.12939
47. Sun, D., Xu, F., Li, Y.: Using learning analytics in understanding students' behavior in block-based and text-based programming modality. In: Proceedings of the 10th International Conference of Educational Innovation through Technology, pp. 271–275. IEEE, Chongqing (2021). https://doi.org/10.1109/EITT53287.2021.00060
48. Syahidi, A.A., Supianto, A.A., Hirashima, T., Watanobe, Y.: Learner action patterns in the problem-solving process related to program code composition based on tracking system activities. In: Proceedings of the 7th International Conference on Informatics and Computing. IEEE, Virtual (2022). https://doi.org/10.1109/ICIC56845.2022.10006930
49. Tabarsi, B., Reichert, H., Lytle, N., Catete, V., Barnes, T.: Scaffolding novices: analyzing when and how parsons problems impact novice programming in an integrated science assignment. In: Proceedings of the 20th Annual ACM Conference on International Computing Education Research, pp. 42–54. ACM, Melbourne (2024). https://doi.org/10.1145/3632620.3671110
50. Xu, B., Yan, S., Jiang, X., Feng, S.: SCFH: a student analysis model to identify students' programming levels in online judge systems. Symmetry **12**(4), 601 (2020). https://doi.org/10.3390/sym12040601
51. Zhang, S., Wong, G.K.W., Chan, P.C.F.: Achievement and effort in acquiring computational thinking concepts: a log-based analysis in a game-based learning environment. In: Proceedings of the 5th APSCE International Conference on Computational Thinking and STEM Education. Asia Pacific Society for Computers in Education, Virtual (2021)
52. Zhang, W., Zeng, X., Song, L.: Towards an assessment model of college students' computational thinking with text-based programming. Educ. Inf. Technol. **30**(2), 1363–1385 (2025). https://doi.org/10.1007/s10639-024-12872-z

Other References

53. Ahadi, A., Lister, R., Vihavainen, A.: On the number of attempts students made on some online programming exercises during semester and their subsequent performance on final exam questions. In: Proceedings of the 2016 ACM Conference on Innovation and Technology in Computer Science Education, pp. 218–223. ACM, Arequipa (2016). https://doi.org/10.1145/2899415.2899452
54. Arksey, H., O'Malley, L.: Scoping studies: towards a methodological framework. Int. J. Soc. Res. Method. **8**(1), 19–32 (2005). https://doi.org/10.1080/1364557032000119616
55. Blikstein, P.: Using learning analytics to assess students' behavior in open-ended programming tasks. In: Proceedings of the 1st International Conference on Learning Analytics and Knowledge, pp. 110–116. ACM, Banff (2011). https://doi.org/10.1145/2090116.2090132

56. Celik, I.: Exploring the determinants of artificial intelligence (AI) literacy: digital divide, computational thinking. Cogn. Absorption. Telematics Inf. **83**, 102026 (2023). https://doi.org/10.1016/j.tele.2023.102026
57. Cutumisu, M., Adams, C., Lu, C.: A scoping review of empirical research on recent computational thinking assessments. J. Sci. Educ. Technol. **28**(6), 651–676 (2019). https://doi.org/10.1007/s10956-019-09799-3
58. Czerkawski, B.C., Lyman, E.W.: Exploring issues about computational thinking in higher education. TechTrends **59**(2), 57–65 (2015). https://doi.org/10.1007/s11528-015-0840-3
59. Eguíluz, A., Guenaga, M., Garaizar, P., Olivares- Rodríguez, C.: Exploring the progression of early programmers in a set of computational thinking challenges via clickstream analysis. IEEE Trans. Emerg. Top. Comput. **8**(1), 256–261 (2017). https://doi.org/10.1109/TETC.2017.2768550
60. Estey, A., Coady, Y.: Can interaction patterns with supplemental study tools predict outcomes in CS1? In: Proceedings of the 2016 ACM Conference on Innovation and Technology in Computer Science Education, pp. 236–241. ACM, Arequipa (2016). https://doi.org/10.1145/2899415.2899428
61. Goldhammer, F., Zehner, F.: What to make of and how to interpret process data. Measur. Interdisc. Res. Perspect. **15**(3–4), 128–132 (2017). https://doi.org/10.1080/15366367.2017.1411651
62. Hosseini, R., Vihavainen, A., Brusilovsky, P.: Exploring problem solving paths in a Java programming course. In: Proceedings of the Psychology of Programming Interest Group Annual Conference 2014, pp. 65–76. Brighton (2014). http://d-scholarship.pitt.edu/21832/1/Paper_Pages_from_PPIGproceedings.pdf
63. Jadud, M.C.: Methods and tools for exploring novice compilation behaviour. In: Proceedings of the 2nd International Workshop on Computing Education Research, pp. 73–84. ACM, Canterbury (2006). https://doi.org/10.1145/1151588.1151600
64. Lepp, M., Kaimre, J.: Does generative AI help in learning programming: students' perceptions, reported use and relation to performance. Comput. Hum. Behav. Rep. **18**, 100642 (2025). https://doi.org/10.1016/j.chbr.2025.100642
65. Lye, S.Y., Koh, J.H.L.: Review on teaching and learning of computational thinking through programming: what is next for K-12? Comput. Hum. Behav. **41**, 51–61 (2014). https://doi.org/10.1016/j.chb.2014.09.012
66. Page, M.J., McKenzie, J.E., Bossuyt, P.M., Boutron, I., Hoffmann, T.C., Mulrow, C.D., et al.: The PRISMA 2020 statement: an updated guideline for reporting systematic reviews. BMJ (Online) **372**, n71 (2021). https://doi.org/10.1136/bmj.n71
67. Scherer, R.W., Saldanha, I.J.: How should systematic reviewers handle conference abstracts? A view from the trenches. System. Rev. **8**(1), 264 (2019). https://doi.org/10.1186/s13643-019-1188-0
68. Shute, V.J., Sun, C., Asbell-Clarke, J.: Demystifying computational thinking. Educ. Res. Rev. **22**, 142–158 (2017). https://doi.org/10.1016/j.edurev.2017.09.003
69. Spliethoff, L., Abele, S.: Measuring professional competence using computer-generated log data. In: Goller, M., Kyndt, E., Paloniemi, S., Damşa, C. (eds.) Methods for researching professional learning and development : challenges, applications and empirical illustrations, vol. 33, pp. 165–186. Springer, Cham (2022). https://doi.org/10.1007/978-3-031-08518-5_8
70. Tedre, M., & Denning, P. J.: The long quest for computational thinking. In: Proceedings of the 16th Koli Calling International Conference on Computing Education Research, pp. 120–129. ACM, Koli (2016). https://doi.org/10.1145/2999541.2999542
71. Tikva, C., Tambouris, E.: Mapping computational thinking through programming in K-12 education: a conceptual model based on a systematic literature Review. Comput. Educ. **162**, 104083 (2021). https://doi.org/10.1016/j.compedu.2020.104083

72. Wang, K.D., Cock, J.M., Käser, T., Bumbacher, E.: A systematic review of empirical studies using log data from open-ended learning environments to measure science and engineering practices. Br. J. Educ. Technol. **54**(1), 192–221 (2022). https://doi.org/10.1111/bjet.13289
73. Watson, C., Li, F.W.B., Godwin, J.L.: Predicting performance in an introductory programming course by logging and analyzing student programming behavior. In: Proceedings of the 13th International Conference on Advanced Learning Technologies, pp. 319–323. IEEE, Beijing (2013). https://doi.org/10.1109/ICALT.2013.99
74. Wing, J.M.: Computational thinking. Commun. ACM. ACM **49**(3), 33–35 (2006). https://doi.org/10.1145/1118178.111821
75. Wing, J.M.: Computational thinking: What and why? Unpublished manuscript (2010). https://www.cs.cmu.edu/~CompThink/resources/TheLinkWing.pdf

Differences in VLE Adoption: Longitudinal and Large-Scale Analysis of Contextual Effects on French Teachers' TEL Practices

Christine Michel[1(✉)], Laëtitia Pierrot[2(✉)], Frédéric Oru[3], and Olivier Vigneau[3]

[1] University of Poitiers, Techné UR-20297, 86000 Poitiers, France
christine.michel@univ-poitiers.fr
[2] Le Mans University, CREN UR-2661, 72000 Le Mans, France
laetitia.pierrot@univ-lemans.fr
[3] EDIFICE, 75017 Le Mans, France
{frederic.oru,olivier.vigneau}@edifice.io

Abstract. Against the widespread use of virtual learning environments (VLEs) in French schools, this research examines their adoption by primary and secondary school teachers by detecting digital maturity profiles based on activity traces. The aim is to analyze the diversity and intensity of the activities carried out in VLEs to identify these profiles and better understand the conditions of their emergence. Based on the statistical processing of VLE data from 144,900 teachers in three academies over 2 school years, we constructed three indicators (MatU, MatD, MatF) to qualify the use in terms of combination, diversity, and frequency of VLE services used. The results reveal five general profiles that differ according to the academic district, the level of education, or the period in which the VLE was deployed. This shows that digital maturity is strongly linked to contextual variables. These profiles suggest that some contexts favor the adoption of complex, collaborative uses, especially in schools that adopted VLE just after the health crisis. The study thus highlights the role of the institutional framework in structuring and sustaining the use of digital technologies in education.

Keywords: Teaching analytics · Technology Integration in Education · Virtual Learning Environment · Teachers' Digital Usage · TEL Adoption and academic policies

1 Introduction

Expectations for technology-enhanced learning (TEL) have grown steadily since the beginning of the 21st century. Since the first recommendations of the OECD in 2001, which stressed the need to combat the digital divide and to integrate techno-pedagogical skills into teacher training, TEL has been gradually introduced into the school environment [16]. This development has been accompanied by efforts to provide teachers with ongoing training to support their use of these tools [20]. However, despite these initiatives, the effective use of TEL remains uneven and sometimes limited, particularly in teachers' daily practice [2].

K. Tammets et al. (Eds.): EC-TEL 2025, LNCS 16063, pp. 321–336, 2026.
https://doi.org/10.1007/978-3-032-03870-8_22

In France, TEL is implemented at both national and local levels. At the national level, training and equipment plans are the result of ministerial policies[1]. At the local level, the academic regions pilot projects in partnership with local authorities (town halls, departments, regions), schools, and other educational actors, including EdTech. This territorial network is based on steering to ensure consistency between the context and the actions carried out. For example, the deployment of virtual learning environments (VLE) follows this logic: nationally, it is governed by a master plan, but locally, different solutions can be chosen according to the choices made directly by schools, municipalities, departments, regions, or academies [11]. However, this strategy is not guaranteed to be adopted by teachers. Previous studies [17, 21] have shown that teachers' use of VLE replicates that were previously observed for other online services such as digital textbooks. Communication practices are mainly developed here, especially with families [17, 21]. On the other hand, other VLE functionalities, such as peer-to-peer resource sharing and assessment, are little used [11].

In this context of the widespread use of VLE, a more detailed understanding of the actual practices of user teachers is needed. Our study therefore aims to understand how French teachers from different academic backgrounds use VLE through 3 questions: RQ1-Which VLE services do teachers use most? RQ2 -What are the most detrimental effects (contextual, institutional, personal) on their use? RQ3 - What usage strategies or teacher profiles can be identified in terms of their use of VLE? This paper adopts an instrumental case study approach [24], analysing the institutionalised use of VLEs in the French education system to understand the dynamics of TEL adoption. The aim is not to statistically generalise the results, but rather to highlight profiles, dynamics and conditions of use that can provide insight into broader issues of public policy deployment and professional development.

2 Background

Teachers' use of VLE and, more generally, TELs has been examined in studies that focus mainly on the integration of these technologies into their teaching practices. To a lesser extent, studies document the factors explaining use, but in a fragmented way. Section 2.1 examines the main specificities of use in primary and secondary education, Sect. 2.2 the impact of geographical and socio-economic contexts, Sect. 2.3 the reconfiguration of use following COVID-19, and Sect. 2.4 the institutional logics that influence this use.

TEL Uses in Primary and Secondary Education. According to the national audience measurement system for VLE set up by the French Ministry of Education[2], there are significant differences between primary and secondary school teachers. The 2022 report notes that primary school teachers focus mainly on the collaborative production of teaching resources, management of class information, and communication with families [13]. In secondary schools, where VLEs are more prevalent, uses include student assessment in addition to communication with students and families and scheduling. This type of report allows the measurement of the extent of the services used by counting their usage

[1] https://www.education.gouv.fr/strategie-du-numerique-pour-L-education-2023-2027-344263.

[2] https://www.data.gouv.fr/fr/datasets/dnma-metriques-par-uai-croisees-par-les-services/.

frequency: primary school teachers prefer services offering digital textbooks (31.5% of users), followed by e-mail (8.8%), while secondary school teachers alternate between textbook (25.6%), school life (21.6%) and e-mail (18.1%). However, these frequencies of use do not give a clear picture of the purposes of use.

The literature has explored the relationship between service and purpose. For example, the first studies of VLE services in France identified the goal of bringing schools and families closer together through VLE [21]. Outside the French context, the same communication objective is pursued by teachers using blog or forum-type services, primarily in primary schools, to centralize useful information (timetables, school activity information, links to educational resources) [4].

Other studies focus specifically on the creation of resources by teachers [7, 26]. These studies emphasize the opportunities for collaboration, interactivity, and personalization that TELs provide, although the resource formats vary. Assessment, primarily summative, is perceived as facilitated by TELs, but although teachers recognize their usefulness in personalizing activities and providing automatic feedback, few explore quizzes, tests, and other portfolios [27]. However, there are two limitations to these studies. First, the distinction between primary and secondary education is not systematically explored, even though class sizes, schools, disciplines, or organizational logic may differ [18]. Moreover, primary education includes schools that serve students aged 3 to 11, with clearly distinct needs and priorities. The same is true for secondary schools. Second, digital services are rarely studied in combination (e.g., assessment and communication), which limits our understanding of the integrative pedagogical logic at work in teachers' practices.

TEL Uses in-Context. Teaching contexts - particularly the territorial (rural, peri-urban, urban) and socio-economic dimensions - are likely to have a significant impact on teachers' digital use.

The frequency of TEL use is directly related to the geographical context: in the US, teachers in urban schools are less likely to use TELs, whereas those in rural or peri-urban areas use them more, particularly for assessment, resource sharing, or communication with students. The latter also benefit in some cases from better infrastructure, especially in peri-urban areas [8]. Conversely, use is less developed in China's rural areas [28]. In rural schools, teachers are interested in using services for communication purposes.

More recently, other studies have highlighted the obstacles faced by rural teachers in other countries [6, 25]. Isolation and low population density force teachers to develop diversified uses to compensate for these constraints.

In general, geographical distribution is associated with a distribution of socio-economic status. Several studies have looked at the socio-economic status of families, highlighting the disparity observed in TEL deployment in schools with a majority of students from disadvantaged families [15, 22]. In response to these challenges, equipment and training plans may be prioritized in rural areas and/or where the majority of students come from less privileged backgrounds [9].

TEL Uses During and Post-Covid-19. The Covid-19 pandemic forced schools to make a sudden shift to distance learning, supported by a variety of technologies. This extraordinary sequence highlighted the dynamics of technology adoption by teachers while revealing differences in teaching practices and contexts [11].

A longitudinal study [19] examined the evolution of teachers' use of educational technologies before, during, and after the pandemic. The results showed that although technology adoption accelerated during the containment period, this integration was not sustained once teachers returned to face-to-face teaching. Teachers often perceived these tools as temporary fixes rather than integrated elements of their teaching practice. However, since 2021, teachers have had a better perception of TELs and are using them more extensively for learning-centered activities.

These findings are consistent with another study that analyzed the digital practices of elementary school teachers during and after the lockdown [12]. This research highlights that, despite the increased use of VLE services during the crisis, their use decreased once schools reopened. Some practices stabilized, mainly related to pedagogical approaches focused on teaching (communication, creation, and dissemination of resources). Moreover, profiles of users have emerged, mainly including teachers who reproduce so-called "traditional" practices and others who combine them with learning-centered activities.

TEL Uses and Policies. Just as the use of VLEs in schools depends on educational policy decisions, so does the integration of technologies. Educational policies can be applied at different levels: at the school level or more broadly.

At school, individual factors are decisive in TEL use. Specifically, digital skills also influence technology adoption [3]. TEL mastery is highly variable and uneven, depending on professional experience, beliefs, and previous training, despite the availability of tools. But school policies and projects can promote the use of TELs and, more broadly, innovative teaching approaches [27]. Conversely, a lack of institutional support is an obstacle to their adoption. More generally, the 'school culture' [23], whether it values collaboration between teachers or relies on more conservative practices, can impact actual teaching practices. Outside of school, several drivers and barriers have been identified [14], such as the accessibility of equipment, the quality of infrastructure, and the nature of support policies offered. Regular training and the provision of technical support are facilitators. Conversely, a lack of training or recurring technical issues are barriers.

France seems to prefer mainly centralized policies aimed at standardizing the level of services and equipment provided in schools, as in the case of VLE [5]. However, these plans are accompanied by great inequalities in certain geographical areas, whether rural or urban, in areas classified as educational priorities with limited access. Moreover, this deployment, based on directives issued by ministerial departments, is sometimes perceived by teachers as too top-down and far removed from practices on the ground.

3 Research Method

Study Context. Table 1 describes the general characteristics of the data collected. The data correspond to the traces of activity on the academic VLEs of 144,900 teachers observed over 2 school years (61,597 in 2022–2023 and 83,303 in 2023–2024). Most teachers (87–94%) remained in the same establishment over the two years.

The VLEs are mainly deployed in the Lille Academic district (56%), followed by Amiens (29%) and Paris (15%). The distribution is fairly balanced across primary, secondary, and sixth-form colleges in the Lille Academic district, while it is mainly in

Table 1. General features of the data collected

Region	Hauts-de-France		Ile-de-France	
Academic district	Amiens	Lille	Paris	Total
2016–2019	61%	62%	48%	86 613
2020–2021	39%	38%	29%	53 449
2022–2024	0%	0%	22%	4 838
Kindergarten	6%	9%	20%	14 258
Elementary School	32%	34%	47%	50 768
Middle School	27%	27%	32%	40 110
Hight School	35%	30%	0%	39 764
No priority	81%	73%	63%	10 7313
REP	11%	16%	32%	24 196
REP +	7%	11%	5%	13 391
Not defined	3%	0%	0%	1 180
Rural	7%	2%	0%	4 662
Intermediate	43%	16%	0%	31 279
Urban	47%	82%	100%	107 779
Total	42 718	81 157	21 025	144 900
	29%	56%	15%	

middle schools in Amiens (35%) and primarily in elementary schools in Paris (47%). The use of VLEs has been established for a long time in all three areas. All establishments were equipped shortly after the health crisis in Lille and Amiens, while 22% of establishments in Paris are still becoming familiar with the solution.

Regarding social characteristics, the REP and REP + zones correspond to neighborhoods characterized by social difficulties that strongly impact academic success. Teachers have special conditions for exercising their profession, which make it possible to develop and facilitate collective work and continuing education. Rural and intermediate areas are characterized by lower population density or difficulty accessing schools. To limit the effects of this, the state encourages the hiring of staff to offer a wider range of extracurricular activities and invests as a priority in high-speed Internet connection and actions to stimulate digital uses to promote learning.

The Lille and Paris Academic districts have the highest proportion of teachers working in disadvantaged social areas: REP in Paris (32%) and REP/REP + in Lille (16% + 11%). The Amiens academy is the most rural, with half of the teachers working in intermediate (43%) or rural (7%) areas. Paris is a completely urban area.

Data Acquisition and Modelling. The data used in this study comes from the activity traces of teachers using either VLE ONE or NEO, as deployed in their academic district. This data takes the form of activity logs compiled over a specific period. Each log contains information on the number of actions performed on a VLE service by each user, according to their institution. 32 services are observed (see Table 2). The use of the data, made possible through pseudonymization, is authorized by the academies as part of their public interest missions.

Table 2. Diversity (MatD), uses combination (MatU), and frequency of use (MatF) scales

MatD	Diversity	MatU	Uses combination	MatF	Frequency of use
0	No use	0	No use	0	No use
1		1	Activity without connection *(for example consultation by following a link in an email)*	1	1–2 per year
2		2	Connection without activity	2	2–8 per year
3	1 objective	3	Communication	3	1–4 per month
4	2 objectives	4	Communication, resource creation & selection	4	1–2 per week
		5	Communication, management	5	2–5 per week
		6	Communication, collaboration	6	1–2 per day
5	3 objectives	7	Communication, resource creation & selection, management	7	2–8 per day
		8	Communication, resource creation & selection, collaboration	8	1–2 per hour
		9	Communication, collaboration, management	9	2–4 per hour
6	4 objectives	10	All the services	10	More than 4 per hour

The data has been modeled to reveal different usage objectives depending on the type and combinations of the VLE services used (see Table 2): *connection, consultation, communication, creation & selection of resources, management, and collaboration* [10]. A second corpus was built based on activity logs to characterize the diversity of uses regardless of their frequency. It is composed of 1 and 0 depending on whether the service was used at least once by the teacher during the period, and 0 otherwise.

A hierarchical ascending classification method was used on the first and second corpus to construct user classes according to the objectives achieved. The classes were characterized using three indicators: MatD, MatU, and MatF (see Table 2). MatD characterizes the classes of the binary corpus and measures the diversity of uses according to the number of objectives achieved with the VLE. MatD quantifies the uses, ranging from non-use (class 0) to the most complete use (class 6, 4 objectives achieved). MatU is a more detailed version of MatD and measures the combination of services used. MatF characterizes the classes of the initial corpus according to the frequency of use, ranging from non-use (class 0) to use several times a day (class 10).

Data and Context Understanding. To visualize teacher usage, we calculated the average number of actions performed on each VLE service and grouped these actions based on key pedagogical objectives. This count was done for each academy to compare the main uses between different schools. To explain the maturity levels obtained from the classifications, correlation analyses were performed between usage objectives and maturity levels using Chi-squared tests. Cramér's V-score was used to measure the strength of the association between variables.

To complement these analyses, a two-dimensional visualization of the observed maturity levels was created to facilitate the interpretation of the results. This approach is based on an analysis method developed in a previous study carried out at the Académie de Paris [10]. One of the contributions of this study is the design of a dashboard with bubble chart-style graphs that allow the identification of maturity levels according to MatD, MatU, and MatF indicators. These indicators are grouped into two main dimensions: the intensity and diversity of teachers' digital maturity. These graphs are therefore useful for identifying the main maturity groups and identifying different strategies.

4 Results

Uses of the VLE Services. Figure 1 shows the average usage of teachers according to the academic districts. It can be seen that usage is broadly similar from one academic district to another, particularly about connection rates or the sending of individual messages (see Table 3).

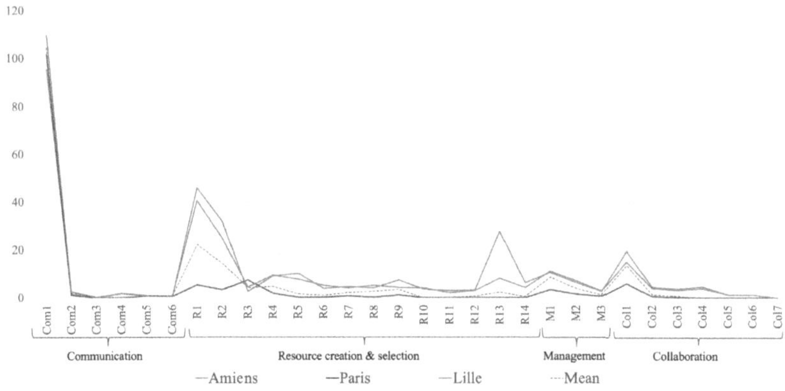

Fig. 1. Teacher uses by academy (n = 144,900)

Disparities appear in more complex uses: for example, teachers in the Paris academic district have a less developed use of collaborative features and resource creation. Conversely, in the Lille and Amiens academic districts, the blog service is less invested in than in Paris, in favor of notebooks, textbooks, and forums.

Table 3. Frequency of services uses according to academic district

Usage	Var	Amiens	Lille	Paris	Mean
0 - Connection	Cx1	381.25	403.65	396.66	396.53
8 - Connection (mobile app)	Cx2	268.35	328.19	144.02	255.27
2 - Individual message (send)	Com1	95.57	110.00	101.80	104.67
50 - Contact book (publish words)	Com2	1.62	2.59	1.27	2.18
11 - Contact book (share at least 2 words)	Com3	0.15	0.26	0.07	0.21
5 - Profile (change currency)	Com4	1.82	1.96	0.06	0.23
1 - Account activation	Com5	0.88	0.93	0.84	0.90
4 - Profile photo (update)	Com6	0.63	0.74	0.62	0.69
35 - Multimedia notebook (create page)	R1	45.92	40.51	5.43	22.24
48 - Document area (share document/file)	R2	31.88	24.92	3.31	14.58
64 - Blog (post publication)	R3	2.65	4.49	7.53	4.18
38 - Video or sound upload	R4	9.14	9.50	1.89	4.80
39 - Sound/video capture ()	R5	10.16	7.87	0.29	1.73
26 - Integration (video. Sound)	R6	4.03	5.23	0.33	1.00
40 - Pad. Timeline. Wall. Wiki. Mind map. Pages (create resources)	R7	4.61	4.21	0.80	2.17
10 - Textbook (share)	R8	4.14	5.20	0.25	2.77
9 - Blog (sharing)	R9	7.45	4.25	1.14	3.44
51 - Textbook (insert multimedia content)	R10	3.67	4.10	0.00	0.02
28 - Mediacentre (consult)	R11	3.08	2.10	0.02	0.10
36 - Exercise (distribution)	R12	3.26	2.99	0.13	0.64
63 - Academic Moodle (access)	R13	27.60	8.13	0.00	2.45
65 - Forum (create discussion with students)	R14	6.33	4.30	0.05	0.62
66 - Class settings (access)	M1	10.70	11.15	3.39	8.61
67 - Administration actions	M2	6.42	7.06	1.47	3.95
24 - Statistics (consult)	M3	2.66	2.84	0.57	1.33

(continued)

Table 3. (*continued*)

Usage	Var	Amiens	Lille	Paris	Mean
17 - Share content (any type with teacher(s))	Col1	19.45	15.12	5.93	13.68
14 - Library (consult)	Col2	4.56	3.89	0.54	1.51
15 - Library (retrieve)	Col3	3.72	3.12	0.19	0.64
19 - Library (publish)	Col4	4.75	3.89	0.01	0.01
16 - Library (comment)	Col5	1.39	1.41	0.00	0.01
22 - Library (reply to comment)	Col6	1.39	1.41	0.00	0.01
21 - Library (subscribe to a teacher)	Col7	0.00	0.00	0.00	0.00

Factors Explaining Maturity Levels. Table 4 presents the significant links (with a threshold of $\alpha = 99\%$) between one of the maturity levels (MatU, MatD, MatF) and the context variables. Cramer's V coefficient measures the intensity of the link between the variables and is interpreted as follows: $V < 0.1$: very weak relationship; $0.1 < V < 0.2$: weak relationship; $0.2 < V < 0.3$: average relationship; $V > 0.3$: strong relationship.

According to Cramer's V coefficient, the F, D, and U maturity levels are mainly linked to the Academic district, Level of education, and VLE Deployment period variables ($V = 0.24$ and 0.36 in Table 4). The Priority education and Geographical area variables significantly affect digital maturity, but in a weaker relationship ($V = 0.08$ and 0.07 in Table 4).

Table 5 presents the average levels of maturity for the different modalities of the 3 context variables: *Academic district, Level of education,* and *VLE Deployment period.*

The Lille Academic district has an overall higher average maturity level (MatU = 4.83; MatD = 3.59; MatF = 5.67) than Amiens and Paris. In addition, usage is more developed in terms of complexity and diversity in elementary schools (MatU = 5.99, MatD = 4.01) and kindergartens (MatU = 5.50; MatD = 3.71) than in high schools (MatU = 3.15; MatD = 2.75) and middle schools (MatU = 3.95; Mat D = 3.26). The intensity levels are comparable, with a maximum value for middle schools (MatF = 5.68). Regarding the VLE Deployment variable, schools that have had the VLE for a short time (since 22–23) have the simplest and least frequent uses (Mat U = 3.82; Mat D = 2.69; MatF = 2.78). It is surprising to note that establishments that deployed the VLE during and just after the COVID health crisis period have more developed uses in complexity and diversity (Mat U = 5.58; Mat D = 3.87) than those that have had it for a long time (since 16–19) (Mat U = 4.03; Mat D = 3.19). On the other hand, the frequency of use is equivalent when the VLE has been present for a long time (MatF = 5.12) or since the Covid crisis (MatF = 5.16). It is interesting to note that these average values do not correspond to homogeneous behavior among teachers according to Academic district, Level of education, and VLE Deployment. Indeed, the standard

Table 4. Measurement of the relationship between maturity variables and context variables

Relations	p-value	Chi-squared	Cramer's V
Academic district*MatF	0.00	36607.17	0.36
Level of education*MatU	0.00	51281.91	0.34
Level of education*MatD	0.00	42643.90	0.31
VLE Deployment*MatU	0.00	19465.19	0.26
VLE Deployment*MatD	0.00	16732.80	0.24
VLE Deployment*MatF	0.00	2963.48	0.17
Level of education*MatF	0.00	11240.38	0.16
Academic district *MatU	0.00	3878.37	0.12
Academic district *MatD	0.00	3432.98	0.11
Priority education*MatU	0.00	1997.91	0.08
Geographical area*MatF	0.00	2963.48	0.08
Priority education*MatF	0.00	1550.95	0.07
Priority education*MatD	0.00	1457.64	0.07
Geographical area *MatU	0.00	1963.08	0.07
Geographical area *MatD	0.00	1861.92	0.07

Table 5. Average of maturity measurements according to contextual characteristics.

	Average			Standard Deviation		
	MatU	MatD	MatF	MatU	MatD	MatF
Academic district Amiens	4.30	3.23	4.17	3.28	1.85	2.31
Lille	4.83	3.59	5.67	3.23	1.69	2.02
Paris	4.31	3.18	4.50	3.37	1.94	2.64
Level of education Kindergarten	5.50	3.71	4.45	3.88	2.19	2.38
Elementary school	5.99	4.01	4.88	3.75	2.04	2.22
Middle school	3.95	3.26	5.68	2.37	1.27	2.14
High school	3.15	2.75	4.87	2.20	1.42	2.45
VLE Deployment period 16–19	4.03	3.19	5.12	2.88	1.61	2.32
20–21	5.58	3.87	5.16	3.58	1.91	2.19
22–23	3.82	2.69	2.78	3.84	2.34	2.39

deviation values are relatively high, with a minimum value of 1.27 for the diversity of use in middle schools and a maximum value of 3.88 for kindergartens.

Teachers' Strategies of Use According to Context Variables. To analyze the variability of usage linked to the three most impactful context variables, Figs. 2, 3, and 4 present, in the form of bubble graphs, the number of teachers according to usage strategies based on uses combination (MatU) and intensity (MatF).

The distinctions in maturity profiles according to the academic districts (see Fig. 2) highlight the particularity of the Lille academic district, with a large majority of teachers making frequent use of 2–8 per day (MatF = 7), for simple communication purposes (MatU = 3), communication, creation and collaboration (MatU = 8) or all purposes (MatU = 10). The Amiens academic district is characterized by lower levels of use, with the majority of teachers using the VLE to communicate very occasionally, i.e. on average 1–4 per month (MatU = 3, MatF = 3). Teachers in the Paris academic district have a variety of strategies. There is a relatively well-balanced distribution between teachers with low levels of maturity (MatU = [0;3], MatF = [0;3]) and high levels of maturity (MatU = [7;10], MatF = [7;10]).

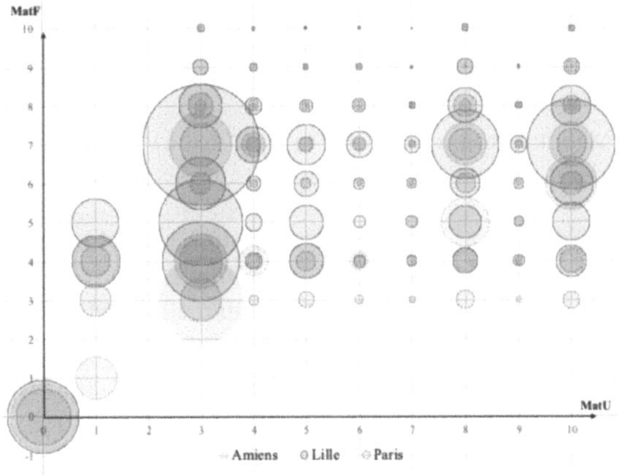

Fig. 2. Teachers' Maturity Profile According to the academic district

Figure 3 illustrates the segmentation of uses according to level of education. Elementary school teachers have particularly advanced uses: most of them are at the MatU = 10 maturity level, i.e. they use the VLE to achieve the 4 identified objectives (communication, creation and selection of educational resources, management, and collaboration) at high frequencies, i.e. 2–8 per day (MatF = 7) or 1–2 per day (MatF = 6). The majority of middle and high school teachers also have frequent usage of 2–8 per day (MatF = 7), but many of them also have less frequent usage ranging from 2–5 per week (MatF = 5) to 1–4 per month (MatF = 3). In addition, this usage is centered on communication objectives (MatU = 3).

An analysis of teachers' maturity profiles according to the deployment period of the VLE in the institution (see Fig. 4) shows that the teachers with the highest maturity levels are those who started using the VLE just after the COVID health crisis with MatU

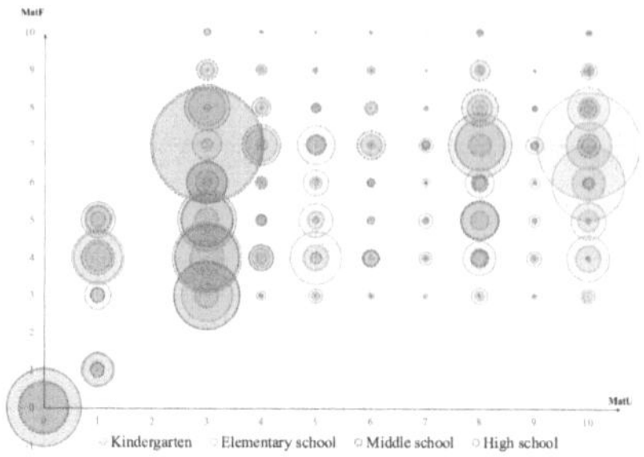

Fig. 3. Teachers' Maturity Profile According to the level of education

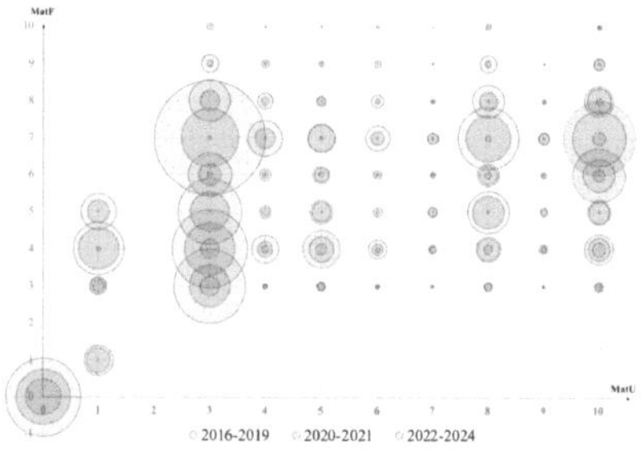

Fig. 4. Teachers' Maturity Profile According to the Date of VLE Deployment in the School

= 10 and MatU = 8 levels, i.e. characterized by strategies of collaboration with other teachers. Teachers who have had the VLE for a long time (16–19), especially before the COVID crisis, mainly use it for simple communication (MatU = 3) and at varying frequencies, between 2–8 per day (MatF = 7) and 1–4 per month (MatF = 3). Certain teachers develop strategies of collaboration with other teachers (MatU = 8), but they are in the minority.

Detail of Teacher's Uses According to Contextual Variables. Figure 5 shows the frequency of use of the most popular services for resource creation and selection, management, and collaboration, compared by academy, deployment period, and academic level. The greatest differences in use between the academic districts concern the following services: Multimedia notebook (create page) (R1), Document area (share document/file) (R2), Academic Moodle (access) (R13), Class settings (access) (M1), Share content (any type with teacher(s)) (Col1). When the data is compared according to the period, the uses of R13 are more similar. Comparison by school level shows other differences. As before, there are still variations in the use of R1, R2, and Col1, but also in the use of Video or sound upload (R4), Pad/Timeline/Wall/Wiki/Mind map/Pages (create resources) (R7), Blog (sharing) (R9), Administration actions (M2). These initial trends must be analyzed in more detail, using measures of diversity and intensity of use to better understand how these services combine.

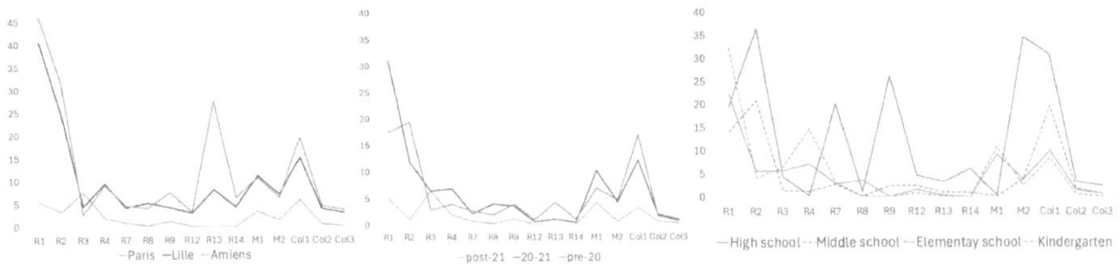

Fig. 5. Teacher's uses (resource creation and selection, management, and collaboration services) according to contextual variables

5 Discussion

RQ1&RQ2. Most Contextual Effects on VLE Services Use. Regarding the differences in use between levels of education, our results are consistent with those indicating that primary and secondary teachers have different uses, but our results are more precise. Our work shows that while teachers focus primarily on the collaborative production of educational resources, classroom information management, and communication with families [13], they do so in differentiated ways: one group of teachers does only communication (MatU = 3, Fig. 3), one group combines communication with classroom management (MatU = 5, Fig. 3), and the third group achieves all 4 objectives (MatU = 10, Fig. 3). The most frequently used applications allow the use of multimedia resources by uploading them to the platform (R4, Fig. 5) or sharing them in a multimedia notebook (R1, Fig. 5). Uses of multimedia notebooks are also realized in secondary schools but with text resources whereas in primary school multimedia content is shared. Moreover, within each group, there is a variation in the intensity of use (MatF from 3 to 7, Fig. 3), but the most observed frequency of use is 2–8 times a day (MatF = 7).

In secondary education, our results are not entirely consistent with the literature. A very large proportion of the population only uses e-mail communication (MatU = 3). On the fringes, teachers use other VLE services in an advanced way to: do administration actions (M2, Fig. 5), share documents or content to inform learners (with document sharing and blog), or organize collaboration with them (with Pad/Timeline/Wall/Wiki/Mind map/Pages) (R2, R7, R9, Fig. 5) and also to collaborate with other teachersCol1, Fig. 5), but not to carry out assessments. These differences are undoubtedly related to the fact that there are two types of VLE in France: one focused on administrative activities (Pronote) and the VLEs we analyze (ONE and NEO) that integrate collaborative functionalities. When teachers have access to peer collaboration features, they develop these uses.

In terms of the length of time teachers have been using the VLE, our results highlight a greater integration of digital services among teachers who discovered the tool shortly after the health crisis. This suggests that, given the limitations of COVID-19, teachers had to develop collaborative strategies, with learners (to teach) and their colleagues (to collaborate), that became established over time. This contrasts with the results of the post-Covid study, which emphasized that the dynamics initiated during the health crisis had little persistence and were characterized by their transitory dimension (Pozo et al. 2024). On the other hand, another of our findings is similar to that study: teachers who used TEL well before the restrictions now present less mature profiles, with relatively low levels of MatU and use devoted mainly to communication. Thus, although TEL use increased temporarily, this adoption did not lead to widespread use after the crisis. This raises the question of long-term adoption of TEL in general and VLE in particular: how can we maintain the momentum of use over the long term? In addition to positive individual attitudes towards technology, the studies underline the importance of an institutional framework that encourages exploration of TEL, with plans to support collaboration and sharing of practice [1].

At this stage, it is difficult to interpret the differences between the academic districts because they result from different policy choices in terms of training, equipment, or communication with teachers. Qualitative studies are needed to understand them better. Nevertheless, it can be seen that these choices have an impact on the adoption of VLE, which shows that public policies have observable effects. Similarly, geographical area or social differences have effects on usage, but they are not strong. A specific analysis of these variables will make it possible to identify more precisely how these constraints affect usage.

RQ3. Teachers' Usage Strategies of VLE. Figures 2, 3, and 4 show that there are 5 categories of users: *A-Non-users* (MatU = [0;2]), B-Communicators (MatU = 3), C-Communicator-controllers-organizers (MatU = 5), D-Communicators who create resources and collaborate (MatU = 8), E-Complete profiles (MatU = 10). Within these categories, the frequencies of use vary but use 2–8 times a day is the most representative (MatF = 7).

This result is transversal to all the contexts observed, which shows that it is linked to the values or individual choices of the teachers. Further studies are needed to understand precisely why some teachers choose to work according to one category or another. These results can be put into perspective with formalizations such as DigCompEdu to illustrate, for example, whether and how C profiles use the organization and control of learners' work, or how D profiles adapt the creation of resources according to teaching disciplines or learners' characteristics in their classes. In addition, it will be interesting to compare profiles A and E, particularly in terms of teachers' sense of efficacy and satisfaction, but also about effective learning in the classroom.

6 Conclusion

This study aimed to explore the use of VLE by French teachers, examining the diversity and intensity of their use as observed through their activity logs (n = 144,900). The analysis of a corpus covering three academic districts and two school years allowed us to identify the most widely used services, revealing various usage profiles. While communication and the sharing of educational resources are widespread, notable variations emerge. One of the aims of the study was to identify these variations to create a profile of teachers, taking into account their usage frequency and strategies for combining services, and, by extension, their level of digital maturity.

The results show variations mainly related to the educational context (primary, secondary). Other contextual effects are also evident: TEL deployment and prioritization policies influence the dynamics of use, with variations depending on the geographic and institutional characteristics of the academic districts. Although the three districts selected in this corpus have distinct socio-geographical characteristics, they are all located within mainland France. An extension of the study could include schools using the same VLE in the outermost regions to better understand the impact of contextual effects. Finally, the study identifies a typology of teachers, ranging from non-users to teachers with more mature profiles. These profiles are directly related to the observed use of the VLE, as measured by our maturity indicators. A more in-depth analysis would allow us to qualify teachers' pedagogical goals and approaches. In particular, exploring elements of pedagogical effectiveness assessment would provide a better understanding of the links between digital maturity and usage goals.

References

1. Adhya, D., Panda, S.: Teacher educators' attitude towards technology-enabled learning and its incorporation into teaching-learning during and post-pandemic. EMI. **59**, 1–19 (2022). https://doi.org/10.1080/09523987.2022.2101204
2. Akram, H. et al.: Teachers' Perceptions of Technology Integration in Teaching-Learning Practices: A Systematic Review. Front. Psych.. 13, (2022)
3. Claro, M., et al.: Teaching in a digital environment (TIDE): defining and measuring teachers' capacity to develop students' digital information and communication skills. Comput. Educ. **121**, 162–174 (2018). https://doi.org/10.1016/j.compedu.2018.03.001
4. Colwell, J., Hutchison, A.: Supporting teachers in integrating digital technology into language arts instruction to promote literacy. JDLTE. **31**, 56–63 (2015). https://doi.org/10.1080/21532974.2014.991813
5. Cordier, A., Collin, S.: Politiques publiques d'intégration du numérique en éducation : France-Québec, regards croisés. Education comparée. ECI. **19** (2018)
6. Fernández-Arias, P., et al.: Digital competence of rural teachers in depopulated regions of Spain: a bibliometric review. EJIHPE. **15**(1), 5 (2025). https://doi.org/10.3390/ejihpe15010005
7. Haleem, A., et al.: Understanding the role of digital technologies in education: a review. Sus. Op. Comp. **3**, 275–285 (2022). https://doi.org/10.1016/j.susoc.2022.05.004
8. Kormos, E., Julio, L.: Contrasting instructional technology adoption in K-12 education to promote digital equity. IJWBLTT. **15**, 19–30 (2020). https://doi.org/10.4018/IJWLTT.2020070102
9. Mané, C.E.: The effect of school socioeconomic status and teachers' perception of school culture on teachers' proficiency with information and communications technology tools in the classroom. University of Georgia (2019)
10. Michel, C., Pierrot, L., Oru, F., Vigneau, O.: The challenge of modeling the complexity of use for the measurement of digital maturity in education. In: Ferreira Mello, R., Rummel, N., Jivet, I., Pishtari, G., and Ruipérez Valiente, J.A. (eds.) Technology Enhanced Learning for Inclusive and Equitable Quality Education, pp. 268–283. Springer, Cham (2024)
11. Michel, C. et al.: VLE limits and perspectives for digital integration in teaching practices. In: De Laet, T. et al. (eds.) Technology-Enhanced Learning for a Free, Safe, and Sustainable World, pp. 96–109 Springer, Cham (2021). https://doi.org/10.1007/978-3-030-86436-1_8
12. Michel, C., Pierrot, L.: Towards modelling the technology integration in elementary school. A diachronic study of teachers' digital practices during and after covid-19 lockdown. In: Hilliger, I. et al. (eds.) Educating for a New Future: Making Sense of Technology-Enhanced Learning Adoption, pp. 201–214. Springer, Cham (2022). https://doi.org/10.1007/978-3-031-16290-9_15

13. Ministère de l'Éducation nationale: Les ENT face aux nouveaux défis 2022. éduscol (2022)
14. Nelson, M.J., et al.: Mediating factors that influence the technology integration practices of teacher educators. Comput. Educ. **128**, 330–344 (2019). https://doi.org/10.1016/j.compedu.2018.09.023
15. Njeri, M., Taym, A.: Analysing the power of socioeconomic status on access to technology-enhanced learning in secondary schools. RSELTL. **2**(4), 223–250 (2024). https://doi.org/10.62583/rseltl.v2i4.55
16. OECD: Les nouvelles technologies à l'école. OECD (2001)
17. Pacurar, E., Abbas, N.: Analysis of French secondary school teachers' intention to integrate digital work environments into their teaching practices. Educ. Inf. Technol. **20**(3), 537–557 (2015)
18. Parsons, T.: The School Class as a Social System: Some of Its Functions in American Society. In: Exploring Education. Routledge (2017)
19. Pozo, J.-I. et al.: Has the educational use of digital technologies changed after the pandemic? A longitudinal study. Plos One. **19**(12), e0311695 (2024). https://doi.org/10.1371/journal.pone.0311695
20. Redecker, C.: European Framework for the Digital Competence of Educators: DigCompEdu. Punie, Y. Publications Office of the European Union, Luxembourg (2017)
21. Schaming, C., Marquet, P.: ENT et coéducation école/famille: La politique éducative d'un établissement peut-elle influencer l'appropriation de l'ENT ? Spirale. **63**, 37 (2019). https://doi.org/10.3917/spir.063.0037
22. Scherer, R., Siddiq, F.: The relation between students' socioeconomic status and ICT literacy: findings from a meta-analysis. Comput. Educ. **138**, 13–32 (2019). https://doi.org/10.1016/j.compedu.2019.04.011
23. Spiteri, M., Chang Rundgren, S.-N.: Literature review on the factors affecting primary teachers' use of digital technology. Tech Know Learn. **25**(1), 115–128 (2020). https://doi.org/10.1007/s10758-018-9376-x
24. Stake, R.E.: The Art of Case Study Research. Sage Publications, Thousand Oaks (1995)
25. Timotheou, S., et al.: Impacts of digital technologies on education and factors influencing schools' digital capacity and transformation: a literature review. Educ. Inf. Technol. **28**(6), 6695–6726 (2023). https://doi.org/10.1007/s10639-022-11431-8
26. Torrens, I. et al.: Digital tools for interactive learning: a systematic mapping. RENOTE. **21**, 403–412 (2023). https://doi.org/10.22456/1679-1916.137776
27. Yin, S.S.Y., Mohamad, M.: Unleashing the potential: a systematic review of teachers' perspectives on enhancing teaching practices through digital tools. IJARBSS. **13**(8), 1105–1117 (2023)
28. Zhao, Y., et al.: Analysis of urban-rural discrepancies in primary and secondary school teachers' ICT application ability in teaching and research in China. In: (ISET), pp. 131–134 (2017). https://doi.org/10.1109/ISET.2017.38

Impact of Immediate Feedback on Students' Learning in a Virtual Reality Environment for Chemical Education

Valentin Midez[1(✉)], Audrey Serna[1], Florent Diet[1], Victor Oliva Torres[1], and Élise Lavoué[1,2]

[1] INSA Lyon, CNRS, Universite Claude Bernard Lyon 1, LIRIS, UMR5205, 69621 Villeurbanne, France
{valentin.midez,audrey.serna,victor.oliva-torres}@insa-lyon.fr, elise.lavoue@univ-lyon3.fr

[2] University Jean Moulin Lyon 3, iaelyon School of Management, Lyon, France

Abstract. Virtual Reality offers the opportunity to create immersive environments for safe, practice-based learning, but its intense immersion can limit critical thinking. This study explores the impact of immediate feedback on chemistry learning in an immersive environment. It involved 46 participants divided into two conditions, with and without immediate feedback. We assessed their performance, including correct answers and procedures performed, as well as perceived cognitive load. The results show that immediate feedback does not increase the perceived cognitive load, but its effect on learning depends on the tasks performed. They can be detrimental to performance for a single task, whereas they lead to significant improvements for repeated tasks. These observations highlight their usefulness in repetitive scenarios while underlining the need for appropriate design to avoid adverse effects on learning.

Keywords: Virtual reality · Feedback · Reflection · Immersive learning · Chemical education

1 Introduction

Virtual reality (VR) can be used to simulate complex, interactive environments, providing immersive, engaging experiences for learning and training activities [2]. Several studies have shown that VR is particularly effective in supporting active learning and practical application [4]. It provides a safe environment where learners can experiment and develop practical skills without risk while enhancing their engagement. Immersive simulations offer embodied, realistic, and repeatable experiences that help learners explore strategies for managing complex situations and develop their skills [12].

However, some studies have shown that such immersive environments can hinder learners' ability to reflect critically on their actions [11]. To improve the effectiveness of VR environments in educational contexts, Roussou and Slater

K. Tammets et al. (Eds.): EC-TEL 2025, LNCS 16063, pp. 337–351, 2026.
https://doi.org/10.1007/978-3-032-03870-8_23

[16] emphasize the importance of supporting learners' reflection during task execution. To address this issue, several studies have explored the integration of immediate feedback, reporting positive outcomes on learners' engagement, critical reflection, and performance [1,13,14]. Others, however, point to more mixed effects, particularly regarding learners' perceived cognitive load depending on the complexity of the feedback [15,21]. The design and pedagogical role of such feedback thus remain key challenges to explore.

In this study, we focus on chemistry education, where part of the learning objectives involves performing laboratory-based tasks and procedures, which can be trained in immersive environments. In this context, we investigate whether integrating immediate feedback in a VR learning environment has an effect on the learning experience. We conducted a comparative study with 46 participants, randomly assigned to two conditions: with or without immediate feedback. We analyzed the impact of immediate feedback on both performance (regarding expected answers and completed procedures) and perceived cognitive load in different types of tasks (single vs. repeated). The results show that immediate feedback does not increase perceived cognitive load, but its effect on performance depends on the nature of the task. These findings suggest that integrating immediate feedback into VR environments can be beneficial if carefully designed according to the learning scenario.

2 Related Work

2.1 Virtual Reality in Education

In education, virtual reality technologies offer immersive and interactive environments that allow learners to practice without physical or ethical risks [1,6]. These environments can enhance learners' attention by fostering a sense of presence, defined as the subjective experience of being in the virtual environment [16]. VR can improve retention of both knowledge and procedural skills, especially when traditional methods such as physical demonstrations or classroom simulations are difficult to implement due to material, time, or safety constraints [1]. It allows learners to experiment and correct their mistakes without real-world consequences freely [8]. In their meta-analysis, Cromley et al. [5] highlight that immersive environments in VR promote knowledge acquisition and learners' engagement, which can limit their ability to reflect on their actions. Jiang and Ahmadpour [11] point out that the intense immersion and flow state experienced in VR reduce self-awareness, thus hindering reflexivity about the actions performed.

According to Elaish et al. [7], the successful integration of VR in education requires an instructional design that aligns immersion with learning objectives, ensuring that virtual environments provide real educational value. Roussou and Slater [16] further recommend combining the interactive features of VR with support for reflective processes. They suggest that immersive and interactive environments, combined with explicit feedback to inform, confirm, or correct learners' actions, can encourage critical reflection and prevent potential errors while reducing the risk of cognitive overload. These theoretical insights underscore the importance of examining how reflective processes can be effectively supported in VR-based learning environments.

2.2 Reflective Processes and Feedback in Virtual Reality

Reflective processes involve reflecting on how the task was carried out, in order to reevaluate the initial objectives and the strategies used to achieve them [24]. Reflecting on their own learning, learners become aware of their learning processes and identify possible alternative strategies [18]. This introspective work enables them to adjust existing practices, develop new ones, or redefine their meaning [23]. Schön [17] expands this notion by distinguishing between reflection-in-action, which supports immediate adjustments, and reflection-on-action, which allows for retrospective and critical analysis. Reflection-in-action can lead to constructing new understandings and real-time adaptation during task execution.

One way to support reflective processes is to provide feedback during the task (reflection-in-action) or after it (reflection-on-action). Hattie and Timperley [10] identify three levels of feedback: task-level feedback (specific information on performance), process-level feedback (guidance on strategies used), and self-regulation feedback (supporting learners' ability to self-assess). This study focuses on feedback related to task execution in immersive VR environments. Recent systematic reviews have emphasized the importance of feedback in immersive learning environments. Lee et al. [14] highlight the role of feedback in serious games using virtual, augmented, or mixed reality to foster reflection, increase engagement, and support the development of complex cognitive skills. Similarly, Lampropoulos et al. [13] show that combining VR with gamification elements such as levels, badges, and scores helps learners engage in critical thinking by providing immediate feedback on their actions.

Several comparative studies have also investigated the impact of immediate feedback in VR-based training. Almousa et al. [1] found that visual and auditory cues helped learners evaluate and adjust their performance in real-time while practicing cardiopulmonary resuscitation. In a study on breastfeeding training, Tang et al. [21] showed that adding a progress bar, badges, scores, and auditory prompts maintained engagement and supported learners' reflection on their performance. Van Ginkel et al. [22] used VR to support the development of public speaking skills, showing that real-time indicators (e.g., prolonged eye contact or fast speech) enabled immediate correction and improved presentation skills.

However, despite these benefits, concerns remain about the cognitive load induced by immediate feedback in VR. Cognitive load refers to the balance between task demands and the cognitive resources available to the learner [20]. Ma et al. [15] found that providing complex or multiple feedback cues can overload cognitive resources and reduce learning effectiveness. Furthermore, Tang et al. [21] reported a significant increase in time pressure and mental effort caused by immediate feedback.

In conclusion, while VR has shown its potential to support learning, the specific role of immediate feedback remains underexplored. Although promising results have been reported, the issue of cognitive load induced by real-time feedback still needs to be addressed to ensure optimal learning conditions.

3 Research Questions

This study examines whether adding immediate feedback in a virtual reality learning environment influences learning outcomes. We focus specifically on the acquisition of chemistry-related skills involved in laboratory manipulations. We address the following two research questions:

- **RQ1**: Does integrating immediate feedback into the VR environment affect learners' performance in learning activities? In terms of performance, we analyze the relevance of the answers provided and the procedures performed by the learners about the target skills defined in the learning scenario.
- **RQ2**: Does integrating immediate feedback into the VR environment impact learners' perceived cognitive load?

We explore these questions on different types of tasks (single vs. repeated tasks) using a dedicated scenario. In the following sections, we describe the VR environment, the learning scenario and the integration of feedback designed to support learners' reflexivity.

4 Virtual Reality Environment for Learning Chemistry

As part of the Renforce project, we developed a virtual reality (VR) learning environment for chemistry education. Some of the targeted skills relate to the practice of scientific reasoning: proposing hypotheses to answer a scientific question, designing experiments to test them, measuring physical quantities directly or indirectly, interpreting experimental results, drawing conclusions, and communicating them with arguments. Other targeted skills focus on the adoption of ethical and responsible behavior, particularly in relation to safety rules and procedures related to chemical handling. VR environments allow training these skills, especially gestures and practical manipulations (e.g., pouring a liquid from one beaker to another).

The VR environment, developed using Unity, is a virtual laboratory that reproduces all the necessary elements for chemical manipulations (workbench, fume hood, taps, glassware, flasks, and measurement equipment). It also integrates a liquid management system to prepare mixtures (Fig. 1).

Fig. 1. Virtual chemistry laboratory environment.

4.1 Learning Scenario

To address our research questions, we designed a learning scenario covering basic chemistry skills: observing, experimenting, and measuring. The scenario focuses on the organization and transformation of matter, specifically on identifying whether a solution is acidic or basic using pH measurement. This topic, introduced in lower secondary school in the French curriculum, offers a simple context that requires no prior knowledge and is accessible to various profiles of learners.

A tutorial video presented to participants introduces the key knowledge and skills covered in the scenario, including identifying the acidic or basic nature of a solution based on the presence of H^+ and OH^- ions; understanding chemical transformations in different contexts (e.g., daily life, environment); using several methods to measure pH (pH strips, pH meter, pH indicators); identifying reactions between acidic and basic solutions; and applying appropriate procedures during chemical manipulations.

The scenario consists of two manipulations, each designed to assess the activation of chemistry-related knowledge and skills across two dimensions: the relevance of the learners' answers and the proper execution of the expected procedures. To examine the effects of immediate feedback on various types of tasks, each manipulation included either single tasks (manipulation 1) or a sequence of repeated tasks (task 1 followed by task 2 in manipulation 2).

- **Manipulation 1:** Learners have to identify whether five solutions (distilled water, coffee, lemon juice, seawater, and bleach) are acidic, basic, or neutral. They use pH strips and a reference chart to measure and classify each solution. This task involves pipetting the liquid, applying it to a strip, observing the color change, and classifying the solution accordingly. **Targeted skills:** measuring pH using pH strips; classifying solutions as acidic, basic, or neutral. **Expected answers:** 2 acidic (lemon juice, coffee), 1 neutral (distilled water), 2 basic (seawater, bleach). **Required procedures:** use one strip per solution; discard each strip after use; rinse the pipette between measurements.
- **Manipulation 2:** Learners have to repeat the same acid-base reaction task twice. These two tasks aim to reach a specific pH using a combination of acidic

and basic solutions and a colored indicator to assess the pH reached. In Task 1, they transform an acidic solution (white vinegar) into a basic solution with a pH of 8. In Task 2, they transform a basic solution (ammonia) into an acidic solution with a pH of 6. Learners have to select the appropriate titration solution (a base in Task 1, an acid in Task 2) and choose the correct pH indicator based on its color change range. They observe the color during titration and can use pH strips at any time to verify the pH reached. **Targeted skills:** performing a transformation by selecting a titrant and a pH indicator based on its transition range; reaching a target pH. **Expected answers:** pH indicator (Task 1: phenol red; Task 2: bromothymol blue); titrant (Task 1: sodium hydroxide; Task 2: hydrochloric acid); target pH (Task 1: 8; Task 2: 6). **Required procedures:** respect the correct mixing order (indicator first); monitor the color transition; rinse the pipette before use; use a pH strip to confirm the result; accurately reach the pH value; discard the strip after use.

4.2 Integration of Feedback into the Environment

The feedback system aims to inform learners about their acquisition of the knowledge and skills targeted in the learning scenario. Feedback relies on the assessed answers and the procedures specified for each experimental task.

Immediate feedback combines visual and auditory cues to provide real-time input as learners act, to support reflection-in-action [17] (Fig. 2). For the design of these elements, we draw inspiration from recent studies that propose immediate, game-inspired audiovisual feedback mechanisms [13,21]. For correct answers, feedback takes the form of colored stars that appear accompanied by a sound symbolizing the twinkling of the star. In the case of an incorrect answer, learners also receive immediate feedback in the form of greyed-out stars. This visual cue indicates failure without corrective guidance to avoid disrupting procedural learning dynamics. For procedures, the feedback is represented by a progress bar (or XP bar). Each time a correct procedure is detected, the bar increases and is accompanied by a sound indicating progress.

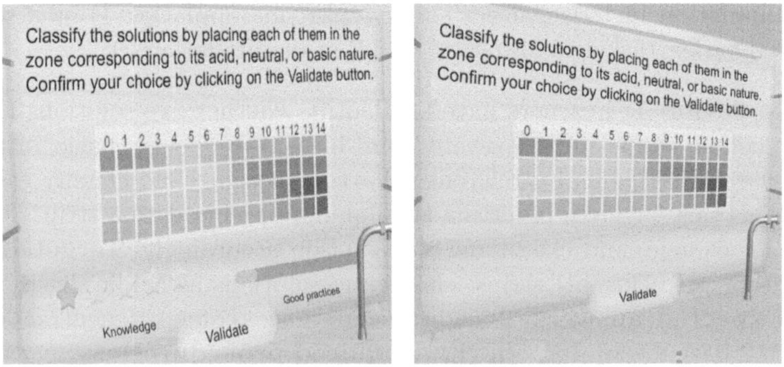

Fig. 2. Instruction panel displayed for each experimental condition for the group with IF on the left (stars and XP bar), and without IF on the right.

To support reflection-on-action [17], a summary of correctly (or incorrectly) performed answers and procedures is displayed at the end of each manipulation. This summary enables learners to review their performance after each task and engage in retrospective reflection. The summary is available to all participants, regardless of their experimental condition.

5 Research Protocol

5.1 Participants

Participants were recruited via a university mailing list. Individuals with prior training or education in chemistry were excluded from the study to ensure homogeneous baseline knowledge across groups. 46 participants, aged between 19 and 36 ($M = 23.4$, $SD = 3.92$), participated in the experiment, including 17 women and 29 men. Participants were randomly assigned to one of two experimental groups of 23 participants each: one group with immediate feedback (With IF) and one group without immediate feedback (Without IF).

We used non-parametric tests to compare the groups due to small sample sizes (Mann–Whitney for quantitative variables and Chi-squared tests for categorical variables). As reported in Table 1, the two groups were well balanced regarding demographic characteristics, with no significant differences in age or gender. We found no significant differences in the number of years of study or participants' prior experience with VR.

Each participant received a €10 gift card as compensation for their time and participation. The research protocol was approved by the Research Ethics Committee from the University of Lyon.

Table 1. Distribution of participants by gender, age, years of study after high school, VR experience frequency, and VR gaming habits between the immediate feedback and no immediate feedback groups. P-values from Mann–Whitney and Chi-squared tests.

Variables	Categories	With IF (n = 23)	Without IF (n = 23)	p-value
Gender	Male	14 (61%)	15 (65%)	1.00
	Female	9 (39%)	8 (35%)	
Age (M ± SD)		23.83 ± 4.93	22.91 ± 2.57	0.80
Years of study after high school (M ± SD)		4.65 ± 1.67	5.35 ± 1.85	0.17
Have you ever worn a VR headset?	Never	10 (61%)	8 (47%)	0.64
	Only once	8 (24%)	11 (33%)	
	Several times	4 (12%)	2 (13%)	
	Regularly	1 (3%)	2 (7%)	
Do you play VR video games?	Never	18 (62%)	19 (58%)	1.00
	Occasionally	5 (38%)	4 (42%)	
	Often	0 (0%)	0 (0%)	

5.2 Experimental Procedure

We set up a dedicated 6 × 6 m room to allow participants to move freely and interact with the VR environment designed for the study. We followed a between-subjects study design, therefore participants were divided between the two experimental conditions and followed the same procedure in the same order. The only difference between the groups was the presence or absence of immediate feedback during the learning tasks. Before starting, all participants signed an informed consent form in accordance with ethical guidelines. They then completed a demographic questionnaire, followed by questions about their previous VR experience and virtual reality gaming habits. Participants were guided through a VR tutorial to familiarize them with the headset (Vive Pro Eye) and the Valve Index controllers. The tutorial included instructions on manipulating virtual objects and navigating the environment. The experimental group also received instructions to understand the functioning of immediate feedback. After the tutorial, a video covering basic acid–base chemistry concepts was shown outside of VR to provide the necessary knowledge while minimizing VR exposure time. Participants were then equipped with the headset to complete the learning scenario consisting in manipulation 1 followed by manipulation 2 in the virtual laboratory. At the end of the session, participants completed the NASA-TLX questionnaire to assess their perceived cognitive load during the manipulations.

5.3 Data Collection and Analysis

All interaction data were collected automatically through simple actions such as "*pouring a solution into a beaker*" or "*grasping a pH strip*". These actions enabled us to analyze participants' performance during each manipulation by verifying the accuracy of their answers or detecting the completion of expected procedures (e.g., "*selecting the correct color indicator*" or "*respecting the correct mixing order*" in Manipulation 2). We identified whether participants provided correct or incorrect answers for each item evaluated in the learning scenario. We thus defined performance as the combination of correct answers and the execution of expected procedures for each manipulation, reflecting the acquisition of procedural skills related to the experimental tasks.

We conducted two types of analyses to address our research questions: an analysis of participants' performance across the different manipulations of the scenario (RQ1) and an analysis of perceived cognitive load (RQ2). We conducted the analyses primarily using Python (*Pandas*, *SciPy*), with complementary analyses run in Jamovi for the NASA-TLX self-assessment questionnaire [9]. For RQ1, as data were not normally distributed, group performances were compared using the Mann-Whitney test based on scores from correct and incorrect answers and scores for completed procedures in each manipulation. For the repeated tasks in Manipulation 2 (Task 1 and Task 2), we used Wilcoxon tests with and without Benjamini-Hochberg correction to analyze within-group differences. Given the small sample size and the non-normal distribution of almost all the data, we used non-parametric tests. For RQ2, we assessed perceived cognitive load using the NASA-TLX, which evaluates six specific dimensions: mental demand, physical demand, temporal demand, effort, perceived performance, and frustration. We used these dimensions to compute a global cognitive load score reflecting participants' subjective experience. We conducted between-group comparisons of these scores using the Mann–Whitney test.

6 Results

6.1 RQ1a: Performance on Expected Answers

In Manipulation 1, participants spent 5.2 min on average in both groups. The group with immediate feedback scored significantly lower on correct answers and higher on incorrect answers than those without immediate feedback (Table 2). The moderate effect size confirms that this difference is noteworthy [3]. We reported both metrics since participants could also choose not to answer.

In Manipulation 2, Task 1 was slightly longer in the group without IF (mean = 4.5 mins), compared to the group with IF (mean = 4.1 mins). Conversely, Task 2 was shorter in the group without IF (mean = 2.4 mins) than in the group with IF (mean = 2.9 mins). Table 3 shows the overall results for this manipulation and the detailed results for each task. We observe no significant difference between the two groups, regardless of whether they received immediate feedback. However, we note a slightly higher number of incorrect answers, close to statistical significance, for the group with immediate feedback during Task 1.

Table 2. Manipulation 1. Mean and standard deviation of correct and incorrect answers (scores out of 5 points) for the experimental group (With IF) and the control group (Without IF). Mann–Whitney test results: p-value and effect size (Cohen's d). Statistical significance at $p < 0.05$ is indicated by an asterisk (*).

	Experimental condition	Mean (SD)	p-value	Effect size
Correct answers	With IF	4.48 (0.59)	0.03*	0.69
	Without IF	4.83 (0.39)		
Incorrect answers	With IF	0.52 (0.59)	0.03*	0.69
	Without IF	0.17 (0.39)		

Table 3. Manipulation 2. Mean and standard deviation of correct and incorrect answers (scores out of 6 points, 3 per task) for the experimental group (With IF) and the control group (Without IF). Mann–Whitney test results: p-value and effect size (Cohen's d).

	Answers	Experimental condition	Mean (SD)	p-value	Effectsize
Entire manipulation	Correct	With IF	4.17 (1.37)	0.72	0.13
		Without IF	4.35 (1.34)		
	Incorrect	With IF	1.61 (1.03)	0.12	0.47
		Without IF	0.13 (1.01)		
Task 1	Correct	With IF	1.78 (0.85)	0.25	0.40
		Without IF	2.09 (0.67)		
	Incorrect	With IF	1.09 (0.67)	0.08	0.54
		Without IF	0.74 (0.62)		
Task 2	Correct	With IF	2.39 (0.84)	0.911	0.14
		Without IF	2.26 (1.05)		
	Incorrect	With IF	0.52 (0.67)	0.34	0.19
		Without IF	0.39 (0.72)		

In contrast, the intra-group analyses presented in Table 4 reveal interesting findings for the group with immediate feedback. Benjamini–Hochberg corrected post-hoc tests show a significant improvement in the number of correct answers between the two tasks and a significant reduction in errors. We observe no such improvement in the group without immediate feedback.

Table 4. Manipulation 2. Results of Wilcoxon post-hoc tests between Task 1 and Task 2: raw p-value, corrected p-value (Benjamini–Hochberg), and effect size (Cohen's d). Statistical significance at $p < 0.05$ is indicated by an asterisk (*).

	Experimental condition	Raw p-value	Corrected p-value	Effect size
Correct answers	With IF	0.001*	0.038*	0.72
	Without IF	0.555	1.0	0.20
Incorrect answers	With IF	0.007*	0.027*	0.85
	Without IF	0.078	0.313	0.52

6.2 RQ1b: Performance on Procedures

We analyzed the performance on procedures for both manipulations. Without considering tasks separately, we observe no significant differences between the two groups for either the first manipulation or the second manipulation.

Table 5 provides the detailed results for each task of Manipulation 2. Before correction, significant differences were observed, with a medium effect size, for two specific procedures: *Monitor the color transition* during Task 1, and *Use a pH strip* during Task 2, both in favor of the group with immediate feedback. However, Benjamini-Hochberg corrected post-hoc tests no longer show statistically significant results, although they remain close to the significance threshold.

Finally, the intra-group analyses presented in Table 6 highlight a significant improvement in the *Accurately reach the pH value* procedure for the group with immediate feedback between Task 1 and Task 2, with a large effect size. After Benjamini-Hochberg corrected post-hoc test, this difference remains marginally significant. No such significant evolution was observed for the group without immediate feedback.

Table 5. Manipulation 2. Inter-group comparison of scores obtained for the procedures in Tasks 1 and 2 (scale from 0 to 1). Mann–Whitney test results: raw and corrected p-values (Benjamini–Hochberg), and effect sizes (Cohen's d). Asterisks (*) indicate statistical significance at $p < 0.05$.

Procedure	Task	With IF Mean (SD)	Without IF Mean (SD)	p-value (raw)	p-value (corrected)	Effect size
Respect the mixing order	T 1	0.86 (0.34)	0.92 (0.22)	0.907	1.000	0.23
	T 2	0.88 (0.29)	0.87 (0.29)	0.552	0.663	0.04
Monitor the color transition	T 1	0.65 (0.49)	0.30 (0.47)	0.020*	0.121	0.73
	T 2	0.57 (0.51)	0.57 (0.51)	1.000	1.000	0.00
Rinse the pipette	T 1	0.87 (0.34)	0.78 (0.42)	0.452	0.978	0.23
	T 2	0.74 (0.45)	0.57 (0.51)	0.226	0.452	0.36
Use a pH strip	T 1	0.91 (0.29)	0.91 (0.29)	1.000	1.000	0.00
	T 2	1.00 (0.00)	0.83 (0.39)	0.041*	0.225	0.63
Accurately reach the pH value	T 1	0.17 (0.39)	0.26 (0.45)	0.489	0.978	0.21
	T 2	0.52 (0.51)	0.26 (0.45)	0.075	0.225	0.54
Discard the used pH strip	T 1	0.78 (0.42)	0.78 (0.52)	0.954	1.000	0.00
	T 2	0.74 (0.45)	0.65 (0.49)	0.535	1.000	0.19

Table 6. Manipulation 2. Intra-group comparison of scores obtained for the procedures in Tasks 1 and 2 (scale from 0 to 1). Wilcoxon test results: raw and corrected p-values (Benjamini–Hochberg), and effect sizes (Cohen's d). Asterisks (*) indicate statistical significance at $p < 0.05$.

Action	Experimental condition	Task 1 Mean (SD)	Task 2 Mean (SD)	p-value (raw)	p-value (corrected)	Effect size
Respect the correct mixing order	With IF	0.86 (0.34)	0.88 (0.29)	0.934	0.934	0.07
	Without IF	0.92 (0.22)	0.87 (0.29)	0.473	0.567	0.21
Monitor the color transition	With IF	0.65 (0.49)	0.57 (0.51)	0.559	0.838	0.17
	Without IF	0.30 (0.47)	0.57 (0.51)	0.080	0.369	0.53
Rinse the pipette	With IF	0.87 (0.34)	0.74 (0.45)	0.277	0.554	0.76
	Without IF	0.78 (0.42)	0.57 (0.51)	0.123	0.369	0.72
Use a pH strip	With IF	0.91 (0.29)	1.00 (0.00)	0.162	0.485	0.43
	Without IF	0.91 (0.29)	0.83 (0.39)	0.397	0.567	0.05
Accurately reach the pH value	With IF	0.17 (0.39)	0.52 (0.51)	0.015*	0.089	0.77
	Without IF	0.26 (0.45)	0.26 (0.45)	1.000	1.000	0.00
Discard the used pH strip	With IF	0.78 (0.42)	0.74 (0.45)	0.744	0.892	0.10
	Without IF	0.78 (0.52)	0.65 (0.49)	0.419	0.567	0.26

6.3 RQ2: Cognitive Load

The comparison of the NASA-TLX scores between the two experimental conditions shows no significant differences in any of the measured variables: mental demand, physical demand, temporal demand, effort, frustration, and self-rated performance (see Table 7). The effect sizes, calculated using rank-biserial correlation, were consistently small across all dimensions. These findings confirm that immediate feedback did not impact participants' perceived cognitive load.

Table 7. Comparison of NASA-TLX scores between the two experimental conditions. Mann-Whitney test results (p-value). Effect size (rank-biserial correlation)

Variable	Experimental Condition	Mean (SD)	Median	p-value	Effect size
Mental demand	Without IF	11.35 (3.81)	12.00	0.817	0.042
	With IF	11.09 (4.94)	12.00		
Physical demand	Without IF	2.91 (3.88)	2.00	0.771	0.051
	With IF	2.70 (3.44)	1.00		
Temporal demand	Without IF	3.52 (4.07)	3.00	0.273	0.183
	With IF	2.48 (3.74)	0.00		
Performance (self-rated)	Without IF	13.61 (3.66)	14.00	0.799	0.045
	With IF	14.09 (3.29)	14.00		
Effort	Without IF	5.96 (2.75)	6.00	0.383	0.151
	With IF	5.43 (4.26)	5.00		
Frustration	Without IF	14.30 (5.27)	16.00	0.178	0.231
	With IF	12.13 (5.86)	13.00		

7 Discussion and Conclusion

In this study, we investigated the impact of immediate feedback on participants' performance in a VR learning environment dedicated to chemical education. This work builds upon previous findings on the role of immediate feedback in performance improvement [1,21,22] by distinguishing its effects on expected answers and completed procedures. Our results tend to nuance the positive outcomes reported in earlier studies.

The findings suggest that immediate feedback, as designed in this study, could be integrated without causing cognitive overload, even in tasks requiring heightened attention and procedural accuracy. This result contradicts the findings of Tang et al. [21], who reported increased temporal demands and effort. We believe that this difference could be explained by the amount of information provided by the feedback and its visualisation, as in [21] the textual overlays on the elements added complexity to the visual scene [15]. This aligns with Souchet et al. [19] who emphasize that cognitive load varies according to several factors, including task complexity and level of interaction required to complete the task, and observed increased performance with heightened cognitive load. Future studies should therefore investigate in more depth the relationship between cognitive load, performance and feedback.

Regarding performance, the results show differentiated effects of immediate feedback depending on the type of task. For single tasks, such as in Manipulation 1, immediate feedback resulted in significantly fewer correct answers compared to the group without feedback, even though we did not observe this effect for completed procedures. This suggests that immediate feedback may increase simultaneous information processing and reduce users' attention, affecting performance for this type of task. In contrast, for repeated tasks in Manipulation 2, the group with immediate feedback improved their correct answer rate while reducing the number of errors. In addition, they significantly (before correction, and a near-significantly after correction) improved one specific procedure.

Conversely, we did not observe such improvement in the group without feedback. These results illustrate the role of immediate feedback in supporting the progressive adjustment of actions and the acquisition of procedures through repetition.

In conclusion, while immediate feedback may restrain performance in single tasks, our findings demonstrate its potential to support learning in repeated tasks without increasing cognitive load. These observations highlight the importance of adapting feedback design to the nature of the task and learners' needs to maximize its effectiveness in immersive educational contexts. This finding aligns with Tang et al. [21], who advocate for a cautious approach to feedback integration, as it may sometimes divert attention from essential aspects of learning. The feedback design and the amount of information provided raise issues that should be further investigated to maximize the balance between cognitive load and performance.

Finally, this study presents several limitations. First, the small sample size limits the strength of the results, and the limited number of task repetitions does not allow for a full exploration of the cumulative effects of immediate feedback. Secondly, the participants' profiles and the specific learning context constrain the generalizability of these findings to other domains. In addition, cognitive load was only assessed using a questionnaire, while Souchet et al. [19] recommend mixed subjective and physiological measures.

Nevertheless, this study opens several promising avenues for future research, such as exploring how immediate feedback can be optimally designed with the relevant amount of information and for various types of tasks. Further research should also be conducted on how different types of immediate feedback—such as task-, process-, self-regulation- or self-level cues [10]—affect cognitive load and performance. Finally, we will investigate the impact of task repetition and feedback role on long-term knowledge retention and skills transfer.

Acknowledgements.. This research was conducted as part of the RENFORCE project (ANR-22-CE38-0008), funded by the French National Research Agency (ANR) and endorsed by the Minalogic competitive cluster. The authors would like to thank all participants for their involvement in the study.

References

1. Almousa, O., et al.: Virtual reality simulation technology for cardiopulmonary resuscitation training: an innovative hybrid system with haptic feedback. Simul. Gaming **50**(1), 6–22 (2019). https://doi.org/10.1177/1046878118820905
2. Checa, D., Bustillo, A.: A review of immersive virtual reality serious games to enhance learning and training. Multimedia Tools Appl. 5501–5527 (2019). https://doi.org/10.1007/s11042-019-08348-9
3. Cohen, J.: Statistical power analysis for the behavioral sciences, Rev. ed. Statistical power analysis for the behavioral sciences, Rev. edn., p. xv, 474. Lawrence Erlbaum Associates, Inc., Hillsdale (1977)
4. Conrad, M., Kablitz, D., Schumann, S.: Learning effectiveness of immersive virtual reality in education and training: a systematic review of findings. Comput. Educ. X Reality **4**, 100053 (2024). https://doi.org/10.1016/j.cexr.2024.100053
5. Cromley, J.G., Chen, R., Lawrence, L.: Meta-analysis of STEM learning using virtual reality: benefits across the board. J. Sci. Educ. Technol. **32**(3), 355–364 (2023). https://doi.org/10.1007/s10956-023-10032-5
6. Di Pasquale, V., Cutolo, P., Esposito, C., Franco, B., Iannone, R., Miranda, S.: Virtual reality for training in assembly and disassembly tasks: a systematic literature review. Machines **12**(8), 528 (2024). https://doi.org/10.3390/machines12080528
7. Elaish, M.M., Yadegaridehkordi, E., Ho, Y.S.: Publication performance and trends in virtual reality research in education fields: a bibliometric analysis. Multimedia Tools Appl. (2024). https://doi.org/10.1007/s11042-024-19238-0
8. Gloy, K., et al.: Immersive anatomy atlas: learning factual medical knowledge in a virtual reality environment. Anat. Sci. Educ. **15**(2), 360–368 (2022). https://doi.org/10.1002/ase.2095
9. Hart, S.G., Staveland, L.E.: Development of NASA-TLX (Task Load Index): results of empirical and theoretical research. In: Hancock, P.A., Meshkati, N. (eds.) Advances in Psychology, Human Mental Workload, North-Holland, vol. 52, pp. 139–183 (1988). https://doi.org/10.1016/S0166-4115(08)62386-9
10. Hattie, J., Timperley, H.: The power of feedback. Rev. Educ. Res. **77**(1), 81–112 (2007). https://doi.org/10.3102/003465430298487
11. Jiang, J., Ahmadpour, N.: Beyond Immersion: designing for reflection in virtual reality. In: Proceedings of the 33rd Australian Conference on Human-Computer Interaction, OzCHI '21, pp. 208–220. Association for Computing Machinery, New York (2022). https://doi.org/10.1145/3520495.3520501
12. Kiegaldie, D., Shaw, L.: Virtual reality simulation for nursing education: effectiveness and feasibility. BMC Nurs. **22**(1), 488 (2023). https://doi.org/10.1186/s12912-023-01639-5
13. Lampropoulos, G.: Kinshuk: virtual reality and gamification in education: a systematic review. Educ. Tech. Res. Dev. **72**(3), 1691–1785 (2024). https://doi.org/10.1007/s11423-024-10351-3
14. Lee, L.K., et al.: A systematic review of the design of serious games for innovative learning: augmented reality, virtual reality, or mixed reality? Electronics **13**(5), 890 (2024). https://doi.org/10.3390/electronics13050890
15. Ma, X., Wijewickrema, S., Zhou, Y., Zhou, S., O'Leary, S., Bailey, J.: Providing effective real-time feedback in simulation-based surgical training. In: Descoteaux, M., Maier-Hein, L., Franz, A., Jannin, P., Collins, D.L., Duchesne, S. (eds.) MICCAI 2017. LNCS, vol. 10434, pp. 566–574. Springer, Cham (2017). https://doi.org/10.1007/978-3-319-66185-8_64

16. Roussou, M., Slater, M.: Comparison of the effect of interactive versus passive virtual reality learning activities in evoking and sustaining conceptual change. IEEE Trans. Emerg. Top. Comput. **8**(1), 233–244 (2020). https://doi.org/10.1109/TETC.2017.2737983
17. Schon, D.A., DeSanctis, V.: The reflective practitioner: how professionals think in action. J. Contin. High. Educ. **34**(3), 29–30 (1986). https://doi.org/10.1080/07377366.1986.10401080
18. Schunk, D., Zimmerman, B.: Self-Regulated Learning: From Teaching to Self-reflective Practice. The Guilford Press, London (1998)
19. Souchet, A.D., Stéphanie, P., Domitile, L., Leroy, L.: Measuring visual fatigue and cognitive load via eye tracking while learning with virtual reality head-mounted displays: a review. Int. J. Hum.-Comput. Interact. **38**(9), 801–824 (2022). https://doi.org/10.1080/10447318.2021.1976509
20. Sweller, J.: Cognitive D. Cogn. Sci. **12**(2), 257–285 (1988). https://doi.org/10.1207/s15516709cog1202_4
21. Tang, K., Gerling, K., Vanden Abeele, V., Geurts, L., Aufheimer, M.: Playful reflection: impact of gamification on a virtual reality simulation of breastfeeding. In: Proceedings of the 2023 CHI Conference on Human Factors in Computing Systems, CHI '23, New York, vol. 783, pp. 1–13 (2023). https://doi.org/10.1145/3544548.3580751
22. Van Ginkel, S., Ruiz, D., Mononen, A., Karaman, C., de Keijzer, A., Sitthiworachart, J.: The impact of computer-mediated immediate feedback on developing oral presentation skills: An exploratory study in virtual reality. J. Comput. Assist. Learn. **36**(3), 412–422 (2020). https://doi.org/10.1111/jcal.12424
23. Verlaine, E.D.: Discovering how to do reflexivity and self-reflexivity: a longitudinal empirical research findings. Adv. Soc. Sci. Res. J. **9**(8), 371–394 (2022). https://doi.org/10.14738/assrj.98.12931
24. Zimmerman, B.J.: Becoming a self-regulated learner: an overview. Theory Pract. **41**(2), 64–70 (2002). https://doi.org/10.1207/s15430421tip4102_2

Generating Video Narratives for Learning Following Subsumption Links

Abrar Mohammed(✉) and Vania Dimitrova

School of Computer Science, University of Leeds, Leeds, UK
abrmoh111@gmail.com, v.g.dimtrova@leeds.ac.uk

Abstract. Video-based learning is becoming a popular platform where learning can happen in various life-related domains. However, learners may lack prior knowledge needed to select appropriate videos and may struggle to identify and link key parts in those videos, leading to frustration and feeling overwhelmed. To address this challenge, we present a novel framework for generating Video Narratives for Learning (VIN-L). A video narrative is a combination of video segments which have been automatically characterised and linked by computer algorithms. VIN-L generates video narratives by using a domain taxonomy to link characterised segments from different videos following Ausubel's Subsumption theory for meaningful learning. Four video narrative types have been generated implementing subsumption links: Derivative, Super Ordinate, Correlative, and Combinational. VIN-L has been applied on a corpus of 60 videos related to health quality of life needs of people living with chronic respiratory illnesses. The resulting video narratives have been evaluated with domain experts and with Amazon Mechanical Turk workers, assessing quality, perceived usefulness, and the potential of using the video narratives to support learning. Domain experts' results show that the generated video narratives are of good quality and have the potential to support learning. The Amazon Mechanical Turk study has shown that the generated video narratives have potential to be useful for learning, helping with identifying and linking key domain terms.

Keywords: Video-based learning · Video Segmentation · Video Characterisation · Video Narratives · Domain taxonomy · Subsumption theory

1 Introduction and Related Work

Videos for learning platforms become a widely used way to find information or share personal knowledge or skills. They are particularly useful in developing soft-skills, which are a collection of interpersonal skills and personal attributes [10]. Using videos for learning plays a key role in informal support for soft skill development [5]. It helps users to pay attention to soft skills details and the relationship between them, as well as to enhance their self-regulation and motivation [6]. Learning such skills requires time and resources management to ensure good quality of learning materials [7].

K. Tammets et al. (Eds.): EC-TEL 2025, LNCS 16063, pp. 352–366, 2026.
https://doi.org/10.1007/978-3-032-03870-8_24

However, there are major challenges that affect user engagement with videos. Learners prefer watching short videos as their concentration span is reduced over time [18,26]. Video content complexity could affect a user's engagement with the video and hence cause confusion or boredom [21]. Furthermore, learners who are new to the domain and lack prior knowledge would not be able to identify key points to look out for in the videos which causes frustration and reduces engagement. This calls for finding new ways to identify the main points in a video and to direct learners to segments that elaborate on specific key points.

To aid the use of videos for learning, researchers have adopted a variety of approaches. Hypermedia tools have been applied in different scenarios, e.g. in [12,27] a smart learning environment has been designed where YouTube videos, web pages and quizzes have been utilised by instructors to set goals and provide their students with personalised resources. Recent video segmentation approaches utilise state-of-the-art tools in natural language processing to identify key domain areas in the videos [8]. The potential of Large Language models (LLMs) for summarising long videos has been explored [1,4]. The key limitation of these approaches is their inability to direct learners to specific concepts from the domain and to help with linking domain concepts.

A way to support learners to explore domain concepts while watching videos is to use concept maps [17]. Semi-automatic concept map approaches, e.g. concept map created by students [24,29], pose challenges since students may be unable to identify the relationship between domain topics and can find building concept maps too time consuming. Automatic concept map approaches facilitate the creation of the concept maps. For example, ConceptGuide [31] uses YouTube videos (transcript and meta data) and Wikipedia glossaries to present the possible related videos with their topics. Similarly, a concept map is designed by [28] where domain concepts are extracted from text questions and students' answers to find relationship between the extracted concepts. While automatic concept maps allow conceptualising the domain and linking concepts in a video, their application on a range of videos would lead to a confusion since the concept space from each video may differ.

The gap detected within the aforementioned approaches includes the following: using long, unsegmented traditional learning videos, LLMs summarising videos with no pedagogical guidance and no underpinning theory, and using general knowledge models when characterising the videos which might not cover specific domain areas, linking the whole videos together but without specifying or locating the key domain areas within the videos.

To address this gap we propose a novel automated approach to generate video narratives that link video snippets and allow exploring domain concepts following pegadogical models. Similarly to automated concept maps and natural language processing methods, we extract concepts and relationships from video content. Distinctively, we use the same knowledge model for all videos and allow linking video snippets in narratives underpinned by a pedagogical model to enable exploring concepts using multiple videos.

Our approach is inspired by work on narratives in learning. Narratives are defined as sequences of ideas or actions that relate to a specific event or topic [13]. Narratives for learning have been implemented in different ways. For example, [23] use stories to set a structure of instructions to be followed by (face to face or remote-students) to learn some principles in engineering design. Similarly, [25] design a narrative experience design canvas to help students set their goals and set learning plans accordingly. Furthermore, [14] find that linking online resources as narratives and presenting them via a knowledge-graph help in filtering irrelevant resources during the search process.

We propose a framework to generate video narratives that link related characterised video segments from different videos following a pedagogical theory. We utilise Ausubel's theory of meaningful learning [2] to link domain concepts and generate video narratives. Ausubel defines the learning of domain concepts as a subsumption in which new material is related to existing cognitive structures. A learners' cognitive structure is a hierarchical organisation of general concepts from which there will be a link to specific sub-concepts. Ausubel has defined four subsumption linking types: *Derivative* (the new learning material is an example of an idea that exists in the cognitive structure); *Super Ordinate-* (the new learning material is related to a generic idea in the cognitive structure); *Correlative* (the new learning material is an elaboration of a previously learned idea); and *Combinational* (the new learning material is not super ordinate or sub ordinate with any existing ideas in the cognitive structure but rather can be learnt in combination with other, more generic, less relevant ideas). Ausubel's theory for meaningful learning includes has been used in concept map approaches [15,16] to group information and connect related learning modules.

This paper contributes to the area of using videos for learning by developing a novel generic framework for generating VIdeo Narratives for Learning (VIN-L) which is based on Ausubel's Subsumption theory of meaningful learning. The main input is a set of characterised video segments, generated using VISC-L which was described in our previous work [20], and a domain taxonomy. VIN-L links the video segments by implementing the Subsumption links. VIN-L has been applied in the Health Related Quality of Life Awareness domains and evaluated with domain experts and learners to answer the following research questions:

RQ1: How to generate good quality narratives to support domain learning?
RQ2: Are the generated narratives useful to support domain learning?

The structure of the paper is as follows: Sect. 2 presents the design and the implementation of the framework in the health domain; Sect. 3 presents the evaluation of the generated video narratives; Sect. 4 presents the results and discussion; and Sect. 5 presents the conclusion and future work.

2 Framework Design and Implementation

Our framework consists of two parts: VISC-L and VIN-L. In this section, we present the implementation of VISC-L and the design and implementation of

VIN-L in the Health Related Quality of Life Awareness domain. According to our data-driven approach, we use VISC-L that utilises a domain taxonomy to collect, segment, and characterise videos. The output of VISC-L is used as an input to VIN-L to generate domain-related video narratives (see Fig. 1). The pseudocode of the algorithms used in VISC-L and VIN-L is presented in [19].

2.1 Preliminaries

Our framework is based on two assumptions: (1) the domain we are tackling is presented with videos associated with their transcripts; and (2) the domain is computationally presented with a taxonomy. Consequently, we use a domain taxonomy (Ω), video segment (VS), characterised video segments (Ch), and video narrative (VN). The domain taxonomy ($\Omega = \{C, H\}$) consists of classes and individuals that belong to these classes. C is a nonempty set of relevant domain classes and individuals which are linked via a hierarchy H (see Fig. 2).

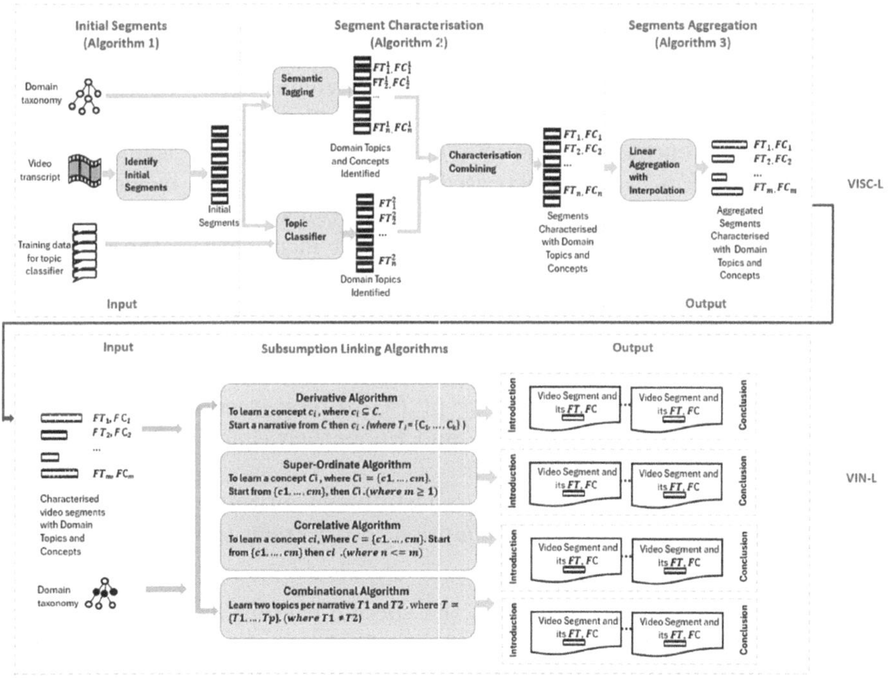

Fig. 1. Generating Video Narrative pipeline that includes applying VISC-L first to generate the characterised video segments, the output from VISC-L is the input to VIN-L. Applying VIN-L which is underpinned by Ausubel's Subsumption Theory helps in generating video narratives.

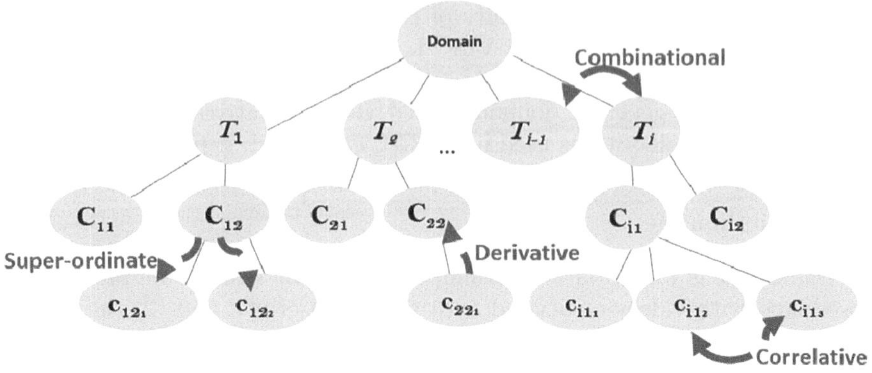

Fig. 2. Domain taxonomy which is a list of topics which are top level in the taxonomy structure T, a list of concepts C and a list of sub-concepts c.

We use $c_i \in C_j$ to denote that c_i is an individual of a class C_j meaning that c_i is directly below C_j in the taxonomy hierarchy. We refer to the immediate classes of the root of the hierarchy as domain topics T_i, where each T_i is a set of classes and each class is a set of its individuals, $T_i = \{C_1, ..., C_m\}$, m > 0. A Video Segment (*VS*) has the following details: ID, start time, end time, and a transcript representing the presenter's utterance in the segments, *VS*= $\langle VS_{\mathrm{Id}}, VS_{\mathrm{s}}, VS_{\mathrm{e}}, VS_{\mathrm{t}} \rangle$. A characterised video segment (*Ch*) includes details about the focus topics FT_i, which are the top concepts in Ω, and the focus concepts Fc_i, belong to the focus topic FT_i that mentioned in the video segments. Every Fc_i from FC_j , $Fc_i \in FT_i$. Hence, *Ch* has the following definition $Ch = \langle VS_{\mathrm{Id}}, VS_{\mathrm{s}}, VS_{\mathrm{e}}, VS_{\mathrm{t}}, FT, FC \rangle$. A Video Narrative (*VN*) is a sequence of characterised video segments (*Ch*) which are linked based on a specific domain linking type *VN*= $\{Ch_1, .., Ch_n\}$, where $n > 0$. *VN* is based on two components, the focus topic FT and the focus concept FC to be learned and a sequence of video segments *Ch* containing this FT and FC in their characterisation and are linked following domain linking.

We have designed four types of video narratives algorithms based on the linking types defined by Ausubel's Subsumption theory (refer to Fig. 2) as follows.

Derivative Linking (D). To learn the specific concept c_{22_1}, the Derivative algorithm first introduces the generic concept C_{22} via a group of video segments which have, as part of their characterisation, the focus Topic T_2 and the focus Concept C_{22}: $Ch = \langle VS_{\mathrm{Id}}, VS_{\mathrm{s}}, VS_{\mathrm{e}}, VS_{\mathrm{t}}, T_2, C_{22} \rangle$ and places these segments at the beginning of the Derivative narrative. Then, the video segments that include in their characterisation the focus Topic T_2 and the focus concept c_{22_1}: $Ch = \langle VS_{\mathrm{Id}}, VS_{\mathrm{s}}, VS_{\mathrm{e}}, VS_{\mathrm{t}}, T_2, c_{22_1} \rangle$ are added to the Derivative narrative.

Super Ordinate Linking (S). To learn the generic concept C_{12}, the Super Ordinate algorithm first introduces the specific concept(s) c_{12_1} and/or c_{12_2} via a group of video segments that have part of their characterisation these concepts: $Ch = \langle VS_{\mathrm{Id}}, VS_{\mathrm{s}}, VS_{\mathrm{e}}, VS_{\mathrm{t}}, T_1, c_{12_1} \rangle$, $Ch = \langle VS_{\mathrm{Id}}, VS_{\mathrm{s}}, VS_{\mathrm{e}}, VS_{\mathrm{t}}, T_1, c_{12_2} \rangle$ and place these segments in the Super Ordinate narrative. Now, the specific concept(s) c_{12_1} and/or c_{12_2} are in the cognitive structure and ready to be bound to their generic concept C_{12}. Then, the Super Ordinate algorithm selecst the video segments that have the generic concept C_{12} as part of their characterisation, where $C_{12} \in T_1$: $Ch = \langle VS_{\mathrm{Id}}, VS_{\mathrm{s}}, VS_{\mathrm{e}}, VS_{\mathrm{t}}, T_1, C_{12} \rangle$ and add these segments to the Super Ordinate narrative.

Correlative Linking (CR). To learn the concept c_{i1_2}, the Correlative algorithm select the video segments that have the focus concepts c_{i1_3} and c_{i1_1} as part of their characterisation: $Ch_1 = \langle VS_{\mathrm{Id}}, VS_{\mathrm{s}}, VS_{\mathrm{e}}, VS_{\mathrm{t}}, T_i, c_{i1_3} \rangle$ and the segment $Ch_2 = \langle VS_{\mathrm{Id}}, VS_{\mathrm{s}}, VS_{\mathrm{e}}, VS_{\mathrm{t}}, T_i, c_{i1_1} \rangle$. Then, place these video segments in the Correlative narrative. Notice that these concepts (c_{i1_3}, c_{i1_1}) are siblings of the target concept c_{i1_2} as they belong to C_{i1}. Now, (c_{i1_3}, c_{i1_1}) are in the cognitive structure and ready to be linked to the target concept c_{i1_2}. Hence, the Correlative algorithm selects a group of video segments that have the concept c_{i1_2} as part of their characterisation $Ch_i = \langle VS_{\mathrm{Id}}, VS_{\mathrm{s}}, VS_{\mathrm{e}}, VS_{\mathrm{t}}, T_i, c_{i1_2} \rangle$ and adds these segments to the Correlative narrative.

Combinational Linking (CO). To learn the topic T_1, it is useful to learn it in conjunction with other topic, e.g. with the topic T_2 where some of their concepts C_{12} and C_{21} are mentioned together in the same segment. Each segment selected to be in the Combinational narrative has the following characterization: $Ch = \langle VS_{\mathrm{Id}}, VS_{\mathrm{s}}, VS_{\mathrm{e}}, VS_{\mathrm{t}}, FT, FC \rangle$. Hence, FT refer to the two topics to be learnt and FC refers to the set of focus concepts that belong to FT.

2.2 Framework Outline

The framework we have presented consists of two parts: VISC-L and VIN-L.

Video Segmentation and Characterisation (VISC-L). The first step of our computational approach is to define ways of segmenting and characterising videos. In order to make it generic to ensure it is applicable in different domains, contexts are independent on the area of learning. This framework, which combines Semantic Tagging characterisation and Topic Classifier characterisation and was presented in detail in [20], consists of: Input, Initial Segments (where the initial segments are generated), Segment Characterisation (where the initial segments are characterised), and Aggregation (where the characterised adjacent video segments are aggregated based on the common domain topic(s) and concept(s)). The output is video segment characterisation that includes the focus topic and the focus concept (see Sect. 2.1) of the video segment which is essential for linking different video segments coming from same or different videos.

Video Narratives (VIN-L). We propose a generic framework for generating video narratives to support learning which is based on Ausubel's Subsumption theory. VIN-L includes three main phases: Input, Subsumption Linking Algorithms and Output. The input is the aggregated video segments (VISC-L output) and the domain taxonomy. The Subsumption Linking The algorithms are designed based on Ausubel's Subsumption theory [19]. The output includes four types of video narratives generated from the four types of subsumption linking. The duration of the generated video narrative is controlled by the algorithms to be ≥ 3 min and ≤ 6 min following the recommendation of suitable video length when used for learning [3].

Application in Healthcare. To generate video narratives, we first applied VISC-L (see Fig. 3) in the health domain. The domain taxonomy [19] was created following the iterative ontology development methodology [11,22]. The taxonomy represent the main aspects of quality of life that can be related to people with chronic respiratiry problems. It includes 212 concepts. The main domain topics are: Physical Health, Psychological Health, Level Of Independence, Social Relationship, Environment, and Personal Values And Beliefs. The taxonomy was used to inform video search on YouTube (as described in [20]) which allowed us to collect 321 videos (60 patient stories and 261 tutorials). These videos have been passed as an input to VISC-L where they have been segmented, during the Initial Segments step, into 1483 from the patient stories videos and 25959 tutorial segments. Both types of segments have been characterised separately using the Semantic Tagging algorithm where we link a video segment transcript to concepts (classes or individuals) in the taxonomy. The semantically characterised tutorial segments have been used to fine-tune the Contextual Classifier which in turn is used to characterise the patient story segments, for which we have combine the output of semantic tagging and Contextual classifier results of the patient video segments where both characterisations focus on the same topic and concept(s). The adjacent segments within the same videos that have the same focus topic and focus concepts are aggregated. The final result is 167 characterised patient video segments which are distributed among the domain topics as follows: Physical Health-80, Psychological Health-16, Level Of Independence-15, Social Relationship-43, Environment-10, and Personal Values And Beliefs-3, (see Fig. 3-Video Segmentation and Characterisation).

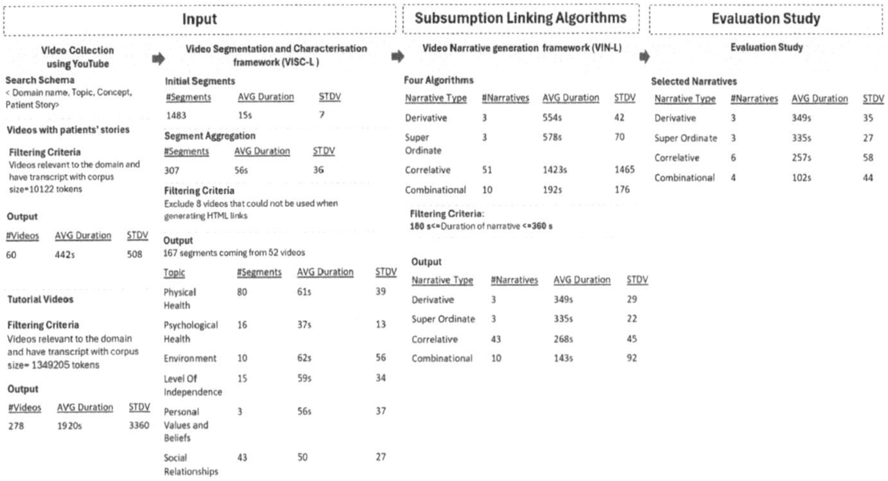

Fig. 3. The output after implementing the Frameworks in the Health Related Quality of Life Awareness domain.

The domain taxonomy and the output from VISC-L has been passed as an input to VIN-L to generate video narratives. Then, the Subsumption Linking Algorithms are implemented to generate 59 video narratives which are distributed among narrative types as follows: Derivative-3, Super Ordinate-3, Correlative-43, and Combinational-10 (see Subsumption Linking Algorithms from Fig. 3). In the third step of VIN-L, we automatically augmented the generated video narratives adding textual linking, using pre-designed templates that included the following: (a) text that clarifies the type of linking followed in the narratives; (b) segment characterisation that includes the video Id and the start time and the duration of each segment within its video; (c) a set of video segments that have been linked together following Ausubel's Subsumption Theory (the video narrative we have generated); and (d) a conclusion statement that summarises the learning intention of the video narrative. Finally, we converted the augmented video narratives into web pages for easy browsing.

3 Evaluation Studies

Aim. We have conducted two studies: study-1 with domain experts and study-2 with Amazon Mechanical Turk workers. Both studies assessed the quality and perceived usefulness of the video narratives. With Amazon Mechanical Turk workers we also assessed the learning effect and the cognitive work load required for exploring the generated video narratives.

Participants. Study-1 included 6 experts, 3 of them were from the European project InAdvance[1], and the other 3 were from the School of Computer Science, University of Leeds. The experts' experience is related either to their profession in the health field (e.g. doctor, nurse) or to their work as researchers focusing on patients' health related quality of life. Study-2 used 192 AMT workers (hereafter referred to as potential learners).

Materials and Procedure. The materials and procedure are presented in detail in [19]. The web pages with video narratives were included in Google forms and shared with the participants. The Google forms' structure was the same in both studies and included: a consent form, a section to collect user profiles and then the video narrative section. The video narrative section in the form used by experts was divided into four groups where each group represented a narrative type. Instead, in the forms used by AMT users the video narrative section included one narrative type per a form (i.e. we used four different Google forms, one for each narrative linking type). After each video narrative section, in the experts and AMT forms there were two parts (1) evaluating the quality of the video narrative categories, and (2) indicating the perceived usefulness after watching the video narrative type(s). The video narrative quality used LIKERT response labels [30]. The perceived usefulness of the generated narratives was assessed adapting Technoology Acceptance Model (TAM) questionnaire [9]. At the end of each form, participants sere asked for free text feedback to identify possible positive and negative aspects of using the video narratives. The total number of video narratives used was 28. We excluded video narratives where most segments are shorter than 30 s. We also excluded the duplicated video narratives where the same video narrative was generated for all the siblings of the specific concept (this case occurred only with Correlative video narratives).

4 Results and Discussion

We have aggregated the outcome of both studies: in study-1 we use two Google forms used with two groups of experts, and in study-2 we used four Google forms, a form for each narrative type.

4.1 Quality of the Narratives

To be able to answer RQ1, we have evaluated the quality of the video narratives by: comparing between the quality categories, and comparing between the video narrative types (see Fig. 4)

[1] https://www.inadvanceproject.eu/about.

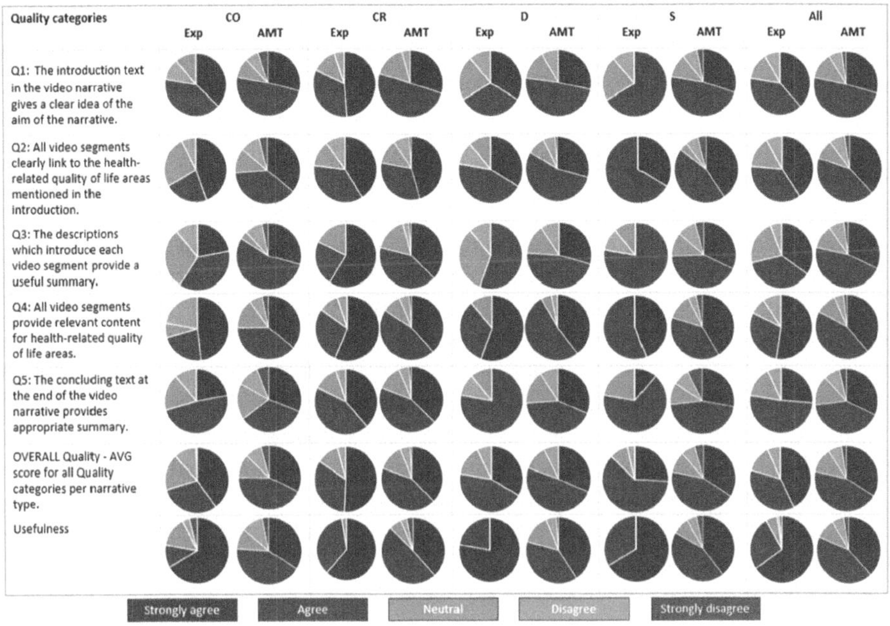

Fig. 4. Quality of the generated narratives in the Health Related quality of Life Awareness domain as evaluated by experts and Amazon Mechanical Turk workers. The number of responses per narratives type represented as (number of experts, number of AMT learners) is as follow: Combinational (27,100), Correlative (39,94), Derivative (9,96), Super Ordinate(9,94), and All responses are (84,384).

Comparison Between the Quality Categories of the Video Narratives Referring to the column (All) in Fig. 4 we can get an overview of the quality of all responses. The experts and the potential learners found that the majority of the video segments within each video narrative provided content related to the domain (Q4). As a result, the video segments were also found to be clearly linked to the health domain areas defined in the introduction of the video narrative (Q2). Based on that, the experts and potential learners found that the video narrative introduction part clarified the aim of the narratives (Q1), indicated that the quality of the description (characterisation) of the segments (Q3) enabled them to identify the domain areas mentioned in the introduction (Q1) and in the conclusion (Q5) of the video narratives. The assessment of the overall video narrative quality indicated that the experts and potential learners found the generated video narratives to be of a good quality.

Comparison Between the Narrative Types In this comparison we refer to the columns in Fig. 4 and relate them to the definition of the video narratives mentioned in Sect. 2.1.

The experts found no difference in the quality of the D, S and CR narrative types, whereas the potential learners found CR to be the most preferable narratives to be used for learning over the CO, D or S narratives. This could be explained with the design of CR narratives, as the link between the concepts in CR narratives is clear and all the concepts within a narrative belong to the same focus topic. Both experts and potential learners agreed that the link between concepts in the CO narratives was less obvious (possibly because the concepts belonged to different topics). The difference between the quality of narrative types was not statistically significant (Kruskal-Wallis). To compare between pairs of narrative types based on the quality categories (Q1-Q5) results, we ran Mann Whitney U-Test. The experts' results showed that the difference between the CR and CO narratives was statistically significant. The experts found that having two focus concepts per video segments affected the quality of the introduction section in the video narrative (**Q3**). However, this is not the case with the potential learners, where the difference between pairs of narratives types was not statistically significant (Man Whitney U-Test). Additionally, in both experts' and potential learners' results the difference between the quality categories and the usefulness of the video narratives was not statistically significant (Spearman $rs = -0.10541$).

4.2 Perceived Usefulness

To answer RQ2, we analysed the perceived usefulness of the generated video narratives based on the aggregated experts' and potential learners' responses. Referring to the column (All) in Fig. 5, the experts found that the generated narratives (CR, D and S) were quite likely to help learners to be aware of key topics and concepts (PU3) and to identify key points related to the domain (PU1). Hence, the experts found that the video narratives would help to focus on key points (PU2) and link them together (PU4). This can be referred to the design of the CR, D and S narratives which focus on specific concepts within one topic. Meanwhile, the CO narratives could be used to raise awareness of the domain concepts as they linked different concepts from different topics. This is not the case with the potential learners who scored CO narratives the highest since CO would enable them to identify key domain areas (PU1), focus on them (PU2), and link them together (PU4). The potential learners found that CO and D narrative types could have a similar effect on enabling learners to identify the focus topic and concept (PU3). The difference in perceived usefulness was not statistically significant at ($p <= 0.05$, Mann Whitney U-test) according to the experts' and potential learners' results.

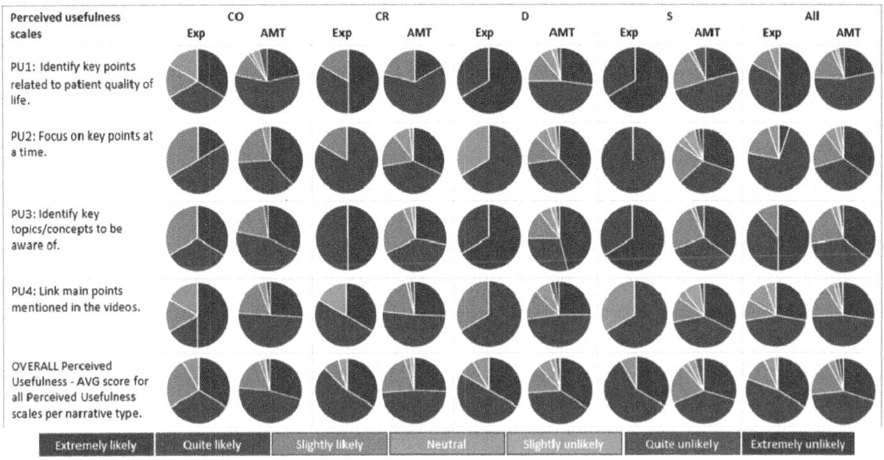

Fig. 5. Perceived usefulness of the generated narratives in the Health Related quality of Life Awareness domain as evaluated by experts and Amazon Mechanical Turk workers. The number of responses per narratives type represented as (number of experts, number of AMT learners) is as follow: Combinational (6,50), Correlative (6,47), Derivative (3,48), Super Ordinate(3,47), and All responses are (18,192). Perceived usefulness evaluation is done after watching each narrative type. The number of participants who evaluated each narrative type is varied as presented above.

4.3 Learning Effect

We assessed the learning effect of the video narratives with the potential learners only. In study-2 (AMT potential learners) we added a pre-test before watching the video narratives and a post-test after watching the video narratives to assess domain awareness. The results showed that potential learners managed to recall new domain terms after watching the video narratives. This aligns with the quality and perceived usefulness scores of potential learners, who found the video narratives of good quality and useful for domain learning.

4.4 Cognitive Load

To clarify in more depth the difference between the narrative types, we analysed the learners' feedback on their cognitive load of using the video narratives to support domain learning. We have analysed the responses of the learners on the NASA-TLX sub-scale items after watching the video narratives to evaluate: the Mental Work load, Effort, Frustration and Performance sub-scale. The results were close to each other among all types of narratives, and the Performance scale was the highest, which shows that video narratives had a potential to raise awareness of health-related quality of life when used with learners.

4.5 Qualitative Feedback

We summarise below the experts' and potential learners' textual feedback when asked what they found positive and negative about the video narratives.

Positive. Experts found the video narratives focusing and linking key concepts that could be helpful for different levels of needs. For example, *"you can easily focus on specific segments of a video rather than going through the entire videos, which can at times be quite lengthy."*. The potential learners found all types of video narratives were informative, engaging and highlighting key domain concepts. For example, *"It provides information about the feelings and needs of the patient. One gets to know what life is like from their perspective. It engages the viewer to understand the issues faced by the patients living with respiratory illnesses."*.

Negative. There were issues associated with using some of the example video narratives as noticed by experts and potential learners. Experts commented that some video narratives caused confusion and did not provide enough elaboration in the text linking video snippets. For example, *"In some cases, one issue is mentioned much more than the other. as a result, the video is mostly focused on one of the two issues and not necessarily the link between them."*. The potential learners found some video narratives not engaging because of the content shown in the videos. For example, *"The medical people seemed a little business-like instead of compassionate."*. Assessing the quality of the videos was outside the scope of our work; this is an interesting problem that requires further research.

5 Conclusion

We have designed and implement a novel generic framework for generating video narratives to support learning. The paper has shown how a pedagogical theory, namely Ausubel's subsumption theory for meaningful learning, can be utilised to turn text analysis and linking models, that have not been designed nor developed for learning, to generate pedagogically underpinned narratives. Four types of video narratives were generated. Two evaluation studies were conducted - with experts and with potential learners (using AMT). The participants found the video narratives of a good quality and useful for learning. They also led to enhancing domain knowledge (when used by potential learners). Some insights have been inferred when analysing the evaluation responses from both experts and potential learners. The experts found that the video narratives offered a good focus on key domain areas and supported the linking between these areas. The potential learners also noticed some strengths in the video narratives: the videos provided a clear linking of key points in the domain, and the transition between the segments helped them notice the link between the concepts.

Further improvements of the narratives, as recommended by the participants in the evaluation studies include: selecting more video segments from the same videos that have the same Focus topic and Focus concept, increasing the segment size to enable the segments to provide more elaboration on the focus topic and concept, improving the text used to augment the video narratives to clarify the relationship between the Focus topic(s) and Focus concept(s). Further studies can explore how to improve the textual augmentation, e.g. LLMs can be used for generating more informative textual explanations in the narrative introduction, conclusion, and to explain video segment linking.

Acknowledgments. The authors thank Professor Tanja Mitrovic and Dr Lydia Lau for their support and feedback; as well as the researchers from the University of Leeds, the experts from the InAdvance project, and the Amazon Mechanical Turk workers for their participation in the evaluation studies.

References

1. Argaw, D.M., et al.: Scaling up video summarization pretraining with large language models. In: Proceedings of the IEEE/CVF Conference on Computer Vision and Pattern Recognition, pp. 8332–8341 (2024)
2. Ausubel, D.P., Novak, J.D., Hanesian, H., et al.: Educational psychology: A cognitive view, vol. 6. Holt, Einehart and Winston New York (1968)
3. Brame, C.J.: Effective educational videos: principles and guidelines for maximizing student learning from video content. CBE—Life Sci. Educ. **15**(4), es6 (2016)
4. Chen, G., et al.: Videollm: modeling video sequence with large language models. arXiv preprint arXiv:2305.13292 (2023)
5. Cinque, M.: MOOCs and soft skills: a comparison of different courses on creativity. J. E-learn. Knowl. Soc. **13**(3) (2017)
6. Conkey, C.A., Bowers, C., Cannon-Bowers, J., Sanchez, A.: Machinima and video-based soft-skills training for frontline healthcare workers. Games Health: Res. Dev. Clin. Appl. **2**(1), 39–43 (2013)
7. Crosbie, R.: Learning the soft skills of leadership. Ind. Commer. Train. **37**(1), 45–51 (2005)
8. Das, A., Das, P.P.: Automatic semantic segmentation and annotation of MOOC lecture videos. In: Jatowt, A., Maeda, A., Syn, S.Y. (eds.) ICADL 2019. LNCS, vol. 11853, pp. 181–188. Springer, Cham (2019). https://doi.org/10.1007/978-3-030-34058-2_17
9. Davis, F.D.: Perceived usefulness, perceived ease of use, and user acceptance of information technology. MIS Q. 319–340 (1989)
10. Dixon, J., Belnap, C., Albrecht, C., Lee, K.: The importance of soft skills. Corp. Finan. Rev. **14**(6), 35 (2010)
11. Fernández-López, M.: Overview of methodologies for building ontologies (1999)
12. Fessl, A., Maitz, K., Dennerlein, S., Pammer-Schindler, V.: The impact of explicating learning goals on teaching and learning in higher education: evaluating a learning goal visualization. In: De Laet, T., Klemke, R., Alario-Hoyos, C., Hilliger, I., Ortega-Arranz, A. (eds.) EC-TEL 2021. LNCS, vol. 12884, pp. 1–15. Springer, Cham (2021). https://doi.org/10.1007/978-3-030-86436-1_1
13. Greenhalgh, T., Hurwitz, B.: Why study narrative? BMJ **318**(7175), 48–50 (1999)
14. Hao, J., Zhao, L., Milisavljevic-Syed, J., Ming, Z.: Integrating and navigating engineering design decision-related knowledge using decision knowledge graph. Adv. Eng. Inf. **50**, 101366 (2021)

15. Katagall, R., Dadde, R., Goudar, R., Rao, S.: Concept mapping in education and semantic knowledge representation: an illustrative survey. Procedia Comput. Sci. **48**, 638–643 (2015)
16. Liu, C., Kim, J., Wang, H.C.: Conceptscape: collaborative concept mapping for video learning. In: Proceedings of the 2018 CHI Conference on Human Factors in Computing Systems, pp. 1–12 (2018)
17. Machado, C.T., Carvalho, A.A.: Concept mapping: benefits and challenges in higher education. J. Contin. High. Educ. **68**(1), 38–53 (2020)
18. Meseguer-Martinez, A., Ros-Galvez, A., Rosa-Garcia, A.: Satisfaction with online teaching videos: a quantitative approach. Innov. Educ. Teach. Int. **54**(1), 62–67 (2017)
19. Mohammed, A.: Generating video narratives to support learning. Ph.D. thesis, University of Leeds (2024)
20. Mohammed, A., Dimitrova, V.: Video segmentation and characterisation to support learning. In: European Conference on Technology Enhanced Learning, pp. 229–242. Springer, Heidelberg (2022). https://doi.org/10.1007/978-3-031-16290-9_17
21. Mongkhonvanit, K., Kanopka, K., Lang, D.: Deep knowledge tracing and engagement with MOOCs. In: Proceedings of the 9th International Conference on Learning Analytics & Knowledge, pp. 340–342 (2019)
22. Noy, N.F., McGuinness, D.L., et al.: Ontology development 101: a guide to creating your first ontology (2001)
23. Pina, J., et al.: Adapting a narrative curriculum to a remote format in the context of socially distanced middle school education resulting from covid-19. J. Pre-Coll. Eng. Educ. Res. (J-PEER) **12**(2), 4 (2022)
24. Pinandito, A., Prasetya, D.D., Khudhur, N., Hayashi, Y., Hirashima, T.: The effectiveness of collaborative concept map recomposition and discussion with kit-build concept map in online learning (2021)
25. Recke, M.P., Perna, S.: Emergent narratives in remote learning experiences for project based education. Electron. J. e-Learn. **19**(2), 59–70 (2021)
26. Risko, E.F., Anderson, N., Sarwal, A., Engelhardt, M., Kingstone, A.: Everyday attention: variation in mind wandering and memory in a lecture. Appl. Cogn. Psychol. **26**(2), 234–242 (2012)
27. Serrano-Iglesias, S., Gómez-Sánchez, E., Bote-Lorenzo, M.L., Asensio-Pérez, J.I., Ruiz-Calleja, A., Vega-Gorgojo, G.: Demonstration of SCARLETT: a smart learning environment to support learners across formal and informal contexts. In: De Laet, T., Klemke, R., Alario-Hoyos, C., Hilliger, I., Ortega-Arranz, A. (eds.) EC-TEL 2021. LNCS, vol. 12884, pp. 404–408. Springer, Cham (2021). https://doi.org/10.1007/978-3-030-86436-1_44
28. Shao, Z., Li, Y., Wang, X., Zhao, X., Guo, Y.: Research on a new automatic generation algorithm of concept map based on text analysis and association rules mining. J. Ambient. Intell. Humaniz. Comput. **11**, 539–551 (2020)
29. Spicer, D.B., Thompson, K.H., Kilgallen, S.M.: Making the connection: using concept mapping to bring the basic sciences to the diagnosis. J. Am. Osteopath. Assoc. **120**(8), 524–528 (2020)
30. Taherdoost, H.: What is the best response scale for survey and questionnaire design; review of different lengths of rating scale/attitude scale/likert scale. In: Hamed Taherdoost, pp. 1–10 (2019)
31. Tang, C.L., Liao, J., Wang, H.C., Sung, C.Y., Lin, W.C.: Conceptguide: supporting online video learning with concept map-based recommendation of learning path. In: Proceedings of the Web Conference 2021, pp. 2757–2768 (2021)

Integrating Generative AI into Instructional Design Practice: Effects on Graduate Student Learning and Self-Efficacy

Steven Moore[1](✉), Lydia Eckstein[2], Christine Kwon[1], and John Stamper[1]

[1] Carnegie Mellon University, Pittsburgh, PA 15213, USA
StevenJamesMoore@gmail.com

[2] Eberly Center Teaching Excellence & Educational Innovation, Pittsburgh, PA 15213, USA

Abstract. Generative AI (genAI) tools are increasingly being integrated into instructional design workflows for content creation, assessment development, and lesson planning. For novice designers, it is critical to understand whether this integration supports the design process without compromising underlying pedagogical learning. This study addresses this gap through an ecologically valid field experiment within a 14-week graduate course training novice instructional designers. Using a counterbalanced A/B design embedded in authentic coursework, students created eight microlessons, alternating genAI assistance with independent work. Learning of pedagogical principles was assessed via module pre/post-tests and self-efficacy, in teaching practices and genAI use, was measured via course-level pre/post-surveys. Results showed no evidence that genAI use hindered learning, as post-test scores on module content remained stable or improved, despite variations in test form difficulty. Students demonstrated substantial and statistically significant gains by over 10% in self-efficacy related to both their teaching practices and their ability to leverage genAI. By evaluating genAI within sustained and authentic instructional design activities, this study demonstrates that thoughtfully integrated AI tools can effectively support novice designers, enhancing their confidence and professional growth without compromising foundational pedagogical learning.

Keywords: Instructional Design · Design for Learning · Generative AI · Self-Efficacy · A/B Study

1 Introduction

Generative AI (genAI) tools are transforming educational environments, influencing both student work quality and the learning process itself [9, 10]. While offering benefits like idea generation and real-time feedback, genAI may shift cognitive demands of academic tasks [24]. This is particularly salient in project-based learning environments, where students are expected to apply pedagogical principles to design educational materials. In such contexts, genAI can increase efficiency and streamline production, but

K. Tammets et al. (Eds.): EC-TEL 2025, LNCS 16063, pp. 367–381, 2026.
https://doi.org/10.1007/978-3-032-03870-8_25

may simultaneously reduce opportunities for deep engagement and conceptual understanding [37]. At the same time, it may shape students' confidence in their capabilities by enhancing self-efficacy when used successfully or diminishing it if students become overly reliant on AI-generated content [38]. As educators and institutions begin integrating genAI into the classroom, it is essential to understand its implications not only for productivity, but for learner growth.

However, the use of genAI in education may also present challenges, particularly by limiting creativity and, for students, impeding deeper learning as they engage superficially with content [39]. Over-reliance on AI can hinder the development of foundational teaching and learning skills, overshadowing the growth of critical thinking and creativity. As more practitioners and educators integrate genAI into assignments to enhance student engagement, students themselves are increasingly using these tools, sometimes even without explicit instruction to do so [19]. This growing reliance on AI may influence how students approach assignments, including microlesson creation, and could impact their confidence in their own abilities as well as their proficiency with these tools as educators.

This study examines genAI's impact on student learning and self-efficacy within a graduate course where students created eight microlessons [35] incorporating distinct learning science principles through an A/B experimental design. For each microlesson, students alternated between using genAI assistance and working independently when generating the learning objectives, assessments, and instructional content. Student learning gains were assessed through pre- and post-tests for each set of microlessons. Additionally, students' self-efficacy as educators and as users of genAI was measured through pre- and post-course assessments. We investigated the following two research questions:

RQ1: In what ways does employing genAI during the creation of microlessons affect students' learning of fundamental teaching and learning principles?
RQ2: How do graduate students' self-efficacy as educators and users of genAI change over the duration of a graduate-level course that integrates genAI tasks?

Through the investigation of these research questions, this work makes the following contributions: First, we show that employing genAI does not compromise students' learning of teaching principles. Second, we provide evidence that students' self-efficacy in both teaching practices and genAI usage increases significantly when they engage with genAI-assisted instructional design. Third, we present a novel, ecologically valid implementation of genAI within a graduate-level course on instructional design. This research offers insights into how future instructional designers learn and evolve with AI tools in authentic, real-world contexts.

2 Related Work

2.1 Learning and Self-Efficacy

Engaging students in the creation of microlessons is not just a practical skill-building exercise, it is also a powerful strategy for learning [13]. Design-based pedagogies, such as project- and problem-based learning require students to apply theoretical knowledge to authentic tasks, promoting deeper cognitive engagement and knowledge transfer [17, 21]. When students are asked to create instructional content, they must analyze subject matter, structure ideas coherently, and consider how others will interact with the material. These processes enhance metacognitive awareness and encourage students to transform information into usable knowledge [2]. Beyond cognitive benefits, design-based learning tasks also support the development of self-efficacy, students' beliefs in their ability to perform specific tasks successfully. Social cognitive theory identifies mastery experiences as the most influential source of self-efficacy, and instructional design activities often provide precisely these experiences [32]. By working through iterative cycles of creation, revision, and feedback, students gain confidence in both their subject-matter understanding and their professional identity as educators or designers [28, 40].

However, the integration of genAI into the design process complicates these dynamics. While AI-enhanced tools can support students by reducing cognitive load or enhancing surface-level quality, they may also alter the conditions under which self-efficacy develops. For instance, if students attribute successful performance to the genAI rather than their own effort or understanding, their self-efficacy may stagnate or even decline [26]. Conversely, students who learn to use genAI critically, by evaluating and refining outputs rather than passively accepting them, may gain confidence in both their instructional judgment and their capacity to harness emerging technologies effectively [25]. Understanding genAI's impact on learning and self-efficacy in design-based educational settings is essential, as student interpretation of progress within AI-enhanced environments significantly affects learning outcomes [36].

2.2 GenAI's Influence on Instructional Design

GenAI is transforming instructional design by enhancing creativity, streamlining planning, and providing personalized feedback while catalyzing idea generation for diverse learning needs [8, 11]. AI tools expedite design processes through innovative suggestions for lessons, assessments, and materials while improving quality through efficient iteration and refinement [22, 29]. Recent studies have explored genAI applications in instructional design, such as using tools like ChatGPT to create course materials [7, 15]. For example, Choi et al. [8] found that experienced instructional designers using ChatGPT for course mapping identified it as providing solid baselines for creating effective and efficient course structures, though still requiring domain expertise for accuracy and contextual relevance. Another investigation assessed ChatGPT's potential in developing lesson plans, showing that the tool could offer valuable starting points by generating general structures, ideas, and resources, which is an especially useful feature for novice educators [3]. Since teachers must evaluate the AI-generated content to ensure its alignment with learning objectives, researchers suggested that engaging with ChatGPT might also enhance teachers' critical thinking skills in lesson planning [14].

2.3 Evolving Roles in Instructional Design

The role of instructional designers is undergoing a significant transformation with the rise of genAI. Krushinskaia et al. [22] proposed a study to explore the potential of genAI as a co-designer in instructional settings, focusing on how teachers could collaborate with LLMs fine-tuned for educational purposes, such as Google's LearnLM [34]. Their research aims to investigate whether such partnerships could provide students with more personalized and effective learning opportunities. Despite consensus on ChatGPT's utility for instructional design [5, 12], designers must critically assess AI outputs using foundational knowledge to ensure pedagogical alignment [3]. This reliance highlights a key challenge that successful collaboration with AI requires a strong grasp of instructional design principles, yet research shows that even experienced educators often lack robust instructional design proficiency. This gap becomes even more pronounced for novice educators and learning engineers, who may struggle to effectively evaluate and refine AI-generated content [16].

3 Methods

The study was conducted as part of a 14-week graduate-level course on Tools for Online Learning during the spring 2024 semester at a large university in the northeastern United States. This course covers the topics of educational technology and learning science principles. The course met twice a week for 80 min in-person class sessions, which typically consisted of lectures supported by a slide deck, group discussion, and active learning activities. Outside of class, students completed biweekly projects providing hands-on experience with different pieces of educational technology and completed online course materials, consisting of instructional content and low-stakes assessments, before class time. Our intervention in this course spanned four week-long modules covering the following topics: Universal Design for Learning (UDL) [27], Guided Discovery (GD) [18], Fostering Help-Seeking (FHS) [31], and Collaborative Learning (CL) [23].

3.1 Participants

Participants were 27 s-semester master's students (ages 22–36) enrolled in a master's level Educational Technology and Applied Learning Sciences program. All students had foundational knowledge from first-semester coursework and prior genAI experience, representing emerging instructional design practitioners.

3.2 Learning Platform

The four modules from the course used in this study were part of the online materials students completed before class time, delivered via the Open Learning Initiative (OLI) platform, a well-established open-ended learning environment that offers courses across various domains, including anatomy, foreign language, and statistics [4]. The study modules were delivered via the Open Learning Initiative (OLI) platform, which integrates instructional content with both low-stakes formative and high-stakes summative assessments. Each module in the course was designed to be completed over approximately one week and was structured similarly to textbook chapters, containing three to six related topics. The instructional content was presented across multiple pages, including text and brief instructional videos. Interspersed throughout were formative activities, such as multiple-choice and short-answer questions, which provided students with opportunities for practice and feedback. Students could attempt these optional activities multiple times, receiving instant feedback with each attempt. Each module contained prompts for students to create and submit two microlessons for a total of eight microlessons overall.

3.3 Design

This study investigated the impact of integrating genAI into a core instructional design activity embedded within an authentic graduate course. We utilized the required coursework task of creating microlessons as the specific context to explore how genAI assistance influences student learning of pedagogical principles and their self-efficacy regarding both instructional design and genAI use. The study followed an A/B counterbalanced experimental design [20], where students created eight microlessons across four course modules. For each module's pair of microlessons, students were randomly assigned to use ChatGPT (built upon GPT-4) as an assistant for one microlesson (treatment condition) and to complete the other without AI assistance (control condition). The condition assignment alternated across modules in a counterbalanced manner, ensuring that by the end of the course, each student had completed four microlessons with AI support and four without. This within-subjects design allowed for direct comparison of outcomes associated with using genAI during the instructional design process versus traditional methods.

The creation of each microlesson served as a practical exercise in lesson planning and construction, following the fundamental instructional design principle of backwards design. Students developed their microlessons within the course's learning management system, Canvas, following a four-step scaffolded process. Each step was associated with an essay question that allowed students to enter and format text. At the outset, students selected a topic for their microlesson and were reminded of the specific learning science principle they were required to incorporate. In the next step, they formulated one or more learning objectives, ensuring that these objectives were actionable, measurable, and student-centered. In the third step, students created at least three assessments in any format they preferred, such as multiple-choice or short-answer questions. Finally, they wrote one to five paragraphs of instructional content aligned with their chosen topic and learning objectives, integrating a strategy to apply the designated learning science principle.

Each microlesson was required to incorporate a specific learning science principle covered in the corresponding module, in either the instructional paragraphs or through the three assessment items. For example, in the first module on UDL, the two microlessons students created needed to incorporate one of the seven principles or one of the eight steps of UDL [6, 33]. A list of the eight learning science principles incorporated into the different microlessons shown in order can be seen in Table 1.

Table 1. Overview of the four modules paired with the eight learning science principles used for micro-lesson development.

Module Topic	Principle	Description
Universal Design for Learning	Seven Principles	Seven principles of UDL that can be applied as a rubric
	Eight Steps	Eight steps that demonstrate the process of adopting UDL
Guided Discovery	Contrasting Cases	Using different examples to highlight nuances between key concepts
	Tell-then-Practice	Presenting information followed by applied practice opportunities
Fostering Help-Seeking	Strategies to Improve	Guiding students on strategies to improve their help-seeking behaviors
	Leveraging Prior Knowledge	Focusing on the connection between prior learning and current challenges
Collaborative Learning	Cooperative Learning	Structured group work with shared responsibilities
	Peer Learning	Learning through interaction and feedback between fellow learners

3.4 Generative AI Usage by Students

For microlessons completed under the genAI condition, students were explicitly guided to use ChatGPT to support their design process, simulating realistic human-AI collaboration in instructional design. Instructions accompanying each genAI-assigned microlesson prompted students to leverage ChatGPT for specific tasks across the design process: (1) constructing actionable, measurable learning objectives, (2) brainstorming applications of the designated learning science principle within assessments or instruction, (3) creating or refining formative assessment questions related to the objectives, and (4) drafting or editing instructional text, focusing on clarity and appropriate tone. To document this collaboration, students were required to submit a transcript of their ChatGPT conversation via shareable link or text document. While a detailed analysis of these interaction logs is beyond the scope of this paper, Table 2 provides illustrative examples of common student prompting strategies observed during this process.

Table 2. Examples of prompts used by students and their intended purpose.

Purpose	Student Prompt Examples
Brainstorming learning objectives	What might be a few learning objectives for a lesson on conjugating verbs in Spanish?

(continued)

Table 2. (*continued*)

Purpose	Student Prompt Examples
Simplifying complex concept	Explain the testing effect and stereotype threat to someone with no background in psychology
Creating analogies or examples	Please give me a real world example for the concept of interleaved practice
Drafting lesson text	Write an introduction to a 5-min lesson on indexing into a list in python programming
Refining quiz questions	Write three multiple choice questions with distractors for a lesson on the effects of marine life on…
Revising explanations	Make this explanation clearer: 'Learners remember better when they…'
Prompt chaining for quality	That example was too confusing can you give a more concrete one?

To maintain a focus on pedagogical intentionality, students were continually reminded to critically evaluate all AI-generated outputs for accuracy, pedagogical soundness, and alignment with learning objectives. The instructions emphasized that genAI should serve as a tool to assist their instructional design decisions, not replace their critical judgment. To maintain ecological validity and capture authentic usage patterns within this real-course setting, we deliberately allowed flexibility, as no constraints were imposed on the number of student-AI interactions, nor were specific prompt structures mandated.

Additionally, for microlessons assigned to the non-genAI (control) condition, students received explicit instructions not to use any genAI tools. To encourage adherence in this setting, we implemented several measures to help keep the students honest. Students confirmed compliance via a checkbox upon submission and were reassured that assignments would not be penalized for lacking surface polish, such as the use of informal language or the presence of minor typos, in attempts to reduce potential incentives to use AI purely for refinement. Instructors also qualitatively reviewed submissions noting typical stylistic differences, such as simpler sentence structures and less elaborate phrasing in the non-genAI work, which provided some indication of adherence. Despite these measures, we acknowledge the inherent limitation that total adherence to the non-genAI condition cannot be guaranteed outside a controlled laboratory environment, which is considered in the interpretation of our findings.

3.5 Data Sources

Self-Efficacy. The course also incorporated an assessment of students' self-efficacy in both using AI tools and applying learning science principles in teaching both at the beginning and the end of the course. Students were presented with six statements (3 measuring AI self-efficacy, 3 measuring self-efficacy on their ability to design educational lessons using learning principles) and asked to indicate their level of confidence in their abilities on a 100-point scale (in increments of 10) with higher numbers expressing a higher degree of self-perceived confidence. The same set of questions was used in both the pre-test and post-test, allowing for a direct comparison over time.

Knowledge Checks. Additionally, at the beginning of each module, students completed a pre-test consisting of five multiple-choice questions intended to assess students' knowledge of the module's key concepts. Upon completing the module, they took a post-test with a different set of five questions targeting the same concepts (i.e., these items were designed to be isomorphic). For these pre- and post-tests, an A/B design was implemented, where half the students received version A of the pre-test and version B of the post-test, while the other half received version B of the pre-test and version A of the post-test. These four sets of pre/post-tests served as a measure of learning gains as students progressed through the given modules. Two questions on each module's pre- and post-test specifically assessed understanding of the learning science principles applied in that module's microlessons. Since students used genAI for one of the microlessons per module, these targeted questions enabled comparing learning outcomes between the AI-assisted and non-AI conditions for each principle.

4 Results

4.1 Student Learning with GenAI

Student learning gains were evaluated using a 2 (pre–post) $\times$ 2 (test form sequencing: A $\rightarrow$ B vs. B $\rightarrow$ A) mixed-model ANOVA. In this design, half the students received test form A at pre-test and form B at post-test, while the remaining half experienced the reverse order. Assignment to test order was independent of the genAI conditions. The average scores by test form sequence across all four modules can be seen in Fig. 1.

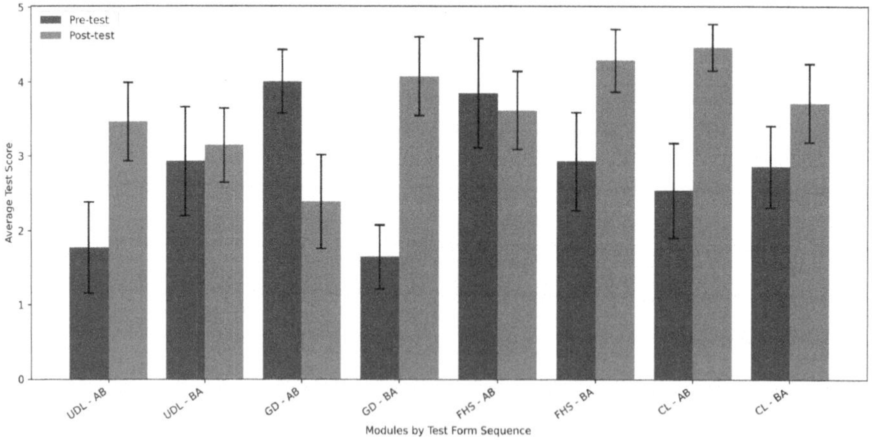

Fig. 1. Pre- and post-test average total scores across all four modules, segmented by test form sequence (AB or BA).

Analyses revealed significant interactions between time and test sequence across modules, complicating interpretations due to likely test form difficulty differences (see Table 3). For UDL, overall improvement was significant but driven only by the A → B group, with pre-test scores suggesting Form A was harder. For GD, no overall time effect was found, but an interaction showed the B → A group improved while A → B declined, with pre-tests suggesting Form A was easier. Similarly, FHS showed overall improvement, but the interaction indicated only the B → A group gained significantly (again, pre-tests suggested Form A was easier). Conversely, the CL module showed strong overall gains, with an interaction favoring the A → B group, leading to significant post-test differences. These complex interactions consistently highlight test form difficulty as a likely confound in observed learning gains.

Table 3. ANOVA results for quiz scores by module, * indicates significance at $p < .05$.

Module	Time Effect	Test Order Effect	Interaction
Universal Design for Learning (UDL)	12.47, p = .002* (η^2_p = .33)	2.16, p = .15 (η^2p = .08)	7.50, p = .01* (η^2p = .23)
Guided Discovery (GD)	1.89, p = .18 (η^2p = .33)	3.35, p = .08 (marginal; η^2p = .12)	59.38, p < .001* (η^2p = .70)
Fostering Help-Seeking (FHS)	4.70, p = .04* (η^2p = .16)	0.19, p = .67 (η^2p = .007)	9.33, p = .005* (η^2p = .27)
Collaborative Learning (CL)	37.61, p < .001* (η^2p = .60)	0.71, p = .41 (η^2p = .03)	5.53, p = .03* (η^2p = .18)

Targeted MCQs to Assess Impact of genAI on Knowledge of Learning Science Principles. To assess the impact of genAI assistance on knowledge of specific learning science principles targeted in each module, we analyzed pre-post change scores (improvement, no change, or decline) on two specific multiple-choice questions included in the pre- and post-tests for each module. These questions directly assessed understanding of the principle students were required to implement in their corresponding microlessons for that module. We conducted Mann-Whitney U-tests comparing the change scores on each targeted item between the group that used genAI for the associated microlesson and the group that did not. The results of these comparisons are presented in Table 4.

Table 4. A comparison of pre/post-test change scores on targeted module questions using Mann-Whitney U-Tests, where a * denotes a significant difference.

Module Topic	Principle	U Value	*p*-Value
Universal Design for Learning (UDL)	Seven Principles	123	0.13
	Eight Steps	74	0.43
Guided Discovery (GD)	Contrasting Cases	124.5	0.10

(continued)

Table 4. (*continued*)

Module Topic	Principle	U Value	*p*-Value
	Tell-then-Practice	136.5	0.03*
Fostering Help-Seeking (FHS)	Strategies to Improve	96.5	0.79
	Leveraging Prior Knowledge	153	0.002*
Collaborative Learning (CL)	Cooperative Learning	74.5	0.43
	Peer Learning	42	0.02*

As shown in Table 4, the results examining the impact of genAI use on learning specific principles were mixed. Significant differences favoring the genAI group emerged for the second microlesson items in the FHS ($p = .002$) and CL ($p = .02$) modules, with a marginal difference favoring the AI group for the first GD item ($p = .10$). However, for the second GD item, the non-genAI group showed significantly greater improvement ($p = .03$). Several comparisons yielded no significant differences between the groups. While these findings point to some potential benefits of using genAI during the instructional design process for learning the targeted principles, we remain cautious in their interpretation. In each case where a significant difference was found, the group that performed better at post-test also happened to have the easier test form for that specific item, making it difficult to attribute improvements solely to genAI use. Nonetheless, these trends suggest this is a promising area for further investigation, ideally employing more standardized assessment measures to isolate the effect of genAI on learning core pedagogical concepts.

4.2 Students Self-Efficacy

We assessed student self-efficacy using a six-item survey administered at the start (pre-test) and end (post-test) of the course. The survey comprised two three-item subscales: one focused on teaching practices and the other on the use of genAI. Internal consistency reliability for both subscales was evaluated using McDonald's omega (ω) and found to be acceptable at both pre- and post-test. To evaluate changes in self-efficacy over the semester, paired t-tests were conducted comparing pre-test and post-test scores for each subscale. Table 5 presents the descriptive statistics, reliability coefficients, and the results of these paired t-test analyses across the 27 students.

Table 5. Descriptive statistics, reliability, and pre/post-test changes in self-efficacy measures.

Self-Efficacy Measure	Pre-Test Mean (SD)	Post-Test Mean (SD)	Pre-Test ω	Post-Test ω	Pre/Post Change	Effect Size (Hedges' g)
Teaching Practices	68.02 (14.18)	78.52 (11.67)	.84	.74	$t(26) = -5.53$, $p < .001$	1.03
genAI Use	69.75 (18.58)	81.72 (12.38)	.91	.71	$t(26) = -5.03$, $p < .001$	0.94

Students reported statistically significant increases in self-efficacy from pre-test to post-test for both teaching practices and the use of genAI, with large effect sizes observed for both changes (Hedges' $g = 1.03$ and 0.94, respectively). On average, scores for both measures increased by more than 10 points over the semester. Additionally, we compared the two types of self-efficacy within participants at each time point using paired t-tests. There was no significant difference between teaching practice self-efficacy and genAI use self-efficacy at the start of the course ($t(26) = -0.89$, $p = .38$, Hedges' $g = -0.17$), nor was there a significant difference between them at the end of the course ($t(26) = -1.37$, $p = .18$, Hedges' $g = -0.26$). Students showed substantial, comparable self-efficacy growth in both domains throughout the semester.

5 Discussion

This study investigated how novice instructional designers and learning engineers used genAI to design microlessons within an authentic graduate-level course setting. Across four week-long modules, students collaborated with or without genAI to create instructional materials, while engaging in a parallel learning experience about core learning science principles. Our findings indicate that students generally improved on quizzes assessing fundamental learning and learning science principles from pre to post across the four modules. However, variations in test form difficulty warrant caution in drawing definitive conclusions about content mastery. Additionally, students reported significant gains in self-efficacy from the beginning to the end of the course, both in their teaching practices and their ability to integrate genAI into the lesson design workflow. These results suggest that structured integration of genAI into instructional design coursework can occur without hindering student learning of core principles, while simultaneously enhancing confidence in both pedagogical skills and AI tool utilization.

A key contribution of this study lies in its integration of genAI into an authentic semester-long graduate course setting. This environment moves beyond short-term or simulated use cases to examine how genAI is integrated into the actual workflow of novice instructional designers dealing with real course requirements, deadlines, and iterative feedback. This provides ecologically valid insights into how emerging instructional designers engage with genAI tools over time. We simultaneously evaluated the impact of genAI assistance on (a) learning outcomes related to core pedagogical principles using targeted pre-post assessments, (b) student self-efficacy concerning both instructional design practices and genAI use, and (c) the instructional design process itself via a counter-balanced A/B design comparing AI-assisted vs. non-AI work on the same types of tasks. The work provides a holistic picture of genAI's role during instructional design, going beyond a single dimension such as output quality or user perception. It provides specific evidence regarding how future professionals in education technology and learning sciences develop skills and confidence when learning with and about genAI tools integrated into their core training.

Interpreting these results requires considering factors like prior knowledge, engagement, experience, and particularly confounding variations in test form difficulty. While this prevents definitive causal claims about genAI enhancing knowledge based solely on quiz scores, the stable or improved post-test performance, combined with increased self-efficacy, suggests genAI support did not impede learning. A key finding is that the structured use of generative AI did not hinder students' learning of core pedagogical principles. Although post-test scores were stable or improved, our analysis did not show consistent, statistically significant learning gains attributable to the genAI condition, a result confounded by variations in test form difficulty. It is possible that the primary benefit of the AI intervention was allowing students to focus on higher-order tasks like structuring and refinement, an advantage not fully captured by our knowledge-based assessments. This suggests that while genAI can be safely integrated, its main contribution may be in enhancing the design workflow rather than directly accelerating conceptual understanding. This finding aligns with research showing that creating educational content fosters understanding [1, 30]. The use of genAI might facilitate this by allowing students to focus more on higher-order tasks like structuring and refinement. Nonetheless, effective instructional design still hinges on pedagogical expertise for critically evaluating and adapting AI-generated materials to ensure quality and contextual fit [29]. Our findings, while positive regarding learning outcomes, do not eliminate concerns that over-reliance on genAI could hinder the development of foundational pedagogical skills. Although students' improved post-test performance and increased self-efficacy are promising, this work highlights a potential gap in skill development. Facilitating this growth may require strategies like thoughtful reflection and critical evaluation of AI-generated materials.

The self-efficacy pre-post tests revealed significant growth in students' confidence both as educators and as users of genAI. Although the study lacks a control group entirely unexposed to genAI, as all students participated in the course rotation, this consistent increase across two distinct self-efficacy measures provides strong indicative evidence of positive development. This is particularly relevant as tools like ChatGPT become commonplace in professional lesson planning [3]. While such tools offer efficiency in instructional design, concerns remain about whether novice designers can maintain quality control and retain agency over AI-generated content. However, our results suggest that integrating genAI into microlesson development strengthened students' confidence in both pedagogical strategy and AI use. This gain was reflected in the student self-efficacy reports, supporting the idea that well-designed AI integration can be a catalyst for professional growth among instructional designers.

6 Limitations and Future Work

In our research, we conducted an A/B field study in a real class for novice instructional designers and learning engineers. However, we acknowledge this work was conducted in a single course with a relatively small sample size, which may restrict the generalizability of our findings. The ecological validity inherent in this field study design presents challenges in ensuring perfect experimental control. Specifically, we must acknowledge the possibility of control condition leakage, where students instructed not to use genAI might have done so despite monitoring efforts (detailed previously in the Methods section). In our experimental design, we deliberately used different test forms at pre- and post-test to reduce practice effects and assess generalizable learning gains. Unfortunately, these test forms ended up differing in difficulty, leading to a potential ceiling effect in pre-test scores that complicates the interpretation of content mastery in certain modules. Additionally, while self-efficacy improvements were observed, the absence of a control group for this measure limited our ability to draw firm conclusions about the sustained impact of genAI on confidence with instructional design skills relative to a group with no AI exposure at all. Although our counter-balanced, within-subjects design let every student serve as their own control, every participant ultimately engaged with genAI for half of the microlessons. This raises concerns regarding spill-over, where strategies or content created with genAI may have influenced work in the nominal no-genAI condition, and course-level motivational effects that cannot be disentangled from genAI exposure.

In future research, we aim to address these limitations by incorporating a larger, more diverse sample across multiple courses and educational settings. Longitudinal studies tracking both educational artifact quality and self-efficacy over time can help determine whether improvements continue as students gain more experience with genAI. We plan to investigate how specific rubric criteria differ between genAI-assisted and non-assisted designs, such as the quality of learning objectives, to provide more nuanced insights into the effects of genAI integration. These efforts will help clarify the pedagogical benefits and potential trade-offs of incorporating genAI into the instructional design process.

7 Conclusion

This study investigated the integration of genAI into authentic instructional design tasks within a graduate course for novice instructional designers. Our findings demonstrate that structured use of genAI for creating microlessons did not impede students' learning of core pedagogical principles, while significantly boosting their self-efficacy in both general teaching practices and the specific use of AI tools for instructional design. Our approach embedded AI use within real coursework over a semester and employed a comparative approach to assess learning alongside self-efficacy. This yielded ecologically valid insights regarding the ways emerging professionals engage with AI tools and develop confidence through practice. These results suggest that thoughtful genAI integration can support novice instructional designers' development, enhancing their confidence and potentially streamlining design processes without sacrificing foundational knowledge. This work demonstrates the potential for genAI to function as a valuable collaborator in instructional design, fostering growth when implemented within authentic, pedagogically sound learning experiences that balance technological assistance with human expertise.

Acknowledgments. We thank the Eberly Center for Teaching Excellence and Educational Innovation for their support via the Generative Artificial Intelligence Teaching as Research initiative.

Disclosure of Interests. The authors have no competing interests to declare that are relevant to the content of this article.

References

1. Aflalo, E.: Students generating questions as a way of learning. Act. Learn. High. Educ. **22**(1), 63–75 (2021)
2. Barron, B., Darling-Hammond, L.: Teaching for meaningful learning: a review of research on inquiry-based and cooperative learning. Book excerpt. Educ. Found. (2008)
3. van den Berg, G., du Plessis, E.: ChatGPT and generative AI: possibilities for its contribution to lesson planning, critical thinking and openness in teacher education. Educ. Sci. **13**(10), 998 (2023)
4. Bier, N., et al.: OLI Torus: a next-generation, open platform for adaptive courseware development, delivery, and research. In: Companion Proceedings of the 13th International Learning Analytics and Knowledge Conference. (2023)
5. Bolick, A.D., Da Silva, R.L.: Exploring artificial intelligence tools and their potential impact to instructional design workflows. TechTrends **68**(1), 91–100 (2024)
6. Burgstahler, S.: Universal Design: Process, Principles, and Applications. -IT. (2009)
7. Chen, W., et al.: A survey study of kindergarten teachers' use of ChatGPT to support instructional design. J. Educ. Technol. Innov. **6**, 3 (2024)
8. Choi, G.W., et al.: Utilizing generative AI for instructional design: exploring strengths, weaknesses, opportunities, and threats. TechTrends **68**(4), 832–844 (2024)
9. Cipriano, B.P., et al.: A picture is worth a thousand words: exploring diagram and video-based OOP exercises to counter LLM over-reliance. In: Ferreira Mello, R. et al. (eds.) Technology Enhanced Learning for Inclusive and Equitable Quality Education, pp. 75–89 Springer, Cham (2024)
10. Denny, P. et al.: Generative AI for education (GAIED): advances, opportunities, and challenges (2024). https://doi.org/10.48550/arXiv.2402.01580
11. Farrokhnia, M., et al.: A SWOT analysis of ChatGPT: implications for educational practice and research. Innov. Educ. Teach. Int. **61**(3), 460–474 (2024). https://doi.org/10.1080/14703297.2023.2195846
12. Grassini, S.: Shaping the future of education: exploring the potential and consequences of AI and ChatGPT in educational settings. Educ. Sci. **13**(7), 692 (2023)
13. Handayani, R.D.: Online microteaching lesson study: a recipe to enhance prospective physics teachers' pedagogical knowledge. Int. J. Lesson Learn. Stud. 221–234 (2022)
14. Hodges, C.B., Kirschner, P.A.: Innovation of instructional design and assessment in the age of generative artificial intelligence. TechTrends **68**(1), 195–199 (2024). https://doi.org/10.1007/s11528-023-00926-x
15. Hu, B., et al.: Teaching plan generation and evaluation with GPT-4: unleashing the potential of LLM in instructional design. IEEE Trans. Learn. Technol. (2024)
16. Huizinga, T., et al.: Teacher involvement in curriculum design: need for support to enhance teachers' design expertise. J. Curric. Stud. **46**(1), 33–57 (2014). https://doi.org/10.1080/00220272.2013.834077
17. Hung, W. et al.: Problem-based learning. In: Handbook of Research on Educational Communications and Technology, pp. 485–506 Routledge (2008)
18. Janssen, F.J., et al.: How to make guided discovery learning practical for student teachers. Instr. Sci. **42**, 67–90 (2014)
19. Kazemitabaar, M., et al.: CodeAid: evaluating a classroom deployment of an LLM-based programming assistant that balances student and educator needs. In: Proceedings of the CHI Conference on Human Factors in Computing Systems, pp. 1–20 ACM, Honolulu HI USA (2024). https://doi.org/10.1145/3613904.3642773
20. Kohavi, R., Longbotham, R.: Online controlled experiments and A/B tests. Encycl. Mach. Learn. Data Min. 1–11 (2015)

21. Kolodner, J.L., et al.: Problem-based learning meets case-based reasoning in the middle-school science classroom: putting learning by design (tm) into practice. J. Learn. Sci. **12**(4), 495–547 (2003)
22. Krushinskaia, K., et al.: Effects of generative artificial intelligence on instructional design outcomes and the mediating role of pre-service teachers' prior knowledge of different types of instructional design tasks. In: Olney, A.M. et al. (eds.) Artificial Intelligence in Education. Posters and Late Breaking Results, Workshops and Tutorials, Industry and Innovation Tracks, Practitioners, Doctoral Consortium and Blue Sky, pp. 395–400 Springer, Switzerland, (2024). https://doi.org/10.1007/978-3-031-64312-5_49
23. Laal, M., Laal, M.: Collaborative learning: what is it? Procedia-Soc. Behav. Sci. **31**, 491–495 (2012)
24. Nazaretsky, T., et al.: AI or human? Evaluating student feedback perceptions in higher education. In: Ferreira Mello, R. et al. (eds.) Technology Enhanced Learning for Inclusive and Equitable Quality Education, pp. 284–298 Springer, Cham (2024). https://doi.org/10.1007/978-3-031-72315-5_20
25. Power, R.: Evaluating graduate education students' self-efficacy with the use of artificial intelligence agents: a case study. J. Educ. Inform. **5**(1), 3–19 (2024)
26. Rodríguez-Ruiz, J., et al.: Is artificial intelligence use related to self-control, self-esteem and self-efficacy among university students? Educ. Inf. Technol. **30**(2), 2507–2524 (2025)
27. Rose, D.: Universal design for learning. J. Spec. Educ. Technol. **15**(4), 47–51 (2000). https://doi.org/10.1177/016264340001500407
28. Roytek, M.A.: Enhancing instructional design efficiency: methodologies employed by instructional designers. Br. J. Educ. Technol. **41**(2), 170–180 (2010)
29. Ruiz-Rojas, L.I., et al.: Empowering education with generative artificial intelligence tools: approach with an instructional design matrix. Sustainability. **15**(15), 11524 (2023)
30. Singh, A., et al.: What's in it for the learners? Evidence from a randomized field experiment on learnersourcing questions in a MOOC. In: Proceedings of the Eighth ACM Conference on Learning @ Scale. pp. 221–233 ACM, Virtual Event Germany (2021). https://doi.org/10.1145/3430895.3460142
31. Stahl, E., Bromme, R.: Not everybody needs help to seek help: surprising effects of metacognitive instructions to foster help-seeking in an online-learning environment. Comput. Educ. **53**(4), 1020–1028 (2009)
32. Stajkovic, A.D., Luthans, F.: Social cognitive theory and self-efficacy: goin beyond traditional motivational and behavioral approaches. Organ. Dyn. **26**(4), 62–74 (1998)
33. Story, M.F.: Principles of universal design. Univers. Des. Handb. 2, (2001)
34. Team, L. et al.: LearnLM: Improving Gemini for Learning (2024). https://doi.org/10.48550/arXiv.2412.16429
35. Torres, K.M.: Transforming higher education with microlessons. In: Global Perspectives on Micro-Learning and Micro-Credentials in Higher Education, pp. 59–74 (2024)
36. Xu, Z.: AI in education: enhancing learning experiences and student outcomes. Appl. Comput. Eng. **51**(1), 104–111 (2024)
37. Yan, L., et al.: Promises and challenges of generative artificial intelligence for human learning. Nat. Hum. Behav. **8**(10), 1839–1850 (2024)
38. Yilmaz, R., Yilmaz, F.G.K.: The effect of generative artificial intelligence (AI)-based tool use on students' computational thinking skills, programming self-efficacy and motivation. Comput. Educ. Artif. Intell. **4**, 100147 (2023)
39. Zdravkova, K., et al.: Unveiling the impact of large language models on student learning: a comprehensive case study. In: 2024 IEEE Global Engineering Education Conference (EDUCON), pp. 1–8. IEEE (2024)
40. Zimmerman, B.J.: Self-efficacy: an essential motive to learn. Contemp. Educ. Psychol. **25**(1), 82–91 (2000)

Exploring the Impact of LLM-Based Scaffolding on Academic Performance and the Mediating Roles of AI Literacy and Prior Knowledge

André C. A. Nascimento[1,2](✉), Mar Pérez-Sanagustín[3], J. F. Parmentier[4], Isabel Hilliger[5,5], Gabriel Ferrettini[3], and Rafael Ferreira Mello[1,2,2]

[1] UFRPE, Recife, Brazil
{andre.camara,rafael.mello}@ufrpe.br
[2] Cesar School, Recife, Brazil
[3] Université de Toulouse, IRIT, Toulouse, France
{mar.perez-sanagustin,gabriel.ferrettini}@irit.fr
[4] IPSA, IRIT, Paris, France
jean-francois.parmentier@irit.fr
[5] Pontificia Universidad Católica de Chile, Santiago, Chile
ihillige@uc.cl

Abstract. Large Language Models (LLMs) have rapidly gained popularity among university students for tasks such as essay writing, virtual tutoring, and coding exercises. Although the number of studies applying LLM-based solutions in educational contexts has grown significantly, researchers emphasize the need for empirical studies to evaluate the effectiveness of these tools to support teaching and learning. To address this gap, this paper presents a study analyzing the effects of an LLM-based system designed to support students' self-reflection. The study compares the grades and course outcomes of two groups of students enrolled in the same Thermodynamics course during two academic years (2023 and 2024, 234 students in total), but only the 2024 cohort had access to an LLM-based chatbot specifically designed to support self-reflection. The data showed no significant correlation between students' AI literacy profiles, their prior experience with generative AI, and the adoption of the tool. However, an analysis of engagement with the tool in the 2024 cohort revealed that students who interacted more extensively with the chatbot—particularly medium and high achievers (based on prior academic performance)—demonstrated a significant improvement in their final grades.

Keywords: Large Language Models · Self-reflection · Quasi-experiment · Higher Education

1 Introduction

Large Language Models (LLMs), such as ChatGPT, have seen rapid adoption among university students [1]. Students are increasingly leveraging these tools to compose essays and address programming tasks. However, the extent to which such tools contribute to

K. Tammets et al. (Eds.): EC-TEL 2025, LNCS 16063, pp. 382–396, 2026.
https://doi.org/10.1007/978-3-032-03870-8_26

the learning process remains a topic of considerable debate [2]. Advocates highlight the educational affordances of generative AI, while detractors raise concerns about its potential misuse, often framing it as a tool for academic dishonesty. These divergent perspectives have resulted in polarized views. Nonetheless, the proliferation of generative AI across various domains appears irreversible. It is therefore upon the academic community to critically examine how students are engaging with these technologies and to assess their implications for teaching and learning.

Several studies have emerged in the past year examining student engagement with LLM-based agents in diverse educational settings. This work primarily analyzes interaction patterns—such as turn-taking dynamics and word counts—to quantify how learners communicate with AI [3, 4]. While such research provides preliminary insights into human-AI interaction, recent findings also highlight risks of cognitive offloading, where overreliance on AI tools may erode essential student competencies, including critical thinking [5]. In response, scholars have shifted focus toward leveraging LLMs to foster metacognitive skills and structured self-reflection [6, 7], with early results demonstrating promise.

Despite these advances, critical questions remain unresolved. Prior research identifies moderating factors—such as AI literacy and prior knowledge [6, 7]—that may influence the efficacy of LLM-based interventions, yet their impact on metacognitive outcomes remains underexplored. Still, empirical evidence is scarce on whether LLM-supported self-reflection activities yield superior metacognitive outcomes compared to traditional (non-LLM) approaches. These gaps underscore the need for rigorous, comparative studies to evaluate the effectiveness of LLMs as metacognitive scaffolds while accounting for learner-specific variables.

To address this need, this paper presents a quasi-experiment examining the effects of integrating an LLM-based tool into a Thermodynamics course to support student self-reflection over five weeks ($n = 131$). In this setting, LLM scaffolding refers to structured activities designed to promote self-reflection. Academic performance was compared with those of students from the same course 2023 and 2024 academic years. Data collection included: (a) student-LLM conversational logs, (b) course grades, (c) reflection activity grades, (d) a questionnaire capturing students' prior knowledge in a mid-term exam, and (e) a self-reported questionnaire on AI literacy, and (f) perceived utility of the tool (for cohort 2024) and prior knowledge on the course topics. These datasets were cross-analyzed to address two **research questions**:

- **RQ1**. To what extent does the LLM-based scaffolding tool enhance students' academic performance, measured by final course and reflection activity grades?
- **RQ2**. How do variations in students' (a) AI Literacy and (b) Prior Knowledge of the subject mediate their engagement patterns with the tool?

2 State of the Art

2.1 Supporting Self-Reflection with LLMs

Self-reflection constitutes a fundamental component of metacognitive processes, enabling learners to identify misconceptions, refine their skills, and critically evaluate their learning outcomes [8]. The pedagogical effectiveness of self-reflection is further amplified when supported by well-designed prompts and methodologies, which foster a more profound and adaptable application of knowledge across diverse learning contexts.

The integration of large language models (LLMs) into educational settings has opened new avenues for enhancing and scaling self-reflective practices. Unlike human tutors, LLMs can provide instant, personalized reflection support at scale, making them uniquely positioned to address accessibility challenges in education. Emerging empirical evidence suggests that when LLMs are carefully engineered with pedagogical prompts, they can effectively guide students through structured reflection, thereby supporting metacognitive development and improving learning outcomes. For instance, [9] conducted a comparative study examining LLM-guided self-reflection against traditional methods, such as questionnaire-based reflection and passive review of lecture slides. Their findings indicated that both LLM-assisted ($d = 0.42$) and questionnaire-based approaches ($d = 0.39$) yielded statistically significant improvements in subsequent assessment performance compared to passive review methods ($d = 0.12$). However, no significant differences were observed between the two active reflection techniques. In a complementary study, [10] demonstrated, albeit with a small sample size ($n = 19$), that strategically designed prompts could enable LLMs to achieve an 82% inter-rater reliability with human tutors when assessing reflective outputs, highlighting their potential as adaptive tools for both guidance and evaluation. These studies collectively underscore the potential of LLMs to serve as scalable and effective scaffolds for self-reflection when aligned with sound pedagogical principles.

Despite these encouraging findings, critical gaps remain in the current literature. While existing studies, such as those by [9], suggest that LLM-supported reflection can be as effective as traditional methods, little research is directly comparing the metacognitive gains achieved through LLM-mediated reflection versus non-LLM approaches. Such comparative analyses are essential to determine whether LLMs offer unique advantages or merely replicate the benefits of established reflective practices. Second, the real-world implications of LLM-supported reflection—including potential risks such as over-reliance on AI tools —remain underexplored. A recent review of AI's role in metacognition and critical thinking highlights the urgent need for empirical studies investigating these dynamics in authentic educational settings [8]. All this underscores the necessity for further research to elucidate the conditions under which LLM-supported reflection is most beneficial, as well as the potential pitfalls associated with its use.

2.2 Factors Influencing Student-LLMs Interactions Engagement

AI literacy has been diversely conceptualized in the literature, with definitions ranging from techno-centric [11] to human-centered perspectives [12]. The framework proposed by [13] has emerged as particularly influential, defining AI literacy as the competencies that enable individuals to evaluate AI technologies critically, collaborate with these technologies effectively, and use them as a tool in any context (online, home, and at the workplace). This comprehensive conceptualization is especially pertinent for examining student-LLM interactions, as it emphasizes the dual capacity to leverage AI's potential while maintaining a critical awareness of its limitations - a crucial balance in educational contexts where cognitive agency must be preserved.

The growing recognition of AI literacy's importance has led to the development of various instruments for measuring these skills, in addition to empirical studies examining its influence on LLM usage patterns. [6] have contributed to this effort through their Generative AI Literacy Assessment Test (GLAT), a 20-item multiple-choice instrument that demonstrated AI literacy levels significantly predict student performance in GenAI-supported tasks. Complementary research by [14] reveals how AI literacy intersects with broader digital competencies and attitudes toward technology, while [11] developed a multidimensional assessment framework for secondary students that incorporates cognitive factors (knowledge and understanding), affective components (intrinsic motivation, self-efficacy, and anxiety), and behavioral dimensions (engagement and usage intention). In a similar line, [15] identified anxiety, perceived usefulness, and positive attitudes toward AI as key psychological factors influencing students' intention to engage with AI technologies. These studies show that AI literacy operates through interactions between technical understanding, emotional dispositions, and practical engagement patterns that could influence student-LLMs interactions.

While existing research has established clear relationships between AI literacy and general LLM usage, significant gaps remain regarding how these factors operate when these tools are used to support self-reflection activities. This oversight is particularly critical because self-reflection tasks inherently require sustained cognitive effort—a process likely mediated by AI literacy dimensions [11]. Furthermore, AI literacy skills should also be examined in relation to prior domain knowledge, given its established importance in learning outcomes. Our study will take this prior knowledge into account and investigate how AI literacy profiles, in conjunction with subject matter expertise, shape the effectiveness of LLM-supported metacognitive activities in authentic educational settings.

3 Study

3.1 Study Context and Design

This study employed a quasi-experimental design to examine the effects of an LLM-supported self-reflection intervention in an undergraduate Thermodynamics course. The course forms part of the second-year curriculum in Aerospace Science Curriculum, spanning 5 weeks with weekly sessions comprising 2 h of theoretical instruction and 2 h of practical exercises. The same instructor was responsible for all teaching materials and delivery in the two years in which this study was conducted (2023 and 2024). In both years, students completed mandatory self-reflection activities through the institutional Moodle platform each week (five activities in total). These activities require students to identify and summarize 2–5 key concepts learned each week and specify those areas or concepts in which they still have doubts. While these reflections do not contribute to final grades, submissions were not compulsory except for weeks 4 and 5. That's why, for this study, we focused specifically on data from these weeks.

The research compared two student cohorts: a **control** group from the 2023 offering ($n = 110$), who completed traditional reflection activities, and an **intervention** group from 2024 ($n = 103$), who had access to a custom OpenAI-based LLM web-based tool[1]

[1] Demo video of the platform: https://tinyurl.com/3prsfktc.

[16] designed to scaffold their reflective practice (based on GPT4o-mini). The tool, introduced in the first week of the course, was optional for students to use when preparing their weekly summaries. The instructor configured the tool with specific pedagogical constraints: it was programmed to avoid providing direct answers, instead generating questions to prompt deeper reflection aligned with weekly learning objectives. The system incorporated course materials and topic lists provided by the instructor, transforming these into structured prompts that maintained a supportive yet focused interaction style (see Supp. Materials for detailed prompt configuration). Students accessed these guided reflection sessions through a dedicated URL for each weekly activity.

This study ensures methodological rigor while preserving validity in real educational contexts. Both cohorts received identical core course content and materials, were taught by the same instructor, and completed examinations of comparable formats designed to assess the same learning objectives. This quasi-experimental approach allowed for a meaningful comparison between traditional and LLM-supported reflection methods within an authentic educational context.

3.2 Data Gathering Methods

The data collected for this study are summarized in Table 1, with all anonymized datasets available upon request. Participation required informed consent, and only data from consenting students were included in the analysis.

Two self-reported instruments were employed: (1) the AI Literacy Questionnaire for defining students' AI literacy Skills, (2) the Perceived Utility Questionnaire, for capturing students' perception about the usefulness of the tool for the activity. The AI Literacy Questionnaire was adapted from validated measures targeting dimensions relevant to LLM-supported self-reflection: AI awareness (Wang et al., 2023), behavioral engagement with AI (Ng et al., 2023), and affective factors including anxiety, perceived usefulness, and attitudes toward AI (Chai et al., 2020). An exploratory factor analysis revealed three well-defined constructs: AI Anxiety (apprehension about AI use), AI Attitude (positive disposition toward AI), and AI Usefulness (perceived utility of AI).

The Usefulness Questionnaire, co-designed with the instructor to address specific pedagogical interests, comprised five 7-point Likert scale items (1 = strongly disagree, 7 = strongly agree): (1) "Using the tool was engaging"; (2) "The tool helped me master course concepts"; (3) "I was absorbed in using the tool"; (4) "The tool was essential for understanding course content"; and (5) "I would recommend this tool to other students."

Complete instrumentation details, including the full item set and validation statistics, are available at the Supplementary Materials.

Table 1. Data gathering techniques

Name and Label	Description
Prior Knowledge	Students' grade in an exam with questions about the main concepts of the course taken on the **third week** for evaluating prior knowledge on the course

(continued)

Table 1. *(continued)*

Name and Label	Description
Final grade,	Students' final grades in the course
Self-reflection activity Grades,	Self-reflection activity Grades for week 4 (W4) and week 5 (W5) graded in a 0–3 rubric score, adapted from [17] and normalized in a 0–1 scale
Perceived Utility	Questionnaire for capturing the perceived utility of the tool provided (Five 7-point likert scale questions). Students filled in the questionnaire in W2
AI Literacy	Questionnaire composed by 17 questions directly extracted from existing questionnaires organized into 5 items: AI Awareness (3 questions); AI Behavioral Intention for working with AI (3 questions); AI Anxiety (4 questions); AI Usefulness (4 questions); AI Attitude (3 questions) define the students' AI literacy profile
Conversation Traces	Trace data about students' conversations with the GenAI-based chatbot

3.3 Data Gathering Methods

To **examine the effects of the LLM-based tool on students' final grades and summary grades (RQ1)**, we performed a two-phase analytical approach.

Phase 1. We employed a comparative analytical approach to evaluate differences in **students' final grades and summary grades between cohorts**. First, we normalized course final grades using *z*-score transformation to enable fair comparison across years, accounting for potential variations in assessment difficulty (Fig. 1). Before comparing performance between cohorts, we established baseline equivalence by examining **Prior Knowledge** grade distributions (Fig. 2). The null hypothesis stated no significant difference in Prior Knowledge performance means between cohorts ($\alpha = 0.05$). Using Prior Knowledge scores as a stratification variable, we categorized students into four performance quartiles: low performers (q0-q25), medium-low performers (q25-q50), medium-high performers (q50-q75), and high performers (q75-q100). This stratification enabled subgroup analyses while controlling for prior knowledge. Then, for each performance quartile, we conducted between-cohort comparisons of final grades and summary grades using independent sample *t*-tests. Effect sizes were calculated using Cohen's *d* to quantify the magnitude of observed differences. All analyses were performed using Scipy [18], with statistical significance set at $p < 0.05$.

Phase 2. We examined **how engagement with the LLM tool influenced students' final and summary grades in the 2024 cohort**. We operationalized engagement through two behavioral indicators: (1) the number of activities students engaged with the tool, since it wasn't mandatory; and (2) the number of messages exchanged with the tool.

First, we calculated, for each quartile, the number of activities they engaged with and the number of messages. Second, we used the number of activities students engaged in, and the total number of messages for categorizing students into low ($n = 52$) and high engagement ($n = 51$) groups using the following criteria: more/less than 10 messages exchanged and more/less than 3 activities performed. This classification yielded balanced groups for comparison (52 **low-engaged students** labelled with low engagement, and 51 **high-engaged**). Finally, we run comparisons of students' final grades (dependent variable) between the two engagement groups using Propensity score Matching ($k = 1$) controlling by Prior Knowledge grades (independent variable). We used the Causal Inference library in Python[2] and calculating the Average Treatment Effect (ATE). We considered the highly-engaged students as the treatment group while the low-engaged students were the control group.

To examine how students' engagement level and course outcomes vary based on students' levels of AI literacy (hereinafter AI Literacy profiles) and prior experience using GenAI (RQ2), we conducted the following analysis**.** First, we calculated the average values for questions related to Perceived Utility, AI Usefulness, AI Attitude and AI Anxiety. Then, we calculated a correlation matrix between these variables against the two behavioral engagement indicators defined (number of activities and number of messages), the students' summary grades in W4 and W5, and students' final grades.

Second, we clustered students by the AI literacy indicators (AI Usefulness, AI Attitude and AI anxiety) and analyzed their characteristics according to their Perceived Utility. Only students who have filled at least one of the questionnaires were considered ($n = 93$) and missing values were imputed by the kNN ($k = 5$) method. The number of clusters K, was defined through Elbow analysis, indicating $k = 3$ as the balanced trade-off between model complexity and intra-cluster variance. We obtained three different clusters: C0 with 38 students, C1 with 31 and C2 with 24 students. Then, to characterize each Cluster, we analyzed their behavior using the engagement and the Perceived Utility indicators. Then, we calculated the percentage of students in each quartile within each cluster to explore whether specific clusters were associated with prior knowledge. To assess patterns of tool usage, we analyzed the proportion of high- and low-engagement students across clusters, aiming to identify whether specific clusters were more actively engaged.

4 Results

4.1 Final and Summary Grades Comparison: 2023 vs. 2024 Cohorts with and Without LLM Support (RQ1)

Concerning final and activity summary grades, data showed that the observed raw final grades showed a reduction from 2023 to 2024 ($M_{(2023)} = 14.47$ vs $M_{(2024)} = 10.43$), but after normalization (described in Sect. 3.3), no significant changes were observed, across all quartiles (Supp. Table 2C). Although no significant differences were found in the average grades of students' summaries for the reflection activity in Week 4 across quartiles (Table 2), some differences emerged in Week 5 (Supp. Table 2B). Specifically, the results show a small but statistically significant difference in summary grades for Week 5 between the 2023 and 2024 cohorts for Q0 ($M_{(2023)} = 0.41$; $M_{(2024)} = 0.48$)

[2] https://github.com/laurencium/causalinference.

and Q50 ($M_{(2023)} = 0.42$; $M_{(2024)} = 0.49$), with higher mean scores observed in the 2024 cohort.

Table 2. Differences between the final grades and summary grades for W4 in 2023 and 2024 cohorts

Prior Knowledge Quartile	Mean (std) 2023		Mean (std) 2024		Difference	*p*-value
Summary Grades (W4)						
q0	0.471988	(±0.076557)	0.458966	(±0.106330)	–0.013022	0.63697
q25	0.468343	(±0.059552)	0.457095	(±0.114657)	–0.011248	0.672386
q50	0.487753	(±0.039996)	0.480149	(±0.130560)	–0.007603	0.782329
q75	0.506396	(±0.041046)	0.503515	(±0.127128)	–0.002881	0.921524

Concerning the 2024 cohort's engagement with the tool, Fig. 1(a) shows notable differences in students' engagement levels across quartiles. Specifically, Table 3 indicates that students in Q25 (M = 3.36 activities) and Q50 (M = 3.50 activities) demonstrated the highest levels of engagement in terms of the number of activities completed. This pattern is further supported by the number of messages exchanged with the chatbot, with students in Q25 averaging 18.80 messages and those in Q50 averaging 19.53 messages, suggesting more sustained interaction with the tool. In contrast, students in Q0 and Q75 were the least engaged, both in terms of participation in activities and messages exchanged. However, students in Q75 showed slightly higher engagement than those in Q0, particularly in the number of messages exchanged.

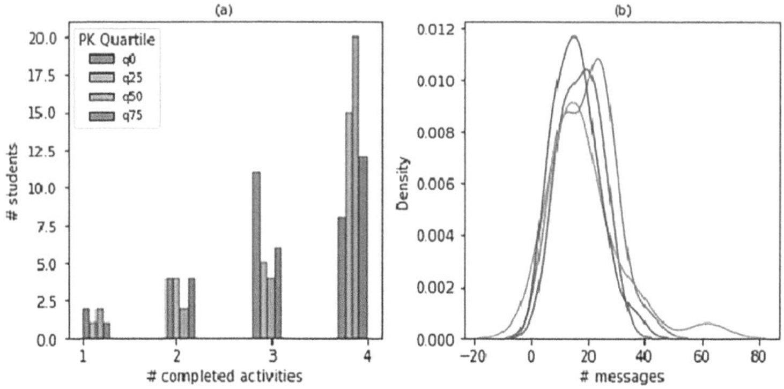

Fig. 1. Level of interactions stratified by prior knowledge (PK) quartiles: (a) histogram of the number of completed activities by the students; (b) density plot of the number of messages sent by the students

Table 3. Average number of activities and messages per Prior Knowledge quartile.

Prior Knowledge Quartile	Avg Number of Activities (std)		Avg. Number of Messages (std)	
q0	3.00	(±0.912870)	15.80	(±7.686568)
q25	**3.36**	(±0.907377)	**18.80**	(±12.819256)
q50	**3.50**	(±0.922958)	**19.53**	(±8.904772)
q75	3.26	(±0.915393)	17.56	(±6.985869)

When **analyzing students' engagement with the tool in relation to their final course grades** in Fig. 2, we observed notable differences. The Average Treatment Effect (ATE), controlling for prior knowledge (PK), indicates that students with high engagement achieved, on average, 2.49 points higher on the final exam than those with minimal tool usage (SE = 0.898). This effect is statistically significant, $p = 0.006$, with a 95% confidence interval ranging from 0.73 to 4.25 points. However, as illustrated in Fig. 2, no significant difference was found in **summary grades** cohort when comparing high and low engagement groups. The observed average effect was an increase of only 0.012 points, with a large p-value (p = 0.718) and a 95% confidence interval ranging from − 0.054 to 0.078, suggesting that this difference is likely attributable to random variation.

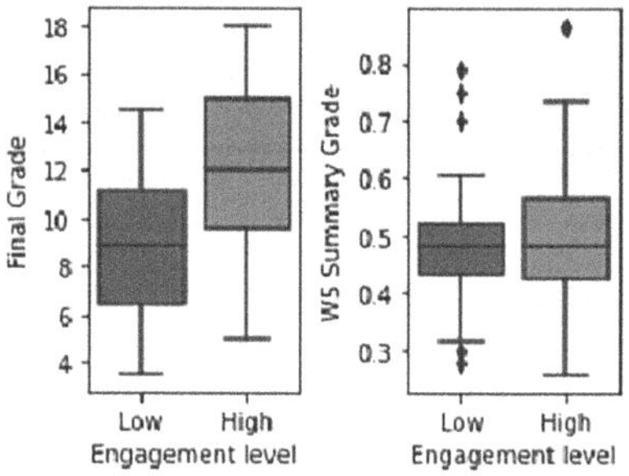

Fig. 2. Academic performance measurements between high and low engagement groups.

4.2 Relationships Between Engagement, AI Literacy, and Perceived Utility (RQ2)

For the 2024 cohort, no significant correlations were found between students' engagement levels, their AI literacy profiles, and their perceived utility of the tool (see Fig. 3). An overview of cluster profiles is presented in Fig. 4, which can be described as following: **Cluster 0** presents moderate levels of *AI Usefulness* (M = 3.16) and *AI Attitude* (M = 3.71), and moderate to high levels of *AI Anxiety* (M = 3.65), but still shows strong perceived utility of the tool (M = 4.80). **Cluster 1** demonstrates moderate perceptions of *AI Usefulness* (M = 4.78) and *AI Attitude* (M = 5.55, along with relatively low levels of *AI Anxiety* (M = 2.52). Students in this cluster show medium levels of perceived utility of the tool. **Cluster 2** shows higher mean scores in both *AI Usefulness* (M = 5.47) and

AI Attitude (M = 5.50) compared to the other clusters, but still feel anxious about using it (M = 5.31). Students in this cluster reported the least perceived utility values.

5 Findings

5.1 Findings on the Effects of an LLM-Based Scaffolding Tool on Students' Academic Performance (RQ1)

Our analysis revealed two findings **regarding the intervention with the tool on students' academic performance**. First, **comparing the 2023 and 2024 cohorts showed that the tool intervention did not lead to any measurable changes in students' final grades (Finding 1.1)**. This behavior is observed across the four strata defined by the quartiles of Prior Knowledge grades. Even though there was a small increase in the medium achievers ($\Delta_{q25} = 0.06$ and $\Delta_{q50} = 0.16$), we did not find this difference to be significant ($p > 0.05$). Second, **differences in summary grades were observed only in week 5, with no significant variations in the other week (Finding 1.2).** Our analysis revealed a significant positive effect on summary grades in quartiles Q0 and Q50 during week 5. One possible explanation is that, by this point, students had gained confidence in using the tool and had developed the competencies required to engage with it effectively. Still, although the increases in Q25 and Q75 were not statistically significant, the upward trend across all quartiles suggests that even limited engagement with the tool may enhance the quality of students' self-reflection work. However, there is no supporting data to confirm that these factors directly contributed to the observed increase in grades.

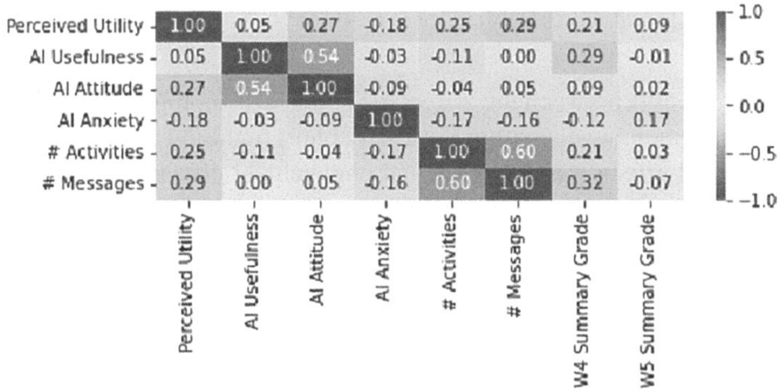

Fig. 3. AI Literacy Spearman correlation to AI tool usage.

Concerning the **2024 cohort's engagement with the tool and its relationship to final and summary grades**, our analysis revealed 2 findings. First, the results indicate that **q25 and q50 Prior Knowledge quartiles showed more interactions with the tool on average than the others (Fig. 1) (Finding 1.3)**. Second, **high-engaged students show better results in the course's final grades (Finding 1.4)**. The Average Treatment Effect (ATE), controlling by prior knowledge (PK), reveals that high-engagement students achieved, on average, 2.49 points higher on the final exam than those with minimal tool usage (*Standard Error = 0.898*). These results reinforce the finding that longer and more frequent interactions with the LLM are associated with a statistically significant and positive impact on students' overall course performance. However, given the absence of significant differences in summary grades between high- and low-engagement students within the 2024 cohort, the benefits of using AI as a learning support may manifest more clearly over the long term. This suggests that encouraging students to engage more extensively with the LLM across multiple activities and throughout different academic courses may contribute to improved final grade outcomes. Moreover, although we controlled for prior knowledge, this finding does not imply causality. Further analysis is needed to compare it with other engagement measures related to different course activities, which were not available at the time of the study.

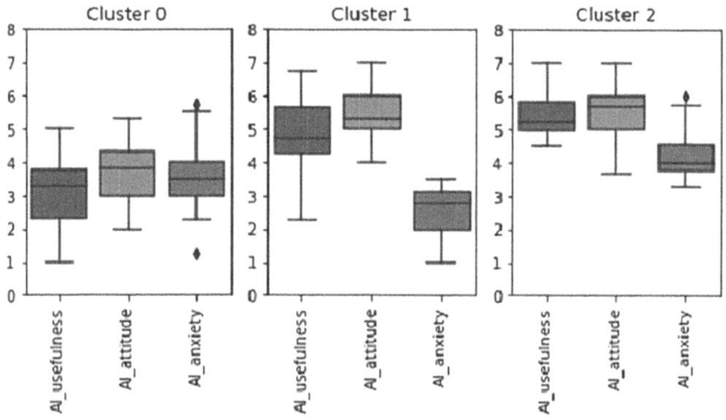

Fig. 4. Box plots showing the characteristics of the cluster per the AI Literacy indicators (AI Usefulness, AI Attitude and AI Anxiety).

The differing results between the 2023–2024 comparison, together with the analysis of students' engagement levels within the 2024 cohort highlight two distinct dynamics: overall cohort-level effects versus individual engagement effects. One possible explanation is that the average levels of tool usage and interaction across the entire 2024 group were not sufficient to produce a measurable cohort-wide impact. This suggests that introducing an AI tool for supporting certain pedagogical activities would not be sufficient for improving academic performance for all students. The integration of these tools should be carefully prepared and pedagogically informed. Factors such as varying levels of engagement with the tool, differences in how students adapt to its use, and individual learning behaviors may affect the overall observed effects. Recent research on the design of strategies for LLM engagement reinforces that such an aspect is extremely relevant to improve learning outcomes [9].

These findings emphasize the importance of fostering meaningful engagement with AI tools to maximize their educational benefits. Encouraging strategies that promote higher interaction levels could lead to improved learning experiences and outcomes, particularly in enhancing students' metacognitive abilities, leading to improved final course grades.

5.2 AI Literacy, Prior Knowledge, and Their Influence on Student Engagement with LLM-Based Scaffolded Activity (RQ2)

Regarding the **relationship between students' engagement levels with the tool and their AI literacy and perceived utility indicators**, we identified three key findings. First, **no significant correlations were observed between students' AI literacy profiles or their perceived utility of the tool and the engagement indicators (see Fig. 3) (Finding 2.1)**. According to the literature, AI literacy encompasses the knowledge and skills required to interact effectively with AI technologies, including an understanding of core AI concepts, the ability to critically evaluate AI systems, and the capacity to use AI tools responsibly and ethically across various contexts (Jin et al., 2024). Although there has been an increase in the availability of instruments to assess AI literacy, these tools are predominantly based on self-reported data. As noted by Lintner (2024), self-report measures may introduce bias and fail to accurately capture an individual's actual level of literacy. This limitation may account for the lack of correlation observed between AI literacy and both perceived utility and engagement indicators in our study. Our findings suggest that the AI literacy assessment employed may not be sufficiently robust to detect students' predisposition to engage with an AI tutor within the analyzed cohort. Notice that, even if the instrument was validated, our questionnaire for capturing students' AI profile was composed of items from different questionnaires, which could have negatively impact the data collected and the results we obtained.

Second, **our analysis reveals that students in different clusters display distinct AI literacy profiles and perceptions of tool usefulness as well as engagement levels (Finding 2.2)**. We characterized students in **Cluster 0** as ***"Skeptical but Curious."*** These students reported moderate perceptions of AI usefulness and moderate to high levels of AI anxiety, yet they also expressed a generally positive perception of the AI tool used in the study. This finding suggests that despite self-reporting a certain degree of skepticism toward AI, students may still recognize and appreciate its pedagogical value when introduced in a purposeful and structured learning context.

We labeled students in **Cluster 1** as ***"Enthusiastic."*** These students self-reported strong positive attitudes toward AI and AI usefulness, along with low levels of AI anxiety. However, their reported perceived utility of the specific tool used in the study was moderate. This result suggests that these students may hold a less critical perspective on AI, viewing the use of AI-based tools for learning as expected or commonplace. As a result, their perception of the tool's utility may be tempered by familiarity rather than novelty or pedagogical impact.

We characterized students in **Cluster 2** as ***"Hopeful but Anxious."*** These students exhibited the highest scores in both AI Attitude and perceived AI Usefulness, yet also reported the highest levels of AI anxiety. Interestingly, they also reported the lowest levels of perceived utility for the tool used in the study. These findings suggest that, while these students appear to accept the integration of AI into society, their elevated anxiety may hinder their ability to fully benefit from AI-based educational interventions.

Third, **our analysis did not reveal any prevalence of a specific Prior Knowledge quartile or engagement profile within any particular cluster (Finding 2.3)**. Although prior knowledge often influences grades and, at times, engagement with course activities, this was not the case here. This might be due to the fact that, in the second year of the program, prior knowledge does not sufficiently differentiate students' involvement with the course content. Other indicators, such as GPA, may provide a more accurate measure; however, GPA data was not available for this study.

6 Conclusions, Limitations and Future Work

This study explored the integration of a Large Language Model (LLM)-based scaffolding tool in a Thermodynamics course, aiming to support student self-reflection over a five-week period. Through a quasi-experimental design, we investigated the impact of the tool on academic performance by comparing outcomes from two cohorts (2023 without LLM support and 2024 with LLM support). Using a multi-source dataset—including conversational logs, course and activity grades, AI literacy profiles, and perceived utility—we examined two key questions: (1) whether the LLM-based tool enhanced students' academic performance (RQ1), and (2) how students' AI literacy and prior knowledge influenced their engagement with the tool. The findings contribute to a deeper understanding of the pedagogical potential of GenAI in higher education settings.

First, findings related with the first research question offer insights into the conditions under which LLM-based scaffolding tools can influence student performance and engagement in educational contexts. While the intervention did not lead to statistically significant improvements at the cohort level, the positive association between individual engagement and academic performance highlights the importance of promoting sustained and meaningful interactions with AI tools. This supports growing evidence that the pedagogical value of GenAI depends not only on access to the technology but also on how it is embedded in instructional design and how students engage with it over time [9]. The fact that we only observed performance gains in Week 5 of the summary activity aligns with studies suggesting that students require time to develop trust, confidence, and effective strategies when interacting with GenAI systems. Moreover, the nuanced relationship between engagement and outcomes underlines the need for adaptive scaffolding and context-aware integration approaches that respond to students' prior knowledge, cognitive needs, and learning goals. Moving forward, future research should investigate how different instructional strategies, levels of guidance, and types of metacognitive prompts can optimize the educational impact of GenAI tools, while also accounting for individual learner variability and long-term effects. Additionally, further analysis will be needed to investigate students' engagement with the LLM-based activities in relation to their engagement with other course activities (e.g., those in the Learning Management System), in order to better isolate the observed effects.

Second, our findings did not reveal a direct correlation between students' AI literacy profiles and their engagement with the LLM-based tool. The clustering analysis, however, highlights meaningful differences in how students perceive the utility of the tool based on their attitudes and anxieties toward AI. This suggests that students' subjective experiences with AI—shaped by their emotional and cognitive orientations—may influence how they interpret and value AI-based educational interventions, even if such dispositions do not translate directly into behavioral engagement. This nuanced relationship aligns with recent studies emphasizing that AI literacy is not only a matter of skills and knowledge, but also of affective and contextual factors that shape users' interaction with AI systems. Moreover, our findings underscore the importance of moving beyond generalized assessments of AI literacy to consider how specific forms of AI—such as generative AI in education—may require distinct competencies and foster varied perceptions of utility and trust. Future research should consider integrating multimodal assessments and context-sensitive instruments to better capture the complex interplay between AI literacy, perception, and meaningful engagement in educational settings.

This study presents several limitations that should be acknowledged. First, although the intervention focused on a self-reflection activity, we did not employ any instrument to assess changes in students' self-reflection skills over time. This was due to both the nature of the course and the constraints typical of ecological experiments conducted in authentic classroom settings. Future research should explicitly measure self-reflection skill development to better understand how LLM-based tools can support metacognitive growth. Second, the course duration was limited to five weeks, which restricts our ability to draw conclusions about the long-term effects of the intervention. Longitudinal studies are needed to evaluate the sustained impact of LLM-based scaffolding on academic outcomes and learning behaviors. Third, at the time of the study, there were no validated instruments specifically designed to measure students' AI literacy in relation to generative AI in educational contexts. As a result, we relied on existing validated instruments that address AI literacy more generally. This may have limited the precision of our analysis and its alignment with the unique competencies required for effective GenAI engagement. Future studies should consider using more targeted, pedagogically grounded instruments to capture students' readiness and capacity to interact meaningfully with GenAI tools in learning environments.

Supplementary Materials. https://osf.io/37anh/?view_only=76b827a4d10a4d08b00550cdc3a607ef.

Acknowledgments. This paper has been partially funded by the ANR LASER (156322) and the LAFE project, Millennium Nucleus, Student Experience in Higher Education in Chile: Expectations and Realities (NCS2021–083), Fondecyt (11230827).

Declaration of Gen AI and AI-assisted Technologies in the Writing Process. During the preparation of the paper, the authors used ChatGPT-40 and DeepSeek to check grammar and improve readability and language. After using this tool, authors reviewed and edited the content as needed and take full responsibility for the final publication.

Disclosure of Interests. The authors have no competing interests to declare that are relevant to the content of this article.

References

1. Kuhail, M.A., et al.: Interacting with educational chatbots: a systematic review. Educ. Inf. Technol. **28**(1), 973–1018 (2023)
2. Lim, W.M., et al.: Generative AI and the future of education: Ragnarök or reformation? A paradoxical perspective from management educators. Int. J. Manag. Educ. **21**(2), 100790 (2023)

3. Wang, Y., Wang, X.: A study of the developmental trajectory of students' interactive dialogue model in middle school information technology course: an epistemic network analysis.Educ. Inf. Technol. (2024)
4. Su, H., Tong, Y., Zhang, X., Fan, Y.: Uncovering students' processing tactics towards ChatGPT's feedback in EFL education using learning analytics. In: Ma, W.W.K., Li, C., Fan, C.W., U, L.H., Lu, A. (eds.) Blended Learning. Intelligent Computing in Education. Lecture Notes in Computer Science, vol. 14797. Springer, Singapore (2024)
5. Stadler, M., Bannert, M., Sailer, M.: Cognitive ease at a cost: LLMs reduce mental effort but compromise depth in student scientific inquiry. Comput. Hum. Behav. **160**, 108386 (2024)
6. Jin, Y., Martinez-Maldonado, R., Gašević, D., Yan, L.: GLAT: the generative AI literacy assessment test (2024). https://arxiv.org/abs/2411.00283
7. Ng, D.T.K., Leung, J.K.L., Chu, S.K.W., Qiao, M.S.: Conceptualizing AI literacy: an exploratory review. Comput. Educ. Artif. Intell. **2**, 100041 (2021)
8. Goyal, A.: AI as a cognitive partner: a systematic review of the influence of AI on metacognition and self-reflection in critical thinking. Int. J. Innov. Sci. Res. Technol. **10**(3), 1231–1238 (2025)
9. Kumar, H., et al.: Impact of guidance and interaction strategies for LLM use on learner performance and perception. In: Proceedings of ACM Human-Computer Interaction, vol. 8 (2024)
10. Yuan, B., Hu, J.: Generative AI as a tool for enhancing reflective learning in students. ArXiv Prepr. ArXiv:2412.02603 (2024)
11. Ng, D.T.K., et al.: Artificial Intelligence (AI) literacy questionnaire with confirmatory factor analysis. In: 2023 IEEE International Conference on Advanced Learning Technologies (ICALT), pp. 233–235. IEEE (2023)
12. Luckin, R., et al.: Empowering educators to be AI-ready. Comput. Educ. Artif. Intell. **3**, 100076 (2022)
13. Long, D., Magerko, B.: What is AI literacy? competencies and design considerations. In: Proceedings of the 2020 CHI Conference on Human Factors in Computing Systems, in CHI '20. Association for Computing Machinery, New York (2020)
14. Wang, B., et al.: Measuring user competence in using artificial intelligence: validity and reliability of artificial intelligence literacy scale. Behav. Inf. Technol. **42**(9), 1324–1337 (2023)
15. Chai, C.S., Wang, X., Xu, C.: An extended theory of planned behavior for the modelling of Chinese secondary school students' intention to learn artificial intelligence. Mathematics **8**(11), 2089 (2020)
16. Ferrettini, G., Nascimento, A.C.A., Pérez-Sanagustín, M., Hilliger, I.: SIMBA : creating chatbots for students tutoring. In: Proceedings of the 20th European Conference on Technology Enhanced Learning (ECTEL) (2025)
17. Miller, K., et al.: Analysis of student engagement in an online annotation system in the context of a flipped introductory physics class. Phys. Rev. Phys. Educ. Res. **12**(2) (2016)
18. Virtanen, P., et al.: SciPy 1.0: fundamental algorithms for scientific computing in python. Nat. Methods **17**, 261–272 (2020)

Towards Automated Characterization of Revision Events in Student Writing

Léo Nebel[1,2(✉)], François Bouchet[1], Vanda Luengo[1], and Mathilde Couraud[2]

[1] Sorbonne Université, CNRS, LIP6, 75005 Paris, France
leo.nebel@lip6.fr
[2] EvidenceB, Paris, France

Abstract. Writing is an iterative process, yet traditional assessments often prioritize the final product over the transformations that shape it. This study investigates the complex nature of revision in student writing through computational modeling, leveraging keystroke data to capture and analyze revision behaviors. Focusing on a dataset of 1,975 annotated revision events from 10th-grade French students, we assess multiple methodological approaches, including rule-based heuristics, machine learning classifiers, and large language models (LLMs). While previous research has demonstrated the feasibility of automated revision detection, we extend these efforts by introducing a novel framework for identifying embedded revisions, i.e. instances where a revision occurs within another. By comparing the efficacy of different computational strategies, our findings reveal key insights into how revisions unfold in real-time writing. Annotations evaluated by agreement measures underline the complexity of the task. This work not only enhances the precision of automated revision classification but also lays the groundwork for intelligent writing support systems that provide targeted feedback to students, fostering a deeper engagement with the revision process.

Keywords: Writing · Revision · Keystroke Logging

1 Introduction

When students write a text, teachers typically provide feedback only on the final product. Assessing the writing process itself is far more challenging, yet it has the potential to enable a whole new kind of helpful feedback. Intelligent Tutoring Systems (ITS) offer an opportunity to address this gap by analyzing online keystroke data, enabling feedback not only on the written content but also on the writing process. This feedback can be a great asset for students to improve their writing strategy and, therefore, their overall writing product quality.

The writing process is typically divided into three interwoven episode types: planning, formulating, and reviewing [11]. Planning overlaps with self-regulation, aligning with the first stage of Zimmerman's self-regulation cycle [24], and has

K. Tammets et al. (Eds.): EC-TEL 2025, LNCS 16063, pp. 397–411, 2026.
https://doi.org/10.1007/978-3-032-03870-8_27

been studied through think-aloud protocols and self-reports [3]. In contrast, formulating and reviewing can be analyzed non-intrusively via keystroke data, enabling large-scale studies. This paper focuses on reviewing episodes, aiming to automatically detect revision events (by predicting their beginnings and ends) within the writing process. Keystrokes outside these events are considered part of the formulation. This work enables future research on revision sequences, their impact on text quality, and the development of a feedback system to support students' revision behaviors.

A fully autonomous revision characterization pipeline would enable real-time analysis and immediate feedback on students' writing strategies. The revision detection methods presented here could support feedback that promotes extensive revisions after larger writing units (e.g., paragraphs), rather than limiting edits to minor, in-process changes – an approach linked to proficient writers [6,15] (see *Revision A* in Fig. 1). Further classification of revision types – dependent on this initial step – would allow strategy-specific feedback, aligning revision behavior with text weaknesses (e.g., structural revisions for unclear reasoning, surface revisions for grammar or spelling). This approach moves beyond product-focused feedback by incorporating insights into task processing and self-regulation – two key feedback levels shown to significantly enhance learning [13].

The next section presents the state of the art and the research questions. The third section details our method and the models trained and compared. The fourth section covers the results, while the fifth discusses them.

2 Related Work

In the three-phase writing process (planning, formulating, and reviewing), Flower and Hayes [11] considered reviewing could be broken down into two key actions: evaluating the text without modifying it (internal revision), and making textual changes (external revision). This study focuses solely on *external revision*, as it is the only observable component through keystroke analysis. Internal revision typically requires eye-tracking data [21] or methods like think-aloud protocols which may introduce biases we seek to avoid. Moreover, these two types of data are rarely available in a real-world setting, and so are difficult to scale up outside of a lab context.

Previous research has examined the link between revision and text quality. Breetvelt [5] found a negative correlation when revisions occurred in the early writing phases, although this finding is limited by the small sample size ($n = 20$), lack of revision type analysis, and potential think-aloud protocol biases. However, the relationship between writing proficiency and revision frequency remains unclear. Some studies suggest skilled writers revise more often [18], while others argue they require fewer revisions due to more accurate drafts [15]. Despite these discrepancies, research agrees that skilled writers revise at the meaning level after extended writing bursts, whereas less-skilled writers focus on surface-level changes with frequent short pauses [6,12]. This indicates that text quality depends not only on the amount of revision [1], but also on a balance of revision type, frequency, and distribution. To explore these relationships, we aim to develop an automatic revision characterization, first requiring automated detection of revision events.

Previous studies have explored the automatic extraction of revision events from keystroke data. Conijn et al. [7] identified revisions by marking their beginning (e.g., a first backspace key or a cursor move within the typed text, see Fig. 1) and end (completion of the correction). Rule-based methods effectively detect revision onsets, typically triggered by deletions or cursor movements away from the leading edge [4]. To identify revision endpoints, they trained binary classifiers, assuming a revision ends, at the latest, when the next one begins. The results of this approach are provided in Table 1. However, this work has some limitations. First, to the authors' knowledge, their analyses have been conducted only in the aforementioned paper in terms of population (graduate and undergraduate students) and language (English). Replication is therefore needed.

Additionally, a key limitation is the definition of revision events, which does not account for embedded revisions, i.e. cases where a revision occurs within the character range of a prior revision (cf. Sect. 3.1 for an example) [8]. To illustrate how the lack of a model of embedded revision can distort the interpretation of the writer's intent, thus preventing precise feedback, one can consider the same keystroke sequences displayed on Fig. 2. In Fig. 2b, the first revision clearly adds specificity, while when embedded revisions are not considered, the revisions are analyzed as shown on Fig. 2a, where the intent is unclear due to early truncation. Therefore it is clear that recognizing embedded revisions as episodes enables a deeper and more precise analysis of revision sequences. For example, being able to identify overlapping tasks like spelling corrections during reformulation can inform feedback encouraging sequential editing to reduce cognitive load.

Table 1. Results from Conijn's et al.

Model	Performance Metrics			Distance (chars)	Accuracy (-)
	Accuracy	Precision	Recall	Avg/STD	1-off
Random Forest	0.713	0.987	0.986	3.5/9.0	0.830
Decision Tree	0.240	0.991	0.837	4.1/6.9	0.420
SVM	0.473	0.975	0.974	3.5/9.0	0.645

This analysis of the state of the art led us to attempt to expand the work of [7] to include embedded revisions, on a different population with a different language. More precisely, we tried to answer the following research questions:

- Can new models better identify revision events through keystroke data?
- How well do the existing approaches perform when replicating them on our different datasets (language and students' level)?
- How well are these models performing to identify the more complex phenomenon of embedded revisions through keystroke data?

Revision A

Climate change is an isue|
Climate change is an isu|
...
Climate change is an issue|

Revision B

Climate change is an issue|
Climate change is an i| issue
...
Climate change is an important issue|

Fig. 1. Example of a revision beginning caused by a deletion (*Revision A*) and another caused by a cursor move inside the text (*Revision B*)

Although framed differently, several studies have shown the feasibility of automatically predicting revision types [9,14]. However, these have been relying on manually extracted revision events or aligned sentences between different drafts (e.g. 2 or 3 snapshots of the students' written text and not a continuous recording). By addressing our research questions, we contribute a key step toward a fully automatized revision characterization pipeline.

3 Methods

3.1 Model, Context and Dataset

Model. We first reproduced Conijn's et al.'s model [7], then extended it by allowing unrestricted revision endpoints to capture embedded revisions [8,17], such as correcting a typo while reformulating a larger text segment (see Fig. 2). These accounted for a significant share of annotated revisions (404 out of 1975, see Table 2). We kept unchanged the rule-based approach [7] for detecting revision events' beginning points, as it works both for embedded and non-embedded revisions, but tried different methods for detecting revision end (cf. Sect. 3.3).

Context. We collected data using an online tool integrated into a broader Intelligent Tutoring System designed to help French 10th-grade students bridge learning gaps before entering high school. This tool assesses students' essays using a multi-criteria approach, out of the scope of this paper, while recording keystroke data for research purposes. We conducted experiments with four classes from different high schools in a large metropolitan area, involving 112 students. Each class participated in 1 to 3 sessions ($M = 2.15$, $SD = 0.89$), totaling $N = 295$ texts. In each session, students completed only one of two randomly chosen exercises between two different themes, but in all exercises, the task was the same: students were tasked with composing an argumentative text that coherently connected a given introduction and conclusion. The sessions, held in a classroom setting, lasted 90 min, which the task designers considered sufficient. Observations confirmed that all students submitted their texts before the session ended. Parents of participating students provided informed consent for data collection and research use. Additionally, all texts were reviewed multiple

```
This exercise is complicated.|
This exercise is f| complicated.
-> beginning 1st revision
This exercise is fo| complicated.
-> end 1st revision
This exercise is f| complicated.
-> beginning 2nd revision
This exercise is fa| complicated.
This exercise is far| complicated.
-> end 2nd revision
This exercise is far | complicated.
This exercise is far t| complicated.
This exercise is far to| complicated.
This exercise is far too| complicated.

This exercise is far too complicated.|
...
```

(a) Without ER modeling

```
This exercise is complicated.|
This exercise is f| complicated.
-> beginning 1st revision
This exercise is fo| complicated.

This exercise is f| complicated.
-> beginning 2nd revision
This exercise is fa| complicated.
This exercise is far| complicated.
-> end 2nd revision
This exercise is far | complicated.
This exercise is far t| complicated.
This exercise is far to| complicated.
This exercise is far too| complicated.
-> end 1st revision
This exercise is far too complicated.|
...
```

(b) With ER modeling

Fig. 2. Example of a same multiple revisions episode considering (a) or not (b) embedded revisions (ER) in the model

times to ensure they contained no sensitive information that could compromise author anonymity.

Datasets. The dataset for the revision study was a subset of the original, consisting of 23 texts and 1975 revision events (extracted through the rule-based approach to detect revision beginning points as described earlier), picked among all classes and sessions to avoid bias. We split the data into an 80% training set and a 20% test set, ensuring that each revision event remained entirely within one set, though events from the same text could be in different sets. Table 2 shows the distribution of rows and events across the sets, revealing that the datasets are highly imbalanced: there is the same number of true revision endpoints as the number of revisions among all the rows (i.e. 1975 "1" labels), the others being "0" labels.

To replicate the work of Conijn et al., we used a subset of our original dataset created by adding the constraint that a revision ends when the next one begins, thus reducing from about 1,500,000 rows to 33,000 in subset $\mathcal{A}$ (see Table 2), maintaining 1,975 revision events and 395 for the test set. Moreover, for the analyses that consider the cases of embedded revisions (where a revision can end after the next one begins), it complicates the task, as more keystrokes could be regarded as revision endpoints. To address this, we used a mixed approach to simplify the task for our classifiers and create subset $\mathcal{B}$ (see Table 2). We retained the rule that the latest possible end of a revision is the keystroke where the cursor moves to the leading edge after the revision begins. This rule reduces the dataset size, minimizing model errors while still allowing embedded revisions. This approach reduced the dataset from 1,500,000 to 490,000 keystrokes in subset

Table 2. Dataset Overview for Full, Training, and Test Sets ($N = 295$ texts for all)

Subset	Total Rows	# of revisions	# of embedded revisions
Full Dataset	1,500,000	1,975	404
→ Training Set	1,200,000	1,580	355
→ Test Set	300,000	395	49
Subset $\mathcal{A}$	33,000	1,975	404
→ Training Set	26,500	1,580	355
→ Test Set	6,500	395	49
Subset $\mathcal{B}$	490,000	1,975	404
→ Training Set	397,000	1,580	355
→ Test Set	93,000	395	49

$\mathcal{B}$, while retaining the 1,975 revision events (395 for the test dataset). So, overall we have: $\mathcal{A} \subset \mathcal{B} \subset full$

3.2 Labeling and Evaluation Metrics

Labeling with Human Annotation. To evaluate our revision endpoint prediction models, ground truth labels were required. Three annotators were trained using detailed guidelines and 2–3 iterations on a small text corpus before annotating 23 texts, each covering a different subset via a custom script. Each text was reviewed by at least two annotators. The script navigated to revision start points (identified by the rule-based method) and replayed keystrokes one by one, allowing annotators to mark revision endpoints. This setup also enabled the annotation of embedded revisions – unlike prior work – and allowed reverting to Conijn et al.'s method by limiting revision ends to the onset of the next. We assessed inter-rater agreement using Cohen's kappa, Krippendorff's alpha, and revision distance. Although Krippendorff's alpha is better suited for multiple annotators and missing or ordinal data [2,16], both metrics yielded similar results here due to the binary nature of labels and the predominance of two annotators per instance.

Evaluation Metrics. We evaluated model performance using accuracy, precision, and distance metrics (average, standard deviation, min, max). Since each revision event has one predicted endpoint, recall equaled precision; both were retained for clarity. To capture near-miss predictions, we also reported 1-off and 3-off precision. Due to the dataset's size (1.5M rows) and imbalance, training was conducted on two subsets: $\mathcal{A}$, which follows Conijn et al.'s constraint of non-overlapping revisions, and $\mathcal{B}$, based on our rule-based restriction (see Sect. 3.1). Subset sizes are shown in Table 2.

3.3 Revision End Detection Techniques and Evaluation

Baseline Approach. The baseline model here consists of randomly selecting a revision end from all keystrokes within a given revision event. It is worth noting that it differs from Conijn et al.'s who considered that revision ends when the same number of characters has been inserted as the number of characters deleted.

Rule-Based Approach. We first implemented a rule-based approach derived through inductive reasoning, using simple rules aligned with annotator logic. The dataset's diversity—texts from various students and topics—helped limit overfitting by covering a range of revision behaviors. If a revision starts with a deletion, it ends once a non-backspace is followed by a space and the typed characters roughly match the deleted ones (± 5). If it starts with a cursor move, the revision ends at the next cursor movement. This method, detailed in Algorithms 1–3, was evaluated on the same test sets as the models (subsets $\mathcal{A}$ in 4.2 and $\mathcal{B}$ in 4.3), despite requiring no training. Results were nearly identical on the full dataset ($\pm 1\%$ across metrics).

Algorithm 1. Detect Revision End

```
Require: List of revision events, List of keystrokes
Ensure: List of detected revision endpoints
for all revision_event in revision_events do
    reason ← DetermineBeginningReason(revision_event)
  ▷ "cursor_move", "deletion", or "both"
    if reason = "cursor_move" or reason = "both" then
        revision_end ← FindEndofRevisionMove(revision_event, keystrokes)
    else if reason = "deletion" then
        revision_end ← FindEndOfRevisionDeletion(revision_event, keystrokes)
    end if
    Store revision_end
end for
return detected revision endpoints
```

Algorithm 2. Find End of Revision Move

```
Require: revision_event, List of keystrokes
Ensure: revision_end (position of next cursor move)
for all keystroke in KeystrokesAfter(revision_event) do
    if keystroke is a cursor move then
        return keystroke.id
    end if
end for
return keystroke.id
```

Algorithm 3. Find End of Revision Deletion

```
Require: revision_event, List of keystrokes
Ensure: revision_end (position where deletion sequence ends)
typed_chars ← 0, deleted_chars ← 0
for all keystroke in KeystrokesAfter(revision_event) do
    if keystroke is a character then
        typed_chars ← typed_chars + 1
    else if keystroke is a deletion then
        deleted_chars ← deleted_chars + 1
    end if
    if |typed_chars - deleted_chars| ≤ 5 and keystroke is a space then
        return keystroke.id
    end if
end for
return keystroke.id
```

Binary Classifiers. We also tested revision endpoint prediction using the same classic binary classifiers and keystroke-derived features as in Conijn et al. [7], without incorporating textual input. Four models (SVM, Decision Tree, Random Forest, and XGBoost) were trained using ten-fold stratified cross-validation. Hyperparameters were optimized via Bayesian grid search based on F1 score. Each model outputs a probability for a keystroke being a revision end; the one with the highest probability above an empirically chosen threshold (0.1) is selected. To address dataset imbalance (Table 2), we applied SMOTE during training, omitting some features to preserve plausible synthetic samples.

BERT Fine-Tuning. We also fine-tuned a French BERT model, distilcamembert-base[1], to predict revision endpoints using only text input. Each instance included the text before and after a keystroke, as well as the text at the revision's onset, reflecting the information shown to annotators. Similar to the classifier-based method, the model outputs a probability per keystroke, and the highest value above a threshold is selected as the revision end. A sigmoid layer, thresholding, and maximum selection were applied. Training used binary cross-entropy loss with class weights, dropout for regularization, and was run for three epochs.

Prompting of GPT-4o. We explored predicting revision endpoints using GPT-4o mini via direct prompting [20]. Prompts included the pre- and post-revision text, the text at the keystroke, and the revision reason (deletion, cursor movement, or both), as defined by our rule-based method. To improve efficiency, we batched prompts in groups of ten to minimize system prompt redundancy (see Fig. 3).

[1] https://huggingface.co/cmarkea/distilcamembert-base.

Task Description: A revision occurs when a student deletes, corrects, or reformulates a text, and is considered ended once the change is fully incorporated. If the revision is still in progress, the student has not finished modifying the text. A revision cannot end with an unfinished word.

Input Format:

- **Reason for revision beginning:** `{row['logic_begin']}`
- **Initial text:** `{row['text_start']}`
- **Current text:** `{row['text_end']}`
- **Next text:** `{row['text_next']}`

Response Format (strictly adhere to this format):

```
{ "prediction": 0  or  1,
 "confidence":  a precise float between 0.00 and 1.00 }
```

Example 1:

- Reason for revision beginning: Cursor movement
- Initial text: `"Ths is a test."`
- Current text: `"This is a test."`
- Next text: `"This is a test. "`
- Expected Output: `{ "prediction": 1, "confidence": 0.95 }`

Example 2:

- Reason for revision beginning: Cursor movement
- Initial text: `"I going to school."`
- Current text: `"I a going to school."`
- Next text: `"I am going to school."`
- Expected Output: `{ "prediction": 0, "confidence": 0.10 }`

Example 3:

- Reason for revision beginning: Deletion
- Initial text: `"I am going to school."`
- Current text: `"I am going to scho"`
- Next text: `"I am going to sch"`
- Expected Output: `{ "prediction": 0, "confidence": 0.05 }`

Confidence Guidelines:

- 0.95–1.00: Strong certainty that revision is complete.
- 0.50–0.94: Uncertain cases where completion is not fully clear.
- 0.00–0.49: Strong certainty that revision is ongoing.

Fig. 3. Prompts used for predicting revision ends with GPT-4o mini

4 Results

4.1 Annotation

The dataset of 23 texts was split into five batches and annotated by three annotators. Two showed strong agreement (Cohen's $\kappa = 0.77$), with an average difference of 2 characters between annotated revision ends ($\sigma = 5.5$) and 0.86 agreement within three characters. The third annotator showed lower agreement with the others ($\kappa = 0.40$ and 0.41), with larger endpoint discrepancies and 0.56 and 0.55 agreement within three characters.

4.2 Without Embedded Revisions

Due to the threshold approach, some cases may have no predicted revision end. To ensure models would not perform well by targeting only a subset, we also computed coverage rates (not shown in Table 3). All models exceeded 90% coverage, except the SVM (82%) and the LLM-based model (30%). The rule-based model performed best, predicting the exact keystroke end in 73% of cases, with an average error of 1.45 characters and 90% of ends detected within three keystrokes. Among classifiers, XGBoost led, followed by Random Forest (Conijn's best model). The LLM-based model showed potential but was limited by low coverage. Improvements in prompting (e.g., Chain-of-Thought), model selection, or fine-tuning may enhance it. The BERT-based model performed no better than the random baseline, failing to balance overfitting and learning despite class imbalance.

Table 3. Performance and distance metrics of different models - Subset $\mathcal{A}$

Model	Performance Metrics			Distance (chars)	Precision (-)
	Accuracy	Precision [a]	Recall (See footnote 2)	Avg/STD/Max	1-off/3-off
Baseline	0.90	0.14	0.14	6.30/9.50/89	0.32/0.54
Rule-based	0.97	**0.73**	0.73	1.45/5.12/51	0.83/0.90
Random Forest	0.94	0.46	0.46	2.07/3.63/33	0.63/0.83
Decision Tree	0.93	0.34	0.34	3.17/6.80/99	0.49/0.75
XGBoost	0.94	0.49	0.49	1.96/3.65/32	0.65/0.84
SVM	0.93	0.29	0.29	3.57/7.17/78	0.49/0.72
Bert-Based	0.91	0.14	0.14	7.15/9.57/58	0.29/0.51
LLM-based	0.89	0.39	0.39	2.41/4.12/29	0.60/0.79

[a] See 3.2 for the explanation about precision and recall being equal

4.3 Including Embedded Revisions

This subsection reports results on subset $\mathcal{B}$, which includes embedded revisions (Table 4). Accuracy generally improves, mainly from better prediction of non-revision endpoints. Despite lower precision, top models perform comparably to previous results, even with additional endpoint candidates. The rule-based model remains the best, with XGBoost as the top binary classifier. The LLM-based model performs similarly to Random Forest but still suffers from low coverage (31%).

Table 4. Comparison of different models including embedded revisions-Subset $\mathcal{B}$

Model	Performance Metrics			Distance (chars)	Precision (-)
	Accuracy	Precision (See footnote 2)	Recall (See footnote 2)	Avg/STD/Max	1-off/3-off
Baseline	0.99	0.06	0.06	122.5/178.3/1256	0.13/0.19
Rule-based	0.99	**0.69**	0.69	7.00/38.01/604	0.73/0.79
Random Forest	0.99	0.41	0.41	3.02/5.57/49	0.54/0.74
Decision Tree	0.99	0.30	0.30	4.65/7.14/59	0.39/0.61
XGBoost	0.99	0.44	0.44	2.55/4.87/43	0.58/0.79
SVM	0.99	0.24	0.24	4.83/8.07/92	0.36/0.58
Bert-Based	0.99	0.05	0.05	147.8/190.0/1274	0.11/0.14
LLM-based	0.91	0.31	0.31	3.57/5.40/39	0.51/0.69

Table 5. Comparison of different models predicting embedded revisions only.

Model	Performance Metrics			Distance (chars)	Precision (-)
	Accuracy	Precision (See footnote 2)	Recall (See footnote 2)	Avg/STD/Max	1-off/3-off
Baseline	0.99	0.06	0.06	114.3/163.12/666	0.16/ 0.20
Rule-based	0.99	**0.79**	0.79	5.14/19.19/110	0.82/0.86
Random Forest	0.99	0.50	0.50	2.45/3.86/18	0.53/0.79
Decision Tree	0.99	0.49	0.49	2.65/4.62/18	0.58/0.79
XGBoost	0.99	0.50	0.50	2.32/3.83/18	0.57/0.81
SVM	0.99	0.41	0.41	3.10/4.85/24	0.52/0.79
Bert-Based	0.99	0.03	0.03	133.8/197.7/760	0.11/0.21
LLM-based	0.93	0.27	0.27	5.14/9.85/39	0.50/0.71

Evaluating only embedded revisions from subset $\mathcal{B}$ (49 events) helps assess their detectability (Table 5). Results are slightly better than on the full dataset across most models, with the rule-based model achieving even higher precision than in Table 3, suggesting embedded revisions are not harder to detect. While the rule-based model consistently yields the best precision, it shows larger errors due to lacking a notion of revision duration, unlike binary classifiers.

5 Discussion

The first observation, to answer our first research question, is that the language models as we used them here, without combination with external model, do not seem to outperform more traditional classifier-based approaches. A limitation of our LLM- and BERT-based models is the need to restrict input size around the cursor, hindering full-context interpretation.. Additionally, the imbalanced data issue persists with the BERT model, and while this does not invalidate the approach, the task is difficult with the proposed data representation. Strict boundaries improve performance logically, while the high performance of the rule-based model, even with embedded revisions, offers practical insights and real-world applicability [8,17]. Its explainability is especially valuable, particularly for providing feedback to students on their revision processes.

Regarding our second research question, initial comparisons suggest our binary classifier results differ from those of Conijn et al. However, their model selects all keystrokes above a threshold as possible revision ends, often yielding multiple ends per event, unlike real scenarios with a single true endpoint. In contrast, we predict a single revision end per event. Their reported accuracy is also ambiguous; for instance, "71% of revision ends predicted at the exact location" likely corresponds to precision in our terms. Theoretically, high accuracy is expected due to class imbalance, which inflates true negatives and favors accuracy over precision or recall. Comparing our best 1-off precision (0.83 with the rule-based approach) to their best 1-off accuracy (0.83), our performance appears comparable, though the metrics may not align. Dataset differences may also play a role – Conijn's corpus includes graduate students, likely exhibiting more advanced revision patterns than our high school participants.

Finally, regarding our last research question, we successfully integrated embedded revisions without significantly compromising model performance. This, combined with precise keystroke-level extraction, is essential for accurately identifying revision types. Lacking such granularity can lead to misclassification (e.g., mistaking a long reformulation for a short surface-level revision, as in Conijn et al.). These recurring errors hinder targeted feedback, whether for surface revisions, to address spelling, grammar, or content-level improvements to address coherence, relevance... Unlike draft-based methods [14], which only permit feedback on the product of revision, keystroke-level methods provide access to process-related features (e.g., timing, frequency). This granularity enables feedback that supports students' self-regulation. Grouping embedded revisions into episodes highlights task overlaps and justifies feedback encouraging sequential editing to reduce cognitive load. A simple model could guide students by prioritizing: "Focus first on meaning, then on grammar.". Such low-level analysis also enables fine-grained, dynamic feedback based on individual progress (e.g.,"You've improved your vocabulary choice post-writing," or "Conjugation errors are reduced, though some grammar issues remain."). It will also enable comparison of how the students may change their revision process over time, based on this feedback, an impossibility when only final drafts are considered. These analyses may themselves refine future feedback (e.g. "Congratulations, you've spent more time revising your text, thus correcting most of your conjugation mistakes").

Beyond our research questions, annotator disagreement merits attention. Discrepancies with the third annotator may stem from difficulties using our annotation script for embedded revisions. However, even annotators who generally agreed faced challenges, reflecting the task's complexity. Some cases are clear (e.g., reformulating mid-text and returning to the leading edge), others are more ambiguous, such as when a student deletes and resumes writing at the same point, making it difficult to find the precise end of the revision.

6 Conclusion

This study investigates techniques for predicting revision event positions within keystrokes. Using a manually annotated dataset of 1,975 revision events from 10th-grade French students, we replicated prior research led in English for university students. We explored rule-based, BERT-based, and LLM approaches to try to improve endpoint detection. Beyond replication, we incorporate the previously ignored yet frequent case of embedded revisions, enabling a finer-grained analysis. Our findings show that various models can capture revision patterns, advancing automated analysis and support for student revision practices.

Among the limitations of our study are the restricted student population, which may not encompass the full range of revision behaviors, and the experimental context, which differs from typical usage where students often work partially autonomously at home. We also did not account for recurring revision strategies used by some students (e.g., consistently deleting and retyping words instead of inserting missing characters), which could help improve revision detection in future texts by the same individuals. Additionally, although our language differs from the original study (French vs. English), both are Indo-European languages, and we can reasonably expect other language families to exhibit distinct revision patterns requiring different approaches. Nonetheless, the rule-based model may generalize to other Indo-European languages and users across age groups and educational settings. While results may vary slightly depending on revision type frequencies—particularly for revisions at the leading edge where deletion and addition lengths differ—the current corpus includes all possible revision ending types. A broader limitation of keystroke-based revision analysis is its focus on observable output, whereas revision also involves internal processes such as error detection and diagnosis [12]. These cognitive operations precede observable changes and involve mentally comparing the current text with intended goals. Keystroke analysis cannot capture whether the student correctly understood the assignment or accurately assessed their text at a given moment. However, it does reveal the outcomes of these internal diagnoses. When revisions do not improve the text, it remains unclear whether this results from a poor diagnosis or an ineffective response to an accurate one.

This study's results constitute an essential preliminary step toward a comprehensive automatic revision characterization model, enabling the development of student revision feedback. Our goal is now to automatically classify each revision's nature using various taxonomies. Product-based taxonomies [10] distinguish surface from text-based revisions, with detailed subcategories [9], while process-based taxonomies characterize revisions according to their timing in the writing process [8,17]. Previous work has demonstrated that such classifications can be achieved using trained classifiers or large language models [14,19]. These approaches enable detailed analysis of revision sequences. We aim to advance by developing a feedback model based on concepts introduced here and assessing its effect on student revisions and text quality. Some work has explored this direction, but with less precise revision characterization—a limitation noted by the authors themselves in understanding which revision aspects contribute to text quality and effective feedback [22,23]. Revision, as a complex cognitive process, requires competencies beyond detection [12], including diagnosing gaps between a text and task expectations and knowing when to apply changes. We plan new experiments to investigate these issues further and reflect on effective revision feedback, as well as the extent to which keystroke analysis can sufficiently capture this complexity to enhance students' revision during writing.

References

1. Alamargot, D., Chanquoy, L.: Through the Models of Writing. Studies in Writing, vol. 9. Springer, Dordrecht (2001). https://doi.org/10.1007/978-94-010-0804-4
2. Antoine, J.-Y., Villaneau, J., Lefeuvre, A.: Weighted Krippendorff's alpha is a more reliable metrics for multi-coders ordinal annotations: experimental studies on emotion, opinion and coreference annotation. In: Proceedings of the 14th Conference of the European Chapter of the Association for Computational Linguistics, Gothenburg, Sweden, pp. 550–559 (2014). https://doi.org/10.3115/v1/E14-1058
3. Azevedo, R., et al.: Lessons learned and future directions of MetaTutor: leveraging multichannel data to scaffold self-regulated learning with an intelligent tutoring system. Front. Psychol. **13**, 813632 (2022). https://doi.org/10.3389/fpsyg.2022.813632
4. Baaijen, V.M., Galbraith, D., de Glopper, K.: Keystroke analysis: reflections on procedures and measures. Written Commun. **29**(3), 246–277 (2012)
5. Breetvelt, I., Van Den Bergh, H., Rijlaarsdam, G.: Relations between writing processes and text quality: when and how? Cogn. Instr. **12**(20), 103–123 (1994). https://doi.org/10.1207/s1532690xci12022
6. Connelly, V., Dockrell, J.E., Walter, K., Critten, S.: Predicting the quality of composition and written language bursts from oral language, spelling, and handwriting skills in children with and without specific language impairment. Written Commun. **29**(3), 278–302 (2012). https://doi.org/10.1177/0741088312451109
7. Conijn, R., Speltz, E.D., Chukharev-Hudilainen, E.: Automated extraction of revision events from keystroke data. Reading Writ. (2021). https://doi.org/10.1007/s11145-021-10222-w
8. Conijn, R., Speltz, E.D.: A product- and process-oriented tagset for revisions in writing. Written Commun
9. Du, W., Raheja, V., Kumar, D., Kim, Z.M., Lopez, M., Kang, D.: Understanding iterative revision from human-written text. In: Proceedings of the 60th Annual Meeting of the Association for Computational Linguistics (Volume 1: Long Papers), pp. 3573–3590 (2022). https://doi.org/10.18653/v1/2022.acl-long.250

10. Faigley, L., Witte, S.: "Analyzing Revision." Coll. Compos. Commun. **32** (1981). https://doi.org/10.2307/356602
11. Flower, L., Hayes, J.R.: A cognitive process theory of writing. Coll. Compos. Commun. **32**(4) (1981). https://doi.org/10.2307/356600
12. Flower, L., Hayes, J.R., Carey, L., Schriver, K., Stratman, J.: Detection, diagnosis, and the strategies of revision. Coll. Compos. Commun. **37**(1), 16 (1986). https://doi.org/10.2307/357381
13. Hattie, J., Timperley, H.: The power of feedback. Rev. Educ. Res. **77**(1), 81–112 (2007). https://doi.org/10.3102/003465430298487
14. Kashefi, O., et al.: ArgRewrite V.2: an annotated argumentative revisions corpus. Lang. Resour. Eval. **56**(3), 881–915 (2022). https://doi.org/10.1007/s10579-021-09567-z
15. Kaufer, D.S., Hayes, J.R., Flower, L.: Composing written sentences. Res. Teach. English, 121–140 (1986)
16. Krippendorff, K.: Content Analysis: An Introduction to its Methodology. (Fourth Edition). Sage (2018)
17. Lindgren, E., Sullivan, K.P.H.: Analysing on-line revision. In: Rijlaarsdam, G., Sullivan, K.P.H., Lindgren, E., (eds.) Studies in Writing. Computer Keystroke Logging: Methods and Applications, vol. 18, pp. 157–188 (2006)
18. Raimes, A.: Language proficiency, writing ability, and composing strategies: a study of ESL college student writers. Lang. Learn. **37**(3), 439–468 (1987)
19. Ruan, Q., Kuznetsov, I., Gurevych, I.: Are large language models good classifiers? A study on edit intent classification in scientific document revisions (2024). arXiv: arXiv:2410.02028. https://doi.org/10.48550/arXiv.2410.02028
20. Schulhoff, S., et al.: The prompt report: a systematic survey of prompting techniques (2024). arXiv: arXiv:2406.06608. https://doi.org/10.48550/arXiv.2406.06608
21. de Smet, M.J.R., Leijten, M., Van Waes, L.: Exploring the process of reading during writing using eye tracking and keystroke logging. Written Commun. **35**(4), 411–447 (2018). https://doi.org/10.1177/0741088318788070
22. Vandermeulen, N., Leijten, M., Van Waes, L.: Reporting writing process feedback in the classroom. using keystroke logging data to reflect on writing processes. J. Writ. Res. **12**(1), 109–140 (2020). https://doi.org/10.17239/jowr-2020.12.01.05
23. Vandermeulen, N., Lindgren, E., Waldmann, C., Levlin, M.: Getting a grip on the writing process: (effective) approaches to write argumentative and narrative texts in L1 and L2. J. Second. Lang. Writ. **65**, 101113 (2024). https://doi.org/10.1016/j.jslw.2024.101113
24. Zimmerman, B.J., Schunk, D.H.: Self-regulated learning and performance: an introduction and an overview. Handbook of self-regulation of learning and performance, pp. 15–26 (2011)

Enhancing Student Focus and Problem-Solving with Real-Time LLM Feedback on Compiler Errors

Maciej Pankiewicz[1,2(✉)] and Ryan S. Baker[1]

[1] University of Pennsylvania, Philadelphia, PA, USA
mpank@upenn.edu
[2] Warsaw University of Life Sciences, Warsaw, Poland

Abstract. Programming syntax is highly complex, which has made it consistently difficult to automate feedback for compiler errors in educational settings. Large language models (LLMs) show promise for addressing this issue at scale by providing personalized feedback tailored to specific code submissions, but the effectiveness of this feedback remains uncertain. This study evaluated the impact of GPT-4o at generating real-time feedback for compiler errors during a randomized controlled trial. A total of 248 CS1 students participated, submitting 22,674 pieces of code to an automated programming assessment platform. Students in the Experimental group received LLM feedback, while the Control group did not. Results showed that students who received LLM feedback rated it highly for usefulness, and submitted fewer non-compiling code attempts. These students also had significantly improved performance in terms of resolving errors in consecutive attempts compared to the Control group. Affective surveys revealed that the LLM feedback group self-reported higher focus and lower levels of "confrustion" (a combination of confusion and frustration) after encountering compiler errors. When LLM feedback was temporarily disabled, students in the Experimental group solved programming problems more quickly and demonstrated significant improvement in resolving errors across attempts. However, no significant differences were observed between groups in terms of final scores on a simulated exam. These findings suggest that LLM-generated feedback can improve students' coding experience, engagement, and problem-solving efficiency in the initial phases of computer science education, though it may not lead to better final performance.

Keywords: Automated Assessment · CS1 · Large Language Models · LLM · GPT · Compiler Errors · Automated Feedback

1 Introduction

Feedback is an important feature of self-paced learning environments [31]. Over the years, it has become a key component of various digital learning platforms, including intelligent tutors [14, 31], online courseware [8, 10], and specialized environments for programming education [9, 23, 27]. Despite wide adoption, its effectiveness varies and

K. Tammets et al. (Eds.): EC-TEL 2025, LNCS 16063, pp. 412–426, 2026.
https://doi.org/10.1007/978-3-032-03870-8_28

studies on the effects of feedback have yielded mixed results: some indicate significant gains in learning outcomes and engagement [1, 34], while others highlight potential issues such as misuse or overuse [2].

Crafting a feedback message to help students fix an error in programming code is a complex task. There are three distinct and very broad error categories: syntax (compiler) errors (when code does not compile), runtime errors (when the code compiles but an exception occurs while the program is running), and logic errors (when the program runs but fails to produce the expected result). Generating feedback for each of these areas poses unique challenges. More detailed overview of feedback in programming education can be found in [20].

This paper focuses on automating feedback for compiler (syntax) errors in an introductory programming course (CS1), because the ability to fix them directly impacts early programming success [5, 11]. Fixing a syntax error may be challenging, because compiler messages are often unclear or overwhelming [33], making it difficult for beginners to understand the source of the problem. But generating meaningful feedback that precisely addresses the issue is complicated because of the extensive number of possible syntax errors, variations in message content across different compilers for the same language, the unique nature of individual student submissions, and the fact that interpreting such feedback may require a level of programming knowledge that novices may not yet possess.

Large language models (LLMs) offer promising avenues for tackling these challenges, because of the vast repositories of programming data used to train them [8] and capacity for contextual awareness [28].

Several recent studies have attempted to evaluate the effectiveness of large language models in generating feedback for programming assignments. A common approach in this line of research involves expert evaluation of the feedback content, often resulting in high ratings of its quality [6, 15, 17, 26]. However, while expert assessments provide a valuable indication of the potential of LLMs, several challenges remain regarding their practical utility in educational settings, particularly for novice programmers in introductory courses.

First, positive expert evaluations of LLM-generated feedback do not necessarily indicate that such feedback effectively supports learners with limited programming experience. Prior research has shown that level of expertise influences how effectively LLM-generated assistance can be used [13, 22]. In an experimental lab study with CS1 students, feedback generated by GPT-4 for compiler errors in the C programming language only occasionally outperformed standard compiler error messages. In contrast, human-written explanations surpassed both LLM-generated and conventional messages in both objective and subjective evaluations [32]. Similarly, a two-month study conducted in a CS1 course using C# reported mixed results for GPT-4-generated feedback [25].

Second, while some evidence points to the potential benefits of long-term usage of LLM-generated feedback, such conclusions have typically been drawn from more advanced courses [24]. These courses assume a certain level of prior knowledge, which likely influences how students interpret and act upon feedback. Given that understanding feedback may be closely tied to programming experience, further investigation is needed to determine whether similarly positive long-term effects can be achieved within a CS1 context, especially among students with minimal or no prior programming background.

Third, much of the current research on LLMs in programming education has focused on their implementation as interactive assistants, where students engage in dialogue with the model [4, 18]. While promising, this approach poses significant integration challenges. Many introductory computer science courses rely on structured pedagogical designs, such as scaffolding and worked-out examples. Transitioning to an assistant-based model requires substantial redesign of the course structure and careful validation of its pedagogical effectiveness. As an alternative, integrating LLM-generated feedback into existing automated assessment platforms may offer a more manageable yet still impactful solution – though not without its own challenges.

Overall, past work suggests that a learner's programming experience may significantly affect the effectiveness of LLM feedback for compiler errors, and its long-term impact on the early stages of programming education warrants further investigation. Thus, it remains an open question whether such feedback can consistently support novices at this stage of their learning.

Therefore, in this study, we focus on two main research questions: (1) How do novice CS1 students perceive the quality of LLM-generated feedback delivered on-the-fly for compiler errors? and (2) What are the long-term effects of this feedback on student performance within a platform and learning outcomes? We specifically investigate whether the limitations previously identified in LLM feedback for compiler errors can be mitigated by using GPT-4o, a more recent and advanced model. To this end, we conducted an experimental study using an automated assessment platform, which delivered GPT-4o-generated feedback for student submissions that contained compiler errors.

2 Methods

Data for this study was collected during the first two months of the four-month winter semester of 2024/2025. The participants were computer science students enrolled in a mandatory first-semester course titled "Introduction to Programming" at a large European university. The course focused on programming in C#. A total of 248 students consented to participate and completed a pre-test (8 items, 1 point each) designed to objectively assess their programming knowledge at the start of the semester.

We utilized the RunCode platform [23] for automated assessment of programming assignments, sharing a total of 149 programming problems with students. Usage of the platform was not mandatory, and performance did not count towards the course grade. The following topics were covered: types and variables (33 problems), conditional statement (28), recursion (28), loops (17), and loops with arrays (43).

Assignment difficulty varied, with the easiest problems such as multiplying two integers, to much more difficult, such as extracting and alphabetically sorting words from a given text. All modules containing programming assignments were initially locked (for both groups), requiring students to first solve a sequence of several micro-tasks – simple coding tasks that focus on one particular aspect of the code and require the user to enter (or edit) only one line of the code. They were designed to help students understand how different programming components work one-by-one. An example of such a task could be: "use the = operator and assign a value to the variable *age*". Though completion of the micro-tasks was required to advance to the programming assignments, neither was required as part of the course grade.

The platform's assessment process involved compiling and testing the submitted code. Submissions that failed to compile were marked as *non-compiling*. Feedback included compiler messages for non-compiling code submissions. For compiling submissions students received results for each unit test executed on the code (with input values and expected outcome for each unit test), and overall score (the percentage of unit tests that ended successfully: 0–100%).

While solving assignments on the platform students self-reported their affective states through a dynamic HTML element presented directly after they received submission results with the question: "Choose the option that best describes how you feel at the moment" with the following response options: *Focused*, *Anxious*, *Confused*, *Frustrated*, *Bored*, *Other* (in this order) and appropriate emoticons to visually highlight each of the available responses. This set of affective states was chosen based on their importance for learning [12]. In previous research, it has been found that unresolved confusion and frustration negatively impact learning outcomes in similar ways [16, 19], and theoretical work has argued that extensive empirical evidence demonstrates that the two affective states form a confrustion constellation, where it matters less whether a student is specifically confused or frustrated than details of the experience (such as resolution, duration, interpretation) which produce common results across both affective states [21, 29]. Hence, we decided to combine these affective states prior to our study (but still asked students to self-report using commonly understood terms). To avoid irritation that could arise from being required to fill out the affect survey too frequently, it was not presented after every submission, but randomly, with a probability of 1/10.

Students in the Experimental (GPT) condition additionally received feedback generated automatically using the OpenAI's GPT-4o model for submissions containing compiler errors. Feedback was created via an API request using the approach to prompt generation described in [25] and consisted of the following parts: 1) general instructions for an assistant, 2) text of a programming assignment, 3) student code, 4) list of detected compiler errors. Feedback examples were not added to the prompt, which resulted in more detailed responses from the utilized GPT-4o model. Feedback was displayed to students as a pop-up immediately after submission. Once the pop-up was closed, the feedback remained accessible below the code editor for further review. To evaluate the usefulness of GPT-generated feedback, students in the Experimental group were also presented with a dynamic HTML element prompting them to rate the usefulness of the feedback they received. The rating was collected using a 5-point Likert scale, ranging from "1 – Not useful at all" to "5 – Extremely useful." This survey appeared after every fifth instance of GPT feedback provided to the student. To assess programming competency, a non-graded simulated exam was organized in the middle of the semester (after 2 months), featuring two programming assignments drawn from previous exams: the first focused on loops and numerical arrays, and the second on loops and string operations. These assignments were made available on the platform, and students had the opportunity to complete them within a fixed 60-min timeframe from home, similar to their regular use of the platform. While multiple attempts were allowed, the platform only displayed the total score and did not provide details of the unit tests executed on the code. However, if compiler errors were detected, they were presented to students, just as they would be if the tasks were solved locally on their computers. For these assignments GPT feedback was not provided.

3 Results

In this section, we analyze the reception of the GPT feedback and examine its impact on affect based on student reports after the submission of code containing compiler errors. We further assess student performance on the platform, and for assignments with GPT feedback disabled for the Experimental group.

3.1 Pre-test Scores

To verify that both groups had comparable baseline knowledge prior to the intervention, a Mann-Whitney U test was conducted to compare pre-test scores between the Experimental ($N = 121$, $Mdn = 4$) and Control ($N = 127$, $Mdn = 4$) groups. The results showed no statistically significant difference in pre-test performance between the two groups, ($W = 7502$, $p = 0.748$).

3.2 Usefulness of the GPT Feedback

To evaluate the perceived usefulness of the GPT generated hints, a total of 1036 responses were collected from $N = 62$ students within the Experimental (GPT) group throughout the duration of the study (as a reminder, use of the tool was not mandatory). The Control group did not have access to the GPT feedback; therefore, no responses were recorded from this group. Figure 1 displays the histogram of the frequency of students according to the median rating they gave to received feedback, with the x-axis representing the median of the feedback rating for a student. The majority of students (81%) rated the feedback they received as *very* or *extremely* useful – this shows a positive reception of the GPT feedback feature by students. The usefulness of feedback was rated significantly higher than the neutral midpoint of 3 ($Mdn = 4.5$), as indicated by a one-sample Wilcoxon signed-rank test ($W = 1424.5$, $p < 0.001$).

3.3 Affective States

To understand the impact of the GPT feedback feature on student affect, we performed an analysis of responses in the affect survey displayed after receiving the results for the submission. The most frequently reported state in both conditions was *focused* (56%). A total of 2788 survey responses were collected (Experimental: 1288, Control: 1500) from 117 students (Experimental: 60, Control: 57) during the period of study.

Out of these responses, 1300 (Experimental: 583, Control: 717) were reported directly after receiving feedback for a non-compiling submission. In the following analysis we excluded students with less than 3 responses. To compare differences in

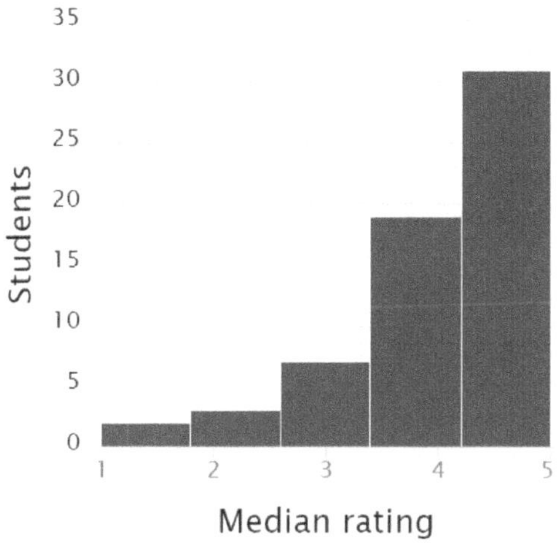

Fig. 1. Distribution of students according to the median rating for received GPT feedback.

the proportions of the affective states reported by each student after a non-compiling submission, non-parametric Mann-Whitney U tests were calculated, due violation of normality assumptions. To control the false discovery rate resulting from multiple comparisons, the Benjamini-Hochberg alpha correction was applied. Two affective states showed marginally significant differences between conditions. For *focused*, students in the Experimental group reported higher rates (Mdn = 0.66, N = 50) than those in the Control group (Mdn = 0.4, N = 46), (W = 1471.5, adjusted $\alpha = 0.0125$, $p = 0.018$, for a non-parametric Mann-Whitney U test). For *confrustion*, students in the Experimental group reported lower rates (Mdn = 0.13) than those in the Control group (Mdn = 0.22), (W = 866.5, adjusted $\alpha = 0.025$, $p = 0.037$, for a non-parametric Mann-Whitney U test). For *anxiety*, the Experimental group reported a median that was not significantly different (Mdn = 0, Mean = 0.04) from the Control group (Mdn = 0, Mean = 0.06), (W = 1054, adjusted $\alpha = 0.05$, $p = 0.364$, for a non-parametric Mann-Whitney U test). The same was true for *boredom* (Exp. Mdn = 0, Mean = 0.05 vs. Contr. Mdn = 0, Mean = 0.04), (W = 1188.5, adjusted $\alpha = 0.075$, $p = 0.694$, for a non-parametric Mann-Whitney U test). The means reflect that there was some small amount of anxiety and boredom despite medians being 0.

3.4 Student Progress on the Platform

During the study period, students performed 22,674 code submissions for programming assignments in modules: types and variables, conditional statement, arrays and loops: in the Control group: 12,226 (N = 78), and in the Experimental (GPT) group: 10,448 (N = 71), with an average of 152.2 submissions per student (Contr. = 157, Exp. = 147.1). There were 9,304 (41%) non-compiling submissions (Contr. = 5,369, Exp. = 3,935). The number of students who submitted code at least once is lower than the total number of students in the experiment, as not all participants joined the platform.

To understand the impact of the automated GPT feedback on student progress within the platform, we analyzed the rate at which students completed programming assignments. We compared the number of successfully solved tasks within the first 200 submissions on the platform, averaging the number of tasks solved per student in each condition. Students supported by GPT feedback for compiler errors seemed to perform slightly better in terms of the number of completed assignments within the first 200 submissions (Fig. 2).

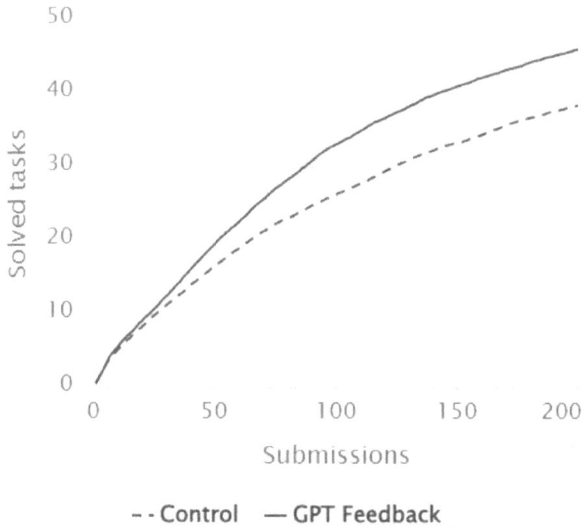

Fig. 2. Relationship between the number of submissions and tasks solved for GPT Feedback and Control Groups (first 200 submissions).

We also compared the total number of completed assignments between both groups. This difference was not statistically significant (GPT Mdn = 50.5, Control Mdn = 41, W = 2900.5, $p = 0.426$ for a non-parametric Mann-Whitney U test).

A rank-based regression analysis was conducted to assess the impact of GPT feedback on the frequency of submissions containing compiler errors, controlling for pre-test scores. The results revealed a significant reduction in the average frequency of non-compiling submissions for participants in the GPT group compared to the Control group ($\beta = -0.049$, $t(145) = -2.01$, $p = 0.047$). Pre-test scores also had a significant negative association with the frequency of errors ($\beta = -0.041$, $t(145) = -7.35$, $p < 0.001$), indicating that higher pre-test scores were linked to fewer errors. The model explained approximately 29.3% of the variation in the frequency of compiler errors ($R^2_{robust} = 0.293$) and was statistically significant overall ($F = 29.47$, $p < 0.001$). These findings suggest that availability of GPT feedback contributed to a measurable reduction in submissions containing compiler errors.

To better understand the trajectory of the intervention's impact, we also compared the frequency of non-compiling submissions across the first 7 attempts on each task for both groups. Frequency was calculated as the ratio of non-compiling submissions to the total number of submissions. For each attempt, we calculated error frequency cumulatively including all submissions up to this attempt. A linear mixed-effects model was conducted to examine the effects of group (GPT vs. Control), attempt, and their interaction on the frequency of non-compiling submissions. The random intercept for participants accounted for variability between students ($\sigma2 = 0.03$), and residual variability was small ($\sigma2 = 0.002$). The results showed that the GPT and Control groups did not differ significantly in their mean frequency of non-compiling submissions at the first attempt (GPT: Mean = 0.43; Control: Mean = 0.39; b = 0.040, SE = 0.029, $t(146) = 1.36$, $p = 0.175$). Additionally, there was no significant main effect of attempt (b = 0.001, SE = 0.001, $t(886) = 1.45$, $p = 0.148$), suggesting that the frequency of non-compiling submissions did not consistently change across attempts. However, a significant interaction between group and attempt (b = −0.011, SE = 0.001, $t(886) = -7.44$, $p < 0.001$) indicated that the GPT group improved over time, with frequency of non-compiling submissions decreasing significantly faster than in the Control group (Fig. 3). These findings highlight the effectiveness of the intervention in reducing non-compiling submissions over consecutive attempts.

3.5 Performance After GPT Feedback Disabled

To understand the potential impact of GPT feedback feature on student performance even after it is no longer available, we analyzed submissions made on a non-graded simulated exam, featuring two programming assignments drawn from previous exams: the first (T1) focused on loops and numerical arrays, and the second (T2) on loops and string operations. For these tasks, GPT feedback was disabled for the Experimental group.

N = 82 students attempted the first task (T1) with 39 students correctly solving the assignment (Control: 21, Experimental: 18) and 74% average score. N = 55 students (Control: 27, Experimental: 28) attempted the second task (T2) and 21 students correctly solved the assignment (Control: 9, Experimental: 12) with 55% average score.

We calculated the total score as the sum of the highest scores obtained for each task and conducted a rank-based regression analysis to examine the effect of group assignment on total scores, while controlling for pre-test scores. The pre-test scores had a positive and significant effect on final scores ($\beta = 0.100$, $t(80) = 4.667$) $p < 0.001$), indicating that higher pre-test scores are associated with higher final scores. However, assignment to the GPT group ($\beta = -0.082$, $t(80) = -0.799$, $p = 0.427$) did not show a statistically significant effect on final scores.

To evaluate differences in terms of non-compiling submissions, we conducted a rank-based regression analysis to examine the effect of group assignment on the frequency of non-compiling submissions, while controlling for pre-test scores. The analysis revealed that pre-test scores had a significant negative effect on the frequency of non-compiling submissions ($\beta = -0.095$, $t(80) = -8.099$, $p < 0.001$), indicating that higher pre-test scores were associated with fewer non-compiling submissions. In contrast, assignment to the GPT group did not have a statistically significant effect ($\beta = 0.043$, $t(80) = 0.772$, $p = 0.442$).

A linear mixed-effects model was conducted to examine the effects of group (GPT vs. Control), attempt, and their interaction on the frequency of non-compiling submissions. The random intercept for participants accounted for variability between students ($\sigma2 =$

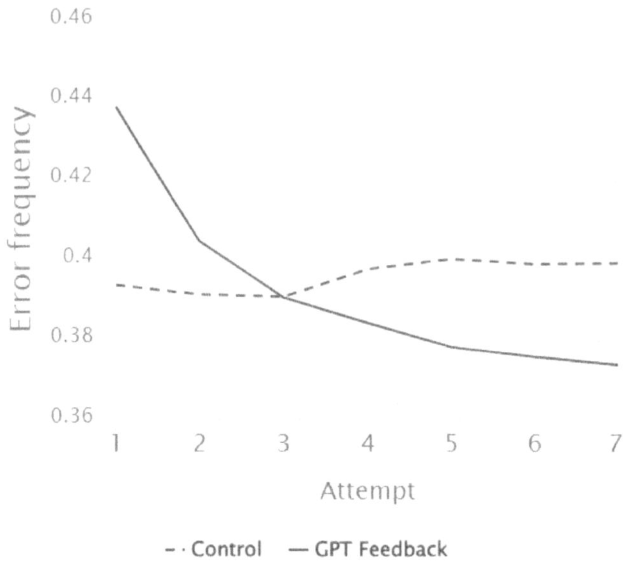

Fig. 3. Error frequency across consecutive attempts for GPT Feedback and Control Groups (assignments with GPT feedback enabled).

0.14), and residual variability was small ($\sigma 2 = 0.01$). The results indicated that there was no significant difference in frequency of non-compiling submissions between the GPT group (Mean = 0.57) and the Control group (Mean = 0.48; b = 0.084, SE = 0.083, $t(83) = 1.02$, $p = 0.312$). However, there was a significant main effect of attempt, with frequency of non-compiling submissions decreasing over time (b = −0.010, SE = 0.003, $t(508) = -3.67$, $p < 0.001$). Importantly, a significant interaction was found between group and attempt (b = −0.013, SE = 0.004, $t(508) = -3.12$, $p = 0.002$), indicating that the GPT group improved at a faster rate than the Control group (Fig. 4).

These findings suggest that even after the GPT feedback was not available, students in the Experimental condition had a reduced frequency of non-compiling submissions over time compared to the Control condition.

3.6 GPT Feedback Disabled – Time to Solve

We further compared both groups in terms of time performance and conducted a rank-based regression analysis to examine the time required to solve each assignment (T1 and T2), controlling for pre-test scores.

For the first task (T1), the analysis revealed that condition significantly predicted the time needed to complete the assignment, with participants in the GPT condition showing a significant reduction in completion time compared to those in the Control condition ($\beta = -567.81$, $t(36) = -2.832$, $p = 0.007$). Pre-test scores, however, did not have a significant effect on ranked assignment completion time, ($\beta = -38.448$, $t(36) = -0.888$, $p = 0.38$).

To complement the rank-based regression results, we calculated the means of completion times: 1645 s (27 m) for the Experimental (GPT) group and 1992 s (33 m) for the

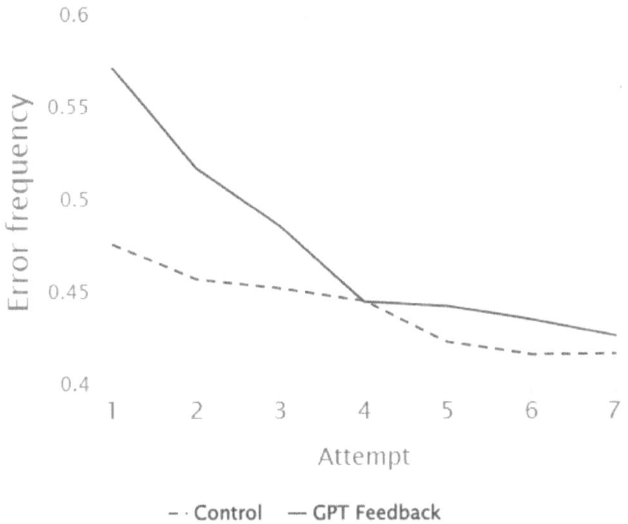

Fig. 4. Error frequency across consecutive attempts for GPT Feedback and Control Groups (GPT feedback disabled).

Control group. While rank-based regression is robust to outliers, its coefficients reflect relative differences in ranks rather than absolute values, limiting interpretability on the original scale. Means provide a clearer sense of the practical differences between groups.

For the second task (T2), we applied the same rank-based regression method. The results indicated a marginal effect of group membership, with participants in the GPT condition showing a potential (marginally significant) reduction in ranked completion time compared to the Control group ($\beta = -642.94$, $t(18) = -2.037$, $p = 0.057$). Pre-test scores again did not significantly predict ranked completion time ($\beta = -92.93$, $t(18) = -0.985$, $p = 0.337$). The mean completion time for the GPT condition was 1489 s (25 m), while the Control group had a mean completion time of 1854 s. (31 m). These findings suggest that, after controlling for pre-test scores, condition was a significant factor influencing assignment completion time in terms of rank order, with participants in the GPT condition generally completing the assignment faster than those in the Control group. On average, in the GPT group it took 20 m 22 s to perform the first submission for task T1, and 21 m 43 s in the Control condition. For task T2, GPT condition needed 22 m 43 s, and Control group 26 m 21 s to perform the first submissions. For both tasks, consecutive submissions happened earlier in the GPT condition than in the Control group. Results are presented on Fig. 5.

These findings suggest that, after controlling for pre-test scores, the earlier presence of GPT feedback was a significant factor influencing later assignment completion time (without GPT feedback), with participants in the GPT group generally completing the assignment faster than those in the Control group. This finding is similar to [24], where a significant improvement in terms of time needed to solve was observed for assignments on which GPT feedback was disabled.

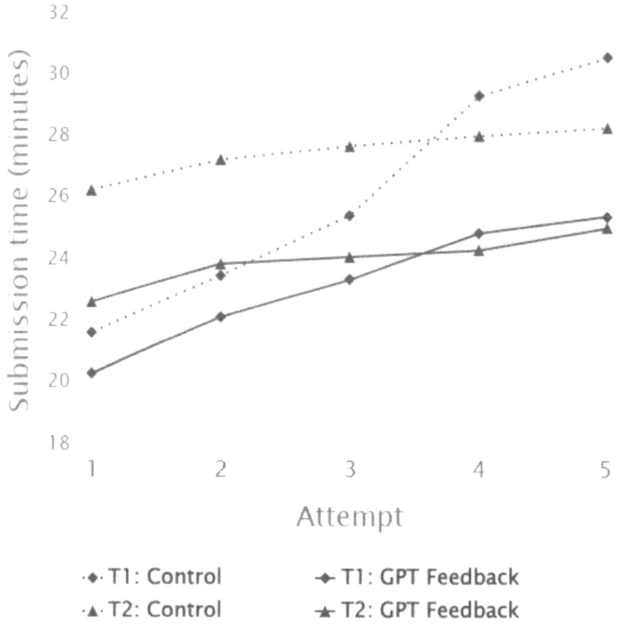

Fig. 5. Submission time across attempts for tasks T1 and T2 in GPT Feedback and Control Groups.

4 Discussion

In this study, GPT-4o was used to automate feedback generation for non-compiling submissions on the platform for automated assessment of programming assignments. According to survey responses, a significant majority of students (81%) rated the usefulness of feedback positively and only 8% did not find it beneficial. The student ratings were significantly higher than the neutral midpoint and better than in past studies involving GPT feedback for programming assignments [24, 25].

Compared to previous studies, our method differed in several ways: 1) the use of the GPT-4o model, improved compared to the older GPT-4 and GPT-3.5 models, 2) a more extended intervention, involving a wide range of assignments of various difficulty, 3) rather than turning off GPT feedback at the halfway point and evaluating performance after that point (as in [25]), we tested the effectiveness of the intervention on a separate set of tasks, at the same time for all students.

We found that students in the GPT condition significantly less frequently submitted non-compiling code when GPT feedback was available. Additionally, the frequency of non-compiling submissions decreased significantly faster in GPT group. For assignments with GPT disabled for the Experimental group, this effect persisted, and the GPT condition again resulted in significantly faster decrease in the frequency of non-compiling submissions across consecutive attempts, compared to the Control group. Additionally, we observed that students in the GPT condition needed significantly less time to complete assignments when GPT was disabled. However, these shorter-term benefits did not result in higher final scores on a simulated exam for the GPT condition, and neither condition was at ceiling, suggesting that the GPT condition was not successful at producing better learning that transferred to an external task.

According to student self-reports, the availability of GPT feedback led to significant differences in terms of higher levels of focus and lower levels of *confrustion*. This was a positive outcome of the intervention – according to the literature, increased focus has been often found to be positively associated with learning [7, 30], while *confrustion* has a more complex and often negative relationship to learning [3].

Previous studies on GPT feedback for programming assignments in CS1 showed mixed results. It has been reported that GPT-4 feedback for the C language outperformed standard compiler messages only in 1 out of 6 tasks, measured by student's time-to-fix each problem, and handwritten explanations outperformed the LLM messages [32]. According to [25], GPT-4 messages for C# language also were not equally good in addressing all compiler errors and did not effectively help students resolve errors requiring deeper understanding of data types.

In this study, we utilized the newest GPT-4o model, to investigate whether it led to better results than its predecessor. We offered GPT feedback for a larger set of CS1 assignments of more varied difficulty. We attempted to provide a thorough evaluation of the observed impact from many different angles: feedback reception (perceived usefulness), effectiveness (ability to improve non-compiling submissions in consecutive attempts), and learning transfer and outcomes (if the effect of the intervention persists to later tasks where the feedback is no longer given). Our study demonstrates the potential of the GPT-4o model to significantly enhance the learning experience in introductory programming courses by producing a persisting reduction of non-compiling submissions, fostering focus, and decreasing confusion/frustration, while suggesting that the ultimate goal of better learning outcomes has still not been reached.

This study has several limitations that will necessitate further investigation. It was conducted over a period of only two months, covering half of the four-month semester. Future research should investigate the long-term effects of GPT feedback on student performance and learning outcomes across semesters or academic years. Another limitation is the sample size and single setting, which may impact the robustness and generalizability of the findings. Future studies should replicate this intervention with larger and more diverse participant groups to enhance external validity. Additionally, this study focused solely on C#, while introductory computer science courses often involve other programming languages, such as Java and C++. Expanding future research to include a wider range of programming languages and more demanding courses, such as data structures and algorithms, would provide a more comprehensive understanding of the efficacy and applicability of GPT feedback across different CS contexts.

Overall, this study suggests that using an LLM to automate feedback generation can offer benefits for both performance and emotional engagement in the initial phases of programming education, potentially reducing barriers and making CS education more accessible. However, there remains considerable room for improvement.

References

1. Aleven, V., et al.: Example-tracing tutors: intelligent tutor development for non-programmers. Int. J. Artif. Intell. Educ. **26**, 224–269 (2016)
2. Aleven, V., et al.: Help helps, but only so much: research on help seeking with intelligent tutoring systems. Int. J. Artif. Intell. Educ. **26**, 205–223 (2016)
3. Baker, R.S., et al.: The Confrustion Constellation: A New Way of Looking at Confusion and Frustration. https://osf.io/4rgtk, https://doi.org/10.35542/osf.io/4rgtk
4. Bassner, P., et al.: Iris: an AI-driven virtual tutor for computer science education. In: Proceedings of the 2024 on Innovation and Technology in Computer Science Education, vol. 1, pp. 394–400. Association for Computing Machinery, New York, NY, USA (2024). https://doi.org/10.1145/3649217.3653543
5. Becker, B.A., et al.: Compiler error messages considered unhelpful: the landscape of text-based programming error message research. In: Proceedings of the Working Group Reports on Innovation and Technology in Computer Science Education. pp. 177–210. Association for Computing Machinery, New York, NY, USA (2019). https://doi.org/10.1145/3344429.3372508
6. Chapagain, J., et al.: A study of LLM generated line-by-line explanations in the context of conversational program comprehension tutoring systems. In: Ferreira Mello, R., et al. (eds.) Technology Enhanced Learning for Inclusive and Equitable Quality Education. EC-TEL 2024. LNCS, vol. 15159, pp. 64–74. Springer, Cham (2024). https://doi.org/10.1007/978-3-031-72315-5_5
7. Fancsali, S.: Causal discovery with models: behavior, affect, and learning in cognitive tutor algebra. In: Educational Data Mining 2014 (2014)
8. Finnie-Ansley, J., et al.: The robots are coming: exploring the implications of OpenAI codex on introductory programming. In: Proceedings of the 24th Australasian Computing Education Conference, pp. 10–19 ACM, New York, NY, USA (2022). https://doi.org/10.1145/3511861.3511863
9. Gabbay, H., Cohen, A.: Exploring the connections between the use of an automated feedback system and learning behavior in a MOOC for programming. In: Hilliger, I., Muñoz-Merino, P.J., De Laet, T., Ortega-Arranz, A., Farrell, T. (eds.) Educating for a New Future: Making Sense of Technology-Enhanced Learning Adoption. EC-TEL 2022. LNCS, vol. 13450, pp. 116–130. Springer, Cham (2022). https://doi.org/10.1007/978-3-031-16290-9_9
10. Goldin, I., et al.: Hints: you can't have just one. In: Educational Data Mining 2013. (2013)
11. Jadud, M.C., Dorn, B.: Aggregate compilation behavior. In: Proceedings of the eleventh annual International Conference on International Computing Education Research, pp. 131–139 ACM, New York, NY, USA (2015). https://doi.org/10.1145/2787622.2787718
12. Karumbaiah, S., et al.: How does students' affect in virtual learning relate to their outcomes? A systematic review challenging the positive-negative dichotomy. In: Proceedings of the International Learning Analytics and Knowledge Conference, pp. 24–33 (2022)
13. Kiesler, N., et al.: Novice learners of programming and generative AI - prior knowledge matters. In: Proceedings of the 24th Koli Calling International Conference on Computing Education Research. Association for Computing Machinery, New York, NY, USA (2024). https://doi.org/10.1145/3699538.3699580
14. Koedinger, K.R., Corbett, A.: Cognitive tutors. Cambridge Handb. Learn. Sci. 61–78 (2005). https://doi.org/10.1017/CBO9780511816833.006
15. Koutcheme, C. et al.: Open source language models can provide feedback: evaluating LLMs' ability to help students Using GPT-4-As-A-Judge. In: Proceedings of the 2024 on Innovation and Technology in Computer Science Education, vol. 1, pp. 52–58. Association for Computing Machinery, New York, NY, USA (2024). https://doi.org/10.1145/3649217.3653612

16. Lee, D.M.C., et al.: Exploring the relationship between novice programmer confusion and achievement. In: Affective Computing and Intelligent Interaction: 4th International Conference, ACII 2011, Memphis, TN, USA, pp. 175–184 (2011)
17. Leinonen, J., et al.: Using large language models to enhance programming error messages. In: Proceedings of the 54th ACM Technical Symposium on Computer Science Education, vol. 1, pp. 563–569. Association for Computing Machinery, New York, NY, USA (2023). https://doi.org/10.1145/3545945.3569770
18. Liu, R., et al.: Teaching CS50 with AI: leveraging generative artificial intelligence in computer science education. In: Proceedings of the 55th ACM Technical Symposium on Computer Science Education, vol. 1, pp. 750–756 Association for Computing Machinery, New York, NY, USA (2024). https://doi.org/10.1145/3626252.3630938
19. Liu, Z., et al.: Sequences of frustration and confusion, and learning. In: Proceedings of the 6th International Conference on Educational Data Mining, pp. 114–120 (2013)
20. Lohr, D., et al.: You're (Not) my type- can LLMs generate feedback of specific types for introductory programming tasks? J. Comput. Assist. Learn. **41**(1), e13107 (2025). https://doi.org/10.1111/jcal.13107
21. Mogessie, M., et al.: Confrustion and gaming while learning with erroneous examples in a decimals game. In: Artificial Intelligence in Education: 21st International Conference, AIED 2020, pp. 208–213 (2020)
22. Moradi Dakhel, A., et al.: GitHub copilot AI pair programmer: asset or liability? J. Syst. Softw. **203**, 111734 (2023). https://doi.org/10.1016/j.jss.2023.111734
23. Pankiewicz, M., et al.: Using intelligent tutoring on the first steps of learning to program: affective and learning outcomes. In: Artificial Intelligence in Education: 24th International Conference, AIED 2023, pp. 593–598 (2023). https://doi.org/10.1007/978-3-031-36336-8_92
24. Pankiewicz, M., Baker, R.S.: Large Language Models (GPT) for automating feedback on programming assignments. In: 31st International Conference on Computers in Education Conference Proceedings, Volume I, pp. 68–77 (2023)
25. Pankiewicz, M., Baker, R.S.: Navigating compiler errors with AI assistance - a study of GPT hints in an introductory programming course. In: Proceedings of the 2024 on Innovation and Technology in Computer Science Education, vol. 1, pp. 94–100. Association for Computing Machinery, New York, NY, USA (2024). https://doi.org/10.1145/3649217.3653608
26. Phung, T., et al.: Generating high-precision feedback for programming syntax errors using large language models. In: Feng, M., et al. (eds.) Proceedings of the 16th International Conference on Educational Data Mining, pp. 370–377 International Educational Data Mining Society, Bengaluru, India (2023). https://doi.org/10.5281/zenodo.8115653
27. Price, T.W., et al.: iSnap: towards intelligent tutoring in novice programming environments. In: Proceedings of the 2017 ACM SIGCSE Technical Symposium on Computer Science Education, pp. 483–488 (2017)
28. Radford, A., et al.: Language models are unsupervised multitask learners. OpenAI blog **1**(8), 9 (2019)
29. Richey, J.E., et al.: Gaming and confrustion explains learning advantages for a math digital learning game. In: Proceedings of the International Conference on Artificial Intelligence and Education (2021)
30. Rodrigo, M.M.T., et al.: Affective and behavioral predictors of novice programmer achievement. In: Proceedings of the 14th Annual ACM SIGCSE Conference on Innovation and Technology in Computer Science Education, pp. 156–160 Association for Computing Machinery, New York, NY, USA (2009). https://doi.org/10.1145/1562877.1562929
31. Roll, I., et al.: Improving students' help-seeking skills using metacognitive feedback in an intelligent tutoring system. Learn. Instr. **21**(2), 267–280 (2011)

32. Santos, E.A., Becker, B.A.: Not the silver bullet: LLM-enhanced programming error messages are ineffective in practice. In: Proceedings of the 2024 Conference on United Kingdom \& Ireland Computing Education Research. Association for Computing Machinery, New York, NY, USA (2024). https://doi.org/10.1145/3689535.3689554
33. Traver, V.J.: On compiler error messages: what they say and what they mean. Adv. Hum.-Comp. Int. **2010** (2010). https://doi.org/10.1155/2010/602570
34. VanLehn, K.: The relative effectiveness of human tutoring, intelligent tutoring systems, and other tutoring systems. Educ. Psychol. **46**(4), 197–221 (2011)

Code-Aware LLM Prompting in Deductive Qualitative Analysis: A Study in Multi-framework Analysis of Learning Designs

María Jesús Rodríguez Triana[1(✉)], Mohamed Saban[1], Juan I. Asensio-Pérez[1], Luis P. Prieto[1], Inmaculada Haba-Ortuo[1], Cristina Villa-Torrano[1], and Denis Gillet[2]

[1] GSIC-EMIC, Universidad de Valladolid, Valladolid, Spain
{mjrodtri,mohamed.saban,luispablo.prieto,ic.haba.ortuno}@uva.es, juaase@tel.uva.es, cristina@gsic.uva.es

[2] REACT, École Polytechnique Fédérale de Lausanne, Lausanne, Switzerland
denis.gillet@epfl.ch

Abstract. Large Language Models (LLMs) have demonstrated potential for (semi-)automating the qualitative analysis of unstructured data, particularly in deductive qualitative coding using codebooks. While prior research has shown the feasibility of this technology, model performance seems to vary depending on the nature of the constructs being coded. However, existing approaches typically apply a single LLM prompting strategy across entire datasets, often of discourse transcripts or questionnaire data, using a single coding scheme or theoretical frame. This paper introduces an adaptive prompting approach where LLM prompts are customized based on researcher-defined or data-driven rules for specific codes. We apply this approach to analyze the description of 35 multimedia learning designs (comprising 758 items/activities) created by teachers in an inquiry-based learning digital platform. Two human coders and an open-weights LLM (Llama 3.3) coded the dataset attending to three different pedagogical frameworks. Our results indicate that data-driven adaptive prompting outperforms uniform prompting approaches (namely, zero-shot, few-shot with/without context) in terms of agreement with human coders and cost. While the improvement is not statistically significant, the approach offers potential advantages for large datasets (especially, considering the costs), highlighting opportunities for human-AI collaboration in educational data analysis.

Keywords: Qualitative coding · Large Language Models · Human-AI collaboration · Learning Design · Learning Analytics

1 Introduction

Large Language Models (LLMs) have shown promise in assisting humans when coding qualitative data, a key task ind educational research known for its high

K. Tammets et al. (Eds.): EC-TEL 2025, LNCS 16063, pp. 427–441, 2026.
https://doi.org/10.1007/978-3-032-03870-8_29

workloads and reliability concerns [17]. Based on the use of LLMs, novel models of Human-AI collaboration are being explored for qualitative codebook development in thematic analysis (see, e.g., [4,5]) or for sharing the burden of the actual coding of large datasets (see, e.g., [2,20]). Frameworks have also emerged to evaluate codebook utility as well as coding reliability and consistency using LLMs [1]. Much of this research focuses on the performance of LLMs when using different prompting strategies. In the specific case of so-called deductive coding [7], where datasets are analyzed using a predefined set of codes (typically derived from theoretical frameworks of interest), previous research has explored different dimensions of LLM prompting strategies. For example, [20] and [13] analyze the impact of the number of examples included in the prompt (comparing zero-shot vs. few-shot). Other works, such as [6] and [2], evaluate prompts that implement the chain-of-thought approach [18], where the LLM decomposes the coding task into smaller sub-tasks and provides the rationale for each coding result. However, to the best of our knowledge, all reported studies about the use of LLMs for qualitative coding use a single prompting strategy to apply the codebook to the target dataset. In some cases, such as in [2], different prompts are built for different datasets but the same prompt is applied for all the codes that need to be identified in each of the datasets. Only in [13], a work recently expanded in [12], the authors look at the code differences (regarding clarity, concreteness, objectivity, granularity, and specificity) to analyze the obtained results when applying a particular prompting strategy. While the authors apply the same prompt to all the codes in each coding run, their results suggests that the effectiveness of different LLM prompting strategies seems to vary depending on the nature of the code/construct being coded. Yet, to the best of our knowledge, no research in educational technology has used an *adaptive* prompting strategy for deductive qualitative coding, adjusting the prompting strategy based on the specific code/construct, assessed the implications in coding accuracy and resource consumption (e.g., time and computing demands).

To fill the aforementioned gap, this paper explores the following research question: **can a code-specific prompting strategy improve deductive coding of qualitative educational data carried out by LLMs, compared to using a single prompt for all codes?** In this context, "improvement" means higher agreement between a human-agreed "ground truth" and LLM coding results, balanced against the resources required by each prompting strategy.

This paper explores two code-specific adaptive prompting strategies –human expert-derived and data-driven–on a dataset of 35 multimedia learning designs (comprising 758 items/activities) created in Graasp, a tool especially devoted to supporting inquiry-based learning (IBL). The analysis uses a 13-code codebook from three theoretical frameworks about student engagement, the social level of the learning activity [11], and the associated IBL phases [14]. In the expert-derived adaptive prompting, expert human coders selected one of three prompting strategies (zero-shot, few-shot, and few-shot with context prompting [13]) for each code based on information needs and difficulty experienced during the analysis of each code. The adaptive data-driven approach used a sub-dataset (of 2 designs and 89 items, purposefully selected by experts) to assess the agreement with human coders of each one of the strategies, to inform which strategy to use for each code in the full dataset. LLM coding results with adaptive code-specific prompting were compared against three uniform prompting strategies applied across all codes. Agreement between human coders and LLMs, as well as the cost in tokens and time, were measured. The paper discusses the benefits of each strategy and highlights implications for deductive coding of large educational datasets, offering insights for researchers using LLMs for such purposes.

2 Methods

2.1 Coding Task, Dataset, and Codebook

This paper is part of a larger project analyzing over 17,000 Inquiry-Based Learning (IBL) designs created by educators in English. As a first step towards the automation of such analysis, here we focus on a content analysis task aimed at understanding whether a representative subset of those designs actually scaffold inquiry, promote engagement, and support collaboration among learners (see [15] for a detailed description of the original coding task).

The current coding task analyzes 35 multimedia learning designs created in English by primary and secondary teachers using Graasp[1], an authoring tool developed in the context of the Go-Lab European Initiative[2] to promote IBL. Learning designs created with Graasp are usually structured according to well-established phases of an inquiry process (orientation, conceptualization, investigation, conclusion, and discussion) and enriched by the teachers with multimedia items made of instructions and embedded artefacts (e.g., images, videos, external websites) or apps (e.g., IBL-specific apps, labs, or third party tools) to help students with learning activities. The 35 analyzed learning designs comprise a total of 758 such items. In our previous work, we tried to code the designs using either the whole design or its phases as units of analysis. However, it was difficult to spot the pieces of evidence that led us to allocate the different codes. Thus, we decided to use the *item* as the unit of analysis and later aggregate the item codes to enable the analyses at the phase or the design level.

One key aspect of the our dataset is the items complexity. Unlike previous TEL studies focus on purely textual (e.g., transcript) data, where each item corresponds with a piece of the discourse, each item here is characterized by several fields (see Fig. 1), including the learning design where they belong, the item name, its type (i.e., whether its a phase, a resource or an app), its description and content (in case of embedded resources such as documents), the item MIME type (in case of embedded resources) and its URL (in case of embedded resources/apps). Since processing all this information could be challenging and time-consuming for both humans and LLMs, we excluded certain fields and pre-processed others to facilitate the coding. First, we extracted the *task description*

[1] https://graasp.org (formerly https://graasp.eu).
[2] https://www.golabz.eu.

by concatenating the item description and its content. Then, to have a better understanding of the embedded artifacts, we provided a textual description of the MIME type, extracted the artifact description if available in the project repository, and provided a domain description for the rest of the URLs. With these three fields, we generated the *embedded artifact description*, extracting the repository description if available, using domain descriptions for the rest of the URLs, and the media type description if the domain description was unavailable.

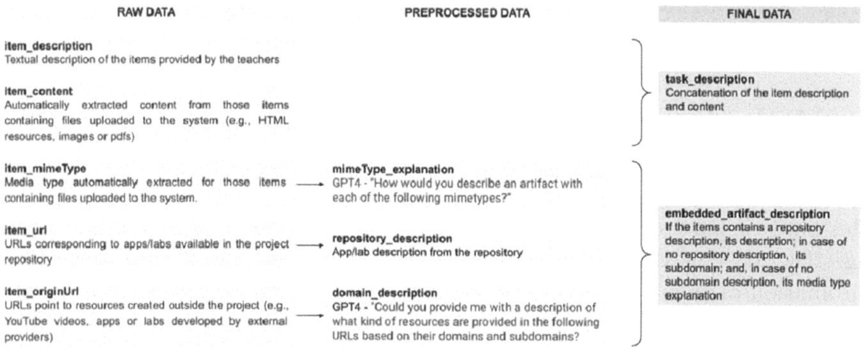

Fig. 1. Overview of the raw data extracted for each item (left), how it was preprocessed (middle), and which fields were finally included in the prompts (right).

For the content analysis of the 758 items, the researchers in [15] developed a codebook composed of 13 codes grounded on three different theoretical frameworks modelling the student engagement [3] (passive, active, constructive and interactive), the social level of the learning activities [11] (individual activity, individual product, collective activity, and collective product), and the phases of IBL scaffolding [14] (orientation, conceptualization, investigation, conclusion and discussion). Table 1 shows a description of these codes.

Two researchers (referred to, from now on, as the "human experts") with previous experience in deductive coding and knowledge of the aforementioned frameworks, independently coded the 758 items, taking them 254 and 256 min, respectively. Table 1 shows the agreement between human coder for each code. The codes vary in prevalence (from 35 to 249 appearances across the 758 items) and coding difficulty (with Cohen's Kappa between 0.536 and 0.796, and Gwet's AC1 between 0.811 and 0.966). Calculated Gwet's AC1 inter-rater reliability coefficients tend to be higher than those calculated with Cohen's Kappa. This may happen because the data is highly imbalanced, a well-known problem when using Cohen's Kappa (see, e.g., [19] or [9]). Thus, while we report both metrics for comparison with other studies, we used Gwet's AC1 as the main metric to assess the agreement between humans and LLMs, and to guide our decisions about the prompting. After the coding process reported in Table 1 was completed, the researchers discussed each disagreement and reached a joint decision. These agreed-upon decisions served as our "ground truth".

During the coding process, the experts noted that some codes required frequent checks of examples to better understand inclusion/exclusion criteria, particularly for passive learning, orientation, investigation, conclusion, and discussion. Additionally, the human coders initially attempted to code each item in an isolated manner and, later, taking into account what had already happened in previous items of the learning design. In this process, they noticed that having that additional context in mind made the coding much easier and increased the frequency of certain codes (namely, passive, constructive, interactive, individual activity, individual product, and discussion). These needs reported by the experts ("context-awareness" or "examples") are summarized in Table 1.

2.2 LLM Coding Procedure

The experiments were conducted using Llama 3.3:70b, an open-source model, on a server with an Intel Xeon Silver 4210, 120 GB RAM, and two QUADRO RTX5000 16 GB GPUs hosted in our premises. This setup allowed for data privacy, full control over the environment, and reproducibility of the experiments. Prompts were adapted from those proposed by [13] for zero-shot, few-shot and with context, tailored to the coding goals and resulting in the following ones:

- **Prompt for zero-shot**: This method took each code one at a time, along with the corresponding definition, and then asked the LLM to code each item using the following prompt:

```
"You are a qualitative coding expert. You are assessing the student
engagement of learning activities created by teachers in an inquiry-
based learning digital platform. These activities may have different
media content including text and embedded artifacts (e.g., images,
videos, apps, labs). Please review the provided activity description
and code it based on the construct: {construct}.
The definition of this construct is {definition}.
After reviewing the text, assign a code of '1' if you believe the
text exemplifies {construct}, or a '0' if it does not. Your response
should only be '1' or '0'."
```

- **Prompt for few-shot**: This approach used the same prompt as the zero-shot, but including annotated examples for each of the constructs. Below are three annotated examples for the construct *collective product*.

```
"[...] Please review the provided activity description and code it
based on the construct: collective product.
The definition of this construct is: Learners are asked to produce
an artifact with other people (e.g., other peers, teacher, parents,
external people).
Here you have some examples:
   TASK DESCRIPTION:
   English text devoted to students that:
   1) requires collective artifact generation with peers such
   as joint reports, slides, concept maps, ... For example:
   "In groups, create a report [...]"; "Prepare a joint presentation
   [...]"
```

Table 1. Code overview based on their frequency (out of 758 items), human inter-rater reliability measures (Cohen's Kappa and Gwet's AC1), and experts' needs while coding.

Codes	Description	Frequency (out of 758 items)	Human coders' Kappa	Human coders' Gwet AC1	Coders' needs
passive	Learners being oriented toward and receiving information from the instructional materials without overtly doing anything else related to learning.	171	0.767	0.874	context-awareness
active	Learners do some form of overt motoric action or physical manipulation without necessarily entailing the production of an artifact.	49	0.594	0.939	–
constructive	Learners generate or produce additional externalized outputs or products beyond what was provided in the learning materials.	214	0.762	0.834	context-awareness
interactive	Learners dialogue with another person, device, learning environment, or system (e.g., a chatbot). Also, if a learning environment or computer-based system expects a response from the user, and provides feedback to that response. It does not necessarily entail the creation of an artifact.	97	0.770	0.934	context-awareness
individual activity	Learners are asked to accomplish certain activities individually, not involving the creation of an artifact.	227	0.756	0.822	context-awareness
individual product	The participating students were asked to produce an individual artifact.	249	0.762	0.811	context-awareness
collective activity	Learners are asked to only accomplish certain activities with other people (e.g., other peers, teachers, parents, external people), not involving the creation of an artifact.	36	0.536	0.947	–
collective product	Learners are asked to produce an artifact with other people (e.g., other peers, teacher, parents, external people)	35	0.577	0.963	–
orientation	The process of stimulating curiosity about a topic and addressing a learning challenge through a problem statement.	166	0.712	0.852	examples
conceptualisation	The process of generating research questions and/or hypotheses regarding a stated problem.	45	0.737	0.966	–
investigation	The process of planning exploration or experimentation, collecting and analyzing data based on the experimental design or exploration.	122	0.666	0.875	examples
conclusion	The process of drawing conclusions from the data. Comparing inferences made based on data with hypotheses or research questions.	43	0.597	0.953	examples
discussion	The process of presenting findings of particular phases or the whole inquiry cycle by communicating with others and/or engaging in reflective activities about the whole learning process or its phases.	137	0.796	0.919	context-awareness

```
    Caution:
    1) items not requesting collaboration with other peers but
    with other stakeholders shout NOT be coded "Collective product",
    as in "ask your teacher for an account"
    2) If creating the product in groups is optional, shout NOT
    be coded "Collective product"
[...]"
```

- **Prompt for few-shot with context**: In this case, we added context to the construct definition and annotated examples. As mentioned previously, the experts realized that having the context (i.e., information from the previous items of the same learning design) made the coding much easier and accurate. Therefore, we included a summary of the three previous items. The summary was previously obtained by asking Llama to generate a summary of the task description and the embedded artifacts of the selected items, using no more than 50 words. Below is an example of this approach:

```
"[...] Please review the provided activity description and code it
based on the construct: individual product.
The definition of this construct is: The participating students were
asked to produce an individual artifact.
Here you have some examples:
    TASK DESCRIPTION:
    English text devoted to students that:
    1) requires individual artifact generation. For example:
    "Write down your measurements in the following table"; "Through
    the different objects and report your observations in the
    following tool"; "Answer the following questions"; "Create
    a report summarizing your investigation";
    2) prompt the students to verbalize their ideas/thoughts.
    For example: "Draw your initial thoughts and ideas"; "Share
    your thoughts/ideas/suggestions of [...]"
    Caution:
    1) If the text also entails collective product generation
    should NOT be coded as "individual product".
For additional context, here is a summary of the 3 previous items:
    Students received tasks with descriptions and used Golabz
    apps like SpeakUp and Input Box for interactive discussions
    and note-taking.
[...]"
```

Then, to answer our RQ, we followed three different coding strategies, as illustrated in Fig. 2:

- *Uniform prompt for all codes*: This is the common approach observed in the literature, where the same prompt (zero-shot, few-shot and few-shot with context) is used for all the codes.
- *Expert-driven prompt selection per code*: In this case, for each code, the two expert coders selected the prompt that they considered more suitable

according to their needs in terms of examples and context awareness (as reported in Table 1). The few-shot prompt was applied to codes requiring examples, while the few-shot with context was used in the case of codes requiring context. The zero-shot prompt was applied to the remaining codes.

- *Data-driven prompt selection per code*: In this strategy, the code selection is based on a preliminary analysis of a subset of two designs (purposefully selected to contain examples of each code) with a total of 89 items. For this subset, we coded each item with the three prompts. Then, for each code, we selected the best-performing prompt (in terms of agreement, see Fig. 3) and, in case of a tie, the simplest prompt was selected (zero-shot > few-shot > few-shot with context). Once the prompts were selected for each code, the whole dataset was coded by the LLM.

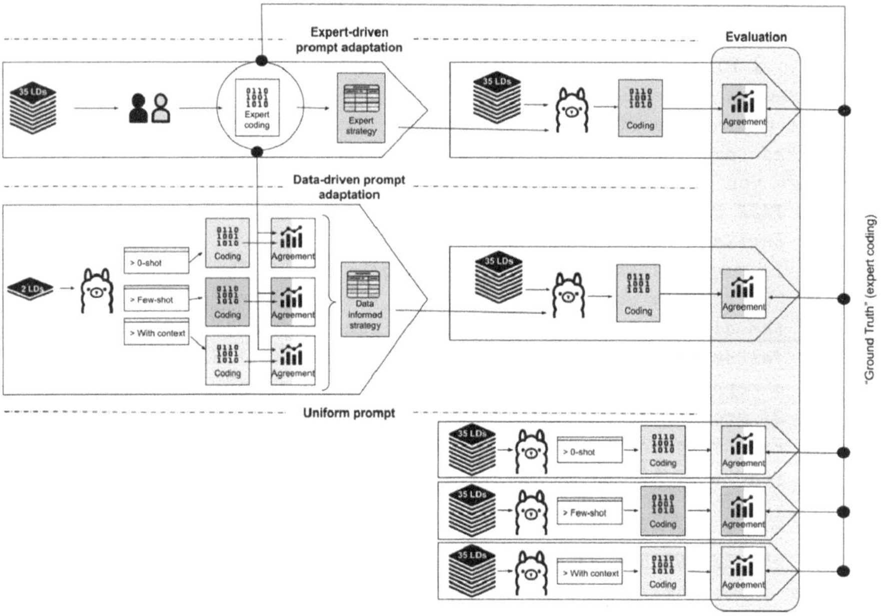

Fig. 2. Overview of the workflow followed in each coding strategy. The agreement is calculated between the expert's coding and the coding generated by Llama using the expert-driven, data-driven or uniform prompt strategies.

Moreover, to assess whether the LLMs return consistent results, we ran the coding task three times per code with the subset of two designs. The results show high consistency, obtaining >97% unanimity for most cases, except for passive learning, where the unanimity went down to 93%. In light of this consistency, we decided to execute the analysis of the entire dataset only once.

To evaluate the agreement between the humans and each of the aforementioned coding strategies, we calculated Gwet's AC1 and Cohen's Kappa (the

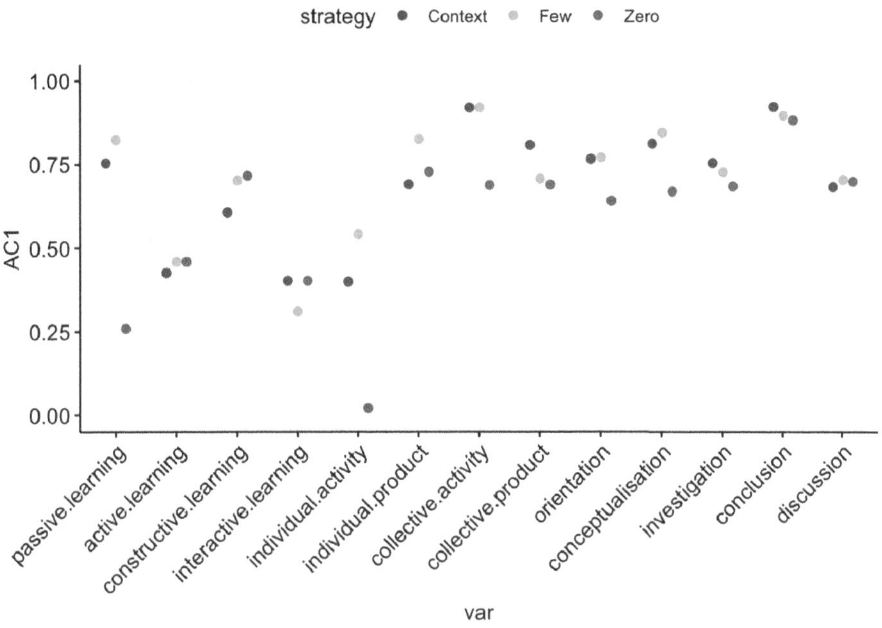

Fig. 3. Agreement between the humans and Llama using zero-shot, few-shot and few-shot with context prompts, in coding a sub-dataset of 89 learning design items.

latter is provided in the suplementary material [16] just to enable comparison with other studies). Furthermore, we have obtained the times and tokens used in each of the strategies to estimate their costs (since that is also the preferred metric to estimate billing costs by LLM services such as OpenAI's).

Descriptive statistics have been used to visualize and compare the different levels of agreement (AC1/Kappa). Median AC1 agreement was used to determine which coding strategy to use for the data-driven adaptive prompting. The resulting agreement/performance of the LLMs for the different strategies was compared using ANOVA, followed by post-hoc analysis with Tukey's HSD (Honest Significant Differences), after testing for normality (Shapiro-Wilk) and homogeneity of variance (Levene). Conger's version of Cohen's Kappa and AC1 were calculated using the *irrCAC* package in the R statistical software, which was also used to calculate ANOVA, Shapiro-Wilk and Tukey HSD tests. Levene tests were done using the *car* package.

The codebook, preprocesed dataset, prompts, results of the qualitative coding (by humans and Llama) and a report with the levels of agreement are all available in the additional material [16].

3 Results

Sub-dataset (2 designs) Coding by LLMs. As noted above, we coded a sub-dataset of two purposefully-selected learning designs using all codes from the three conceptual frameworks. For each of the 89 items, Llama's final judgment was determined by majority vote across three trials. Figure 3 shows how LLM agreement with the human's agreed judgment varied across three uniform prompting strategies. Few-shot prompting with context performed best overall (median AC1 = 0.754, median Kappa = 0.469), followed by few-shot without context (median AC1 = 0.726; median Kappa = 0.384), with zero-shot performing worst on average (median AC1 = 0.684; median Kappa = 0.27). However, this ranking varied by code/construct: zero-shot outperformed others on most ICAP codes (except passive learning), few-shot performed the best in eight of the codes, and few-shot with context led in five (with some ties). The best-performing strategy for each code—favoring shorter, lower-cost prompts—was then used for adaptive, data-driven coding of the full dataset (see next section).

Full Dataset (35 designs) Coding by LLMs. The comparison between the human-LLM agreement of different prompting strategies per code can be seen in Figs. 4 and 5. Looking at the uniform prompting strategies, most of the times, the few-shot strategy performed better (median AC1 = 0.818, median Kappa = 0.509) than the other strategies (zero-shot median AC1 = 0.753; few-shot with context median AC1 = 0.787), although there are a few codes for which zero-shot (active and interactive learning) and few-shot with context (collective product and orientation) outperformed it.

If we compare the uniform prompting strategies with the adaptive strategies, it seems the data-driven adaptive prompt selection performed better (median AC1 = 0.824; median Kappa = 0.516) than either of the single-prompt strategies above, and better than the expert-driven adaptive prompt (median AC1 = 0.771; median Kappa = 0.484). On the other hand, the expert-driven adaptive prompt actually performed *worse* than the single-prompt strategies (except zero-shot, which is clearly the worst-performing). This may mean that, in this case, human (expert) intuitions about the best coding strategies were not in line with the LLMs best-performing strategies and, therefore, were not as good indicators for code-aware prompt selection as those obtained by coding a small sub-dataset.

Nevertheless, although the data-driven adaptive prompting strategy led to higher AC1 and Kappa scores, the differences were not statistically significant (also considering that 13 codes per group is a small sample size). Beyond agreement levels with human coders, prompting strategies also affected resource consumption, including token usage and processing time. As shown in Table 2, adaptive strategies –aside from zero-shot– consumed the fewest tokens (5.897% fewer tokens in data-driven adaptive than in few-shot). Surprisingly, zero-shot and few-shot prompts had similar execution times (9 h vs. 18 h for the context-rich approach), despite few-shot using three times more tokens. This was unexpected, as we anticipated the additional examples in few-shot prompts would significantly increase processing time.

Something to note is that, while the number of tokens and execution time naturally increased when moving from zero-shot to more context-rich prompting strategies, this growth was not homogeneous across all codes. The increase was especially high for those codes presenting more and longer examples (e.g.,

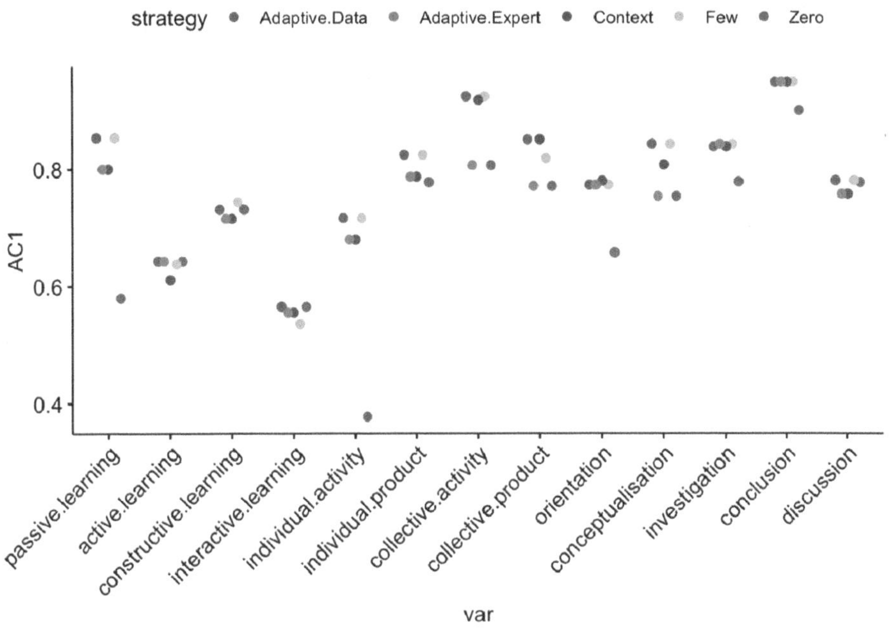

Fig. 4. Agreement between the humans and Llama using the different strategies with the whole data set.

Orientation, Investigation, and Discussion). Thus, those codes requiring more (and more elaborate) examples for humans (as per the codebook definition) also required the model to process a higher number of tokens and, consequently, more execution time.

4 Discussion

This study aimed to explore whether a code-specific prompting strategy improves the deductive coding of qualitative educational data carried out by LLMs when compared with the use of a single prompt for all codes. In our study, we used three different frameworks related to the expected learner engagement [3], the social level of the learning activities [11], and the IBL phases [14] to code the 758 items of 35 learning designs. To answer our research question, we compared different coding strategies: using a single prompt for all codes (namely, zero-shot, few-shot, and few-shot with context), or adapting the prompt strategy per code based on expert-driven and data-driven rules. The results obtained using Llama showed that even within the codes belonging to the same framework, the best-performing codes varied, and that not always the most complex prompt performed best. This aligns with previous studies (e.g., [13]), which found that although some prompts may perform better on average, no single prompt strategy consistently outperforms others across all codes. In [13], researchers noticed that few-shot

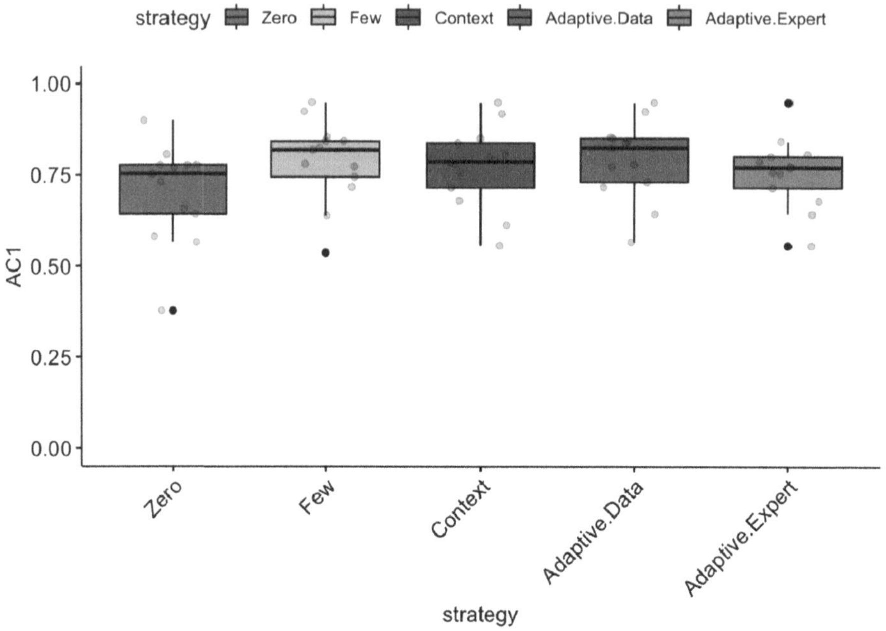

Fig. 5. Comparison of the different prompting strategies with the whole data set.

and with context prompting worked well for codes where experts considered examples or context were needed. In contrast, we found that the expert-driven prompting strategy performed worse than a uniform few-shot approach applied to all codes. These results suggest that an adaptive prompting strategy guided by prompt performance for individual codes on a small –purposefully selected by experts– subset of data may lead to better outcomes in deductive coding.

While the improvement in human-LLM agreement in our case was not statistically significant, considering both agreement *and costs* (time and tokens) may have relevant implications, especially for large datasets. We therefore recommend running a small-scale preliminary analysis to inform the choice of prompting strategy before scaling up. This result also has wider implications for the nature of the human-AI collaboration that can be set up to automate the deductive coding of large-scale datasets (having experts purposefully select a sub-dataset vs. set up the prompting rules manually, based on their experience).

Still, our findings should be interpreted with caution. The results we obtained with Llama 3.3:70b may be context-dependent. While the best performing prompts were similar in the small subset and the whole dataset (see Figs. 3 and 4), different LLMs (e.g., different Llama versions, Gemma 2 2B, InternLM or GPT4) may yield different results per code. Similarly, while one of the novelties of this paper is the type of dataset (learning designs instead of discourse data) and its complexity (made of several fields to be taken into consideration instead of an "utterance" within a discourse), also these differences may entail

Table 2. Input tokens for each code and prompting strategy, for the full dataset (35 designs, 758 items).

Codes	Zero-shot	Few-shot	With context	Adaptive (data-driven)	Adaptive (expert)
	Tokens	Tokens	Tokens	Tokens	Tokens
Passive learning	255,217	560,691	611,088	560,691	611,088
Active learning	255,217	442,443	492,840	255,217	255,217
Constructive learning	252,943	428,799	479,196	252,943	479,196
Interactive learning	281,747	490,197	540,594	281,747	540,594
Individual activity	251,427	557,659	608,056	557,659	608,056
Individual product	246,121	406,817	457,214	406,817	457,214
Collective activity	262,039	431,831	482,228	431,831	262,039
Collective product	254,459	390,899	441,296	441,296	254,459
Orientation	252,943	825,233	875,630	825,233	825,233
Conceptualisation	249,153	467,457	517,854	467,457	249,153
Investigation	300,697	788,849	839,246	839,246	788,849
Conclusion	255,217	528,097	578,494	578,494	528,097
Discussion	315,099	808,557	858,954	808,557	858,954
Total	3,432,279	7,127,529	7,782,690	6,707,188	6,718,149

that our findings do not generalize to other datasets and structures. Thus, when using different and/or more advanced LLMs, prompting pipelines or datasets, it would be advisable to run the exploratory phase again on a small sample to guide prompt selection.

Also, we should not forget that we have only explored 13 codes from three frameworks, and other frameworks may work differently. Moreover, our "ground truth" is based on the human-agreed coding, which has its own limitations. Given the subjectivity of coding, different coders –or even the same coder at different times– may produce varying results [8, p. 20] [10]. Understanding where the LLM fails (e.g., construct ambiguity, reliance on external knowledge) could provide insight for refining both prompts and codebooks.

Finally, our results on agreement and cost raise the question of whether we can reliably offload the coding task to an LLM. In our case, we would aim for higher performance before relying on the automatic coding. In terms of speed, human coders were actually faster than the quickest Llama prompt. Yet, as processing time varies depending on server setup and LLM used, token usage may offer a more consistent way to estimate costs. Using token costs as a metric, analyzing the platform's database of over 17,000 learning designs with OpenAI's GPT-4 Turbo would exceed 30,000 USD, as of this writing. Using the data-driven adaptive prompting described above, there would be close to a 6% (around 2,000 USD) saving. This highlights the need for further prompt (and maybe codebook) improvements to enhance accuracy and cost-efficiency.

5 Conclusions

The varying information needs and difficulty experienced by human experts/coders across the constructs at hand led us to the hypothesis of adapting the prompting strategy for LLMs coding. However, we have observed that LLMs do not mirror human performance patterns or "information needs". Thus, it is currently hard to fathom how to best structure a human-AI collaboration process without such shared ground. For now, conducting an exploratory study to find the best-performing prompts per code on a sub-dataset appears beneficial, improving both agreement and associated costs (e.g., time and tokens).

As our results might be context-dependent, in future studies we will explore the use of this adaptive prompting strategy with datasets of different nature (e.g., learning designs, dialogues, diary entries...), different codebooks, and LLMs (e.g., GPT4). Moreover, we will expand the analysis, refining the prompt (and the codebook) using specific examples of LLM-human discrepancies to improve the performance, as proposed by [1,4].

Acknowledgments. This research was partially funded by: MCIU/AEI/10.13039/50 1100011033 together with ESF+ (RYC2022-037806-I), the European Union's "Next GenerationEU/PRTR" (RYC2021-032273-I) and ERDF (PID2023-146692OB-C32); and the Regional Government of Castile and Leon and FEDER (VA176P23).

References

1. Barany, A., et al.: ChatGPT for education research: exploring the potential of large language models for qualitative codebook development. In: Olney, A.M., Chounta, I.A., Liu, Z., Santos, O.C., Bittencourt, I.I. (eds.) Artificial Intelligence in Education. AIED 2024. LNCS, vol. 14830, pp. 134–149. Springer, Cham (2024). https://doi.org/10.1007/978-3-031-64299-9_10
2. Chew, R., Bollenbacher, J., Wenger, M., Speer, J., Kim, A.: LLM-assisted content analysis: using large language models to support deductive coding. arXiv preprint (2023). https://doi.org/10.48550/arXiv.2306.14924
3. Chi, M.T., Wylie, R.: The ICAP framework: linking cognitive engagement to active learning outcomes. Educ. Psychol. **49**(4), 219–243 (2014). https://doi.org/10.1080/00461520.2014.965823
4. Dai, S.C., Xiong, A., Ku, L.W.: LLM-in-the-loop: leveraging large language model for thematic analysis. In: Bouamor, H., Pino, J., Bali, K. (eds.) Findings of the Association for Computational Linguistics: EMNLP 2023, pp. 9993–10001. Association for Computational Linguistics (December 2023). https://doi.org/10.18653/v1/2023.findings-emnlp.669
5. De Paoli, S.: Performing an inductive thematic analysis of semi-structured interviews with a large language model: an exploration and provocation on the limits of the approach. Soc. Sci. Comput. Rev. **42**(4), 997–1019 (2024). https://doi.org/10.1177/08944393231220483
6. Dunivin, Z.O.: Scalable qualitative coding with LLMs: chain-of-thought reasoning matches human performance in some hermeneutic tasks. arXiv preprint (2024). https://doi.org/10.48550/arXiv.2401.15170

7. Fereday, J., Muir-Cochrane, E.: Demonstrating rigor using thematic analysis: a hybrid approach of inductive and deductive coding and theme development. Int. J. Qual. Methods **5**(1), 80–92 (2006). https://doi.org/10.1177/160940690600500107
8. Gwet, K.L.: Handbook of Inter-Rater Reliability: The Definitive Guide to Measuring the Extent of Agreement Among Raters. Advanced Analytics, LLC, USA (2014)
9. Gwet, K.L.: Computing inter-rater reliability and its variance in the presence of high agreement. Br. J. Math. Stat. Psychol. **61**(1), 29–48 (2008). https://doi.org/10.1348/000711006X126600
10. Kitto, K., Manly, C.A., Ferguson, R., Poquet, O.: Towards more replicable content analysis for learning analytics. In: LAK23: 13th International Learning Analytics and Knowledge Conference, pp. 303–314. LAK2023, Association for Computing Machinery, New York, NY, USA (2023). https://doi.org/10.1145/3576050.3576096
11. Lakkala, M., Lallimo, J., Hakkarainen, K.: Teachers' pedagogical designs for technology-supported collective inquiry: a national case study. Comput. Educ. **45**(3), 337–356 (2005). https://doi.org/10.1016/j.compedu.2005.04.010
12. Liu, X., et al.: Qualitative coding with GPT-4: where it works better. J. Learn. Anal. **12**(1), 169–185 (2025). https://doi.org/10.18608/jla.2025.8575
13. Liu, X., Zhang, J., Barany, A., Pankiewicz, M., Baker, R.S.: Assessing the potential and limits of large language models in qualitative coding. In: Kim, Y.J., Swiecki, Z. (eds.) Advances in Quantitative Ethnography. icqe 2024. CCIS, vol. 2278, pp. 89–103. Springer, Cham (2024). https://doi.org/10.1007/978-3-031-76335-9_7
14. Pedaste, M., et al.: Phases of inquiry-based learning: definitions and the inquiry cycle. Educ. Res. Rev. **14**, 47–61 (2015). https://doi.org/10.1016/j.edurev.2015.02.003
15. Rodríguez-Triana, M.J., Prieto, L.P., Pishtari, G.: What do learning designs show about pedagogical adoption? An analysis approach and a case study on inquiry-based learning. In: De Laet, T., Klemke, R., Alario-Hoyos, C., Hilliger, I., Ortega-Arranz, A. (eds.) EC-TEL 2021. LNCS, vol. 12884, pp. 275–288. Springer, Cham (2021). https://doi.org/10.1007/978-3-030-86436-1_21
16. Rodríguez-Triana, M.J., et al.: Code-aware llm prompting in deductive qualitative analysis: codebook, dataset, prompts, qualitative coding, and agreement report (June 2025). https://doi.org/10.5281/zenodo.15698094
17. Saldaña, J.: The Coding Manual for Qualitative Researchers. SAGE publications Ltd., New York (2021)
18. Wei, J., et al.: Chain-of-thought prompting elicits reasoning in large language models. Adv. Neural Inf. Process. Syst. **35**, 24824–24837 (2022). https://proceedings.neurips.cc/paper_files/paper/2022
19. Westover, A.M., Westover, T.M., Westover, M.B.: Interrater reliability estimation via maximum likelihood for Gwet's chance agreement model. Open J. Stat. **14**(5), 481–491 (2024). https://doi.org/10.4236/ojs.2024.145021
20. Xiao, Z., Yuan, X., Liao, Q.V., Abdelghani, R., Oudeyer, P.Y.: Supporting qualitative analysis with large language models: combining codebook with GPT-3 for deductive coding. In: Companion Proceedings of the 28th International Conference on Intelligent User Interfaces, pp. 75–78 (2023). https://doi.org/10.1145/3581754.3584136

Empowering Teachers to Enhance Student High Order Thinking Skills with Artificial Intelligence Educational Tools

Merike Saar[1(✉)], Aleksandra Ljalikova[1], Emily Theophilou[2], Shatha N. Alkhasawneh[2], and Davinia Hernández-Leo[2]

[1] Tallinn University, Narva Mnt 25, Tallinn, Estonia
merike.saar@gmail.com
[2] Pompeu Fabra University, c/Roc Boronat 138, 08018 Barcelona, Spain

Abstract. Artificial Intelligence Educational Tools (AIED) are poised to transform educational practices by enabling personalised learning, automating administrative tasks, and delivering real-time feedback. However, the ethical and constructive implementation of AIED in K-12 education remains a pressing concern, particularly among teachers. Even when teachers view AIED as a highly transformative tool, they often remain reluctant to experiment with it in the classroom, primarily because they feel unprepared and lack confidence in using AIED effectively. This study aims to address these gaps by exploring the constructive applications of AIED to empower teachers in enhancing students' cognitive engagement (based on ICAP framework) and higher-order thinking skills (HOTS). A five-month teacher training course was conducted, incorporating pre- and post-surveys to assess teachers' confidence, knowledge, and appropriation of AIED. Teachers engaged in training on AI-related risks and tools, designed lessons that integrated AIED, and gathered student feedback. Teacher training surveys (N = 17) were analysed with paired samples T-tests; deductive content analysis focusing on HOTS and the role of AIED was conducted based on ten lesson plans. For triangulation, descriptive analysis was applied to the student feedback survey (N = 240) about their perception of such learning activities. Overall, the study shows that teacher training empowered teachers in using AIED; the alignment of lesson activities with ICAP principles might depend on the learning community; and AI-supported learning can foster HOTS depending on the type of learning activities and the AIED role.

Keywords: Artificial Intelligence Educational Tools · High Order Thinking Skills · ICAP Framework · Student Engagement · Teachers' Knowledge Appropriation

1 Introduction

Artificial Intelligence (AI) is revolutionising education by transforming teaching and learning processes. From personalised learning systems and intelligent tutoring tools to administrative support and predictive analytics, AI applications in education promise

K. Tammets et al. (Eds.): EC-TEL 2025, LNCS 16063, pp. 442–456, 2026.
https://doi.org/10.1007/978-3-032-03870-8_30

enhanced outcomes through tailored experiences, automation of routine tasks, and real-time feedback for students and educators (Cardona et al., 2023; Almasri, 2024). However, in addition to capabilities to enhance teaching and learning practices, hasty adoption of AIED might also pose dangers (Giannakos et al., 2024), while the successful integration of AI hinges on teachers' perceptions and attitudes.

On the one hand, research shows that educators recognise benefits like reduced administrative burdens and personalised learning opportunities but harbour concerns regarding the technology's impact on their professional roles and the quality of education delivered (Gökçearslan, 2024; Yim & Wegerif, 2024). Although teachers often perceive AI as useful and accessible, they face challenges such as limited technical knowledge, inadequate infrastructure, and fears of job displacement (Alwaqdani, 2025). Moreover, the ethical implications of AI—spanning data privacy, algorithmic bias, and the erosion of the human element in teaching—remain significant hurdles to trust and acceptance (Yim & Wegerif, 2024).

On the other hand, AI's influence on teaching extends beyond administrative efficiency, requiring educators to shift from content providers to facilitators of learning (Karpouzis, 2024). This role transition is supported by AI tools that foster engaging, personalised, and higher-order learning experiences, often taking on various roles such as co-designer or study buddy (Sabzalieva & Valentini, 2023). However, equipping teachers to adapt effectively demands comprehensive professional development initiatives addressing both technical skills and ethical considerations. Current training programmes, however, fall short of preparing teachers to navigate these changes confidently and ethically (Cardona et al., 2023).

Also, teachers' evolving roles underscore the importance of designing learning experiences that promote deep student engagement and higher-order thinking skills (HOTS). HOTS are advanced cognitive abilities beyond simple memorisation and recall, involving skills like analysis, evaluation, and synthesis, which are essential for problem-solving and decision-making. Researchers emphasise the importance of HOTS in education and highlight critical thinking as a core component (Conklin, 2012; Ghanizadeh et al., 2020). Bloom's Taxonomy (Bloom et al., 1956; Krathwohl, 2002) is often used to demonstrate how learners progress from understanding and knowledge recall (involving lower-order thinking skills/LOTS) to higher-level cognitive engagement. Although teachers' awareness of HOTS is improving (Retnawati et al., 2018), the majority of teacher-developed assessment items indicate a focus on lower levels of Bloom's Taxonomy (Abosalem, 2016). At the same time, research also shows a relationship between HOTS and students' engagement (Alsowat, 2016).

Cognitive engagement, in turn, can be explored through the lens of the ICAP framework (Chi & Boucher, 2023), which posits that "the levels of learning outcomes are predicted by the ordering Interactive > Constructive > Active > Passive" modes of engagement in classroom activities (p. 97). Physical activities linked to passive engagement are difficult to determine, as the student's engagement during a reading or listening activity is not visible (so, self-reporting can be used for data collection). Active engagement involves simple manipulation of the learning material (underlining, copy-pasting, etc.), while constructive engagement is linked to the generation of novel outputs (e.g., explanation of a concept in one's own words). Interactive engagement entails turn-taking and the co-generation of new knowledge with peers. The last two are associated with deep learning. ICAP can, therefore, help teachers pick AIED learning activities that enhance cognitive engagement and deep learning. However, as Chi and Wylie (2014) caution, not all uses of technology in learning are truly interactive. Depending on how it is implemented, technology can engage students in passive, active, or constructive ways, each varying in cognitive depth.

So, AI has great potential to boost HOTS, and activities enabling them should be included in teachers' learning designs. However, the inclusion of such affordances in AI-enhanced education remains underexplored. This study aims to investigate the effects of a training course focused on ethical and constructive AI use and lesson planning aligned with HOTS and ICAP principles. Specifically, it examines how such training influences teachers' AI adoption confidence and expectations for enhancing students' engagement and higher-order thinking skills with AI. The research questions are:

1) How does teachers' adoption of AI change after participating in a collaborative training course on the ethical and constructive use of AIED?
2) What engagement modes (based on ICAP) do teachers plan into their lessons with AIED?
3) What HOTS do teachers expect to enhance by using AIED in their lessons?
4) How do students perceive their cognitive engagement in AIED activities?

2 Methodology

2.1 Participants and Context

The research project took place within the framework of school–university partnerships (SUP) in Estonia, Spain, and Portugal. It is part of a long-term Erasmus + initiative involving a university or a teacher-training association and one school from each country. The project aimed to support teachers in developing shared, evidence-based knowledge about the constructive use of AIED in K-12 settings.

The professional development design for teachers was based on the knowledge appropriation model (KAM) (Ley et al., 2022) and implemented in two rounds. In the first round, two teachers per school, along with university didactics experts and researchers, participated in two three-day learning, teaching, and training (LTT) sessions held in Spain and Estonia. During the initial LTT session, the research group and teachers collaboratively discussed key issues related to AIED and began co-designing a training course for learning activities integrating AIED.

Participants in the first round co-created innovative practices involving AIED, implemented them with their students, and reflected on the outcomes during the second LTT session. These shared experiences and discussions highlighted diverse approaches to using AIED. Compared to the start of the project, teachers reported feeling more empowered by their new experiences with AIED (Saar et al., 2024). Adjustments to lesson plans were proposed to enhance students' cognitive engagement, drawing on the ICAP model. Additionally, the research team identified a need for more structured methods of student data collection. Teachers received guidance on conducting surveys on student engagement and disseminating their new knowledge within school communities.

This paper focuses on the second round of teacher training, in which teachers from the first round—together with university researchers—supported the training of colleagues from their school communities. A group of teachers from each school participated in collaborative lesson design sessions. The AIED session themes focused on the constructive and ethical use of AI, addressing issues such as environmental impact, social inequality, and plagiarism. After designing the materials, teachers implemented them in their classrooms, gathered student feedback, and collected evidence about learning. In subsequent sessions, they reflected on their experience and worked together to enhance students' learning outcomes with AIED. This evolving knowledge was then formalized and standardized through a collaborative digital platform, where teachers shared their lesson plans, insights, and comments. The teacher training programme aimed to bridge individual and collective knowledge creation, fostering the development of a learning community within schools and across institutions (Ley et al., 2020).

In total, 45 in-service teachers across various school subjects engaged in a five-month training programme conducted at each school. Of these, 17 teachers completed all three stages of the knowledge appropriation process: knowledge maturation, scaffolding, and appropriation. However, several teachers with younger students could not have their students use AI because of privacy concerns. Instead, the teachers used AI to prepare lesson plans and materials. They just demonstrated AI use to students – for example, inserting student-created prompts into AI (using the teacher account so that students did not have access to AI) to create pictures. Therefore, only ten lesson plans, with corresponding student feedback on AI use, are analysed in this paper.

2.2 Ethics

Before the start of the long-term project, the entire process of data collection and analysis was reviewed and approved by the Institutional Committee for the Ethical Review of Projects (CIREP) at Pompeu Fabra University.

Teacher participation in the research was entirely voluntary. All participants provided written informed consent and were informed of their right to withdraw from the study without any consequences. Following the regulations of each participating school, written informed consent was also obtained from the students and their parents or legal guardians.

To ensure data protection and privacy, teacher data were anonymised, and student data were collected and processed anonymously. No personally identifiable information was included in the research outputs. All data handling complied with relevant ethical guidelines and data protection regulations, including the General Data Protection Regulation (GDPR).

2.3 Data Collection Methods

Pre- and post-surveys were conducted in September 2024 and January 2025, respectively, at the beginning and end of the five-month teacher training programme (second round of the long-term project).

The pre-survey included questions regarding teachers' socio-demographic backgrounds. The second part of the questionnaire was based on the KAM developed and validated by Ley and colleagues (2022), with items adapted to fit the specific context of the current project. All items were rated using a five-point Likert scale, where 1 indicated "Strongly disagree" and 5 indicated "Strongly agree". The pre-survey included four components: *Intended Adoption* (5 items), *Self-efficacy* (4 items), *Belongingness* (2 items), and *Ownership* (2 items).

The post-survey consisted of two parts: the ICAP (5 items) and the post-KAM (17 items), which included four sections from the pre-KAM—intended adoption, self-efficacy, belongingness, and ownership. In addition, a new set of items was included to assess teachers' knowledge appropriation practices. This addition aimed to capture how teachers applied and integrated the newly acquired knowledge into their teaching.

Attempts to enhance students' cognitive engagement with AI-supported lesson activities were explored through four questions based on the ICAP framework. The survey questions (five-point Likert scale) were intentionally worded to explore student engagement concerning AI use, not other classroom activities in the lesson:

In my learning designs that make use of AI

1) my students look and listen to how to use AI (Passive mode);
2) my students insert prompts and copy-paste AI responses (Active mode);
3) my students reformulate or expand on AI-produced content (Constructive);
4) my students communicate with AI (ask for further info, details, dispute the responses of AI, etc.) (Interactive mode, interaction with AI).

In addition, a question about Critical thinking was added (expecting collaborative activities with peers), as lesson plans from the first pilot indicated a high rate of critical thinking activities in AI-related lessons:

5) my students discuss and critique AI responses (compare with other sources) (Interactive mode, interaction with peers).

The final section of the post-survey focused on the frequency of AI tool usage and the specific tools teachers reported using in their teaching practice.

Lesson Plans. As part of the training, teachers were instructed to upload their lesson designs to a digital platform (https://trails.upf.edu/). Within the platform, teachers reported on the AIED tools used, lesson activities, materials, learning objectives, and key insights. This process aimed to curate a collection of best practices for integrating AIED into classroom instruction. Lesson plans enabled comparisons of teachers' lesson designs based on the ICAP framework and activities to enhance HOTS (Ghanizadeh et al., 2020). Additionally, it allowed the authors to link student experiences directly with the lesson designs, facilitating data triangulation.

The student feedback survey asked questions about their background (age group, lesson subject and AI tool used) and ICAP-related items (5-point Likert scale), which were similar to the ones in the teacher survey:

1) I looked and listened to how to use AI (Passive mode);
2) I inserted prompts and copy-pasted AI responses (to edit text, etc.) (Active);
3) I reformulated or expanded AI-produced content (or asked further questions) (Constructive mode);
4) I communicated with AI (asked for further info, details, disputed the responses of AI, etc.) (Interactive mode with AI).

5) I discussed with others and critiqued AI responses (compared with other sources). (Interactive mode with peers)

The student survey also included items on students' perceived engagement (based on Fuller et al., 2018) (5-point Likert scale):

1) During this activity, I used my full potential to learn
2) During this activity, I only pretended to learn
3) During this activity, I felt confused/worried
4) During this activity, I felt excited/confident
5) During this activity, I learned something (new)
6) During this activity, I learned something in a new way

As the training course was on ethical and constructive use of AI, one item was added to explore students' attitudes towards using AI:

7) During this activity, I felt I might have cheated.

2.4 Analysis

To address the first research question, both descriptive and inferential statistical analyses were performed on the KAM survey. To compare teachers' adoption of AIED before and after the training programme, paired samples tests were used. A significance level of $p < .05$ was applied to determine statistical differences.

Given that the sample size was fewer than 50 participants, the Shapiro–Wilk test was employed to assess the normality assumption required for parametric testing. In several cases, violations of normality were observed. For these items, the non-parametric Wilcoxon Signed-Rank test was conducted as an appropriate alternative. Effect sizes were calculated to estimate the magnitude of change across all tested variables.

Teachers' Knowledge Appropriation practices and Students' survey results were analysed using descriptive statistics. Negatively worded items were reverse scored. Pearson's correlation coefficients were used to assess the strength and direction of associations between variables related to self-reported AI practices in teaching. All assumptions for parametric correlation analysis were checked and met, and an alpha level of .05 was used for the correlation test. All tests were conducted using Jamovi version 2.6 (Retrieved from https://www.jamovi.org).

Additionally, we analysed the lesson designs implemented by teachers using three categorisation approaches: the level of cognitive complexity following Bloom's taxonomy, the range of HOTS that can potentially be fostered through AI integration, and the role of the AIED tool in each lesson design (Ghanizadeh et al., 2020; Sabzalieva & Valentini, 2023). Since some lesson plans included multiple activities involving AIED tools, they were assigned to different Bloom's taxonomy levels.

3 Findings

3.1 Teachers' Appropriation of AI

The results of the paired samples t-test ($N = 17$) confirm that the five-month teacher training programme—delivered by teacher mentors in collaboration with universities—led to a significant improvement in teachers' *self-efficacy* regarding the adoption of

AI in teaching and learning. The programme consisted of collaborative lesson design, co-developed with mentors and peers, and validation through classroom implementation with students, allowing for direct, experiential engagement with AI-integrated pedagogy. Specifically:

Self-reported knowledge about AI increased from M = 2.41, SD = 0.04 before the training to M = 3.71, SD = 0.77 after it. This difference was statistically significant with a large effect size: $t(16) = -4.22$, $p < .001$, $d = -1.03$. Confidence in implementing AI-related activities also improved significantly, with the mean rising from M = 2.47, SD = 1.33 to M = 3.53, SD = 0.80. The difference was significant with a large effect size: $t(16) = -3.65$, $p = .002$, $d = -0.88$. In addition, confidence in discussing AI in education increased from M = 2.41, SD = 1.00 to M = 3.12, SD = 0.86, and was also statistically significant: $t(16) = -2.40$, $p = .029$, $d = -0.58$. A stronger sense of *belonging* to the AI learning community was reported after the training, with scores rising from M = 2.76, SD = 0.97 to M = 3.76, SD = 1.03. The difference was significant with a large effect size: $t(16) = -3.52$, $p = .003$, $d = -0.85$. Enjoyment in being part of the AI community also increased significantly from M = 3.29, SD = 1.10 to M = 4.00, SD = 0.94, and was statistically significant: $t(16) = -2.51$, $p = .023$, $d = -0.61$. The sense of *ownership* toward AI was also strengthened. Notably, participants' willingness to defend AI use in response to criticism increased from M = 2.76, SD = 1.09 to M = 3.59, SD = 0.80, was statistically significant and had a large effect size: $t(16) = -3.35$, $p = .004$, $d = -0.81$. Lastly, teachers' *intention to promote AI* in their school showed a moderate yet statistically significant increase, from M = 3.12, SD = 1.67 to M = 3.71, SD = 0.77, $t(16) = -2.58$, $p = .020$, $d = -0.63$.

Due to the violation of the assumption of normality (as assessed by the Shapiro–Wilk test previously), the non-parametric Wilcoxon Signed-Rank test was employed for six items. Intention to use AI in teaching increased significantly from M = 3.47, SD = 0.94 to M = 4.35, SD = 0.86. W = 6.00, $p = .002$, rank biserial $r = -0.886$. A belief that AI will influence teaching long-term rose from M = 3.41, SD = 1.06 to M = 4.06, SD = 0.75. W = 2.50, $p = .033$, $r = -0.861$. Perception of AI as an effective teaching tool improved from M = 2.82, SD = 0.95 to M = 3.71, SD = 0.85. W = 0.00, $p = .002$, $r = -1.000$. Frequency of AI use in teaching increased from M = 2.35, SD = 1.06 to M = 3.18, SD = 0.95. W = 9.00, $p = .009$, $r = -0.802$. The ability to evaluate the effectiveness of AI activities rose from M = 2.29, SD = 0.99 to M = 3.41, SD = 0.71. W = 10.00, $p = .007$, $r = -0.810$. The sense of ownership of AI success increased from M = 3.18, SD = 1.13 to M = 4.06, SD = 0.83. W = 5.00, $p = .006$, $r = -0.872$. All these differences between teachers' answers before and after training are statistically significant and have a large effect size.

To examine the relationships between key self-reported aspects of AI integration in teaching, Pearson's correlation coefficients were calculated. The results revealed a moderate, statistically significant positive correlation between the perception that AI use raises awareness of new teaching and learning methods and the tendency to modify study materials and teaching methods based on personal initiative, $r = .52$, $p = .028$. A strong positive correlation was observed between the same perception of AI use and the understanding of AI's effectiveness in education, $r = .82$, $p < .001$. Finally, a moderate-to-strong positive correlation was also found between modifying teaching practices and understanding the effectiveness of AI use, r = .64, p = .004. These results suggest that greater awareness of AI's educational potential is associated with pedagogical flexibility and deeper insight into its impact on teaching and learning.

3.2 Teachers' Self-Reported AIED Learning Design Activities

Interesting patterns can be observed between schools. For example, in School 2, there is a clear preference for a more passive approach (see Table 1), where AI tools are primarily presented to students (Passive: M = 4.00, SD = 0.71), while constructive and interactive approaches are less frequently reported (Constructive: M = 2.20, SD = 0.84; Interactive: M = 2.4, SD = 0.55).

Table 1. Descriptive Statistics of Learning Activities in which Students Engage with AI.

ICAP framework	School	M	SD	N
Passive: Students look and listen to how to use AI	S1	3.50	0.55	6
	S2	4.00	0.71	5
	S3	3.43	0.79	7
Active: Students insert prompts and copy-paste AI responses	S1	3.00	1.10	6
	S2	3.20	1.64	5
	S3	3.00	1.29	7
Constructive: Students reformulate or expand on AI-produced content	S1	3.17	0.75	6
	S2	2.20	0.84	5
	S3	3.29	1.38	7
Interactive: Students communicate with AI (ask for further info, details, dispute the responses of AI)	S1	3.50	1.22	6
	S2	2.40	0.55	5
	S3	3.00	1.15	7
Critical Thinking: Students discuss and critique AI responses (compare with other sources)	S1	3.67	1.03	6
	S2	2.20	0.84	5
	S3	2.71	1.11	7

Note: Mean (M), Standard deviation (SD), Sample size (N)

3.3 Lesson Plans

From the ten teacher-designed lesson plans analysed, we extracted specific classroom activities to categorize them according to HOTS, Bloom's Taxonomy, and the roles of AIED (see Table 2 for a sample of the activities collected). For instance, Lesson Plan 1 focused on creating presentations in an English course, and we have identified the following sequence of activities: students first learnt how to use Gamma.ai to create presentations, then developed their own, and finally analysed the AI-generated content for accuracy and relevance. We followed a similar process for all ten lesson plans, and 17 different lesson activities could be detected.

Within these lesson activities, we detected that 65% (11 out of 17) promoted HOTS, such as critical thinking, creativity, argumentation, and transformation of knowledge, while the remaining 35% (6 out of 17) focused on LOTS. Among the 11 activities promoting HOTS, we observed different types. Creativity was fostered in 3 out of 11 activities, such as using ChatGPT to generate character and space descriptions. Critical thinking appeared most frequently – in 5 out of 11 activities, including tasks where students were asked to discuss and critique the output of AIED tools. Transformation of knowledge was present in 2 out of 11 activities—for example, when students created tutorials on mathematical properties. Lastly, argumentation was encouraged in 1 out of 11 activities, where students practised debating using AIED.

Table 2. A sample of the collected lesson activities, summarising the HOTS, Bloom's taxonomy level of cognitive complexity, and AIED roles

Example lesson activities	AIED tool	HOTS	Bloom's Taxonomy	AIED Role
Analysing/criticising the AI response for accuracy and suitability	Gamma.ai	Critical thinking	Evaluating	Co-designer
Revising history (AI asks questions about a topic and provides explanations on confusing concepts)	Mizou	LOTS (memorisation and drill)	Applying	Study buddy
Creating texts and images to construct real scenarios and fictional historical characters	ChatGPT, Copilot	Creativity	Creating	Co-designer
Practicing debate (making claims and supporting these claims, rebutting AI claims)	Brisk Teaching	Argumentation	Creating	Socratic Opponent
Students create a tutorial about mathematical properties. They give proof of the properties and give examples of use	Fliki	Transformation of knowledge	Creating	Co-designer

Regarding the roles assigned to AIED within the lesson activities (Sabzalieva & Valentini, 2023), we found that the Co-designer role was the most common, appearing in 7 out of 17 activities, where students worked alongside AI tools to create or develop content. The Exploratorium and Information provider roles each appeared in 2 activities, supporting learners in exploring ideas. Similarly, AIED served as a Personal tutor in 2 activities, offering guidance. Less frequently, AI took on more roles, such as a Study buddy (1), a Socratic opponent (1), a Possibility engine (1), and a Storyteller (1).

Activities supporting HOTS most commonly featured the Co-designer role, aligning with Bloom's Taxonomy level of Creating. In contrast, while LOTS activities also included the Co-designer role, it appeared primarily under the Applying level of Bloom's taxonomy. Overall, the activities showed varying levels of Bloom's Taxonomy engagement: Creating appeared in six activities, followed by Applying with five, Analysing with three, Evaluating with two, and Understanding with one.

3.4 Student Responses

Student responses (N = 240) about their experience with AI in ten different classrooms reveal that AI use promotes interaction and engagement. Passive learning activities with AIED prevailed only in two of the ten lessons, where students were asked to create presentations with the help of Gamma.ai and critically analyse the outcome (M = 4.09 on a 5-point Likert scale) or read science theory and solve tasks based on it (M = 4.27). The passive mode can be directly linked to listening to the teacher's instructions on how to use the introduced AI platform. However, in these two lessons, interactive activities (with AI or peers) scored as high (M = 4.09; M = 4.27). In six lessons, interactive activities (with AI or peers), which enhance deep learning, prevailed (M = above 4.05 in all cases). Also, active tasks (simple manipulations of the learning material) scored rather low, remaining below M = 3 in four cases and above M = 4 in one lesson. This shows that in our lesson designs, learning with AI tends to promote constructive (above M = 3 in nine cases) and interactive activities (above M = 3 in all lessons) that support deep learning.

Students' perceived engagement in lessons with the use of AI is also high, ranging from M = 3.0 to M = 4.32 for behavioural engagement, from M = 3.47 to M = 4.12 for emotional engagement, and from M = 2.33 to M = 4.31 for cognitive engagement (on a 5-point Likert scale). See some examples in Table 3 from higher-secondary students (16–20 age group).

Interesting observations can be made from comparing the teachers' AIED lesson designs with student feedback. First, when AI is used just as a co-designer (to create text, pictures, presentations, and videos), there is not much deep learning, as the data for constructive and interactive modes of engagement appear relatively low – from 2.2 to 3.83 and 2.82 to 3.71, respectively. Also, students perceived cognitive engagement in such activities is not very high (between 2.33 and 3.86 on a five-point Likert scale). However, when a critical analysis task was added (e.g., to critique the AI output with peers, Lesson 1), the interactive mode of engagement rose to 4.09, the perceived behavioural engagement to 4.32 and cognitive engagement to 4.2.

Table 3. Examples from the student survey (ICAP and engagement).

Sts (N =)	Lesson	AI tool + role	P	A	C	I with AI	I with peers	B	E	C
22	Making presentations and analysing AI output for accuracy	Gamma.ai Co-designer	4.09	3.23	3.23	2.82	4.09	4.32	3.8	4.20
16	Creating maths materials with examples, solving tasks and comparing the solutions with AI solutions)	Perplexity Co-designer & personal tutor	2.81	4.38	4.69	4.63	3.81	3.28	3.53	3.72
58	Revising history (AI asks questions or explains)	Mizou Study buddy	3.33	1.98	3.67	4.31	2.90	4.19	3.47	4.31

Note. Modes: P - passive; A - active; C - constructive; I - interactive (with AI or peers); B - behavioural engagement; E - emotional engagement; C - cognitive engagement

In our study, the highest cognitive engagement was achieved when AI was used as a personal tutor or study buddy, for example, in mathematics and science lessons where students created materials with the help of AI, solved tasks and compared their solutions with AI-provided solutions. This triggered lots of discussion and learning from mistakes. The constructive and interactive modes in these lessons reached the highest (3.67–4.69 and 4.27–4.63, respectively), though the perceived engagement varied: 3.28–4.19. The use of AI as a Socratic opponent (in a debate) also demonstrated high perceived engagement – behavioural 4.24 and emotional 4.12 (constructive was 3.55, as students did not learn new things but developed their argumentation skills).

4 Discussion and Conclusions

AIED, regardless of how interactive, multifunctional, or affordable it may be, requires teaching practices that are purposefully aligned with its use. Compared to previous educational technologies, implementing AIED in the classroom calls for a more critical approach from teachers and students, highlighting the importance of keeping humans "in the loop" (Hattie & Donoghue, 2016). Following the teacher training program led by mentor teachers, improvements were observed in teachers' self-efficacy and their sense of belonging and ownership related to AI integration in education. The self-reported frequency of AI use and the intention to use AI for teaching and learning also showed noticeable increases.

Contrary to Alwaqdani (2025), who emphasises the challenges teachers face in adopting AIED—such as the effort required for training, fears of job displacement, diminished creativity and critical thinking, unintended consequences, and overreliance on AI's perceived accuracy—our findings suggest that the constructive use of AIED has the potential to enhance student creativity, critical thinking and other HOTS. This is achievable when AIED is integrated through well-defined pedagogical roles (Sabzalieva & Valentini, 2023) that support active learning strategies. Our research further confirms that teachers who demonstrate a stronger awareness of critical thinking pedagogy and innovative educational practices are more likely to recognise the effectiveness of AIED tools. These teachers also show a greater willingness to adapt both their instructional approaches and learning materials to align with the potential of AIED.

However, the constructive use of AI—where teachers actively transform or adapt AI outputs—is less evident. Teachers' data on learning activities involving student engagement with AI reveal a rather heterogeneous pattern. Notably, the role of learning communities appears to be important in shaping how teachers plan AI-supported lessons. The observation that teachers in School 2 tend to present AIED tools to students (indicating a passive mode of cognitive engagement) rather than encouraging interaction with these tools (an interactive mode of engagement) may be interpreted in two ways: it could reflect a need to develop new pedagogical approaches (Chichekian & Benteux, 2022), or it may be influenced by concerns related to data privacy and age restrictions for student use (Akgun & Greenhow, 2022).

It could also be observed that in one school, all teachers used AI to enhance critical thinking (through discussions with AI or peers), while in two other schools, AI was most often used as a co-designer (to produce either text, pictures or videos), and only in one lesson plan did interactive activities prevail. However, student engagement rose considerably when interactive critical thinking activities were included in the lesson design. Thus, encouraging peer-to-peer interaction focused on critically evaluating the AI output can support the development of students' critical thinking skills. However, critical thinking is not a generic, transferable skill; it is context-specific and must be developed within distinct disciplinary domains (Hattie & Donoghue, 2016; McPeck, 2016).

Our study shows that teachers use a variety of AIED activities (based on ICAP) to engage students and boost HOTS. All ICAP engagement modes involving AIED were represented in the lesson plans. Interactive AIED activities that involve critical thinking and other HOTS are perceived as more engaging by students than simple co-creation tasks with AI. This is in line with Fuller et al. (2018), who claim that engagement often depends on how interesting the topic or activity is for a student. For example, watching a boring video does not engage students, while a TED Talk on a captivating topic can be very engaging (Fuller et al., 2018).

The integration of AI into various aspects of lessons in this study highlights its potential to enhance student engagement and promote HOTS. In most lesson plans, teachers employed AIED as a co-designer. However, our findings indicated that students were more engaged when AI assumed roles such as a study buddy, Socratic opponent, or personal tutor rather than just a co-designer. When used in the co-designer role, AIED did not always foster HOTS, which could explain the low engagement rates of students.

In some cases, students were asked to use AI solely to produce content, such as images, to visualise a text, without directly manipulating or analysing the generated material. As a result, these activities primarily supported LOTS rather than promoting HOTS. In this regard, we recommend that activities where AIED acts as a co-designer be followed by tasks that encourage HOTS, such as discussions, evaluations, or analysis of the generated content.

All in all, by providing personalised support and fostering creativity, AI can help students connect theoretical knowledge through practical application, making learning more relevant and impactful. However, AIED must be implemented constructively in the classroom, as when overused, it can negatively impact problem-solving skills (Lee et al., 2025) and imagination (Karl et al., 2025). Moreover, its use raises important ethical considerations. For instance, issues such as data bias, misinformation, and GDPR compliance must be carefully addressed (Farooqi et al., 2024; Yim & Wegerif, 2024). Additionally, teachers' supervision is essential when integrating AIED into classrooms to ensure its effective and ethical use (Karpouzis, 2024). While this is crucial, it also presents a challenge, as it could contribute to the already significant workload that educators face. Lastly, the environmental impact of AI tools, particularly in terms of their high CO_2 emissions, should not be overlooked (Bashir et al., 2024). Effective teacher training on the constructive and ethical use of AI will be essential in mitigating these potential risks.

5 Limitations and Further Studies

Though the study provides an initial overview of how AIED can be used to promote student HOTS and engagement, it is based on a small sample of three schools in Europe. All the teachers volunteered to participate in the training or surveys and might have had a positive prior attitude towards AIED. Also, obtaining the consent from parents was seen as an additional challenge and limited the number of student responses.

The results were also affected by AIED privacy regulations and school policies (in some cases teachers could not use AIED with younger students for age restrictions, etc.) Also, students' positive responses might be due to the innovation aspect of AI use in the lesson (excitement) and could yield different results when AIED becomes commonplace in lessons.

Therefore, further studies are necessary to explore the impact of AIED on student engagement and affordances to enhance HOTS. Teachers' AIED adoption and perceptions of its impact will also change rapidly now that so many new AIED tools are available.

Acknowledgements. Supported by Eramus+ 2023-1-ES01-KA220-SCH-000157262 and PID2023-146692OB-C33 - MICIU/AEI/https://doi.org/10.13039/501100011033. DHL (Serra Húnter) acknowledges ICREA Academia.

References

Abosalem, Y.: Assessment techniques and students' higher-order thinking skills. Int. J. Second. Educ. **4**(1), 1 (2016)

Akgun, S., Greenhow, C.: Artificial intelligence in education: addressing ethical challenges in K-12 settings. AI Ethics **2**(3), 431–440 (2022)

Almasri, F.: Exploring the impact of artificial intelligence in teaching and learning of science: a systematic review of empirical research. Res. Sci. Educ. **54**(5), 977–997 (2024)

Alsowat, H.: An EFL flipped classroom teaching model: effects on english language higher-order thinking skills, student engagement and satisfaction. J. Educ. Pract. **7**(9), 108–121 (2016)

Alwaqdani, M.: Investigating teachers' perceptions of artificial intelligence tools in education: potential and difficulties. Educ. Inf. Technol. **30**, 2737–2755 (2025). https://doi.org/10.1007/s10639-024-12903-9

Bashir, N., et al.: The climate and sustainability implications of generative AI. In: An MIT Exploration of Generative AI (2024). https://doi.org/10.21428/e4baedd9.9070dfe7

Bloom, B.S., Engelhart, M.D., Furst, E.J., Hill, W.H., Krathwohl, D.R.: Handbook I: Cognitive Domain. David McKay, New York (1956)

Cardona, M.A., Rodríguez, R.J., Ishmael, K.: Artificial intelligence and the future of teaching and learning: Insights and recommendations (2023)

Chi, M.T., Boucher, N.S.: Applying the ICAP framework to improve classroom learning. In: In their Own Words: What Scholars and Teachers Want You to Know About Why and How to Apply the Science of Learning in Your Academic Setting, pp. 94–110 (2023)

Chi, M.T., Wylie, R.: The ICAP framework: linking cognitive engagement to active learning outcomes. Educ. Psychol. **49**(4), 219–243 (2014)

Chichekian, T., Benteux, B.: The potential of learning with (and not from) artificial intelligence in education. Front. Artif. Intell. **5**, 903051 (2022). https://doi.org/10.3389/frai.2022.903051

Conklin, W.: Strategies for Developing Higher-Order Thinking Skills Grades 6–12. Teacher Created Materials (2012)

Farooqi, M.T., Amanat, I., Awan, S.M.: Ethical considerations and challenges in the integration of artificial intelligence in education: a systematic review. J. Excell. Manag. Sci. **3**, 35–50 (2024)

Fuller, K.A., et al.: Development of a self-report instrument for measuring in-class student engagement reveals that pretending to engage is a significant unrecognized problem. PLoS ONE **13**(10), e0205828 (2018)

Ghanizadeh, A., Al-Hoorie, A.H., Jahedizadeh, S.: Higher order thinking skills. In: Higher Order Thinking Skills in the Language Classroom: A Concise Guide. Second Language Learning and Teaching, pp. 1–51. Springer, Cham (2020). https://doi.org/10.1007/978-3-030-56711-8_1

Giannakos, M., et al.: The promise and challenges of generative AI in education. Behav. Inf. Technol. 1–27 (2024)

Gökçearslan, S., Tosun, C., Erdemir, Z.G.: Benefits, challenges, and methods of artificial intelligence (AI) chatbots in education: a systematic literature review. Int. J. Technol. Educ. **7**(1), 19–39 (2024)

Hattie, J.A., Donoghue, G.M.: Learning strategies: a synthesis and conceptual model. npj Sci. Learn. **1**(1), 1–13 (2016)

Karl, A.A., Theophilou, E., Hernández-Leo, D.: Artificial fantasy: the effect of generative AI on cognitive empathy in creative problem solving. In: Proceedings of the 26th International Conference on Artificial Intelligence in Education, pp. 1–23 (2025)

Karpouzis, K.: Artificial intelligence in education: ethical considerations and insights from ancient Greek philosophy. In: Proceedings of the 13th Hellenic Conference on Artificial Intelligence (SETN '24), Article 57, p. 7. Association for Computing Machinery (2024). https://doi.org/10.1145/3688671.3688772

Krathwohl, D.R.: A revision of Bloom's taxonomy: an overview. Theory Pract. **41**(4), 212–218 (2002)

Lee, H.-P., Set al.: The impact of generative AI on critical thinking: Self-reported reductions in cognitive effort and confidence effects from a survey of knowledge workers. In: CHI Conference on Human Factors in Computing Systems (CHI '25), pp. 1–23. ACM, Yokohama (2025). https://doi.org/10.1145/3706598.3713778

Ley, T., Maier, R., Thalmann, S., Waizenegger, L., Pata, K., Ruiz-Calleja, A.: A knowledge appropriation model to connect scaffolded learning and knowledge maturation in workplace learning settings. Vocat. Learn. **13**, 91–112 (2020)

Ley, T., Tammets, K., Sarmiento-Márquez, E.M., Leoste, J., Hallik, M., Poom-Valickis, K.: Adopting technology in schools: modelling, measuring and supporting knowledge appropriation. Eur. J. Teach. Educ. **45**(4), 548–571 (2022)

McPeck, J.E.: Critical Thinking and Education. Routledge, London (2016)

Retnawati, H., Djidu, H., Apino, E., Anazifa, R.D.: Teachers' knowledge about higher-order thinking skills and its learning strategy. Prob. Educ. 21st Century **76**(2), 215–230 (2018)

Saar, M., Ljalikova, A., Beardsley, M.Y.: CLIL and EFL teacher perspectives on AI-EdTech: an exploration of opportunities and concerns. In: European Conference on Technology Enhanced Learning, pp. 390–405. Springer, Cham (2024)

Sabzalieva, E., Valentini, A.: ChatGPT and artificial intelligence in higher education: Quick start guide. UNESCO Digital Library (2023). https://unesdoc.unesco.org/ark:/48223/pf0000385146

Yim, I.H.Y., Wegerif, R.: Teachers' perceptions, attitudes, and acceptance of artificial intelligence (AI) educational learning tools: an exploratory study on AI literacy for young students. Fut. Educ. Res. **2**(4), 318–345 (2024)

Using Log Data to Analyze the Impact of Adaptive Support on Self-Regulated Learning in Adult Online Education

Katharina Teich[1,2](✉), Conrad Borchers[3], and Nikol Rummel[1,2]

[1] Center for Advanced Internet Studies, Bochum, Germany
katharina.teich@cais-research.de
[2] Ruhr University Bochum, Bochum, Germany
nikol.rummel@rub.de
[3] Carnegie Mellon University, Pittsburgh, PA, USA
cborcher@cs.cmu.edu

Abstract. Successful self-regulated learning (SRL) is essential for online learning, where learners must independently manage their activities with minimal guidance. This is particularly important for adult learners, who often have to balance learning with professional and personal commitments. A pervasive SRL challenge in this context is effective time management, including issues such as procrastination and inconsistent engagement, which highlights the need for support. While adaptive SRL interventions can support learners in navigating self-paced learning, little is known about the mechanisms underlying their effectiveness. A hypothesis from recent work suggests that engaging in learning behaviors in consistent time intervals, as identified through log data, positively influences learning outcomes. We study this hypothesis in a novel context, where $N = 89$ adult learners in an online course were experimentally assigned to one of two conditions, either with or without adaptive time management support. We generate insights into when and with what frequency learners engage in SRL activities inside the course's learning management system (LMS), and how these activities impact their learning outcomes. Results show that adaptive support significantly increased the regularity and frequency of engagement with the LMS. Regularity was marginally associated with improved learning outcomes, consistent with the spacing effect, which predicts better memory retrieval when practice is evenly spaced. Compared to past research, we contribute novel evidence that SRL support can increase regularity in study behavior derived from log data, and that regularity can help adult learners benefit from self-paced online learning.

Keywords: self-regulated learning · time management · procrastination · regularity · LMS · log data · adaptive support

K. Tammets et al. (Eds.): EC-TEL 2025, LNCS 16063, pp. 457–472, 2026.
https://doi.org/10.1007/978-3-032-03870-8_31

1 Introduction and Related Work

In adult online education, where learners are required to manage their learning alongside competing responsibilities, successful self-regulated learning (SRL) is a particular challenge, but also essential. One of the most critical challenges in this context is time management. Poor time management can lead to procrastination and irregular engagement patterns, all of which can negatively affect learning outcomes. In recent years, the temporal dimension of SRL, specifically, how consistently and at what times learners engage with learning activities, has become a growing focus in technology-enhanced learning research [3]. Such research often uses behavioral log data, such as login timestamps, content views, or assignment submissions, to analyze engagement delays and the spacing of study sessions as indicators of time management and procrastination tendencies [3]. This line of research has been applied to various contexts and data sets, including course enrollment records, assignment completion, and engagement in intelligent tutoring systems [6,7,14].

Seminal theories describe SRL as a cyclical process, whereby learners engage in the stages of processing information, monitoring, evaluating, and adjusting their learning [35]. Derived from this, an emerging hypothesis is that learners who engage in consistent SRL behavior exhibit better learning outcomes, and recent research has provided evidence for this hypothesis using log data [6,19]. More broadly, this hypothesis predicts that consistent learning patterns, characterized by a regular distribution of learning activities, indicate effective use of SRL strategies and predict improved learning outcomes.

In online learning environments, engaging in regular learning activities is particularly challenging. A lack of instructional support and a formal learning environment places substantial responsibility on learners to self-regulate their learning. These challenges are particularly pronounced in the context of **adult online education**, where learners have to additionally balance competing responsibilities, such as work and family, alongside their studies [26]. In this understudied context, SRL strategies, such as time management, are essential but often poorly used due to time constraints [27,32]. SRL support is important to address this challenge. Adaptive support systems tailored to learners' needs have proven particularly valuable in this regard in contexts such as higher education [2] but not in adult online education. These systems help to overcome common SRL challenges, such as irregular learning patterns, by encouraging more consistent and structured SRL behavior [33]. Despite the known effectiveness of SRL interventions, the mechanisms that underlie their effectiveness remain poorly understood. Previous research has related differences in SRL regularity to differences in learning performance, typically through post-hoc clustering of learners [8,20]. However, such studies have not experimentally manipulated SRL support to directly compare support and no-support conditions. In the rare exceptions where SRL support is studied through log data, they are usually studied through a single adaptive learning system as opposed to comparing traces to a business-as-usual control condition with little or no support (e.g., [21]) or have focused on studied learning gain differences as opposed to studying regularity from log data [1]. As a result, it remains unclear whether differences in SRL behavior are a direct consequence of given support. In contrast, correlational evidence suggests that learners who engage more regularly tend to achieve better learning outcomes [5,19]. This suggests that the effectiveness of SRL interventions may lie in their ability to promote regular engagement, thereby shaping learners' SRL strategies and ultimately improving learning outcomes. However, this hypothesis has not been systematically tested in a hypothesis-driven approach that compares engagement patterns across conditions with and without support.

To test the regularity hypothesis, we are building on research on log data-based approaches to studying SRL behaviors [3,6]. In the present paper, we analyze an existing dataset of a previous study [29], comparing an SRL support condition to a no-support condition. We use Moodle log data to explore how adaptive time management support, aimed at promoting regular learning patterns, influences SRL processes in terms of improving the regularity and frequency of engagement. We also assess the support's effectiveness in improving learning outcomes. By analyzing regularity based on an SRL support intervention study with a control-group design, we provide novel evidence that structured interventions can enhance consistent study behaviors in adult online learning.

1.1 Regularity and Time Management in SRL

Engagement regularity is defined as the consistent and spaced distribution of study sessions within learning activities or online courses [8]. This definition relates to the spacing effect, which shows that spreading learning activities over time improves long-term retention and knowledge acquisition [10,18]. One of the most important SRL strategies related to regularity is time management [22]. Successful time management involves planning and allocating time to tasks, enabling learners to prioritize activities, maintain consistent progress, and reduce stress [27,32]. However, a related area of interest is mining behavioral data to capture unsuccessful time management, for instance, through the lens of procrastination, which is defined as delays in completing tasks [24]. For example, [5] mined student course enrollment logs and found links between delayed enrollment and subsequent late course dropping. Procrastination leads to irregular patterns of learning that not only disrupt the pace of learning but also limit opportunities for feedback and reflection, which are critical components of SRL [35]. Research has shown that procrastination is a widespread problem in online learning, where increased autonomy exacerbates its effects [24,34].

1.2 Using Log Data to Study SRL

Understanding time management and the regularity of learning activities is crucial for researching SRL in online learning environments. Despite the clear relevance of these aspects to online SRL [18], research into their impact remains methodologically challenging. Previous research has largely focused on self-reported time management [32], which offers valuable insight into learners' metacognitive reasoning, intentions, and motivations. These reports are especially useful for capturing SRL processes, such as strategic planning, which often occur outside the learning platform. However, self-reports cannot capture the real-time dynamics and evolving nature of SRL processes [13]. Because these reports rely on retrospective reporting, they are prone to biases and social desirability effects and, therefore, provide a more static view of learners' SRL. To address these limitations, analyzing behavioral data has become an important approach in studying SRL [3]. Log data capture real-time behaviors such as login frequency, task transitions, and engagement sequences, allowing researchers to map these actions to SRL processes [16]. For example, regular logins and timely task completion may reflect effective time management [33], while longer periods of inactivity may signal procrastination. Nonetheless, without grounding the interpretations in a theoretical SRL framework (e.g., [35]), inferences about learners' strategies can remain speculative. Some SRL processes, such as reflection and motivation, may not manifest as observable behaviors and thus remain hidden from trace data. Despite these challenges, log data provide a more objective method of analyzing temporal learning behaviors, especially in large-scale or longitudinal studies where self-reports would be impractical. Through a theoretical lens, they allow researchers to uncover learning-relevant behavioral patterns that were previously difficult to capture.

1.3 Adaptive SRL Support

Recent research has shown that adaptive SRL support systems can improve engagement and success in online courses [12,33]. These systems use learner data to scaffold key SRL strategies, such as planning, monitoring, and goal setting [35]. The benefit of these systems lies in their ability to promote SRL processes positively correlated with learning outcomes [9]. For example, tools that help learners create and track study plans have been shown to increase engagement and improve performance [12]. In addition, intelligent tutoring systems that provide personalized feedback and guidance have also been shown to improve SRL and learning outcomes through scaffolding that adapts to learning needs in real-time [1,6,7]. However, evaluating the effectiveness of such systems depends on the availability of behavioral data capturing learner-system interactions and adapting SRL support in response. Similarly, by analyzing behavioral data, researchers can assess how an intervention affected engagement patterns over time. For example, log data allow for a fine-grained differentiation between learners with different self-regulation profiles [7], facilitating more adaptive and data-driven support mechanisms. Without this granular data, the mechanisms by which adaptive support influences SRL remain unclear, which complicates efforts to design and optimize interventions [16]. While previous studies have often examined differences in SRL behaviors between high and low performers [7], fewer studies have explicitly tested the hypothesis that promoting engagement regularity through adaptive support improves SRL and learning outcomes. Our research contributes to this emerging field by using a hypothesis-driven approach to examine the effectiveness of an intervention using log data. To achieve this, an existing dataset of learners' interactions within the Moodle LMS from an adult learning online course was analyzed, providing a unique insight into SRL behaviors with and without adaptive support. Given the critical challenge of time management in adult learning and the focus of the adaptive intervention on addressing this issue, we investigated the following research questions:

- **RQ1a:** Does the adaptive support intervention lead to a more consistent time investment, as measured by Moodle logs, for learners in the support condition compared to those in the no-support condition?
- **RQ1b:** Does the adaptive support intervention lead to a more frequent time investment, as measured by Moodle logs, for learners in the support condition compared to those in the no-support condition?
- **RQ2:** Is the regularity of learning activities in an online course, as measured by the timing and frequency of learner interactions with the course, associated with better learning outcomes, as measured by performance on course quizzes?

We hypothesize that (**H1**) learners in the support condition will demonstrate greater regularity of engagement, reflected in (**H1a**) longer and more consistent time intervals between learning activities and (**H1b**) a higher frequency of learning activities. We further expect that (**H2**) learners who show greater regularity in their SRL behavior will achieve better learning outcomes, with the support condition achieving higher overall performance than the no-support condition.

2 Methods

2.1 Study Context

To investigate the effect of an SRL support intervention on the regularity of learning behaviors, we analyze an existing dataset from a previous experimental study. This study examined the SRL of German adult online learners in a continuing education course on the topic of quality management. Course participants were professionals in fields such as engineering and project management. The course was attended by five cohorts of learners, amounting to a total of $N = 89$ adult learners. All participants attended a three-month hybrid course, which included two online self-study phases (each lasting six weeks) and two in-person phases (each lasting two days). The course was supported by the Moodle LMS, which logged participant interactions with the learning materials and activities with timestamps. The learning materials included videos, texts, and quiz activities (single- and multiple-choice questions). The experimental study compared two conditions to investigate the effects of adaptive SRL support on the SRL of adult learners: Participants were attending the course in either a no-support condition (cohorts 1–3, $n = 48$) or a support condition (cohort 4–5, $n = 41$), that received adaptive time management support (Table 1). Informed consent was obtained from all participants.

Table 1. Distribution of Participants Among the Conditions

Condition	Cohort	Timeframe of the courses	n of Participants
No-Support	1	Mar 2021 – May 2021	15 (12 male, 3 female)
No-Support	2	Oct 2021 – Dec 2021	16 (7 male, 9 female)
No-Support	3	Apr 2022 – Jun 2022	17 (11 male, 6 female)
Support	4	Dec 2022 – Feb 2023	20 (14 male, 6 female)
Support	5	Feb 2023 – Apr 2023	21 (18 male, 3 female)

In the no-support condition, learners accessed course materials through a hierarchical structure, where selecting a module revealed its associated materials. Participants in the support condition engaged in an enhanced learning environment with adaptive SRL support, which was designed to address time management challenges. The intervention provided personalized support tailored to the individual learner as determined by a diagnostic pre-questionnaire. This questionnaire assessed learners' prior knowledge through a multiple-choice test per course topic. It also measured familiarity with self-paced learning (i.e., the number of previous online courses completed and the time since the last course). The adaptive SRL intervention implemented in the support condition integrated three key components into the Moodle course interface (Fig. 1).

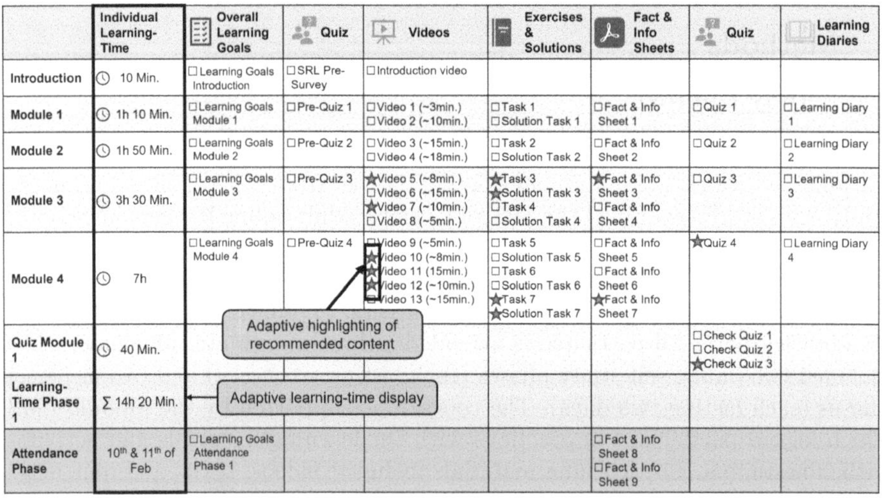

Fig. 1. Design Draft of the Adaptive SRL Support Intervention

The intervention was designed to address individual and contextual differences in learners' self-regulation with a particular focus on time management and regular engagement. Informed by principles of adaptive learning design (e.g.,

[25]) and the first two cycles of a design-based research process [28], the intervention provided flexible, personalized support aligned with learners' needs and prior experience. The system offered three key support features: The (1) **course overview** organized materials by topic and media format, allowing learners to navigate the course efficiently and track their progress through embedded progress bars. The (2) **adaptive learning-time display** estimated the time for each module based on prior knowledge and experience, helping learners allocate time efficiently and avoid last-minute studying. Finally, the (3) **adaptive highlighting of recommended content** directed learners to key material by identifying knowledge gaps, encouraging structured study habits, and preventing inefficient use of time. Together, these features were designed to encourage consistent engagement, support the development of structured learning routines, and minimize irregular study behavior, thereby enhancing learners' SRL.

2.2 Data Set

The log data consisted of timestamped events capturing student interactions with the Moodle LMS. We preprocessed the logs for subsequent analyses as follows: First, we categorized events into action types to ensure analytical focus on meaningful learner-initiated interactions that capture differences in time management. We included activity types directly related to learning, such as completing tasks, as well as transition activities that captured how learners navigated through the course. Activities related to quiz sections were excluded, as not every course iteration included the same number of quiz activities. This categorization ensured that the interpretation of results would be related to deliberate student actions comparable across all five course iterations. This step removed 24.6% of the recorded log data. Second, we classified activities by time of day to capture engagement patterns. Events were categorized into working hours (weekdays 8 AM to 5 PM), weekday evenings (after 5 PM), and weekends. These classifications facilitated an exploratory analysis of when students engaged with the LMS. After these preprocessing steps, the unit of analysis of our dataset represented individual, timestamped learner actions in the LMS. In total, it comprised 139,200 actions by 89 learners (Table 2).

Table 2. Overview of Log Data Set

Condition	Total Logs	Logs after Data Cleaning
No-Support	97,522	63,088 (64.7% of total logs)
Support	87,020	76,112 (87.5% of total logs)
Total	**184,542**	**139,200 (75.4% of total logs)**

2.3 Data Analysis

To investigate **RQ1a**, whether SRL support leads to more regular LMS activity, we calculated time differences between activities for each user. These differences were log-transformed to normalize the distribution, and intervals shorter than 15 min were excluded to capture distinct study activity sessions. The threshold of 15 min was determined based on visual inspections of the time difference distribution. In the following, we refer to unique episodes of LMS activity with gaps of more than 15 min as *sessions*, where appropriate. A mixed-effects regression model with a Gaussian link was fitted to infer engagement regularity, represented as the average difference between LMS activity sessions. Linear mixed models adjust for multiple measurements per student, which would otherwise inflate p-values, per individualized student intercepts capturing variation in the baseline proclivity in the outcome. All models were estimated using the `lme4` package for the R statistical software [4].

Our first hypothesis (**H1a**) conjectured that learners would exhibit a higher regularity of activity in the intervention condition. To estimate this effect, we specified and tested a main effect of condition (Eq. 1):

$$\texttt{regularity}_{ij} = \beta_0 + \beta_1 \texttt{intervention}_i + u_i + \epsilon_{ij}, \tag{1}$$

where $\texttt{regularity}_{ij}$ represents the regularity score for student i at observation (i.e., session) j, β_0 is the fixed intercept, and β_1 captures the fixed effect of being in the intervention group ($\texttt{intervention}_i = 1$ for students in the intervention, 0 otherwise). The term u_i denotes a random intercept for each student, accounting for individual differences in baseline regularity, and ϵ_{ij} is the residual error for each observation.

For **RQ1b**, we examined whether improvements in regularity were due to increased activity levels or changes in the distribution of existing activities. Both alternative explanations can be compared by estimating whether the intervention, in addition to differences in regularity, leads to more activity in general, represented in the number of sessions students exhibited LMS activity in. After aggregating session counts by user and intervention group, a generalized linear model with a Poisson link was used to model the number of sessions (n) as a function of the intervention condition (Eq. 2):

$$n_i = \exp(\beta_0 + \beta_1 \texttt{intervention}_i) + \epsilon_{ij} \tag{2}$$

To address **RQ2**, we evaluated whether regularity in LMS activity was associated with quiz performance. Quiz scores were standardized by dividing by the maximum possible score, with mean imputation applied for missing values. Median regularity scores during learning phases associated with quizzes were aggregated per student and phase and standardized to a mean of 0 and a standard deviation of 1 to aid model coefficient interpretation. A linear mixed-effects model, adjusting for multiple phases per student, tested the relationship between regularity and quiz performance:

$$\texttt{quiz score}_{ij} = \beta_0 + \beta_1 \texttt{regularity}_i + u_i + \epsilon_{ij}. \tag{3}$$

All data analysis code is available via the study's supplementary Git repository.[1]

3 Results

3.1 RQ1a: Does SRL Support Lead to More Regular Activity?

Results revealed that learners in the support condition statistically significantly demonstrated more regular LMS activity, characterized by longer and more consistent time intervals between consecutive sessions of LMS activity. The mixed-effects model showed a significant effect of the intervention group ($\beta_1 = 0.322$, $SE = 0.137$, $z = 2.357$, $p = .018$), with the estimated mean log-transformed time difference for the support condition being $9.465 + 0.322$ compared to 9.465 in the control condition. This effect size is computed on the log-transformed scale of the outcome. Hence, by re-transformation (computed as $(\exp(9.465 + 0.322) - \exp(9.465))/\exp(9.465) \approx 38\%$, the effect corresponds to an approximate 38% increase in average time intervals between activities in the support condition. These findings support **H1a** and suggest that the SRL support intervention effectively fosters greater regularity in learner engagement with the LMS. The effect of support on activity regularity was robust across different times of the week. Specifically, there were no significant interactions between the support condition and time periods, including weekends ($p = .478$) and weekdays during working hours ($p = .605$). These results suggest that the support's impact on engagement regularity was consistent regardless of the time of week.

3.2 RQ1b: Does SRL Support Lead to More Frequent Activity?

The generalized linear model revealed that learners in the SRL support condition engaged in significantly more sessions overall, with a 32.4% increase in the average number of activity sessions compared to the control condition ($\beta_1 = 0.281$, $SE = 0.006$, $z = 48.536$, $p < .001$). This increase indicates that the intervention not only influenced the regularity of engagement but also led to a higher volume of overall activity. The density plot in Fig. 2 shows the distribution of time intervals between LMS activity sessions for learners in the control and intervention groups. The x-axis represents the time difference in minutes between sessions, while the y-axis denotes the estimated density of session intervals. The intervention group exhibits higher densities overall, indicating a greater number of activity sessions compared to the control group. Additionally, the distribution in the support condition is less skewed, with a more even spread across time intervals. This difference in skew is visible in the density of longer time intervals between sessions, which is especially elevated in the support condition, reflecting more regular engagement. These visual trends align with the statistical findings, demonstrating that SRL support not only increases the frequency of engagement but also helps regulate session timing.

[1] https://github.com/conradborchers/srl-regularity-experiment/.

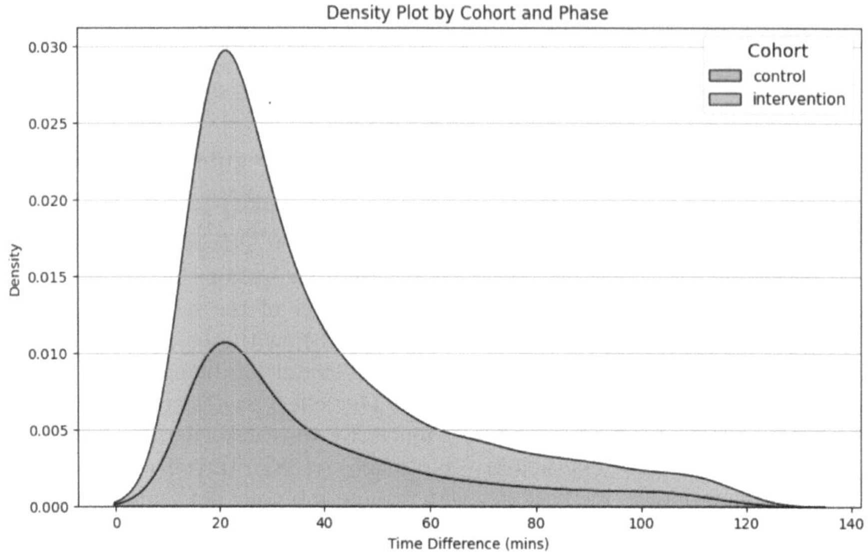

Fig. 2. Estimated density plot of time intervals between LMS activity sessions for no-support and support condition.

We note that, although learners in the support condition had longer average intervals between sessions, they also engaged more frequently. This exemplifies that frequency and regularity can vary independently of each other (e.g., a student might engage a little every day, or a lot in a single day).

3.3 RQ2: Is Regularity Associated with Higher Quiz Scores?

Results revealed a positive, albeit non-significant, association between engagement regularity and quiz performance ($\beta_1 = 0.127$, $SE = 0.077$, $z = 1.652$, $p = .099$). While the effect size suggests that greater regularity may lead to improved learning outcomes, the confidence interval indicates uncertainty ($[-0.024, 0.279]$). One reason for this uncertainty in estimation stems from a potential ceiling effect in quiz scores: all but two students exhibited quiz scores of above 80% and the majority scored above 90%, indicating distributional skew. These findings suggest that learners with more regular activity may perform better on quizzes, though support for **H2** remains inconclusive.

4 Discussion

This paper investigated whether adaptive SRL support promotes regular engagement and improves learning outcomes by analyzing log data from a previous experimental study comparing a no-support and a support condition. While recent studies in the log data-based analysis of SRL differences have found links between engagement regularity and academic performance [8,18], evidence so far has been correlational rather than experimental. This paper addressed this gap by testing the hypothesis that SRL support increases regular engagement and, consequently, learning outcomes by analyzing log data from a previous study that employed an experimental control-group design.

4.1 Increased Regularity in Support Condition (H1)

For **RQ1a**, which investigated whether adaptive SRL support led to more regular engagement, results showed that supported learners engaged in more consistent study patterns (i.e., showed more evenly distributed intervals). This effect was stable across different days of the week and times of day, suggesting that structured support improved learners' ability to regulate their study schedules.

The results for **RQ1b**, which additionally focused on the frequency of engagement, showed that adaptive support also led to greater overall interaction with course materials. Together, these findings indicate that adaptive SRL support encouraged both more regular and frequent engagement, which are two key aspects of effective time management in online learning. While these results might seem contradictory at first, showing both longer intervals between sessions and increased frequency, they capture different engagement dimensions: Regularity reflects how evenly sessions are spaced over time, while frequency reflects how often engagement occurs. A learner may engage frequently but irregularly (e.g., five times in one day and then not at all for a week) or less frequently but regularly (e.g., twice weekly at stable intervals). Our results suggest that adaptive support helped learners both engage more frequently and spread their efforts more evenly across the course timeline. These findings are in line with SRL theory, which emphasizes the role of cyclical, consistent engagement in tracking progress and refining strategies [35]. They also highlight the importance of supporting time management in adult online learning, where effective time management is critical to academic success [22,27]. Consistent engagement also serves as a protective factor against procrastination [24], which often leads to last-minute cramming, cognitive overload, and reduced knowledge retention, which ultimately affects learning outcomes and increases stress [24,30]. By promoting structured engagement patterns, adaptive SRL support can help learners avoid these negative cycles [30] and foster more effective study habits.

The methodological approach strengthens our findings: Assigning participants to different conditions allowed us to isolate the effect of adaptive support on engagement regularity. The identification of distributed engagement patterns was only possible through log data analysis, which provided time stamps of learner interactions [31]. Taking this methodological approach revealed that adaptive SRL support promotes not only temporary increases in activity but also measurable, long-term improvements in engagement.

4.2 Regularity and the Spacing Effect (H2)

For (**RQ2**), the results suggested a positive but non-significant relationship between engagement regularity and learning outcomes. This trend aligns with the spacing effect, which suggests that learning is more effective when spread out over time rather than concentrated in short, intense periods [10]. When learners engage at regular intervals, they benefit from retrieval practice, which strengthens memory retention and facilitates the transfer of knowledge across contexts [10]. The increased regularity observed in the support condition suggests that learners engaged in more spaced study sessions, which promotes deeper processing and long-term retention, which should, in turn, theoretically improve their learning outcomes, even if this is not directly reflected in the quiz results.

In addition, the observed regularity may also reflect differences in learners' procrastination tendencies. Although we did not psychometrically measure procrastination, our log-based regularity metric approximates behavioral indicators of procrastination, which are linked to lower performance and persistence [15]. Research has shown that temporal engagement features can reliably signal procrastination and demonstrate correlations with self-report measures [5]. While not equivalent to validated survey scales, these behavioral proxies provide insight into differences among learners that influence engagement and outcomes.

However, the lack of a significant effect on quiz scores raises some questions. One interpretation of the inconclusive results is that there are between-student differences in how time management relates to learning outcomes. While regular engagement is generally considered ideal, research suggests that time management strategies can take different forms [32]. Traditionally, procrastination has been considered a negative factor affecting learning success [30]. However, research suggests that procrastination can be an adaptive form of time management, particularly for learners who strategically delay tasks to optimize efficiency [11]. This concept, known as active procrastination, challenges the assumption that all learners benefit from rigid study routines [11]. For adult learners balancing multiple responsibilities, strategic delays may sometimes be necessary for efficient time management. In this context, irregular study patterns may not reflect poor SRL, but rather an alternative SRL strategy for some students.

4.3 Implications for Adaptive SRL Support

The findings highlight both the effectiveness and limitations of adaptive SRL support in promoting regular engagement. While the intervention successfully increased regularity, the inherent heterogeneity of adult learners' [17] raises important questions about whether consistent engagement should be universally encouraged: A one-size-fits-all approach to time management support may not fully meet the needs of all learners. Some learners may benefit from scheduling tools to promote consistent study patterns [12], while others may use alternative time management strategies, such as active procrastination [11], that allow them to strategically delay tasks without negatively impacting performance. This tension between promoting regularity and recognizing individual learning rhythms underlines the need for adaptive SRL support that is responsive to learner characteristics and contextual factors such as prior experience with online learning and external time pressures. Although the intervention was effective in promoting regular engagement overall, learners' individual circumstances likely influenced how they reacted to the support. While irregular engagement is often interpreted as procrastination, research suggests that deliberate delays can represent a strategic time management approach for certain learners [11]. This highlights the need for adaptive interventions that can distinguish between unproductive and deliberate procrastination. In this regard, behavioral data are essential: Predictive modeling with log data could identify different engagement patterns [34], allowing adaptive systems to support structured engagement for some learners while recommending active procrastination strategies for others.

Furthermore, the results for **RQ2** suggest that while the intervention increased engagement regularity, its impact on short-term learning outcomes remains inconclusive. To fully benefit from the spacing effect, support should incorporate features that encourage retrieval-based learning [10]. This could, for instance, include time-sensitive review tasks that reinforce knowledge retention over time. In addition, providing learners with real-time visualizations of their engagement patterns [23] could enhance self-awareness and encourage reflection on study behavior, enabling them to adjust their learning strategies proactively.

4.4 Limitations and Future Work

We acknowledge that the ceiling effect in our assessment has masked stronger associations between regularity and learning outcomes. Almost all learners scored above 80%, reducing variability. As the quiz was based on multiple-choice, short-recall questions, it may not have been sensitive enough to reflect deeper learning or long-term retention. To better capture the effects of regular engagement, future studies could incorporate alternative assessments, such as delayed post-tests or applied tasks. A second limitation concerns the reliance on log data only. While log data provide objective, timestamped insights into behavioral patterns, they do not fully capture learners' cognitive strategies or perceptions of the effectiveness of time management. Future research is needed to triangulate behavioral data with other measures, such as questionnaires or structured interviews, to develop a more comprehensive understanding of SRL processes [13]. Finally, the generalizability of our findings needs to be explored in different online learning contexts. This study was conducted in an adult learning course, where adults balanced learning with multiple responsibilities. Future research should investigate if similar effects are observed in other settings, such as universities, to determine how adaptive interventions can be tailored to different learner populations.

5 Conclusion

This study provides novel insights into how adaptive SRL support influences the engagement regularity and frequency, and how these measures relate to learning outcomes. Adaptive SRL support significantly increased both the regularity and frequency of engagement: Learners in the support condition showed a 38% increase in average time intervals between activities and a 32% increase in the number of activity sessions. Additionally, this research also contributes to understanding how regularity relates to learning outcomes. While the results for RQ2 did not show a statistical significant relationship, the observed trend aligns with the spacing effect, suggesting that distributing study sessions over time supports better knowledge retention. The contribution of this research lies in novel experimental contrasts of a no-support and a support condition, offering evidence that adaptive support shapes learner engagement in the understudied context of adult education. Going beyond observational analyses of learner differences, this study highlights the value of experimental condition assignment and log data in evaluating adaptive SRL support, gathering new evidence for the hypothesis that regular study behavior corresponds to better learning outcomes.

Acknowledgments. This research was funded by the German Federal Ministry of Education and Research (BMBF) under grant number 01JD1907A.

References

1. Azevedo, R., et al.: Lessons learned and future directions of metatutor: leveraging multichannel data to scaffold self-regulated learning with an intelligent tutoring system. Front. Psychol. **13**, 813632 (2022)
2. Azevedo, R., Hadwin, A.F.: Scaffolding self-regulated learning and metacognition-implications for the design of computer-based scaffolds. Instr. Sci. **33**(5/6), 367–379 (2005)
3. Baker, R., et al.: The benefits and caveats of using clickstream data to understand student self-regulatory behaviors: opening the black box of learning processes. Int. J. Educ. Technol. High. Educ. **17**, 1–24 (2020)
4. Bates, D.: Fitting linear mixed-effects models using lme4. arXiv preprint arXiv:1406.5823 (2014)
5. Borchers, C., Xu, Y., Pardos, Z.A.: Workload overload? Late enrollment leads to course dropout. J. Educ. Data Min. **17**(1), 126–156 (2025)
6. Borchers, C., Zhang, J., Baker, R.S., Aleven, V.: Using think-aloud data to understand relations between self-regulation cycle characteristics and student performance in intelligent tutoring systems. In: Proceedings of the 14th Learning Analytics and Knowledge Conference, pp. 529–539 (2024)
7. Bouchet, F., Harley, J.M., Trevors, G.J., Azevedo, R.: Clustering and profiling students according to their interactions with an intelligent tutoring system fostering self-regulated learning. J. Educ. Data Min. **5**(1), 104–146 (2013)
8. Bourguet, M.L.: Demonstrating the impact of study regularity on academic success using learning analytics. In: Proceedings of the 14th Learning Analytics and Knowledge Conference, pp. 736–741 (2024)
9. Broadbent, J., Poon, W.L.: Self-regulated learning strategies & academic achievement in online higher education learning environments: a systematic review. Internet High. Educ. **27**, 1–13 (2015)

10. Cepeda, N.J., Vul, E., Rohrer, D., Wixted, J.T., Pashler, H.: Spacing effects in learning: a temporal ridgeline of optimal retention. Psychol. Sci. **19**(11), 1095–1102 (2008)
11. Chun Chu, A.H., Choi, J.N.: Rethinking procrastination: positive effects of "active" procrastination behavior on attitudes and performance. J. Soc. Psychol. **145**(3), 245–264 (2005)
12. Davis, D., Triglianos, V., Hauff, C., Houben, G.-J.: SRLx: a personalized learner interface for MOOCs. In: Pammer-Schindler, V., Pérez-Sanagustín, M., Drachsler, H., Elferink, R., Scheffel, M. (eds.) EC-TEL 2018. LNCS, vol. 11082, pp. 122–135. Springer, Cham (2018). https://doi.org/10.1007/978-3-319-98572-5_10
13. Du, J., Hew, K.F., Liu, L.: What can online traces tell us about students' self-regulated learning? A systematic review of online trace data analysis. Comput. Educ. **201**, 104828 (2023)
14. Fischer, C., et al.: Mining big data in education: affordances and challenges. Rev. Res. Educ. **44**(1), 130–160 (2020)
15. Gurung, A., et al.: Starting seatwork earlier as a valid measure of student engagement. arXiv preprint arXiv:2505.13341 (2025)
16. Hadwin, A.F., Nesbit, J.C., Jamieson-Noel, D., Code, J., Winne, P.H.: Examining trace data to explore self-regulated learning. Metacogn. Learn. **2**, 107–124 (2007)
17. Huang, H.M.: Toward constructivism for adult learners in online learning environments. Br. J. Educ. Technol. **33**(1), 27–37 (2002)
18. Jovanovic, J., Mirriahi, N., Gašević, D., Dawson, S., Pardo, A.: Predictive power of regularity of pre-class activities in a flipped classroom. Comput. Educ. **134**, 156–168 (2019)
19. Kim, J., Li, Q., Jiang, Z., Xu, D.: Not all delay is procrastination: analyzing subpatterns of academic delayers in online learning. In: Proceedings of the 15th International Learning Analytics and Knowledge Conference, pp. 977–983 (2025)
20. Li, S., Zheng, J., Huang, X., Xie, C.: Self-regulated learning as a complex dynamical system: examining students' stem learning in a simulation environment. Learn. Individ. Differ. **95**, 102144 (2022)
21. Li, X., et al.: The flora engine: using analytics to measure and facilitate learners' own regulation activities. arXiv preprint arXiv:2412.09763 (2024)
22. Mejia-Domenzain, P., Marras, M., Giang, C., Cattaneo, A., Käser, T.: Evolutionary clustering of apprentices' self-regulated learning behavior in learning journals. IEEE Trans. Learn. Technol. **15**(5), 579–593 (2022)
23. Molenaar, I., Horvers, A., Dijkstra, R., Baker, R.S.: Personalized visualizations to promote young learners' SRL: the learning path app. In: Proceedings of the Tenth International Conference on Learning Analytics & Knowledge, pp. 330–339 (2020)
24. Park, J., Yu, R., Rodriguez, F., Baker, R., Smyth, P., Warschauer, M.: Understanding student procrastination via mixture models. Int. Educ. Data Min. Soc. (2018)
25. Plass, J.L., Pawar, S.: Toward a taxonomy of adaptivity for learning. J. Res. Technol. Educ. **52**(3), 275–300 (2020)
26. Schulz, M., Roßnagel, C.S.: Informal workplace learning: an exploration of age differences in learning competence. Learn. Instr. **20**(5), 383–399 (2010)
27. Sitzmann, T., Ely, K.: A meta-analysis of self-regulated learning in work-related training and educational attainment: what we know and where we need to go. Psychol. Bull. **137**(3), 421 (2011)
28. Teich, K., Loock, V., Rummel, N.: User-centered design of adaptive support in a continuing education online course: findings from a design-based research process.

In: Zaphiris, P., Ioannou, A. (eds.) HCII 2024. LNCS, vol. 14722, pp. 103–123. Springer, Cham (2024). https://doi.org/10.1007/978-3-031-61672-3_8
29. Teich, K., Loock, V.S., Rummel, N.: Meeting the challenges of continuing education online courses: can we promote self-regulated learning strategies with adaptive support? Br. J. Edu. Technol. **55**(4), 1437–1455 (2024)
30. Wäschle, K., Allgaier, A., Lachner, A., Fink, S., Nückles, M.: Procrastination and self-efficacy: tracing vicious and virtuous circles in self-regulated learning. Learn. Instr. **29**, 103–114 (2014)
31. Winne, P.H., Baker, R.S.: The potentials of educational data mining for researching metacognition, motivation and self-regulated learning. J. Educ. Data Min. **5**(1), 1–8 (2013)
32. Wolters, C.A., Won, S., Hussain, M.: Examining the relations of time management and procrastination within a model of self-regulated learning. Metacogn. Learn. **12**, 381–399 (2017)
33. Wong, J., Khalil, M., Baars, M., de Koning, B.B., Paas, F.: Exploring sequences of learner activities in relation to self-regulated learning in a massive open online course. Comput. Educ. **140**, 103595 (2019)
34. You, J.W.: Examining the effect of academic procrastination on achievement using LMS data in e-learning. J. Educ. Technol. Soc. **18**(3), 64–74 (2015)
35. Zimmerman, B.J.: A social cognitive view of self-regulated academic learning. J. Educ. Psychol. **81**(3), 329 (1989)

Evaluating the Impact of Debriefing Techniques on Student Outcomes After CSCL Activities

Carola Theißen[1(✉)] and Davinia Hernández-Leo[2]

[1] University of Education Heidelberg, Heidelberg, Germany
theissen.carola@gmx.de

[2] ICT Department, Universitat Pompeu Fabra, Barcelona, Spain

Abstract. This design-based research investigates the impact of different debriefing techniques on student learning following Collaborative Learning Flow Patterns (CLFP). Following a literature review, findings were incorporated into the design phase, ensuring alignment with multimedia principles. In five experimental cycles participants engaged in tasks following the Pyramid CLFP, generating 328 analyzable data sets. The study explored various debriefing techniques, including Debriefing Scripts and visualizing student artifacts using Word Clouds, Quotes with Emphasis, Heatmaps, and Concept Maps. Results indicate that structured and visual debriefing methods notably enhance student learning outcome. Word Clouds facilitated broad discussions in open-ended tasks but lacked structural depth. Concept Maps provided clear representations of complex relationships, proving highly effective for structured tasks. Quotes with Emphasis supported student reflection but risked reinforcing misconceptions, while Heatmaps illustrated collective tendencies but lacked relational detail. These findings highlight the importance of carefully designed debriefing techniques in optimizing student learning outcomes and provide the basis for further advancing the implementation of these in pyramid collaborative learning.

Keywords: Teacher-led debriefing · Computer-Supported Collaborative Learning · Collaborative Learning Flow Pattern · Design-based research

1 Introduction

Debriefing is a structured discussion that takes place after a learning activity. It is a way to analyze experiences, extract insights, and identify areas for future improvement. The knowledge that students take away from learning activities is often subjective, shaped by their prior understanding and the specific interactions they engage in during the learning process [1]. In this context, the goal of debriefing is to explore the individual knowledge that students have constructed. The teacher, as the debriefer, facilitates this exchange of perspectives, providing a complex coordination task that involves summarizing and reflecting on the learning process in real-time [2].

Technological tools can assist teachers in managing the debriefing process, but they also increase the cognitive load on the teacher [3]. Consequently, understanding how

K. Tammets et al. (Eds.): EC-TEL 2025, LNCS 16063, pp. 473–488, 2026.
https://doi.org/10.1007/978-3-032-03870-8_32

to best support teacher-led debriefing is critical to optimizing learning outcomes in collaborative settings.

In this study, debriefing methods were tested after Pyramid CLFP facilitated through a Computer-Supported Collaborative Learning (CSCL) tool called PyramidApp. In the web-based application, students engage in progressively larger groups as they move through different levels of activity. First, they are asked to enter an individual answer to a task posed (individual level). Students are then randomly allocated into groups where they evaluate their peers' submissions and engage in discussion to collaboratively improve a joint answer. Optionally, a second group level can be promoted when the groups merge into larger ones and students rate and improve the options further. Meanwhile, the teacher is provided with a dashboard to monitor students' engagement that aims to support orchestration [2]. At the end of the activity, the teacher is encouraged to debrief the students by a pop-up window.

Up to now, debriefing has been carried out on the fly, challenging the teacher to summarize what the students have learned and to guide a reflective discussion. Therefore, debriefing methods should be found and developed that enable the teacher to structure and facilitate the debriefing to support the students' learning in the most effective way.

2 Related Work

Debriefing has been widely recognized as a crucial component of effective learning, particularly in constructivist and collaborative settings [2, 4, 5]. While much of the early research focused on simulation-based learning in healthcare [6–8], recent studies have expanded its application to classroom-based group learning and active learning strategies [3, 9].

Barrett et al. [9] found that addressing both correct and incorrect responses during debriefing enhances conceptual understanding, especially in tasks involving higher-order thinking. These findings align with Butler et al. [10], who emphasize that explanation-based feedback promotes deeper comprehension and supports conceptual transfer. In contrast, research suggests that the effectiveness of debriefing is less dependent on the specific method used and more on the instructor's ability to facilitate meaningful reflection and discussion [8, 11].

3 Methods

A design-based research (DBR) approach was chosen as it aims to develop and investigate didactic innovations in real teaching-learning contexts. DBR focuses on both developing practical solutions and generating theoretical insights [12].

In the preparation phase, a comprehensive literature review was conducted to establish a theoretical foundation. Due to space constraints, this phase is not described in detail. During the design phase, insights from the literature review were used to develop initial methods for teacher-led debriefing in collaborative learning settings. Furthermore, data collection and evaluation strategies were designed. Initial classroom observations of PyramidApp in use were conducted, followed by discussions with the facilitator to refine the approach. In the third phase, the interventions were developed and evaluated in five iterative cycles and recommendations for designing instructional strategies and action were derived. The results of the retrospective analysis fed the respective following design phase.

3.1 Data Collection and Evaluation Methods

The research was conducted during the autumn semester 2024 at a university in Spain. Participants were students from undergraduate (N = 257) as well as postgraduate programs (N = 71) in the School of Engineering in courses held by one teacher.

The empirical experiments follow a mixed methods approach, in which the data collection and analysis are both qualitative and quantitative. Data collection takes place during and after the teaching experiment and includes students work, questionnaires before and after the debriefing, field notes and 'mini-interviews' with students and the teacher [13]. Depending on the student task and type of question (open- vs. close-end) in each cycle the tests are analyzed.

In the 'empirical experiments' phase, a pre-posttest design is used in which the students' answers to the question posed in the respective cycle are queried at different points in time. The students' individual submissions to PyramidApp are used as a pretest. To be able to differentiate the learning outcome between collaborative learning and the final debriefing, the questionnaires are completed both before and after the teacher-led debriefing. The data collection point before the debriefing is therefore referred to as the mid-test. Mid- and posttests are collected with the help of Google Forms.

Data from pre-, mid- and posttests is analyzed depending on the student task. If necessary, all data is first translated into English with the help of Google Translate. For open-end tasks, a qualitative content analysis according to Mayring [14] is carried out with the help of MAXQDA24 [15]. For closed tasks, students' submissions are assessed, and statistical tests are computed in Jamovi [16] looking for significant improvement through the debriefing interventions in students' performance and comparing their effect on learning outcomes.

4 Initial Design Phase of Possible Debriefing Methods

The literature review indicated a lack of research regarding debriefing Collaborative Learning activities. Second, the review gave insight into various approaches on how a debriefing can be structured and carried out. As the debriefing strategy can be classified as immediate or delayed, oral in class [1], several techniques can be applicable. Additionally, having access to students' submissions opens opportunities to incorporate them into the debriefing discussion.

The debriefing methods designed and investigated in this study can be categorized into three distinct approaches: (1) a control condition with no structured debriefing, (2) debriefing using a scripted framework called "Debriefing Script", and (3) debriefing incorporating a visual representation of students' artifacts. Each method is described in detail below.

4.1 Control Condition

The teacher that was part of this study already had experience in orchestrating and facilitating the debriefing. They made a judgement based on the situation and their experience whether the students should take some time to look at the winning options in PyramidApp or even displayed given answers that struck them. In cycle four, this method is discussed as the control condition as the aim of the study is to explore possible improvements to this intuitive method and to standardize the process for other facilitators too.

4.2 Debriefing Script

The literature review found that debriefing processes are often structured into different phases and identified the formats for Lederman's phase model [1]. The first phase of debriefing involved an invitation to talk by the teacher and/or questions regarding what occurred during the learning activity. The second phase focused on recognizing the effects of the activity, with questions addressing students' experiences and emotions. Finally, the third phase provided space for discussing implications, applications, and clarifications of key facts, concepts, or principles. These three phases were then adapted into a script for the present research. Each of the phases is introduced by an exemplary question and can be extended by optional follow-up questions. A particular emphasis in the design phase of the Debriefing Script was placed on the language of the questions to encourage student engagement and motivation in expressing their thoughts and feelings. Particularly the optional follow-up questions of the Debriefing Script, were developed based on the framework *Debriefing with Good Judgement* [17]. It should foster a safe environment where students can share their perspectives without uncertainty regarding the instructors' intent. At the same time, this approach addresses misconceptions while avoiding negative emotions and defensiveness utilizing "advocacy-inquiry" (ibid., 53). The Debriefing Script that was tailored to debriefing discussions following the activities in this study can be seen in Table 1.

Table 1. Debriefing Script for three-phase debriefing discussion

Initial Questions	Optional follow-up questions
"How did you like this learning activity?"	Anyone else have a thought? Are there any other options?

(continued)

Table 1. (*continued*)

Initial Questions	Optional follow-up questions
"What have you learned during this activity? Are there any new insights you have gained in communicating with your peers?"	I saw that many of you answered....So I am curious: Where did you hear about this?/Can you help me understand how you came to this conclusion? In my experience I have observed...I was wondering what you all think about that? I see some have submitted...as an answer. Given my view, I don't get it. What am I missing here? **Was there something that surprised you in your peers' answers?*
"Can someone please summarize what we have learned and how you would answer my initial question now?"	Does someone want to add something?

* This follow-up question was included during the fourth cycle as students were hesitant to engage in the debriefing discussion. The facilitator posed it intuitively, in cycle five a similar phrasing obtained active response as well.

4.3 Visualizations Using Student's Artifacts

The third debriefing method was also derived from the literature review, where numerous studies were found that utilized students' artifacts in the broadest sense to facilitate debriefing. Since PyramidApp already provides the facilitator with written responses from students regarding their tasks, this method aims to leverage that data. To explore possible approaches for presenting the data, relevant literature on data visualization was consulted [18, 19] and Mayer's Principles of Multimedia Learning [20] were considered. The creation of these visualizations was approached openly and was an integral part of the study. The visualizations tested in this study (Word Clouds, Heatmaps, Quotes with Emphasis, and Concept Maps) are included as exemplary illustrations and have been translated into English if possible.

5 Empirical Experiments

Each cycle aimed to compare different debriefing methods to determine the most effective approach for enhancing student learning outcomes and overall experience across various task types. Table 2 presents the tasks for each of the cycles with their educational objectives based on Krathwohl's Taxonomy [21].

Table 2. Tasks in Empirical Experiments

Cycle	Student Task	Task Type	Educational objectives
1: Topics of debate in ICT	Topics of debate/controversy in Information and Communication Technology (ICT)	Associative open-ended task	**Remember**: Identify key issues or topics in the field of ICT that are often debated or controversial
2: Scientific Credibility	By only looking at this bibliographic data (not checking the actual documents), which of the following information sources would have higher levels of scientific credibility and why? [List of references]	Analytical open-ended task	**Evaluate**: Compare and contrast the credibility of the listed sources based on bibliographic information and articulate reasoning
3: Personal Data	Which of the following are personal data? Name, Nickname, register, writing, Notes report, age, attendance list, class photo, medical record, text message, mailing address, school name, class schedule, mobile phone bill	Closed task	**Apply**: Categorize the provided list of items as either personal data or not based on the definition

(continued)

Table 2. (*continued*)

Cycle	Student Task	Task Type	Educational objectives
4: Credit Scoring	Imagine you have millions of events from WhatsApp messages. Of each event you have the following info: Telephone number that sends the message, Telephone number that receives the message, Localization, Message address, Message length (in characters), Date of the message From these data, we ask you to create the most relevant user features oriented towards financial risk: which features could you extract from these events?	Guided open-ended task	**Analyze**: Generate a set of new user features that could be used to assess financial risk effectively, considering the given data
5: Servlet Code	Identify and explain three errors in the following servlet which aims to implement a change in its behaviour depending on the webpage from which it is liked to	Closed task	**Apply:** Identify, explain and solve errors

The cycles were carried out in different higher education classrooms in the Department of Engineering. Table 3 gives an overview of the runs in each cycle, their population and the analyzed data sets.

Table 3. Overview Empirical Experiments with Intervention Groups and Key Data for the Debriefing Discussion

Cycle/Group	Debriefing Condition	Duration of debriefing (min)	No. Students	Data sets	Teaching language
1A	Debriefing Script with Word Cloud	8	59	53	Spanish/Catalan

(*continued*)

Table 3. (*continued*)

Cycle/Group	Debriefing Condition	Duration of debriefing (min)	No. Students	Data sets	Teaching language
1B	Debriefing Script	9	49	40	Spanish/Catalan
2A	Focus Group	12	12	12	English
2B	Distributed Visualizations: Quotes with Emphasis, Heatmap, Concept Map	15	32 + 4 online	33	English
2C	(see 2B)	18	18	14	English
3A	Heatmap + Quotes with Emphasis	4	45	36	Spanish/Catalan
3B	Concept Map	3	48	40	Spanish/Catalan
4A	Control	4	50	36	English
4B	Debriefing Script	8	24	17	Spanish/Catalan
4C	Concept Map	4	41	35	Spanish/Catalan
5A	Debriefing Script	5	8	6	English
5B	Concept Map	3	6	6	English

5.1 Results

This section presents the results of the empirical experiments in chronological order and compares students' outcomes in the tested interventions. These serve as a basis to refine the designed debriefing techniques and to give recommendations on future research as well as their implementation in debriefing practices following Pyramid CLFP.

Cycle 1. The task in the first cycle prompted students to freely associate their ideas. In group 1A a word cloud (Fig. 1) represented students' submissions to PyramidApp on the individual level. In comparison to the debriefing that was structured by the Debriefing Script only, this method encouraged a broader range of topics, reflecting a deeper exploration of ICT-related issues. Group 1A mentioned an average of 4.34 topics per student, while Group 1B mentioned an average of 3.00 in the posttest.

In Group 1A, the continued prominence of *Artificial Intelligence (AI)* that was observed in both groups over pre-, mid- and posttest, was accompanied by new topics such as *Social Networks* and *Infrastructure* which were drawn from the Word Cloud, and *Cybersecurity*, which emerged during the debriefing discussion. In contrast, group 1B showed a stronger focus on *Sustainability*, which gained prominence in the posttest responses, highlighting the influence of the debriefing discussion on shaping students' understanding of emerging issues.

These findings suggest that the combination of collaborative learning and debriefing activities, particularly with visual tools like word clouds, can significantly enhance students' understanding of complex topics. The Word Cloud not only provided a visual representation of key themes but also encouraged broader discussion and deeper reflection. However, students' opinions continued to vary, and the issues discussed were rated differently.

Fig. 1. Word Cloud of Students' Submissions in Individual Level in Group 1A generated with ChatGPT 4.o [22].

Cycle 2. Consequently, in the second cycle a focus group discussion of possible visualizations of students' artifacts was held. For this analytical open-ended task, six different visualizations were prepared for the debriefing: Word Cloud, Quotes with Emphasis, Word Tree, Concept Map, Heatmap and Ranking. Based on the focus group discussion, the three winning options were chosen for the upcoming runs. The Quotes with Empasis visualization was liked for its concreteness; the Concept Map was perceived as a holistic representation that helped them clarify their thoughts and the Heatmap gave them confidence in their answers. The three visualizations were randomly distributed for a self-guided debriefing in groups 2B and 2C with pre- and posttest data collection.

The analysis has shown that the visualization of misconceptions under the condition "Quotes with Emphasis" can mislead students. Although some of the misunderstandings may have been resolved in the following oral debriefing, previous tests have shown that some students may miss these important oral clues that give context to what is presented to them visually. Providing students with only self-directed learning resources, without clear directions or guidance on self-debriefing, increases reliance solely on their personal learning experiences and reflection skills [23–25]. On the other hand, students experience that this kind of visualization helps them to find meaning in the preceding learning activity. This could be because - as mentioned by the focus group - it is a concrete phrase taken from the students' responses and therefore makes them see a connection between the task, the collaborative learning activity and the following debriefing.

The Heatmap may have led to several consistent misconceptions. Nonetheless, there are some advantages like the visibility of class tendencies that could support student's confidence in their answer due to the Prototypical Majority Effect [26]. One way to resolve this dilemma could be to give the Heatmap more context by examples or detail. For the upcoming experiment it was considered to merge the two visualization methods Quotes with Emphasis and Heatmap into one hoping to combine the advantages while cancelling out the misleading potential that came to light in this cycle.

The Concept Map poses a coherent overview itself which was also reflected in the qualitative content analysis of posttest responses. The ongoing challenge of this method is the organization and compilation of knowledge under time constraints.

Cycle 3. The third cycle posed a closed task for the students. Pre-, mid- and posttest answers were assessed with a maximum of 14 points for each test, and statistical analysis revealed a significant improvement for both debriefing interventions – Heatmap + Quotes with Emphasis (HM) (Fig. 2) and Concept Map (CM) – in students' performance.

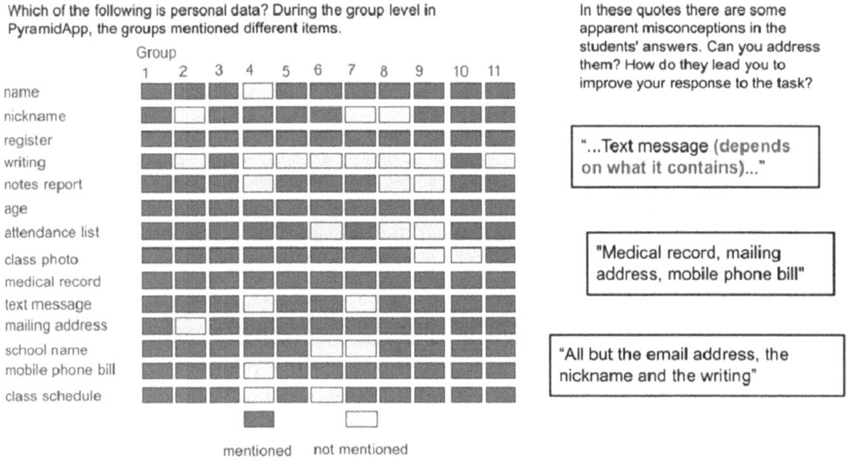

Fig. 2. Heatmap + Quote with Emphasis visualization for Debriefing in Group 3A

A paired-samples t-test (Table 4) was conducted to compare performance between the midtest and posttest for the intervention with Concept Map. The results showed a significant increase from mid- to posttest, $t(39) = -2.395$, $p = .011$, $d = 0.379$. These findings suggest that the intervention led to a small but significant improvement in scores.

Table 4. Paired-Samples T-Test for Mid- and Post-test Scores in Intervention with Heatmap (HM) and Concept Map + Quotes with Emphasis (CM)

			Statistic	df	p		Effect Size
HMmid	HMpost	Student's t	−4.224	35.000	< .001	Cohens d	−0.704
CMmid	CMpost	Student's t	−2.395	39.000	0.011	Cohens d	−0.379

Note: $H_a\ \mu_{M1-M2} < 0$

Table 5. Independent Samples T-Test for Difference Score Mid- to Post-Test

		Statistic	df	p		Effect Size
Difference Score	Student's t	0.988	74.000	0.326	Cohens d	0.227

Note: $H_a\ \mu_{HM} \neq \mu_{CM}$

An independent-sample t-test was conducted to compare the change in performance between the Heatmap + Quotes with Emphasis (HM) and Concept Map (CM) interventions (Table 5). The results showed no significant difference between the two groups, $t(74) = 0.988$, $p = .326$, $d = 0.227$. These findings suggest that both interventions led to similar improvements in performance (Table 5).

With respect to the upcoming study cycle, only the visualization Concept Map was chosen to go further in the research and be compared with other debriefing methods.

Cycle 4. For the guided open-ended task in the fourth cycle, the debriefing methods Debriefing Script and Concept Map (Fig. 3) were compared with an intuitive 'on the fly' debriefing (Control Condition).

Across all three conditions pre- and midtest submissions were often similar, while posttest responses demonstrated a higher frequency of newly introduced aspects. In the Control Condition, posttest responses more frequently included descriptions of features rather than isolated characteristics. Students predominantly repeated peer answers that had been displayed and discussed during the debriefing session, with the topics of living conditions and travel opportunities being the most frequently mentioned. This was followed by generalizations derived from the discussion. This group demonstrated the highest level of reflection in their submissions; however, misconceptions were also most prevalent. Additionally, ten students in this condition indicated that they felt there was nothing to add to their initial answers (20,00%).

Among students who received the Debriefing Script intervention, seven also stood by their initial answers after the CSCL activity; compared to the other conditions the most frequent (41,67%). Another seven repeated a peer response that had been shared during the debriefing. Additionally, they were the least likely to draw generalizations from the debriefing discussion as only two responses demonstrated that. Students in this condition most frequently identified individual data points in their posttest responses, suggesting a lower ability to conceptualize feature creation as required by the task. Their answers primarily consisted of peer response repetitions, followed by specific examples of inferences related to financial risk.

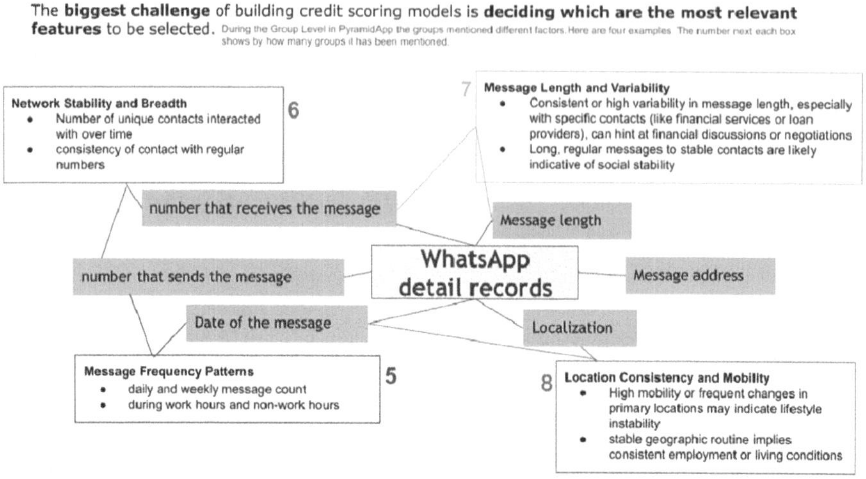

Fig. 3. Concept Map visualization for debriefing in group 4C.

Students in the Concept Map condition identified the highest number of features in their posttest submissions. Features that hadn't been presented in the visualization slightly outnumbered the features that were presented. Compared to the other groups, fewer students in this condition expressed no change in understanding. However, this group also reflected the least on their learning process in their written responses. This experimental cycle demonstrated that the effectiveness of debriefing interventions is influenced by both the structure of the method and the role of the teacher in guiding the discussion. The Debriefing Script and freestyle debriefing approaches were highly dependent on students' initial responses and the teacher's ability to facilitate meaningful conversations. In contrast, the Concept Map served as both a diagnostic tool for the teacher—highlighting areas where further clarification was needed—and a structured reference point for students, providing a sample solution to support their understanding. However, the use of visualizations in complex tasks like this one presents certain limitations. While the Concept Map provided clarity in feature formation, it necessarily focused on selected aspects of the task, potentially narrowing the scope of the discussion. This suggests that in future implementations, classroom conversations may need to be intentionally aligned with the visualized elements, ensuring that key concepts are reinforced while maintaining space for broader exploration. In the last cycle these findings should be consolidated in a closed task.

Cycle 5. The fifth cycle compared interventions with Debriefing Script versus Concept Map again. Pre-, mid- and posttest answers (including a transfer task) were assessed with a maximum of 3 points per test. Statistical analysis revealed no significant improvement in student performance following either debriefing method (Table 6).

Table 6. Paired-Samples T-Test of Mid- to Post-Test Results

			Statistic	df	p		Effect Size
DSmid	DSpost	Student's t	−1.464	5.000	0.203	Cohens d	−0.598
CMmid	CMpost	Student's t	−1.581	5.000	0.175	Cohens d	−0.645

Note: H_a $\mu_{M1-M2} < 0$

Table 7. Independent T-Test for Debriefing Methods with Improvement Score from Mid- to Post-test Score and Gain Score from Pre-test to Transfer Task Score

		Statistic	df	p		Effect Size
Difference Score	Student's t	0.415	10.000	0.687	Cohens d	0.240
Gain Score	Student's t	0.183	10.000	0.858	Cohens d	0.106

Note: H_a $\mu_{DS} \neq \mu_{CM}$

An independent t-test comparing mid- and posttest scores (Table 7) confirmed no significant learning gains overall: $t(10) = 0.415, p = .687, d = 0.240$. The mean improvement was slightly higher for the Debriefing Script ($M = 0.500$) compared to the Concept Map ($M = 0.333$), though neither effect was substantial.

An independent t-test comparing gain scores from the pretest to the performance in the transfer task between the two groups also showed no significant difference (Table 7). While qualitative observations suggest that students benefited from the debriefing discussions, these improvements were not reflected in the statistical analysis. The small effect size ($d = 0.240$) suggests a minimal impact of the interventions. While the mean improvement was slightly greater for the Debriefing Script intervention compared to the Concept Map, the difference was not meaningful in statistical terms. The large variability in scores within the Debriefing Script group may have influenced the results. The small sample size in both conditions (six students per condition) likely had an impact on the results.

6 Discussion

This study analyzed five experimental cycles to examine how different debriefing techniques impact students' learning after Pyramid CLFP. A total of 396 students participated, with 328 datasets analyzed. Results highlight that debriefing methods influence conceptual understanding and engagement, though no significant perfor-mance differences were found across techniques.

The introduction of debriefing techniques using Word Clouds revealed that visual tools can encourage broader discussions by making key themes more visible. While it helped students expand their reflections, their unordered nature introduced a risk of misconceptions. The research focus shifted toward testing alternative visual representations, including Quotes with Emphasis, Heatmaps, and Concept Maps. Quotes with Emphasis helped students connect their thoughts to learning tasks but sometimes reinforced misunderstandings when not sufficiently contextualized. Heatmaps simplified complex concepts and highlighted collective tendencies but also contributed to misconceptions without explanatory context. Combining Heatmaps and Quotes with Emphasis aimed to balance strengths and mitigate limitations. In a comparative analysis with a Concept Map both interventions improved student performance, though no significant difference was detected. Concept Maps proved especially useful for structuring knowledge and visualizing relationships, though they required considerable instructor effort. While they help resolve uncertainties, they may constrain open-ended discussions by limiting exploration of alternative perspectives.

The structured Debriefing Script provided consistency but often led to rigid engagement, limiting students' ability to synthesize broader conceptual connections. In the fourth cycle, an added open-ended question prompted reflection on surprising peer responses. This deviated from the advocacy-inquiry approach and proved useful where students already had a high understanding or faced complex topics.

This study's findings suggest that selecting a debriefing method should depend on the learning objectives. For lower-level learning tasks, structured debriefing scripts may suffice, whereas for higher-order cognitive skills, concept mapping or other visualization techniques may be more effective. Prior research [27] reinforces this, showing that multimedia-supported debriefing methods contribute to deeper knowledge gains. Additionally, collaborative debriefing has been shown to improve learning outcomes compared to individual debriefing [25], a trend also observed in this study's second cycle, where individually debriefed students exhibited persistent misconceptions.

Limitations include a small sample size, especially in the fifth cycle, potential biases from single-researcher analysis, and translation challenges that may have affected data interpretation. Variability in classroom settings and the absence of sociodemographic data further limit generalizability. Despite these factors, the study offers valuable insights into collaborative learning and debriefing methods for practitioners and further research.

7 Conclusion and Future Research

While no significant differences were found between debriefing methods, this study clarifies their strengths and limitations, offering a foundation for further research in CSCL environments. Effective debriefing depends on task type, cognitive demands, and available resources. Freestyle debriefing fosters rich discussions but requires skilled facilitation, while Debriefing Scripts ensure consistency but may limit deeper exploration. Visualizing student artifacts enhances transparency and engagement. A hybrid approach combining structured visuals with guided discussion may be most effective.

Despite the benefits of structured debriefing, challenges remain in automating these techniques for wider application. Future research should explore AI-supported debriefing tools to facilitate real-time visualization of student artifacts and improve scalability.

Acknowledgements. Supported by PID2023-146692OB-C33 - MICIU/AEI/https://doi.org/10.13039/501100011033 and Eramus+ KA220-HED-D8B72E6A. DHL (Serra Húnter) acknowledges ICREA Academia.

References

1. Lederman, L.C.: Debriefing: Toward a Systematic Assessment of Theory and Practice (1992). https://doi.org/10.1177/1046878192232003
2. Amarasinghe, I., Hernández-Leo, D., Manathunga, K., Pérez, J.C., Dimitriadis, Y.: Teacher-led debriefing in computer-supported collaborative learning pyramid scripts (2022)
3. Amarasinghe, I., Hernández-Leo, D., Hoppe, H.U.: Deconstructing orchestration load: comparing teacher support through mirroring and guiding. Int. J. Comput.-Support. Collaborative Learn (2021). https://doi.org/10.1007/s11412-021-09351-9
4. OECD: OECD Digital Education Outlook 2021: Pushing the Frontiers with Artificial Intelligence, Blockchain and Robots. OECD (2021). https://doi.org/10.1787/589b283f-en
5. Mariani, B., Cantrell, M.A., Meakim, C., Prieto, P., Dreifuerst, K.T.: Structured debriefing and students' clinical judgment abilities in simulation. Clin. Simul. Nurs. **9**(5), e147–e155 (2013). https://doi.org/10.1016/j.ecns.2011.11.009
6. Dreifuerst, K.: The essentials of debriefing in simulation learning: a concept analysis. Nurs. Educ. Perspect. (2009). https://www.semanticscholar.org/paper/THE-ESSENTIALS-of-DEBRIEFING-in-Simulation-A-Dreifuerst/7e8730200a482e3b70a39ae5f5320e74212617de
7. Dieckmann, P., Molin Friis, S., Lippert, A., Østergaard, D.: The art and science of debriefing in simulation: ideal and practice. Med. Teach. **31**(7), e287–e294 (2009). https://doi.org/10.1080/01421590902866218
8. Dufrene, C., Young, A.: Successful debriefing—best methods to achieve positive learning outcomes: a literature review. Nurse Educ. Today **34**(3), 372–376 (2014). https://doi.org/10.1016/j.nedt.2013.06.026
9. Barrett, M., Hershock, C., McCarthy, M., Melville, M., Mertz, J.: What type of debrief is best for learning during think-pair-shares? Teach. Learn. Inq. 9(1), 1 (2021). https://doi.org/10.20343/teachlearninqu.9.1.5
10. Butler, A.C., Godbole, N., Marsh, E.J.: Explanation feedback is better than correct answer feedback for promoting transfer of learning. J. Educ. Psychol. **105**(2), 290–298 (2013). https://doi.org/10.1037/a0031026
11. Tannenbaum, S.I., Cerasoli, C.P.: Do team and individual debriefs enhance performance? A Meta-Analysis. Hum. Factors **55**(1), 231–245 (2013). https://doi.org/10.1177/0018720812448394
12. Kerres, M.: Gestaltungsorientierte Mediendidaktik und ihr Verhältnis zur Allgemeinen Didaktik. In: Dieckmann, B., Stadtfeld, P. (eds.) Allgemeine Didaktik im Wandel, pp. 1–13. Klinkhardt Verlag, Bad Heilbrunn (2004)
13. Bakker, A., Van Eerde, D.: An introduction to design-based research with an example from statistics education. In: Bikner-Ahsbahs, A., Knipping, C., Presmeg, N. (eds.) Approaches to Qualitative Research in Mathematics Education, pp. 429–466. Springer, Netherlands (2015). https://doi.org/10.1007/978-94-017-9181-6_16
14. Mayring, P.: Qualitative content analysis: theoretical foundation, basic procedures and software solution. Klagenfurt (2014). https://nbn-resolving.org/urn:nbn:de:0168-ssoar-395173
15. MAXQDA 2024, [software], Berlin, VERBI Software (2024). maxqda.com
16. The jamovi project. jamovi (Version 2.3.21.0) [Computer Software] (2024). https://www.jamovi.org
17. Rudolph, J.W., Simon, R., Dufresne, R.L., Raemer, D.B.: There's no such thing as "Nonjudgmental" debriefing: a theory and method for debriefing with good judgment. Simul. Healthc. **1**(1), 49 (2006)
18. Azzam, T., Evergreen, S., Germuth, A.A., Kistler, S.J.: Data visualization and evaluation. New Dir. Eval. **2013**(139), 7–32 (2013). https://doi.org/10.1002/ev.20065

19. Evergreen, S., Metzner, C.: Design principles for data visualization in evaluation. New Dir. Eval. **2013**(140), 5–20 (2013). https://doi.org/10.1002/ev.20071
20. Mayer, R.E.: Multimedia Learning. Cambridge University Press (2020). https://doi.org/10.1017/9781316941355
21. Krathwohl, D.R.: A revision of bloom's taxonomy: an overview. Theory Pract. **41**(4), 212–218 (2002). https://doi.org/10.1207/s15430421tip4104_2
22. OpenAI. ChatGPT (4.o version) [Large language model] (2024). https://chat.openai.com/chat
23. Fanning, R.M., Gaba, D.M.: The role of debriefing in simulation-based learning. Simul. Healthc. **2**(2), 115–125 (2007). https://doi.org/10.1097/SIH.0b013e3180315539
24. Lapum, J.L., Verkuyl, M., Hughes, M., Romaniuk, D., McCulloch, T., Mastrilli, P.: Self-debriefing in virtual simulation. Nurse Educ. **44**(6), E6–E8 (2019). https://doi.org/10.1097/NNE.0000000000000639
25. Verkuyl, M., et al.: Comparison of self-debriefing alone or in combination with group debrief. Clin. Simul. Nurs. **37**, 32–39 (2019). https://doi.org/10.1016/J.ECNS.2019.08.005
26. Koriat, A., Undorf, M., Schwarz, N.: The effects of group conformity on the prototypical majority effect for confidence and response latency. Soc. Cogn. **38**, 447–469 (2020)
27. Poompimol, S., Panjaburee, P., Yasri, P., Buaraphan, K.: Effects of board game with different debriefing preferences on cyberbullying prevention. IAFOR J. Educ. **11**(3), 207–234 (2023)

LLM-Generated Feedback Supports Learning if Learners Choose to Use it

Danielle R. Thomas(✉), Conrad Borchers, Shambhavi Bhushan, Erin Gatz, Shivang Gupta, and Kenneth R. Koedinger

Carnegie Mellon University, Pittsburgh, USA
{drthomas,cborchers,shivangg,koedinger}@cmu.edu,
{egatz,shambhab}@andrew.cmu.edu

Abstract. Large language models (LLMs) are increasingly used to generate feedback, yet their impact on learning remains underexplored, especially compared to existing feedback methods. This study investigates how on-demand LLM-generated explanatory feedback influences learning in seven scenario-based tutor training lessons. Analyzing over 2,600 lesson completions from 885 tutor learners, we compare posttest performance among learners across three groups: learners who received feedback generated by `gpt-3.5-turbo`, those who declined it, and those without access. All groups received non-LLM corrective feedback. To address potential selection bias—where higher-performing learners may be more inclined to use LLM feedback—we applied propensity scoring. Learners with a higher predicted likelihood of engaging with LLM feedback scored significantly higher at posttest than those with lower propensity. After adjusting for this effect, two out of seven lessons showed statistically significant learning benefits from LLM feedback with standardized effect sizes of 0.28 and 0.33. These moderate effects suggest that the effectiveness of LLM feedback depends on the learners' tendency to seek support. Importantly, LLM feedback did not significantly increase completion time, and learners overwhelmingly rated it as helpful. These findings highlight LLM feedback's potential as a low-cost and scalable way to improve learning on open-ended tasks, particularly in existing systems already providing feedback without LLMs. This work contributes open datasets, LLM prompts, and rubrics to support reproducibility.

Keywords: AI-generated feedback · Large language models · Assessment

1 Introduction

Feedback is one of the most powerful methods to enhance learning [14,31]. Although extensive research has examined the effects of feedback created by humans in educational settings [14], comparatively little attention has been paid to the role of feedback generated by generative AI, in the form of large language models (LLMs), particularly within scenario-based online learning.

K. Tammets et al. (Eds.): EC-TEL 2025, LNCS 16063, pp. 489–503, 2026.
https://doi.org/10.1007/978-3-032-03870-8_33

The effectiveness of feedback depends on several factors, including timing, type, and task complexity [19]. Among the most impactful forms of feedback is informational feedback—guidance that not only evaluates a learner's response but also provides actionable suggestions for improvement [14]. Research indicates that feedback is more effective when it provides correct, as opposed to incorrect, responses and is immediate, as opposed to delayed [14]. Elaborated feedback, such as providing an explanation, yields larger effects on learning than feedback on the correctness of an answer or revealing the answer itself [19]. This study builds on these insights by examining the impact of immediate, *explanatory* feedback within online learning with the feedback generated by LLMs.

Recent research on the use of generative AI, such as LLMs, for feedback generation has demonstrated promising results in educational contexts. For example, the use of ChatGPT-generated hints has been shown to produce learning gains comparable to human tutor-authored help in improving math skills [21]. Similarly, a randomized controlled trial of high-school English language learners found that LLM-generated feedback led to improved essay revision scores and increased motivation compared to students who did not receive such feedback [20]. Research on LLM feedback is in its infancy, with previous work showing that LLM-generated content adequately mirrors human-generated content [9,10], but little is known about learners' perceptions and the actual learning effects.

This study focuses on LLM-generated help in the form of explanatory feedback with *tutors as learners* participating in online training. Tutor learners receive explanatory feedback on their open responses. Uniquely, it involves developing tutoring skills instead of focusing on student math learning or writing, which adds to the novelty of this work. To assess the impact and efficiency of LLM-generated feedback, or simply *LLM feedback*, we investigate the following research questions, focusing on both learning outcomes and learners' perceptions:

RQ1: What differences exist in tutor learning, as evidenced by posttest performance, among tutor learners receiving LLM-generated explanatory feedback within instruction compared to learners not receiving it?

RQ2: How does learners' accuracy and efficiency compare among those who receive LLM-generated feedback compared to those who do not receive LLM-generated feedback?

RQ3: Among learners who received the LLM-generated feedback and rated it, what were their perceptions of the feedback, i.e., *helpful*, *not helpful*, or *incorrect*?

2 Related Work

2.1 LLM-Generated Feedback on Learning

Automated feedback using techniques, such as natural language processing (NLP), has demonstrated positive [5,8] and negative [13,15] learning effects. More recently, general-purpose LLMs such as Claude [4] and GPT models [1] have shown promise in generating high-quality feedback for learners. ChatGPT has been found to effectively generate detailed, coherent, and process-focused feedback to university students, aligning well with human instructors in providing feedback that may support students' learning skills [7]. A randomized controlled trial found that ChatGPT-generated feedback improved the quality of pre-service teachers' writing compared to human expert-written feedback [15]. Pre-service teachers in the LLM-generated feedback condition spent more time processing the feedback and wrote longer texts, indicating deeper engagement with both the feedback and the task. Moreover, they rated the feedback as more useful and interesting than static feedback. However, it remains unclear which specific components of the LLM-generated feedback contributed to these perceptions.

Closer to this work, involving *tutors as learners*, binary coding systems using `GPT-4o` to generate templated feedback to tutors have shown performance matching humans [18]. Sequence labeling has been used to identify elements of correct and incorrect responses to assist with feedback generation [17]. Although previous work has focused mainly on the technical implementation of LLM feedback generation, much less attention has been paid to ensuring a robust pedagogical structure that improves learning [25]. The present work aims to address this gap by investigating the effectiveness of LLM-generated explanatory feedback on tutor learning and tutor perceptions of the feedback.

2.2 Scenario-Based Lesson Design

Scenario-based learning allows learners to develop skills in real-world contexts through guided practice [3]. This situational learning offers low-risk environments for teachers and tutors to build expertise [28–30]. Previous studies have shown approximately 20% learning gain from pretest to posttest in key tutoring skills, such as giving effective praise and responding to student errors [27]. We employ a modified *predict-observe-explain* model, shown in Fig. 1, which is a cyclical instructional approach that structures learning through experience [12]. First, tutor learners are presented with a scenario (e.g., a student making a math error) asking them to *predict* how to best respond within 1) an open-response question and 2) a multiple-choice question (MCQ). Learners assigned the treatment condition have the option to receive LLM-generated feedback on their open response (shown in red). Next, they *explain* their reasoning through another set of questions: 3) an open-ended question and 4) a MCQ. The learners then 5) *observe* research-based recommendations and receive delayed corrective feedback (shown in blue) before they 6) *explain* the reasoning behind what they observed. Finally, learners complete a posttest (receiving no feedback), in which they are presented an analogous tutoring scenario and complete the same sequence of predicting the best responses and explaining their rationale (7–10). The posttest contains four possible points (two MCQs and two open-response questions), which are used to compare the performance of learners under treatment and control conditions.

2.3 Providing Explanatory AI-Generated Feedback

Past work on automated tutor feedback used NLP, including sequence labeling, to identify key elements in responses and generate templated feedback [17,32].

These approaches show moderate success but struggle with tutoring nuances, as many skills defy simple correct/incorrect categorization, and key elements often misalign with correctness. This present study takes a different approach, incorporating a predefined schema to provide LLM-generated rephrasing, enabling automated assessment and feedback. To enhance the accuracy of its evaluations, the model is primed using few-shot prompting. These examples enable the model, namely `GPT-3.5-turbo`, to recognize elements of high-quality tutor responses while identifying common misconceptions.

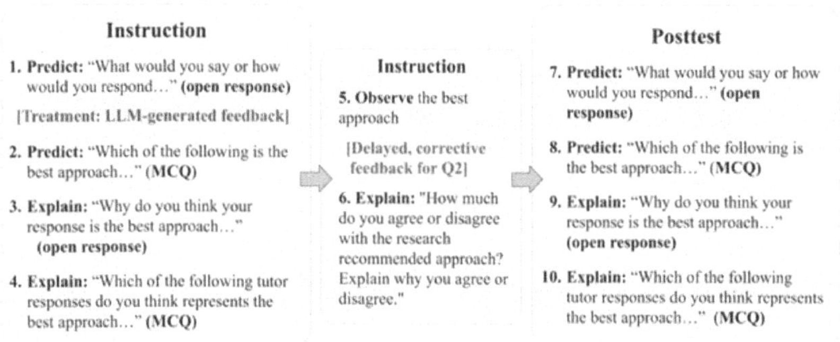

Fig. 1. Scenario-based lesson design displaying the option of tutors in the treatment to receive LLM-generated feedback (shown in red) and all participants receiving delayed, corrective feedback (shown in blue) during instruction. (Color figure online)

When a tutor learner submits a response, such as the one shown in Fig. 2, the system classifies it as either *correct* or *incorrect* based on its alignment with the predefined schema (e.g., research-backed tutoring strategies). *Correct* responses, which demonstrate effective use of instructional strategies, receive reinforcement feedback that acknowledges their alignment with best practices. In contrast, *incorrect* responses trigger the generation of targeted feedback that not only identifies weaknesses, but also provides a rephrased version generated by the LLM that adheres better to the research-aligned tutoring skill. The model is explicitly instructed to make minimal modifications to incorrect responses, retaining the original structure and intent while improving clarity, specificity, or alignment with instructional goals. Figure 2 illustrates a tutor inputting an incorrect open response to predict the best approach (i.e., *"Aaron, I see you made a mistake in the first step"*). In line with research-supported effective feedback practices, system-generated feedback suggests how the response could be improved (that is, "... *by avoiding explicit mention of the student's mistake"*) and provides an alternative correct response (that is, ...*"Let's take a closer look together at the first step"*). Tutors can then attempt the problem again, up to three times, and can also provide feedback on the usefulness of the feedback.

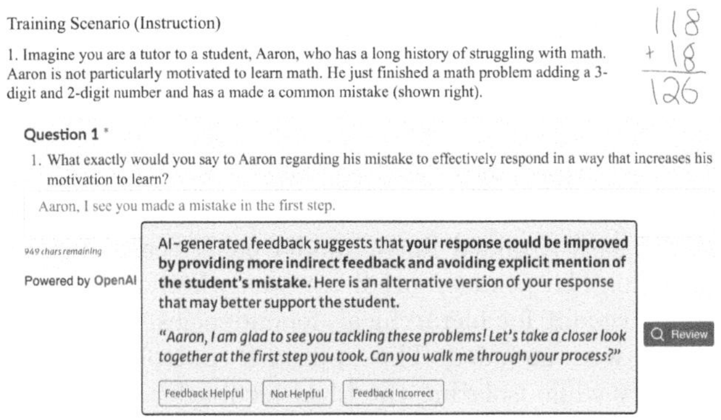

Fig. 2. Example of a human tutor receiving LLM-generated, explanatory feedback on their open response (from the *Reacting to Errors* lesson).

3 Methods

3.1 Participants and Setting

A total of 885 college-student tutors accounting for 2,648 lesson completions, completed at least one of the seven lessons titled *Giving Effective Praise*, *Reacting to Errors*, *Determining What Students Know*, *Helping Students Manage Inequity*, *Using Motivational Strategies*, *Supporting a Growth Mindset*, and *Responding to Negative Self-Talk*. The typical participant completed an average of M = 3.42 lessons (SD = 2.13). Delivered through an online tutoring platform, these lessons align with key tutoring competencies [6]. The tutor lesson data was recorded in DataShop, a widely used repository of educational data in learning analytics research [16]. Participant privacy was maintained in compliance with IRB protocols. Lesson log data are accessible through the GitHub.[1]

3.2 Research Design and Analysis Plan

Learners were randomly assigned to one of two conditions for each lesson: the **Control** condition, where no LLM-generated feedback was available, or the **Intent-to-Treat (ITT)** condition, where they had the option to receive LLM-generated explanatory feedback on how to best respond during instruction (Q1 in Fig. 1). Use of LLM feedback was on-demand. The learners assigned the ITT condition who chose to receive LLM-generated feedback on Q1 formed a third condition, the **Treatment-on-the-Treated (TOT)** condition.

The on-demand use of LLM feedback within the ITT group introduces a self-selection effect. As a result, the study incorporates both TOT and ITT analyses. For some lessons, all learners were assigned to the ITT condition for a period, leading to an unequal distribution of participants between the ITT and the Control condition. Learners were assigned conditions at lesson level,

[1] https://github.com/conradborchers/ai-feedback-exp/.

meaning the same learner could experience various conditions across lessons. This within-subject design reduces variability and enhances statistical power by allowing learners to serve as their own controls.

In addressing RQ1 within the TOT, we examined the learning differences, measured at posttest performance, between the learners who received LLM feedback (*TOT*) to those in the *Control* and *ITT* conditions who opt not to use the LLM feedback. We used a mixed linear model using scaled posttest scores as the outcome variable. The primary predictor was whether the learner received LLM feedback. To account for hierarchical dependencies, random intercepts for learners and lessons were included. This approach controlled for individual and contextual variability while isolating the LLM feedback effect.

In addressing RQ1 within the ITT, we investigated the impact of LLM feedback availability on tutor learning. We conducted an *Intent-to-Treat (ITT)* analysis, comparing tutors assigned to the LLM feedback condition with those in the *Control*. Posttest performance, expressed as standard deviations, served as the primary outcome variable. A linear mixed model was used to estimate the effect of LLM feedback assignment, regardless of whether the tutors opted to receive feedback. Random intercepts for both learners and lessons account for hierarchical dependencies and individual variability. Given that some tutors in the ITT condition did not receive LLM feedback–either by choice or due to system failures–we applied *principal stratification* to control for potential selection bias [23]. We engineered engagement-related features to predict the likelihood that a learner will request LLM feedback. An elasticNet regression model with 10-fold cross-validation was used to infer feedback propensity [33]. The resulting predictive model was applied to the Control to create a propensity-matched comparison. This approach allowed us to estimate the effect of LLM feedback more accurately by comparing tutors who were likely to request LLM feedback (had it been available) to those who actually received it. We tested the interaction between feedback propensity and condition to assess whether LLM feedback was particularly beneficial for high-propensity learners.

3.3 Assessing Tutor Learner Posttest Performance

Tutor posttest performance on each lesson was calculated by summing the binary score (i.e., 0/1) for Q7–Q10 (see Fig. 1), yielding a maximum score of four points. Q8 and Q10 were multiple choice. Q7 and Q9 were open responses and were evaluated using `GPT-4o`. Each lesson included two scenarios: one presented during instruction and one at posttest. To control for difficulty, the scenarios were randomly assigned and counterbalanced between the participants.[2]

[2] We note that, in experimental learning research, posttest performance is often used as a proxy for learning. By comparing posttest scores across randomly assigned conditions—which is expected, on average, to even out prior knowledge differences—researchers can infer differences in the amount of learning that occurred during the intervention. This approach assumes that higher post-test performance reflects greater knowledge acquisition attributable to the experimental manipulation.

Human Annotation, Interrater Reliability, and Item-level Reliability. To evaluate learner's open responses at posttest (Q7 and Q9 in Fig. 1), we implemented a few-shot learning approach using learner-generated responses in conjunction with human-scored examples to help generate accurate assessments. The prompts were designed to evaluate *predict* (Q7) and *explain* (Q9) open-response types. Prompt development was an iterative process, refined through multiple feedback cycles. Strategies included context framing (e.g., "*... You are a tutor evaluator ...*"), incorporating human-coded response examples, and using chain-of-thought prompting to encourage reasoning. To ensure consistency, the model's temperature was set to 0, and responses were capped at 300 tokens to maintain conciseness. Inter-rater reliability (IRR) was established in prior open-source work for most lessons. For lessons where IRR was not previously established, 50 tutor responses were randomly chosen, and two experienced human coders scored the responses. The IRR for all lessons ranged from 0.64–0.88 for *predict* and 0.65–0.91 for *explain* open responses. Annotation rubrics and lesson-specific reliability are provided in the GitHub. Three MCQ items were found to be unreliable and removed: *Determining What Students Know* (explain); *Reacting to Errors* (explain); and *Responding to Negative Self-Talk* (predict). The results were robust against the exclusion of these items.[3]

4 Results

The descriptive statistics are shown in Table 1 showing the average posttest score by condition, the number of learners, and the average completion time. The average posttest scores where the TOT condition was the highest among conditions are shown in bold. In five of the seven lessons, the TOT condition had the highest average posttest score compared to the other conditions.

4.1 RQ1: Impact of LLM-Generated Feedback on Learning

Treatment-On-The-Treated (TOT) Condition vs No Treatment Assigned or Used. To address RQ1, we examined differences in tutor learning, as evidenced by posttest performance, among learners *actually* receiving LLM-generated feedback compared to those who did not (combined Control and ITT, who opted not to receive LLM feedback.) We used a linear mixed model based on scaled posttest scores, expressed in standard deviations. The primary predictor of interest was whether students received LLM-generated feedback. Random intercepts were included for both learners and lessons to account for the hierarchical structure and variability at these levels. This approach allowed us to model individual and contextual factors while isolating the effect of LLM feedback on performance.

[3] The results were similar and robust with or without the exclusion of three unreliable items, which improved reliability by over 0.05 in Cronbach's alpha.

Table 1. Lesson Descriptive Statistics. Average posttest scores where the TOT condition was the highest among conditions are shown in bold.

Lesson	Feedback Offered: Intent-to-Treat (ITT) Was LLM Feedback Used?		No LLM Feedback Assigned (Control)
	Yes (TOT)	No Feedback Used	
Effective Praise	**89.57%** (76), 7.9 min	85.95% (120), 8.38 min	87.92% (151), 11.42 min
Manage Inequity	82.89% (38), 8.58 min	83.88% (76), 6.87 min	81.46% (120), 10.05 min
What Students Know	**82.67%** (25), 4.31 min	80.56% (102), 5.23 min	78.52% (97), 8.55 min
Reacting to Errors	64.24% (188), 10.44 min	56.48% (386), 8.9 min	73.4% (94), 14.16 min
Negative Self-Talk	**75.76%** (33), 5.54 min	72.69% (72), 7.05 min	65.01% (121), 9.67 min
Growth Mindset	**81.88%** (63), 6.28 min	75.21% (118), 7.81 min	77.18% (84), 7.62 min
Motivational Strategies	**79.94%** (145), 10.66 min	78.35% (229), 11.08 min	78.33% (75), 7.58 min

The results indicate that receiving LLM feedback was associated with significantly higher posttest performance, with an estimated effect of 0.10 SD (95% CI [0.01, 0.19], $p = .023$). The intraclass correlation coefficient (ICC) showed that 26.9% of the variability in posttest performance was attributable to individual learner differences and 8.8% to lesson-level differences. To further investigate the impact of LLM-generated feedback at the lesson level, we fitted models for individual lessons to estimate effect sizes. Effect size estimates ranged from 0.02 to 0.27 SD, with the largest effect observed in the *Responding to Negative Self-Talk* (Estimate = 0.27) and the smallest in the *Helping Students Manage Inequity* (Estimate = 0.02). However, sample sizes within individual lessons were insufficient to reliably test these effects with adequate statistical power.

Adjusting for Selection Bias via Principal Stratification and Propensity Modeling. Approximately one-third (33.2%) of lesson completions in the assigned LLM-generated feedback condition did not receive feedback, either because the learners did not request it or due to occasional system failures, raising potential bias in estimating effects. To address this, we used principal stratification to create a more fair control group that resembles the tutors likely to request LLM feedback with similar tutors in the control group. Following [23], we engineered features to match tutors with a high proclivity to request LLM feedback to similar tutors in the control, specifically leveraging metrics related to general engagement, response behaviors, and session characteristics during tutor training relevant to both conditions. These features included the total attempts of each tutor in the questions and the unique problems attempted. Time-based metrics such as the total duration of training, the average duration, and the range of attempt durations were also considered.

Additionally, we examined input length of features (e.g., min, max, and average input length) of open-ended responses and session-based navigation behaviors (e.g., average time between attempts). We then used these characteristics to predict the tendency of a tutor to request LLM feedback under the intervention condition, represented by the total number of times they had requested LLM-generated feedback. We then performed a 10-fold cross-validation using an ElasticNet regression model to infer the number of times a tutor requested LLM feedback in the intervention condition. The ElasticNet model regularizes parameters for variable selection using weighted absolute value (L1) and quadratic (L2) penalties to shrink estimates toward 0. Both the weighting of both penalties and the strength of the penalty can be independently tuned [33]. During cross-validation, we tuned hyperparameters alpha (the weight of L1 and L2 penalties) and lambda (the penalty strength). Following [24], we also averaged cross-validation ROC-AUC through a median split of labels and prediction in correctly predicting this outcome across folds, achieving satisfactory accuracy across folds (M = 0.75), which is fair for this method [24]. We then applied this prediction model to the control condition, generating a covariate that adjusts for selection effects by estimating the number of LLM feedback requests learners in the control condition would likely have made. Effectively, this process then adjusts learners' posttest scores who requested and received generative LLM feedback to those our model *predicted to have used* LLM feedback in the control condition, counteracting potential selection effects. More details on the range of features and code from the statistical analyses can be accessed in the GitHub. Table 2 shows model results after including the predicted number of LLM feedback requests as a covariate.

Table 2. Model coefficients of the LLM feedback intervention effect after adjusting for learners' predicted propensity to request feedback. All coefficients and posttest scores are standardized to a mean of 0 and standard deviation of 1.

	Estimates	95% CI	p-value
Intercept	0.05	–0.18–0.28	.666
Intent-to-Treat (ITT)	–0.08	–0.17–0.01	.102
Control Propensity to Request LLM Feedback	0.06	0.00–0.12	**.040**
ITT Interaction with Propensity	0.04	–0.04–0.12	.307

The model (Table 2) revealed a significant selection effect, where the Control condition's predicted propensity to request LLM feedback was positively associated with posttest scores ($\beta = 0.06$, 95% CI [0.00, 0.12], $p = .040$). A positive but non-significant interaction between the ITT condition and propensity to request feedback ($\beta = 0.04$, 95% CI [–0.04, 0.12], $p = .307$) indicated that learners engaging in LLM-generated feedback benefited from it, though not significantly so. There were no significant condition differences, in line with our random assignment ($\beta = -0.08$, 95% CI [−0.17, 0.01], $p = .102$), though the negative trend could signal imprecision in the stratification method used to generate the propensity covariate. Looking at lessons individually, we gathered some evidence that LLM feedback contributed to performance, even after accounting for selection effects. The propensity-adjusted treatment effects (corresponding to the ITT interaction effect with propensity in Table 2), estimated through separate regressions for each lesson, indicate that two lessons—*Giving Effective Praise* ($\beta = 0.33$) and *Supporting a Growth Mindset* ($\beta = 0.28$)—demonstrate small to moderate, statistically significant effects ($p < .05$). No other treatment effects were statistically significant, ranging from −0.15 *SD* (*Helping Students Manage Inequity*) to 0.20 *SD* (*Using Motivational Strategies*).

Notably, simply being assigned the possibility of requesting LLM-generated feedback (ITT) did not significantly improve posttest performance, as the main effect of the ITT condition was not significant (see previous paragraph). This suggests that the potential to request LLM-generated feedback alone was insufficient to enhance performance outcomes, highlighting the importance of actual engagement with LLM-generated feedback to realize its benefits. Figure 3 illustrates the posttest scores by condition, adjusting for the learner's propensity to request LLM feedback to account for treatment selection effects. Among learners who were offered LLM feedback (blue), those who were more likely to use the LLM feedback were predicted to score higher at posttest. Learners who were not offered LLM feedback (red) did not show much difference in posttest score regardless of their predicted likelihood of using the feedback. This aligns with a positive treatment effect after adjusting for self-selection bias.

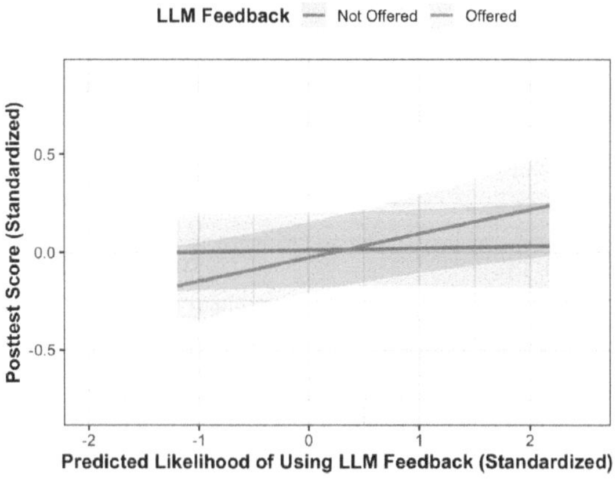

Fig. 3. Posttest scores by condition, adjusting for learner propensity to request LLM feedback to adjust for treatment selection effects, including 95% confidence intervals estimated through model coefficient standard errors. (Color figure online)

4.2 RQ2: Influence of LLM Feedback on Lesson Efficiency

To address RQ2, we investigated the influence of LLM-generated feedback on lesson efficiency. We analyzed the time it took tutors to complete lessons among learners in the TOT condition (those receiving LLM feedback) compared to the Control and ITT conditions, who did not receive LLM feedback. The analysis focused on log-transformed time data to normalize the distribution and ensure desirable outcome distributions for regression modeling. A linear mixed model was fitted with log-transformed time taken as the dependent variable, AI-generated feedback as the primary predictor, and random intercepts for learners and lessons to account for nested data, similar to RQ1.

Results indicate no statistically significant effect of receiving LLM feedback on the time taken to complete lessons (Estimate = 0.00, 95% CI [-0.08, 0.08], p = .999). Indeed, the conditions were surprisingly similar, with learners receiving feedback taking an average of 5.75 min to complete lessons, while others took an average of 5.59 min, which is a difference of merely 9 s. The intraclass correlation coefficient (ICC) shows that 33% of the variance in time taken was attributable to differences between learners, while only 2% of the variance was due to differences between lessons. These findings suggest that receiving LLM feedback did not meaningfully alter the time spent on lessons, and individual differences were the primary driver of variation in lesson efficiency.

4.3 RQ3: Learner Perceptions of LLM-Generated Feedback

We analyzed learner perceptions of LLM feedback based on an optional, single-survey response collected at the tutor level. Among the 568 lessons completed (TOT), 332 learners chose to provide feedback on their perceptions of the feedback. The results show that the vast majority of learners classified it as helpful 312 (93.98%), while 14 (4.22%) found it not helpful, and only 6 (1.81%) categorized it as incorrect. These findings showed overwhelmingly positive perceptions.

5 Discussion

Small Learning Gains from LLM-generated Feedback, Moderated by Learners' Tendency to Seek Support. Learners with a higher propensity to request LLM-generated feedback performed significantly better on posttest compared to those who did not. After adjusting for this selection effect, the main effect of LLM-generated feedback was positive, though there was heterogeneity across lessons. Given the significant positive effect among the group that used the feedback, we conclude that learners most likely to seek feedback learned more, which is likely associated with receiving LLM-generated feedback. In all cases, we estimate the true effect of LLM feedback to be small and possibly dependent on the specific content being practiced, warranting further research. These findings are important as they show improvements over a realistic existing system that was already providing feedback without LLMs (see Fig. 1).

Besides the question of whether LLM-generated feedback is effective or not, the key lesson learned from the present study is that even if the LLM feedback was effective, its effectiveness hinges on the willingness of learners to request and engage with it. Learners who actively engage with the feedback derive greater benefits, yet this engagement may also reflect preexisting learning differences or greater intrinsic motivation. In line with prior research on scaffolding in tutoring systems [2], it is possible that proactive help-seeking behaviors may constrain the broader impact of LLM-generated feedback. Research on help-seeking behavior has shown that learners who ask for help more effectively, particularly by recognizing when and how to seek help, experience significant improvements in learning outcomes [2,22]. It is possible, though subject to future research, that, if learners were required to request LLM feedback benefits would be larger.

LLM-generated Feedback does not Take more Time. Learners engaging with LLM feedback did not take statistically significantly more time compared to the control condition of not receiving such feedback. This suggests that providing LLM-generated feedback to learners is a low-cost instructional addition to short scenario-based lessons or even professional development training for teachers, tutors, and alike. However, in some cases, the feedback generated was rather long, making it more likely that not all learners are reading the feedback. Nevertheless, upon adjusting for self-selection, there were learning benefits to receiving LLM feedback, so at least some learners process the feedback. We suspect that the lack of completion time differences could be due to increased fluency through marginal learning: Learners benefit from receiving feedback and completing the posttest in a short period of time due to increased fluency.

Another alternative explanation for the lack of completion time differences by condition is that learners receiving LLM feedback (*treatment-on-the-treated* condition) used generative AI to generate their open responses at posttest, shortening the time required to produce a response and producing marginally higher posttest performance. A follow-up analysis revealed that learners who received LLM feedback during instruction (in Q1, see Fig. 1) produced significantly longer responses at posttest (in Q9), six words longer on average. While longer responses may indicate better learning, it is also possible that some learners copied or adapted the LLM-generated feedback from Q1, which could have inflated their performance. According to Fan et al. [11], the use of LLMs may encourage learner dependence on the technology contributing to metacognitive "laziness," hindering learners' ability to generate, critically reflect on, and effectively learn from their responses when needed. Although we cannot rule out such misuse of genAI, we posit that such cases were rare, as our lessons are low-stakes assessments and take learners a short time to complete (averaging $<$6 min).

Learners Found the LLM-generated Feedback Helpful. Most of the learners in the LLM feedback condition (*treatment-on-the-treated*) rated the feedback as *helpful*, echoing the findings of Kinder et al. [15]. While this positive reception is encouraging, we also acknowledge the potential for self-selection bias: learners who chose to engage with the feedback may already have been more motivated or open to support. However, the overwhelmingly positive responses warrant another interpretation: Learners' positive ratings may reflect both genuine appreciation of the feedback and a possible influence of social desirability. The lack of optional textual comments leaves open whether learners had nuanced reactions they did not express. Nonetheless, the overwhelmingly positive ratings point to a strong initial acceptance of LLM-generated feedback as a useful instructional tool. While liking does not always equate to learning [26], the positive perceptions observed here suggest that LLM feedback has the potential to enhance learning—particularly when learners are inclined to engage with it.

6 Limitations, Future Work, and Conclusion

There are several limitations. We strived to correct for possible selection bias within the *treatment-on-the-treated* group but there is a possibility that bias still exists, given that the propensity scoring method in itself is imperfect. Calls to the OpenAI API failed occasionally, with 15.7% of requests for LLM feedback failing, with some tutors assigned the LLM-generated feedback condition opting for feedback but not able to receive it. We suspect that this reduced the overall use of LLM feedback, but it may also have undermined learner trust in the feedback, which could be investigated more closely in future research. Future work will analyze log data for time spent reading LLM feedback versus skipping ahead and examine carryover effects in AI-generated responses. Future work will also explore why lessons on motivation showed stronger effects, while equity lessons did not—potentially due to content complexity or feedback alignment.

In sum, this study highlights the promise of LLMs for generating explanatory feedback to enhance learning outcomes in scenario-based training. As our key empirical finding, the effectiveness of such feedback depends not only on its quality, but also on learners' willingness to seek and engage with it. Analyzing over 2,000 lesson completions, we found that learners who opted to receive LLM-generated feedback consistently outperformed those who did not. After adjusting for self-selection using propensity scoring methods, we observed a small effect of LLM feedback on posttest performance. Notably, this learning benefit came without a significant increase in lesson completion time. We contribute an open dataset, annotation rubrics, and LLM scoring prompts, enhancing future research, which may explore how to maximize the impact of LLM feedback through better and more adaptive help-seeking support.

Acknowledgments. This work was made possible with the support of the Learning Engineering Virtual Institute. The opinions, findings and conclusions expressed in this material are those of the authors.

References

1. Achiam, J., et al.: Gpt-4 technical report. arXiv preprint arXiv:2303.08774 (2023)
2. Aleven, V., Mclaren, B., Roll, I., Koedinger, K.: Toward meta-cognitive tutoring: a model of help seeking with a cognitive tutor. Int. J. Artif. Intell. Educ. **16**(2), 101–128 (2006)

3. Bardach, L., Klassen, R.M., Durksen, T.L., Rushby, J.V., Bostwick, K.C., Sheridan, L.: The power of feedback and reflection: testing an online scenario-based learning intervention for student teachers. Comput. Educ. **169**, 104194 (2021)
4. Caruccio, L., Cirillo, S., Polese, G., Solimando, G., Sundaramurthy, S., Tortora, G.: Claude 2.0 large language model: tackling a real-world classification problem with a new iterative prompt engineering approach. Intell. Syst. Appl. **21**, 200336 (2024)
5. Cavalcanti, A.P., et al.: Automatic feedback in online learning environments: a systematic literature review. Comput. Educ. Artif. Intell. **2**, 100027 (2021)
6. Chhabra, P., Chine, D., Adeniran, A., Gupta, S., Koedinger, K.: An evaluation of perceptions regarding mentor competencies for technology-based personalized learning. In: Society for Information Technology & Teacher Education International Conference, pp. 1812–1817. Association for the Advancement of Computing in Education (AACE) (2022)
7. Dai, W., et al.: Can large language models provide feedback to students? A case study on chatgpt. In: 2023 IEEE International Conference on Advanced Learning Technologies (ICALT), pp. 323–325. IEEE (2023)
8. Demszky, D., Liu, J., Hill, H.C., Jurafsky, D., Piech, C.: Can automated feedback improve teachers' uptake of student ideas? Evidence from a randomized controlled trial in a large-scale online course. edworkingpaper no. 21-483. Annenberg Institute for School Reform at Brown University (2021)
9. Denny, P., Khosravi, H., Hellas, A., Leinonen, J., Sarsa, S.: Can we trust llm-generated educational content? Comparative analysis of human and llm-generated learning resources. arXiv preprint arXiv:2306.10509 (2023)
10. Escalante, J., Pack, A., Barrett, A.: Llm-generated feedback on writing: insights into efficacy and enl student preference. Int. J. Educ. Technol. High. Educ. **20**(1), 57 (2023)
11. Fan, Y., et al.: Beware of metacognitive laziness: effects of generative artificial intelligence on learning motivation, processes, and performance. Br. J. Educ. Technol. (2024)
12. Gibbs, G.: Learning by doing: A guide to teaching and learning methods. Further Education Unit (1988)
13. Gurung, A., et al.: Identification, exploration, and remediation: can teachers predict common wrong answers? In: LAK23: 13th International Learning Analytics and Knowledge Conference, pp. 399–410 (2023)
14. Hattie, J., Timperley, H.: The power of feedback. Rev. Educ. Res. **77**(1), 81–112 (2007)
15. Kinder, A., et al.: Effects of adaptive feedback generated by a large language model: a case study in teacher education. Comput. Educ. Artif. Intell. **8**, 100349 (2025)
16. Koedinger, K.R., Baker, R.S., Cunningham, K., Skogsholm, A., Leber, B., Stamper, J.: A data repository for the edm community: the pslc datashop. Handb. Educ. Data Min. **43**, 43–56 (2010)
17. Lin, J., et al.: How can i improve? Using gpt to highlight the desired and undesired parts of open-ended responses. arXiv preprint arXiv:2405.00291 (2024)
18. Lin, J., et al.: How can i get it right? Using gpt to rephrase incorrect trainee responses. Int. J. Artif. Intell. Educ. 1–27 (2024)
19. Mertens, U., Finn, B., Lindner, M.A.: Effects of computer-based feedback on lower- and higher-order learning outcomes: a network meta-analysis. J. Educ. Psychol. **114**(8), 1743 (2022)

20. Meyer, J., et al.: Using llms to bring evidence-based feedback into the classroom: llm-generated feedback increases secondary students' text revision, motivation, and positive emotions. Comput. Educ. Artif. Intell. **6**, 100199 (2024)
21. Pardos, Z.A., Bhandari, S.: Chatgpt-generated help produces learning gains equivalent to human tutor-authored help on mathematics skills. PLoS ONE **19**(5), e0304013 (2024)
22. Roll, I., Aleven, V., McLaren, B.M., Koedinger, K.R.: Improving students' help-seeking skills using metacognitive feedback in an intelligent tutoring system. Learn. Instr. **21**(2), 267–280 (2011)
23. Sales, A.C., Pane, J.F.: The role of mastery learning in an intelligent tutoring system: principal stratification on a latent variable (2019)
24. Sales, A.C., Vanacore, K.P., Ottmar, E.R.: Geepers: principal stratification using principal scores and stacked estimating equations. arXiv preprint arXiv:2212.10406 (2022)
25. Stamper, J., Xiao, R., Hou, X.: Enhancing LLM-based feedback: insights from intelligent tutoring systems and the learning sciences. In: Olney, A.M., Chounta, I.A., Liu, Z., Santos, O.C., Bittencourt, I.I. (eds.) Artificial Intelligence in Education. Posters and Late Breaking Results, Workshops and Tutorials, Industry and Innovation Tracks, Practitioners, Doctoral Consortium and Blue Sky. AIED 2024. CCIS, vol. 2150, pp. 32–43. Springer, Cham (2024). https://doi.org/10.1007/978-3-031-64315-6_3
26. Sung, E., Mayer, R.E.: When graphics improve liking but not learning from online lessons. Comput. Hum. Behav. **28**(5), 1618–1625 (2012)
27. Thomas, D., Yang, X., Gupta, S., Adeniran, A., Mclaughlin, E., Koedinger, K.: When the tutor becomes the student: design and evaluation of efficient scenario-based lessons for tutors. In: LAK23: 13th International Learning Analytics and Knowledge Conference, pp. 250–261 (2023)
28. Thomas, D.R., et al.: Do tutors learn from equity training and can generative ai assess it? arXiv preprint arXiv:2412.11255 (2024)
29. Thomas, D.R., et al.: Learning and ai evaluation of tutors responding to students engaging in negative self-talk. In: Proceedings of the Eleventh ACM Conference on Learning@ Scale, pp. 481–485 (2024)
30. Thompson, M., Owho-Ovuakporie, K., Robinson, K., Kim, Y.J., Slama, R., Reich, J.: Teacher moments: a digital simulation for preservice teachers to approximate parent-teacher conversations. J. Digit. Learn. Teach. Educ. **35**(3), 144–164 (2019)
31. Wisniewski, B., Zierer, K., Hattie, J.: The power of feedback revisited: a meta-analysis of educational feedback research. Front. Psychol. **10**, 487662 (2020)
32. Xu, C., Lin, J., Wu, T., Aleven, V., Koedinger, K.R.: Improving automated feedback systems for tutor training in low-resource scenarios through data augmentation. arXiv preprint arXiv:2501.09824 (2025)
33. Zou, H., Hastie, T.: Regularization and variable selection via the elastic net. J. R. Stat. Soc. Ser. B Stat. Methodol. **67**(2), 301–320 (2005)

Automated Approaches for Concept Map Assessment: A Systematic Review

Laís Pisetta Van Vossen[1(✉)], Joice Luiz Jeronimo[1], Elaine Harada Teixeira de Oliveira[2], and Isabela Gasparini[1]

[1] Santa Catarina State University (UDESC), Joinville, Brazil
{lais.vossen,joice.jeronimo}@edu.udesc.br, isabela.gasparini@udesc.br
[2] Federal University of Amazonas (UFAM), Manaus, Brazil
elaine@icomp.ufam.edu.br

Abstract. As concept maps gain prominence in education, ensuring reliable and efficient assessment methods becomes increasingly important. However, automating this process remains a complex problem. Due to their free-form nature, assessing a concept map is subjective, as there is no single "correct" way to design one for a given topic. To address these challenges, this systematic literature review identifies techniques and criteria currently employed to automate the evaluation of concept maps. In addition to conventional systematic review methods, the study utilized DeepSeek as an auxiliary tool for paper selection, validating its results against selections made by two independent researchers via the Kappa test. The findings highlight recent advancements in evaluation techniques for using AI in qualitative assessment. Still, gaps persist in assessing collaborative and multilevel educational contexts. Additionally, the field lacks standardized evaluation criteria, including established datasets or universally accepted metrics for comparing the performance of different automated assessment approaches. By synthesizing current practices in automated concept map evaluation, this study aims to foster discussions on standardizing evaluation metrics and to provide a comprehensive overview of the state of the art in this evolving domain.

Keywords: Concept Map · Systematic Literature Review · Automated Assessment

1 Introduction

Concept Maps (CMs) are robust tools for organizing and visually representing knowledge on a given subject. This tool, created by Novak, consists of concepts, typically enclosed in circles or boxes, and relationships between concepts indicated by connecting lines [26]. Moreover, CMs have some essential elements, which include hierarchy, cross-links, and examples [26]. Hierarchy is a concept that defines how the map is organized, progressing from a more general term to a more specific one, which may vary depending on the context. Meanwhile, cross-links represent connections between different knowledge domains within the concept map. Examples include the incorporation of practical instances related to

K. Tammets et al. (Eds.): EC-TEL 2025, LNCS 16063, pp. 504–518, 2026.
https://doi.org/10.1007/978-3-032-03870-8_34

the concept being explored, which aids comprehension and makes it less abstract. However, with the popularization of concept maps, several other elements and features have been incorporated [9]:

Despite the variety of features that compose modern CMs, at first glance, they may appear as a simple arrangement of words in a hierarchy. However, according to [26], "when care is used in organizing the concepts represented by the words, and the propositions or ideas are formed with well-chosen linking words, one begins to see that a good concept map is at once simple, but also elegantly complex with profound meanings", and this complexity and profound meaning are being explored in various ways, such as for assessments [30], or even as a study tool to observe students' knowledge and identify content they may struggle to assimilate [9].

When used correctly, CM analysis can provide insights into students' learning levels, highlighting strengths and knowledge gaps, making CMs a powerful diagnostic tool for educators [13]. However, their evaluation imposes a significant cognitive load on educators, rendering the use of CMs as knowledge assessment tools impractical for large student groups. Therefore, to understand the processes for automating CM evaluation, this paper aims to identify how the literature is implementing these evaluation methods, seeking to understand the scope of the techniques employed and how their quality is being assessed, as well as in which contexts and which characteristics are being considered in this automated evaluation process. To this end, the following research questions are proposed: **Q1)** What methods or techniques for automated evaluation are being applied to concept maps? **Q2)** What criteria are used to assess the quality of the evaluations? **Q3)** Which characteristics of concept maps are considered during the evaluation process? **Q4)** In what contexts is the automation of concept maps assessment being implemented?

2 Related Work

The work of [1] provides an *overview* of methods and schemes for assessing concept maps (CMs), with a focus on computer-automated evaluation systems. The study classifies evaluation systems into five groups:

1. Type of evaluation: quantitative, qualitative, or a combination;
2. Evaluation method: structural, relational, or a combination;
3. Evaluation with or without the support of an expert-based reference CM;
4. Which evaluation scheme is used: automated or manual assessment;
5. Whether there are restrictions on the application of the proposed method for evaluating CMs.

Finally, [1] reiterates the difficulty of creating an automated CM evaluation system, noting that even tools employing advanced assessment methods are not adaptive enough to accommodate the wide variety of existing scenarios. The authors also raise the issue of interpreting these evaluations, as many criteria used in the analyzed studies concern the number of concepts and the relationships between their connections, making it difficult for students to understand the assessment.

The work of [30] also provides an *overview* of the use of concept maps as tools for assessing student knowledge. The main objective of the study is to analyze different CM-based tasks and the criteria used to evaluate them.

Among the evaluation methods explored, the authors note that only one-third of the methods applied to open-ended CMs were automated in some way. The freedom to choose words and structural patterns was identified as a factor complicating this automation. Thus, Strautmane (2012) [30] emphasizes the importance of an automated evaluation system that provides a score or grade without teacher intervention, thereby reducing the workload in CM assessment.

The paper [9] presents a systematic literature review, exploring which analysis methods are being used for open-ended CMs and how each method relates to the measured characteristics of these maps. To this end, the authors surveyed studies presenting some form of CM analysis or evaluation since 1984 (the year the term "concept map" was established), resulting in a total of 25 papers for full reading after applying inclusion and exclusion criteria.

As a result, [9] presents a survey of the types of conclusions that can be drawn by analyzing each characteristic of a concept map using one of the four identified analysis methods: qualitative, quantitative, holistic, or similarity-based. Additionally, the authors highlight that many studies in the field associate an increase in specific analyzed parameters (e.g., the number of connections between concepts) with student development and learning. However, this relationship is not always valid. Another concern for the field is the ambiguity of the terms used, which, according to [9], may hinder transparency and interpretation of studies in the area.

The paper [16] performs a systematic literature review on the applications of concept maps as an educational assessment tool in engineering. In the study, 53 papers were analyzed regarding sample size, discipline of focus, interdisciplinary, research methodology, concept map metrics, topic, type of activity and software, scoring method, expert map usage, automated scoring, validity, and repeatability. Of the 53 papers, only 8 used automated scoring methods, with 6 using a direct expert map comparison technique. The study discusses that while automated methods streamline scoring and enable faster feedback with maintained accuracy, they often fail to evaluate content correctness or quality.

This paper distinguishes itself from others by providing an exclusive focus on the analysis of automating the evaluation of CMs. Although this feature has appeared in more recent studies, the analysis of these automated methods lacks depth. Despite the paper by [1] focusing on this issue, an update is necessary, as it was published 16 years ago, and new methods and papers on the topic have since been published. Additionally, this paper covers aspects not present in others, such as evaluating the sample size of the tests conducted and the criteria used to validate the proposed methods.

3 Methodology

The entire systematic review process was conducted on the platform Parsifal[1] and followed the guidelines for systematic reviews from Kitchenham and Charters (2007) [18]. After determining the research questions, the first step was to design a search query using the PICOC [4] method and the questions presented in Sect. 1. This approach was selected because it facilitates the conversion of the research objectives into keywords for the search string, therefore the following PICOC components were used in the process:

- Population: Concept map
- Intervention: Automatic evaluation of concept maps
- Outcome: Assessment, evaluation or measurement of the concept map
- Context: Educational context, using concept maps as a teaching and learning tool

With these keywords representing the main research topic, the following query was used due to the number of papers it yielded and their relevance: ("concept map" OR "concept mapping" OR "concept maps" OR "conceptual map" OR "conceptual mapping" OR "conceptual maps") AND (automation OR automated OR automatic OR automatically OR "computer assisted" OR "computer based" OR computer-assisted OR computer-based) AND (assessment OR Measurement OR evaluate OR evaluating OR evaluation OR feedback OR measuring OR score OR scoring). The query was adapted for each database it was applied to, conforming to the patterns and rules they have. Moreover, the words related to concept maps were searched in the title of the papers, while the others related to automation or assessment were searched in all the papers' metadata. This was done to ensure the results would clearly focus on concept maps.

The query was applied on February 11, 2025, to 5 databases considered relevant for this research area and used in previous related research, with two focusing on computing (ACM and IEE Xplore), one in education (ERIC) and the other two in a vast range of disciplines (Scopus and Web of Science). No year constraint was applied to the databases, meaning that it captured papers from a wide range of years, with the oldest being 1994 and the newest from 2025. This review's stages are represented by Fig. 1, which shows the selected databases and their number of returned papers.

The search string resulted in 505 papers, 170 duplicate papers, and 261 that didn't meet the inclusion and exclusion criteria. In addition to that, 3 new papers were included by the Snowball Sampling method, which looked for papers that cited or were cited by the related work in Sect. 2 and that implemented an automated CM assessment. Regarding the inclusion criteria, 9 papers were removed because they were unavailable for full-text reading. As for the exclusion criteria, 207 papers were excluded for not performing automated assessments of concept maps, 34 for not using concept maps as a teaching and learning tool, 8 for not being primary papers, 2 for being gray literature, and 1 for being a conference

[1] https://parsif.al/.

abstract or editorial paper. The first author applied the exclusion criteria based only on the title, abstract, and keywords of each paper, resulting in 77 papers. To check the quality of the filtering by selection criteria done by the first author, the second author selected 30 random papers for filtering. The title and summary of those same 30 papers were used in a prompt for DeepSeek, available in GitHub[2], to get another "opinion" on the selection process. The DeepSeek and researchers 1 and 2 selection results for those 30 papers were compared using Fleiss' Kappa measure, resulting in a value of 0.63, indicating substantial agreement [21].

The resulting 77 papers underwent a quality assessment, during which the authors downloaded all the papers and checked the following questions:

- Does the automated method proposed assess CMs made by students? This question aims to remove papers that evaluate the quality of automatic generated concept maps
- Does the proposed assessment method provide feedback, score, or any type of evaluation regarding the CM quality? The objective is to eliminate papers that don't evaluate something regarding the quality of the map but other aspects (e.g., collaboration in CM construction)
- Does the paper clearly describe the automated assessment method proposed? Eliminates papers that don't explain the entire assessment method
- Does the paper test the automated evaluation method proposed and provide the results? This question aims to remove papers that only proposed a new assessment method but didn't test it on real data.
- Does the paper present an evaluation method for the automated assessment proposed? Eliminates papers that didn't compare the proposed method with results from any other method.

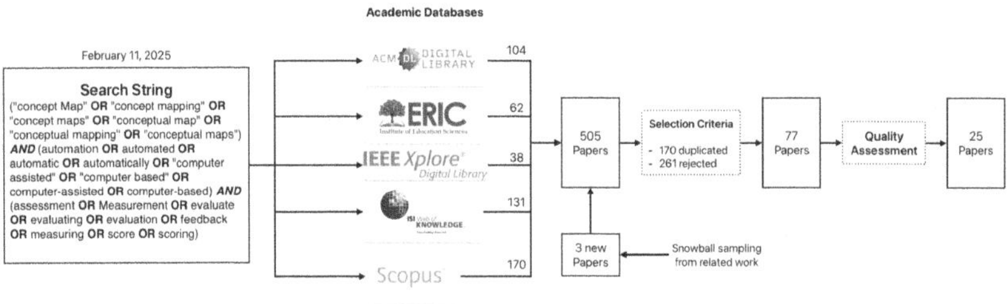

Fig. 1. Stages of the Systematic Review.

All the papers that didn't check all the quality criteria determined were excluded from further analysis. There was one exception, with a particular case involving papers describing the Kit-Build system, that met the criteria but were

[2] https://github.com/Laispvv/Automated-Approaches-for-Concept-Map-Assessment.

removed to avoid repetition in the analyses. Since they referred to the same system, only the most recent paper retrieved was considered, even though more than 10 papers related to the Kit-Build system reached the quality assessment stage. In the final stage of the systematic review, data extraction was performed on the remaining 25 papers that met the quality criteria. Predetermined information was extracted from them as outlined in the form available on GitHub[3].

4 Results

This section presents the analyses conducted on the papers resulting from the selection process to answer the research questions established in Sect. 1.

4.1 What Methods or Techniques for Automated Evaluation are Being Applied to Concept Maps?

Table 1. Technics and methods applied by each paper.

Technique	Method	Papers
Graph Theory	Similarity	Only Similarity: [22] Quantitative: [14,19], Quantitative + Qualitative: [33]
	Not Similarity	Quantitative + Qualitative: [6]
AI	Similarity	Only Similarity: [25] Quantitative: [17] Qualitative: [23,29] Quantitative + Qualitative: [8]
	Not Similarity	Quantitative: [3] Qualitative: [32] Quantitative + Qualitative: [2]
Specialized algorithm	Similarity	Only Similarity: [7,20,27,34] Quantitative: [5,15,28,31] Qualitative: [24]
	Not Similarity	Quantitative: [10–12]

Table 1 categorizes the selected papers based on the automated concept map assessment techniques and the evaluation methods applied. It shows a strong association between similarity-based approaches and the use of specialized algorithms.

[3] https://github.com/Laispvv/Automated-Approaches-for-Concept-Map-Assessment.

To understand which methods or techniques are being used for the automated assessment of CM, we grouped the papers' techniques into three categories: Graph Theory, Artificial Intelligence (AI), and Specialized Algorithm. Within each technique, there is a division between papers that use the similarity method between two CMs to perform the evaluation and those that do not. Additionally, some papers employ combined methods, as in the case of [33], which uses similarity, quantitative, and qualitative methods along with the Graph Theory technique to assess the concept maps. The Graph Theory and AI categories are characterized by papers that employ these techniques in their evaluations. However, this doesn't mean they don't use specialized algorithms alongside them, as evaluating a concept map typically requires an algorithm specifically designed for that scenario.

It is also noticeable that different techniques were used more frequently for specific methods than others. Some examples include the predominance of similarity evaluation associated with specialized algorithms and the more significant presence of qualitative analysis linked to the use of AI techniques. This was mainly due to the use of Natural Language Processing algorithms, which enabled semantic analysis of the terms used in the CMs.

Although, among the resulting papers, not many employed AI as their technique, in Fig. 2, the increase in the number of papers using AI techniques is noticeable starting from 2021. With further exploration of these algorithms for evaluating CMs in future papers, new ways of automating qualitative evaluations may emerge.

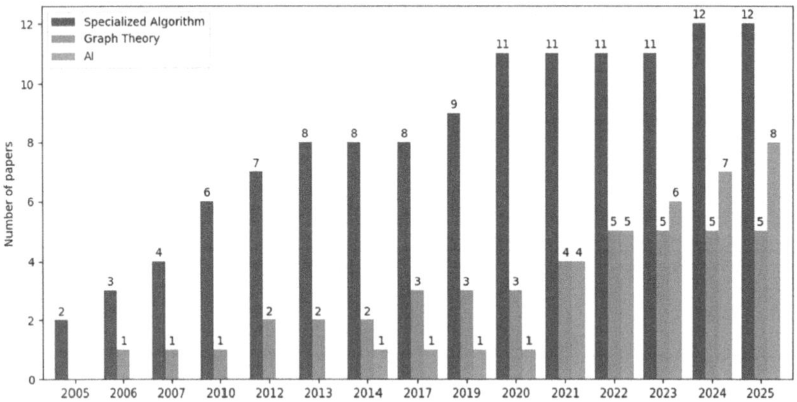

Fig. 2. Cumulative sum of technics used by year of paper publication.

4.2 What Criteria are Used to Assess the Quality of the Evaluations?

This question aims to understand how the papers validate the accuracy of the proposed automated assessments of CMs. We identified, as shown in Table 2, four types of metrics used for result comparison: comparison with manual evaluations conducted by experts, comparison with automated assessments from other CM evaluation algorithms, comparison with grades obtained through other types of tests (e.g., exams, essays), and others, for metrics that did not fit the previous categories.

Table 2. Metrics used for comparison and type of evaluation done by each paper.

Metric for comparison	Papers
Manual evaluation of the CM by an expert by any criteria	Similarity between two CM: [7,23,25,29,31] Quality assessment: [6] (scoring rubric based on size and strength of CM), [14,19,34] (criteria used: completeness and interconnectedness), [15] (rubric used to grade concepts on good, better, or best), [33] (Existencial, Relational and Holistic score - to calculate some of these metrics uses an expert map for comparison), [3] (rating scheme with four categories), [32] (Classification of CM structure in spoke, net or chain) Manual calculation of metrics that the system calculates automatically: [2,8] (manually calculated the Waterloo rubric[a] and compared with the automated calculation)
Scores calculated by other automatic CM evaluation algorithm	[11] (TaxS), [28] (coefficient of correspondence), [10] (compared to the Waterloo rubric[4] calculated by [2] on a public available dataset)
Score from other kinds of tests	[12] (marks achieved on open-answer final test), [27] (posttest score, delayed-test score and learning gain), [17] (correlation with homework scores), [5] (relation with score on achievement test)
Others	[23] (Jaccard[b] e Neighbors[c]), [22] (Jaccard[b]), [20] (comparing the participants' reordered CM with the expert CM), [28] (compared attributes before and after learning), [24] (interview with students regarding effectiveness of the algorithms)

[a] Available at: https://uwaterloo.ca/centre-for-teaching-excellence/catalogs/tip-sheets/rubric-assessing-concept-maps. [b] Statistic used to measure the similarity between two sample sets. [c] Computes "closeness" between CMs based on the analysis of neighborhood sets.

The expert manual evaluation metric was undoubtedly the most widely used to validate the effectiveness of the proposed algorithms. This manual assessment can measure the similarity between two CMs, determine quality, assign a grade, or classify a CM. Furthermore, two papers relied on experts to manually calculate the same metrics that their proposed algorithms computed automatically.

For instance, [2] introduced an algorithm to calculate the Waterloo rubric automatically and validated it by comparing the results with those obtained from manual calculations.

Another frequently used metric involved correlating CM evaluations with performance in traditional educational assessments, such as exam grades or responses to essay questions. This type of metric allows for observing the correlation between a CM's score and grades from more familiar evaluation systems for educators. It also eliminates the need for teachers to have in-depth knowledge of assessing concept maps, reducing potential research bias.

An observed evaluation gap is the lack of comparison between automated assessment algorithms from different papers. There is little dialogue between different systems, making it challenging to compare proposed methods and hindering a comparative analysis of assessment accuracy across different systems. Whether due to different contexts, challenges in reproducing algorithms from other papers, or the absence of a public benchmark dataset, the field as a whole struggles to determine its progress in the quality of CM evaluation due to this lack of comparability between the methods.

4.3 Which Characteristics of Concept Maps are Considered During the Evaluation Process?

The type of proposed activity significantly influences the automated assessment method that can be employed for CMs. In this analysis, activities were divided into two types. "Fill-in-the-map" activities provide some set of information for constructing the CM, whether it be linking phrases, concepts, or both. In this activity, the student is not free to create the map from scratch, as they must use the provided information. This reduces certain complexities in assessment since the terms used can be predetermined, avoiding issues such as determining term similarity. On the other hand, in "Construct-the-map" activities, the student has complete freedom to choose the concepts, linking phrases, and structure of the map, building it from the ground up.

Table 3. Characteristics of the CM and type of task evaluated.

Characteristics of the CM	Type of Task
Only propositions	Fill-in-the-map: [3,7,34] Construct-the-map: [12,25,29]
Calculated metrics based on concept map foundation characteristics	Fill-in-the-map: [5,15,28] Construct-the-map: [6,8,10,14,17,19,22,24,31–33]
Only concept map foundation characteristics	Fill-in-the-map: [20,27] Construct-the-map: [2,23]
Metrics regarding concept map creation process	Construct-the-map: [11]

It is important to note that assessment methods that did not restrict their evaluation to "Fill-in-the-map" activities were classified as "Construct-the-map". However, they are not necessarily limited to this type of activity. This is because a method capable of assessing free-form maps can more easily evaluate a map with predefined elements than the reverse. Accordingly, in Table 3, the activity type was associated with map characteristics and divided into four categories.

The first category comprises methods that rely solely on the propositions formed in the CMs, with a proposition being the sentence composed of the triad concept-linking phrase-concept.

The second category consists of algorithms that compute their metrics based on the fundamental characteristics of conceptual maps. Most papers fall into this category. Examples include the work of [28], which calculated the ruggedness metric (related to fragmentation into sub-maps), and the study by [22], which employed pedagogically based metrics such as Prerequisite Constraints, assessing the knowledge prerequisites of a concept.

The third category comprises papers that used fundamental metrics of a conceptual map, including concepts, linking phrases, propositions, and the CM's organizational structure. For instance, [20] employed the position of concepts and links as a metric since these elements were already provided for CM creation, making the assessment focus on validating correct term placement. Meanwhile, [2] applied the Waterloo Rubric as an assessment algorithm, requiring fundamental map features such as terms used in concepts and linking phrases, concept count, propositions, and others.

Finally, only one paper incorporated metrics collected during the conceptual map creation process. This was done in the paper [11], which utilized logs of creation, deletion, addition, and other actions recorded by the system during the student's CM construction process.

4.4 In What Contexts is the Automation of Concept Maps Assessment Being Implemented?

Table 4 was created to address the context in which automated methods for evaluating concept maps (CMs) are employed. For this purpose, two variables were analyzed: the size of the sample of maps evaluated by the proposed method in the papers and the educational level at which the method was applied. Only five papers used samples of fewer than 10 maps, with most being at an unspecified educational level due to the origin of these maps, which were sourced from the internet [23,25,29].

One issue that stands out in Table 4 is that only a single paper [33] has developed and tested an automated assessment algorithm across more than one educational context. Restricting studies to evaluating their algorithms within a single educational level may introduce biases in the analyses and findings, as the developed assessment method could become tailored exclusively to that specific scenario.

Table 4. Context and sample sizes of tests by automated CMs assessment systems.

Sample size	Papers
Less than 10	Not specified: [22,23,25,29] Elementary School: [12]
10–30	Higher Education: [6,7,15,17,24] Postgraduate: [11]
31–100	High School: [5,14,28] Higher Education: [2,8,10,27,31,34] Postgraduate: [20]
More than 100	Middle School: [19] High School: [3,32] Higher Education, Postgraduate: [33]

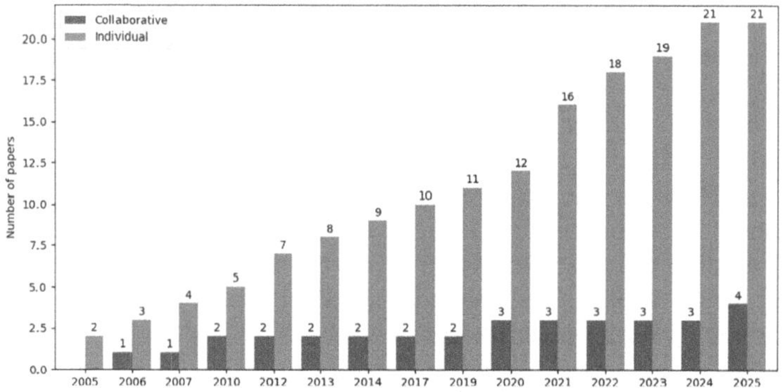

Fig. 3. Cumulative sum of collaborative and individual CM creation tasks by year.

Another aspect of the context was whether the applied methods evaluated concept maps created individually or collaboratively. Figure 3 shows the cumulative sum of papers in each category over the years. It is important to note that studies were classified as collaborative if they evaluated concept maps developed by larger groups, such as in [15] and [32], or by pairs, as in [28] and [6]. However, even though these studies were considered collaborative, they did not collect metrics during the collaborative process of creating concept maps (CMs). In other words, the collaborative aspect was not incorporated into the automated assessment algorithm design, and the developed systems did not differentiate feedback based on each student's contribution to the proposed activity. This remains a significant challenge for the field, which has produced few papers that considered collaborative environments in their evaluations.

5 Discussion

Among all the analyzed papers, the most prevalent educational context was Higher Education, with 12 papers using CMs created by students at this educational level. Additionally, there is a gap in the evaluation of maps made by Middle School students, with only the work of [19] examining this context. Another notable issue is that only the study by [33] analyzed multiple educational settings. This lack of diversity in students' educational levels may introduce biases in the analyses, limit the results of automated evaluation algorithms to only the tested context, and, more broadly, constrain the proposed methods to a single environment, making it difficult to assess their adaptability.

The systematic analysis reveals significant advances in automated assessment approaches for CMs but also exposes critical challenges requiring attention from the scientific community. A key challenge is the lack of consensus on evaluation techniques, criteria, and metrics, as detailed in Subsects. 4.1, 4.2, and 4.3. For instance, while some studies validate results through comparison with expert manual evaluations (Table 2), others correlate findings with traditional exam scores, making cross-method comparisons challenging and possibly introducing bias in the analysis. The absence of public datasets or universally accepted metrics, as noted in Sect. 4.2, perpetuates this fragmentation, limiting reproducibility and collective progress. This disparity reflects the inherent subjectivity of CMs, but also underscores the need for standardized guidelines to steer future research.

Furthermore, another research gap lies in the restricted application of developed techniques, predominantly in Higher Education contexts (Table 4). This limitation introduces bias, as algorithms designed for controlled scenarios or specific activities may lack adaptability to dynamic environments or diverse age groups. Another underrepresented context is the assessment of CMs created collaboratively. The lack of methods to analyze group dynamics prevents automation from capturing the complexity of collaborative learning. This omission is concerning, as modern educational environments often encourage teamwork, and the absence of suitable tools limits the diagnostic potential of CMs in these scenarios.

Additionally, the predominance of methods relying on similarity to a reference CM confines automation to partially manual evaluation since creating reference maps still requires human intervention. This approach also limits independent student use of CM tools for self-directed learning.

Since 2021, there has been a marked surge in AI adoption, particularly NLP and deep learning. In this context, text embedding and neural network techniques could prove valuable for assessing qualitative aspects of CMs, such as semantic relevance. However, the potential of AI remains underexploited. For example, Generative AI models, such as GPT-4, could create dynamic reference maps to reduce reliance on experts, create CMs to assemble a benchmark or even simulate the manual evaluation done by an expert, while social network analysis techniques might evaluate collaboration on CM creation. Despite progress, significant opportunities remain for applying diverse AI methodologies in this research domain.

6 Conclusion

The present study analyzed the methodologies and techniques applied in the automated assessment of concept maps, addressing fundamental aspects such as the techniques used, the quality criteria for assessing the automation method proposed, which CMs characteristics were used for evaluation, and application contexts. The results indicate that the assessment of CMs remains a challenge, with limited contexts, with the majority of papers testing in only one educational level, and a significant dependency on similarity methods. Besides that, assessment techniques have evolved in more recent years, with a rise of studies employing AI techniques, such as natural language processing (NLP), machine learning, and deep learning, to help with a more qualitative evaluation of the CMs.

In summary, the reviewed literature highlights underexplored aspects of the CM automated assessment, with a more recent exploration of AI techniques. However, there is still room for improvement, particularly in developing any benchmark or diverse dataset for use as metrics for validating the accuracy of automated assessment methods. These contributions could help the entire community improve its solutions and build a more robust but adaptative solution for CM assessment.

Acknowledgements. This study was financed in part by the Coordenação de Aperfeiçoamento de Pessoal de Nível Superior - Brasil (CAPES) - Finance Code 001, and also partially supported by CNPq grant 302959/2023-8 (DT2) and 303443/2023-5 (DT2), FAPESC Edital n° 60/2024 research project "Metodologias inovadoras e technologies educacionais para o processo de ensino e aprendizagem", PROMOP/UDESC.

Disclosure of Interests. The authors have no competing interests to declare that are relevant to the content of this article.

References

1. Anohina, A., Grundspenkis, J.: Scoring concept maps: an overview. In: Proceedings of the International Conference on Computer Systems and Technologies and Workshop for PhD Students in Computing, pp. 1–6. Association for Computing Machinery, New York (2009). https://doi.org/10.1145/1731740.1731824
2. Bhatia, S., Bhatia, S., Ahmed, I.: Automated waterloo rubric for concept map grading. IEEE Access **9**, 148590–148598 (2021). https://doi.org/10.1109/ACCESS.2021.3124672
3. Bleckmann, T., Friege, G.: Concept maps for formative assessment: creation and implementation of an automatic and intelligent evaluation method. Knowl. Manage. E-Learn. **15**, 433–447 (2023)
4. Carrera-Rivera, A., Ochoa, W., Larrinaga, F., Lasa, G.: How-to conduct a systematic literature review: a quick guide for computer science research. MethodsX **9**, 101895 (2022). https://doi.org/10.1016/j.mex.2022.101895
5. Chang, K.E., Sung, Y.T., Chang, R.B., Lin, S.C.: A new assessment for computer-based concept mapping. Educ. Technol. Soc. **8**, 138–148 (2005)

6. Clariana, R.B., Koul, R., Salehi, R.: The criterion-related validity of a computer-based approach for scoring concept maps. Int. J. Instr. Media **33**, 317–325 (2006)
7. Cline, B.E., Brewster, C.C., Fell, R.D.: A rule-based system for automatically evaluating student concept maps. Expert Syst. Appl. **37**, 2282–2291 (2010). https://doi.org/10.1016/j.eswa.2009.07.044
8. Dahir, M.A., Qasim, S.A., Ahmed, I.: Cronus: an automated feedback tool for concept maps. IEEE Access **9**, 119564–119577 (2021). https://doi.org/10.1109/ACCESS.2021.3106509
9. de Ries, K.E., Schaap, H., van Loon, A.-M.M.J.A.P., Kral, M.M.H., Meijer, P.C.: A literature review of open-ended concept maps as a research instrument to study knowledge and learning. Qual. Quant. **56**(1), 73–107 (2021). https://doi.org/10.1007/s11135-021-01113-x
10. Deshpande, P., Ahmed, I.: Topological scoring of concept maps for cybersecurity education. In: Proceedings of the 50th ACM Technical Symposium on Computer Science Education, pp. 731–737. ACM, Minneapolis (2019). https://doi.org/10.1145/3287324.3287495
11. Dias, S.B., Dolianiti, F.S., Hadjileontiadou, S.J., Diniz, J.A., Hadjileontiadis, L.J.: On modeling the quality of concept mapping toward more intelligent online learning feedback: a fuzzy logic-based approach. Univ. Access Inf. Soc. **19**(3), 485–498 (2019). https://doi.org/10.1007/s10209-019-00656-z
12. Giovannella, C., Selva, P.E., Fraioli, S.: Mapevaluator in action: a comparative test on the efficiency of the quantitative concept map evaluation in a primary school. In: Seventh IEEE International Conference on Advanced Learning Technologies (ICALT 2007), pp. 566–570 (2007). https://doi.org/10.1109/ICALT.2007.184
13. Hay, D.B., Kinchin, I.M.: Using concept maps to reveal conceptual typologies. Educ. + Train. **48**, 127–142 (2006). https://doi.org/10.1108/00400910610651764
14. Hoppe, H.U., Engler, J., Weinbrenner, S.: The impact of structural characteristics of concept maps on automatic quality measurement. In: Proceedings of the 10th International Conference of the Learning Sciences: The Future of Learning, ICLS 2012 (2012)
15. Hubal, R., et al.: Testing of a program to automatically analyze students' concept maps. Pharmacy **8**(4), 209 (2020). https://doi.org/10.3390/pharmacy8040209
16. Jackson, A., Barrella, E., Bodnar, C.: Application of concept maps as an assessment tool in engineering education: systematic literature review. J. Eng. Educ. **113**, 752–766 (2024). https://doi.org/10.1002/jee.20548
17. Jain, G.P., Gurupur, V.P., Schroeder, J.L., Faulkenberry, E.D.: Artificial intelligence-based student learning evaluation: a concept map-based approach for analyzing a student's understanding of a topic. IEEE Trans. Learn. Technol. **7**, 267–279 (2014)
18. Kitchenham, B., Charters, S.: Guidelines for performing systematic literature reviews in software engineering. Technical report 2 (2007)
19. Kroeze, K.A., van den Berg, S.M., Veldkamp, B.P., de Jong, T.: Automated assessment of and feedback on concept maps during inquiry learning. IEEE Trans. Learn. Technol. **14**, 460–473 (2021). https://doi.org/10.1109/TLT.2021.3103331
20. Kumar, R., Sarukesi, K., Uma, G.V.: OAMS-a game based online formative knowledge assessment system using concept map. J. Theor. Appl. Inf. Technol. **53**, 150–156 (2013)
21. Landis, J.R., Koch, G.G.: The measurement of observer agreement for categorical data. Biometrics **33**, 159 (1977). https://doi.org/10.2307/2529310

22. Limongelli, C., Marani, A., Sciarrone, F., Temperini, M.: Measuring the similarity of concept maps according to pedagogical criteria. IEEE Access **10**, 27655–27669 (2022). https://doi.org/10.1109/ACCESS.2022.3156662
23. Limongelli, C., Schicchi, D., Taibi, D.: Enriching didactic similarity measures of concept maps by a deep learning based approach. In: Proceedings of the International Conference on Information Visualisation (2021). https://doi.org/10.1109/IV53921.2021.00049
24. Liu, C.C., Don, P.H., Tsai, C.M.: Assessment based on linkage patterns in concept maps. J. Inf. Sci. Eng. (2005)
25. Montanaro, A.G., Sciarrone, F., Temperini, M.: A deep learning approach to concept maps similarity. In: Proceedings of the International Conference on Information Visualisation (2022). https://doi.org/10.1109/IV56949.2022.00048
26. Novak, J.D., Cañas, A.J.: The theory underlying concept maps and how to construct and use them. Technical report, IHMC CmapTools (2008)
27. Rismanto, R., Pinandito, A., Andoko, B.S., Hayashi, Y., Hirashima, T.: Evaluating the kit-build concept mapping process using sub-map scoring. Res. Pract. Technol. Enhanc. Learn. **19** (2024). https://doi.org/10.58459/rptel.2024.19021
28. Schaal, S., Bogner, F.X., Girwidz, R.: Concept mapping assessment of media assisted learning in interdisciplinary science education. Res. Sci. Educ. **40**, 339–352 (2010)
29. Sciarrone, F., Temperini, M.: A sentence-embedding-based dashboard to support teacher analysis of learner concept maps. Electronics **13** (2024). https://doi.org/10.3390/electronics13091756
30. Strautmane, M.: Concept map-based knowledge assessment tasks and their scoring criteria: an overview. In: Concept Maps: Theory, Methodology, Technology. Proceedings of the fifth International Conference on Concept Mapping, pp. 80–88 (2012)
31. Taricani, E.M., Clariana, R.B.: A technique for automatically scoring open-ended concept maps. Educ. Tech. Res. Dev. **54**, 65–82 (2006)
32. Vossen, L., et al.: Concept map assessment through structure classification. arXiv preprint arXiv:2503.22741 (2025). https://doi.org/10.48550/arXiv.2503.22741
33. Wei, W., Yue, K.B.: Integrating concept mapping into information systems education for meaningful learning and assessment. Inf. Syst. Educ. J. **15**, 4–16 (2017)
34. Wu, P.H., Hwang, G.J., Milrad, M., Ke, H.R., Huang, Y.M.: An innovative concept map approach for improving students' learning performance with an instant feedback mechanism. Br. J. Educ. Technol. **43**, 217–232 (2012). https://doi.org/10.1111/j.1467-8535.2010.01167.x

Challenges and Design Opportunities for AI-Based Tutoring and Assessment Software in Special Education: An Interview Study with Teachers

C. Naomie Williams[1(✉)], Margaret Ellen Seehorn[2], Haiyi Zhu[1], and Vincent Aleven[1]

[1] Carnegie Mellon University, Pittsburgh, PA 15213, USA
{naomiew,haiyiz}@cmu.edu, aleven@cs.cmu.edu
[2] Grinnell College, Grinnell, IA 50112, USA
seehorne@grinnell.edu

Abstract. Approximately 240 million children, 10% of children worldwide, have disabilities. However, few studies have investigated requirements for AI-based tutoring and assessment for this population within a real-world context. It is unclear how special education classrooms experience these emergent tools in practice. We therefore conducted interviews with 18 special education teachers in the United States about the usage, challenges, and perceived benefits of AI in their classrooms. The interviews reveal tensions between special education's need for personalized learning systems and difficulty integrating existing techno-solutions due to: (1) poor interface and curriculum adaptations for students with learning disabilities, (2) under-consideration of special education's additional form of academic assessment when differentiating students, and (3) criteria for subject mastery incompatible with special education students' personalized learning plans. Nevertheless, special education teachers remain optimistic towards AI's promise of flexible instruction for students requiring accessible digital interfaces. From these findings, we conclude with design implications and potential research directions to better synergize emerging techno-solutions with special education classrooms' needs. This work envisions tangible pathways towards inclusive AI for students with disabilities and a more equitable classroom of tomorrow.

Keywords: AI in Special Education · Accessibility · Narrative Interview

1 Introduction

Education promised to be the great equalizer. Technology became the medium to improve access to education and catapult students to better futures. However, the extent this promise has come to fruition for students with learning disabilities is unclear. Literature reviews spanning the last decade emphasize the need for more real-world studies examining the use of AI in special education [1–3]. Prior scholarship for AI in special education has contributed innovative case studies and theoretical approaches to support

K. Tammets et al. (Eds.): EC-TEL 2025, LNCS 16063, pp. 519–533, 2026.
https://doi.org/10.1007/978-3-032-03870-8_35

students with disabilities [1, 3–5]. However, contributions in this domain received critique for lacking the longitudinal data to enhance statistical robustness and real-world relevance" [3]. Notwithstanding limitations, AI-based tutoring and assessment software maintain promise for special education.

AI-based tutoring and assessment technologies such as: iReady, IXL, MATHia, and ALEKS, refer to learning software where the interface and curriculum are personalized for each user based on the student's behavior and academic performance [6]. Typically, these systems help students practice complex problems, provide adaptive (individualized) step-level guidance within these problems, select problems that involve unmastered material, and support individualized placement. Several meta-analyses show that students learn better when using AI-based tutoring and assessment technologies than without [7]. This suggests that such software may be particularly beneficial for underserved students with disabilities, though the study did not focus on this population [8].

Special education, envisioned and mandated in the US as an inclusive, school-based learning environment for students with disabilities, shares AI-based tutors' ethos for personalized instruction. In the United States, public schools are required to have an Individualized Education Program, or IEP, for each student receiving special education services. IEPs are living documents co-designed by teachers, parents, school administrators, and related services personnel. Teachers use the IEP as a guide to determine what curriculum modifications, personalized learning goals, and assistive technologies are necessary for an individual student. A mutual ethos of personalization would suggest the possibility of a promising synergy between AI's capability and goals of special education.

Students in special education have widely differing learning support and technological access needs, often requiring a combination of assistive technologies (e.g. text to speech software and adaptive switch devices as an alternative to mouse and keyboard), personalized learning goals, and curriculum modifications (changes to a student's educational program). The characteristic properties of AI-based tutoring and assessment software would nominally make them suitable for use in special education, with its high demands for personalization and individualized instruction.

Our goal is to expand our understanding of AI in special education by studying teachers' perspectives of AI-based tutoring and assessment within classrooms that serve students with multiple, widely differing, and co-occurring disabilities. Prior scholarship highlights a need for real-world data [7, 9], data that clarifies the extent that education, and the emergent technology facilitating, has equalized opportunity for students with disabilities. As scholarship continues to push the boundaries for inclusive education, it's crucial to understand the ways emerging techno-solutions can reify and expand existing inequities or, if well-designed, limit them. This study's goal is to understand the degree to which that notion is true – and more specifically, the strengths and weaknesses of AI in special education, as seen through the eyes of teachers. We conducted interviews with 18 special education teachers in the United States to gain insights into the usage, challenges, and perceived benefits of AI-based tutoring and assessment software in their classrooms. We present and discuss our findings and conclude with design implications and potential research directions to improve the synergy between AI-based tutoring and assessment software and the needs of special education classrooms.

2 Related Work

2.1 AI-Based Tutoring Systems for Personalization and Accessible Learning

There are two general ways AI-based learning technologies currently serve students with disabilities: customized learning support and fundamental accessibility. Accessibility incorporates the needs of people with disabilities into the development and implementation of mainstream technologies to provide equitable access to exclusionary physical and digital environments that otherwise could not accommodate them, including K–12 education [7, 10]. AI-based tutoring systems use artificial intelligence to personalize learning materials and curriculum pacing, two critical components of special education's IEP. AI-based tutors can take the form of intelligent tutoring systems [11], serious games [12], and other emergent technologies such as smart assistants and interactive robots [9]. AI-based tutors can use algorithms that study student behavior, identify strengths and weaknesses in performance, and suggest areas for improvement. For example, a machine learning model was proposed to identify reading, writing, and memory difficulties for students with dyslexia [13]. Although unevaluated, the proposal highlights novel methodology to customize support for students needing additional reading and writing assistance.

AI-based tutoring and assessment technologies could enable pathways to personalize technology-enhanced learning for students with specific disabilities, should special education teachers incorporate AI in their classrooms. Potential avenues include using computer vision to detect facial expressions and determine which activities increase engagement, robots for social-emotional learning, AI-generated recommendations to reduce teacher effort when personalizing instructions, and interactive simulations with multisensory learning scaffolds [7, 13–19]. These contributions present encouraging opportunities and recommendations to tailor educational techno-solutions for specific disabilities.

However, there is limited understanding of how these techno-solutions work in the daily practice of special education, whether in separate classrooms or mixed within regular classrooms. In special education, individual students often have multiple co-occurring disabilities and will be in classrooms with other students who have widely differing disabilities and support needs. This environment differs from prior scholarship, which has primarily studied personalized support for specific disabilities in isolation [9, 36]. We argue this overgeneralization of smaller studies for specific types of disabilities to broader special education could result in decreased software usability, failure to address crucial learning needs, and increase the amount of teacher labor required for instruction within special education classrooms [20].

2.2 Challenges Within AI-Based Tutoring for Students with Disabilities

Although, as mentioned, there is ample past research on how AI-based tutoring and assessment technologies might be designed to serve students with disabilities, past scholarship has not focused enough on understanding how these technologies would need to function in the daily practice of special education. For example, in 2015, Whyte et al. found that "the existing computer-based interventions have been designed from theoretical models about the science of autism" [2] rather than the real-world experience of teachers and their students with disabilities. Cinquin et al. recommended future research expand beyond case studies to "compare different solutions across a large spectrum of cognitive impairments to assess whether they are able to cope with the diversity of people with disabilities' situations" [1], as existing evaluations of the time were considered too context dependent, with too few learning trials. [2, 21]. In 2019 scholarship for emergent technology for students with disabilities had a limited number of long-term studies where evaluation was modeled in an environment reflective of where the actual e-learning tool would be used [1]. Unfortunately, five years later, "larger sample sizes and longitudinal studies to enhance statistical robustness and real-world relevance" were still needed [3].

Considering the growing adoption of AI-based tutoring and assessment software in classrooms, and limited empirical evaluation, it is imperative we hear from teachers of students with disabilities already utilizing these tools. In this paper we sought answers to the following research questions: **1) How are adaptive tutoring and assessment tools being used in special education classrooms? 2) What factors inform AI-based learning technology's usage, and its perceived benefits, by special education teachers? 3) From the perspective of teachers, have the potential benefits of AI in special education been actualized for students with disabilities?**

3 Methods

To understand how these limitations and unexplored areas of AI-based tutoring and assessment technologies impact students with disabilities, we interviewed 18 special education teachers.

Recruitment: We used Reddit for recruitment, a social media platform of user-organized discussion forums, or subreddits, around specific interests. We reached 63 teachers via education specific subreddits related to our study - r/SpecialEd, r/TeachingResources, r/EdTech, and r/OnlineLearning. Every teacher recruited had experience teaching students with learning disabilities, ranging from 1 year of experience to 30. Selecting 18 special education teachers, representing ~ 30% of total recruited, we used the following criteria: 1) experience using learning technology in their classrooms, and 2) Be a K-12 educator in a public or private school. By selecting teachers from both public and private schools, we aspired to represent a variety of educational contexts, including specialty schools only serving students with disabilities.

Semi-structured Narrative Interviews: Our interview protocol inquired into their school's accommodation practices and sought to uncover the frustrations, and successes using educational technology in their classrooms, with an emphasis on tools with adaptive capability. The interview was 60 min long and semi-structured, with the majority spent on two retrospective contextual inquiries. First teachers were given the opportunity to share the kind of educational technology they had experience with. Examples questions include: *What kinds of educational software do you use with your students?*

Do you use any "adaptive" or intelligent" learning software? How does that software fit into your typical week? Then we pivoted to their school's accommodation practices, where teachers were asked to walk us through a recent experience creating learning accommodations for one of their students, asking questions such as: *In the classes you teach, what percentage of students would you say have learning disabilities? Could you describe how students needing accommodations are identified, who is involved in the process, and what documentation you're provided? Of the accommodations mentioned, which ones are used in combination with software?* Afterwards, teachers shared recent stories of learning technology, not limited to adaptive, being used in their classrooms. In the spirit of a semi-structured interview, the questions varied by teacher. Follow-up questions typically depended on answers to previous questions, as the interview tried to steer the interview to points of interest related to the main theme of the study. Finally, we concluded with some speculative questions, allowing the teacher to look towards the future. Example questions include*: Is there anything about the design of the software you would like to change? If you could have anything to make your experience with teaching better for you and your students with accommodations, what would that be? Consider this your wish list in an ideal world.*

Analysis: After finishing all 18 interviews, we completed a thematic analysis via Interpretation Sessions to analyze approximately 20 h of transcribed audio recordings [22]. 5 coders consisting of the lead author and 4 undergraduate assistants reviewed the transcripts. The first step involved generating codes—labels or short phrases used to assign meaning to pieces of data in the interview transcripts, capturing key observations or insights. Codes represented succinct, essential summaries of utterance in the transcript. The first 3 interviews were qualitatively coded by multiple researchers to establish a baseline and resolve any disagreements in the granularity of the coding [23]. Following the shared coding session, the remaining 15 transcripts were divided among the research team. Each transcript had 2 reviewers and received 2 passes. The first pass examined the data using an inductive lens by deprioritizing "analytic preconceptions" to answer specific research questions [24]. The goal was to understand the experiences of special education teachers through their eyes. The second pass featured a more theoretical thematic analysis aiming to uncover the significance of emerging patterns and broader implications [24]. During this phase, transcripts were analyzed for broader ideas and documenting specific observations related to our research questions. For the second step, we reconvened as a group to analyze the 443 individual codes to complete a bottom-up affinity diagram [22]. The codes were clustered and refined into 3 levels of themes in an iterative process. The first level clustered our 443 codes into 61 themes. These were then grouped into 12 s-level themes. The four top-level themes and 13 s level themes correspond to the level two and three headers in the Results section, respectively.

Ethics and Participant Safety: We assured all teachers participation was voluntary, responses would be anonymized, and consent could be revoked at any time. To ensure participants' identities remain unidentifiable to those not within the study team, participant data is reported at an aggregate level with participant IDs. We acknowledge research participatory in nature can have high emotional and time investment, then fail to produce tangible outcomes for participants [25]. We intend to continue collaborating with the special education teachers who participated in this study. As a demonstration of our commitment to maintain communication post-study, we created an opt-in Google Group mailing list that 13 out of 18 teachers have joined.

Positionality: We acknowledge that our perspectives are shaped by our experiences, which influence our research. Our study team is composed of American citizens working in the United States. The first and second author identified as disabled, with the first author having lived experience as a special education student in the American public school system. Our academic backgrounds span interdisciplinary fields within Human-Computer Interaction, including education, accessibility, social computing, and AI.

4 Results

4.1 Special Education Teacher's Current Practices

Participants reported using multiple types of learning software in special education. These tools can be broadly categorized into three groups: AI-based tutoring and assessment systems, assistive technologies, and learning management systems. Table 1 provides examples for each category. For example, Lexia is an AI-based tutor designed to support students' reading development through personalized, adaptive learning paths, while DreamBox personalizes math instruction using an individual student's performance in lesson and overall progress data. These AI-based tutoring and assessment programs are used to help identify disability based on performance, match students to accommodations, and determine which classroom is the appropriate academic level for the student. Assistive technologies such as Clicker, a word processor with pictorial rep-resentations and drag and drop word banks, scaffold sentence building for learners needing additional literacy support. Learning Management systems are used to manage IEP progress and facilitate communication between special education teachers, parents, and other relevant personnel. In contrast to Frontline IEP and YellowFolder, software intended for use within special education, some participants adapted workforce man-agement programs such as ADP Learning and Cornerstone to manage IEPs.

Table 1. Examples of self-reported software from participants

AI-based Tutor & Assessment	Assistive Technology	Learning Management Systems
Lexia	Clicker (Cricksoft)	Frontline IEP
DreamBox	LyriQ Screen Reader	ADP Learning
Mobi Max	Adaptive Switch	CornerStone LMS
TeachTown	Braille Keyboard	Google Classroom
HelpKidzLearn	LiveScribe Pen	YellowFolder

Assessments From AI-Based Tutoring and Assessment Software are Crucial to Identifying Students Who May Need Special Education Services. P3 describes the start of an IEP process, "A student is identified either by parent or a teacher as struggling with whatever…content is being used at that grade level. Maybe the student, hasn't turned in any work, maybe the work that's being turned in is all wrong. Maybe the student's breaking down over the work." Teachers in P1's school refer students who are "far below grade level" to the district psychologist for further evaluation. A student study team is formed; comprised of the general education teacher, special education staff, school administration, district psychologist, and specialists that support specific disabilities such as a speech, occupational, or physical therapist. According to P3, the student study team will "send in an observer to the classroom and run the student through a battery of computer tests. They'll do some reading, math, and may also look at auditory processing. They may ask the nurse to do an auditory test and a vision test to see if the student's having vision problems."

Although Crucial, Technology-Based Assessments are Often Inaccurate, Thus Teachers Use Additional Assessments to Evaluate Students. AI-based tutors and other software provide that adapt based on student performance to determine a student's current academic level. P2 explains how a technology-based assessment adapts for their sixth-grade students, "The placement test would give them sixth-grade computation problems aligned to the state standards. If they get them right, [the test] will keep going to make sure [the student] knows all the skills in that specific area. Whereas if they start to get them wrong, then it bumps them down to…a [lower] grade level."

However, assessment is not limited to measuring subject mastery. Technology-based assessments are used in the form of IQ tests and adaptive behavior scales, to identify disability and determine a student's accommodations. It is imperative the assessments adapt appropriately and produce accurate results, so students needing special education services can receive accommodations timely. However, these examinations are often time consuming and inaccurate. For example, P5 describes how AI-based psychological testing falls short with a student who is nonverbal, "[students] still have to go through all the psychological testing, but a lot of the times they're not able to get an accurate IQ score, because the kids are nonverbal." Consequently, P5 seeks out additional input from parents and therapists to, "determine where they would fit withing the school system and what accommodations are needed".

Student performance data from AI-based tutoring and assessment software assists in matching students with disabilities to the appropriate special education classroom. P9 and P11 also emphasize the importance of these assessments to "make sure the students end up in the right class for them". Students with disabilities are matched to a classroom before receiving personalized instruction.

After classroom placement, AI-based tutoring and assessment usage shifts towards measuring learning goal progress defined in the IEP creation process, as part of the software's guidance to students in their problem-solving exercises. Learning goals are adaptive and based on resources and a student's needs. P9 uses assessments to "understand student capabilities and create goals." P5 expounds, "A list of goals is created based on how they have done in previous and current assessments and their ability level in general, and these goals are added to their IEP. Once a week, their performance towards accomplishing these goals is evaluated and the average of these values becomes their quarterly grades".

4.2 Special Education Teacher's Current Challenges

AI-Based Tutoring and Assessment Software Fall Short in Providing Accurate, Detailed, and Meaningful Assessment. Unfortunately, assessment results from software alone provide insufficient information to measure student growth. P14 says, "[the data] is a general, shallow hint." P3 believes learning technology can provide "a good base-line" but fails to present the data to teachers in a meaningful way. "Teachers will look at those numbers and think a kid is functioning at grade level when they're not...in specific areas...There's not enough categorization of the sub-context to understand the overall scores." P3 explains that their students have higher scores for comprehension when reading passages are fiction, due to additional contextual clues. The software will not distinguish that, placing the student at a higher level. *AI-based tutoring and assessment software fail to consider the intersecting skills between subjects and the literacy levels of students with limited cognitive abilities, resulting in inappropriate shifts between mastery levels.* When the student receives a non-fiction passage, such as an excerpt from a science book or a math word problem, the lack of contextual information reduces comprehension of harder vocabulary words. This misperception of student mastery results in abrupt shifts between levels, instead of gradual change. P1 describes the impact of these oversights in the case of DreamBox, an adaptive math software, "One student who fails a lot of the math questions in DreamBox has a low comprehension level. He has difficulty understanding the math questions. It's not because he has low math skill. It's because his literacy comprehension is bad. DreamBox could not detect this."

AI-based tutoring and assessment software do not consider accessibility barriers on the software and environmental factors when adapting to poor student performance. P18 acknowledges software can show a student is getting poor grades but doesn't consider why. P18 believes, "failure can be because of several things. Maybe they're not interacting with the software. It could be hard for them to use it." For P18, challenges outside the software, within the classroom environment can contribute to low scores. P17 can identify the "local situation" and "trace [it] to this individual [student]". Special education teachers know the issue that is contributing to "low concentration", whereas the software does not. In P7's classroom, "information from the computer is sparse" and teachers are unable to figure out what learning gaps to address solely from that information.

AI-Based Tutoring and Assessment Software Differentiates Students According to Grade Level, While Special Education Uses Performance Level and Accommodations, Adding Challenge to Progress Monitoring. Consequently, students with widely differing needs and disabilities are represented in one classroom. These students may not be of a similar age, adding to the complexity of managing a classroom with students in different developmental stages. According to P4, within the multi-grade classroom, students are further differentiated due to the "notable differences between their levels of need". Strategies for additional differentiation can vary depending on the teacher. P3 "separates students into different tiers, based on how much support they need: general, extra repetition, and full IEP support without an IEP." P1 uses academic performance to "split students into three levels" with the "third level split into more levels". Students within those tiers are "assign[ed] books that are harder or easier to the different levels".

Variance Between Accessibility Needs and Performance Level Results in Multiple AI-Based Tutoring and Assessment in One Classroom, Increasing Complexity of Classroom Instruction. As P1 puts it, "There isn't one AI tool for the entire class. All students work on the same subject, but the app differs between individual students based on proficiency." *However, software differentiation between students is not streamlined.* In contrast to P1, who matches software to students based on performance level, P7 differentiates using accessibility needs. "There is software for students that are visually impaired, for [those] that have a learning disability, or a hearing impairment."

With multiple AI-based tutoring and assessment software, managing individual progress towards learning goals is slow. In P4's classroom students are taught as a group. "Students who have understood the concept are not able to move onto the next topic until the students who were not understanding catch up." *Despite the tiered classroom environment and varying software applications, group learning is crucial.* Likewise, P6 teaches for the slowest learner by "[going] through the classroom activity sessions slowly and at a steady pace to not overwhelm any slower learning students".

AI-based tutoring and assessments are unaware of the additional forms of progress monitoring and personalized learning goals tracked independently from the software, increasing labor for special education teachers. In P5's class "students spend an hour to hour and a half daily receiving one-on-one instruction with a teacher or aide." P2's students with cognitive disabilities "spend more time being pulled out of classes, and that education focuses on vocational training and life skills." P12 creates their own "[assessment and evaluation] on the condition or the status of the student. We usually question the student verbally and get more information from the parent." For P7 there is "not enough time for one-on-one evaluation and discovery so work is done at home." Special education teachers rely on other forms of data collection to understand student growth and redefine subject mastery outside of the software being used. Moreover, tracking individual student data can be tedious. P1 explains, "despite many teachers standardizing assessments and material using assistive technology, student data and progress is tracked in a non-standardized, pen and paper format." P3 expounds, "[Each class] I do weekly progress monitoring, which is on a sheet. [Each student] is on a different grade level for that too. I [track] what they're doing, which questions they're missing one-week, which ones they got right next week, and which questions they need more of that way too." But using this information to assess student progress is difficult when this must be done for each student in every class.

Slow bureaucratic process within special education and discovery of new technology often falls to teachers, making adoption of more effective AI-based tutoring and assessment technologies difficult. P7 further explains that in addition to teaching, teachers identify student needs and discover software solutions if unavailable. "You just have to discover what your students need, and make sure that you get the services provided for them." Special education teachers advocate for the adoption of new techno-solutions with their school's administrators but are often limited by slow bureaucracy. P9 laments, "when you give some suggestions on [what] you want introduced to the school, or [say] you want this kind of resource, [administration] doesn't respond immediately with immediate action. That is the lack of support or cooperation from the institution's management." Other teachers, such as P6, desire better software, but are forced to use whatever the school decides. "I am just a teacher; I didn't make the decision to use it. This is the system they're using to learn, so I had to start using the software." When teacher-advocated software is approved and desired for renewal, financial costs are a barrier to continued use. P5 recounts their experience, "Our supervisor wasn't going to pay to have it renewed. Because somehow, the price increased, and our department just freaked out. And... Everybody said how much they needed and liked it and then they agreed to continue paying for it." Without institutional support, teachers absorb the costs, or their students go without. "If we're not using technology, then we're just using paper... And it may sound silly, but printers aren't always available, and we can't even print in color. I have to do that at home."

4.3 Benefits of AI-Based Tutoring and Assessment Software in Special Education

Despite these challenges, special education teachers view AI-based tutoring and assessments as beneficial. **AI-based tutoring and assessment software can accommodate assistive technology**. P4 has students who are blind and nonverbal in one class. The class solely communicates digitally using braille keyboards. "Every student has their own braille keyboard which is always connected with the computer. It's easy for them to read and understand what I'm trying to say... it's the only means of communication we can do." Technology-enhanced learning in P10's classroom supports LiveScribe, a smart pen designed for students with disabilities. P10 describes how LiveScribe works, "[it] reads aloud any text it physically passes over and a student can then go over the written words or sentences. The pen remembers the text it has read. The playback speed is controlled for maximum comprehension. The student or I can reduce the speed."

Students with Disabilities are More Engaged When the Software is Highly Interactive and Incorporates Gamified Elements. When P18 tries to teach traditionally, "it's simpler using the software. Because I'm teaching verbally, I'm not able to use visual representations. I'm not able to present the kids with games and everythingP12 uses a software that supports customizable multimedia—they can present teaching materials and communicate using videos and images. P16's classroom enjoys a technology that, "presents mathematics problems in form of games. [I]t also can be used for group activities as well as individual activities." P16 continues to describe the added benefit of technology supporting their multi-lingual classroom environment with the Spanish and English language options. P6 uses learning software on a tablet that has, "stories, [students] can listen to. They also have mathematical examples, physical examples using animations, which is easy for the kids to understand and learn first." Agreeing with P18, "software is simpler, it's easier" for P6. Although P2 had software with progress monitoring, they switched to improve engagement, "I use Prodigy mostly for my sixth and seventh graders because it's a reward for them. They're more willing to use it. And MobyMax... Became a chore because it wasn't very fun."

4.4 Special Education Teacher's Aspirations for Future AI-Based Tutoring and Assessment Software

Special Education Teachers Want an All-Inclusive AI-Based Tutoring and Assessment Software That Support Multiple, Widely Differing Disabilities. P6 explains, "I wish I could have an all-inclusive technological package that…. Would serve all my students at once and wouldn't make anyone feel left out, is really going to be a dream come true." P5 wants more options on what their students can do in class, but currently, needs different types of devices to accommodate all students.

AI-Based Tutoring and Assessment Technologies Should Track Student Progress More Holistically, While Communicating Key Learner Insights For Special Education Teachers and Parents, In an Easy-To-Understand Format. P1 wants a software that, "can track all of a student's progress…including their attendance grade, assignments accuracy, assessments, and performance." Technology Enhanced Learning should facilitate communication between special education teachers and parents. P18 wants a software that, "keeps families informed about their children progress through the practice questions that we…assign them to do at home." *However, progress data needs to be easily digestible with recommendations for achieving a student's specific goals.* P3 feels, "computers don't necessarily give me suggestions on how to reteach this. Obviously, I need to reteach the area because the kid's not getting it."

5 Discussion

Understanding how learning technologies, especially adaptive tools, are used by special education teachers is crucial for iterating on the design and goals for future systems. AI-based tutoring and assessment software specifically, have significant promise to support students with disabilities. In this paper we contribute the first comprehensive window into how teachers use these systems within special education, their perceived benefits, current challenges, and desires for future technologies. AI for education has received increased attention broadly [26]; however, there is still limited empirical data about its practical uses, benefits, and challenges for students with disabilities [3]. Prior scholarship has contributed critical theoretical work that explores ways AI-based tutoring systems and assessments could support specific disabilities individually [1, 3]. Our work affirms that teachers see value in intelligent serious games and multi-sensory learning mediums [7, 12, 17], desire holistic progress tracking that includes social-behavioral goals [15] -- such as those found in students IEPs, comprehensive learning analytics [5], and assistance from AI recommendations [13, 16].

Nevertheless, we uncovered AI-based tutoring and assessment software fail to meet the needs of students already in special education, while simultaneously having a critical role identifying students who may need (but not receive) special education services – resulting in increased labor for special education teachers. AI-based tutoring and assessment technologies provide inadequate progress monitoring, often shifting levels abruptly with large jumps in difficulty. Special education teachers' credit this to AI-based tutoring and assessments' failure to consider the literacy levels of students with limited cognitive abilities and intersecting skills between subjects (Subsect. 3.2). Additionally, AI-based tutoring and assessment technologies do not provide streamlined accessibility support for the range of disabilities represented in classrooms. Special education classrooms are not grouped according to grade level, rather performance and accessibility needs. Consequently, teachers find themselves using multiple AI-based tutoring and assessment software in one class to accommodate students' assistive technologies, personalized learning goals, and curriculum modifications defined in each IEP (Subsect. 3.2). The variety of AI-based tutors, disabilities, and performance levels in one classroom results in unreliable learning analytics and recommendations from the software, difficulty maintaining curriculum pacing on a class level, and need for additional progress monitoring, data management systems separate from the AI-based tutors. Despite these challenges, teachers continue to dedicate significant time outside of work to find new technology, because the promise of personalization is worth struggling for.

Future technology-enhanced learning studies should **evaluate effectiveness and accessibility across multiple disabilities.** It is difficult for special education teachers to maintain instructional pace that attends to varying support needs, while allowing higher achieving students to reach their full potential (P7, P12, P18). Additionally, onboarding students with disabilities to a new e-learning environment is challenging—teachers report a period of struggle introducing new technologies. Students with disabilities may not adapt in an expected way to technical errors or an interface they find unintuitive. It's imperative to evaluate the system with a sample target population to identify areas of improvement and limit the amount of software updates.

Special education teachers have limited resources and institutional support, making it difficult for teachers to locate and implement resources that could potentially be useful in their classrooms. Teachers are often forced to use software provided by their school or school district. **Although emerging techno-solutions could be helpful, special education teachers may be unable to adopt it.** Therefore, it is imperative that existing techno-solutions have the empirical support in their design and implementation, while maintaining flexibility to support a wide range of widely differing disabilities that can be present in one classroom or possessed by one student. Designing a technology-enhanced learning system for a specific disability or task will be insufficient to support the needs of special education teachers and their students.

Effective Techno-Solutions Facilitate Parent-Teacher Communication. Special education teachers want parents to contribute to defining and evaluating learning goals and accommodations by providing insight into the at-home learning experience (P10, P7, P9, P18). Despite the potential benefit of providing more holistic assessments for student with disabilities' progress, teachers are concerned about overreliance on software outside of the classroom. Many students within special education have few technological resources and minimal parental involvement. Future studies should consider these concerns in the design of new and existing systems, while soliciting teacher and student input throughout the development life cycle. Existing scholarship has highlighted excellent opportunities for emergent technology to help students with disabilities; however, these opportunities are theoretical or from case studies, with limited empirical evidence from intended teachers, students, and parents who could benefit.

Considering the variety of tools special education teachers use with their students, the mixed-ability nature of Special education classrooms, and additional learning goals from the IEP, a priority research direction should **uncover mechanisms to reduce the burden teachers face creating and organizing student personalization data.** We imagine a future system where teachers could provide information from a student's IEP, including but not limited to accessible formats and mastery criteria for learning goals. The AI-based tutoring and assessment system would adjust the default user experience and student progress data would be re-standardized for easy interpretation by teachers. If multiple software systems are needed, a comprehensive dashboard could legibly centralize all student's data, potentially reducing special education teachers' currently numerous forms of data management. To aid in the streamlining of personalization data, we envision a tool that combines special education's tactical in the classroom learning with technology-enhanced practice to track student progress, fulfilling teachers' desire for technology to supplement rather than replace.

Acknowledgements. This study is supported by the National Science Foundation grant awards: #DGE1745016 and #DGE2140739.

Disclosure of Interests. The authors have no competing interests to declare that are relevant to the content of this article.

References

1. Cinquin, P.-A., Guitton, P., Sauzéon, H.: Online e-learning and cognitive disabilities: a systematic review. Comput. Educ. **130**, 152–167 (2019). https://doi.org/10.1016/j.compedu.2018.12.004
2. Whyte, E.M., Smyth, J.M., Scherf, K.S.: Designing serious game interventions for individuals with autism. J. Autism Dev. Disord. **45**, 3820–3832 (2015). https://doi.org/10.1007/s10803-014-2333-1
3. Yang, Y., Chen, L., He, W., Sun, D., Salas-Pilco, S.Z.: Artificial intelligence for enhancing special education for k-12: a decade of trends, themes, and global insights (2013–2023). Int. J. Artif. Intell. Educ. (2024). https://doi.org/10.1007/s40593-024-00422-0
4. Kohnke, S., Zaugg, T.: Artificial intelligence: an untapped opportunity for equity and access in STEM education. Educ. Sci. **15**, 68 (2025). https://doi.org/10.3390/educsci15010068
5. Nguyen, A., Gardner, L.A., Sheridan, D.: A framework for applying learning analytics in serious games for people with intellectual disabilities. Br. J. Educ. Technol. **49**, 673–689 (2018). https://doi.org/10.1111/bjet.12625
6. du Boulay, B.: Recent Meta-reviews and Meta–analyses of AIED systems. Int. J. Artif. Intell. Educ. **26**(1), 536–537 (2015). https://doi.org/10.1007/s40593-015-0060-1
7. Chang, C.-H.S.: Design and evaluation of a multi-sensory scaffolding gamification science course with mobile technology for learners with total blindness. Comput. Hum. Behav. (2022)
8. Christle, C.A., Yell, M.L.: Individualized education programs: legal requirements and research findings. Exceptionality **18**, 109–123 (2010). https://doi.org/10.1080/09362835.2010.491740
9. Panjwani-Charania, S., Zhai, X.: AI for students with learning disabilities: a systematic review (2023). https://papers.ssrn.com/abstract=4617715
10. García, A.M., De Bra, P., Stash, N., Fletcher, G.H.L., Fabri, M., Pechenizkiy, M.: Adaptive web-based educational application for autistic students. CEUR Workshop Proc. **1628** (2016)
11. Nagashima, T., et al.: Designing playful intelligent tutoring software to support engaging and effective algebra learning. In: Hilliger, I., Muñoz-Merino, P.J., De Laet, T., Ortega-Arranz, A., and Farrell, T. (eds.) Educating for a New Future: Making Sense of Technology-Enhanced

Learning Adoption, pp. 258–271. Springer International Publishing, Cham (2022). https://doi.org/10.1007/978-3-031-16290-9_19
12. Flogie, A., Aberšek, B., Aberšek, M.K., Lanyi, C.S., Pesek, I.: Development and evaluation of intelligent serious games for children with learning difficulties: observational Study. JMIR Serious Games **8**, e13190 (2020). https://doi.org/10.2196/13190
13. Sharif, M.S., Elmedany, W.: A proposed machine learning based approach to support students with learning difficulties in the post-pandemic norm. In: 2022 IEEE Global Engineering Education Conference (EDUCON), pp. 1988–1993 (2022). https://doi.org/10.1109/EDUCON52537.2022.9766690
14. Abdul Hamid, S.S., Admodisastro, N., Manshor, N., Kamaruddin, A., Ghani, A.A.A.: Dyslexia adaptive learning model: student engagement prediction using machine learning approach. In: Ghazali, R., Deris, M.M., Nawi, N.M., and Abawajy, J.H. (eds.) Recent Advances on Soft Computing and Data Mining. pp. 372–384. Springer International Publishing, Cham (2018). https://doi.org/10.1007/978-3-319-72550-5_36
15. Garnier, P., Martel, K., Dachez, J., Audry, P., Bourgoin, P., Stawinski, F.: Educators' perspectives on working with a humanoid robot in a French preschool class for autistic children. J. Res. Spec. Educ. Needs **23**, 163–174 (2023). https://doi.org/10.1111/1471-3802.12588
16. Hamid, S.S.A., Admodisastro, N., Manshor, N., Ghani, A.A.A., Kamaruddin, A.: Engagement prediction in the adaptive learning model for students with dyslexia. In: Proceedings of the 4th International Conference on Human-Computer Interaction and User Experience in Indonesia, CHIuXiD '18, pp. 66–73. ACM, Yogyakarta Indonesia (2018). https://doi.org/10.1145/3205946.3205956
17. Khamparia, A., Pandey, B., Mishra, B.P.: Effects of microworld game-based approach on neuromuscular disabled students learning performance in elementary basic science courses. Educ. Inf. Technol. **25**, 3881–3896 (2020). https://doi.org/10.1007/s10639-020-10142-2
18. Ouherrou, N., Elhammoumi, O., Benmarrakchi, F., El Kafi, J.: Comparative study on emotions analysis from facial expressions in children with and without learning disabilities in virtual learning environment. Educ. Inf. Technol. **24**, 1777–1792 (2019). https://doi.org/10.1007/s10639-018-09852-5
19. Zingoni, A., et al.: Investigating issues and needs of dyslexic students at university: proof of concept of an artificial intelligence and virtual reality-based supporting platform and preliminary results. Appl. Sci. **11**, 4624 (2021). https://doi.org/10.3390/app11104624
20. Fryia, G.D., Wachowiak-Smolikova, R., Wachowiak, M.P.: Web accessibility in the development of an e-Learning system for individuals with cognitive and learning disabilities. In: 2009 First International Conference on Networked Digital Technologies, pp. 153–158 (2009). https://doi.org/10.1109/NDT.2009.5272167
21. Grynszpan, O., Weiss, P.L. (Tamar), Perez-Diaz, F., Gal, E.: Innovative technology-based interventions for autism spectrum disorders: a meta-analysis. Autism. **18**, 346–361 (2014). https://doi.org/10.1177/1362361313476767
22. Beyer, H., Holtzblatt, K.: Contextual design. Interactions **6**, 32–42 (1999). https://doi.org/10.1145/291224.291229
23. McDonald, N., Schoenebeck, S., Forte, A.: Reliability and inter-rater reliability in qualitative research: norms and guidelines for CSCW and HCI practice. Proc. ACM Hum.-Comput. Interact. **3**, 1–23 (2019). https://doi.org/10.1145/3359174
24. Braun, V., Clarke, V.: Using thematic analysis in psychology. Qual. Res. Psychol. **3**, 77–101 (2006). https://doi.org/10.1191/1478088706qp063oa

25. Pierre, J., Crooks, R., Currie, M., Paris, B., Pasquetto, I.: Getting ourselves together: data-centered participatory design research & epistemic burden. In: Proceedings of the 2021 CHI Conference on Human Factors in Computing Systems, pp. 1–11. Association for Computing Machinery, New York (2021). https://doi.org/10.1145/3411764.3445103
26. Allman, B., Kimmons, R., Wang, W., Bao, H., Rosenberg, J.M., Koehler, M.J.: Trends and topics in educational technology. TechTrends. **68**, 402–410 (2024). https://doi.org/10.1007/s11528-024-00950-5

Human Teacher vs. LLM-Generated Feedback in Secondary Education: A Comparative Study on Student Perceptions

Cleon Xavier[1(✉)], Newarney Torrezão da Costa[1,4], Ana Karoline Valdo[1], Gabriel Alves[3], Luiz Rodrigues[2,4], Luiz Fernando Rodrigues[3], Matheus Silva[1], Rodrigues Neto[3], Taciana Pontual Falcão[3], Dragan Gasevic[5], and Rafael Ferreira Mello[3,4]

[1] Instituto Federal Goiano – IF Goiano, Iporá, Goiás, Brazil
{cleon.junior,newarney,ana.valdo,matheus.vieira}@ifgoiano.edu.br
[2] Federal Technological University of Paraná (UTFPR), Apucarana, Brazil
luizrodrigues@utfpr.edu.br
[3] Federal Rural University of Pernambuco – UFRPE, Recife, Pernambuco, Brazil
{gabriel.alves,taciana.pontual,rafael.mello}@ufrpe.br
[4] CESAR School, Recife, Pernambuco, Brazil
[5] Monash University, Melbourne, Australia
dragan.gasevic@monash.edu

Abstract. While providing feedback is a critical task in education, assessing open-ended responses and crafting personalized feedback for each student is time-consuming and challenging. Large Language Models (LLM) can be used to support this process by leveraging their natural language understanding capabilities to evaluate open-ended answers and generate automated feedback. However, in real-world learning environments, empirical gaps remain regarding: I) How do students perceive LLM-generated feedback compared to teacher-provided feedback? and II) What impact does LLM assistance have on instructor feedback practices? Thus, this paper presents a controlled experiment with 60 secondary school students in Brazil, comparing traditional teacher feedback with LLM-assisted feedback using the Tutoria platform. Results showed no significant difference in students' perceptions of feedback quality between the two approaches, with 85% unable to distinguish LLM-generated feedback from teacher feedback. Notably, LLM assistance produced feedback messages 2.6 times longer ($p < 0.001$) without significantly increasing grading time ($p = 0.047$, $ES = 0.09$).

Keywords: Large Language Model · Automated Feedback · Student Perception

1 Introduction

In the educational process, feedback is one of the key strategies to enhance learning outcomes [4]. Students across different educational levels and modalities—

K. Tammets et al. (Eds.): EC-TEL 2025, LNCS 16063, pp. 534–548, 2026.
https://doi.org/10.1007/978-3-032-03870-8_36

whether in-person or distance—rely on feedback as a support mechanism. Typically delivered via text or voice messages, feedback serves as a method to monitor learning progress, clarify individual doubts, explore alternative problem-solving approaches, or correct specific activities [18]. While researchers define feedback in various ways, it can be broadly understood as an interactive exchange process between a student and an agent [15].

With the advancement of Artificial Intelligence (AI) techniques, the feedback process can significantly be enhanced, primarily through the use of machine learning algorithms [6]. Machine learning enables both the processing of text datasets to assess whether instructor-provided support adheres to expected feedback practices in distance education and the facilitation of teaching-learning processes by generating individualized, real-time feedback [30].

The emergence of Large Language Models (LLMs) has prompted a rethinking of feedback paradigms [9]. LLMs' ability to synthesize human-like textual outputs has spurred innovations in Artificial Intelligence in Education (AIED), including adaptive feedback systems [2]. Recent studies demonstrate LLMs' efficacy in diverse educational settings: from secondary education, where they improve writing skills and motivation [17], to higher education, where they rival instructor feedback in quality and clarity [10].

The implications of AI adoption may significantly transform teachers' professional practices [8]. A critical workload challenge involves providing formative feedback on open-ended responses [34]. Recent advancements demonstrate that LLMs can deliver human-like, comprehensive evaluations of student-generated text [9], suggesting their potential to streamline educators' assessment burden while maintaining pedagogical quality [34].

Despite this progress, critical gaps remain in the literature. While prior work has compared LLM-generated feedback to no feedback [17] or teacher-provided feedback [10], to the best of our knowledge, no study has examined how these automated systems contribute to teachers' effort to generate meaningful feedback messages and how students perceive these AI-generated messages in secondary education contexts. This study addresses this gap by evaluating how students perceive LLM-generated feedback relative to traditional teacher feedback in a secondary school learning environment, along with an investigation of how this support contributes to teachers' performances. Our analysis contributes to the literature by presenting a study on the use of LLMs for textual feedback support in secondary education. The research compares scenarios with and without LLM assistance, while examining both student perceptions and variables that may impact teachers' workload.

2 Theoretical Framework

The integration of AI-supported feedback in online learning environments has demonstrated dual benefits for educational stakeholders [5]. For learners, it can enhance metacognitive skills through immediate, formative feedback on task performance, while increasing engagement via personalized guidance [32]. For educators, it can reduce workload by automating repetitive assessment tasks and provide actionable learning analytics to inform adaptive teaching strategies [5]. Building on these proven benefits, generative AI – particularly LLMs – offers potential for feedback creation, whether by fully automating the process or assisting educators in tailoring responses to individual learner needs [14]. Furthermore, the personalization of feedback in question-answering systems has been supported by LLMs' capabilities of reliably answering various types of educational questions, highlighting advantages from being supported by LLMs [22]. Key implications include real-time assistance for educators and learners, adaptive learning aligned with individual pacing and needs, instantaneous feedback delivery, and equitable support for all students [24].

Feedback co-creation, the collaborative process between humans and generative AI for feedback production, represents an emerging field with significant potential in learning contexts [14]. In this paradigm, AI can save one's time by generating initial feedback drafts, while teachers' expertise remains crucial to ensure pedagogical relevance and sensitivity [14]. The relevance of feedback co-creation is supported by Rüdian et al. [25], who investigate student perceptions of LLM-generated feedback compared to teacher-created feedback. Whereas students struggle to distinguish between LLM- and teacher-produced feedback in anonymous evaluation, their perception shifts markedly negative when aware of the automated origin – particularly regarding emotional and social dimensions. This highlights the need for careful, transparent implementation of LLMs in educational feedback, with active teacher involvement remaining critical [25].

The research by Escalante et al. [10] presented two studies in the context of teaching English as a new language to university students. The first study compared students receiving feedback from GPT-4 with a control group receiving feedback from instructors. This study found no significant difference in learning outcomes between the two groups. The second study examined the perceptions of a different group, consisting of 43 English as a New Language (ENL) students who received feedback from both GPT and a human tutor. The results revealed an almost equal split in preference between AI-generated and human feedback.

The study by Meyer et al. [17] primarily investigated the effectiveness of LLM-generated feedback on students' text revision performance, motivation, and positive emotions. The study compared feedback generated by an LLM with no feedback (the control group received only general instructions). The experiment was conducted in secondary school classrooms in Germany, focusing on argumentative writing tasks in English as a foreign language. The results showed that LLM-generated feedback improved text revision performance and increased student motivation for future tasks compared to the no-feedback group.

Similarly, Chan et al. [7] compared LLM-based feedback with a general guide previously produced by the teacher, referred to as traditional feedback, in the context of English as a Second Language (ESL) essay revisions. This study involved university students, where the control group received feedback without LLM assistance. The group that received LLM-based feedback showed improvement in revision, higher motivation, and greater engagement. However, emotional responses were mixed, with no statistically significant differences observed.

Regarding the analysis of instructor workload, the study by Qiao et al. [21] examined the use of LLMs to support moderation in online discussion for a programming course. The developed system, based on a co-creation approach, generated draft responses for instructor approval. The results demonstrated that LLM-assisted forum moderation enhanced productivity, as most generated responses required only minimal edits, though challenges persisted for complex or context-dependent questions. Notably, the study did not quantitatively compare response lengths or time savings with versus without LLM assistance, focusing instead on qualitative instructor experiences and workflow integration.

2.1 Research Questions

While AI-supported feedback demonstrates benefits for enhancing metacognitive skills for learners and reducing cognitive load for educators [10,14,21,22], critical questions remain about its optimal implementation in real-world educational settings. The potential of LLMs in feedback generation must be balanced with nuanced pedagogical considerations, particularly in how students perceive automated feedback and how instructors benefit from its use. In light of these considerations, two guiding research questions are proposed for this study:

- Research Question 1 (RQ1): *How do secondary education students perceive LLM-generated feedback compared to teacher-provided feedback, and to what extent can students distinguish between the two types of feedback?*
- Research Question 2 (RQ2): *To what extent does LLM-assisted feedback generation impact instructor feedback practices, considering output length, time efficiency, and instructor acceptance?*

Regarding RQ1, feedback should be analyzed considering student perceptions across aspects of knowledge, motivation, goals, tactics, outcomes and actions, progress monitoring, and teacher-student interaction. These metrics are commonly evaluated in learning processes, particularly in the analysis of self-regulated learning [4,19]. In relation to RQ2, time is an objective demand when analyzing workload [20], and previous studies can be found that investigate the relationship between feedback length and its potential impact on quality [9,29].

3 AI Platform for Feedback

Tutoria is a platform designed to support instructors in the evaluation of activities submitted through learning management systems (LMS) such as Moodle, with a particular emphasis on open-ended questions. It offers AI-powered assistance for composing textual feedback, aiming to reduce the instructor's workload in manual effort required during the grading process. A central feature of the system is its tagging mechanism, which enables instructors to classify segments or entire students' responses as correct, partially correct, or incorrect. Instructors can create or reuse existing tags, each linked to an explanatory message [11,12]. The system also provides tag recommendations based on prior assessments, continuously refining its suggestions through usage. Figure 1 illustrates a representative workflow: after tags were applied to Student 1's response, the system recommended a tag for Student 2's response (highlighted by the green marker), which was accepted and incorporated into the assessment. In addition to the tagging mechanism, the platform encourages instructors to provide textual feedback that justifies the evaluation and enhances students' understanding. To streamline this process, Tutoria integrates an LLM to automatically generate feedback suggestions, thereby reducing the instructor's workload. The model adapts to the tone and style previously used by the instructor in manually provided feedback, promoting consistency and alignment with their teaching approach.

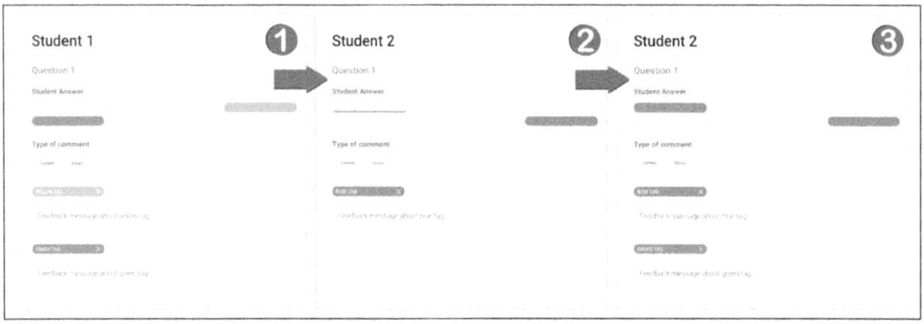

Fig. 1. Tag recommendation from Tutoria.

The LLM integration in Tutoria adheres to prompt engineering best practices, employing direct instructions, structured formatting, and illustrative examples. For each tag created, the system generates a corresponding textual feedback suggestion, which instructors can either edit or adopt as-is. Because feedback messages are linked to tags, they can be reused in future assessments, promoting consistency and efficiency in the grading process. This tag-based recommendation and automated feedback workflow streamlines the evaluation of open-ended questions across various knowledge domains, making the system adaptable to a wide range of educational contexts. Moreover, Tutoria can be integrated with widely adopted learning management systems such as Moodle and Google Classroom to collect student responses.

4 Method

This study investigated the impact of LLM-generated feedback compared to instructor-provided feedback in chemistry assessments for secondary school students. Students from two classes were randomly divided into two groups (Group

A and Group B, see Fig. 2) and each student completed two assessments based on open-ended questions delivered via Moodle. A counterbalanced design was employed to mitigate order-effects [33]: Group A received LLM-generated feedback on the first assessment and instructor feedback on the second, then groups were reversed in the next assessment.

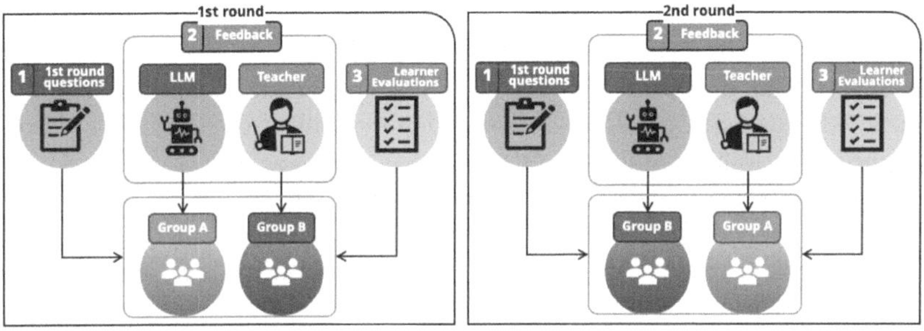

Fig. 2. Overview of the experimental study

For this, two classes were involved in the experiment. The students in the first class (n = 36) were between 14 and 15 years old, and those in the second class (n = 31) were between 16 and 17 years old. To answer RQ1, we followed guidelines aimed to increase the validity of empirical studies [33] and excluded students who: (i) failed to complete any assessment (n = 7); (ii) did not respond to the feedback perception questionnaires (n = 20); or (iii) did not authorize the use of their data (n = 0). The final dataset included data from 40 students for analysis and this data were used to answer the RQ1. A total of 29 students identified as female and 11 as male. For the purposes of the study, students were randomly assigned to Group A or Group B, regardless of their original class. All participants were regularly enrolled in Brazilian secondary education, where chemistry is a mandatory subject.

To answer RQ2, data from students who did not respond to the feedback perception questionnaires were also included, given that RQ2 was about teachers' practices. In this case, we analyzed the feedback given to 60 students (i.e., the students who completed the assessments). Unlike previous studies that primarily employed LLMs for textual feedback on essays and English language learning [7,10,17], our selection aimed to introduce this technology into Natural Sciences education through Chemistry, focusing on supporting short-answer responses to open-ended questions in Brazilian Portuguese. In Natural Sciences (such as Chemistry, Physics, and Biology), teaching typically relies on the definition of fundamental concepts [13,27]. For example, when discussing atoms, it is first necessary to define what atoms are, then introduce the theoretical models used to represent them.

4.1 Data Collection Instruments

The study employed the school's Moodle platform with an integrated feedback tool for data collection (Tutoria). The school uses Moodle as an integral part of its hybrid teaching infrastructure. It is used both to complement in-person activities—such as distributing supplementary materials, administering digital quizzes in the classroom, and managing assignment submissions—and to fulfill the mandatory 20% workload in distance education. This prior adoption of Moodle as the school platform facilitated the process, as participants were already familiar with the platform's interface. The experimental conditions reflected authentic educational workflows, and the deployment of the Tutoria system did not require additional training for students.

The two selected classes had the same chemistry teacher. Therefore, the teacher prepared two assessments for each class, resulting in a total of four assessments, each containing five short-answer questions about chemistry concepts covered in previous lectures. Students answered questions such as "*What do chemical elements in the same period have in common?*" or "*Electronegativity is an example of a periodic property - explain what electronegativity means and its trend in the periodic table*". For assessment grading, two evaluators used the tool: the secondary school chemistry teacher (who was also the course instructor) and a final-year undergraduate student majoring in chemistry education. Both evaluators received standardized training covering the tool's operations, including external question bank import functionality, Moodle course page integration, and interface navigation. They also had access to tutorial videos and a dedicated familiarization period before operational deployment. For grading, they applied tags (correct, incorrect, or partially correct) to student answers and designed feedback messages either manually or with the tool's integrated LLM (i.e., DeepSeek V-3).

Next, students were invited to complete questionnaires about their perception and experience of the received feedback. Table 1 presents the questionnaire items and their corresponding thematic areas, which have been used in prior research [28]. The questionnaire was developed based on prominent feedback literature [4, 19]. Moreover, additional data collected through the instructor support feedback tool included: the time taken to generate each feedback message, the length of the message provided, and the extent to which instructors modified the LLM-generated feedback. These metrics were used to evaluate both the efficiency of the automated system and the human oversight required.

4.2 Procedure

We structured the procedure in three phases: assessment administration, feedback generation, and perception evaluation. We first deployed two curriculum-aligned assessments per class through the institutional Moodle platform, with students completing them in consecutive sessions. After this assessment round, instructors utilized the feedback tool for grading and feedback generation.

Table 1. Questions to evaluate Feedback experience and perceptions

Theme	Question	Sub-theme
Knowledge & beliefs	1. The course feedback that I have received is easily understandable	Interpretation
	2. I can connect the course feedback that I have received with the desired goals (standards) of my course tasks	Where am I going - judgement
	3. The course feedback that I have received helps me understand the course tasks better	Task-level
Domain knowledge	4. The course feedback that I have received deepens my domain knowledge	Understanding
Motivational beliefs	5. The course feedback that I have received motivates me to work towards a desired goal.	Managing affect
	6. The course feedback that I have received helps build my self-confidence	Managing affect/self-level
Set goals	7. The course feedback that I have received helps me adjust my own goals of the course tasks	Self-regulation
Tactics & strategies	8. The course feedback that I have received helps me develop and adjust my learning strategies	Self-regulation/process-level
Products	9. The course feedback that I have received gives advice on what I can do to achieve the desired performance	Where to next?/Process-level
	10. I feel confident carrying out the learning strategies suggested by the course feedback	Agency/action
Monitoring	11. The course feedback that I have received shows me my current progress	How am I doing/task-level
Teacher-student interactions	12. The course feedback that I have received encourages dialogue between me and the instructor	Learning support
	13. The course feedback that I have received shows that my instructor understands my strengths and weakness	Teacher knowledge/trust
	14. The course feedback that I have received makes me feel that my instructor cares about me	Trust

Regarding the grading and feedback phase, responses were first tagged as correct, partially correct, or incorrect. While the tool supported both partial and complete response tagging, we standardized the process by applying tags to entire responses only. In addition to tagging, instructors provided manual feedback to randomly selected students in each assessment round. Following manual feedback assignment, instructors proceeded with the automated feedback generation. Upon completing corrections for the first assessment round (see Fig. 2), students were prompted to complete the feedback perception questionnaire.

After evaluating the first-round feedback, instructors released the second-round assessment results and administered the feedback perception questionnaire again. This iteration included an additional question asking students whether they thought the feedback originated from an AI system or their instructor. Following both assessment rounds, we compiled all data for subsequent analysis.

4.3 Data Analysis

We employed robust inferential tests to answer our two RQs. Robust tests mitigate the impact of common assumption violations, such as non-normality and heteroscedasticity, while traditional parametric approaches like the t-test often fail under these conditions, potentially leading to biased or invalid conclusions [3]. Therefore, to ensure the validity of findings, we utilized the robust Yuen's test from the Wilcox Robust Statistics (WRS) package, specifically designed to handle such violations, to answer our RQs. This test extends the traditional t-test framework by using trimmed means and a bootstrapping method to compare central tendencies across conditions while minimizing the influence of outliers and non-constant variance [16].

Additionally, in relation to RQ1, we employed the Chi-square test of independence to understand students' opinions on whether they received teacher or LLM-generated feedback. Given that this is a nominal scale, we compared whether the proportion of students who received teacher-generated feedback differed from that of students who received LLM-generated feedback in terms of identifying if the received feedback was human or AI-generated. In relation to RQ2, for the LLM-generated feedback, we compared the original LLM-generated text with the final version revised by teachers using the *paraphrase-multilingual-mpnet-base-v2* model, an SBERT model based on the Masked and Permuted Language Modeling (MPNet) [23,26] We adopted the standard 95% confidence interval for all tests. Also, we followed research recommendations and did not adjust alpha/p-values, given that we performed a small number of previously planned comparisons [1].

5 Results

5.1 RQ1: How Do Secondary Education Students Perceive LLM-Generated Feedback?

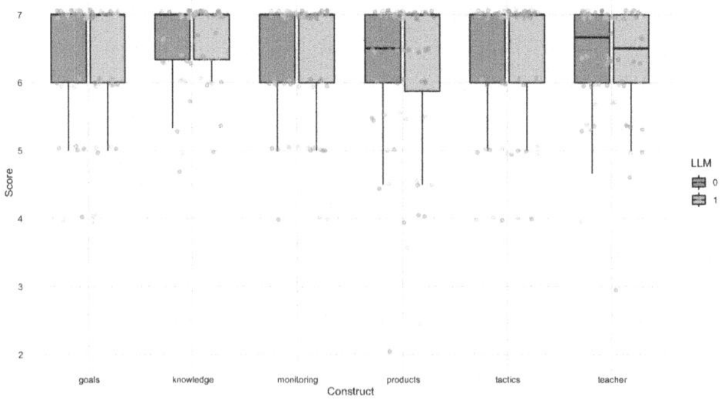

Fig. 3. Students' perceptions on the feedback they received, which was either generated with LLM support (1) or not (0).

Figure 3 presents students' opinions on the feedback they received. Overall, students had a highly positive perception, given that the median value (i.e., the box's bold line) was between six and seven – on a one-to-seven scale – for all metrics. Additionally, the figure suggests students' perceptions were similar regardless of the teacher having LLM support (1) or not (0) while designing the feedback. This insight was supported by the inferential statistics, which confirmed that there were no statistically significant differences in students' opinions about the feedback when comparing those provided by the teacher with LLM support to those offered without the LLM support (see Table 2).

Table 2. Results from the robust tests for two dependent groups (feedback generated with/without LLM support). All tests had the same sample size (80), degrees of freedom (23), and confidence level (95%).

Construct	Stat.	p-value	Difference (95% CI)
Knowledge	−0.128	0.900	−0.014 (−0.239, 0.212)
Motivational	0.509	0.616	0.125 (−0.383, 0.633)
Goals	0.253	0.803	0.042 (−0.299, 0.382)
Tactics	−0.933	0.360	−0.167 (−0.536, 0.203)
Products	−0.168	0.868	−0.042 (−0.555, 0.472)
Monitoring	0.000	1.000	0.000 (−0.573, 0.573)
Teacher	−0.169	0.867	−0.028 (−0.367, 0.312)

Finally, we also investigated whether students identified the feedback as being generated by the LLM, rather than by the teacher, after the second application. From the 13 students (out of 40) who received LLM-generated feedback, 11 (85%) believed the teacher generated the feedback they received. Among the remaining 27 students, who received teacher-generated feedback, 20 (80%) correctly identified it as teacher-generated, while two of them did not answer this item. These proportions are not significantly different based on the chi-squared test ($\chi < 0.001$; df = 1; p = 1). Hence, this finding suggests a substantial proportion of the students perceived the LLM-generated feedback similarly to that generated by two experienced teachers.

5.2 RQ2: To What Extent Does LLM-Assisted Feedback Generation Impact Instructor Feedback Practices?

Henceforth, all analysis was conducted using R[1], specifically the *WRS2* package [16]. A standard 95% confidence interval (CI) was adopted to determine statistical significance. Hypothesis testing was performed using Yuen's test for trimmed means [35], with a 20% trim level. Effect sizes were calculated based on Pearson's

[1] https://www.r-project.org/.

correlation, as proposed by Wilcox [31], where values of approximately 0.1, 0.3, and 0.5 indicate small, medium, and large effects, respectively.

Table 3 presents descriptive statistics of the feedback provision process. It demonstrates that feedback messages were of significantly greater length when the teachers had LLM's support for generating feedback. Since the 95% confidence intervals for the two conditions did not overlap and the p-value for the hypothesis test on feedback length equality was effectively zero, we reject the null hypothesis that both conditions produced equal feedback lengths. Furthermore, statistical tests showed a large effect size (0.79) on the feedback length when using LLM.

Nevertheless, the use of an LLM did not appear to have had a substantial effect on correction time. The overlap between the 95% confidence intervals for both conditions, combined with the p-value of 0.18992, indicated insufficient evidence to reject the null hypothesis that the correction times under both conditions are equal. Hence, adding LLM support contributed to teachers delivering longer, and supposedly higher quality, feedback messages with no practical increase in the time needed to do so. Furthermore, nearly all feedback generated by the LLM was longer than that produced without LLM support and was either fully accepted or only slightly modified by teachers.

Table 3. Descriptive statistics regarding the feedback provision process.

Condition	Length (characters)		Time	
	Mean (SD)	95% CI	Mean (SD)	95% CI
With LLM	262.70 (112.41)	(252.51, 272.80)	59.12 (54.53)	(53.53, 64.70)
Without LLM	118.10 (76.53)	(112.57, 123.69)	55.03 (53.77)	(50.97, 59.08)

Length Test: 21.4556 (df = 405.85), p-value = 0.00, eff. size = 0.79
Time Test: 1.3128 (df = 447.78), p-value = 0.19, eff. size = 0.06

Notably, teachers were largely receptive to LLM-generated suggestions, with 56% of the feedback messages forwarded to students without modifications. For the remaining 44%, we compared the original LLM-generated text with the final version revised by teachers. The cosine similarity achieved a mean of 0.9416 (SD = 0.0873) with a 95% CI of $(0.9273, 0.9560)$, indicating a high similarity and reflecting general teacher agreement with the LLM-generated content.

6 Discussion

Our study took place in a secondary school setting and was guided by two research questions: one focused on students' perceptions of the feedback they received, and the other examined the impacts on teachers' work based on a co-creation model for feedback. Our results show that, overall, students had a positive perception of the feedback, whether it was generated solely by teachers or in collaboration with AI. There was no significant difference in feedback quality from the students' perspective. Additionally, using an LLM to assist in feedback creation produced texts 2.6 times longer for students without a significant increase in grading time. Finally, 56% of the AI's suggestions were accepted in full by instructors, while 44% underwent minor adjustments.

From RQ1, we were able to assess students' perceptions regarding themes such as knowledge and beliefs, domain mastery, goals, and others. Our findings align with the study by Escalante et al. [10], who analyzed students' perceptions of feedback generated by ChatGPT versus humans, with both receiving positive evaluations. A key contribution of our work is that, unlike prior studies [10,17], our research provides a comparative analysis of feedback generated by LLMs in collaboration with instructors versus feedback generated solely by instructors for secondary education. The similar evaluation of feedback (with and without LLM support) may encourage further research on LLM-assisted co-creation, as it does not appear to impact students' perceptions negatively.

Still regarding RQ1 and students' perceptions of the feedback they received, most were unable to identify whether the feedback was generated with LLM assistance. The use of the virtual learning environment already adopted by the institution for pedagogical practices—complementing in-person instruction and supporting some classes—without requiring layout changes for Tutoria integration is a positive aspect of our study. By conducting the study in a setting that was part of their regular pedagogical routine, we aimed to minimize biases that could influence students' perceptions. Although participants consented to be part of a study involving AI-assisted feedback, the finding that most respondents believed the feedback was generated by instructors—even when it was predominantly produced by the LLM with subtle instructor contributions—supports the strong promise of AI-assisted collaborative feedback technologies. This aligns with prior research [25]. However, this also raises important ethical considerations about transparency and the conditions under which students should be informed of AI involvement, as the inability to distinguish sources does not negate the need for disclosure.

Regarding RQ2, the study's primary objective was to determine whether AI systems, through textual feedback on short-answer open-ended questions, could support teachers' work, particularly by alleviating their workload. One of the variables analyzed in relation to workload was the time spent on the activity, though this was not the only metric. In our study, we observed that time was not reduced when using an LLM for feedback creation. One contributing factor was that since the LLM generated more detailed texts, instructors had to spend time reviewing them for confirmation and potential contributions. However, while the time spent may have been equivalent, this does not necessarily mean the cognitive workload was the same, as reviewing does not always demand the same effort as writing.

While our results demonstrate that LLM-assisted feedback was consistently longer and largely accepted by instructors, this finding warrants detailed interpretation. As prior work shows [9], longer AI-generated feedback tends to be more readable, but length alone doesn't guarantee pedagogical effectiveness. Our study didn't measure how students processed these longer messages.

7 Limitations and Directions for Future Research

Although this study provides valuable insights into LLM-assisted feedback co-creation in secondary education, several limitations should be acknowledged. First, the study was conducted in a single disciplinary context (Chemistry) with relatively small sample sizes (N = 40 for RQ1, N = 60 for RQ2), which may limit the generalizability of our findings to other STEM subjects or educational levels. Second, the short-term nature of the intervention (two assessment cycles) prevents conclusions about longitudinal effects on learning outcomes or instructor workload sustainability. Third, our workload analysis focused primarily on temporal metrics; future studies could incorporate physiological measures to better quantify cognitive load differences between manual feedback generation and LLM-assisted review processes.

Future work should include longitudinal studies to investigate whether metrics such as feedback time using LLMs undergo significant changes over extended use. Additionally, qualitative studies with instructors are needed to better understand the workload impact from other perspectives. Regarding students, longer-term implementations should examine potential learning outcome improvements resulting from the more feedback typically generated by LLMs. Qualitative investigations should examine the balance between feedback length, precision, and usability, particularly whether students perceive longer LLM-generated feedback as more helpful or overwhelming. About ethics, future research should explore how and when to disclose AI involvement to students without undermining trust or engagement. There is also a need for cross-disciplinary applications to determine whether consistent behavioral patterns emerge or if outcomes vary depending on the educational context.

Acknowledgments. The authors of this study would like to thank the Instituto Federal Goiano and the Centro de Estudos e Sistemas Avançados do Recife for their support in the development of this research.

Disclosure of Interests. The authors have no competing interests to declare that are relevant to the content of this article.

References

1. Armstrong, R.A.: When to use the Bonferroni correction. Ophthalmic Physiol. Opt. **34**(5), 502–508 (2014)
2. Bandi, A., Adapa, P.V.S.R., Kuchi, Y.E.V.P.K.: The power of generative AI: a review of requirements, models, input–output formats, evaluation metrics, and challenges. Future Internet **15**(8), 260 (2023)
3. Cairns, P.: Doing Better Statistics in Human-Computer Interaction. Cambridge University Press (2019)

4. Carless, D., Boud, D.: The development of student feedback literacy: enabling uptake of feedback. Assess. Eval. High. Educ. **43**(8), 1315–1325 (2018)
5. Cavalcanti, A.P., et al.: Automatic feedback in online learning environments: a systematic literature review. Comput. Educ.: Artif. Intell. **2**, 100027 (2021)
6. Cavalcanti, A.P., de Mello, R.F.L., Rolim, V., André, M., Freitas, F., Gaševic, D.: An analysis of the use of good feedback practices in online learning courses. In: 2019 IEEE 19th International Conference on Advanced Learning Technologies (ICALT), vol. 2161, pp. 153–157. IEEE (2019)
7. Chan, S., Lo, N., Wong, A.: Leveraging generative AI for enhancing university-level English writing: comparative insights on automated feedback and student engagement. Cogent Educ. **12**(1), 2440182 (2025)
8. Collie, R.J., Martin, A.J., Gasevic, D.: Teachers' generative AI self-efficacy, valuing, and integration at work: examining job resources and demands. Comput. Educ.: Artif. Intell. **7**, 100333 (2024)
9. Dai, W., et al.: Assessing the proficiency of large language models in automatic feedback generation: an evaluation study. Comput. Educ.: Artif. Intell. **7**, 100299 (2024)
10. Escalante, J., Pack, A., Barrett, A.: Ai-generated feedback on writing: insights into efficacy and ENL student preference. Int. J. Educ. Technol. High. Educ. **20**(1), 57 (2023)
11. Falcão, T.P., et al.: Tutoria: a software platform to improve feedback in education. J. Interact. Syst. **14**(1), 383–393 (2023)
12. Falcao, T.P., et al.: Tutoria: supporting good practices for providing written educational feedback. In: Simpósio Brasileiro de Informática na Educação (SBIE), pp. 668–679. SBC (2022)
13. Ghassan, S.: Learning difficulties in chemistry: an overview. J. Turk. Sci. Educ. **4**(2), 2 (2007)
14. Giannakos, M., et al.: The promise and challenges of generative AI in education. Behav. Inf. Technol. 1–27 (2024)
15. Lipnevich, A.A., Panadero, E.: A review of feedback models and theories: descriptions, definitions, and conclusions. Front. Educ. **6** (2021)
16. Mair, P., Wilcox, R.: Robust statistical methods using WRS2. The WRS2 package (2019)
17. Meyer, J., et al.: Using LLMs to bring evidence-based feedback into the classroom: AI-generated feedback increases secondary students' text revision, motivation, and positive emotions. Comput. Educ.: Artif. Intell. **6**, 100199 (2024)
18. Morris, R., Perry, T., Wardle, L.: Formative assessment and feedback for learning in higher education: a systematic review. Rev. Educ. **9**(3), e3292 (2021)
19. Nicol, D.J., and, D.M.: Formative assessment and self-regulated learning: a model and seven principles of good feedback practice. Stud. High. Educ. **31**(2), 199–218 (2006). https://doi.org/10.1080/03075070600572090
20. Philipp, A., Kunter, M.: How do teachers spend their time? A study on teachers' strategies of selection, optimisation, and compensation over their career cycle. Teach. Teach. Educ. **35**, 1–12 (2013)
21. Qiao, S., Denny, P., Giacaman, N.: Oversight in action: experiences with instructor-moderated LLM responses in an online discussion forum. In: Proceedings of the 27th Australasian Computing Education Conference, pp. 95–104 (2025)
22. Razafinirina, M.A., Dimbisoa, W.G., Mahatody, T.: Pedagogical alignment of large language models (LLM) for personalized learning: a survey, trends and challenges. J. Intell. Learn. Syst. Appl. **16**(4), 448–480 (2024)

23. Reimers, N., Gurevych, I.: Sentence-BERT: sentence embeddings using siamese BERT-networks. In: Proceedings of the 2019 Conference on Empirical Methods in Natural Language Processing. Association for Computational Linguistics (2019)
24. Rodrigues, L., et al.: LLMs performance in answering educational questions in Brazilian Portuguese: a preliminary analysis on LLMs potential to support diverse educational needs. In: Proceedings of the 15th International Learning Analytics and Knowledge Conference, LAK 2025, p. 865–871. Association for Computing Machinery, New York (2025)
25. Rüdian, S., Podelo, J., Kužílek, J., Pinkwart, N.: Feedback on feedback: student's perceptions for feedback from teachers and few-shot LLMs. In: Proceedings of the 15th International Learning Analytics and Knowledge Conference, pp. 82–92 (2025)
26. Song, K., Tan, X., Qin, T., Lu, J., Liu, T.Y.: MPNet: masked and permuted pre-training for language understanding. Adv. Neural. Inf. Process. Syst. **33**, 16857–16867 (2020)
27. Taber, K.: Chemistry lessons for universities?: a review of constructivist ideas. Univ. Chem. Educ. **4**(2), 63 (2000)
28. Tsai, Y.S., Ferreira Mello, R., Jovanović, J., Gašević, D.: Student appreciation of data-driven feedback: a pilot study on task. In: LAK21: 11th International Learning Analytics and Knowledge Conference, pp. 511–517 (2021)
29. Wang, L., Chen, X., Wang, C., Xu, L., Shadiev, R., Li, Y.: ChatGPT's capabilities in providing feedback on undergraduate students' argumentation: a case study. Thinking Skills Creat. **51**, 101440 (2024)
30. Waqas, A., et al.: Revolutionizing digital pathology with the power of generative artificial intelligence and foundation models. Lab. Invest. 100255 (2023)
31. Wilcox, R.R.: Introduction to Robust Estimation and Hypothesis Testing. Academic press (2011)
32. Wisniewski, B., Zierer, K., Hattie, J.: The power of feedback revisited: a meta-analysis of educational feedback research. Front. Psychol. **10**, 487662 (2020)
33. Wohlin, C., et al.: Experimentation in Software Engineering, vol. 236. Springer (2012)
34. Yan, L., Martinez-Maldonado, R., Gasevic, D.: Generative artificial intelligence in learning analytics: contextualising opportunities and challenges through the learning analytics cycle. In: Proceedings of the 14th Learning Analytics and Knowledge Conference, pp. 101–111 (2024)
35. Yuen, K.K.: The two-sample trimmed T for unequal population variances. Biometrika **61**(1), 165–170 (1974)

Optimizing Mastery Learning by Fast-Forwarding Over-Practice Steps

Meng Xia[1], Robin Schmucker[2], Conrad Borchers[2(✉)], and Vincent Aleven[2]

[1] Texas A&M University, College Station, USA
mengxia@tamu.edu
[2] Carnegie Mellon University, Pittsburgh, USA
{rschmuck,cborcher,aleven}@cs.cmu.edu

Abstract. Mastery learning improves learning proficiency and efficiency. However, the overpractice of skills–students spending time on skills they have already mastered–remains a fundamental challenge for tutoring systems. Previous research has reduced overpractice through the development of better problem selection algorithms and the authoring of focused practice tasks. However, few efforts have concentrated on reducing overpractice through step-level adaptivity, which can avoid resource-intensive curriculum redesign. We propose and evaluate Fast-Forwarding as a technique that enhances existing problem selection algorithms. Based on simulation studies informed by learner models and problem-solving pathways derived from real student data, Fast-Forwarding can reduce overpractice by up to one-third, as it does not require students to complete problem-solving steps if all remaining pathways are fully mastered. Fast-Forwarding is a flexible method that enhances any problem selection algorithm, though its effectiveness is highest for algorithms that preferentially select difficult problems. Therefore, our findings suggest that while Fast-Forwarding may improve student practice efficiency, the size of its practical impact may also depend on students' ability to stay motivated and engaged at higher levels of difficulty.

Keywords: mastery learning · knowledge tracing · problem selection · intelligent tutoring systems · data-driven optimization

1 Introduction

The field of technology-enhanced learning has successfully optimized problem selection strategies and improved learning efficiency through methods such as Bayesian Knowledge Tracing (BKT) [8]. BKT, one of the most widely used knowledge tracing algorithms, has proven effective in modeling student knowledge acquisition, enabling tutoring systems to adaptively select practice problems with relevant and adequately difficult skills. In addition, several extensions to BKT have been proposed, including deep learning- (e.g., [26,33] and

M. Xia, R. Schmucker and C. Borchers—Equal contribution.

K. Tammets et al. (Eds.): EC-TEL 2025, LNCS 16063, pp. 549–563, 2026.
https://doi.org/10.1007/978-3-032-03870-8_37

regression-based approaches such as AFM, PFA and AugmentedLR (e.g., [25, 29]).

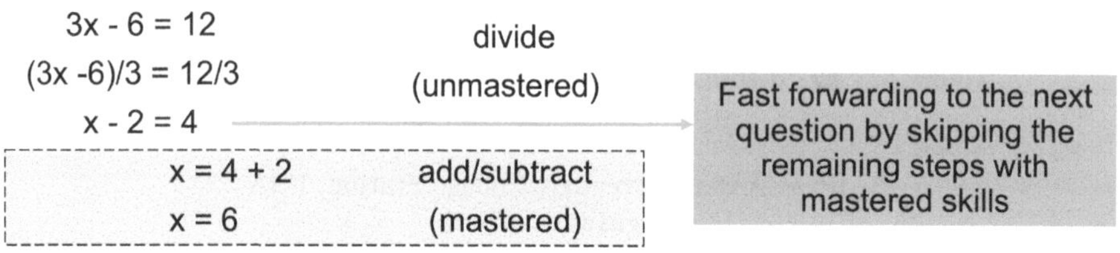

Fig. 1. Fast-Forwarding reduces overpractice by avoiding problem-solving paths students have fully mastered. Linear equation-solving steps in gray are known to be mastered by the student and can be fast-forwarded to reduce overpractice.

Adaptive problem selectors are informed by knowledge tracing and grounded in mastery learning [4]. Mastery learning assumes that learning and instruction can be divided into atomic skills that students acquire by exercising distinct cognitive operations and receiving feedback from which they learn. This idea aligns with large-scale evidence from several datasets [15] and has improved student performance at scale [27]. Mastery learning underlies the design of many contemporary tutoring systems and the idea that students require several practice repetitions–learning opportunities–to master each skill. On average, they require seven [15]. However, when tasks or activity sequences are poorly designed, practice activities might lead to *overpractice* and *underpractice* of individual skills.

Overpractice occurs when students practice skills they have already mastered, which is undesirable for learning efficiency if students have not yet mastered other skills [7]. Overpractice typically occurs when students practice static problem sets where problems include multiple skills, and there is little variability in what skills the problems target. In contrast, underpractice can be due to limited problem pools, meaning students do not master content upon completing a problem set or have insufficient time to practice. While curricular redesign based on learning analytics has been suggested as one method to mitigate over- and underpractice [7], avoiding both remains a fundamental challenge in adaptive learning, with learning analytics frameworks on the data-driven redesign of adaptive learning systems considering problem selection a core dimension for design improvement [12]. In particular, the consequences of reducing overpractice on learning are known to be positive: empirical research has shown that reducing overpractice in CognitiveTutor geometry decreased practice time without impacting learning outcomes [7], and such reductions have thus far required a careful and labor-intensive curricular redesign. In the present study, we study whether overpractice can be reduced through more automated means, based on optimization of step-level adaptivity ("inner loop" [3]) and having the system take over the mastered steps under some conditions. Such optimization balances the allocation of repetitions, giving students time to master challenging skills.

One reason why overpractice is an open problem is that serving practice problems with a single skill is not a viable solution, as multi-step problems give learners important opportunities to learn, most notably when practicing two skills together is more challenging than practicing them in isolation [10]. Hence, it is important to develop novel ways for students to master the skills required to learn while optimizing practice time *and* retaining multi-step problem solving.

An emerging approach to improve adaptive problem selection efficiency is called *focused practice*. This approach involves isolating specific skills that the learner currently lacks. Recent problem selection algorithms consider the overall redundancy in mastery of knowledge and the degree of isolation of unmastered skills in problem selection [11]. However, this approach still necessitates the availability of a diverse pool of problems with sufficient breadth and variation in skill density. Additionally, the requirement of designing focused tasks that exercise a limited number of skills necessitates additional content authoring time.

Can a general-purpose, problem pool agnostic, and selector agnostic method for focused practice increase student learning efficiency as measured in overpractice? We propose Fast-Forwarding (Fig. 1), which allows learners to complete multi-step problems up to the point where all remaining problem-solving steps are mastered, thereby contributing only to overpractice. Compared to prior approaches to focused practice [7,12], Fast-Forwarding **neither requires a specific problem selection mechanism nor depends on curricular redesign** while retaining multi-step problem solving. We quantify the effectiveness of Fast-Forwarding across various contemporary problem selection algorithms in intelligent tutoring systems through simulation studies. We ask:

RQ1: How does learning efficiency as measured in overpractice benefit from Fast-Forwarding in a mastery problem selector given limited practice time?
RQ2: How much overpractice does Fast-Forwarding reduce until content mastery across different problem selection regimes?

We conducted experiments through simulations based on solution pathways and parameters estimated from open-source data system. We chose equation solving as a domain due to its recursive nature: foundational skills are often repeated at the end of solving for X. However, we note that the **methods studied here apply to numerous other domains of instruction with step-level problem solving, for which tutoring systems are available** [2]. In STEM problem solving, science domain decisions tend to happen first (e.g., selecting physics principles), while later steps involve algebra or arithmetic, which many students may have mastered. In all of these domains, fast-forwarding could remove overpracticed steps by completing mastered steps on behalf of the learner.

2 Related Work

2.1 Learner Models and Problem Selectors

Various learner models have been developed to model students' learning and problem-solving behaviors. Bayesian knowledge tracing, arguably the most widely used model in adaptive learning systems today, models learners' latent knowledge of distinct skills as a probability of knowing each [8]. Other dynamic probabilistic models have been proposed to model the dependency of different learning concepts. For example, Learning Factor Analysis [6] models learner knowledge states via logistic regression to deal with learning concepts at different levels, and Performance Factor Analysis [25] fits distinct learning rates for correct and incorrect responses. Other models, such as deep knowledge tracing, use neural network architectures to model and predict learner performance [26]. These learner models assess learners' mastery of various skills and how they evolve with provided practice opportunities.

Many problem selection algorithms use estimated content mastery in adaptive learning in diverse ways. Contemporary mastery problem selection algorithms used in Cognitive Tutor typically select the problem with the most unmastered skills (mastery hard) [2,14]. Problem selection algorithms in TutorShop [1] also offer a similar regime that selects problems with the least, but at least one, mastered skills (mastery easy). However, all these selectors, while generally reducing student practice time [27], are limited in that they require a static pool of content and skills. Few notable exceptions exist, where tutoring systems have been designed to adaptively take over specific, commonly overpracticed steps [16,28]. Other researchers proposed to supplement problem sets with focused tasks to reduce overpractice, which are problems that target a few skills simultaneously. They particularly designed practice problems that involve only a focused set of skills that students have not mastered and then selected these focused tasks with higher probability [11,12]. However, designing focused tasks is time-consuming and requires content authoring. Fast-Forwarding, the method proposed in this study, in contrast, can be applied to any existing question pool and dynamically monitors whether certain steps can be skipped based on mastery estimates to mitigate overpractice.

2.2 Learner Simulation

Simulating learner data to study learning processes and outcomes is a core method in the field, particularly where obtaining real-world data is challenging, expensive, or impractical [13]. These simulations leverage cognitive learning theories to generate performance patterns that can be used to refine instructional methods. For instance, past research has employed simulated learners to identify skill models based on performance patterns, which were subsequently validated on real learner data, leading to improved instruction tailored to these identified skills [19]. Similar refinements have been applied to analyzing error types [31]. Recent research using Generative Adversarial Networks (GANs) has also been applied to enhance the assessment of student knowledge through simulation: Zhang et al. [33] augmented log data from tutoring systems using GANs, which improved the reliability of knowledge estimates.

However, despite these advances in simulations for refining knowledge tracing and instruction, there is a lack of simulated learner experiments that quantify the impact of problem selection algorithms on practice time and efficiency. Previous work has primarily focused on simulating the effects of setting mastery thresholds for error types [9] or on performance prediction given different mastery levels [24]. In addition, validating simulated learners on outcomes of interest remains a key research challenge. According to a recent literature review by Käser and Alexandron [13], a major issue in previous research using simulated learner data is the lack of systematic studies on the validity of synthetic data. However, there are exceptions, such as the work that used simulated student data in tutoring systems to predict real student performance [22]. Similarly, recent studies have increasingly used synthetic data to improve predictive models and predictive validity [33]. Our research simulates the practice efficiency of different problem-selection strategies in tutoring systems. We incorporate empirical estimates of learning rates and solution pathways into our simulations to improve validity.

3 Methods

3.1 Study Context and Dataset

We utilize an open-source dataset from APTA, a collaborative tutoring system for middle school equation-solving, available on PSLC DataShop (datasets #5549 and #5604) [17]. The study sample consists of data from IRB-approved classroom studies conducted in math classes at two public suburban middle schools in a mid-sized city in the eastern U.S. Overall, 164 6th- to 8th-grade students engaged with a series of multi-step linear equation-solving problems [5].

We analyzed the data comprising 10,937 entries (N = 10,937) of completed and timestamped problem-solving steps using the DataShop student step rollup tool [17]. The log data provide a detailed description of the student solution paths, meaning the order of operations used to solve individual problems. This allows for a fine-grained analysis of skills (e.g., add constant) students employ to derive solutions, offering deeper insights into their step-level problem-solving processes and serving as reference pathways for our simulation studies.

We only considered students' first attempts, as they reflect the students' initial response to solving linear equation steps without tutor assistance. Steps exhibiting hint usage were classified as incorrect attempts [17].

3.2 Computation of Overpractice

We define overpractice on a skill as the number of practice opportunities (e.g., problem-solving steps) on a skill given a predicted error rate on that skill below 0.05, in line with the mastery criteria in the Lynnette tutor [21]. Table 1 reveals several key findings regarding student performance and practice behavior across different skills. **This analysis served as a baseline for how much overpractice was present in our dataset from real students.** Simulations, as described below, were then used to determine how much students could potentially save if they had unlimited practice time and under different, alternative problem-solving regimes.

Table 1. Student mastery rates, practice and overpractice opportunities for each skill based on student data. The first row shows the % of students who mastered each skill, the second row the average number of problem-solving steps per skill, and the third row the number of steps taken after mastery (overpractice).

	cancel-const	cancel-var	comb-const	comb-var	division-complex	division-simple	simplify-division	add/subtr-const	add/subtr-var
Mastered (%)	74.4	6.7	73.8	6.7	26.8	79.3	79.3	68.9	6.7
Avg Opps.	15.9	1.1	16.2	0.9	4.1	15.4	18.3	16.3	1.2
Avg Overpr.	6.4	0.5	6.7	0.5	1.5	7.8	9.8	6.2	0.5

Varied Skill Mastery and Practice Engagement. The "Mastered" column indicates the proportion of students who achieved mastery for each skill, while the "Avg Opps" column denotes the average number of completed practice opportunities per skill. Average practice engagement varies significantly, with some skills having a higher average number of completed practice opportunities than others, such as *division-simple.*

Severe Overpractice. The column "Avg Overpr." delineates the average number of practice opportunities associated with overpractice for each skill. A considerable number of students experience overpractice across all skills. While more students overpractice the skills, some students achieve mastery of them.

3.3 Fast-Forwarding

Fast-Forwarding is a novel technique introduced in Fig. 1 that terminates practice problems early and forwards students to the next problem during the active problem-solving process ("inner loop" [30]). Fast-Forwarding is a flexible technique that can augment existing problem selection algorithms. Its only requirement is access to a pool of multi-step practice problems–a precondition for any step-level adaptation.

Fast-Forwarding optimizes practice efficiency by focusing on problem-solving steps that are unmastered, allowing students to achieve proficiency more quickly without redundant practice of already mastered skills (i.e., overpractice). However, a key consideration was to exclude skills from the solution pathway **if and only if all remaining skills had already been mastered**. This decision is informed by the literature on the composition effect [10], which is explained below.

Specifically, we did not adopt a model that would fast-forward students through problem-solving steps for *any* skill they had already mastered in the middle of the problem. Advancing students this way might limit the benefits of practicing combinations of skills in multi-step problem solving; in that case, unmastered in combination with mastered skills. This effect, known as the composition effect, suggests that a skill can be more challenging when practiced alongside a second skill and may require integrated practice [10]. Thus, Fast-Forwarding ensures students continue to practice skill combinations until all involved skills are mastered, preventing premature advancement that could leave important compositions unpracticed or systematically underpracticed.

3.4 Simulation Methodology

We simulate student performance (AFM; [6]) and trace student knowledge (BKT; [8]) through two distinct models. AFM and BKT work together to simulate student responses and different problem-selection regimes. Our simulations focus on problem-solving processes at the step-level, in line with AFM [6] and prior analyses of our study data [5]. Besides the present description, we promote method adoption and reproducibility by open-sourcing our code on GitHub[1].

Knowledge Tracing: Mimicking the knowledge tracing within the Lynnette tutoring system, we employ BKT [8] to analyze student responses and consider mastery to be achieved at a threshold of 95%, which is the threshold in our study data's Lynnette tutoring system [21]. BKT models student learning as a hidden Markov process where each skill is represented by a binary latent state (learned or unlearned). The model updates the probability of mastery based on observed correct and incorrect responses, using four key parameters: prior knowledge (p_{init}), the initial probability that a student knows the skill before any practice, learning rate (p_{learn}), the probability of transitioning from the unlearned to the learned state on each opportunity, guess rate (p_{guess}), the probability of answering correctly by guessing when the skill is unlearned, and slip rate (p_{slip}), the probability of answering incorrectly due to a mistake when the skill is learned. Given an observed response, BKT applies Bayes' rule to update the posterior probability of mastery. If a student answers correctly, the model increases the mastery probability, accounting for possible guessing. If they answer incorrectly, it decreases the probability, adjusting for slips. Mastery is typically declared when the posterior probability of a student being in the learned state exceeds a predefined threshold (here, 95%). For our simulations, we used standard TutorShop BKT parameters for all skills ($p_{init} = 0.25$, $p_{learn} = 0.2$, $p_{guess} = 0.2$, $p_{slip} = 0.1$), ensuring consistency with typical cognitive tutor implementations [1]. For this study, we simulate 10,000 simulated students that exhibit a normal distribution in initial AFM proficiency levels. This sample size is expected to yield sufficiently reliable results. We note that statistical significance testing our context is not meaningful, as more simulation samples will always tend to produce significant differences, no matter the minuteness of effect sizes.

Student Simulation: We simulate student learning data using AFM [6], a logistic regression model of knowledge acquisition (represented as the probability of getting a specific problem-solving step requiring specific skills correct) as a function of learners' initial proficiency levels, skill-specific difficulty, and skill-specific learning rates. To promote the validity of our methodology, we fit the standard AFM model [6] to our open source dataset (see Sect. 3.1) to obtain estimates of student acquisition rates across different skills, which then serve the simulation of performance in our experiments. Skill-level learning rates used for simulation are encoded in interactions between the learning opportunity count and the skill exercised at a given problem-solving step. This AFM learning rate should not be confused with the BKT parameters for knowledge tracing serving

[1] https://github.com/rschmucker/fast-forwarding.

problem selection, where we use standard default settings from Lynnette, which assume constant skill learning rates across all skills (see above) to mimic student experiences in the original study.

We define prototypical solution paths for each practice problem based on the most frequent skill-application path for each problem in our data. At each step in the simulation, we sample a student response based on the correctness probability estimated by the AFM model. We update the AFM simulation and BKT models before moving to the next step or practice problem. In line with Lynnette [21], BKT mastery estimates provide a basis for all problem-selection algorithms–including the proposed Fast-Forwarding method. To address RQ2, we implement a mechanism that replenishes the problem pool after it has been exhausted, meaning that the problem pool is reset to its initial state. This mechanism ensures that the simulation only terminates once all skills are mastered.

Problem-Selection Algorithms. Fast-Forwarding offers a flexible method for enhancing the efficiency of existing problem-selection algorithms. To verify its capabilities, this study integrates Fast-Forwarding into diverse problem selectors:

Random: Selects problems from the pool at random without replacement.
Deterministic: Selects problems following a domain expert-defined order taken directly from the standard Lynnette set suite [21] designed to surface increasingly difficult and complex problems over time.
Mastery Easy [2]**:** Employs student mastery estimates to select problems by averaging the difficulty of all available opportunities and serving the problem with the *lowest* difficulty based on mastery estimates while ensuring that the problem has at least one unmastered skill.
Mastery Hard [2]**:** Employs student mastery estimates to select problems by averaging the difficulty of all available opportunities and serving the problem with the greatest difficulty, usually featuring the most unmastered skills. This selector is the standard problem selector in Lynnette [21] and is evaluated in RQ1.
Focused Practice [11]**:** More recent selection algorithm that considers problem difficulty while preferentially sampling problems with few skills via multinomial sampling.

4 Results

4.1 Learning Efficiency Benefits (RQ1)

For the legacy mastery-based problem selector, Fast-Forwarding reduced overpractice by 35.7% across the simulated students, as measured in learning opportunities to apply mastered skills. Assuming a median number of steps, underpractice was not changed by Fast-Forwarding (M = 0.44 for Fast-Forwarding vs. M = 0.43 without). Hence, Fast-Forwarding mitigates overpractice while not introducing more underpractice, meaning that overall mastery levels do not suffer.

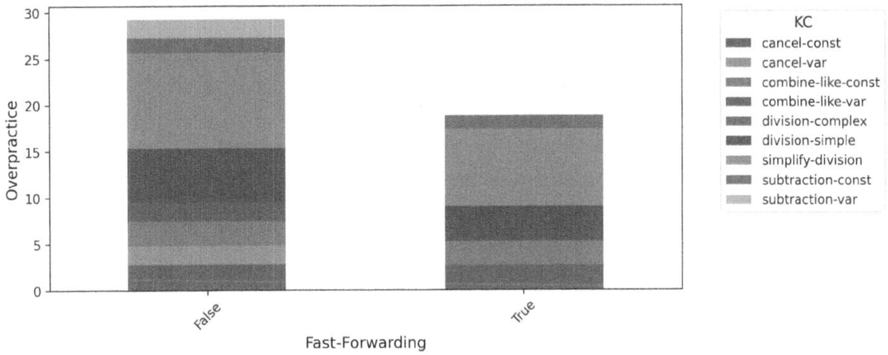

Fig. 2. Stacked bar plot showing the reduction in overpractice across individual skills when Fast-Forwarding is applied.

Figure 2 shows the sum of overpractice across various skills averaged across students. Overall, without Fast-Forwarding, overpractice is substantially higher, which can be attributed to continuing practice without early termination of fully mastered pathways. Notably, Fast-Forwarding removes overpractice entirely from some skills. For example, in our sample, Fast-Forwarding removed overpractice from the skills "subtract variable", "combining like variables", and "cancel variable", These are skills that typically appear at the end of practice problems. The same is true for skills involving handling constants. However, these skills may also be required to set up more advanced skills through transformation, such as division. These "setup" skills may not always be eliminated by Fast-Forwarding. For example, $3x - 2 = 4$ requires first subtracting as division by 3 upfront is not permitted in Lynnette, which only accepts whole numbers [21]).

4.2 Effects Across Problem Selectors (RQ2)

One strength of Fast-Forwarding is that it does not depend on the specific problem-selection algorithm used. Figure 3 shows the impact of applying Fast-Forwarding on overpractice across various problem selection regimes. This simulation aimed to determine how much overpractice students would encounter to reach mastery, assuming unlimited time. Notably, Fast-Forwarding consistently reduced overpractice across all problem selectors, ranging from 0.1% to 35.7%. The largest reduction for the legacy mastery hard problem selector aligns with RQ1 findings, but with the difference that no learning opportunity limit was imposed here, reducing overpractice somewhat more.

As error bars in Fig. 3 indicate, between-student variation in overpractice differed across problem selectors. As expected, random scheduling led to the largest variation, and deterministic scheduling led to the second-lowest variation. Despite this variation, Fast-Forwarding still led to a notable reduction in overpractice of 0.67 *SD* for this problem selector. Surprisingly, mastery easy led to the lowest variation in overpractice and only marginal overpractice reductions from Fast-Forwarding. Notably, the modest reduction in the focused practice problem selector was concurrent with the second-largest variation in overpractice across students (7.9%, corresponding to a reduction of 0.41 SD). We suspect this variation stems from increased randomness in the problem selector, both choosing skills *and* problems randomly. Accordingly, the mastery hard problem selector was more desirable based on the reported largest reduction in overpractice (35.7%; RQ1) *and* lower between-student variation, corresponding to a substantial effect size of 3.4 SD.

Finally, given the content unit being designed to include sufficient problems to allow all students to master content, the deterministic problem selector, requiring all problems, was associated with substantial overpractice, over ten times larger than mastery-based problem selectors. Overall, assuming students exert continued practice effort, mastery is obtained with the least overpractice for problem selectors with Fast-Forwarding, especially those who preferentially serve difficult problems.

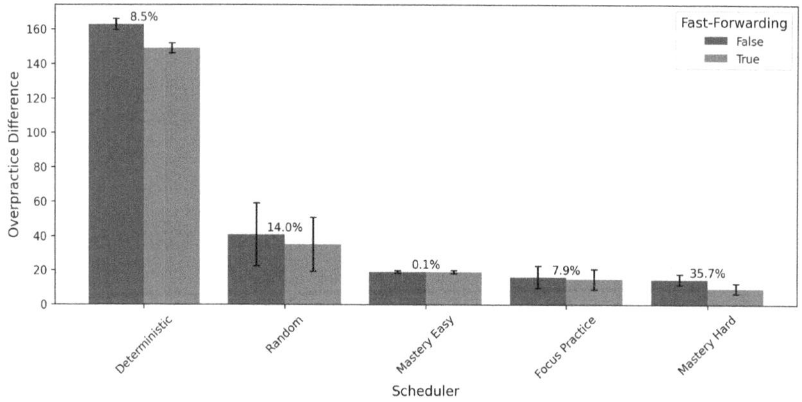

Fig. 3. Overpractice difference across problem selectors for Fast-Forwarding, including % decreases when Fast-Forwarding is applied. Error bars are 2 SD across students.

5 Discussion

Mastery learning makes learners improve efficiently [27]. Problem selection is key in improving learning analytics applications that support mastery learning, most notably tutoring systems [12]. The objective of the present study was to evaluate a novel method that promises to improve the efficiency of mastery learning as measured in overpractice [6] while preserving multi-step problem solving and its benefits to learning [10]. Through simulation based on parameters informed by real student data, we applied our method, Fast-Forwarding, to mitigate overpractice across contemporary and legacy methods for problem selection in a tutoring system.

5.1 Fast-Forwarding Under Legacy Practice Conditions (RQ1)

RQ1 focused on learning efficiency gains in a legacy mastery problem selector, prioritizing hard problems given limited practice time. Informing practice time by average step completions of students in an open-source dataset and using learning parameters from the same data, our analysis aimed at closely estimating how much practice students could save by our Fast-Forwarding method. Under limited practice time, our findings indicate that students could save up to about a third of overpractice in a linear equation-solving tutor [21] by Fast-Forwarding. In particular, this overpractice benefit was not accompanied by an underpractice deficit, indicating that the overall efficiency of practice improved.

Our findings pose two central questions for future research. First, while Fast-Forwarding is generally applicable to any mastery-based problem selector and content unit, equation solving is a task domain that naturally affords a high level of overpractice: More complex problems require more steps than simple problems, and intermediate problem states are similar to simpler problems, whose problem steps are repeated. Some of these "foundational steps" at the end of equations were eliminated from overpractice through Fast-Forwarding, for example, combining variables. However, other task domains might not have such hierarchical problem structures, such that Fast-Forwarding could potentially be less effective for such domains, which merits future research. Specifically, our method contributes a novel method of overpractice reduction in addition to curricular redesign [7] and problem selection optimization [12]. It is possible that each of these methods may be most effective across different domains. However, we argue that our method can be most readily applied to any multi-step problem-solving domain with knowledge tracing [1], including any problem selector.

Notably, Fast-Forwarding could not eliminate *all* underpractice in equation solving, potentially because some steps are required to set up more complex, unmastered operations, such as division, where students first need to subtract constants (a more foundational skill) to divide adequately (e.g., in $3x - 2 = 4$, where division by 3 upfront, leading to non-integers, is not permitted in Lynnette [21]). While Lynnette could fast-forward students to the state $3x = 6$ to just practice division, dealing with constants, in this case, may pose an important learning opportunity, assuming a composition effect whereby the same skill is more or less difficult depending on co-occurring skills [10]. Although Fast-Forwarding currently preserves such learning opportunities, future research may investigate to what extent learners could benefit from intermediate forwarding.

5.2 Fast-Forwarding is Effective for High-Difficulty Selectors (RQ2)

Assuming unlimited practice time, RQ2 focused on the effectiveness of Fast-Forwarding flexibly applied to different contemporary and legacy problem selection regimes. We find that, in a content pool with enough problems to allow all students to master all skills, mastery learning as such already substantially reduces overpractice compared to deterministic problem selectors that require learners to fully complete a unit before moving on. However, for all mastery-based algorithms, including recent ones that try to create more opportunities for focused practice and less overpractice [11], Fast-Forwarding further reduced overpractice. However, it was especially effective for selectors that prioritized difficult problems while minimizing overpractice differences between students, which may be desirable for creating practice regimes that are equally effective for all students [15]. One interpretation of this finding is that mastery algorithms that prefer harder problems tend to serve problems with many skills (i.e., the mastery hard algorithm used in this study tends to maximize the number of unmastered skills in a problem). In contrast, the mastery easy algorithm tends to serve problems with fewer skills (with at least one unmastered skill) [14]. It is hence expected that longer problems allow for more opportunities for the Fast-Forwarding mechanism to fast-forward the student, reducing overpractice to a larger extent. Second, selectors that preferred harder problems in our selection also led to the least problem selection overall. This is perhaps because, unlike Mastery Easy, such selectors more heavily punish problems that include mastered knowledge, as Mastery Easy only requires at least one skill in a problem to be unmastered.

5.3 Considerations Towards Applying Fast-Forwarding in Practice

While our findings suggest that Fast-Forwarding alongside selecting hard problems reduces overpractice most (based on simulation assumptions about learning based on real student data; a key issue identified in past research [13]), it is not self-evident that such problem selection regimes will be most effective for learning in practice. Although mastery learning is effective [27], it can be difficult for students to maintain the effort required to engage in practice. Studies published in the 1970s documented that student participation in computer-assisted instruction decreased with difficulties below 80% expected accuracy and was high when problems were easy [23]. While motivational theory suggests that a moderate level of difficulty is the most desirable level for motivation, more recent research also suggests that novelty and variation in learning tasks can compensate for some of the adverse effects of high difficulty on motivation [20]. Engagement in practice is crucial for the learning benefits of tutoring systems [15]. Therefore, potentially more important than practice efficiency (i.e., much practice with a little overpractice will usually result in more learning than little or no practice with no overpractice), future research is required to determine to what extent Fast-Forwarding can benefit students and their learning most. Although our findings suggest that Fast-Forwarding is especially helpful in reducing overpractice in problem selectors prioritizing hard problems, increasing difficulty (i.e., removing mastered skills) even further through Fast-Forwarding may not always be desirable for student motivation and engagement. Increasing the novelty of tasks to potentially and partially offset this effect [20] could be realized through authoring additional focused tasks [18] or potentially only executing Fast-Forwarding sometimes and at random, which would also lower overall practice difficulty by occasionally including mastered skills. Independently, current mastery thresholds (i.e., 95%) might be better if they were higher to account for forgetting, an interesting question outside the scope of our paper with some nascent evidence [32]. These design considerations, including how to best introduce and realize Fast-Forwarding in the tutoring system interface, are beyond the scope of the present study and subject to future research.

5.4 Limitations and Future Work

First, our findings are limited to a single domain (i.e., equation solving). Given the portability of Fast-Forwarding to any problem selector and problem domain with empirically derived student solution pathways, our findings merit future research into more domains of tutoring, which our open-source code enables.

Second, our Fast-Forwarding implementation was limited because Bayesian Knowledge Tracing (BKT) parameters were not fitted for individual students, which may have impacted the precision of skill mastery predictions. Although our BKT values used aligned with actual Lynnette settings [21], future research should consider individual fitting BKT parameters to learner data for more precise problem selection and simulation.

Third, our findings are limited to a single skill model, while potential difficulty factors in complex skill models may better describe the learner data [21]. A risk of using Fast-Forwarding when applied to coarse-grained skill models is taking away practice from difficult, hidden skills. Although skill model refinement is a key challenge in data-driven tutoring system improvement [11], future research may study what effects Fast-Forwarding has on more coarse-grained skill models.

6 Conclusion

This study introduced the generalizable Fast-Forwarding method to enhance mastery learning efficiency by reducing overpractice while preserving the benefits of multi-step problem solving. Our simulation studies showed that Fast-Forwarding reduces overpractice by up to one-third, particularly in selectors prioritizing harder problems. This improvement makes it a promising tool for optimizing tutoring systems, a key application area of technology-enhanced learning. These findings suggest that balancing efficiency with task difficulty, which may reduce student engagement if too high, should be a key consideration in future research to improve learning in practice.

Acknowledgments. This research was funded by the Institute of Education Sciences (IES) of the U.S. Department of Education (Award #R305A220386).

References

1. Aleven, V., et al.: An integrated platform for studying learning with intelligent tutoring systems: CTAT+TutorShop. arXiv preprint arXiv:2502.10395 (2025)

2. Aleven, V., Mclaren, B.M., Sewall, J., Koedinger, K.R.: A new paradigm for intelligent tutoring systems: example-tracing tutors. Int. J. Artif. Intell. Educ. **19**(2), 105–154 (2009)
3. Aleven, V., McLaughlin, E.A., Glenn, R.A., Koedinger, K.R.: Instruction based on adaptive learning technologies. Handb. Res. Learn. Instruct. **2**, 522–560 (2016)
4. Bloom, B.S.: A response to Slavin's mastery learning reconsidered. Rev. Educ. Res. **57**(4), 507–508 (1987)
5. Borchers, C., Yang, K., Lin, J., Rummel, N., Koedinger, K.R., Aleven, V.: Combining dialog acts and skill modeling: what chat interactions enhance learning rates during AI-supported peer tutoring? In: Proceedings of the 17th International Conference on Educational Data Mining (2024)
6. Cen, H., Koedinger, K., Junker, B.: Learning factors analysis – a general method for cognitive model evaluation and improvement. In: Ikeda, M., Ashley, K.D., Chan, T.-W. (eds.) ITS 2006. LNCS, vol. 4053, pp. 164–175. Springer, Heidelberg (2006). https://doi.org/10.1007/11774303_17
7. Cen, H., Koedinger, K.R., Junker, B.: Is over practice necessary?-improving learning efficiency with the cognitive tutor through educational data mining. Front. Artif. Intell. Appl. **158**, 511 (2007)
8. Corbett, A.T., Anderson, J.R.: Knowledge tracing: modeling the acquisition of procedural knowledge. User Model. User-Adap. Inter. **4**, 253–278 (1994)
9. Fancsali, S., Nixon, T., Ritter, S.: Optimal and worst-case performance of mastery learning assessment with Bayesian knowledge tracing. In: Educational Data Mining 2013 (2013)
10. Heffernan, N.T., Koedinger, K.R.: A developmental model for algebra symbolization: the results of a difficulty factors assessment. In: Proceedings of the Twentieth Annual Conference of the Cognitive Science Society, pp. 484–489. Routledge (1998)
11. Huang, Y.: Learner modeling for integration skills in programming. Ph.D. thesis, University of Pittsburgh (2018)
12. Huang, Y., et al.: A general multi-method approach to data-driven redesign of tutoring systems. In: LAK21: 11th International Learning Analytics and Knowledge Conference, pp. 161–172 (2021)
13. Käser, T., Alexandron, G.: Simulated learners in educational technology: a systematic literature review and a turing-like test. Int. J. Artif. Intell. Educ. **34**(2), 545–585 (2024)
14. Koedinger, K., Pavlik Jr, P.I., Stamper, J., Nixon, T., Ritter, S.: Avoiding problem selection thrashing with conjunctive knowledge tracing. In: Educational data mining 2011 (2010)
15. Koedinger, K.R., Carvalho, P.F., Liu, R., McLaughlin, E.A.: An astonishing regularity in student learning rate. Proc. Natl. Acad. Sci. **120**(13), e2221311120 (2023)
16. Koedinger, K.R., Corbett, A.: Cognitive tutors. In: Smart Machines in Education, pp. 145–167 (2001)
17. Koedinger, K.R., D'Mello, S., McLaughlin, E.A., Pardos, Z.A., Rosé, C.P.: Data mining and education. Wiley Interdisc. Rev.: Cogn. Sci. **6**(4), 333–353 (2015)
18. Koedinger, K.R., McLaughlin, E.A.: Closing the loop with quantitative cognitive task analysis. In: International Educational Data Mining Society (2016)
19. Li, N., Stampfer, E., Cohen, W., Koedinger, K.: General and efficient cognitive model discovery using a simulated student. In: Proceedings of the Annual Meeting of the Cognitive Science Society, vol. 35 (2013)
20. Lomas, J.D.: Optimizing motivation and learning with large-scale game design experiments. Ph.D. thesis, Human-Computer Interaction Institute, School of Computer Science, Carnegie Mellon University (2014)

21. Long, Y., Holstein, K., Aleven, V.: What exactly do students learn when they practice equation solving? Refining knowledge components with the additive factors model. In: Proceedings of the 8th International Conference on Learning Analytics and Knowledge, pp. 399–408 (2018)
22. Matsuda, N., Cohen, W.W., Sewall, J., Lacerda, G., Koedinger, K.R.: Predicting students' performance with simstudent: learning cognitive skills from observation. Front. Artif. Intell. Appl. **158**, 467 (2007)
23. Miller, R., Hess, R.D.: The effects upon students' motivation of fit between student ability and level of difficulty of CAI programs. Technical report, Stanford University, School of Education, Stanford, Calif. (1972)
24. Pardos, Z.A., Yudelson, M.V.: Towards moment of learning accuracy. In: AIED 2013 Workshops Proceedings Volume, vol. 4, p. 3. Citeseer (2013)
25. Pavlik Jr, P.I., Cen, H., Koedinger, K.R.: Performance factors analysis–a new alternative to knowledge tracing. Online Submission (2009)
26. Piech, C., et al.: Deep knowledge tracing. In: Advances in Neural Information Processing Systems, pp. 505–513 (2015)
27. Ritter, S., Yudelson, M., Fancsali, S.E., Berman, S.R.: How mastery learning works at scale. In: Proceedings of the Third (2016) ACM Conference on Learning@ Scale, pp. 71–79 (2016)
28. Ritter, S., Anderson, J.R.: Calculation and strategy in the equation solving tutor. In: Proceedings of the Annual Meeting of the Cognitive Science Society, vol. 17 (1995)
29. Schmucker, R., Wang, J., Hu, S., Mitchell, T.: Assessing the knowledge state of online students - new data, new approaches, improved accuracy. J. Educ. Data Min. **14**(1), 1–45 (2022)
30. VanLehn, K.: The behavior of tutoring systems. Int. J. Artif. Intell. Educ. **16**(3), 227–265 (2006)
31. Weitekamp, D., Ye, Z., Rachatasumrit, N., Harpstead, E., Koedinger, K.: Investigating differential error types between human and simulated learners. In: Bittencourt, I.I., Cukurova, M., Muldner, K., Luckin, R., Millán, E. (eds.) AIED 2020, Part I. LNCS (LNAI), vol. 12163, pp. 586–597. Springer, Cham (2020). https://doi.org/10.1007/978-3-030-52237-7_47
32. Zhang, J., Vanacore, K., Baker, R.S., Ch, N., Mills, C., Henkel, O.: How much mastery is enough mastery? The relationship between mastery in a lesson and the performance on the subsequent lesson. In: Proceedings of the International Conference on Educational Data Mining (2025)
33. Zhang, L., Lin, J., Borchers, C., Cao, M., Hu, X.: 3DG: a framework for using generative AI for handling sparse learner performance data from intelligent tutoring systems. arXiv preprint arXiv:2402.01746 (2024)

Author Index

K. Tammets et al. (Eds.): EC-TEL 2025, LNCS 16063, pp. 565–569, 2026.
https://doi.org/10.1007/978-3-032-03870-8

The manufacturer's authorised representative in the EU is Springer Nature Customer Service Centre GmbH, Europaplatz 3, 69115 Heidelberg, Germany. If you have any concerns regarding our products, please contact ProductSafety@springernature.com

Printed and bound by CPI Group (UK) Ltd, Croydon, CR0 4YY
01/10/2026
02225952-0020